ENCYCLOPEDIA OF INDIAN PHILOSOPHIES

ENCYCLOPEDIA OF INDIAN PHILOSOPHIES

The Philosophy of the Grammarians

HAROLD G. COWARD
and
K. KUNJUNNI RAJA

PRINCETON UNIVERSITY PRESS
Princeton, New Jersey

Published by Princeton University Press, 41 William Street,
Princeton, New Jersey 08540
In the United Kingdom: Princeton University Press, Oxford

Library of Congress Cataloging-in-Publication Data

The Philosophy of the Grammarians / edited by Harold G. Coward
and K. Kunjunni Raja.
p. cm.—(Encyclopedia of Indian philosophies ; v. 5)
Includes bibliographical references and index.
ISBN 0-691-07331-7 (alk. paper)
1. Bhartṛhari. Vākyapadīya. 2. Pāṇini. Aṣṭadhyāyī.
3. Patañjali. Mahābhāṣya. 4. Sanskrit language—Philosophy.
5. Sanskrit language—Grammar—History. 6. Indo-Aryan languages—Grammar—History. 7. Sanskritists—India. I. Coward,
Harold G.
II. Kunjunni Raja, K. III. Series: Encyclopedia of Indian
philosophies (Princeton, N.J.) ; vol. 5.

PK475.P48 1990 181'.4—dc20 90-47434 CIP

This book was composed in India by Jainendra Prakash Jain
at Shri Jainendra Press, New Delhi

Princeton University Press books are printed on acid-free paper,
and meet the guidelines for permanence and durability of the
Committee on Production Guidelines for Book Longevity of the
Council on Library Resources

Printed in the United States of America
by Princeton University Press, Princeton, New Jersey

10 9 8 7 6 5 4 3 2 1

Contributors :

Ashok Aklujkar, University of British Columbia
John G. Arapura, McMaster University
S. R. Bannerjee,
S. D. Joshi, University of Poona
Shoryu Katsura, Hiroshima University
G. B. Palsule, University of Poona
Karl H. Potter, University of Washington
V. K. S. N. Raghavan, University of Madras
K. A. Subramania Iyer, Lucknow University

CONTENTS

PREFACE xi

PART ONE :
INTRODUCTION TO THE PHILOSOPHY OF THE GRAMMARIANS

(*Harold G. Coward and K. Kunjunni Raja*)

1. Historical Résumé 3
2. Metaphysics 33
3. Epistemology 51
4. Word Meaning 63
5. Sentence Meaning 83

PART TWO :
SURVEY OF THE LITERATURE OF GRAMMARIAN PHILOSOPHY

1. Philosophical Elements in Vedic Literature 101
   (*John G. Arapura and K. Kunjunni Raja*)
2. Philosophical Elements in Yāska's *Nirukta* 107
   (*K. Kunjunni Raja*)
3. Philosophical Elements in Pāṇini's *Aṣṭādhyāyi* 111
   (*K. Kunjunni Raja*)
4. Philosophical Elements in Patañjali's *Mahābhāṣya* 115
   (*K. Kunjunni Raja*)
5. Bhartṛhari 121
   Trikāṇḍi or *Vākyapadīya*, with *Vṛtti* on Books 1 and 2
   (*Ashok Aklujkar*)
   Ṭikā on Patañjali's *Mahābhāṣya* (*K. Kunjunni Raja*)
6. Durvinīta or Avinīta 175
7. Dharmapāla 177
8. Hari Vṛṣabha or Vṛṣabhadeva 179
   (*Ashok Aklujkar*)
9. Maṇḍana Miśra 181
   Sphoṭasiddhi (*G. B. Palsule, Harold G. Coward, and Karl H. Potter*)

10. Helārāja 193
Commentary on Bhartṛhari's *Trikāṇḍī* (*K. Kunjunni Raja*)
11. *Prameyasaṃgraha* 199
12. Puṇyarāja 201
13. Kaiyaṭa 203
Pradīpa on Patañjali's *Mahābhāṣya* (*S. R. Bannerjee* and *K. Kunjunni Raja*)
14. Jyeṣṭhakalāśa 205
15. Maitreya Rakṣita 207
16. Puruṣottamadeva 209
17. Dhaneśvara 211
18. (Ṛṣiputra) Parameśvara II 213
Sphoṭasiddhigopālikā (*K. A. Subramania Iyer*)
19. Śeṣa Kṛṣṇa 215
Sphoṭatattvanirūpaṇa (*G. B. Palsule*)
20. Satyānanda or Rāmacandra Sarasvatī 219
21. Śeṣa Cintāmaṇi 221
22. Śeṣa Vīreśvara or Rāmeśvara 223
23. Śeṣa Nārāyaṇa Bhaṭṭa 225
24. Viṣṇumitra 227
25. Īśvarānanda or Īśvarīdatta Sarasvatī 229
26. Bharata Miśra 231
Sphoṭasiddhi (*G. B. Palsule*)
27. *Sphoṭasiddhinyāyavicāra* (*G. B. Palsule*) 235
28. Annambhaṭṭa 237
29. Appayya Dīkṣita I 239
30. Bhaṭṭoji Dīkṣita 241
Śabdakaustubha
31. Śeṣa Viṣṇu 243
32. Śivarāmendra Sarasvatī 245
33. (Śeṣa) Cakrapāṇi (Datta) 247
34. Mallaya Yajvan 249
35. Nīlakaṇṭha Śukla 251
36. Nārāyaṇa (Śāstrin) 253
37. Koṇḍa (or Kauṇḍa) Bhaṭṭa 255
Vaiyākaraṇabhūṣaṇa and *Vaiyākaraṇabhūṣaṇasāra* (*S. D. Joshi*)
38. Tāraka Brahmānanda Sarasvatī 309
39. Cokkanātha or Śokanātha Dīkṣita 311
40. Tirumala Yajvan 313
41. (Rāma) Nārāyaṇa (Śarman) (Vandyopādhyāya) 315
42. Sadāśiva 317
43. Hari Dīkṣita 319

44. Rāmabhadra Dīkṣita 321
Ṣaḍdarśinīsiddhānta saṃgraha (*Vyākaraṇa* Section) (*K. Kunjunni Raja*)
Śabdabhedanirūpaṇa (*K. Kunjunni Raja*)
45. Nāgeśa (or Nāgoji) Bhaṭṭa 323
Paramalaghumañjūṣā (*K. Kunjunni Raja*)
Mahābhāṣyapradīpoddyota (*V. K. S. N. Raghavan*)
Sphoṭavāda (*K. Kunjunni Raja*)
46. Jñānendra Sarasvatī 351
47. Gopālakṛṣṇa Śāstrin 353
48. Dharaṇīdhara 355
49. Vaidyanātha Payaguṇḍa 357
50. Satyapriya Tīrtha Svāmin 359
51. Jayakṛṣṇa Maunin 361
52. Harivallabha 363
53. Vāsudeva Dīkṣita 365
54. Śrīkṛṣṇa Bhaṭṭa Maunin 367
Sphoṭacandrikā (*G. B. Palsule*)
55. Umāmaheśvara or Abhinava Kālidāsa 371
56. Nīlakaṇṭha Dīkṣita 373
57. Āśādhara Bhaṭṭa 375
58. Rāmasevaka 377
59. Indradatta Upādhyāya 379
60. Kṛṣṇamitrācārya or Durbalācārya 381
61. Haribhaṭṭa 383
62. Dharaṇīdhara (II) 385
63. Mannudeva or Manyudeva or Gopāladeva 387
64. Bhairava Miśra 389
65. Kumāra Tātaya 391
66. Satārā Rāghavendrācārya (Gajendragadkar) 393
67. Gaṅgādhara Kavirāja 395
68. Tārānātha Tarkavācaspati 397
69. Khuddi Jhā (Śarman) 399
70. Nityānanda Panta Parvatīya 401
71. Dravyeśa Jhā 403
72. Sūryanārāyaṇa Śukla 405
73. Gopāla Śāstrī Nene 407
74. P. S. Anantanārāyaṇa Śāstrī 409
75. Brahmadeva 411
76. V. Kṛṣṇamācārya 413
77. Sadāśiva Śāstrī (Śarman) 415
78. Bāla Kṛṣṇa Pañcolī 417
79. Rāma Prasāda Tripāṭhī 419
80. Rudradhara Jhā Śarman 421

81. Kālikā Prasāda Śukla 423
82. Śabhāpati Śarman Upādhyāya 425
83. Raghunātha Śarman 427
84. Satyakāma Varmā 429
85. Rāmājñā Pāṇḍeya 431

BIBLIOGRAPHY ON GRAMMAR (*Vyākaraṇa*) (*Karl H. Potter*) 433

Part 1 : Authors Whose Dates Are (More or Less) Known 439

Part 2 : Authors and Works Whose Dates Are Unknown 517

Part 3 : Secondary Literature on *Vyākaraṇa*

NOTES 549

CUMULATIVE INDEX 563

PREFACE

This volume, the fifth in the *Encyclopedia of Indian Philosophies*, is devoted to the philosophy of the Grammarians. The introductory essay is intended to set their school in its context and to summarize the main Grammarian teachings. The summaries of primary sources that follow the introduction aim at making available the substance of the main philosophical ideas contained in these works, so that philosophers who are unable to read the original Sanskrit and who find difficulty in understanding and finding their way about in the translations (where such exist) can get an idea of the positions taken and arguments offered. The summaries, then, are intended primarily for philosophers and only secondarily for indologists. Certain sections of the works have been omitted or treated sketchily because they are repetitions or deemed less interesting for philosophers, though they may be of great interest to Sanskritists. The summaries are not likely to make interesting consecutive reading: they are provided in the spirit of a reference work. The appendix, which contains a lengthy bibliography of original and secondary writings on the philosophy of Grammar, is also presented as an aid to research.

References in the footnotes such as "G273" are to the bibliography presented in the appendix. References such as "RB10337" are to the first volume of this encyclopedia, 2nd edition (1984). Abbreviations used are listed at the beginning of the appendix.

Preparation of this volume has been made possible by grants from the American Institute of Indian Studies and the University of Calgary. These grants made possible the obtaining of the summaries and funded the travel that the editorial work required. The editors wish to thank Pradip R. Mehendiratta for his good offices. A debt of gratitude is also owed to the late Professor T. R. V. Murti, who gave generously of his time in working with Harold Coward in the volume's planning stages. A research followship awarded to K. Kunjunni Raja by the Calgary Institute for the Humanities enabled the two editors to work together in completing the project. Special gratitude is due to Karl H. Potter, editor of the *Encyclopedia of Indian Philosophies*, for his many contributions, which have added greatly to the value of this volume.

1987

HAROLD G. COWARD
K. KUNJUNNI RAJA

PART ONE

INTRODUCTION TO THE PHILOSOPHY OF THE GRAMMARIANS

1

HISTORICAL RÉSUMÉ

1. The Place of Language in Indian Philosophy

Language has been one of the fundamental concerns of Indian philosophy and has attracted the serious attention of all thinkers from the outset. In India the study of language has never been the monopoly of the Grammarians or the Rhetoricians. All schools of thought began their philosophical discussions from the fundamental problem of communication. The poet-philosophers of the *Ṛg Veda* were greatly concerned with the powers and limitations of language as a means of communicating their mystic, personal experiences of an ecstatic nature to their fellows and they tried to stretch the power of language by various means. They praised language as a powerful and benign deity (*vāc*), ever ready to bestow favors on her devotees. The entire creation of the world was attributed by some sages to divine language, and it was generally recognized that the ordinary speech of mortals was only a fraction of that language.

Among the six accessories to the study of the Vedas (*Vedāṅgas*) two are directly concerned with language: grammar (*vyākaraṇa*), or linguistic analysis, and etymology (*nirukta*), or interpretation of the meanings of selected words in the Vedas through etymological methods. Another accessory, metrics (*chandas*), is concerned with prosody.

Among the systems of Indian philosophy (*darśana*), Pūrvamīmāṃsā is called *vākyaśāstra* or the science of sentence interpretation, and the Nyāya system was also intrinsically language oriented. The Buddhist and Jain schools of thought have also devoted considerable attention to the working of language. Grammar and literary criticism (*sāhitya*) are directly interested in language problems, including semantic and philosophical issues, and Grammarians have claimed the status of an independent *darśana* for themselves.

The Indian approach to the study of language and linguistic problems has been characterized by both analysis and synthesis. On the one hand, a systematic attempt was made to analyze speech utterance in terms of sentences and words, stems and suffixes, morphemes and phonemes. The verbal root was considered as the core element to which preverbs, primary suffixes, and secondary suffixes, as well as nominal or verbal terminations, were added to evolve the word. On the other hand, rules of coalescence (*saṃdhi*) between these various elements and between words in a compound word or a sentence were studied and systematized. Rules of syntax were also studied carefully and attempts made to identify the cementing factors helping to form an integral unit.

The analytical method was older and more popular. The Sanskrit term for grammar, *vyākaraṇa*, means literally "linguistic analysis". Kumārila Bhaṭṭa, in the beginning of the seventh century, said that "we cannot think of any point of time totally devoid of some work or other dealing with the grammatical rules treating of the different kinds of roots and suffixes."[1] Śākalya's *Padapāṭha* of the *Ṛg Veda* was one of the early attempts in the direction of analysis; he broke down the *saṃhitā* text of the *Ṛg Veda* into words, identifying even the separate elements of compound words. The *Bṛhaddevatā*, attributed to Śaunaka, says that a sentence is made up of words, and words are made up of phonemes (*varṇa*).[2] Pāṇini, who flourished about the fifth century B.C., brought the descriptive grammar of the Sanskrit language to its highest perfection in his *Aṣṭādhyāyī*, which has been praised by Leonard Bloomfield, the father of modern linguistics, as "the greatest monument of human intelligence."[3] Pāṇini's primary concern was the building up of Sanskrit words, both Vedic and classical, from verbal roots, preverbs, primary and secondary suffixes, and nominal and verbal terminations; but he was also interested in syntactic problems involved in the formation of compound words and the relationship of the nouns in a sentence with the action indicated by the verb. Pāṇini did not neglect meaning, but he was aware of the fact that meaning was likely to change over time and that the final authorities regarding meaning are the people who speak the language.

It was the etymological school of Yāska, author of the *Nirukta* commentary on the *Nighaṇṭu* list of select words in Vedic literature, that undertook a semantic analysis of words with their components in order to explain their meanings in the contexts of their occurrence. This school generally subscribed to the view that nouns are derived from verbal roots. The *Uṇādisūtras* follow this view and attempt to find derivations for even apparently integral words.

Mīmāṃsā, called *vākyaśāstra*, was mainly concerned with the methodology of textual interpretation in order to give a cogent explanation of prescriptive scriptural texts. It had to deal with apparent absurdities, inconsistencies, and contradictions, besides ambiguities, and evolved rules of interpretation that were accepted generally by all schools of thought and were used freely in legal practice and in commentaries. The Mīmāṃsakas used both analysis and synthesis in their approach to textual problems. They gave a semantic definition of the sentence, evolving the concepts of mutual expectancy (*ākāṅkṣā*), consistency (*yogyatā*), and contiguity (*āsatti*) as factors necessary for the existence of a sentence. It was the Mīmāṃsā school that developed the theory of metaphor to explain the apparent absurdities and inconsistencies in Vedic texts.

The Nyāya school, mainly interested in the theory of knowledge and the truth or falsity of judgments, had to be concerned with the theory of meaning, because understanding the proposition was a primary requirement for making any significant study about it.

The literary critics who were concerned with the understanding and appreciation of literature were very much interested in the stylistic analysis of language and in finding out the deviance of literary language from ordinary language, in order to see how far poets have been able to communicate their vision of beauty and emotional experience through the medium of words.

It is clear that for centuries the various schools of thought in India have carried out studies that have produced insights into the working of language. The Grammarians' interest was not confined to the description and analysis of a particular language, but extended to the true nature and potentialities of language, including its role in effecting liberation.

2. The Basic Problems of Philosophy of Language

A. Linguistic Elements

One of the fundamental problems discussed is the relation between the linguistic elements (*śabda*) and their meanings (*artha*). The term *śabda* is normally used by the Grammarians to refer to a linguistic element, a meaningful unit of speech.[4] Patañjali's definition is that *śabda* is that which, when articulated, is seen to convey the idea of the referent. Maṇḍana Miśra defines it in his *Sphoṭasiddhi* as the cause that produces the idea of its meaning. In any case, it is the meaning bearer. In ordinary parlance people may use the word *śabda* to mean sound, as pointed out by Patañjali himself, but for the Grammarian it is the meaning-bearing unit.

Is it the articulated sound, or the phoneme (*varṇa*), or the word (*pada*), or the sentence (*vākya*) that is referred to by the term *śabda*? According to the *sphoṭa* theory of Bhartṛhari it is the complete utterance of the sentence that is the unit, and it is called *vākyasphoṭa*; but at a lower analytical level the word can be considered as the unit, for which the term *padasphoṭa* is used by the Grammarian. Those who know the language very well think and speak in units of sentences and also hear whole sentences. It is only those who do not know the language properly who hear words or phonemes or bits of sounds and have to struggle with them to get the connected sentence meaning. But in grammatical texts the words are taken as the unit for the sake of easy understanding.

This view is not acceptable to the Mīmāṃsakas, who consider the letter (permanent articulated sound-unit) or phoneme (*varṇa*) to be the *śabda* or unit of language and the meaning bearer. They assume phonemes to be permanent and each utterance to be their realization. To the Naiyāyikas *śabda* means sound produced by the speaker and heard by the listener, and it is impermanent; *pada* means a morpheme (meaningful unit).

B. Meaning (*Artha*)

What is meant by *artha* or meaning? Is it the universal that is intended, or the particular? According to Kātyāyana and Patañjali, two different positions were held by two ancient Grammarians, Vyāḍi and Vājapyāyana, the former holding that words refer to *dravya*, "substance" or "individual", and the latter holding that words (including proper names) refer to *jāti*, "universal" or "attribute". Pāṇini seems to have left the question open, holding that words could refer to individuals or to the universals. The Mīmāṃsakas held that the primary meaning of a word is the universal and the sense of the particular in a sentence is obtained either through secondary significative power (according to Bhāṭṭa Mīmāṃsakas) or through both the universal and the particular being grasped by the same perceptive effort simultaneously (according to the Prābhākaras). The early Naiyāyikas considered the meaning of words as comprising universal (*jāti*), configuration (*ākṛti*), and particular;[5] later Naiyāyikas held that the primary meaning of words is the individual as qualified by the universal (*jātiviśiṣṭavyakti*). The Buddhists of Dignāga's school held that the meaning is *vikalpa*, a mental construct that has no direct correspondence with the real, its nature being to exclude other things (*anyāpoha*). The function of a word or a name is the exclusion of other possibilities.

C. Significative Power (*Śakti*)

The significative power of words (*śakti*) is based on the relation that exists between a word and its meaning. The Grammarians hold that in the case of ordinary words in everyday speech it is permanent; but in the case of technical terms it is based on the convention. The Mīmāṃsakas consider the relation as "original" (*autpattika*), that is, as permanent or eternal. The Grammarians explain this permanence in two ways: *pravāhanityatā* and *yogyatānityatā*. We learn language from our elders; they in turn learned it from their forefathers; thus it could be traced back to any conceivable period of human society. This type of permanence is *pravāhanityatā*. The other view is based on the innate capacity of words to express any meaning; this capacity (*yogyatā*) is restricted by convention. Patañjali made a distinction between absolute eternality (*kūṭasthanityatā*), by which an item is not liable to any modification, and the perennial nature as used through generations of speakers (*pravāhanityatā*).

D. Polysemy

It is generally believed that in an ideal language a word must have only one meaning, and a sense must have only one word to express it. This binary relationship between a word and its meaning is accepted in principle by all schools of thought. It is also believed that this relationship, which is the basis for the significative power of words, is stable and constant because linguistic communication would be impossible without it. If there is no general understanding of the meaning of words shared by the speaker and listener there will be chaos and mutual comprehension will be jeopardized.

The existence of polysemy is recognized in actual practice, however. Two words may have the same form, and the same word may develop more than one meaning. The problem of homophones and homonyms has been discussed by scholars like Bhartṛhari. Yāska's discussion about the principle of word derivation in Sanskrit also sheds considerable light on the problem of synonyms. Nouns are normally derived from verbal roots. If all nouns are so derived from verbal roots denoting action, every object will have as many names as the actions with which it is associated, and by the same token each noun could be applied to as many objects as are associated with that action indicated by that verbal root. Yāska's answer to the problem is that there are no restrictions. Language designates things in an incomplete manner; it can choose only one of the many activities associated with an object. Hence there is some sort of permanent relation between a word and its meaning.

It is accepted that even the primary meaning of a word is not definitely circumscribed and that the boundaries of the meaning often change on the basis of contextual factors, not only in the case of ambiguous words but even in that of ordinary words: thus "man is mortal" does not mean "woman is immortal"; but in the phrase "man and woman", "man" does not include "woman". When there is conflict between the correct etymological meaning and the popular usage, the meaning current in popular usage among the educated elite is to be accepted. Grammatical analysis and etymological interpretations are only means of approach; the final authority is the popular usage of the cultured.

E. Secondary Meaning (*Lakṣaṇā*)

Even though it is accepted that every word has a primary stable meaning core, in actual practice shifts in meaning, metaphoric transfers, and secondary usages are quite common. If there is discrepancy in sense when the primary meaning is taken, the passage will have to be explained by resorting to the secondary meaning. There are three conditions considered necessary for resorting to secondary meaning. The first, is inconsistency or incongruity of the words taken in the literal sense. A sentence like "He is an ass" or "He is a firebrand" cannot be taken in the literal sense because the human being referred to cannot be an animal or an inanimate object. A sentence like "The house is in the river" does not make sense, because a house cannot exist in the river. In such cases the primary meaning of the word has to be given up and another meaning used. The second condition is that the actual meaning and the primary meaning must be related in some way; it may be on the basis of similarity or common quality or it may be on the basis of some other relationship like proximity. The example "He is an ass" can be explained if the term "ass" is interpreted as "a fool" (as the donkey is notorious for its dullness). The example of the house on the river has to be explained by taking "river" to mean the bank of the river on the basis of proximity. The third condition for resorting to secondary significance is either sanction by popular usage, as in the case of faded metaphors, or a special purpose for which it is resorted to, as in the case of intentional metaphors. The inconsistency of primary meaning can mean impossibility of syntactic connection from the point of view of meaning, or it can mean inconsistency in the context. As an example, in "see that crows do not spoil the curd" "crows" implies all beings, including a dog, who might spoil it.

Literary critics like Ānandavardhana proposed the element of purpose in intentional metaphors and pointed out its importance in enriching literature's content.

F. Conditions for Syntactic Relation

How can we get a connected meaning from a sentence if each word gives only its isolated sense, which is of a universal nature? This problem has been discussed in India since ancient times, and three main factors have been pointed out as unifying of sentence meaning: expectancy (*ākāṅkṣā*), consistency (*yogyatā*), and contiguity (*āsatti*). Words in a sentence must have mutual expectancy. Pāṇini hinted as much when he stressed the need for *sāmarthya* or capacity among the meanings of words for mutual connection, mainly in compound words.[6] This *sāmarthya* has been interpreted as similar to *ākāṅkṣā* or mutual expectancy and unity of sense. Later the Mīmāṃsakas developed this concept, and the logicians made further modifications. Mutual expectancy consists in a word being unable to convey a complete sense in the absence of another word. Literally it is the desire on the part of the listeners to know the other words in the sentence in order to complete the sense. A word is said to have expectancy for another if it cannot, without the latter, produce knowledge of its interconnection in an utterance. The Mīmāṃsakas were more interested in psychological expectancy, while the logicians and the Grammarians stressed the need for syntactic expectancy.

To this primary condition were added two more, *yogyatā* or consistency of sense and *āsatti* or the contiguity of the words. Grammarians did not emphasize the importance of *yogyatā* for to them it is enough for a sentence to give a syntactically connected meaning. Its veracity is not a condition. From the Grammarian's point of view *lakṣaṇā*, secondary meaning, is also of little interest. "He is a boy" and "He is an ass" are equally valid for them. Even empty phrases like "the child of a barren woman" are linguistically valid to them, for Grammarians are not concerned with the real existence of the thing meant by an expression. *Yogyatā* involves a judgment on the sense or nonsense of a sentence. There is difference of opinion about whether it should be taken as a positive condition. If the lack of *yogyatā*—inconsistency—is only apparent and can be explained away by resorting to the metaphorical meaning of a word in the sentence, there is no difficulty in understanding the sentence's meaning.

Āsatti or contiguity is the uninterrupted utterance or the unbroken apprehension of the words in a sentence. In the case of elliptical sentences, one school believes that the syntactic relation is known by supplying the necessary meaning, while another school insists that the missing words have to be supplied and the meaning obtained. Some take *tātparya*, the intention of the speaker known from contextual factors, as a fourth condition for understanding the meaning of a sentence.

G. Sentence Meaning

Regarding the comprehension of the sentence meaning there are two main theories, called *anvitābhidhāna* and *abhihitānvaya*. Speech is purposive in nature. People use words with the intention of conveying a connected, unified sense. Hence from the use of words in juxtaposition it is assumed that the speaker has uttered them with the intention of conveying a connected sense. Expectancy, consistency, and contiguity help in this comprehension of a unified sentence meaning. The sentence meaning is something more than the sum of the word meanings. Besides the word meanings, the syntactic connection of the word meanings has to be conveyed. The *abhihitānvaya* theory says that in a sentence each word gives out its individual isolated meaning (which is universal) and their significative power is exhausted with that. Then with the help of *lakṣaṇā* (secondary significative power) the syntactic relationship is obtained, and thus the sentence meaning is understood. According to the *anvitābhidhāna* school, by contrast, each word in a sentence conveys not only its isolated meaning but also the syntactic element. The words convey the meaning of the universal and simultaneously the meaning as referring to the particular. The words themselves also give the syntactic relationship. Thus the entire sentence meaning is conveyed by the words themselves. The Naiyāyikas, who believe that the words in a sentence denote primary meanings that are particulars as qualified by universal traits, contend that the sentence meaning is an association of the word meanings (*saṃsargamaryādā*).

H. *Sphoṭa* Theory

Even in ancient India there were some scholars who emphasized the unreal nature of words and advocated the need for taking the sentence as a whole. In the *Nirukta* Yāska refers to Audumbarāyaṇa's theory that it is the statement as a whole that is regularly present in the perceptive faculty of the hearer.[7] The *sphoṭa* theory, fully promulgated by Bhartṛhari in the fifth century of the Christian era, is one of the most important contributions of India to the problem of meaning. He insisted that the fundamental linguistic fact is the complete utterance or sentence. Just as a letter or a phoneme has no parts, so also the word and the sentence are to be taken as complete integral units, not as made up of smaller elements. Bhartṛhari says that although linguistic analysis—splitting sentences into words and further into roots and suffixes and into phonemes—may be a useful means for studying language, it has no reality. In a speech situation, communication is always through complete utterances. The speaker thinks and the listener understands the utterance as a single unit. It is only those who do not know the language thoroughly who analyze it into words, and further bits, in order to get a connected meaning. Those who know the language will conceive the idea and the expression as a single unit and express it; and the listener likewise comprehends it as a whole, the understanding is as an instantaneous flash of insight (*pratibhā*). The fact that the expression has to be through the medium of phonemes, through a temporal or spatial series, does not warrant our considering it as made up of parts. When a painter conceives a picture in his mind and paints it on a canvas, he may use various colors, and make various strokes; that does not mean that the picture is not a unit. And we see the picture as a unit, not as different colors and strokes. Just as the meaning is unitary, integral, and indivisible, the symbol that signifies it must also be unitary and indivisible. This concept is called *sphoṭa*—the sentence taken as an integral symbol, in which its apparent parts are irrelevant to it as parts. It is not something hypothetically assumed to explain language behavior; it is actually experienced and known through perception. On hearing a sentence those who know the language well hear the sentence, not the phonemes or sound bits or even words. Those who do not know the language may hear only the sound bits. The *sphoṭa* theory says that hearing the whole sentence is the real experience, while the apparent experience of hearing the sound bits is only for those who do not know the language.

I. Componential Analysis of Word Meaning

It may be noted that even the so-called unity of meaning is often an illusion, for it is the language that makes the unity. Yāska in the fifth century B.C. and, following him, Bhartṛhari in the fifth century of the Christian era have pointed out that a verb conveys a series of operations or activities taking place in a particular temporal sequence. Thus the word "cooks" conveys the idea of a series of activities—preparing the fire, putting the vessel on it, pouring water in the vessel, washing the rice, putting it in the water, blowing the fire to make it burn properly, putting out the fire, removing the excess water, and so on. It is the word "cooks" that collects all of these activities into a unitary, integral action. Each of these activities can be further analyzed into a series of activities taking place in time.

Later philosophers of language made further componential analysis of words from the semantic point of view and declared that every verbal root (*dhātu*) involved two semantic factors, activity (*vyāpāra*) and goal or result (*phala*). The verb "he cooks" means an activity directed toward the softening of the rice, and so forth. There is a difference of opinion about whether both are primary meanings of the verbal root or one can be taken as the main meaning and the other as subsidiary. The verb was divided into the root and the suffix, and separate meaning bits assigned to them. Maṇḍana Miśra said that the meaning of the root is the result, and it is the suffix that indicates the activity. With the addition of preverbs the meaning changes considerably in Sanskrit, and there have been discussions of whether all the meanings are present in a latent form in the root, to be revealed by the preverbs, or these preverbs can be assigned specific meanings.

J. Suggestion (*vyañjanā*)

The theory of literal (primary) and metaphoric (secondary) meaning developed by the Nyāya and Mīmāṃsā schools of sentence interpretation in ancient India was extended farther by Ānandavardhana in the second half of the ninth century to include emotive and other associative meanings under linguistic meaning. He did not attack the usual division of speech into words, into stems and suffixes and the distinction between the primary and secondary meanings of words. He accepted all of these concepts, but in addition he postulated a third capability of language, which he called *vyañjanā* or the capacity to suggest meaning other than its literal or metaphoric meaning. Ānandavardhana pointed out that this suggestive function of language has a vital role to play in literature.

K. Time

The concept of time and its divisions were discussed by such Grammarians as Patañjali and Bhartṛhari. The division of time into past, present, and future has a place in grammar, but the rules of usage given are not strictly followed in actual practice. The present tense (*laṭ*) is used to indicate the entire stretch of time included from the beginning of the action till its completion. "He is cooking" can mean he has started cooking and the operations are not yet completed. The present need not be momentary. Usages like "the mountains are standing" and "the rivers are flowing" mean that they continue to stand or flow.

Bhartṛhari considers time to be the most important power of Śabda Brahman, relatively more independent than other powers, and to be responsible for regulating them. The ancient authority Vārṣāyani said that becoming (*bhāva*) has six stages from birth to decay.[8]

L. Gender

Grammatical gender has attracted much speculation because in Sanskrit the grammatical gender does not coincide with sex, and words referring to the same object may occur in different genders.

3. The Literature on Grammar

Grammar (*vyākaraṇa*) was recognized from the earliest times in India as a distinct science, a field of knowledge with its own parameters that distinguished it from other sciences such as astronomy (*jyotiṣa*), architecture (*śilpaśāstra*), agriculture (*kṛṣiśāstra*), and the like. The coverage in this encyclopedia thus presents a peculiar problem somewhat different from that faced in dealing with the literature of other philosophical systems. Whereas in the cases of those other systems the "philosophical" literature is confined to that material which relates to the overall aim of liberation and those treatises which discuss theoretical issues pertinent to that aim in a polemical context, in the case of the grammatical literature the coverage has been widened to include those works which deal with theory of meaning and the related issues discussed in the previous section. As a result, the literature that is summarized here in the subsequent pages represents a selection from the total corpus of *vyākaraṇa* literature classified as such in India. For that reason it seems appropriate to attempt at this point to place the writers treated in the body of this volume within the total roster of authors whose works constitute the entire corpus of grammatical literature.

To this end we have provided as an appendix a bibliography of *vyākaraṇa* works and authors that covers what is currently known of the literature on grammar in general. Within the confines of this literature the present volume provides summaries of some works that are (1) in print and (2) especially relevant to the concerns touched on in the preceding section. Many of the works that are not summarized do, without doubt, bear on these topics. The distinction drawn must seem from the standpoint of Indian tradition rather artificial. We can only remind our readers that the entire project of this encyclopedia is directed toward a readership that comprises in the main those trained in philosophy as understood in the western world. The bibliography will suggest to such readers the extent of classical writings on grammar in general. From these writings we have selected the ones that seem most informative concerning matters of general philosophical interest, as "philosophy" has been understood for the purpose of this entire encyclopedic project.

The origin of grammar in India, as with so much else, is unclear. What is clear is that it was recognized as a field of study from a very early time. Pāṇini and Yāska, who must represent a stage of thought several centuries prior to the Christian era, both refer to a number of grammatical authorities and their views. In some cases the names cited by both writers are identical. According to a statement in the Brāhmaṇas it was the god Indra who first analyzed a speech utterance in terms of its parts.[9] Some scholars speak of an "Aindra" school of Grammarians in locating the origins of grammar. Patañjali refers to a tradition involving the futile attempt of Bṛhaspati to teach the language by enumerating its words and their meanings.[10] The earliest historical figure who dealt with linguistic study seems to be Śākalya, author of the *Padapāṭha* of the *Ṛg Veda*, who is mentioned by Pāṇini. According to Bhartṛhari, the sage Audumbarāyaṇa (also mentioned by Yāska), together with Vārttākṣa, seems to have held views similar to the *sphoṭa* theory.[11] A late tradition makes Sphoṭāyana, mentioned by Pāṇini, the founder of the *sphoṭa* theory.[12] Śakaṭāyana held the view that all words must be derived from verbal roots; some people consider him to be the author of the *Uṇādisūtras*. Gārgya and others held the view that not all nouns can be traced to verbal roots. But no authenticated works of any of these pre-Pāṇinian writers have come down to us, and it is difficult if not impossible to say which, if any, of Pāṇini's rules may have been taken from his predecessors.

Yāska and Pāṇini are the two great early writers on language. They belong to a period several centuries before Christ, possibly the fifth century. Yāska is generally considered to be earlier than Pāṇini, but Paul Thieme holds that Yāska knew Pāṇini.[13] George Cardona thinks it wise to leave the problem open.[14] The two writers are classified into different genres of literature by the Indian tradition. Yāska's *Nirukta* provides the name for a discipline of etymology counted as separate from grammar (*vyākaraṇa*), the discipline for which Pāṇini stands as the major seminal figure. (The bibliography appended to this volume confines itself to works classed in the latter discipline.)

A. Pāṇini's *Aṣṭādhyāyī*

Pāṇini's basic work is merely titled "The Eight-Chaptered" (*Aṣṭādhyāyī*). But a very remarkable work it is, providing a model for recent and contemporary work in descriptive linguistics that can stand with the best efforts of modern analysts. The eight chapters constitute a complete descriptive analytical grammar of the Sanskrit language, comprising about four thousand rules called *sūtras* preceded by a list of sounds divided into fourteen groups, which are called the *śiva-*, *pratyāhāra-*, or *maheśvara-sūtras*. In these rules the language is analyzed into verbal and nominal bases, so that the bases have come to be cataloged in two lists known as *dhātupāṭha*—the exhaustive lists of primitive verbal roots—and *gaṇapāṭha*—the selective lists of nouns, verbs, and so on for application in his rules. It is not clear whether one person wrote all these different components of the fundamental Pāṇinian corpus. A further feature of Pāṇini's method is a set of metarules of *paribhāṣās*, which tell us in which order to apply the rules, where exceptions are to be made, and so forth. All of these components are, in any case, made the subject of a grand commentarial tradition extending to the present.

Certain additional materials are ascribed to Pāṇini by the tradition, though scholarship is less agreed on the authenticity of these ascriptions. Among them, one group of *sūtras*, the *Uṇādisūtras*, provides rules for introducing affixes after verbal roots to derive nominal bases. The authorship of these *Uṇādisūtras* is frequently attributed to Śakaṭāyana instead of Pāṇini; and some scholars have found them to date from a later period. It is likely that there is truth in all of these views, in other words, that the *sūtras* represent a development of analysis over a long period.

A second set of ancillary *sūtras* are the *Phiṭsūtras*, which provide principles of accentuation. A feature of these rules is that accents are presupposed for nominal bases, from which the rules derive revisions of accentuation for the wholes of which those bases form a part. Because Pāṇini's rules contain none specifying accents for nominal bases, Cardona reports that "it is clear that the *phiṭsūtras* cannot be attributed to Pāṇini."[15] In fact, they are traditionally ascribed to Sāntanava, a rather later writer. Still, there are scholars who believe the *Phiṭsūtras* date from a pre-Pāṇinian period.

The *Liṅgānuśāsana* rules concern gender; they dictate how to determine the gender of linguistic items based on their structure and meaning. Although some scholars believe that this set of rules antedates Pāṇini and was known to him, Pāṇini in fact had his own rules governing gender, which in some respects complement and in others contradict the rules in the *Liṅgānuśāsana.*

There are also two texts dealing with phonetics called *Pāṇinīyaśikṣā*, one of which has regularly been attributed to Pāṇini. It seems unlikely that either of them is by Pāṇini himself.[16]

Pāṇini's system is remarkable in several respects. It purports to derive all the forms of the Sanskrit language that correspond to correct usage from operations on two kinds of primitives—affixes (*pratyaya*) and bases (*prakṛti*). The bases are of two kinds themselves, verbal (*dhātu*) and nominal (*prātipadika*). The rules indicate how affixes are to be introduced after bases to generate the correct inflected forms of the language. They also tell us what compounds can be formed, and how to derive, for example, active and passive sentences. Some rules tell us under what conditions one form can be substituted for another.

These rules are ordered, though not in a recognizable, systematic fashion throughout. In some cases the actual order in which the rules are given dictates the order in which they are to be applied. In other cases one rule blocks application of another—for example, a particular rule governs its own domain and restricts the scope of a more general one. There are negative rules (*niṣedhasūtra*), which preclude application, as well as definitions (*saṃjñāsūtra*) and metarules (*paribhāṣā*) which serve to interpret and fix the scope of the operational rules (*vidhisūtra*). Still another type of rule is the extension rule (*atideśasūtra*), which extends the scope of a rule beyond its normal bounds.

The remarkably systematic nature of Pāṇini's grammar is further reflected in Pāṇini's use of abbreviated expressions—symbols—to indicate certain recurrent features, notably syntactic functions such as agent, action, and object (known generally as *kārakas*). He also introduces "markers" (Cardona's term for *it*) to provide placeholders for certain functions and to form abbreviations (such as a marker *X* followed by a marker *M* signifies *X* and all the items following in a list up to and including *M*).[17]

B. *Vārttikakāras*

Inevitably, in such a complex undertaking as Pāṇini's system provides, there were attempts to criticize and improve on his rules and definitions. Within what comes to be known as the Pāṇinian school of grammar, comprising those who accept a tradition going back to Pāṇini and not to others to be discussed shortly, the first emendation of the *Aṣṭādhyāyī* of which we know appears to have come in the form of comments (*vārttika*) attributed to Kātyāyana.

Considerable time must have elapsed between Pāṇini and Kātyāyana because there are sufficient differences in their language to account for some of the *Vārttikas*. A similar gap of time has to be assumed between Kātyāyana and Patañjali, author of the *Mahābhāṣya*, so Kātyāyana may be assigned to the third century B.C. Although he is nowadays counted as a Pāṇinian, he may have belonged to a different school.

Various other authors of comments on and criticisms of Pāṇini probably lived in this period, and some names are mentioned that likely include a number of them, such as Śakaṭāyana, Śākalya, Vājapyāyana, Vyāḍi, and Pauṣkarasādi. We know little about their ideas, though a few of Vyāḍi's rules are held traditionally to have come down to us, and Śakaṭāyana is believed to have been the author of the *Uṇādisūtras* accepted by Pāṇini.

C. Patañjali's *Mahābhāṣya*

Kātyāyana's *Vārttikas* come to us as a part of the "great commentary" (*mahābhāṣya*) on Pāṇini ascribed to Patañjali (who may or may not be the same as the author of the *Yogasūtras*). The *Mahābhāṣya* takes the form of dialogues between student and teachers, some of whose solutions to problems are unacceptable, while one provides the final true view (*siddhānta*). Not all of Pāṇini's rules are discussed, and it is not always easy to identify the final view or to differentiate Kātyāyana's contributions from those of Patañjali, not to speak of the possibility of subsequent interpolations. Nevertheless, the *Mahābhāṣya* provides the classical interpretation of Pāṇini's system and is made the subject of subsequent commentaries through the centuries until the present time. Furthermore, in Patañjali's work, especially in its introductory passages, important philosophical ideas are broached, so that the *Mahābhāṣya* is perhaps the earliest philosophical text of the Grammarians.

D. Other Schools of Grammar

For the period between the time of Patañjali (perhaps 150 B.C.) and that of Bhartṛhari (perhaps fifth century after Christ), scholars trace the origins of a number of the other systems of Sanskrit Grammar, including the Digambara school of Jainendra and the Buddhist Cāndra school, as well as the Kātantra tradition.

The *Kātantrasūtras* are traditionally ascribed to Śarvavarman, who is dated by Shripad Krishna Belvalkar without much evidence as having flourished in the first century of the Christian era. The evidence, such as it is, is that Durgāsiṃha, a commentator on these *sūtras* who must have lived around or before A.D. 800, had a text of the *sūtras* that had already undergone considerable transformation or had possibly been lost, as there is a quite distinct version of them current in Kashmir by approximately the same time. The origins of Kātantra seem to have come out of a felt desire for a more popular and easier grammar than Pāṇini's formidable system provides. It has spawned a fairly consistent line of commentators lasting until the present time.

In keeping with the motivations to brevity and simplicity, the *Kātantrasūtras* return to the older method of ordering the syllables (as found in the *Prātiśākhyas*), arrange discussions of things more naturally (similarly to the arrangement later adopted within the Pāṇinian tradition by Bhaṭṭoji Dīkṣita in his *Siddhāntakaumudī*), and omit many of the most difficult rules prescribed by Pāṇini. The result is a work of about fourteen hundred *sūtras* only, in contrast to Pāṇini's four thousand.

As is well known, the Jains were divided from an early period into the Digambara and Śvetāmbara traditions. Each developed its own literature, and not surprisingly each developed its peculiar grammatical tradition.

The Digambara tradition goes back to the *Jainendravyākaraṇa*, which the Jains attribute to Mahāvīra, the Jina (founder of Jainism), who answers questions put to him by Indra, but which is a work that appears to have been composed about A.D. 500 by Pūjyapāda or Devanandin, who is also known as the author of certain fundamental philosophical works (see the first volume of this encyclopedia [2d ed. p. 99]).

According to Belvalkar the Jainendra grammar is a condensation of Pāṇini and the *vārttikas*, a condensation accomplished by the use of short technical terms that make study of the work very complicated. This difficulty may account for the relative dearth of commentaries that have been composed on it, those of Abhayanandin (perhaps 750) and of Somadeva (1250) seeming to be the only ones still extant.

The Śvetāmbara version of grammar stems from a later date. Its basic works are the *Śabdānuśāsana* and *Amoghavṛtti* of Abhinava Śakaṭāyana, not to be confused with the ancient authority by that name. This *Śabdānuśāsana* draws on the work of all the authors discussed so far, as well as on Candragomin's Buddhist tradition; indeed, the dependence on this last tradition is fairly widespread. This system was carried on through the usual commentarial works until it was supplanted for the most part by that of Hemacandra's *Śabdānuśāsana*, also addressed to the Śvetāmbaras.

Buddhist Grammar dates at least from Candragomin, to whom the *Cāndrasūtras* are ascribed, and who appears to have lived about Bhartṛhari's time, in the fourth or fifth century. Once again it depends largely on Pāṇini, Kātyāyana, and Patañjali, though it is somewhat briefer—3,100 *sūtras* in all. There are also accessory lists: a *Dhātupāṭha*, *Liṅgānuśāsana*, *Gaṇapāṭha*, *Upasargavṛtti*, and *Varṇasūtras*, and a commentary on this material written by Candragomin, fragments of which have come down to us. This grammar seems to have been popular, was translated into Tibetan and was circulated throughout Buddhist lands. It is still studied in Tibet, though not in Sri Lanka, where it was later superseded by Kāśyapa's *Bālāvabodha* (ca. 1200).

E. Bhartṛhari (perhaps fifth century)

It was Bhartṛhari who led Grammar into philosophy proper, by making a case for *vyākaraṇa* as a *darśana*, a view about ultimate things, eventually about liberation. He was also the major architect of the *sphoṭa* theory, which is regularly identified as the unique contribution of Grammarians to the philosophical problem of meaning. The locus classicus for his thoughts on these matters is the work popularly called *Vākyapadīya*, but he also wrote a commentary on the *Mahābhāṣya* and possibly other works. We have made the commentarial tradition on Bhartṛhari's *Vākyapadīya* central to the concerns of this volume. The first such commentator was Bhartṛhari himself, it would seem, for he now appears to have been the author of a commentary on at least the first two books of the three that constitute the *Vākyapadīya* or *Trikāṇḍī*.

F. The Fifth Through Tenth Centuries

Attacks were leveled against Bhartṛhari's *sphoṭa* theory by Kumārila Bhaṭṭa, the famous Mīmāṃsaka, and by the Buddhist Dharmakīrti. Maṇḍana Miśra, the great Advaitin and Mīmāṃsaka, wrote an independent work, *Sphoṭasiddhi*, defending *sphoṭa* against these attacks and vindicating Bhartṛhari's position. And just at the end of this period we date Helārāja, probably the most important commentator after Bhartṛhari himself.

This period also features the production of a very influential commentary, the oldest extant complete running commentary, on Pāṇini's grammar, the *Kāśikāvṛtti*. It was composed by two authors, Jayāditya and Vāmana, around the middle of the 7th century. The *Kāśikā* was in turn commented upon by Jinendrabuddhi, a Buddhist known for philosophical works as well as for his grammatical erudition.

To this period likewise belong Abhayanandin, the Jainendra

commentator, Abhinava Śakaṭāyana, author of *Śabdānuśāsana*, and Durgāsiṃha, the Kātantra commentator, all mentioned earlier.

G. Eleventh Through Sixteenth Centuries

We have now arrived at an era in which a number of grammatical traditions were in place. The next few centuries featured in the main commentators explaining and furthering these traditions, with one or two new additions to the field.

Within the Pāṇinian tradition itself the most important commentators early in this period included Kṣīrasvāmin, author of a commentary on Pāṇini's *Dhātupāṭha*; Haradatta, a commentator on the *Kāśikā*; Maitreya Rakṣita, a Bengali Grammarian who wrote on the theory of verbal bases; and most notably, Kaiyaṭa, the major commentator on Patañjali's *Mahābhāṣya*. It is on Kaiyaṭa's *Pradīpa* rather than on the *Mahābhāṣya* itself that the subsequent commentators mainly based their remarks. Kaiyaṭa must have lived about the beginning of the eleventh century. Still other figures of importance are Puruṣottamadeva, author of commentaries on Pāṇini and Patañjali (though the latter has been lost), and Rāmacandra, author of *Prakriyākaumudī*, on Pāṇini.

The period is likewise marked by the composition of various materials stemming from the traditions of Kātantra. In Jainism, as was pointed out before, the field was commandeered, at least within the Śvetāmbara branch, by Hemacandra, a polymath writer who is probably the most important and influential Jain scholar the tradition has ever known. His *Śabdānuśāsana* is even longer than Pāṇini's—some 4,500 *sūtras*—and draws on his predecessors, especially on Śakaṭāyana's work. At least a quarter of the work deals with the various *prākṛta* (Prakrit) languages, the ancestors of the modern regional languages of northern India, which are today beginning to take on their developed form. Hemacandra also composed a commentary, the *Bṛhadvṛtti*, which quotes many writers either to support or to criticize them.

A new school of Grammar, known as the Jaumara school and influential especially in West Bengal even today, takes its rise from a grammar called *Saṃkṣiptasāra*, composed by Kramadīśvara about the middle of the eleventh century. This work again depends on Pāṇini, with a few rules rejected and the *sūtras* rearranged. He makes many innovations both in the method and in the organization. The text as known to Gopīcandra, another influential writer of this system, contains a chapter on Prakrit. The school actually takes its name from Jumaranandin, who revised the *Saṃkṣiptasāra*, probably in the fourteenth century.

Two other new systems are those of the Sārasvata and the Mugdhabodha. The Sārasvata school appears to have been popular in northern

India from its inception in the thirteenth century down to the time of Bhaṭṭoji Dīkṣita, when the revival of the Pāṇinian tradition put most of the other schools of grammar into a decline. The basic work of the system is the *Sārasvatīprakriyā*, composed by Anubhūti Svarūpācārya about 1270. Anubhūti Svarūpācārya also wrote works on Advaita Vedānta. About the same time Vopadeva (or Bopadeva), a native of the Maharashtra country, wrote a grammar known as *Mugdhabodha*, which once more represents an attempt to simplify and abbreviate Pāṇini's system, this time with evidence of a religious purpose. Vopadeva's arrangement, like that of the Kātantra, promised to make his grammar more accessible, but as he also rearranged the order of the syllables and removed all the markers his system was not easily recognizable to Pāṇinians. Nevertheless, the Mugdhabodha system was very popular up to the time of Bhaṭṭoji, who went out of his way to refute it.

The picture, then, of Grammar during the fifteenth and sixteenth centuries is one in which a number of competing grammatical systems flourished with different degrees of popularity in different parts of the subcontinent, and the Pāṇinian system itself was only one among them.

H. The Modern Period: Bhaṭṭoji Dīkṣita, Koṇḍa Bhaṭṭa, and Nāgeśa Bhaṭṭa

The Pāṇinian tradition suffered through the difficulty of its system so that, as we have seen, other traditions grew up over the centuries that rivaled or surpassed Pāṇini's school in popularity and influence. Although some attempts had been made by grammarians who remained within the Pāṇinian tradition to simplify the system, notably Rāmacandra's *Prakriyākaumudī*, it was Bhaṭṭoji Dīkṣita at the end of the sixteenth century who produced a version of the Pāṇinian grammar that made it generally accessible and served to elevate that tradition to its present place of unrivaled eminence. Bhaṭṭoji's work is called *Siddhāntakaumudī*. Cardona, referring to a traditional explanation, notes that *kaumudī* means "moonlight," and just as moonlight brightens and cools, the *kaumudī* works "dispel ignorance while not involving the great effort necessary to understand works like the *Mahābhāṣya*," works that previously had to be mastered in order to grasp the sense of Pāṇini's rules. Bhaṭṭoji also wrote a commentary on the *Siddhāntakaumudī*, the *Prauḍhamanoramā*. The modern commentarial literature concentrates on the *Siddhāntakaumudī* version of the system; the number of commentaries on it and on *Prauḍhamanoramā* far outnumbers the number composed after Bhaṭṭoji on Pāṇini and Patañjali themselves. These commentaries are not always in agreement with Bhaṭṭoji; in addition to abridgment, his approach involved new interpretations of some of the rules, which departed in several instances from the interpretations of the classical Pāṇinians.

Bhaṭṭoji wrote, in addition to the *Siddhāntakaumudī* and its commentary, another work, the *Śabdakaustubha*, in which he collected the interpretations of earlier writers on Pāṇini's rules, especially those of Patañjali. This work is incomplete, dealing only with the first, second, fourth, and part of the third chapters of Pāṇini's eight. In addition, Bhaṭṭoji is responsible for seventy-four verses on grammar, sometimes referred to as the *Vaiyākaraṇamatonmajjana*, which form the text around which Koṇḍa Bhaṭṭa, the next great figure after Bhaṭṭoji, assembles his magnum opus, the *Vaiyākaraṇabhūṣaṇa* with its *sāra*.

Koṇḍa Bhaṭṭa provided in his work of 1630 refutations of rival theories of meaning proposed by other schools, principally the Nyāya and Mīmāṃsā. The work thus stands as the most important treatise after Bhartṛhari's to stem from the Pāṇinian school concerning philosophy as understood for the purpose of this volume. Koṇḍa Bhaṭṭa's *Vaiyākaraṇabhūṣaṇasāra* is an abridged version, presenting the arguments alone without the considerations of other views that accompany them in the *Vaiyākaraṇabhūṣaṇa* itself.

Similarly, Nāgeśa Bhaṭṭa in the early eighteenth century dealt with philosophical matters. Nāgeśa was the pupil of Hari Dīkṣita, author of *Śabdaratna* (or perhaps two *Śabdaratnas*, a longer and a shorter), who in turn was Bhaṭṭoji's grandson. His output was lavish, including commentaries on Bhaṭṭoji and Kaiyaṭa as well as a number of original works. Of the latter, three versions of a *Mañjūṣā* developing from Bhaṭṭoji's verses are particularly pertinent to questions of philosophy. The shortest of them, *Paramalaghumañjūṣā*, is summarized below. Nāgeśa is the most acknowledged grammarian of modern times, though he also wrote treatises on several of the other philosophical systems—Sāṃkhya, Yoga, and Nyāya. There is also a separate work on the *sphoṭa* theory, of great interest for purposes of this discussion.

The foregoing summary mentions only a small number of writers on grammar who have graced the ages in India. The bibliography appended to this volume will suggest to the casual reader the extensive development of this topic and the attention given to it, and it may offer the less casual reader guidance in seeking more detailed information. From among the welter of authors and works mentioned there, this volume concentrates on those who contributed most tellingly to the philosophical aspects of the subject—its theory of meaning and related matters. Although it is hard, and perhaps not really necessary, to distinguish the most philosophically relevant texts from the rest, Table 1.1 will help the reader pick out those authors whose writings promise the most rewards for the philosophically oriented.

TABLE 1.1

Vyākaraṇa Philosophy: Checklist of Authors and Works

This list is not exhaustive and emphasizes writers on philosophy—
See appendix for details

T=Edited and translated

E=Edited, but not translated

M=Not published, but manuscript(s) available

	Name	*Date*	*Place*	*Title*
1.	Patañjali	150 B.C.?	North of Ayodhya?	*Mahābhāṣya* on Pāṇini's *Aṣṭādhyāyī* (T)
2.	Bhartṛhari	A.D. 450?	?	*Vākyapadīya* or *Trikāṇḍī* (T) *Mahābhāṣyadīpikā* or *Tripādī* (E)
3.	Vṛṣabhadeva or Hari Vṛṣabha	650?	?	*Paddhatī* on book 1 of *Vākyapadīya* (E)
4.	Maṇḍana Miśra	690?	?	*Sphoṭasiddhi* (T)
5.	Helārāja	980?	Kashmir	*Prakāśa* on book 3 of *Vākyapadīya* (E)
6.	Puṇyarāja	1000?	?	?*Ṭīkā* on book 2 of *Vākyapadīya* (E)
7.	Kaiyaṭa	1150?	Kashmir	*Mahābhāṣyapradīpa* (E)
8.	(Ṛṣiputra) Parameśvara II	1410	Kerala	*Sphoṭasiddhigopālikā* (E)
9.	Satyānanda or Rāmacandra Sarasvatī	1500	?	*Mahābhāṣyapradīpalaghuvivaraṇa* (E)
10.	Śeṣa Kṛṣṇa	1540	Varanasi	*Sphoṭatattvanirūpaṇa* (E)
11.	Annambhaṭṭa	1540	Andhradesa	*Mahābhāṣyapradīpoddyotana* (E)
12.	(Śeṣa) Nārāyaṇa (Bhaṭṭa)	1546	Varanasi	*Mahābhāṣyasūktiratnākara* (M)
13.	Īśvarānanda or Īśvarīdatta Sarasvatī	1550	?	*Mahābhāṣyapradīpabṛhadvivaraṇa* (E) *Śabdabodhataraṅgiṇī* (M)
14.	Bhārata Miśra	1550	?	*Sphoṭasiddhi* (E)
15.	Author unknown	1550	?	*Sphoṭasiddhinyāyavicāra* (E)
16.	(Śeṣa) Cintāmaṇi	1557	Varanasi	*Mahābhāṣyapradīpaprakāśa* (M)
17.	Bhaṭṭoji Dīkṣita	1590	Andhradesa	*Vaiyākaraṇasiddhāntakārikā* (E)
18.	Śeṣa Viṣṇu	1605	Varanasi?	*Mahābhāṣyaprakāśikā* (M)
19.	Śivarāmendra Sarasvatī	1605	?	*Mahābhāṣyaratnaprakāśa* (E)
20.	Nārāyaṇa (Śāstrin)	1640	?	*Mahābhāṣyapradīpavyākhyā* (E)
21.	Koṇḍa Bhaṭṭa	1640	Varanasi	*Vaiyākaraṇabhūṣaṇa* and *Sāra* (E)
22.	Nārāyaṇa Bhaṭṭatiri	1640	Melputtur (Kerala)	*Apāṇinīyapramāṇatā* (T)
23.	Cokkanātha Dīkṣita	1650	South	*Mahābhāṣyaratnāvali* (M)
24.	Sadāśiva	1667	?	*Mahābhāṣyagūḍhārthadīpanī* (M)
25.	Hari Dīkṣita	1670	Varanasi	*Śabdaratna* (*Bṛhat–* and *Laghu–*) (E)

Name	Date	Place	Title
26. Jagannātha Paṇḍita	1670	Patna	*Prabodhacandrikā* (M)
27. Rāmabhadra Dīkṣita	1700	Tanjore	*Ṣaḍdarśinisiddhāntasaṃgraha* (E) *Śabdabhedanirūpaṇa* (E)
28. Nāgeśa Bhaṭṭa	1714	Maharashtra/ Allahabad; Nāgeśa spent his scholarly life in Varanasi	*Bṛhatmañjūṣā* (M) *Laghumañjūṣā* (E) *Paramalaghumañjūṣā* (part T; E) *Mahābhāṣyapradīpoddyota* (E)
29. Gopālakṛṣṇa Śāstrin	1720	Pudukottah	*Mahābhāṣyaśābdikacintāmaṇi* (M)
30. Dharaṇīdhara	1730	Tiksnajnatiya	*Bodhapaddhati* (M)
31. Vaidyanātha Paiyaguṇḍe	1740	Varanasi	*Mahābhāṣyapradīpoddyotachāyā* (E) *Laghumañjūṣākalā* (E)
32. Kāśīśvara Śarman	1740	?	*Jñānāmṛta* (M)
33. Satyapriya Tīrtha Svāmin	1745	?	*Mahābhāṣyavivaraṇa* (M)
34. Jayakṛṣṇa Maunin	1745	?	*Śabdārthasāramañjarī* (M) *Śabdārthatarkāmṛta* (M)
35. Harivallabha	1747	Gives his native place as Kūrmagiri	*Vaiyākaraṇabhūṣaṇasāradarpaṇa* (M)
36. Śrīkṛṣṇa Bhaṭṭa Maunin	1750	?	*Sphoṭacandrikā* (E) *Tarkacandrikā* (M) *Vṛttidīpikā* (E)
37. Āśādhara Bhaṭṭa	1770	Traditionally considered to have come from Baroda	*Śabdatriveṇikā* (E)
38. Rāmasevaka	1770	?	*Mahābhāṣyapradīpavyākhyā* (M)
39. Indradatta Upādhyāya	1800	?	*Śabdatattvaprakāśa* (M)
40. Kṛṣṇamitrācārya or Durbalācārya	1800	?	*Vaiyākaraṇalaghumañjūṣākuñcikā* (E)
41. Manyudeva	1815	?	*Vaiyākaraṇabhūṣaṇasārakānti* (M)
42. Bhairava Miśra	1824	?	*Sphoṭaparīkṣā* (E) and commentaries on the *Tattvabodhinī, Śabdenduśekhara,* and *Paribhāṣenduśekhara*
43. Kumāra Tatāya	1825	?	*Mahābhāṣyapārijātam nāṭakam* (M)
44. Satāra Rāghavendrācārya Gajendragadkar	1840	?	*Mahābhāṣyatripathagā* (M)
45. Gangādhara Kavirāja	1850	Jessore	*Trikāṇḍaśabdaśāsana* (E) *Trisūtravyākaraṇa* (E)
46. Anantācārya	1906	Musarapakkam	*Śaraṇaśabdārthavicāra* (E)
47. Khuddi Jhā (Śarman)	1910	Varanasi	*Vaiyākaraṇabhūṣaṇasāratiṅarthavādasāra* (E)

Name	*Date*	*Place*	*Title*
48. Nityānanda Panta Parvatīya	1925	?	Commentary on *Paramalaghumañjūṣā* (E)
49. Sūryanārāyaṇa Śukla	1937	?	*Vākyapadīyabhāvapradīpa* (E)
50. Gopāla Śāstri Nene	1940	?	*Vaiyākaraṇabhūṣaṇasārasārala* (E)
51. P.S. Anantanārāyaṇa Śāstri	1940	Trichur	*Vākyatattva* (E)
52. Brahmadeva	1943	?	*Vaiyākaraṇasiddhāntamañjūṣā* (E)
53. V. Kṛṣṇamācārya	1946	Madras	*Sphoṭavāda Upodghāta* (E)
54. Sadāśiva Śāstri Joshi	1946	?	*Paramalaghumāñjūṣārthadīpikā* (E)
55. Bāla Kṛṣṇa Pañcoli	1947	from Gujarat; taught in Varanasi	*Vaiyākaraṇabhūṣaṇasāraprabhā* (E)
56. Madhukānta Śarmā Jhā	1950	?	*Mahābhāṣyaprakāśa* (E)
57. Rāma Prasāda Tripāṭhi	1952	Varanasi	*Vaiyākaraṇabhūṣaṇasārasubodhinī* (E)
58. Rudradhara Jhā Śarman	1954	?	*Mahābhāṣyatattvāloka* (E)
59. Kālika Prasāda Śukla	1951	from Gujarat, worked in Baroda and at Varanasi	*Paramalaghumañjūṣājyotsnā* (E)
60. Sabhāpati Śarman Upādhyāya	1963	?	*Paramalaghumañjūṣāratnaprabhā* (E)
61. Raghunātha Śarman	1970	taught in Varanasi, but came from Chhata in Ballia District, U.P.	*Vākyapadīyāmbakartrī* (E) *Vyākaraṇadarśanabindu* (E)
62. Satyakāma Varma	1970	Delhi	Commentary on *Vākyapadīya* (E)
63. Rāmājñā Pāṇḍeya	1979	Varanasi	*Vyākaraṇadarśanapratimā* (E)

(Because it is difficult to give an exhaustive list of modern scholars, main works are given in the appendix. Dates for modern scholars given above are publication dates for their major works.)

4. Problems of Language Discussed by Other Schools

A. Mīmāṃsā

Mīmāṃsā deals mainly with the interpretation of the Vedic passages that give rules about the various rituals and sacrifices. The Veda consists of metrical hymns (*mantras*) and prose passages (*brāhmaṇas*). The *brāhmaṇas* are classified into two sections: (1) prescriptions, including injunctions (*vidhi*) and prohibitions (*niṣedha*); and (2) supplementary descriptions (*arthavādas*), which are classified into three groups: (a) *guṇavādas*, statements that are contradicted by our experiences in the world and have to be explained figuratively to get a cogent meaning, such as "the mind is a thief" (*stenam manaḥ*), (b) *anuvādas*, involving repetition of ideas already known, such as "fire is the antidote to snow" (*agnir himasya bheṣajam*), and (c) *bhūtārthavādas*, which deal with things that are unknown but may be taken to be true, for example, statements like "Indra killed Vṛtra."

In the *arthavāda* section of Jaimini's *Mīmāṃsāsūtras* the question is raised whether the *arthavāda* passages in the Veda can be considered as authoritative. The aim of the Vedic texts is to bring about action, hence apparently only injunctions and prohibitions can be held to be authoritative; the *arthavāda* passages, not directly related to any command or prohibition, seem to be unauthoritative. But the final view of the Mīmāṃsakas is that the *arthavādas* are also valid instruments of knowledge (*pramāṇa*), because they are supplementary texts to be read along with the injunctions or prohibitions as a unit.

Regarding the interpretation of an injunction itself there is difference of opinion between the two schools of Mīmāṃsā—the Bhāṭṭa, following Kumārila Bhaṭṭa's views, and the Prābhākara, following Prabhākara's views. According to the Bhāṭṭa school the content of an injunction is the realization that the action enjoined will produce some beneficial result. For every Vedic injunction the three basic components that must be indicated are: *sādhya* (what is to be brought about), *sādhana* (the means or *karaṇa*), and *itikartavyatā* (in what way it is to be brought about). In the Bhāṭṭa system the *sādhya* of the *śābdī bhāvanā* is the *ārthī bhāvanā* and the *itikartavyatā* is the *arthavāda* associated with the injunctions. Kumārila says that not even a fool will act without a purpose. There is no need to say who should act, for anyone who is desirous of the fruit will come forward to do it. According to the Prābhākaras, however, the basic components that need to be indicated are: the *viṣaya* (the act enjoined), the *niyojya*, (the person who is enjoined to do it), and the *karaṇa* (the means of doing it). There is no need to indicate the fruit of action for, according to Prabhākara, the Vedic injunction is to be obeyed simply because it is a command. The law is to be obeyed because it is the law, not because of the expectation of any reward or the fear of punishment.

The definition given by the Mīmāṃsakas for a sentence is in *Mīmāṃsāsūtra* 2.1.46. A group of words serving a single purpose (*artha*) forms a sentence, if on analysis the separate words are found to have mutual expectancy (*ākāṅkṣā*). The principle of syntactic unity is that "So long as a single purpose is served by a number of words, which on being separated, are found to be wanting and incapable of effecting the said purpose, they form one syntactical unit—one complete *Yajuṣ-mantra*."[18] Here the sentence definition is based on psychological *ākāṅkṣā* and not syntactic *ākāṅkṣā*. Prabhākara says that in this definition the term *artha* stands for both meaning and purpose and that the two are interrelated. Kumārila Bhaṭṭa says that it is possible to take *artha* as meaning in order to allow a wider scope to the principle, but he does not accept that interpretation himself. Bhartṛhari refers to this definition and says that it is not identical with the definition given by Kātyāyana, that a sentence is that (group of connected words) which contains a single finite verb (*ekatiṅ*).[19]

It was the Mīmāṃsakas who took a leading part in studying the working of *lakṣaṇā* or the secondary significance of words. They had to recognize it in order to explain apparent inconsistencies when words are taken in their literal sense. The main condition of a metaphoric transfer is this inconsistency (*mukhyārthabādha*). The Prābhākaras held that the inconsistency is the impossibility of taking the word in the literal sense, while according to the Bhāṭṭas it is the unsuitability in the context. The role of contextual factors was also recognized by both schools. A sentence may have a secondary meaning according to both the schools, while the Nyāya school allows it only for the individual words.

B. Nyāya

The Nyāya school is greatly interested in problems of language. A considerable portion of Navya-Nyāya is concerned with logical grammar, analyzing and classifying the significant elements of sentences and discovering rules that determine the motion of a meaningful sentence. It is to the Nyāya school that the modern *śābdabodha* studies look for inspiration and help. *Śābdabodha* means "knowledge of the sentence meaning," and it is studied from the listener's point of view.

The Naiyāyikas use the term *pada* (word) for any meaningful unit, not necessarily a free unit; and they use the term *vākya* (sentence) for any syntactically connected "words". Thus for them an expression like *ghaṭaṃ* can be taken to be a "sentence" because it is made up of two "words", *ghaṭa* and *-am*, and is logically complete.

The Naiyāyikas believe that the relation between words and their meanings is not natural, but conventional, being established by the will of God in the case of ordinary words and by the will of man in the case of technical terms. This conventional relation is called significative power (*śakti*). Meaning (*artha*) includes the universal (*jāti*), the configuration (*ākṛti*), and the individual (*vyakti*), according to early Naiyāyikas; but later they considered it to be the individual as qualified by the universal (*jātiviśiṣṭavyakti*).[20]

There is significative power only for primary meaning; secondary meaning is accepted as being related to the primary meaning. The

Naiyāyikas accept secondary meaning only for an individual word in a sentence, not for the sentence as a whole, by contrast to the Mīmāṃsakas, who accept secondary meaning for a sentence. The early Naiyāyikas considered the impossibility of connecting the word meanings in a sentence to be the incompatibility that prompts their having secondary meaning; but according to the Navya-Nyāya school it is the unsuitability of primary sense in view of the sense intended in the context. The three conditions of expectancy, consistency, and contiguity necessary to unify the sentence are accepted by the Naiyāyikas; but to them the expectancy is syntactic, not psychological. Some of the Naiyāyikas accept intention (*tātparya*) as another condition, but not all. Suggestion (*vyañjanā*) is not acceptable to the logicians who include it under inference.

C. Buddhist Logicians[21]

The Buddhist Logicians of Dignāga's school have been very interested in the philosophy of language. How far can verbal communication be successful? Dignāga was greatly influenced by his elder contemporary Bhartṛhari. According to the Buddhist idealists reality consists of unique particulars (*svalakṣaṇa*), which are momentary and in perpetual flux. Perception is the sensation of the unique particulars, but all cognitions are based on concepts that are conceptual constructions (*vikalpa*), which cannot directly grasp reality. Words produce conceptual constructions, and conceptual constructions produce words. The Buddhists do not accept the universal as a reality. The function of a word, that is, a name, is the exclusion or elimination of other possibilities. Construction-free (*nirvikalpaka*) perception of the unique particular alone is real perception; verbal knowledge based on concepts is only inference, according to them, and has no direct correspondence with the real external things.

Bhartṛhari too seems to have held an idealistic view of reality. All verbal discourse is meaningful in terms of our conceptual images and the words that symbolize them. He seems to deny the possibility of a construction-free knowledge beyond the reach of words. All knowledge is interpenetrated with words, and it is impossible to have a cognition free from word association (see *Vākyapadīya* 1.123).

Dignāga's indebtedness to Bhartṛhari can be discovered in his main work, *Pramāṇasamuccayavṛtti* 5, on *apohapariccheda.*[22] Looking for prototype of the theory of *anyāpoha* (exclusion of others), Masaaki Hattori successfully demonstrates that there is a striking resemblance between Dignāga's concept of *apoha* and Bhartṛhari's concept of the universal (*jāti*) discussed in *Vākyapadīya* 3.1, *jātisamuddeśa.*[23]

Dignāga quotes three verses of *Vākyapadīya* in *Pramāṇasamuccayavṛtti* 5 in order to support his arguments. To clarify the grammatical distinctions between two words with different nominal endings and those with identical endings, he quotes *Vākyapadīya* 3.14.8.[24] To support the argument that a universal word (*jātiśabda*) may be applied directly to members of that universal, he quotes *Vākyapadīya* 2.158. To support the argument that a universal word may never be applied to members of that universal, he quotes *Vākyapadīya* 2.155.[25]

Finally, Dignāga declares in *Pramāṇasamuccayavṛtti* that the meaning of a sentence (*vākyārtha*) is "intuition" (*pratibhā*), apparently under the influence of *Vākyapadīya* 2.143ff.: "When abstracted from a sentence, the meaning of a word is discriminated. The meaning of a sentence called *pratibhā* is first produced by it [that is, the meaning of a word]."[26]

D. Literary Criticism

Grammar provided the foundation from which the detailed discussions of literary criticism arose. The importance of emotions with special reference to the theater were stressed in Bhārata's *Nāṭyaśāstra* (third century of the Christian era), which gives detailed directions regarding the communication of emotions by the actors. Ānandavardhana accepted the importance of emotions in all literature and evolved his *dhvani* theory to explain the poet's communication of aesthetic experience through the medium of language by using the method of suggestion.

Ānandavardhana, the author of the *Dhvanyāloka*, flourished in Kashmir under the patronage of King Avantivarman in the later half of the ninth century. The theory of primary and secondary meaning, developed by the Mīmāṃsakas and the Naiyāyikas in ancient India, was further extended by him to include emotive and other associative meanings also under linguistic meaning. He postulated a third potency of language named *vyañjanā*, which he called the capacity to suggest a meaning other than its literal and metaphorical (secondary) meaning. Under the term "meaning" is included not only the information conveyed but the sociocultural significance, the figures of speech, and also the emotion induced; and among the indicators of meaning, Ānandavardhana did not confine himself to the words and sentences, but included all the contextual factors, the intonation and gestures, the sound effect produced, the rhythm and the meter, as well as the literal sense. Although suggestion (*vyañjanā*) is a comprehensive linguistic phenomenon, Ānandavardhana confined his attention to poetic language and studied the problem only from that standpoint. Strictly speaking, the *dhvani* theory of Ānandavardhana is only an extension of the *rasa* theory of Bharata to the domain of literature, as has been pointed out by writers like Abhinavagupta.

Ānandavardhana's basic postulate is that an emotion cannot be evoked in the reader by merely referring to its name or by its bare description. It has to be suggested by describing the situation and contextual factors such as the reactions of the characters. Not only the literal meaning, but also the suggestive possibilities of the expression, such as the sound echoing the sense, rhythm, imagery and symbols, selective exaggeration of the prominent element, and the suppression of the irrelevant, and bringing out the etymological significance through subtle supplementation—all of these devices are to be used for helping to evoke the right response in the reader. Words and expressions are to be selected from those in common usage in such a way as to help evoke the emotional effect desired.

The linguistic speculations of ancient Indians such as the grammarians and logicians generally took a word as the unit of speech and considered a sentence as a combination of words for the purpose of communicating meaning. How is syntactic unity effected from a series of isolated words uttered in a sequence? This question was discussed and various explanations given by different schools of thought. The literal and metaphorical meanings of words were also discussed and the conditions for resorting to a word's metaphorical meaning in a sentence were evolved. But there were some scholars, like Bhartṛhari, who exposed the unsatisfactory nature of a linguistic theory dependent entirely on individual words and their lexical meanings; Bhartṛhari's theory of *sphoṭa* emphasized the importance of taking the whole utterance as a significant unitary linguistic symbol. Ānandavardhana took his cue from Bhartṛhari in developing his theory of suggestion in poetry.

Logicians, interested more in accuracy and precision in the use of words that they want to analyze objectively than in the fullness of expression and the possibilities of extending the range of meanings to the domain of the inexpressible, are satisfied with the normal sense; but poets and critics who deal with the totality of human experience cannot ignore vast areas of human behavior. The suggested meaning is too vague, fleeting, and subjective to have a place among logical meanings; the subtle and subjective suggestions implied in language (*vyañjanā*) do not lend themselves to logical discussion and analysis. The suggested meaning depends on contextual factors, and the same utterance may convey different suggestions to different people depending on their mental makeup and expectations. There is no invariable connection between an expression and the suggestions conveyed. Ānandavardhana included the emotions evoked in the listeners under the rubric of meaning, which naturally necessitates the assumption of a limitless suggestive power for language, for even logicians cannot argue that the emotions induced by language can be included under the literal meaning. Emotions can be evoked by music or dance where no expressed sense is involved; the emotive element in a language cannot be explained in terms of the primary literal meaning or even the metaphorical sense of words.

It is true that intentional metaphors can suggest further ideas; but these suggested meanings have to be assigned to the suggestive power of language. The break in the flow, due to the incompatibility of the expressed sense, in the case of a metaphor is a signal to the listener to stop and think about the possible interpretations and thereby lead him into the sphere of suggestions. Ānandavardhana was concerned only with poetic language and confined his attention to the suggestion of meanings of aesthetic value. His theory of *dhvani* is *vyañjanā* or suggestion as applied to poetry.

It was Ānandavardhana who for the first time enunciated the theory of *aṅgirasa* according to which there should be one predominant sentiment or *rasa* in a literary work such as a drama, epic, or lyric to which all the other *rasas* introduced should be subordinate. Mutually conflicting or supportive emotions could be delineated appropriately in a work, provided there is one *rasa* predominant throughout, the others being kept in the background as subsidiary. Earlier writers like Bharata had not stressed this point but considered that a work such as a drama has to cater to the different tastes of various types of people and must therefore deal with various emotions and *rasas*. Bharata seems to have felt that each character in a play may have one dominant emotion, but he did not consider the need for a predominant *rasa* for the work as a whole. Structural unity in plot was, however, stressed by him. Ānandavardhana perhaps felt that unity in theme implied a predominant *rasa* for the work as a whole and that great classical writers have always taken this idea for granted; so he boldly stated that even the construction of the plot must be made in such a way that there is scope for a predominant *rasa*; incidents and descriptions irrelevant to the development of the main *rasa* should be avoided, and even the introduction of figures of speech and selection of the work's texture should be in keeping with the *rasa* delineated. In all such cases the propriety from the point of view of the *rasa* is the most important factor to be considered.

Another point stressed by Ānandavardhana is that the imaginative sensibility requisite for proper literary appreciation can be acquired only by a close study of classical works and by the constant practice of response to works of art. Because the most important element in the meaning of a poem is the emotion suggested, it can be understood and appreciated only by *sahṛdayas* or men of like sensibility, not by all scholars and logicians, who may only be able to get at the literal meaning through analytical study. The process is one of getting the reader's heart and mind tuned to the same frequency as that of the transmitting artist. Poetry does not give out its full charm to all, only to a select few.

As the *Ṛg Vedic* seer observed, the goddess of speech exposes her full charm and yields herself completely only to the deserving devotee, just as a loving wife does to her husband. Bharata, who had to deal with the problems of the theatrical performances, considered that a drama should please all types of people, not merely the specialists. Ānandavardhana, by contrast, considers that literary taste has to be acquired through practice. Even among connoisseurs tastes differ; some themes such as love stories and adventures may have a wider attraction than stories dealing with the quiet life of a recluse. The ideal *sahṛdaya*, however, is one who can raise himself above his petty prejudices and individual predilections and appreciate things from the poet's point of view.

Ānandavardhana exalts the freedom of the creative writer, which transcends even the powers of nature. He says that in the boundless *saṃsāra* of poetry the poet is the sole creator, the whole world transforms itself depending on his wishes. If the poet is pervaded with *rasa*, the whole world of his creation will be suffused with that *rasa*. A good poet makes even insentient objects act as sentient beings. As Abhinavagupta explains it, the poet's intuitive power (*pratibhā*) enables him to create a world according to his wish. This tendency of infusing life into insentient objects of nature is a special feature of Indian poetry, though it has been criticized by Ruskin as the "pathetic fallacy."[27]

In India even poetics or literary criticism claims to be not only a science (*alaṃkāraśāstra*) but also a *darśana* or philosophy. The main aim of literature and dramaturgy is to give unalloyed pleasure to the readers or the audience by evoking *rasa*. This *rasa* realized and enjoyed has often been compared to the bliss experienced by the mystics on getting a glimpse of the ultimate Reality or Brahman; some have claimed that *rasa*-realization is identical with Brahman-realization; there has also been a claim that it is superior to the bliss the *yogins* get in their deep meditation, for less effort is involved in it.

The *Ṛg Veda* can be considered not only as the earliest religious text, but also as the earliest literary work in India, if not in the world. The Vedic seers were mystic poets fully conscious of language's importance and of the problems of faithfully communicating intimate personal experiences. Some of the concepts that are universally accepted by the critics and are clearly found in the Vedas include:

(1) The need for a vision in the mind, which is integral and pleasurable, as the source for all poetry and philosophy. The term *pratibhā* was not found, but the root *dṛś*, "to see" or "to visualize" is frequently used to convey the idea.

(2) The importance given to craftsmanship in composing poetry. Words have to be selected (from those used in everyday life) and arranged properly, with due regard to the meter used. The words

must be "as sharp as arrows" and the hymn is to be composed carefully, like an artisan constructing a chariot.

(3) Poetry can be understood and appreciated only by the few who are of the same mental nature as the poet (*"sakhāyaḥ sakhyāni jānate"* *Ṛg Veda* 10,71.2c).

Bhaṭṭanāyaka (late ninth and early tenth centuries) seems to have been the first to associate aesthetic experience with mystical experience. The subject is completely dissolved in the object contemplated and the entire surroundings disappear from his attention, because of the concentration on the thing contemplated, in both aesthetic experience and mystical experience. Bhaṭṭanāyaka stated that aesthetic experience is similar to the experience of the Absolute Brahman. Abhinavagupta also accepts Bhaṭṭanāyaka's opinion regarding the similarity between aesthetic experience and the mystic experience of the Absolute.

Bhaṭṭanāyaka seems to have gone one step further to claim the superiority of aesthetic experience to the *yogins*' mystical vision. He says that *rasa* or aesthetic pleasure is poured forth spontaneously by speech like a cow giving forth its milk to its calf; therefore, it is different from (and superior to) that (mystical vision) milked (laboriously) by the *yogins*.

Abhinavagupta recognizes the similarity between aesthetic experience and the mystical experience, but points out the boundary line that separates the two. The mystical experience of the ultimate reality is total and complete, and the *yogin* is far beyond any form of discursive thought. Aesthetic experience gives bliss only temporarily and cannot be considered supreme bliss, though it is superior to the worldly joys. Ānandavardhana was an advocate of *rasa*, but realized its limitations, for in one of his verses quoted in the *Dhvanyāloka* he says that after experimenting with the imaginative poetic vision capable of affording aesthetic experience and also with the intellectual powers for analyzing and understanding the truth about reality, he is exhausted and has realized that the bliss that the devotee gets by contemplation of God is far superior.

Later Jagannātha Paṇḍitarāja, author of the *Rasagaṅgādhara*, states that *rasa* is identical with consciousness (*cit*) or Brahman, and aesthetic experience, in its true sense, is the realization of that consciousness by the removal of the veils covering it.

Rasa is unique and at the ultimate stage there is no plurality. The division of *rasa* into eight or nine is based on the different permanent moods (*sthāyībhāvas*) that lead to the *rasa*. At a still lower level even the *sthāyībhāvas* are sometimes referred to as *rasa*.

2

METAPHYSICS

1. *Vyākaraṇa* as a Philosophical System

The goal of the Indian Grammarians' philosophy, which we here call *vyākaraṇa*, is not mere intellectual knowledge, but direct experience of ultimate truth. Knowledge of grammar resulting in correct speech not only conveys meaning but also enables one to "see" reality. This is the philosophical meaning of the Indian term *darśana*, which literally means "sight". It is this feature that sets Indian philosophy apart from modern western perspectives on language. *Vyākaraṇa* not only addresses itself to the analysis of grammatical rules (though that is certainly important) or to theorizing about the way speech conveys meaning (though that too is achieved), it also insists that one should not be satisfied with mere intellectual conviction but should transform that conviction into direct experience.[1]

From the early Vedas the Indian approach to language has never been narrow or restrictive. Language was examined in relation to consciousness—(the scope of the inquiry) not even limited to human consciousness. All aspects of the world and human experience were regarded as illuminated by language. Indian philosophy also postulated that language had both phenomenal and metaphysical dimensions. It is remarkable that in the ancient hymns of the *Ṛg Veda* a semitechnical vocabulary was already developed to deal with such linguistic matters as grammar, poetic creation, inspiration, illumination, and so on.[2] Although there was careful concern for the phenomenal or outer aspects of language, the Indians always paid equal attention to the inner or metaphysical aspects of language. Indian philosophers of language seem to have successfully avoided the two reductionist mistakes of much western modern language speculation. They did not reduce language to the condition of a merely human convention having only scientific or factual referents; neither did they fall into the error of metaphysical reductionism that so devalues the meanings of human words that language ends up as obscure mysticism.[3] Grammarians like Pāṇini and Patañjali and etymologists like Yāska were clearly concerned with human speech in the everyday empirical world, but they also made room for metaphysical study. Similarly, the great Indian philosopher of language, Bhartṛhari, begins his *Vākyapadīya* with a metaphysical inquiry into the nature and origin of language in relation to Brahman, but then goes on in the second and third chapters to explore technical grammatical points involved in the everyday use of language. In classical Indian thought on language, the study of a particular phenomenon and the contemplation of it as a metaphysical mystery are not mutually exclusive. They are both considered parts of a *darśana* or systematic view of truth.

There is one more aspect of traditional Indian philosophy of language that must be understood by the modern reader. Whereas the contemporary writer often thinks in terms of using language creatively, that is, to create something "original" or "new", the *vyākaraṇa* conception is quite different. The correct or insightful use of language is not seen as conveying new knowledge, but rather as uncovering ancient knowledge that has been obscured due to the accrual of ignorance. The Vedic sage does not produce something new out of his own imagination, but rather relates ordinary things to their forgotten eternal truth. Thus, from the perspective of grammatical philosophy the philosophical study of language and correct grammatical usage are seen as "ignorance-clearing activities", which together open the way to a direct perception of truth.

As a systematic means to knowledge *vyākaraṇa* suffers from certain special difficulties. Language is the object of study in *vyākaraṇa*, yet all thinking about language must, by virtue of human limitations, be done in language itself. One cannot get outside of language so as to examine it objectively. Language must be used to study language from within. *Vyākaraṇa* does not draw back from this difficulty but relishes its challenge; it recognizes that, as Hans-Georg Gadamer puts it, all knowledge of ourselves and all knowledge of the world comes to us through language.[4] Thus the correct knowledge of language is basic to all other approaches to reality—all other *darśanas*.[5]

2. Śabda Brahman and Its Manifestations

It was Bhartṛhari who in *Vākyapadīya* 1.1 first systematically equated Brahman (the Absolute) with language (*śabda*), going on to argue that everything else arises as a manifestation of this one Śabda Brahman.[6] But equating Brahman with language is found much earlier in the Vedic literature. The Asyavāmīya Hymn (*Ṛg Veda* 1.164) states that the ultimate abode of language (*vāc*) is Brahman.[7] Language is described as being at the pinnacle of the universe. Three-quarters of language remain hidden in a cave, while the fourth part fashions creation (*Ṛg Veda* 1.164.10, 41, 45). In *Ṛg Veda* 10.71 it is made clear that the manifestations of Brahman in language are not equally perceived by all people. Those who have purified themselves, namely, the *ṛṣis* or "seers", experience the full manifestation of language. Others, whose ignorance obscures their minds and sense organs, hear little of the fullness of language. The Vedic seers are not considered to be composers of the hymns but rather the "seers" of eternal truth. In *Ṛg Veda* 1.164.37 language is related to cosmic order (*ṛta*) and is understood as logos, which manifests itself as both the uttered word (for use in ritual chanting) and the inner word that reveals truth.

The equation of Brahman with language is also found within the Upaniṣads. In the *Bṛhadāraṇyaka Upaniṣad* 4.1.2 Brahman is identified as the one reality, without a second, which is identical with language. The *Māṇḍūkya Upaniṣad* 3.3 links the unspeakable absolute with the speakable via the symbol of *aum*. *Aum* is described as traversing the phenomenal levels of waking, dreaming, and deep sleep and as reaching out to the absolute. Brahman is identical with language, the basic manifestation of which is *aum*. Bhartṛhari echoes this assertion in *Vākyapadīya* 1.9 in describing *aum* as "the source of all scripture and the common factor of all original causes."[8] *Vyākaraṇa* scholars have focused on those Vedas and Upaniṣads which equate language, Brahman, and absolute reality. Passages that state otherwise are ignored or passed over. This practice, of course, is usual within each of the Indian philosophical schools (*darśanas*)—at least in those which claim to be orthodox (*āstika*) or grounded on the Vedas.

The Vedas occupy a primary place in the manifestation of Śabda Brahman, as well as being the means by which Śabda Brahman may be realized and release experienced. The Veda, though One, is divided into many and spreads out through its various recensions and manifesting sounds (*dhvani*) to the diversity of people. Although the experience of the Vedas may be many, the reality they reveal is the one Śabda Brahman. Vedic language is at once the creator and sustainer of the world cycles and the revealer of the Divine. Language is taken as having Divine origin (*daivī vāk*), as Spirit descending and embodying itself in phenomena, assuming various guises and disclosing its truth to the sensitive soul.[9] As Aurobindo describes it,

> The language of the Veda itself is *śruti*, a rhythm not composed by the intellect but heard, a divine Word that came vibrating out of the Infinite to the inner audience of the man who had

> previously made himself fit for the impersonal knowledge. The words themselves, *dṛṣṭi* and *śruti*, sight and hearing, are Vedic expressions; these and cognate words signify, in the esoteric terminology of the hymns, revelatory knowledge and the contents of inspiration.[10]

In contrast with western views of revelation, there is nothing miraculous in the manifestation of the Vedas to the *ṛṣi*. The *ṛṣi* "sees" the divine truth not because it is given to him in an act of grace, but because he has made himself fit, through heroic practices of self-purification, to "see" the truth directly. He then puts it into spoken words, the Vedic hymns, for the purpose of helping others who are still caught in ignorance to purify themselves until they too have the experience of directly "seeing" Śabda Brahman. *Vyākaraṇa* has the special task of keeping the Vedas uncorrupted so that the manifestation of Śabda Brahman remains available to all in pristine form.[11] Should *vyākaraṇa* fail to provide this service and allow the Vedas to become corrupted through sloppy usage and transmission, then the possibility of realizing truth could be lost for the generations yet to come in this cycle of creation. For this reason *vyākaraṇa* is described by Bhartṛhari as more important than other *darśanas*. As the other schools base themselves on the Vedas, the loss or corruption of the Vedas would render the fruits of their particular approaches useless and misleading.

The fact that Indian philosophy is based on oral traditions[12] is another reason why *vyākaraṇa* takes its teaching to be of primary importance. Because the authoritative manifestation of Śabda Brahman is found first in spoken form and only secondarily in written forms, the role of *vyākaraṇa* in providing the rules and teaching that keeps the oral forms of language pure is of fundamental importance to all other philosophic schools. For example, Pāṇini's *Aṣṭādhyāyī* is a grammar founded upon oral usage rather than upon etymology or derivation.[13] The same stress on language's oral character is found in the discussions offered by Patañjali in his *Mahābhāṣya* and Bhartṛhari in the *Vākyapadīya* of the way uttered words convey meaning. It is perhaps worth noting in passing that for Indian philosophy, the normative form of language is not written but oral and that *vyākaraṇa* plays the important role of keeping the oral form disciplined and pure in its presentation. Without this purity the truth-bearing capacity of language could be restricted and the manifestation of Śabda Brahman obscured. Knowledge of the Vedas is not simply the "book-learning" of main ideas that characterizes modern western scholarship. In the Indian tradition, language is only fully alive when spoken. Thus knowledge of the Vedas includes and requires the ability to speak the words with correct accent and meter. And consistent with the oral emphasis, thinking is seen as internal speaking to which not enough *prāṇa* or breath has been added to make it overt. Writing, the focus of attention for the modern West, is seen by *vyākaraṇa* as a coded recording of the oral, which can never perfectly represent all the nuances of the spoken word and is therefore always secondary. The *vyākaraṇa* approach is opposite to that taken in modern western scholarship. In modern biblical studies, for example, the scholar's aim is to get back to the earliest available written manuscript and then to use it as a criterion against which to check the text that is in use today. The rationale is that errors that have crept in over the years would not be present in the earlier manuscript. In addition, the modern school of Form Criticism has argued that before many of the scriptures (such as the Gospels) were written down there was a period of oral transmission, during which time the text (for example, the original teachings of Jesus) was modified by the needs of the people and the particular conditions under which they lived. This period of oral transmission is judged to be unreliable due to its failure to carry forward the original sayings in a pure and unchanged form.[14]

The *vyākaraṇa* practice is the exact opposite. When India achieved independence in 1947, one of the first acts of the new government was to establish a commission of senior scholars to go from place to place and listen to the assembled Brahmins reciting the Vedas. They would listen for errors in meter, accent, and *saṃdhi* and for any loss or change in words. It was the rigorous practice of the *Prātiśākhyas* that was being checked by the senior scholars. They had mastered the *Prātiśākhyas* and pure presentation of the Vedas through many years of careful oral practice and checking with their teachers. And the teachers of the present senior scholars had acquired their expertise not from books hut from oral practice with the best teachers of the generation before them, who in turn had been taught by the best teachers before them, and so on in an unbroken oral tradition back to the Vedas.

It is not the dead or entombed manuscript but the correct and clear enunciation of the word in the here and now that makes for a living language and scripture. Large numbers of copies of "The Living Bible" stacked in bookstores or reverently placed on personal bookshelves are not true language or living scripture, according to *vyākaraṇa*. Only when a passage is so well learned that it is with one wherever one goes is the word really known. In such a state the words become part of or, even more exactly, *are* one's consciousness in the act of speaking. Books and all written forms are not knowledge in this sense of the word; rather they represent a lower, inferior, second order of language suitable only for the dull or the uneducated. The *vyākaraṇa* provides the training rules for the oral learning of language and for the presentation of the Vedic word in its pure form.

For *vyākaraṇa*, then, spoken language is the medium through which

Śabda Brahman is manifested, and the Vedas are the criterion expression of that manifestation.

3. The Function of Time

In Bhartṛhari's systematization of *vyākaraṇa* philosophy time (*kāla*) is assigned the function of enabling the one Śabda Brahman to appear as the many. This position is consistent with that given time in the *Atharva Veda* and the *Maitrī Upaniṣad*.[15] In *Vākyapadīya* 1.3 Bhartṛhari describes the creation of the objects of the universe as occurring in the first instance through the creative power of Śabda Brahman's *kāla* or time power. *Kāla* is not different from Śabda Brahman but is that aspect of Śabda Brahman which allows manifested sequence to come into being. When such time sequences appear as differentiated objects, then time as a power seems to be different from Śabda Brahman, but really it is not (*Vākyapadīya* 1.2). *Vākyapadīya* 1.3 states that all other powers within the created universe are in the first instance governed by the creative power of time. Through time things come to be and pass away. Time is the efficient cause by which Brahman controls the cycles of the universe.

Two illustrations are offered by Bhartṛhari to make clear his meaning. The power of time in the creative process is like that of the wire-puller in a puppet play (*Vākyapadīya* 3.9.4). Just as the wire-puller is in complete control of the puppet play so *kāla* has full control over the running of the world. Ordinary cause-and-effect processes cannot operate unless *kāla* or time power infuses them with life-force. This control of ordinary cause and effect by time is further illustrated in relation to the strings a hunter ties to the feet of small birds that he uses as bait for larger ones. The small birds can fly over a limited distance but they cannot go beyond the length of their strings. Like the strings controlling the movement of birds, so the objects of the created world are controlled by the "string of time" (*Vākyapadīya* 3.9.15).

It is in *Vākyapadīya* 3.9 that Bhartṛhari presents his detailed analysis of time. Just as number measures material objects, time measures activity (3.9.2). In answer to the question of how activities are measured by time, Bhartṛhari states in verse 3, "In the creation (arising), existence and destruction (of beings) which possess these (activities), time, remaining in a divided state, is said to be the (instrumental) cause."[16] Helārāja, in his commentary, explains the meaning of the verse as follows. Time is the cause of the birth, existence, and decay of everything. Thus we say some things are born in the spring, others in the autumn. The same can be said about their existence and their death. Time, though one, differentiates or sequences things through states of birth, existence, and decay. It is in this sense that time is called the "wire-puller" of the universe. Yet, these everyday changes of state or sequences of action are not the true nature of time but superimpositions. Time in its own nature, as one with Śabda Brahman, is transcendent of all change, yet also its cause.

To one familiar with Advaita Vedānta, the preceding description of time sounds very similar to Śaṃkara's notion of *māyā* in relation to Brahman. This view is certainly held by two eminent contemporary interpreters of the *Vākyapadīya*, Gaurinath Sastri[17] and K. A. Subramania Iyer.[18] As we examine Bhartṛharis' description of *kāla* in *Vākyapadīya* 3.9, we will test this contention.

Verse 14 of *Vākyapadīya* 3.9 is worth careful attention in this regard. It reads, "By means of activities similar to the turning of the waterwheel, the eternal and all-pervasive time turns out (*kalayati*) all the fragments (*kalāḥ* — objects) and thus acquires the name of *kāla* (time)." Like the ever-renewed pushing or lifting up of water by the waterwheel, so the all-pervading and all-penetrating time drives or pushes (*kalayati*) beings or objects, releasing them from their material causes and making them move. That is why time is given the appropriate name of *kāla*. Helārāja goes on to observe that what Bhartṛhari means to say is,

> The soul of the universe is but one, called "*para-Brahman*" i.e., the real Being. This same one, due to its being the agent of manifold actions, is defined as possessing unlimited power. And thus, manifesting successive beings which revolve like the turnings of a wheel, it "drives" (*kalayati*) the beings. Therefore it is called time (*kāla*). This all-pervading one is independent. For this very reason, it has been established as being an independent power in the *Vākyapadīya*.[19]

If Helārāja is right, then Bhartṛhari views time as a power of Śabda Brahman, independent of all beings and objects yet also inherent in them, pushing them through the successive changes of life. Instead of the passive external superimposition of the successive changes upon Brahman (the Advaita model), the image here is more characteristic of urgent change through pregnant forces within Śabda Brahman.

The distinction between Bhartṛhari's conception of time and the Advaita Vedānta view of *māyā* is not that the locus of time or *māyā* is in Brahman (for both schools seem to agree on this point), but rather a question of the ontological power ascribed to time or *māyā*. Bhartṛhari's time doctrine emphasizes the driving (*kalayati*) power inherent in Śabda Brahman, which is the first cause of the bursting forth of worldly phenomena. The Advaita conception of *māyā*, though it does indeed (in the Vivaraṇa tradition, at least) locate *māyā* in Brahman[20] does not attribute to *māyā* the same degree of ontological "pregnancy" or "driving force" as Bhartṛhari ascribes to time. While it is acknowledged that *māyā* has two aspects, obscuring (*āvaraṇa*) and projective (*vikṣepa*), the stress in Advaita interpretation is on the former more than the latter. For the Advaitin, the focus is on *māyā's* obscuring of Brahman; for Bhartṛhari, it is the projective power or driving force of time that occupies center stage. While this difference may at first appear to be merely a question of emphasis, a substantive distinction appears when the ontological status of the phenomenal projection itself is analyzed. While for Advaita the projected world of *māyā* is neither real nor unreal but inexplicable (*anirvacanīya*), the time-driven world of Bhartṛhari, though increasingly impure as it becomes manifested as worldly phenomena, never loses its direct ontological identity with Brahman. The relation between the phenomenal world and Brahman for Bhartṛhari is continuous and does not have the mysterious break of an "all or nothing" sort that Śaṃkara's *māyā* doctrine and its rope-snake analogy requires. Whereas superimposition (*adhyāsa*) is a fitting term for Śaṃkara,[21] it does not seem appropriate to Bhartṛhari. The illustrations offered in the *Vākyapadīya* are more often associated with images of Śabda Brahman bursting forth in illumination (*sphoṭa*), of pregnancy (the peacock egg producing all the colors of creation), and of driving force like the pushing-up or lifting-up action of the waterwheel (*kalayati*).

According to Bhartṛhari, time is a creative power, while for Advaita (the Vivaraṇa Advaitin, at least) the obscuring function of *avidyā* is equated with *māyā*.[22] Bhartṛhari in his commentary on 1.1 describes *avidyā* as the diversity of phenomena created by Śabda Brahman's time power. It is probably open to question whether the term *avidyā* meant the same for Bhartṛhari as it came to be defined by Śaṃkara some centuries later. Modern commentators sometimes incorrectly apply concepts they have learned from Advaita Vedānta when interpreting the *Vākyapadīya*. Notions such as "superimposition" (*adhyāsa*), if seen through Advaita eyes, are probably misleading and unhelpful in understanding Bhartṛhari. We may make more progress by staying with the words of the verses and the clear illustrations offered in the commentary.

Bhartṛhari apparently never wrote a commentary for chapter 3. At present only Helārāja's *Ṭīkā* (ca. A.D. 1050-1100) is available.[23] In *Vākyapadīya* 3.9.62, Bhartṛhari discusses directly the ontological status of time, and Helārāja adds some helpful comments. Bhartṛhari observes that there are different doctrines about time: some call it "power" (*śakti*), some call it "soul" (*ātman*), and others, "deity" (*devatā*). Time is the first (stage) of *avidyā*, and does not exist in knowledge.[24] Helārāja in his *Ṭīkā* further describes time as an independent power of Brahman and discusses its ontological status in relation to *avidyā*: "According to Bhartṛhari, time is the *svātantrya śakti* of Brahman.... Due to *avidyā*, there is, first of all, appearance of diversity. Diversity is temporal and spatial. The former comes first. Consciousness, at the stage called *paśyantī*, is without any sequence. When it becomes associated with *prāṇavṛtti*, it appears to have sequence due to time."[25] As this comment makes clear, there are three ontological levels in Bhartṛhari's thought: Brahman, his powers of time and space, and the diversity of the phenomenal world. Once again he contrasts with Śaṃkara's Advaita, where there is only one ontological level—Brahman—with *māyā* as an epistemological second level (which is neither real nor unreal but inexplicable). For Bhartṛhari the highest ontological level is pure Brahman without sequence or diversity. It is the culmination of our experience of *vāc* or language.[26] Although time is inherent in Śabda Brahman at this stage, no sequence has yet occurred—it is still pure potentiality. The next ontological level, in descending order, is *madhyamā*. It is at this level that time begins to push or drive delimited portions of Śabda Brahman into sequence, which it accomplishes with the help of *prāṇa* or breath. In our experience of language this stage corresponds to the separation of the unitary *sphoṭa* into the mental sequence of thoughts. The full-blown appearance of diversity appears when time has released all the secondary cause-effect relations that have been waiting as stored memory traces (*saṃskāra*) or "seed states" in all the cycles of the universe. It is in this third or *vaikharī* level that the power of time as the sequence evidenced in ordinary cause-effect relations is fully experienced. To return to Bhartṛhari's own analogy, at this stage we see the birds on time's strings flying about to the full limit that their strings allow. Time is thus the governing power of all activity in the universe of manifested objects. It is time that drives or pushes objects into action to the point at which their own secondary cause-effect relations take hold. But it is also the behind-the-scenes activity of time that controls the extent of the secondary actions of objects, along with their moment of decay or withdrawal.

The notion of time functioning by permitting and preventing worldly activity is stated in *Vākyapadīya* 3.9.4 and reappears frequently throughout section 9: "Time has been called the wire-puller of the world Machine. It regulates the universe through prevention and permission."[27] The Sanskrit terms involved are *abhyanujñā* (permission) and *pratibandha* (prevention). As the wire-puller of the universe, time allows some things to appear at a particular time and prevents others from appearing. This scheduling activity is most important, for without it everything would appear simultaneously and there would be mass confusion.[28] The function of time called "permission" allows things to be born and to continue in existence.[29] By its other function, prevention, time obstructs the inherent capacities of objects and "old age" is then experienced. It is in this way that the stages of life and the seasons are ordered. When time is functioning under its impulse of prevention, decay (*jarā*) occurs. Decay and growth (*krama*) operate like pairs of opposites. When decay is active, growth is blocked, and vice versa.[30] But the underlying substratum of all of this activity is the driving impulse of time.[31] Time remains eternal even though the actions of growth and decay come and go.

As a result of the activity of growth and decay, time, which is one, attains the states of past, present, and future. Thus when an action ceases, time, conditioned by that action, is called past. When something is about to happen, time, conditioned by that event, is called future. When action has been initiated but is not yet completed, time is then called present.[32] In this way the one transcendent reality—time—is experienced, through the actions of the secondary causes it releases or restrains, to be sequenced into past, present, and future. Time, says Bhartṛhari, is like the everflowing current of a river, which deposits some things on the river bank and at the same time takes away others.[33] So it is that the seasons change, as symbolized by the motions of the sun and stars. As Helārāja puts it, "The seasons may be looked upon as the abode of time, because it appears as the seasons. The power called 'Freedom' of Brahman is really time and it appears diversified as the different seasons like Spring, etc."[34] Thus the appearance of the universe, which is really without sequence, as something with sequence, is the work of time.[35]

In another analogy, past, present, and future are said to be like three paths on which objects move without any confusion.[36] Helārāja's comment likens this view to the Sāṃkhya-Yoga explanation of time found in Vyāsa's commentary on *Yogasūtra* 2.13. Here the activity of time is equated with the ever-present movement of the *guṇas* on the three paths of being (*adhvan*). The notion that objects and mental states do not all occur simultaneously due to the prevention and permission activities of time is clearly stated. The psychological mechanism involved is that of inherent tendencies or memory traces (*saṃskāra*), which sprout like seeds when the conditions created by the ever-changing *guṇas* are favorable.[37] The point of this parallel between Sāṃkhya-Yoga and *vyākaraṇa* doctrine is to show how the three apparently conflicting qualities can coexist in harmony. As Helārāja puts it,

> Just as the three ingredients, having the characteristics of serenity (*sattva*), activity (*rajas*) and inertia (*tamas*), though existing simultaneously due to their eternity, acquire the subordinate and principal relation and effect beings through their peculiar evo-

> lution, in a proper manner in the splendor of their own course of action, so also, these (three) time-divisions, by the magnificence of their own power (become) capable of effecting sequence in external aspects.[38]

The past and the future hide objects, so they are like *tamas* or darkness (says Bhartṛhari). The present enables us to see the objects, so it is like light or the *sattva* of the Sāṃkhyas. *Rajas* stands for the activity of time itself.[39] For both Sāṃkhya-Yoga and the Grammarian the harmonious coexistence of objects on the three paths of time makes the ordered sequence of the world possible. Time, like an eternal road, is the substratum on which the objects of the world come and go. The road, like time, always remains the same.[40]

The essence of Bhartṛhari's viewpoint is that time is an independent power (*śakti*) of Śabda Brahman. Time is characterized by its two energies of prevention or decay and permission or growth. If we look for the precursors of this doctrine of time, we can find a continuity back through Patañjali's *Mahābhāṣya* to the Vedas. Although Pāṇini is silent on the philosophical aspects of time, Patañjali in his *Mahābhāṣya* discusses time in two places. At 2.2.5, *kāla* is described in terms of the growth or decay of bodies. *Vākyapadīya* 3.9.13 seems to be a direct reference to this passage of the *Mahābhāṣya*. Again, at 4.2.3 of the *Mahābhāṣya*, Patañjali defines time as eternal.[41] But Patañjali does not say whether time is to be taken as a power of Brahman (Bhartṛhari's view) or as a substance (the Nyāya-Vaiśeṣika view).[42] In Nyāya-Vaiśeṣika theory time is viewed as an independent substance. Time is present everywhere as the eternal connecting relations between pairs of objects.[43] Some later Nyāya-Vaiśeṣika theories seem to have followed Bhartṛhari's lead and identified time and space with *ākāśa* and with Brahman.[44]

A direct precursor for Bhartṛhari's view in the *Vākyapadīya* is available in the *Maitrī Upaniṣad* discussion of time. As mentioned earlier, in *Maitrī* 6.15 time is described as the form of Brahman that has parts. These parts (namely, the year, and so on) grow and decay. Time is said to cook all things in the Great Soul (*mahātman*).

Bhartṛhari has on occasion been mistakenly called a Buddhist. The Buddhist (Mādhyamika) view of time, however, is radically different from that of the *Vākyapadīya*. For the Buddhist there is no present time (*vartamānakāla*) apart from the past and future.[45] But the Buddhist emphasis on the constant process of change—and thus the necessary reference to past and future—seems too one-sided when it leaves no room for the present. We do experience the present as an ongoing moment, and this concept Bhartṛhari accommodates successfully.

Bhartṛhari's notion of the dynamic limiting function of time (*kālaśakti*) lies behind the discussion of the levels of language in the *Vākyapadīya*. After setting forth the absolute nature of Brahman as being the one eternal essence of word and consciousness, Bhartṛhari introduces the notion of time as the power or means by which this one unchanging absolute (Śabda Brahman) manifests itself as the dynamic diversity mankind experiences as creation. Time is the creative power of Śabda Brahman and is thus responsible for the birth, death, and continuity of everything in the cosmos. Time is one, but when broken or limited into sequences appears as moments or actions. These segments of time are mentally categorized as seconds or minutes. Such limited segments of time are then mentally unified into day, week, month, and year. In the same fashion notions of past, present, and future are developed. When time is viewed as an action not yet completed, the notion of the present is established. An action that has been completed is time as past, and an action yet to be completed is time as future. All of ordinary life is sequenced by these three powers of time. Yet all the while, declares Bhartṛhari, there is really no sequence at all. From the ultimate viewpoint all three powers of time are constantly present. Time is one. Although the effects of the three powers of time (that is past, present, and future) are mutually contradictory, they function without causing any disorder in the cosmos. They are like three paths on which objects move about without any confusion.

Bhartṛhari enters into this deep discussion of time in relation to the absolute not as a fascinating metaphysical aside, but to explain how the unitary Śabda Brahman manifests itself in experience as the diversity of words called language. As a Grammarian, he is also providing a metaphysical basis for the experience of the tenses past, present, and future in language. And it is past and future that have the veiling function of keeping one apart from the absolute eternal present. In religious terms union with the eternal present is union with the divine, which, for Bhartṛhari, is the inherent goal toward which all language, all grammar, is reaching.

4. *Vyākaraṇa* as a Means of Release (*Śabdapūrvayoga*)

For the Hindu the ultimate goal of philosophy is liberation (*mokṣa*). Before Bhartṛhari, Patañjali in his *Mahābhāṣya* included in the aims of grammatical study (*vyākaraṇa*) the attainment of heaven (*svarga*) through the correct use of words and liberation from bondage (*mokṣa*).[46] While it is clear that for Patañjali liberation is the divine Word, he does not specify how this divine Word is to be achieved. Satyakam Varma solves this problem by assuming that the Patañjali of the *Mahābhāṣya* is the same as the Patañjali of the *Yogasūtras* and that the description of how *yoga* of the Word is to take place is given in the latter work.[47] While not all scholars agree that the same Patañjali authored both the *Mahābhāṣya* and the *Yogasūtras*, Satyakam Varma's suggestion of obtaining help from the *Yogasūtras* has independent merit in the attempt to understand the grammarian concept of *śabdapūrvayoga* or the *yoga* of the Word (literally, *yoga* preceded by the Word). For present purposes, however, an attempt will be made to interpret *śabdapūrvayoga* by using only the *Vākyapadīya*.

Bhartṛhari emphasizes the aim of grammar as leading both to heaven and to liberation not only in the *Vākyapadīya* but also in his commentary on Patañjali's *Mahābhāṣya*.[48] At the beginning of the *Vākyapadīya* Bhartṛhari says that grammar is the door leading to liberation (1.14); it is the straight, royal road for those who desire salvation (1.16); and by means of it one attains the supreme Brahman (1.22). At the end of the first chapter Bhartṛhari returns to the topic and states that "the purification of the word is the means to the attainment of the Supreme Self. One who knows the essence of its activity attains the immortal Brahman" (1.131). The yoga of the Word, then, has the power to take one from the ordinary experience of the word all the way to union with the Divine.

A. *The First Stage*

The first requisite step is the purging of corrupt forms from one's everyday language. While Bhartṛhari allows that corrupt forms of words can convey meaning, spiritual merit can be attained only by the knowledge and use of the correct forms of words, which is the spiritual role of grammar. As Bhartṛhari puts it in the *vṛtti* on 1.131: when speech is purified by the adoption of the grammatically correct forms and all obstruction in the shape of incorrect forms is removed, there results a spiritual merit that brings the experience of well-being (*abhyudaya*). This *abhyudaya* is also translated into English as "moral power" of the sort that begins to move us in the direction of identifying ourselves with the divine.[49] This identification is the first step in the yoga of the Word—the repeated use of grammatically correct language that generates more and more *abhyudaya* until the way is prepared through the lower levels of language (*vaikharī* and *madhyamā vāk*) for the dawning of the mystical vision (*paśyantī*).

For the modern mind it is hard to imagine just how the grammatically correct use of words could be understood as generating moral power, spiritual well-being, and the dawning of the mystical vision. In order for us to empathize with this first step in the yoga of the Word, it will help to remind ourselves how Bhartṛhari understands the function of time in relation to the correct use of words. The appearance of the unitary Śabda Brahman as having parts (words) and sequence (word order) is the work of time.[50] The entire universe is like a puppet show with time as its wire-puller. Time regulates the universe through prevention or decay and permission.[51] Time controls the birth, death, and sequence of all objects, including all words. Time allows some things to appear at a particular time and prevents others from appearing. As the sequencing activity of all experience, time translates into grammar as the rules by which the appearance and disappearance of words in correct linguistic sequence is to take place. Underlying all activity, including all linguistic activity, is the driving impulse of time.[52] Time, as the first power of the divine Word, remains eternal, though the activity of language may come and go.[53]

Incorrect usage results from attempts by humans to change the sequencing of language to suit themselves, without regard for the divine Word. Such ego-centered word use leaves behind memory traces, which serve to conflict and obscure the proper sequencing of Śabda Brahman by its time power. Without the aid of grammar and its purifying rules, such a confused mental state is the usual result. The truth of the Vedic teaching and glimpses of Śabda Brahman are obscured within consciousness by the layers of traces laid down by incorrect word use. Strict adherence to grammar, and its teaching of correct word use, gradually results in removal of these obscuring traces from consciousness. As the proper, non-ego-centered sequencing of language is established, the truth of the Vedic teaching can be seen and responded to. Then increased moral power and the first glimpses of the divine Word are experienced. This achievement is the truly creative function of the Word—not the making of something new by human ego-centered activity (the modern western notion of creativity), but the revelation of the real nature of things through the reflective power of language.[54] Only when the rules of grammar are followed is word use crystalline enough to let the divine show through. Repeated practice of proper word use restores to language its mirrorlike quality, enabling a reflection of the transcendent Word to take place. Such a polishing and purification of the mind and its constituent word structures is the goal of stage one in the yoga of the Word.

B. *The Second Stage*

Stage two occurs when one focuses on the purified reflective power of the word until union with Śabda Brahman is realized. Bhartṛhari quotes some verses describing the process in the *vṛtti* on *Vākyapadīya* 1.131:

> "After taking his stand on the word which lies beyond the activity of breath, after having taken rest in oneself by the union resulting in the suppression of sequence,"

"After having purified speech and after having rested it on the mind, after having broken its bonds and made it bond-free,"
"After having reached the inner light, he with his knots cut, becomes united with the Supreme Light."[55]

The middle passage should be taken first. Speech has been purified (stage one) until the mind is using only correct grammatical structures, which is what the phrase "resting it on the mind" implies. The purging of ego attachment is essential in such a purification and must be carried even farther in stage two. The "breaking of bonds" referred to are the memory traces and their tainted motivations left by egocentric activity—in either spoken words (*vaikharī vāk*) or inner thoughts (*madhyamā vāk*). These ego bonds are removed by meditating on the divine Word (Śabda Brahman) so that the purified forms of language are being clearly reflected. The amount of such meditation required will be equal to the strength needed to negate the egocentric traces stored up within the mind.

The first passage emphasizes the need for "suppression of sequence." The function of time in sequencing the divine Word into thoughts and uttered sounds must now be suppressed. While such sequencing of language is essential in ordinary day-to-day activities, as well as in the understanding of the Vedic teaching, there comes a time when all that must be left behind. Immersion in worldly life as a student or householder, while necessary and good in itself, is not the ultimate goal. Study of the Vedic texts, while necessary, is not to be clung to as if it were the final end. Attachment to language use in either of these areas is only indicative of a failure to go beyond ego. Especially damaging is ego attachment to the Vedic words themselves—a textual literalism or fundamentalism reminiscent of a line from T.S. Eliot's play *Murder in the Cathedral*: "To do the right deed for the wrong reason is the greatest sin."[56] Spiritual pride is always tragic, and spiritual pride attached to the divine Word is especially so. The *vyakāraṇa* practice of *śabdapūrvayoga* guards against such a result by insisting that the sequenced word of scripture be allowed to carry one beyond itself to liberation. This obstacle will undoubtedly be the most difficult one for the grammarian yogi to overcome. After having honed his grammatical style and knowledge of scripture to a fine edge, it will be difficult to let go of that laboriously won achievement. But that is exactly what Bhartṛhari requires, otherwise the traces of ego attachment to the uttered word will block out the reflection of the divine in it.

Giving up attachment to sequenced language, purified though it may be, implies moving from spoken words (*vaikharī*) and inner thoughts (*madhyamā*) to the direct mystical vision (*paśyantī*, *pratibhā*, or *sphoṭa*). As the first passage indicates, the function of breath here is important.

In *vaikharī* breath is very active in producing the sequence of uttered sounds. At the level of inner thought (*madhyamā*) breath is still active, though in a more subtle way, in fashioning sequences of thought. *Paśyantī* lies beyond the activity of breath and sequence.[57] The mind is quiet and focused, allowing the *pratibhā* or intuitive perception of Śabda Brahman. Thus, through *śabdapūrvayoga*, the yoga of the Word, we are to pass on from the gross sequence to the subtle sequence and finally to that stage in which sequence is entirely eliminated. Like a perfectly still pond, consciousness, when stilled from its sequencing activity, clearly reflects the reality before it. For Bhartṛhari, it is Śabda Brahman, the essence of consciousness, that stands revealed at the center of the stilled mind.

The third passage quoted by Bhartṛhari reflects just such an experience: "After having reached the inner light, he, with his knots cut, becomes united with the Supreme Light." Although the "cutting of the knots" is not defined by Bhartṛhari, Vṛṣabha describes it as a cutting of the bonds and knots of "ego sense." Going beyond the ego-sense of "I" and "mine" is obviously a major challenge in the yoga of the Word. It is repeatedly mentioned by Bhartṛhari. For example, in the *vṛtti* on *Vākyapadīya* 1.130 he says that those who know the yoga of the Word break the knots of ego-sense and are merged with the divine Word. If ego attachment in any form remains, the *paśyantī* stage will not be fully realized. In the *vṛtti* on 1.142, *paśyantī* seems to be endowed with a number of phases (of increasingly pure reflection). In the lowest it seems to be still echoing some of the faint sequencing activity of *madhyamā*. At a higher level it assumes a quality in which all word forms are submerged beyond recognition. At the highest level it completely transcends all associations with word forms. Hence *paśyantī* can reflect worldly word forms and can also totally transcend them. Even though it may come into contact with the sequenced and often egocentric word forms of *vaikharī* and *madhyamā*, it remains pure, untouched, and spiritual in nature. To those who are trapped in ego knots and impure word usage, *paśyantī* may appear to be mixed up and contaminated. But in reality it is not. As one adopts correct word forms through a rigorous and reverent study of grammar, one's consciousness is purified and the true inner vision of *paśyantī* revealed. As Bhartṛhari puts it, those whose inner vision is unobstructed (with ego knots) see, without error, the power of words and know the true nature of things.[58] The word forms are seen for what they are, namely, partial manifestations of the one divine Word, which in *paśyantī* stands clearly revealed. The yoga of the Word is the meditational exercise in which the mind is concentrated on the unity of the divine Word and turned away from the diverse thoughts and sounds that manifest it.[59] The whole meditational process, with its culmination in the vision of the divine Word and final reunion with it, is poetically described in the *Ṛg Veda* stanza "Maho devo martyāṃ āviveśa":

> The spiritual aspirant reaches the Essence of Speech—the pure luminous Eternal Verbum, which lies beyond the vital plane (*prāṇavṛttim atikrānte*) by withdrawing his mind from external nature (*ātmānaṃ saṃhṛtya*) and fixing it up on his inner nature (*ātmani*). This entails the dissolution of temporal sequence of thought activity (*krama-saṃhāra-yogena*). The purification of the Verbum results from this and the aspirant enters into it having severed all his ties with the material objective plane. This leads him to the attainment of the internal light and he becomes identical with the undying and undecaying Spirit, the Word Absolute.[60]

Bhartṛhari claims that in the spirituality attained through the practice of the yoga of the Word a greater measure of divine light shines through: "Those persons in whom correct speech exists in a greater measure, in them also resides, in a greater measure, the holy form of the creator."[61] And as long as a grammarian in the state of spirituality is alive, the divine light of the Word resides in him as in a covered vessel. When such a one dies this holy luster merges into Śabda Brahman, its source.[62]

The yoga of the Word demonstrates that the meaningfulness of words is not merely intellectual, it is meaningfulness that has spiritual power. With the proper yoga, words have the power to remove ignorance (*avidyā*), reveal truth (*dharma*), and realize liberation (*mokṣa*). The *vṛtti* on *Vākyapadīya* 1.5 states it clearly: "Just like making gifts, performing austerities and practicing continence are means of attaining heaven. It has been said: When, by practicing the Vedas, the vast darkness is removed, that supreme, bright, imperishable light comes into being in this very birth."[63] It is not only this lofty goal of final release that is claimed for the spiritual power of words, but also the very availability of human reasoning. Without the fixed power of words to convey meaning, inference through words could not take place.[64] Because of the power inherent in *mantras* for both human inference and divine truth, great care must be given to the yoga of words.

In word yoga, the repeated chanting of *mantras* is an instrument of power. The more traces there are to be overcome the more repetitions are needed. *Vākyapadīya* 1.14 *Vṛtti* suggests that repeated use of correct *mantras* removes all impurities, purifies all knowledge, and leads to liberation. The psychological mechanism is described by Bhartṛhari as a holding of the *sphoṭa* in place by continued chanting. Just as from a distance, or in semidarkness, it takes repeated cognition of an object before one sees it correctly, so also repeated chanting of the *mantras* results in the *sphoṭa* being perceived in all its fullness.[65] Maṇḍana Miśra describes it as a series of progressively clearer impressions until a clear and correct apprehension takes place in the end.[66] To begin with, such *mantra* chanting will be mainly at the *vaikharī* or outer word level. But as spiritual improvement is made, the chant will be more and more internalized on the *madhyamā* or inner word level. Eventually all sequenced chanting activity will submerge into the still steady *mantra samādhi* of *paśyantī*, and the final goal of the yoga of the Word will have been realized.

For the *vyākaraṇa* our outer words and inner thoughts are but reflections, more or less perfect, of the one divine Word. The great *ṛṣis* or seers recognized this fact and made themselves empty channels through which the divine Word could reverberate with little distortion. The great Grammarian teachers, basing themselves on the *ṛṣis*' utterances, formulated this wisdom into a teaching informing all of life and even into a pathway to final liberation.

While not all may agree with the spiritual vision of the Hindu Grammarians it must be conceded that we do find here a view of language that makes sense of poetry, revealed scripture, science, and the mystical chanting of *mantras*, and which in addition strongly resonates with our ordinary everyday experience of coffee-cup chat. It is a way of seeing language that effectively explains why it is that sometimes when we listen we do not hear. It also teaches how to remove the obstructions in one's consciousness so that real hearing becomes possible and suggests in a different way the ultimate wisdom of the observation. "In the beginning was the Word, and the Word was with God, and the Word was God" (John 1:1).

3

EPISTEMOLOGY

Recent western thought has focused much attention on the relation between language and knowledge, but it has consistently taken a narrower perspective than *vyākaraṇa* would accept. Within the contemporary school of linguistic philosophy, language seems to be restricted to the printed word and then analyzed for a one-to-one correspondence with objective reality. While the computer-like functions of language must be highly respected, modern linguists and philosophers often seem to consign all other dimensions of the word to the unreality of a mystic's silence.[1] Ernst Cassirer has taken a much broader perspective including the natural sciences, the humanities, and all human cultural activity of language.[2] *Vyākaraṇa* would applaud Cassirer but expand the realm of language even further. According to Bhartṛhari, "There is no cognition without the operation of words; all cognition is shot through and through by the word. All knowledge is illumined through the word."[3] The fundamental epistemological presupposition from Bhartṛhari's perspective is that the problem of meaning is basic. It is through the meaning conveyed by words that all knowledge is experienced. In this sense, then, the philosophy of language is not just another school of philosophy but is the basic foundation for all philosophy. As T.R.V. Murti has so aptly put it, "The problem of what we can know is closely bound up with the question of what we can say. It is only thought as expressed in words that can be understood, communicated and criticized. Language is not an accidental, dispensable garb which could be put on and put off. It grows with thought, or rather thought grows with it. In the ultimate analysis they may be identical."[4] Meaning and cognition are understood to manifest themselves together as expressions of one deep spiritual impulse to know and to communicate. Consciousness (*caitanya*) is identical with speech (*vāc*).[5]

1. *Śabda* AS *Pramāṇa* IN RELATION TO OTHER *Pramāṇas*

Before a discussion of *śabda* or testimony as a means of knowledge (*pramāṇa*), it may be useful to sketch the scholastic Indian conception of knowledge (*pramā*). In Sanskrit the word *jñāna* stands for all kinds of cognition, irrespective of the questions of truth or falsehood. *Pramā*, however, is used to designate only a true cognition (*yathārthajñāna*) as distinct from a false one (*mithyājñāna*). A *pramāṇa* is an active and unique cause of a *pramā* or knowledge.[6] The Sāṃkhya and Yoga schools of Indian philosophy accept three *pramāṇas*: *pratyakṣa* (perception), *anumāna* (inference), and *śabda* (testimony).[7] The Mīmāṃsā school defines six *pramāṇas*: *pratyakṣa, anumāna, śabda, upamāna* (analogy), *arthāpatti* (presumption), and *abhāva* (nonapprehension).[8] The same six *pramāṇas* are also stated by Vedānta.[9] Of course, there are many differences of definition regarding specific *pramāṇas* among the schools.

Within *vyākaraṇa*, Bhartṛhari in his *Mahābhāṣyaṭikā* accepts three *pramāṇas*: perception (*pratyakṣa*), inference (*anumāna*), and scripture (*āgama* or *śabda*). Perception is judged as liable to be erroneous, and at times inference is seen as superior to perception. But *āgama* or *śabda*, which consists of the revealed (*śruti*) and remembered (*smṛti*) scriptures, is a strong *pramāṇa* and is more dependable than inference. Several verses in the *Vākyapadīya* (1.27–43) examine the relations obtaining between the *pramāṇas* of reason and scripture. In Bhartṛhari's view it is not justifiable to replace scripture with inference in nonempirical matters or to hold that philosophical views (*vāda*) can be free from scripture. Inference alone, without the steadying influence of scripture, is an inadequate means of valid knowledge. As *Vākyapadīya* 1.34 puts it, "Whatever is inferred with great effort by clever reasoners is explained otherwise by cleverer ones."[10] Thus *dharma* or right conduct cannot be determined by reasoning without the help of the scriptural tradition (verses 1.30-31). And any attempt to establish the nature of objects by inference will likely fail because their properties differ according to place and time (verse 1.32). Knowledge of this sort can only be derived from the scriptural tradition (*śabda*), and then only after long hours of practice (*abhyāsa*; verse 1.35). The words of the *ṛṣis* convey supersensory knowledge that cannot be set aside by inference, because with their consciousness purged of ignorance (*avidyā*) they have directly perceived divine truth (Śabda Brahman; verse 1.38). The role of *vyākaraṇa* is to safeguard the transmission of this scriptural knowledge and to assist the hearer in realizing the truth of *śabda*.

The early grammarians Pāṇini and Patañjali define *śabda* primarily in terms of the spoken word. In the beginning of his *Mahābhāṣya*, Patañjali defines the word as "That on the utterance of which there is understanding regarding objects (*saṃpratyaya*)."[11] This definition of *śabda* does not identify the word with the uttered sound only. The distinction between word (*śabda*) and sound (*dhvani*) is basic to the understanding of language in Indian philosophy.[12] To take the physical sound as the word is to conflate entities of two different orders, like the confusion of the soul with the body. "The word, like the soul, has a physical embodiment in the sound and is made manifest through the latter, but the conveyance of meaning is the function of the word; the sound only invokes the word."[13] If the word (*śabda*) is only invoked and not constituted by the uttered sounds (*dhvani*), a question then arises about the nature of this *śabda* that is manifested. The Cārvāka, Buddhist, and Jain schools, along with many modern linguists, think all words to be the result of human convention. Where human convention is not allowable, the divine convention of God may be invoked—as is done by the Nyāya, for example. Against this view, and in agreement with the Mīmāṃsā, *vyākaraṇa* maintains that the relation between words and meaning is eternal, underived, and impersonal. The relation between *śabda* and its meaning is not an arbitrary convention established by man or God or both. Not only is there no record of any such convention, says the *vyākaraṇa*, but the very idea of "convention" itself presupposes language—the thing claimed to be derived from convention.[14] Therefore, language must be taken as having existed without beginning.

Murti suggests that the attempt to discover a temporal beginning of language may arise from a confusion of *śabda* with *dhvani*.[15] While speaking sounds and learning how to group sounds into syllables and the like may well be conventional, the fact of verbal communication necessitates the acceptance of *śabda* as a given that the learned sounds manifest but do not constitute. Otherwise, there would be as many different words "cow" as there are people speaking, for each person produces the complex of sounds involved slightly differently, namely, with different accent, speed, and so on. Each single utterance of the word would be unique. The fundamental point of the *vyākaraṇa* position is that in spite of the individual differences in speaking it "cow" is recognized as the same word, "cow". This aspect of *vyākaraṇa* doctrine provides an eastern parallel to the western notion of Platonic forms. The word "cow", like a Platonic form, is identical and immutable even though instances of its utterance may vary. The nub of the argument, as in Plato, is that verbal communication necessitates the acceptance of some kind of eternal word forms. The Platonic problem of the relation of the Idea to the "copies" appears in *vyākaraṇa* as the relation of the immutable word to the many verbal manifestations that evoke it. But *vyākaraṇa* goes beyond just establishing the eternality of *śabda*. It identifies *śabda* with Brahman, so that all words ultimately mean Brahman—

thus the absolute as Śabda Brahman. As Mādhava puts it in his *Sarvadarśanasaṃgraha*,

> Brahman is the one object denoted by all words; and this one object has various differences imposed upon it according to each particular form; but the conventional variety of the differences produced by these illusory conditions is only the result of ignorance. Non-duality is the true state; but through the power of "concealment" (exercised by illusion) at the time of the conventional use of words a manifold expansion takes place.[16]

Thus, knowledge of the meaning of words not only removes ignorance but also leads to the final bliss of identity with Śabda Brahman.

2. Theories of Error

In *vyākaraṇa* as in most other Indian philosophies, error or ignorance (*avidyā*) is ascribed the important function of obstructing the real from view. Although some scholars suggest that Bhartṛhari's theory of error is analogous to Śaṃkara's analysis of the rope-snake illusion,[17] other interpretations, which would distinguish *vyākaraṇa* from Advaita Vedānta, appear viable. Śaṃkara describes error (*avidyā*) as being overcome by a single negation. Bhartṛhari, however, in his *Vākyapadīya* seems to hold that error is overcome positively by an increasingly clear cognition of the word form or *sphoṭa*, which the succeeding perceptions reveal. Whereas the overcoming of error for Śaṃkara takes a negative form, for Bhartṛhari it is positive.

The *vṛtti* on Bhartṛhari's *Vākyapadīya* 1.89 and Maṇḍana's comment on *sūtra* 19 of the *Sphoṭasiddhi* state that the final clear perception of the *sphoṭa* is achieved through a series of errors. The analogy is offered of the way that, from a distance, one may (if one is in India) mistake a tree for an elephant. But if one keeps on looking at it, the tree is ultimately recognized in its true form. In this situation the truth has been arrived at through a series of errors. The sense organ (in this case the eye) has been in contact with the tree throughout. The errors of perception have had the tree as their object, but the cognitions produced by the eye have had an elephant as their form. When the final or true cognition takes place, however, it has the form of the tree itself and is one with its object; but this true cognition has been arrived at by going through the series of erroneous perceptions that preceded it. Now this change from error to true perception cannot be explained by factors such as change in distance, for simply standing in the same spot and gazing with intense concentration often produces the desired result. According to Maṇḍana, "it is the previous cognitions (having tree as the object and the form of the elephant) leaving progressively clearer residual impressions, which become the cause of the clear perception of the tree."[18] There could have been no erroneous cognition of elephant had the tree not been there as an object for the sense organ to contact in the first place. The error, therefore, may be described as misapprehension or vague perception. In Bhartṛhari's theory of language, the *sphoṭa* is similarly said to be the object of the cognitions of each of the letters, and yet it at first appears in the form of a letter. But through the additional cognitions of the subsequent letters, the *sphoṭa* is seen with increasing clarity until, with the uttering of the final letter, the form of the letters has become identical with that of the *sphoṭa*. Here the letters are seen in a position that at first glance seems parallel to the snake in the famous rope-snake illusion of the Advaita Vedāntins. The perception of the rope as snake is error, but it is through negating the erroneous snake perception that the true rope perception is finally realized. And were it not for the prior existence of the rope, the erroneous perception would have lacked the necessary ground for its phenomenal existence. Similarly, in this case, the letters are seen as dependent on the *sphoṭa* for their phenomenal existence, but in that phenomenal existence as being the means by which the noumenal *sphoṭa* may be perceived. This apparent parallel, however, does not hold up under closer analysis. Advaita theory provides for only true or false cognitions and allows no progressive approximation to the real,[19] as is the case in a series of erroneous *sphoṭa* perceptions. Whereas the Advaitin describes his error as being transcended via a single negation (such as when it is realized that "it is not snake"), the grammarian holds that his error (for example, the vagueness of the perception of the whole in the first letter) is positively overcome by the increasingly clear perception of the *sphoṭa* revealed by the succeeding letters. This analysis of the way error is overcome would seem to give further weight to Gaurinath Sastri's suggestion that in some ways the doctrine of reflection (*ābhāsa*) of the Kashmir Trika writers may provide the closest parallel to *sphoṭa* theory.[20] In the Kashmir Trika view consciousness (*caitanya*) is the only reality, and all external manifestation is held to be a reflection on consciousness as on a mirror. Error, in this view, occurs not because the initial perception has no existence but because its reflection of the object captures or includes only a part of its totality and fills in the gaps with other material (traces) taken from the old stock of memory. This error is positively transcended as the form of the reflection is progressively purified of memory material until it perfectly reflects the object. This perfect reflection, which is true knowledge, is further described as a union of the subjective and objective aspects of consciousness—a return to the oneness that is its essential nature.[21] From this brief glance at the Kashmir *ābhāsa* theory, it would seem to provide a helpful parallel supporting the *vyākaraṇa* view of the way in which the mainfest letters erroneously but positively approximate their true object, the *sphoṭa* itself.

To return to Maṇḍana, his explanation of the paradox of the way the indivisible *sphoṭa* appears as the letters, and the letters as the parts of the partless *sphoṭa*, is as follows. He says it is the sounds that resemble one another that are the cause of both the error and the final correct cognition of the *sphoṭa*. If, for the manifestation of two different word-*sphoṭas*, one has to make similar movements of the vocal organs, the letters produced by these movements appear to be parts of both of the indivisible words.[22] This error is fostered by the construction of such artificial devices as alphabet letters or word syllables, usually for teaching purposes. It is precisely because of this kind of confusion, says Maṇḍana, that sentences, words and letters appear to have parts, while in reality they do not.[23] The obverse applies to the *sphoṭa*. From the phenomenal viewpoint the *sphoṭa* "cow", for example, may appear to possess qualities such as accent, speed, loudness, time, place, and person in its utterance. That they are qualities of the phenomenal sounds and not the noumenal *sphoṭa* is what makes possible the common recognition of the word "cow" in spite of its diversity of utterance. From the *sphoṭa* viewpoint, it is this noumenal grounding or basis that makes possible such things as the translation of thought from one phenomenal language to another.

Maṇḍana offers the example of a picture. He points out that in our cognition of a picture, although we may be aware of the different parts and colors, the picture is perceived as a whole over and above its parts.[24] Similarly, when we perceive a piece of cloth our cognition is of the cloth as a whole and is quite distinct from the particular threads and colors involved.[25]

In both of these examples there is a necessary perception of the parts prior to the perception of the whole. This aspect is brought out clearly by Bhartṛhari, who describes the painter as going through three stages when he paints a picture: "When a painter wishes to paint a figure having parts like that of a man, he first sees it gradually in a sequence, then as the object of a single cognition and then paints it on cloth or on a wall in sequence."[26] So also the hearer of a word perceives the word in a sequence of letters, which manifest in him the whole word as the object of a single cognition. As a speaker, however, he utters the whole word in its differentiated appearance as a sequence of letters. It is in this context that the perception of the many letters, before the final perception of the unitary *sphoṭa*, is described as error, illusion, or appearance. But it is a unique kind of error in that it has a fixed sequence and form, ultimately leads to the perception of the truth, and is thus regarded as a universal error.[27] The chief cause of this universal error is described as *avidyā*, the limitation of the individual self-consciousness. A characteristic of this *avidyā* is that it provides no means for cognizing the *sphoṭa* other than the letters. That is why all individual selves universally experience the same error with regard to speech; but it is an error that ultimately leads to cognition of truth. It is only through this error or appearance of differentiation that the individual *sphoṭa* comes within the range of worldly usage so that we ordinary mortals have a way of comprehending it.[28]

With the preceding understanding of Bhartṛhari's *sphoṭa* theory in mind, we are now able to observe its significant difference from Śaṃkara's view of error. Whereas the Advaitin usually describes his error as being transcended via negation (such as when it is said that "it is not snake"), the Grammarian holds that his error (for example, the vagueness of the perception of the whole in the first letter) is positively overcome by the increasingly clear cognition of the *sphoṭa* revealed by the succeeding letters.[29] And the final clear cognition is a case of perfect perception or *pratibhā*—a flash of intuition revealing the *sphoṭa* or whole word.[30] At the more mundane level of psychological functioning, however, the positive process of perfecting the perception is described by Subramania Iyer as follows:

> (The final) clear cognition is a case of perception. The previous cognitions also had the *sphoṭa* as their object, but the cognition of it was vague and that is why they had the form of the sounds. But when the final cognition reveals the *sphoṭa* in all its clarity and distinctness, it no longer has the form of sounds. The error has given place to truth. Such a cognition can only be perception. The object and forms of the cognition are now identical.[31]

Bhartṛhari characterizes the conformity between the object and the form of the cognition in the final intuition as a certain *fitness* (*yogyatā*) between the sounds and the *sphoṭa*, which results in the clear manifestation of the word.[32] The perfect perception in which there is identity between the object (namely, the *sphoṭa*) and the form of its cognition (namely, the letters of sounds) is a special kind of perception that—the modern reader must realize—is held to be a function of the mind[33] rather than of the external sense. The designation of the final cognition of the *sphoṭa* as a case of perception, not of inference, has important logical implications.[34] Maṇḍana expresses the point clearly: "The revelation (of an object) clearly or vaguely is confined to direct perception. In the case of the other means of knowledge there is either apprehension (of the object) or not at all."[35] According to almost all schools of Indian philosophy, the valid means of knowledge (*pramāṇa*) other than perception either reveal the object completely or do not reveal it at all. There can be increasing clarity of revelation only in the case of perception. This point is most important for the *sphoṭa* theory in its contention that the error due to the vagueness of perception of the initial letters may be gradually and positively overcome, as described above. It is also crucial for the *sphoṭa* theory in its contention that the existence of the *sphoṭa* is not a postulation, as the Mīmāṃsakas maintain, but is proved by direct perception.

Śaṃkara in his commentary on *Brahmasūtra* 1.3.28 argues against Bhartṛhari's notion that the *sphoṭa* is directly perceived. According to Śaṃkara, only the individual letters of a word are perceived, and they are combined through the inferential activity of the mind into a word aggregate.[36] Because the psychological process is one of inference instead of perception, there can be no question of degrees of cognition. The inference *pramāṇa* is an all-or-nothing process. The error, if it is to be overcome, must be completely replaced all at once by a new inferential construction of the mind or by a superconscious intuition of Brahman. Thus the position of Bhartṛhari (that the overcoming of error is a perceptual process admitting of degrees of positive approximation) and the position of Śaṃkara (that the overcoming of error is a negative process of inference—admitting of no degrees) are not at all analogous.

3. Theories of Paradoxes

The logical principle "everything is either *P* or not *P*" has its limitations, especially in Indian philosophical discussions. Indian Grammarians and Logicians have classified negation into two types: *prasajyapratiṣedha*, verbally bound negative, and *paryudāsa*, nominally bound negative. The nominally bound negative like *a-brāhmaṇa* ("non-brahmin," generally referring to a *kṣatriya*, or the like) has a positive significance, and the negation is mainly for excluding some from the scope of the term negated. The verbally bound negation is a form of total negation and precludes an activity.

The Mādhyamika Buddhist proposes the fourfold negation (*catuṣkoṭi*) to deny all alternatives to the absolute. The Advaitin's "indescribable," used to indicate the nature of *māyā*, is also not within the "either yes or no" principle. The Mādhyamika thesis "The phenomenal world is indeterminate" means that no predicate is applicable to the world. Now the question is raised, "Is 'indeterminate' a predicate or not?" If it is, then the world is not indeterminate, for at least one predicate is applicable to it. If it is not, then we cannot say that the world is indeterminate. Such paradoxes are met with the reply that "indeterminate" itself is not a predicate.

Bhartṛhari discussed some paradoxes in his *Vākyapadīya*. One is the famous liar's paradox. "I am not telling the truth"; if this statement is true, he is a liar and his statement cannot be true, in which case it is true. Bhartṛhari says that a statement of this type does not refer to itself. Another interesting remark from Bhartṛhari regards the term "indescribable" (*avācya*): "What you consider as *avācya* can at least be referred to by the term *avācya* (indescribable), and then it becomes *vācya* or describable."

4. Levels of Language

The idea that various levels of language and knowing exist is present in several schools of Indian philosophy, but it is an idea that modern scholars in their first encounters with eastern thought either miss or misunderstand. The notion of levels of language is a necessary development in view of Bhartṛhari's absolutism. A monistic hierarchy such as the following necessarily results: just as the phonemes are only unreal abstractions of the word, so also words are unreal abstractions of the sentence, and the sentences are unreal abstractions of the paragraph. Even the paragraph is not the ultimate unity, for it is only an artificial division of the chapter of the book. At the top of this language hierarchy there is only one indivisible reality within our literary self, which, due to our human ignorance or limitation (*avidyā*), can only manifest itself in such unreal forms as the book, the chapter, the paragraph, the sentence, and the word. The underlying principle, maintains Bhartṛhari, is that all difference presupposes a unity (*abhedapūrvako hi bhedaḥ*). Where there is difference or parts there must be an underlying identity, otherwise the one could not be related to the other and each would constitute a world by itself. This concept provides the grounding for Bhartṛhari's metaphysical speculation and for the notion of a hierarchy of levels of languages (*Vākyapadīya* 1.1).

Language can be seen to operate on at least two levels. There is the idea that comes as an inner flash (the cartoon image of the light bulb going on), and there is the outer speaking of words and sentences that attempts to convey the idea to others. The words and sentences are called by Bhartṛhari *vaikharī vāc*—the uttered sounds that combine to make up the sentence, book, or poem. The inner idea or *sphoṭa* is aptly designated as *paśyantī vāc*—the intuitive flash of understanding of the sentence, book, or poem as a whole.[37] Between these two levels there is a middle or *madhyamā vāc*—the level of thought. Here the unitary idea or *sphoṭa* appears separated into its sequence of thoughts, words, and phrases, none of which has yet reached the level of uttered sound. According to Bhartṛhari, *vāc* or language passes through these three levels whenever one speaks. *Śabda*, which is at first quite internal, is gradually externalized for the purpose of speaking. Hearing, of course, operates in the reverse direction. Whether one is dealing with factual scientific language or a poem that can be understood on various levels, Bhartṛhari's *sphoṭa* theory seems to provide an adequate explanation. The complete continuum of cognition is covered. All of these points are in complete accord with Bhartṛhari's basic premise already mentioned, namely, that there is no possible cognition in which language does not figure. Knowledge, consciousness, and the word are all inextricably intertwined.[38] Once this supposition is accepted, the idea of levels of language seems quite logical.

Thought at the *buddhi* or differentiated stage of word sequences is perhaps best understood as internal speaking. And *pratibhā*, intuition, may be seen as a kind of muted speaking. The point being emphasized is that for Bhartṛhari speaking is the essence of consciousness and the means to all knowledge. And it must also be clearly understood that by "speaking," "language," or "thought" what is meant is the conveyance of meaning—"thinking" here does not primarily refer to concept formation, the drawing of inferences, and so on, all of which would exist at the two lowest levels (*vaikharī* and *madhyamā*) only. When "meaning" is identified as intertwined with consciousness (as Bhartṛhari identifies it), it satisfies instances of *pratibhā* as well as instances of more commonplace cognition and can therefore be held to be logically possible at all levels of *vāc*, including even the very highest (namely, the *pramāṇa*).

Let us now examine each level in somewhat more detail.[39] *Vaikharī* is the most external and differentiated level in which *vāc* is commonly uttered by the speaker and heard by the hearer. It is *prāṇa* (breath) that enables the organs of articulation and hearing to produce and perceive sounds in a temporal sequence. *Prāṇa* may therefore be taken as the instrumental cause of *vaikharī vāc*. The chief characteristic of *vaikharī vāc* is that it has a fully developed temporal sequence. At this level a speaker's individual peculiarities (such as accent) are present, along with the linguistically relevant parts of speech. Going further inward, as it were, *madhyamā vāc* is the next level, and its association is chiefly with the mind or intellect (*buddhi*). It is the idea or series of words as conceived by the mind after hearing or before speaking out. It may be regarded as inward speech. All the parts of speech that are linguistically relevant to the sentence are present here in a latent form. At this level a variety of manifestation is possible. The same *sphoṭa* or meaning is capable of being revealed by a variety of forms of *madhyamā*, depending on the language adopted. Although there is not full temporal sequence of the kind experienced in spoken words, word and meaning are still distinct, and word order is present. So temporal sequence must also be present, along with its instrumental cause, *prāṇa*. Traditional yoga is able to demonstrate a subtle but direct connection between breathing and cognition.[40]

The next and innermost stage is *paśyantī vāc*. *Paśyantī* is the direct experience of the *vākya-sphoṭa*—of meaning as a noumenal whole. At this level there is no distinction between the word and the meaning, and there is no temporal sequence. All such phenomenal differentiations drop away with the intuition of the pure meaning in itself. Yet there is present at this level a kind of "going-out" or desire for expression. This impulse is the *pratibhā* "instinct," which in one sense may be said to motivate the phenomenalization into sentences and words of the *paśyantī* vision, so that communication may occur. Thus the Vedic vision or *dhī* of the *ṛṣi*, which in itself is *paśyantī*, becomes phenomenalized so that by its uttered word men might rise above their ignorance and be grasped in their cognition by the revelation of ultimate reality. Therefore, there is a sense in which Veda and *pratibhā* are identified as *paśyantī vāc*. Because *paśyantī* is, by definition, beyond the level of differentiated cognition, it is impossible to define it in word sentences. It occurs at the level of direct intuition and therefore must finally be understood through experience. Nevertheless, there has been no dearth of speculation over the exact nature of *paśyantī* and the possibility of yet a higher level of language, namely *parā vāc*.[41]

4

WORD MEANING

1. Significative Function

Significative power (*śakti*) is defined as the relation that exists between a word (*śabda*) and its meaning (*artha*). This relation is considered to be permanent and stable, so that linguistic discourse be possible. The Naiyāyikas consider this significative power to be conventional, having been established by the will of God. The Grammarians consider the relation to be based on the superimposition of one on the other, creating a sort of identity, one evoking the other. The Buddhist Logicians also consider that there is a causal relation between a word and its meaning. This relation is primary denotative power and is called *abhidhā*.

The function of words for conveying meaning is not restricted to this primary significative power. The binary relationship—every meaning having only one word and every word having only one meaning—may be an ideal, for avoiding confusion and ambiguity. But in all natural languages there are several exceptions to this rule. Even the borders of the meaning are not always fixed and depend on contextual factors, both situational and syntactic. Moreover, unconscious shifts of meaning and figurative usages as well as conscious, intentional devices used by poets and mystics have made the problem of meaning more complex.

Various other functions of language are accepted by different schools of thought to explain the diverse types of language behavior within their field of investigation. The number of functions also varies, depending on the areas meant by *śabda* and *artha*. *Abhidhā*, *lakṣaṇā*, *gauṇī*, *tātparya*, *vyañjanā*, *bhāvakatva*, and *bhojakatva* are the main functions introduced to explain the various types of meaning conveyed by speech. Some are for words, others may be for sentences or for the complete utterance.

Of these types *lakṣaṇā*, secondary significative power, is the most important and popular. Three conditions for a *lakṣaṇā* are generally accepted by all schools. The first is incompatibility or inconsistency of the primary meaning in the context, which produces a break in the flow of thought, forcing the listener to think in order to understand what the speaker has meant by the uncommon usage and why he has used the word in an irregular way. This inconsistency can be either the impossibility of associating the normal meaning with the other word meanings of the sentence or the normal meaning's unsuitability in the context. The second condition is some kind of relation between the primary, normal meaning of the term and its actual meaning intended in the context. This relation can be one of proximity with contrariety or one of similarity or common quality. The latter type is called *gauṇī lakṣaṇā*, which the Mīmāṁsakas treat as an independent function called *gauṇī*; according to them, real *lakṣaṇā* is only of the first type, a relation of proximity with contrariety. The third condition is either acceptance by common usage or a special purpose intended for introducing the *lakṣaṇā*. All faded metaphors (*nirūḍhā lakṣaṇā*) fall into the former category, and metaphoric usages, especially by poets, fall into the latter.

It may be noted here that Pāṇini did not accept *lakṣaṇā* as a separate function in language, though later Grammarians such as Patañjali did so. It was the Mīmāṁsakas who developed it to enable them to explain Vedic passages properly. To them there can be *lakṣaṇā* not only for words, but also for sentences as a whole.[1] The Buddhist who considered that words deal only with mental constructs (*vikalpa*) that have no direct connection with reality considered secondary meanings (*lakṣaṇā*) or metaphor (*upacāra*) as helping language to deal with reality. Dignāga, the promulgator of the *apoha* theory, accepted that words may not have any positive content, but the sentence conveys a meaning that is of the nature of *pratibhā*.

Additionally, Jayanta Bhaṭṭa introduced a new function called *tātparyavṛtti* to explain how individual word meanings in a sentence combined to form a unified sentence meaning. Although he accepted a kind of *abhihitānvaya* (verbal comprehension) theory, he could not resort to *lakṣaṇā* like the Bhāṭṭa Mīmāṁsakas, because Naiyāyikas accept *lakṣaṇā* only for words.

Ānandavardhana, who advocated the *vyañjanā vṛtti*, included the purpose of intentional metaphors under it and pointed out its importance in enriching the contents of literature. To him *śabda* meant not only the words, but contextual factors also, and under *artha* he included not only ideas, but figures of speech and emotions.

Bhaṭṭanāyaka claimed that poetic language has a special function (*vyāpāra*), which he called *bhāvanā* or *bhāvakatva*, that helped in the universalization of the emotions depicted and helped the readers to concentrate. He also claimed another function, *bhojakatva*, for literature;

bhojakatva is the power of making the listener share the poetic emotions. These functions are not accepted by other scholars.

Pāṇini did not accept *lakṣaṇā* as a separate function in language. The so-called incompatibility, either impossibility or unsuitability to the context, on which *lakṣaṇā* is based according to later writers on the various schools, including the Grammarians, he did not consider to be linguistically relevant. "He is an ass" and "he is a boy" are equally correct from the grammatical point of view. His grammar accounts for some of the popular examples of *lakṣaṇā* like "the village on the river" (*gaṅgāyāṃ ghoṣaḥ*) by considering proximity as one of the meanings of the locative case. Similarly, Pāṇini does not mention or provide for the condition of *yogyatā* or consistency, given as one of the conditions for the unity of the sentence. *Agninā siñcati* ("He sprinkles with fire") is grammatically correct, though from the semantic point of view it may not be proper, because sprinkling can be done only with a liquid and not with fire.

These two cases are similar; in both there is an inconsistency or incompatibility either real or apparent. If it is real, there is lack of *yogyatā* and the sentence becomes a nonsentence. If it can be explained by resorting to a transferred meaning for one of the terms, the sentence becomes acceptable as an instance of *lakṣaṇā*. Pāṇini does not make provision for the semantic appropriateness of the utterances derived by his rules. Statements may be true or false intrinsically or extrinsically. The correctness of a statement like the following depends on external factors and has to be checked before decision, for example: "There are fruits on the tree near the river." But there are other statements the correctness of which can be self-evident if one examines the words and their meanings: "He is the son of a barren woman"; "This triangle has four sides"; "The circular square" are all anomalous utterances. If one of the lexical items arrived at by componential analysis of a word in a sentence prevents its co-occurrence with another word in it, it is said to be anomalous. But sentences that have no such resistance are acceptable. "A square has four sides"; "Linguistics is the science dealing with language"; such sentences are intrinsically true. As far as Pāṇini is concerned all of these sentences are grammatically acceptable, and the Grammarian is not concerned with the correctness or compatibility of the meaning.

A metaphoric sentence and a normal sentence cannot be distinguished by their syntactic form. All metaphoric sentences are semantically deviant but syntactically normal. In such cases there is a semantic obstruction based on the violence to the co-occurrence restrictions for one of the lexical items. In the sentence "He is an ass," the word "ass," referring normally to the animal also called a donkey, is syntactically identified with the boy, who is known from the context to be a human being (componential analysis also shows that he is a human being). Semantically this identification is impossible. The apparent anomaly can be solved by interpreting the word properly in the context of utterance. Such intentional deviance is resorted to as a communication device by poets everywhere. If the anomaly cannot be solved the sentence becomes no sentence. But from Pāṇini's point of view all such sentences, metaphoric as well as anomalous ones, are grammatically acceptable.

2. *Sphoṭa* and Word Meaning

In his *Sarvadarśanasaṃgraha* Mādhava describes *sphoṭa* in two ways: first, as that from which the meaning bursts or shines forth; and, second, as an entity that is manifested by the spoken letters or sounds. *Sphoṭa* may thus be conceived as a two-sided coin. On one side it is manifested by the word sound; on the other side it simultaneously reveals word meaning. In more philosophic terminology *sphoṭa* may be described as the transcendent ground in which the spoken syllables and conveyed meaning find themselves united as word or *śabda*. Nāgeśa Bhaṭṭa identifies this theory with a sage Sphoṭāyaṇa, mentioned by Pāṇini in one of his rules. This tradition is unknown to Bhartṛhari, who considers Audumbarāyaṇa (mentioned by Yāska) as having a view similar to subsequent *sphoṭa* theory. The original conception of *sphoṭa* seems to go back to the Vedic period, when *vāc* or speech was considered to be a manifestation of the all-pervading Brahman, and the *praṇava* (*aum*) was regarded as the primordial speech sound from which all forms of *vāc* were supposed to have evolved. *Aum*, the sacred syllable, is said to have flashed forth into the heart of Brahman while he was absorbed in deep meditation and to have given birth to the three Vedas containing all knowledge. Perhaps this claim provided the model upon which the *vyākaraṇa* philosophers based their conception of *sphoṭa*. Indeed, *sphoṭa* is often identified with the *praṇava*.[2]

A. Patañjali's *Sphoṭa*

The Grammarians developed *sphoṭa* theory as they set out to analyze the way word knowledge is manifested and communicated in ordinary experience. Patañjali provides the point of departure for the development of *sphoṭa* theory when, at the beginning of his *Mahābhāṣya*, he asks, "What is the word 'cow'?" and answers, "It is that which, when uttered, brings us knowledge of creatures with dewlap, tail, hump, hooves and horns."[3] Thus Patañjali emphasizes the fact that *knowledge* is the key factor—a word is a word only when it has a meaning. Here he is arguing against the Mīmāṃsā view that a group of letters when spoken is a word, even when there is no meaning or when the meaning is not understood.[4] After discussing the need for something to hold the letters together as they come in temporal sequence so as to provide a cognition of the whole,[5] Patañjali concludes that even though the letters cannot coexist at the time of utterance, they can do so in the mind of the speaker as well as in the minds of the listeners. He distinguishes between *sphoṭa* and *dhvani*. *Sphoṭa* is the permanent element in the word and may be considered the essential word. *Dhvani*—the uttered sounds—is the actualized and ephemeral element and an aspect of the *sphoṭa*.[6] For Patañjali the *sphoṭa* may be a single letter or a fixed pattern of letters. It is the norm that remains unaffected by the peculiarities of the individual speakers. Thus the *sphoṭa* is permanent, unchanging, and is manifested by the changing sounds (*dhvanis*) uttered by the speaker and heard by the listener.

On the basis of Patañjali's thought *sphoṭa*, though one, may be classified as both internal and external. The internal form of *sphoṭa* is its innate expressiveness of the word meaning. The external aspect of *sphoṭa* is the uttered sound (or written word), which is perceived by our sense organs but serves merely to manifest the inner *sphoṭa* with its inherent word meaning.[7]

B. Bhartṛhari's *Sphoṭa* Theory

While Patañjali provided the initial framework, it is in Bhartṛhari's *Vākyapadīya* that *sphoṭa* is given systematic philosophical analysis. *Vākyapadīya* 1.44 states, "In the words which are expressive the Grammarians discern two aspects: the one (the *sphoṭa*) is the cause of the real word (while) the other (*dhvani*) is used to convey the meaning".[8] These two aspects, though they may appear to be essentially different, are really identical. The apparent difference is seen to result from the various external manifestations of the single internal *sphoṭa*. The process is explained as follows. At first the word exists in the mind of the speaker as a unity or *sphoṭa*. When he utters it, he produces a sequence of different sounds so that it appears to have differentiation. The listener, though first hearing a series of sounds, ultimately perceives the utterance as a unity—the same *sphoṭa* with which the speaker began—and then the meaning is conveyed.[9]

In his discussion, Bhartṛhari employs several technical terms: *śabda*/*sphoṭa*, *dhvani*, and *nāda*. By *śabda* and/or *sphoṭa*, he refers to that inner unity which conveys the meaning. The *dhvanis* are described as all-pervasive and imperceptible particles, which, when amassed by the movement of the articulatory organs, become gross and perceptible sounds and are then called *nāda*. These *nādas* function to suggest the word, *sphoṭa*, or *śabda*. Because these *nādas*, which are gross and audible, have division and sequence, it is naturally assumed that the suggested word also has parts when in reality it is changeless and sequenceless.[10] Bhartṛhari offers the illustrative example of reflection in water. Just as an object reflected in water may seem to have movement because of the water's movement, so the word or *sphoṭa* takes on the properties of uttered speech (sequence, loudness or softness, accent, and so on) in which it is manifested.[11]

The question may arise of why this changeless whole or *sphoṭa* should ever come to be expressed in the phenomenal diversity called language. In Bhartṛhari's view, such phenomenalization occurs because the *sphoṭa* itself contains an inner energy (*kratu*) that seeks to burst forth into expression. Thus the unitary *sphoṭa* is seen to contain all the potentialities for diversity, like the seed and the sprout or the egg and the chicken. Bhartṛhari, in his *vṛtti* on *Vākyapadīya* 1.51, explains it as follows:

> The external (audible) word employed in verbal usage is merged in the mind after suppressing all assumption of differentiation, without, however, abandoning the residual force of the differentiation, as in the case of the yolk in the egg of the pea-hen. Just as one single word can merge, so can passages consisting of as many as ten parts. The word, thus merged, with all differentiation suppressed, again assumes differentiation and sequence, when through the speaker's desire to say something, the inner word is awakened and it becomes the sentence or the word, each with its divisions.[12]

Here Bhartṛhari seems to be suggesting two ways in which the energy of speech (*kratu*) causes the phenomenalization of the *sphoṭa*. On the one hand, there is the potentiality for bursting forth pent up in the *sphoṭa* itself, while on the other hand there is the desire of the speaker to communicate. This desire for communication, however, is described as existing solely for the purpose of revealing the *sphoṭa* that is within.[13] Unlike thinkers who conceive of language in conventional or utilitarian terms, Bhartṛhari finds language to contain and reveal its own telos.

C. Maṇḍana Miśra's Defense of Bhartṛhari's *Sphoṭa* Theory

In the *Vākyapadīya* Bhartṛhari masterfully supports his *sphoṭa* theory with illustrations from ordinary life. While they may convince one that the *sphoṭa* theory is not implausible, such examples can hardly be taken as proof of the theory. Maṇḍana Miśra took up this challenge in his *Sphoṭasiddhi*—to demonstrate the existence of the inner word as distinct from its sounds in terms of logical necessity and consistency. His opponent in this task was the skillful Mīmāṃsā philosopher, Kumārila Bhaṭṭa.

The debate begins with a restatement of Patañjali's question, "What is meant by 'word'?" and his answer, *śabda*, or that which has a meaning.[14] Kumārila objects that Patañjali's definition fails by being both too wide and too narrow. The definition of "word" in terms of meaning alone is too wide. Smoke, for example, signifies the meaning fire but is not taken as a word for fire. The definition is too narrow in that it holds *śabda* to be that which is heard. But the ear hears only a group of phonemes or letter sounds, each one of which (according to Patañjali's definition) should be regarded as a word even though it does not signify any external fact. This problem results in the difficulty that in the word "cow," for example, the individual phonemes *c*, *o*, and *w* may be heard by the ear of the young child and therefore qualify as *śabda*, even though the word "cow" as yet carries no meaning for him. This view conflicts with Patañjali's contention that the *śabda* is that significant word-whole which conveys meaning. Consequently, the uttered word "cow" would at the same time be *śabda* and not-*śabda*. It would be *śabda* in the sense that it consists in a commonly understood spoken word. But it would not be *śabda* before its meaning was known—although it would become *śabda* after the meaning is known. For three reasons—first, that smoke should not be called *śabda* even though it causes the cognition fire; second, that phonemes, even though they are audible, should not be called *śabda*; and third, that the same thing should not at one moment be *aśabda* and the next moment *śabda*—Kumārila maintains that Patañjali's definition of *śabda* as interpreted by the Grammarians is not correct.[15] In Kumārila's view, it is the fact of being audible that is the criterion for *śabda*, and the phonemes alone meet this requirement, so it is the phonemes that are commonly accepted as *śabda*. Anything over and above the phonemes (such as *sphoṭa*) does not deserve to be called *śabda*, for there is no such common usage.

Maṇḍana rejects Kumārila's criticism as frivolous misinterpretation. Saying that the signifying power is the criterion for *śabda* does not mean that a word ceases to be a word when it fails to communicate a meaning to an unlearned child. According to the Grammarian, the key point is that the word is capable of conveying meaning—regardless of its being understood or not understood in specific instances. And because the phonemes or letters that constitute a word do not have this capacity individually, they cannot be called *śabda*. Having refuted Kumārila in this summary fashion, Maṇḍana goes on to elucidate the Grammarian interpretation of *śabda* in answer to Patañjali's question: "In that complex cognition expressed by the word 'cow' and which consists of many aspects such as the universal, the particular, quality, action, phonemes, *sphoṭa*, etc., which aspect is it to which the name *śabda* refers?"[16] *Śabda*, maintains Maṇḍana, cannot refer to the individual phonemes because in themselves they convey no meaning. In common experience the whole word is the unit of language that is taken to be meaning-bearing. The common man takes a noun or verb to be a unity signifying meaning—without reference to the plurality of letters and syllables, which are the products of speculative thought. Maṇḍana further criticizes Kumārila's objections and establishes the basis for the *sphoṭa* position as follows:

> As for the definition that a word is what is cognized by the auditory sense-organ, it is vitiated by serious defects. The auditory organ also apprehends qualitative differences of pitch and modulation and such universals as wordhood and the like. These attributes though known through the organ of hearing are not words. Moreover, word is not known only by the auditory organ but also by the mind. So the definition proposed by Kumārila is misleading and apt to create confusion. The verdict of unsophisticated common sense that "cow" is a whole word which yields meaning, ought not to be brushed aside as an uncritical appraisal. The unity of the significant word is a felt fact and no amount of quibbling can conjure it away.[17]

Of the various aspects of the complex cognition "cow," Maṇḍana makes clear that it is the *sphoṭa* or felt word-unity that is capable of conveying meaning and therefore is the essential characteristic—without which it would cease to be what it is. Other aspects of the complex cognition, such as the particular, the quality, the phonemes, and the like, are merely occasional aspects.

The next step in the argument occurs when Kumārila extends his definition of the phonemes as *śabda* to rest not only on their uttered quality but also now on the contention that it is they (and not a so-called *sphoṭa*) that cause the understanding of meaning. "Why not say that the phonemes themselves are the cause of the understanding of meaning and that, when grouped according to units of meaning which are understood, they are called words (*pada*)?"[18]

In rebutting this new contention that it is the phonemes that convey meaning, Maṇḍana reasons as follows. Phonemes cannot singly convey the meaning because, as Kumārila admits, a collection of them in the form of a word or *pada* is needed. Neither can the phonemes coexist as a *pada*, for they are uttered singly and perceived in a certain order. When they are spoken by different speakers or in a different order or at the same time, they do not convey a meaning. At no time can all the phonemes or letters of a word exist together and work together; their individual natures, being eternal and unchanging, are such that no joint simultaneity is possible. Phonemes are necessarily successive and therefore cannot work together to produce a *pada* that conveys a meaning. Therefore, the understanding of meaning, which cannot be due to the phonemes, points to a cause that is something different from the phonemes.[19]

Kumārila counters this rebuttal by giving further development to the Mīmāṃsaka view as stated in the *Śabara Bhāṣya* on *Mīmāṃsāsūtra* 1.1.5. Let it be admitted that the understanding of meaning does not take place from the phonemes in their individual condition. But if, when grouped as *pada*, they are seen to acquire some special efficacy that provides for the conveying of meaning, what then remains to block the acceptance of the collection of phonemes alone as *pada*? Nothing is required but the phonemes. Without them, however, there is no possibility of conveying meaning. In this regard, the case of the phoneme is very much like that of the common seed. The seed will not produce a new effect (a sprout) as long as it is isolated, but when it is helped by a group of other factors such as soil, moisture, and so on, the sprout appears. Now the sprout is commonly judged as being the effect of the seed when combined with a group of helping factors. Similarly, these phonemes, when combined with a group of helping factors (such as being uttered by the same person in a particular sequence), are commonly held to become the cause of the understanding of meaning. As a parting shot, Kumārila invokes a principle of economy: "As long as there is a visible cause and a visible mode of its being, there is no occasion for thinking of an invisible cause."[20]

In reply, Maṇḍana admits that a special efficacy may be shown to be the property of an otherwise ordinary cause but maintains that it is just that special efficacy which has not been demonstrated in the case of phonemes as potential conveyers of meaning. Maṇḍana asks, What is the difference between *o* in the word *go* (cow) and an isolated *o*? The obvious difference is that in one instance the *o* is isolated, while in the word it is accompanied by another phoneme. But can it really be called accompaniment when, by the time of the speaking or hearing of the *o*, the other phoneme is no longer being perceived at all? A previously uttered phoneme, which has ceased to exist leaving no trace, and an unborn phoneme (or one that is as yet unspoken) are on the same footing. If previously spoken phonemes can be said to give help to a successor, then it should also be admitted that unspoken phonemes could also be of help—clearly discrediting the argument. Thus, the previously uttered phoneme *g* cannot in any way help the *o* to produce a special functional effect because it is dead and gone.[21]

Kumārila responds by putting forth yet another explanation. He offers the example of how the new-moon and full-moon sacrifices, along with other rites, have sequence and yet produce their effect together—as do the repeated saying of the Veda for its memorization. In such examples different acts occurring at different times are still found to produce qualitatively and numerically different effects. This same kind of process, he argues, should be accepted in the case of phonemes.[22]

Maṇḍana is quick to note, however, that although these examples may seem plausible they are not parallel to the case of the phonemes. In sequences such as the examples offered, where the resultant is unitary, thinkers agree that the new effect is due to a trace or lasting impression that each part in the series leaves behind and which helps toward the one result. As Maṇḍana puts it, "In new and full moon sacrifices and the like, which have sequence, certain new elements (*apūrva*) which are produced by the acts and which last and are looked upon as powers or functions actually help (in producing the single effect)."[23] In the case of Vedic recitation, the final learning is achieved with the aid of the memory traces left by the preceding repetitions. In the case of both the sacrificial *apūrvas* and the memory traces, there is a kind of continuing existence or simultaneity that allows for co-operation among the serial instances toward a unitary result. But, as Maṇḍana points out, the same is clearly not possible in the case of the phonemes, which have already been described as leaving no trace.

Kumārila counters by allowing that phonemes may indeed leave lasting traces or impressions (*saṃskāras*), and through the traces left by the perceptions of the earlier phonemes and the last phoneme, the unitary meaning of the word may be conveyed.[24] The last phoneme, when helped out by the traces of the previous phonemes, conveys the meaning.

Maṇḍana finds a fallacy in Kumārila's reasoning. He points out that traces that are generated by individual phonemes can only reinstate those same individual phonemes. The memory trace for each phoneme will be present but, just as in the case of the original utterance or hearing, only individually—when the *o* is uttered, or remembered, the trace for the *g* will have ceased to exist. There can only be the cognition of one phoneme at a time, and this principle applies equally to the traces and the original utterance or hearing of the phoneme. Thus, the possibility of the phonemes producing traces gets one no closer to accounting for the generation of a meaning whole.[25]

Kumārila defends his position by once again introducing an argument of economy (that position which resorts to the smallest number of postulated special powers or entities is best). Now it is agreed that each phoneme, whether in its original utterance or hearing or in its trace, cannot coexist with other phonemes so as to give the meaning of the word. Therefore, some cause for the occurrence of meaning must be postulated. The weakness of the *sphoṭa* theory is that it has too many postulations: first, it must postulate the existence of the *sphoṭa* as some kind of unseen entity, and, second, it must then impose upon this postulated *sphoṭa* the capacity to convey meaning. For the *sphoṭa* theorist two things have to be postulated. The upholder of the phoneme, by contrast, has to make only one additional postulation. As has already been made clear, the existence of the trace is accepted by both the disputants. The only point at issue is whether it can be the cause of the understanding of meaning. All that is needed, claims Kumārila, is that a new function be postulated for the trace, which everyone agrees exists. It is the cognition of the final phoneme, accompanied by the special function of the traces of the previous phonemes, that conveys the meaning. Thus only one additional postulation is required, the postulation of a new function for the traces. The *sphoṭa* theorist is in an inferior position because he has to postulate both a new substance (namely, the *sphoṭa*) and a new function (its ability to convey meaning).[26]

To Maṇḍana, Kumārila's explanation seems to be an oversimplification. The memory impression or trace is not seen but is a capacity or function that is inferred from the existence of the original phoneme. The difficulty comes when Kumārila postulates yet another function as resulting from the trace, which is itself already an inferred function. Maṇḍana maintains that the postulation of functions and the like is unacceptable because it results in an infinite regress. In addition to this problem of infinite regress, Maṇḍana finds logical weaknesses in Kumārila's view that it is the cognition of the final phoneme, accompanied by the cognitions of the previous phonemes, that conveys the meaning. This view cannot hold, says Maṇḍana, because the traces left by the letters are the same even when their order is reversed. How is it, then, that the meanings of the words "now" and "won" are not identical? As the letters and traces involved in the two words are identical, their meanings should also be identical, which is clearly not the case.

Letting go of this argument, Kumārila takes up his final and seemingly most potent line of attack. He returns to the proposition that the last phoneme, accompanied by the traces of the previous phonemes, expresses the meaning. To avoid the difficulties encountered earlier, he now defines *saṃskāra* not as a memory trace, but rather as "something else which is brought about by the cognition of the phonemes uttered separately in a fixed order by a particular speaker and leading to the understanding of meaning and it is similar to the effect called *apūrva* (residual force) brought about by the performance of the different rites like a sacrifice and leading to heaven."[27] The distinguishing feature of the trace that causes remembrance is that it causes something similar to that which produced it, which is not, however, the case of *apūrva* in a sacrifice. In a sacrifice, the individual acts performed perish immediately, but the *apūrva* or aftereffect of the whole sacrifice inheres in the self of the sacrificer as a special kind of potency until it brings the reward of heaven. Its result is thus very different from its cause, and this unusual kind of causal relationship is necessitated by scripture's declaration that the performance of a sacrifice produces such a result. In Kumārila's view, the *apūrva* or aftereffect kind of *saṃskāra*, which is left by the different letters upon the subject, is analogous to such religious heaven. Just as in a sacrifice it is the determinate order of performance by a single agent that is responsible for the spiritual leaven, here also the determinate order of the phonemes uttered by a single person is responsible for the unusual result. Therefore, it is when the last phoneme is spoken or heard in the midst of the "leavening" effect of the *saṃskāras* of the previous phonemes that the meaning is conveyed. For Kumārila, *śabda* is the last phoneme being heard or spoken and conveying the meaning (when helped by the *saṃskāras* of the previous phonemes).

The exact nature of this help is that the *saṃskāras* of the previous phonemes become a kind of intermediate cause (*vyāpāra*). They help the last phoneme in its task of conveying meaning. This help does not depreciate the causal value of the previous phonemes in any way, for it is in harmony with their purpose—the phonemes are not uttered just for the sake of pronouncing letters or leaving impressions, but also for the purpose of conveying a meaning. This importance of and necessity for the phonemes as causing the conveyance of meaning must also be admitted by the proponent of the *sphoṭa*, Kumārila claims. The proponent of the *sphoṭa* or undivided word entity has to admit that it is manifested by the phonemes uttered or heard in a definite order. As no single letter can be said to reveal the *sphoṭa*, it must then be revealed by all the phonemes combined with one another. Neither can it be that each phoneme in succession reveals only a part of the *sphoṭa*, because the *sphoṭa*, by definition, is held to be a simple indivisible whole. For the very reasons given by the *sphoṭa* theorist himself, the phonemes of a word existing in a fixed sequence have no way of pooling themselves or their traces so as to result in a unitary whole. Just as the Mīmāṃsaka has been forced to do, so also the *sphoṭa* theorist is forced to postulate some special kind of leaven of a trace by means of which the phonemes reveal the whole meaning. Why then, asks Kumārila (revealing his economy principle once more), does he not attribute the conveying of meaning to a special trace function itself and leave out the extra step of postulating a special kind of trace and then postulating the *sphoṭa*? For these reasons, concludes Kumārila, "it is better to assume that the special trace which has to be postulated conveys the meaning (rather than that it reveals the word)."[28]

Maṇḍana answers the foregoing criticism by making clear that the *sphoṭa* theory does not postulate a new kind of *apūrva* for the conveyance of meaning. *Sphoṭa* theory needs nothing more than the postulation of the ordinary memory trace. It is just the commonly accepted traces (*saṃskāra*) or dispositions (*vāsanā*) that result in the revelation of the *sphoṭa*. The only new thing postulated by *sphoṭa* theory is the *sphoṭa* itself, and in fact even that need not be postulated because it is directly perceptible.[29] Now, maintains Maṇḍana, this position is far superior to Kumārila's, in which the one new thing (namely, the *apūrva*-type trace) cannot be perceived and has to be postulated on the authority of scripture and on analogy to religious merit. Even this analogy is very weak, for although the postulation of *apūrva* or religious merit is necessary to validate the moral law and religious rites, there is no such necessity in the apprehension of the word and its meaning. The cases are not parallel. Also ignored is the common man's intuition, "I understand the meaning from the word," and the teaching of tradition that "the word, the meaning, and their relation are eternal." There is a natural connection between word and meaning that is inalienable. The conventions we learn as children serve only to bring that relation out and to make the meaning present to us. Maṇḍana summarizes his rejection of Kumārila's position as follows: "Because it has been said that the impressions, after all, do not constitute the word, the final phoneme is not expressive, (therefore) a collection of phonemes does not constitute the word and it does not convey any meaning."[30]

In this debate Kumārila's attempt to identify *śabda* with the uttered phoneme seems to be discredited by the reasoning of Maṇḍana, who at the same time has vindicated the identification of *śabda* with *sphoṭa*. Nevertheless, Maṇḍana still has to show how *śabda* as *sphoṭa* may be comprehended using only ordinary memory traces of the phonemes to reveal the *sphoṭa*. He must also show the *sphoṭa* to be not a mere postulation but a perceivable reality, otherwise much of his logical argument simply collapses. These tasks he undertakes in *kārikās* 18 and 19 of the *Sphoṭasiddhi*.

In his explanation Maṇḍana depends on the basic concepts put forward by Bhartṛhari in chapter 1 of his *Vākyapadīya*. The *sphoṭa* is something over and above the phonemes. The phonemes are changeable (capable of variations such as accent, speed, and the like), and when uttered serve only to manifest the changeless *sphoṭa*, which exists within the speaker and is potentially present within every hearer. The phonemes do not convey the meaning, but the *sphoṭa*, once manifested, does so. Between the *sphoṭa* and its word-meaning aspect the relation is that of expression and thing or meaning expressed. It is a natural relationship, and is indestructable and beginningless. Convention only serves to bring it out. Bhartṛhari emphasizes that the *sphoṭa* is an entity that exists within each person. All of us have the capacity instinctively to feel its existence within, and ultimately to perceive it directly with the mind. The contention that the *sphoṭa* may be directly perceived, and is not merely an inference, is one of the key points of *sphoṭa* theory.

Keeping these basic concepts in mind, let us now examine Maṇḍana's detailed description of the way the *sphoṭa* is both cognized and perceived without recourse to any new *apūrva*-type postulations.

Maṇḍana explains the process by which the *sphoṭa* is cognized in his commentary on *kārikā* 18 of the *Sphoṭasiddhi*:

> Each sound individually reveals the whole *sphoṭa*. Nor do the other sounds thus become useless because there is a difference in the revelation. It is like this: All the previous sounds bring about in the listener whose mind is free from any particular residual impression (*saṃskāra*), cognitions in which the word figures vaguely and which sow seeds in the form of residual impressions capable of producing a later clear cognition of the word. The last sound produces a clear cognition in which figures, as it were, clearly the image of the *sphoṭa* caused by all the seeds in the form of residual impressions left by the vague cognitions of the previous sounds.[31]

Maṇḍana offers the analogy of a jeweller who assesses the genuineness of a precious stone. His continuous gaze is really a series of cognitions, each of which perceives the genuineness of the stone but with increasing clarity. Each cognition leaves its *saṃskāra* or common memory trace. The last cognition, helped by the trace of the previous ones, fully perceives the genuineness of the stone; but for the traces of the intervening cognitions, there would be no difference between the last one and the first one. An important point is that the jeweller is described as "expert", meaning that before beginning the examination he already had the image of a precious stone ingrained in his subconscious, and it was this image (like the inherent *sphoṭa*) that was revealed to the jeweller's mind by his series of partial perceptions.

The *sphoṭa* is a unity that already exists in the mind of the speaker. He utters sounds in order to manifest it, and once manifested the *sphoṭa* conveys the meaning. A reasonable explanation of this process by which the *sphoṭa* and its meaning are held to be revealed is offered by Śeṣa Kṛṣṇa in his *Sphoṭatattvanirūpaṇa*. As the phoneme *c* is spoken by someone who intends to say "cow", the hearer grasps not only the phoneme *c* but also the whole word rather vaguely, as it is now known that the speaker is pronouncing a word beginning with *c* and not with any other sound. But there are a multitude of words beginning with *c*, and we do not know which one is going to be uttered; thus the vagueness of our knowledge. But, when the speaker utters the next phoneme, *o*, the field of possible words is further narrowed. All words not having *co* at the beginning are now excluded, and the hearer's knowledge of the whole is less vague. When the final phoneme, *w*, is uttered, all doubt disappears as the *w* unites with the memory traces *co* to manifest the whole *sphoṭa* "cow", which immediately conveys its meaning.[32]

The preceding explanation makes clear the reason behind Maṇḍana's insistence that a speaker's efforts to utter the phonemes will differ according to the *sphoṭa* that he wants to manifest. Even though the phoneme may be the same (for example, the *w* in "won" and "now"), the physical effort involved in vocalizing it will vary according to the position it occupies in the word. Thus the overall physical effort in saying "won" will be markedly different from that involved in saying "now," even though the same three phonemes are involved in each case. Consequently, the *sphoṭa* theorist has a basis for claiming that the *sphoṭas* manifested by the two vocalizations would be different, as would the meanings revealed.

This last point is important in relation to the Mīmāṃsaka contention that, because the phonemes are changeless, no mere difference in order or effort of vocalization can be important to the production of different meanings. Therefore, according to the Mīmāṃsaka, were it not for the postulation of the special "*apūrva*-like effect," the same meaning should result from "now" and "won." From the *sphoṭa* viewpoint, however, it is the *sphoṭa* that is changeless and not the phoneme, and the evident variations in the pronunciation and ordering of phonemes in speaking different words is seen to be consistent with both *sphoṭa* theory and the evidence of experience. "Now" and "won" are composed of the same three phonemes but do require that the vocalization of those phonemes be given different orders and intentions or efforts for the appropriate *sphoṭa* to be manifested and its meaning revealed.

The strength of this *sphoṭa* explanation of the way the word meaning is revealed rests not only on its concurrence with experience but also on the fact that no new kind of trace is postulated. The trace employed is the usual trace providing for the remembrance of the phoneme that originally caused it. "The weak point of the Mīmāṃsaka explanation," as Subramania Iyer puts it, "was that it either postulated a new power for the ordinary kind of residual trace, or postulated a new kind of residual trace in order to explain the fact that, though caused by the cognition of the sound, it does not stop at causing a remembrance of it but causes the understanding of the meaning also."[33] In other words, the trace is supposed to have an object different from that of the cognition that deposited it in the first place, which is, says the *sphoṭa* theorist, a logical impossibility. In his case, the original *sphoṭa* (which lay behind the vocalization of the phonemes by the speaker) and the end *sphoṭa* (which is the object of both the uttered phonemes and their traces) are identical. Consequently, the object (that is, the *sphoṭa*) of the phonemes and the traces is the same, and there is no logical difficulty of the kind that besets the Mīmāṃsaka.

Maṇḍana's explanation of the paradox of the way the indivisible *sphoṭa* appears as the phonemes, and the phonemes as the parts of the partless *sphoṭa,* is as follows. He says it is the sounds that resemble one another which are the cause of both the error and the final correct cognition of the *sphoṭa.* If, for the manifestation of two different word *sphoṭas,* one has to make similar movements of the vocal organs, the phonemes produced by these movements appear to be parts of both of the indivisible words.[34] This error is fostered by the construction of such artificial devices as alphabet letters or word syllables, usually for teaching purposes. It is precisely because of this kind of confusion, says Maṇḍana, that sentences, words, and phonemes appear to have parts where in reality they have none. The obverse applies to the *sphoṭa.* From the phenomenal viewpoint the *sphoṭa* "cow", for example, may appear to possess qualities such as accent, speed, loudness, time, place, and person in its utterance. That these qualities belong to the phenomenal sounds and not to the noumenal *sphoṭa* is what makes possible the common recognition of the word "cow," in spite of its diversity of utterance. From the *sphoṭa* viewpoint, it is this noumenal grounding or basis that makes possible such things as the translation of thought from one phenomenal language to another.

A later scholar of considerable note, Vācaspati Miśra, attempts to reject Maṇḍana's concept of the relation between the phonemes and the *sphoṭa.*[35] This criticism occurs in its fullest form in Vācaspati's *Tattvabindu.* The argument is stated as follows: "The particular sounds which manifest *sphoṭa,* are they different from *sphoṭa* or non-different therefrom?"[36] If nondifferent, says Vācaspati, then each phoneme should manifest the *sphoṭa,* and the remaining phonemes would be futile. If different, then there is no ground for relating the phonemes to the manifestation of the *sphoṭa.* If the phonemes are treated as illusory, then their reality is discredited—yet in experience we undoubtedly cognize individual letters. What is the justification for treating such cognitions as illusory?

In supporting the *sphoṭa* argument of Maṇḍana, S.S. Suryanarayana Sastri effectively answers these criticisms of Vācaspati. To the criticisms regarding difference and nondifference Sastri replies, "Such a question has little application to Maṇḍana's doctrine. To him indeed *sphoṭa* is non-different from the sounds, as a whole is from its parts; and yet it is different too, since the whole is neither each part nor a mere aggregate of parts. The existence of functioning of such wholes can only be denied by defective psychology."[37] As regards the justification for treating cognitions of the phonemes as illusory, Sastri answers:

> The obvious reply is that not the existence of these cognitions but their significance is in question, just as in the case of the reflection.

> The reflection exists without doubt, but it is not real. And sublation in this case consists not in that presentation ceasing to be or giving place to another presentation, but in that presentation *as such* failing to fulfil what is expected of it. If each cognition as an independent part could by combination with other such parts explain the whole, then it would be unsublated; since, however, it fails of its purpose, since it seems to fit in more naturally with a theory which treats it not as a producer but as manifester, it is in so far forth sublated. The reflection is sublated not as a reflection, but as the face; the letter-cognition is sublated not as letter-cognition but as an independent productive constituent of meaning.[38]

Sastri observes that Vācaspati adopts and attempts to develop Kumārila's viewpoint further by trying to show that meaning somehow results from the phonemes entering into a single memory. As Sastri points out, however, such an explanation is untenable in the light of experience. If "cowness" is associated with the remembered letters *c*, *o*, *w*, that meaning should not be recalled except when all three letters are present. How is it, then, that when there is a misprint such as "coe" or a mispronunciation such as "coo" we still correctly apprehend the meaning to be "cow"? The same sort of thing is evident when a letter or sound is omitted in the course of writing or speaking. The explanation in all of these situations would seem to be that we do not pass from part to part but rather apprehend the whole, filling up gaps or correcting errors when they occur.

With regard to memory and sequence, Vācaspati, following Kumārila, maintains that in the memory itself the phonemes have no sequence, being presented together, but that memory follows experience, conforms to it, and the sequence in which the letters are experienced is repeated in memory. This contention, however, does not square with the view that letters, being eternal and pervasive, can have no sequence belonging to themselves. This difficulty is overcome in the *sphoṭa* view, which holds that the sequence is determined by something other than the letters—by the *sphoṭa* intended. It is not the case that the letters in sequence constitute the word; rather, it is the word or *sphoṭa* that determines the sequence. The question may then be asked, Is the word existent or nonexistent prior to the phonemes being apprehended in sequence? In purely empirical terms, this question may be shelved by saying that, though not present in my mind before I learn the sequence, it is present in the mind of another who instructs me; and in this fashion the process may be pushed farther and farther back, there being no authority for postulating the origin of language at any particular time. But such empirical indefiniteness does not seem adequate in the face of the common ground that necessarily appears to underlie all empirical languages—requiring the *sphoṭa* interpretation that the word both is and is not prior to the apprehension of sequence. This paradox is ridiculed by Vācaspati, who describes it as the *sphoṭa* claim that the unreal helps the real. Sastri, in answer, states the *sphoṭa* argument, "It is real, otherwise it could not be manifested in sequence; it is not existent, otherwise there would be no need for manifestation."[39] This solution, Sastri observes, is in line with the solution to the problems of human knowledge and activity in general. "Knowledge is of the novel and yet not of the non-existent. Activity realizes a purpose which is real yet not actual."[40] As both the Advaita Vedānta and the *sphoṭa* theorists point out, the only solution to this paradox, which seems to be universally present in human experience, would seem to be to take the phenomenal as partial and therefore defective and illusory appearances of the unitary real. It is from this viewpoint that *sphoṭa* theory claims that there is a whole (namely, *sphoṭa*) that is increasingly revealed by particular phonemes uttered in sequence. As Sastri concisely puts it, "The succeeding sounds make more clear what was less clearly expressed by the preceding sounds; the latter provides the substructure, former superstructure, while all of them together reveal the one design, which while prompting their utterance is certainly not produced by them."[41]

3. Universal and Particular

In his *Sphoṭasiddhi* Maṇḍana Miśra also analyzes the relation between the universal and the particular. When one perceives the universal of an object, the particular and its qualities are also perceived, yet the essential cognition is that of the universal. To put it another way, when the cognition of the whole takes place we are also aware of the parts that make up the whole, but it is the cognition of the whole that is dominant.[42] Maṇḍana offers the example of a picture. He points out that in our cognition of a picture, although we may be aware of the different parts and colors, the picture is perceived as a whole that is over and above its parts.[43] Similarly, when we perceive a piece of cloth our cognition is of the cloth as a whole and is quite distinct from the particular threads and colors involved.[44]

To illustrate this point, both Bhartṛhari and Maṇḍana refer to the Vaiśeṣika conception that when two things are brought before us we first perceive each one separately, and only on the basis of these separate perceptions does the notion of two arise. This method of perception applies to all higher numbers—their cognition and production is possible only by way of previously cognized lower numbers. So also it is by way of the lower differentiated forms of speech that the higher unities, the word *sphoṭas*, may be understood.[45]

4. Contextual Factors

The need for taking into consideration the contextual factors in determining the exact meaning of an expression has been emphasized by various thinkers in India from very early times. The *Bṛhaddevatā* says that the established rule regarding the meaning of a Vedic passage as well as of an ordinary sentence is that the purpose to be served (*artha*), the subject matter under discussion (*prakaraṇa*), an indication from another place in the text (*liṅga*), its suitability (*aucitya*), the place (*deśa*), and the time (*kāla*) have to be taken into consideration for determining it. Of these terms, *vākya*, *prakaraṇa*, *liṅga*, and *artha* are also known to the Mīmāṁsā school of interpretation. According to them there are six means of proof to be taken into consideration: *śruti* or direct statement, *liṅga* or implication from another word, *vākya* or syntactic connection, *prakaraṇa* or context of situation, *sthāna* or position, and *samākhyā* or the etymological meaning. Of these six, each one is stronger than the succeeding ones. In the *Vākyapadīya* Bhartṛhari gives two lists of contextual factors; the first is almost a paraphrase of the list given in the *Bṛhaddevatā*. The second is a bigger list and is given as contextual factors that determine the exact meaning of a word in the case of ambiguous and equivocal expressions. This second list is discussed in detail by later writers like Nāgeśa, the Grammarian and Ālaṁkārikas like Mammaṭa and Jagannātha Paṇḍitarāja. The contextual factors taken into consideration in determining the meanings of ambiguous expressions include the factors of situational context and the context within the sentence.

Even to understand the purport of an essay or a text as a whole, the Mīmāṁsakas have pointed out certain factors to be taken into account. The six factors for determining the purpose of a text are given thus: consistency in the meaning between the introduction and conclusion; repetition of the main topic; the novelty of the subject matter; the result intended; corroborative and eulogistic remarks, as distinguished from the main theme; and arguments in favor of the main topic. These six *liṅgas* or indications for deciding the purport of a text are accepted by all schools of thought.

Literary critics from the time of Ānandavardhana lay great stress on the importance of contextual factors in conveying suggested meaning. The situational context—such as the speaker, the listener, the time and place, the tone, as well as the social and cultural background—has an important rọle in bringing out the suggestion. It was Bhartṛhari who pointed out that in many cases of language behavior, the literal meaning conveyed by the expression is not the intended meaning and that contextual factors play a vital role in determining the intended sense of a passage. It is because of these contextual and grammatical factors determining the intended sense that homonyms do not introduce the slightest confusion in actual speech.

5

SENTENCE MEANING

1. Factors of Sentence Unity

A. *Ākāṅkṣā*

Those who believe that a sentence is made up of words, each with an independent meaning of its own, will have to explain how a connected and cogent meaning is understood from the sentence. This problem has been discussed by all schools of thought in India, and various theories have evolved. Mīmāṃsā, the *vākyaśāstra*, takes a lead in this field. Bhartṛhari too has discussed various aspects of the problem and made his observations, though his final view is that the partless sentence is the unit of utterance.

Pāṇini uses the term *vākya* in the general sense of an utterance but does not define a sentence. It is Kātyāyana who defines it as that (group of words) containing a finite verb. Pāṇini does not seem to have subscribed to such a view, for his rule *tiṅatiṅaḥ*, referring to the application of the accent of "a finite verb when not followed by another finite verb", shows that he had no difficulty in allowing more than one verb in the same sentence. Pāṇini's view of the sentence seems more akin to that of the Mīmāṃsakas than to that of the Logicians. Even later Grammarians agreed that there can be simple sentences with more than one finite verb if other conditions are fulfilled, for example, *paśya mṛgo dhāvati*, "See the deer is running."[1] The *Nyāyasūtra* does not refer to the sentence or the sentence meaning, though Nyāya is very much interested in the word meanings. Perhaps early Naiyāyikas believed that a sentence is a collection of words and that the sentence meaning is a combination of the word meanings. A formal definition of the sentence is also found in the *Bṛhaddevatā* (2. 117). But it is in the *Mīmāṃsāsūtra* that we first come across this definition: "A group of words serving a single purpose forms a sentence, if on analysis the separate words are found to have *ākāṅkṣā* or mutual expectancy"

(*Mīmāṃsāsūtra* 2.1.46). This definition was mainly for the Yajurveda passages. Here for the first time the importance of *ākāṅkṣā* in unifying the words in a sentence is brought out. In this definition two terms deserve special attention, *arthaikatva* (unity of purpose) and *ākāṅkṣā* (mutual expectancy). The term *arthaikatva* can also be interpreted as unity of meaning; explained in this way it can have an extended application, even to ordinary sentences. The Mīmāṃsā principle of syntactical unity (*ekavākyatā*) states that if a group of words can be interpreted as a single sentence, it is not proper to split it and interpret it as two sentences. A sentence like *paśya mṛgo dhāvati,* "see the deer is running," would be a single sentence according to this principle (not treating it as two: "the deer is running" and "see him").

This condition of mutual expectancy, first promulgated by the Mīmāṃsakas and later accepted by other schools, stresses the necessity of interdependence of words to give a unified sense as in a compound word or a sentence. Pāṇini seems to have accepted something of the sort while mentioning *sāmarthya,* "capacity", as a condition for forming compound words (*Aṣṭādhyāyī* 2.1.1); for *sāmarthya* refers to semantic connection by syntactic elements.[2] Two meanings are given by Kātyāyana for the term *sāmarthya*: first, *ekārthībhāva,* emergence of single integrated meaning, which is similar to *arthaikatva* in the Mīmāṃsā definition of the sentence; and, second, *vyāpekṣā,* which is equivalent to *ākāṅkṣā* in the *Mīmāṃsāsūtra.* It is not clear whether Pāṇini himself intended those meanings or Kātyāyana is reading them in the light of the Mīmāṃsā definition. Strictly speaking, *sāmarthya* is the capacity of the words for mutual association, *vyāpekṣā* is their interdependence, and *ākāṅkṣā* is the need one has for the other in order to complete the sense. Pāṇini is referring to the compound formation while the Mīmāṃsakas are dealing with the Vedic sentence, but the principle involved is the same. Patañjali explains the two views as mutually exclusive and accepts the *ekārthībhāva* point of view as the final one, for according to the Grammarians the elements of a compound give up their individual meanings and acquire a special signification. He thinks that according to the *vyāpekṣā* view the individual members retain their own meanings but are mutually related. Kaiyaṭa points out that the former is a condition for the compound word, and the latter for the sentence. According to Bhartṛhari the sentence is the unit *sphoṭa,* and unity of meaning is certainly necessary. We may say that in all cases there should be unity of meaning when viewed as an integral unit and interdependence when viewed from the point of view of the parts.

Ākāṅkṣā can be seen from two points of view, psychological and syntactic. The Mīmāṃsakas are interested in the psychological expectancy, while the Naiyāyikas take it as a syntactic expectancy. Bhartṛhari actually criticizes the Mīmāṃsā definition of the sentence on the ground that its *ākāṅkṣā* would imply that a passage of several grammatical sentences would have to be considered as one sentence. The Mīmāṃsakas have to solve the problem by referring to the basic psychological expectancy.

Śālikanātha, a follower of Prabhākara, says that *ākāṅkṣā*, being the curiosity on the part of the listeners, has been explained by some as invariable association.[3] This definition will lead to complications, as there is no limit to such mental association. He says that only those that are essential for the accomplishment of the intended purpose need be taken as requirements, not all the *kāraka* associations. "Bring the cow" is complete in itself, but if the phrase "with a stick" is added, that phrase is in need of a verb for completeness, and hence "Bring the cow with a stick" becomes a single sentence. If the phrase were not added, it would mean that the speaker was indifferent to the way the cow was brought.

To the Prābhākara Mīmāṃsakas the three basic requirements for the accomplishment of the intended purpose are: the person who is enjoined to do the act, what to do, and how to do it. If one of these essential requirements is not given in the sentence it has to be assumed as in elliptical sentences. To the Bhāṭṭa Mīmāṃsakas, by contrast, the essential psychological requirements in a sentence are: the act enjoined (*itikartavyatā*), the means (*sādhana* or *karaṇa*), and the fruit of action (*phala* or *prayojana*).

The Grammarians and the Logicians take *ākāṅkṣā* as syntactic, as it is only the need for the syntactic completeness of the sentence. The later Naiyāyikas define *ākāṅkṣā* as a kind of syntactic need that one word has for another in a sentence in order to convey the interrelation of words. It is the *ākāṅkṣā* that leads to the knowledge of the syntactic relation in a sentence. *Ākāṅkṣā* plays an important role in the teaching method of Sanskrit texts. In a sentence the finite verb is taken first and then questions asked to get the necessary words to fill the *kāraka* relations.

Nāgeśa says that *ākāṅkṣā* is the desire on the part of the listeners, on hearing a word in a sentence, to know the idea that can be related in order to get a complete sense; it is only in a figurative sense that the expectancy is attributed to the word.

In the *Vedāntaparibhāṣā* (4.4-7), Dharmarājādhvarīndra says that there are two kinds of *ākāṅkṣā*, natural expectancy (*utthitākāṅkṣā*) and potential expectancy (*utthāpyākāṅkṣā*). *Ākāṅkṣā* can also be mutual or one-sided. In "bring the cow with a stick," the phrase "with a stick" has expectancy toward the verb "bring," but "bring the cow" has no direct expectancy toward the phrase. There is no end to potential expectancy, and the addition of the word to resolve it depends on the speaker's intention.

B. *Yogyatā*

To the primary condition of mutual expectancy were added two more by the Mīmāṃsakas, *yogyatā* (consistency of sense) and *āsatti* or *saṃnidhi*, which stands for the contiguity of the words. These three conditions have been generally accepted by all schools of thought as essential for *śābdabodha*. To them some have added a fourth, namely, the knowledge of *tātparya*, the intention of the speaker or the general purport of the sentence.

Yogyatā is the logical compatibility of the words' consistency in a sentence for mutual association. Really it involves a judgment on a sentence's sense or nonsense. The meaning of a sentence should not be contradicted by experience. "He wets it with water"—here there is *yogyatā*, because wetting is generally done with a liquid; but in a sentence "He wets it with fire" there is no *yogyatā*, because the idea of wetting is incongruous with that of fire.

There is no unanimity of opinion regarding the exact role of *yogyatā* in the comprehension of meaning from a sentence. Some Naiyāyikas hold that a decisive knowledge of *yogyatā* is a prerequisite for verbal cognition. Others say that what is required is only the absence of a knowledge of incompatibility. Kumārila Bhaṭṭa says that incompatibility with the actual facts does not prevent verbal comprehension, but only the validity of the knowledge.[4] Perhaps it is the inconceivability of the mutual association of the word meanings that renders the whole sentence nonsensical; it is not the lack of correlation with the actual facts but the impossibility of connecting the word meanings that stands in the way of verbal comprehension.

Sometimes the lack of *yogyatā* is only apparent and can be explained away by resorting to the metaphorical meaning of a word in the sentence; if the incompatibility can be removed thus and *yogyatā* restored, there is no difficulty in comprehending the meaning of the sentence. The apparent incompatibility of the expressed sense is an essential condition for *lakṣaṇā* (secondary meaning).

C. *Saṃnidhi* or *Āsatti*

Saṃnidhi or *āsatti* is generally explained as the condition that the words in a sentence should be temporally contiguous. It is the uninterrupted utterance or the unbroken comprehension of words when they are in juxtaposition. Kumārila Bhaṭṭa says that it is the continuous moving about of the words in the listener's mind (*buddhau viparivṛtti*). The Prābhākaras also explain it that way. Lack of *saṃnidhi* can occur in two ways—not being uttered together and not being signified by words. The Bhāṭṭa Mīmāṃsakas hold that verbal cognition is possible only when the necessary words are together in the mind. The Prābhākaras consider that only the contiguity of cognition of the sense is necessary. Thus in the case of elliptical sentences, the Bhāṭṭa Mīmāṃsakas want the missing words to be actually supplied.

The Navya-Nyāya school defines *āsatti* as an immediate recollection of the meanings of words through their expressive power or secondary signification (*lakṣaṇā*); even if the words are separated there is *āsatti* if the meanings of the words are recollected without any interruption. This recognition happens in the case of verses. Early Naiyāyikas thought that the knowledge of *āsatti* is the cause of verbal comprehension. The Navya-Nyāya school considers that *āsatti* itself is the cause (*svarūpe sati śābdabodhahetuḥ*).

In the case of elliptical sentences, in which the intended meaning is understood from the context even though some of the words necessary for syntactic completeness are lacking, the Bhāṭṭa Mīmāṃsakas believe that it is necessary to supply the missing words in order to have verbal comprehension of the sentence meaning. The Prābhākaras hold that it is easier to supply the meaning than to presume the missing words as implied.

2. The Role of *Tātparya* or Intention

The term *tātparya* has been used by the different schools of thought in India with varying subtle nuances, depending on the basic standpoint taken by each; but the general idea is quite clear.[5] The term refers to the meaning intended to be conveyed by an utterance, and it can be viewed as the meaning intended by the speaker or as the purport of the utterance. The role of contextual factors in deciding this *tātparya* is also generally accepted by all, along with the importance of *tātparya* in deciding the meaning of a sentence. There is, however, no unanimity of opinion regarding the exact role played by *tātparya* in verbal comprehension.

The meaning of a sentence can be considered from two distinct standpoints, from the point of view of the speaker and from the point of view of the listener. The general western approach has been from the speaker's point of view, while the Indian approach, especially the later *śābdabodha* approach, has been mainly from the listener's point of view.

In a normal speech situation there can be five different aspects of the meaning of an utterance: what is in the mind of the speaker who makes the utterance, what the speaker wants the listener to understand, what the utterance actually conveys, what the listener understands as the meaning of the utterance, and what is in the mind of the listener on hearing the utterance.

In a perfect linguistic communication all five of these meanings must coincide; but often due to various causes there are bound to be differences standing in the way of easy communication. In all cases of successful lying or misdirection, what is in the mind of the speaker at the time of utterance is different from what is intended to be conveyed to the listener. And very often what the listener understands as the meaning of the utterance is different from what the speaker intends to convey; this problem can be caused by the lack of expressive power on the speaker's part or the inability to understand on the listener's part. What is in the speaker's mind before he speaks or in the listener's mind after hearing the utterance is rather intangible and does not easily yield to objective scientific analysis. It is the actual utterance that can be objectively analyzed into its components of words, morphemes, and phonemes, and studied; but that does not mean that the other aspects are less important.

The Mīmāṃsakas and the Naiyāyikas, who take the sentence to be a concatenation of the individual words it contains, have necessarily to depend on the power of *tātparya* to explain how a connected meaning is comprehended from a sentence. Each word in a sentence gives its own isolated meaning; but a string of unconnected isolated senses cannot produce a unified meaning. People use words with the intention of conveying a connected sense; hence from the use of words in juxtaposition (*samabhivyāhāra*) it is assumed that the speaker has uttered them with the intention of conveying a connected sense, for otherwise the simultaneous utterance would be of no avail, but for such an intention *tātparya* works as a general motivating force to help in correlating the word meanings and forming the sentence meaning.

Tātparya is the intention or the desire of the speakers, according to the Naiyāyikas. According to the Mīmāṃsakas, it is the purport of the sentence. This *tātparya* is all-comprehensive, but not all-powerful or absolute. Normally it cannot change the *śakti*, the primary meaning of a word. According to the Mīmāṃsakas, the *śakti* or the relation between a word and its meaning is *autpattika*, innate or permanent; according to the Naiyāyikas, this *śakti* is conventional or *sāṃketika*, but permanent, being based on the will or *icchā* of God in the case of ordinary words and of the authors in the case of technical terms and the like.

According to the Naiyāyika, the *śābdabodha* or understanding of the sentence's meaning is possible only through the knowledge of the words' meanings, which form the immediate cause (*kāraṇa*); the knowledge of the expressive power of *śakti* in the individual words obtained through recollection is the *sahakāri kāraṇa*. Before one considers the question of the speaker's intention, understanding the individual meanings of words on the basis of their *śakti* is essential. It is only in the case of ambiguous words, in which more than one sense is possible, that the speaker's intention or contextual factors are taken into account.

In the case of metaphoric expression, such as "the village on the Ganges," in which the literal meaning is unsuitable, the incompatibility has to be removed by taking one of the word meanings as having been used in a sense different from its normal sense, but somehow related to it. In a particular sentence in which there is contextual incompatibility, it is on the basis of the *tātparya* that the listener decides which of the words is to be taken as metaphorical. Some farfetched relationship can always be assumed between the primary meaning and the intended meaning.

Along with *ākāṅkṣā*, *yogyatā*, and *āsatti*, some Naiyāyikas want to include *tātparya* or a general knowledge of the meaning intended by the speaker, which may be termed "prehension," as an essential factor in all cases of verbal comprehension. Some others believe that the speaker's intention need not be considered as a direct factor, as it could be included in *ākāṅkṣā* itself. *Tātparya* plays a part in deciding *āsatti* also. Gaṅgeśa and Viśvanātha have included *tātparya* as a fourth requisite.

Even though the Mīmāṃsakas do not accept *tātparya* as a separate factor, it is accepted as a general motivating force. According to the Prābhākaras, the *tātparya* enables primary meaning itself to give both its word meaning and the syntactic relation. These *anvitābhidhānavādins* think that the *śakti* of words is understood with reference to a meaning that is related to some *kārya*. All sentences, especially in the Veda, have to be ultimately meaning injunctions or prohibitions. The later theory of Dhanika, who includes *dhvani* under *tātparya*, follows this *anvitābhidhānavāda*.

According to the Bhāṭṭa Mīmāṃsakas, the individual words in a sentence give their isolated meanings, and the sentence meaning is located through *lakṣaṇā*, based on *tātparyānupapatti*. It is Jayanta Bhaṭṭa who in his *Nyāyamañjari* advocates *tātparya* as a separate factor to explain the emergence of the sentence meaning from the associationist point of view. He does not refer to *lakṣaṇā* in this case, because sentence *lakṣaṇā* is not acceptable to the Naiyāyikas. Harisiddhāntavāgīśa, in his commentary on *Sāhityadarpaṇa*, says that this *tātparyaśakti* is the same as the *saṃsargamaryādā* of later Naiyāyikas.

Among Ālaṃkārikas, Ānandavardhana accepts only three functions of words, *abhidhā*, *lakṣaṇā*, and *tātparya*. He mentions the *padārthavākyārthanyāya* but does not refer to it as a function. *Tātparyavṛtti* was accepted for the first time by Abhinavagupta in his *Locana*. He followed Jayanta Bhaṭṭa in this respect. Later Ālaṃkārikas took it as a general view accepted by Dhvanikāra himself. Thus Ruyyaka says wrongly that Dhvanikāra accepted *vyañjanā* as the fourth *vyāpāra*, distinct from *abhidhā*, *lakṣaṇā*, and *tātparya*. Later Ālaṃkārikas took the *tātparyavṛtti* as the view of *abhihitānvayavādins* and confused it with the Bhāṭṭa view, though the Bhāṭṭas have definitely stated that they accept only *lakṣaṇā* and not *tātparya* to explain the emergence of the sentence meaning from the word meanings.

3. *Anvitābhidhāna* and *Abhihitānvaya* Theories

We saw earlier that the two main theories about sentence meaning are the *anvitābhidhāna*, advocated by the Prābhākara Mīmāṃsakas, and the *abhihitānvaya*, held by the Bhāṭṭa Mīmāṃsaka.

Prabhākara and his followers denied that words convey a meaning except in the context of a sentence, even though they regarded words as real and actual constituents of language. Like the Bhāṭṭas, the Prābhākaras have to accept the reality of individual words and their individual meanings, and agree that the primary meaning expressed by the word is a universal (*jāti*). All of these points are specifically stated in the *Mīmāṃsāsūtras*, and no Mīmāṃsaka can doubt its validity. It is also clear that the purpose of words in a sentence is to give a cogent, connected meaning. The difference between the two schools involves the following questions:

(1) Does the unitary sentence meaning arise directly from the words themselves or indirectly through the recollection of the word meanings? The *anvitābhidhāna* theory takes the former view, while the *abhihitānvaya* theory takes the latter.

(2) The meaning of a sentence is made up of the individual word meanings and their mutual relation. Can both of these elements be directly conveyed by the words? The Prābhākaras say that the intention or purport, known from contextual factors, will make the primary, denotative power of the words convey both. But Bhāṭṭas hold that the primary denotative power of words is exhausted by conveying their isolated, individual meanings and stop with that. The connected meaning is conveyed through the secondary power of the sentence (*lakṣaṇā*). The individual meaning is a universal; but in the sentence meaning has to apply to the individual. The latter is also achieved by the power of *lakṣaṇā*.

Some of the Naiyāyikas also accept the *abhihitānvaya* theory, but because according to them the primary meaning of a word is the particular qualified by the universal (*jātiviśiṣṭavyakti*), they do not have to depend on *lakṣaṇā* to get the sentence meaning. To get the syntactic relationship between the words, they cannot resort to *lakṣaṇā*, because they accept it only for words, not for a sentence. One of the Naiyāyikas, Jayanta Bhaṭṭa, proposed a new function of the sentence, *tātparya*, to account for the syntactically connected meaning.

The Prābhākaras stress the natural process by which children learn their language. It is by watching language used and by witnessing the activity of elders in daily life that children come to know the significance of words. Through the substitution method they come to know the meaning of words; this process is natural and subconscious. Later the child comes to understand the meaning of even new sentences. But from the world he knows that words are never used in isolation but have meaning only in the context of a sentence. The constituent words in a sentence convey meaning only as they are related to the sentence meaning. Thus in the sentence "Bring the cow," the word "cow" means not the isolated concept cowness, but cow as related to the action of bringing. So also the word "bring" means the action of bringing in relation to the cow. The words themselves give their own meanings and their syntactic relation, so the sentence meaning is directly conveyed by the sentence.

This view is rejected by the Bhāṭṭa Mīmāṃsaka because of the fallacies of interdependence and complexity. According to them we are able to understand the individual meanings of words, even though we might have learned them by hearing people uttering sentences and watching their reaction. Unlike the words, the sentence does not have an individual meaning of its own. When we hear a sentence, we have first an understanding of the separate meanings of the words one after another; then these word meanings are related on the basis of expectancy and other factors, and we arrive at the unified meaning of the sentence as a whole.

The association of the word meanings is brought about by *lakṣaṇā*, according to Bhāṭṭa Mīmāṃsā, but the Naiyāyikas explain it by resorting to *saṃsargamaryādā*.

4. Sentence *Sphoṭa*

Bhartṛhari identifies Brahman, the ultimate being, with the essence of the speech principle; it is without beginning or end and indestructible. The entire world is an appearance (*vivarta*) of this speech principle. Symbol and meaning are only two aspects of this speech essence. It is the same speech essence that appears in the form of various ideas and meanings on the one hand and their symbols—words and sentences—on the other, and thus constitutes the phenomenal world. This speech essence is of the nature of consciousness: though unchanging and partless, it appears to be evolutionary and pluralistic on the basis of its own powers like time, which, though really identical with it, seems to be different. The eternal, timeless speech principle appears to be changing because of the working of the time factor. Time is an inherent power of the absolute, but it is relatively independent and exerts its influence in bringing about the other powers of the speech essence.

The basic principle of Bhartṛhari's theory of language is that the complete utterance or the sentence is the unit of speech and should be considered as a single, unanalyzable entity. The utterance alone is valid with respect to actual language. The meaning of the utterance or sentence is also integral and indivisible and is of the nature of *pratibhā*, an intuitive flash of insight. This partless expression in the sentence *sphoṭa* manifests in a flash the integral meaning. Sequence and time factor do not really belong to the sentence but are unavoidable as means for revealing the sentence. Sentence *sphoṭa* as the expression (*śabda*) and *pratibhā* as the meaning (*artha*) are the basic factors in linguistic behavior.

In the speaker's mind before he begins to speak and in the listener's mind after hearing, this unity is clear. But because of oui inability to communicate it in an instantaneous flash, the sentence has to be uttered as a sequence of words, each word in its turn being a definite sequence of phonemes or letters. If both the speaker and the listener are quite proficient in the language, as in the case of the mother tongue, they do not feel that they are uttering or hearing articulated sound-bits or words. The speaker utters the sentence and the listener hears it as a sentence. If the language proficiency is meagre, the listener may be hearing the words and trying to organize the meanings into a unit. If the hearer does not know the language, he will hear only a series of articulated sounds or mere sound bits. All analysis of the sentence into lesser meaningful elements such as the word, bases, and affixes may be a convenient fiction. It is true that Grammarians' main work is to analyze the utterance into its component parts in order to help the students understand the meaning, but they are aware that this linguistic analysis has no real validity except as a help to the students.

Even though the *sphoṭa* theory envisages different subdivisions of the *sphoṭa*, Bhartṛhari accepts only the sentence *sphoṭa* as the real unit of speech. Letters and words have only a pragmatic value, as useful units that build up higher units of speech, the sentence. The meaning of this single, indivisible utterance is *pratibhā*, a flash of insight, the real nature of which is indefinable. Its existence is ratified only in the individual's experience of it, and the experiencer himself cannot describe it adequately.

In the discussion of the *sphoṭa* theory it has been pointed out that the actual sounds uttered by the speaker and heard by the listener are the *vaikṛta dhvani*, containing many irrelevant, idiosyncratic, and non-linguistic elements. This *vaikṛta dhvani* reveals the *prākṛta dhvani*, which is the linguistically relevant phonematic pattern of the utterance, free from the variations in intonation, tempo, pitch, and so on, which do not affect the language. Of course in languages in which the tone or pitch or length is relevant, these factors will be part of the *prākṛta dhvani* itself.

In normal linguistic discourse both the speaker and the listener are conscious of the normal phonological or phonematic pattern only. All nonlinguistic matter is eliminated at this stage; but the time sequence is still present. It is this *prākṛta dhvani* that reveals gradually, phoneme by phoneme and word by word, the sentence *sphoṭa*, the integral linguistic symbol. The role of the phonemes (*varṇa*) is only to reveal the word *sphoṭa* and the role of the words to reveal the sentence *sphoṭa*. The smaller elements cannot, individually or collectively, reveal the integral unitary meaning directly because of their appearance in a temporal sequence, because of their not being associated with parts of the meaning; their role is to build up the higher unit until the sentence *sphoṭa* is revealed. This sentence *sphoṭa* gives forth instantaneously in a flash the meaning of the sentence.

Bhartṛhari has stated that the speech principle (*śabdatattva*) has three stages in the course of its manifestation, namely *paśyantī*, *madhyamā*, and *vaikharī*. The *vaikharī* level corresponds to the *vaikṛtadhvani* of the *sphoṭa* theory and is the actualized and manifested speech, the sounds spoken by the speaker and heard by the listener. The *madhyamā* level seems to correspond to the *prākṛta dhvani*, because the linguistically relevant elements, including the sequence, are present in both. The next stage, *paśyantī*, has been identified with *pratibhā* indicated by the *vākyasphoṭa*. When we speak of the *vākyasphoṭa* as the meaning revealer and of *pratibhā* as the meaning, the two seem to be different; but actually they are only two aspects of the same entity. Whether Bhartṛhari considered the Śabda Brahman as a level higher than the *paśyantī* is not certain, for scholars are not unanimous on this point. He says that grammar is the highest place for *vāc* in its threefold aspect—*paśyantī*, *madhyamā*, and *vaikharī*. That claim does not preclude the possibility of a higher level about which one cannot say anything. According to some scholars the *paśyantī* level has two aspects, the higher being also called *parā paśyantī*, at which all distinctions are obliterated.

Even though Bhartṛhari considered the sentence to be the only unit of expression in actual life, he was fully conscious of the importance of linguistic analysis into words and other units as a useful means for understanding the languages. This awareness is apparent from the third book of the *Vākyapadīya*, where various problems are discussed on the basis of morphemes and phonemes that make up the sentence.

5. *Śābdabodha*

Indian thinkers on language belonging to the different schools of thought considered language behavior in a linguistic situation not only from the speaker's point of view but also from the listener's. The various theories of *śābdabodha* or judgment consider the process of cognition of the sentence meaning from the listener's point of view.

The modern technique of *śābdabodha* was developed and perfected by the school of Navya-Nyāya, founded by Gaṅgeśa about A.D. 1320 using technical terms for specifying the meaning of a sentence precisely and accurately. Literally the term *śābdabodha* means "verbal comprehension" or "verbal cognition"; it is used to indicate the meaning of a sentence as understood by the listeners. In modern works the term is used to refer to the linguistic paraphrase of the sentence, in which the exact denotation of each element in the sentence is clearly and precisely indicated. The *śābdabodha* approach of understanding a sentence meaning is intended to avoid syntactic ambiguity by specifying the exact relations among the various elements in a sentence. The vagaries of the sentence's surface structure will be absent in the *śābdabodha* paraphrase, and the linguistic analysis at the syntactic level will become precise.

The *śābdabodha* approach of analyzing the meaning of a sentence is analogous to the deep-structure level in Noan Chomsky's analysis of a sentence. He distinguishes between the surface level and the deep-structure level.[6] The underlying relations between the elements of a sentence at the *śābdabodha* level need not always be the apparent relations at the surface level. Thus *ghaṭasya nirmitiḥ*, "making the pot," and *caitrasya nirmitiḥ*, "creation by Caitra," though similar in Sanskrit at the surface level, have different *śābdabodhas*. The genitive case in the first phrase indicates the object of the verb, while in the second expression the genitive case indicates the agent; the former is *ghaṭakarmikā nirmitiḥ*, creation that has the pot as its object, but the latter is *caitrakartṛkā nirmitiḥ*, creation that has *caitra* as its agent.

The technique of *śābdabodha* was also adopted by later workers in the various other schools of thought. But on the basis of the difference in their basic assumptions there is difference in the emphasis, and the same sentence or expression has different *śābdabodha* paraphrases in the different schools, Nyāya, Mīmāṃsā, and Grammarians. They differ particularly about which element in a sentence should be regarded as predominant. The Logicians (the Naiyāyikas) are mainly interested in analyzing propositional sentences from a static point of view, so they consider the substantive (in the nominative case) to be the most important element. The Grammarians, as well as the early etymological schools, consider the sentence from the dynamic point of view and take the finite verb to be the most important element. The followers of the Mīmāṃsā school, mainly concerned with the interpretation of Vedic injunctions, try to analyze the implications of imperative sentences. The same Sanskrit sentence may be interpreted differently at the deep-structure level in the *śābdabodha* by the different schools of thought, because they differ in their basic standpoints.

The sentence *caitraḥ ghaṭaṃ karoti*, "Caitra makes a pot," will be interpreted by the Grammarians as "ekatvāvacchinnacaitrakartṛkaḥ ekatvāvacchinnaghaṭakarmakaḥ vartamānakālakaḥ kāraṇavyāpāraḥ, the operation or activity of making, in the present tense, which has Caitra in the singular number as its agent and pot in the singular number as its object. To the Naiyāyika or the logician the same sentence will mean "ghaṭakarmakakāraṇakṛtimān caitraḥ," Caitra who has the activity of making which has pot as its object. These interpretations could be further elaborated by pointing out all the implications of the sentence. The passive sentence "caitreṇa ghaṭaḥ kriyate" (a pot is being made by Caitra) could be analyzed in the same way, because from the *śābdabodha* point of view there is little difference in meaning between the active sentence and its passive form, according to the Grammarians. The Naiyāyikas, however, make a clear distinction between the two.

Among ancient writers neither Pāṇini nor Gautama was interested in discussing the sentence. Jayanta Bhaṭṭa says in his *Nyāyamañjarī* that the absence of any reference to the sentence in the *Nyāyasūtras* shows that the early Naiyāyikas considered the sentence to be merely a combination of words. Among Indian Grammarians it was Kātyāyana who first defined a sentence as *ekatiṅ*, that which has one finite verb. Pāṇini seems to have held the view that a sentence may contain more than one finite verb, for his rule *tiṅ atiṅaḥ* ordains the acute accent to a verb when it follows a nonverb (in a sentence). Later Grammarians have also accepted such sentences. Strictly from the formal surface-level approach, as advocated by Kātyāyana, such a sentence may be considered a complex sentence made up of two sentences, but at the deep-structure level, from the semantic point of view, they constitute a single sentence.

We have already seen that the Mīmāṃsakas first promulgated and the other schools later accepted the theory that the writing of the sentence is based on the three factors of mutual expectancy or interdependence of the meanings of the words in it, compatibility or absence of incompatibility, and proximity. The Mīmāṃsakas considered mutual expectancy to be psychological, while the Logicians and Grammarians took it to be syntactical. Between the two schools of Mīmāṃsā, the Bhāṭṭa and the Prābhākara, there is difference in view about the factors involved in an injunctive sentence. According to Kumārila Bhaṭṭa, every command to do something raises three questions: What should be done? How is it to be done? and Who is to do it? A command or law should be obeyed because it is a law, not because of any profit motive or fear of punishment. Kumārila's view was that nobody would act without a purpose. According to the two schools of Mīmāṃsā, every complete sentence must satisfy these basic psychological requirements.

The Mīmāṃsā schools held that the finite verb is the central element in a sentence. It consists of two elements: the verbal root (*dhātu*) and the verbal suffix (*pratyaya*). Of these two, the Mīmāṃsakas held that the verbal suffix is semantically more important than the root. The verbal suffix denotes *bhāvanā* or the efficient force, which is defined as that activity which brings something into being, "bhavitur bhāvānukūlaḥ bhāvakavyāpāraviśeṣaḥ," the operation of the operator conducive to the production of the result. *Bhāvanā* in turn is of two kinds: *śābdī bhāvanā* and *ārthī bhāvanā*. The injunctive sentence induces the hearer to perform some action, which is denoted by the optative suffix *liṅ*; this type is the *śābdī bhāvanā*. The *ārthī bhāvanā* is based on it and is the activity of the agent that leads to the result. In the *Bhāvanāviveka*, Maṇḍana Miśra defines *bhāvanā* as the absence of inactivity in general (*audāsīnyavicchittisāmānyarūpa*).

The Mīmāṃsakas and the Naiyāyikas accepted individual words and their independent meanings. The Bhāṭṭa schools accepted the *abhihitānvaya* theory of verbal comprehension, according to which the words in a sentence escape their isolated meanings and the syntactic connection among them is found through secondary meaning. The Prābhākara school held that the words themselves conveyed their individual meanings and the syntactic relation (the *anvitābhidhāna* theory). The Nyāya school espoused the association theory of verbal comprehension and held that the syntactic connection among word meanings is obtained through the *saṃsargamaryādā*, the power of mutual association.

In *nīlo ghaṭaḥ*, "a black pot", the syntactic relation between the two word meanings is identity; it is conveyed through the power of association, called *saṃsargamaryādā* by the Logicians. It is not directly conveyed by any element in the sentence. If the underlying syntactic relation between the elements in a sentence is conveyed through some morphemic element in the surface structure itself, it is called *prakāra*. Thus in the phrase *dhānyena dhanavān*, "possessed of wealth in the form of grains," the relation of identity of *dhānya* and *dhana* is conveyed by the instrumental ending *ena* (*dhānyābhinnadhanavān*). Thus a distinction is made between the two types, one in which the syntactic relation is inherent in the constituent elements and the other in which this relation is absent and has to be found through implication or suggestion.

Every verbal root consists of two elements: *phala*, "the result," and *vyāpāra*, "an activity." Thus the meaning of every root can be analyzed as a kind of activity producing some result. Thus *pac*, "to cook," means *viklithyānukūla vyāpāra*, an activity conducive to the softening. In a transitive sentence the activity pertains to the agent (*kartṛ*) and the result of the operation accrues to the object.

In this chapter and the preceding ones we have shown how the

Grammarian philosophers developed a consistent system for handling technical grammatical issues as well as epistemology and metaphysics. True to the Indian tradition the philosophy of Grammar has shown itself to be both a means of theoretical knowledge and a spiritual discipline leading to *mokṣa* or release. The Grammarians began simply with the investigations of words, of how to manipulate and acquire them. But this systematic study of overt speech led to an awareness of higher and higher levels of language until the Word Absolute, Śabda Brahman, was discovered. From this metaphysical perspective, Śabda Brahman is the underlying principle of unity that makes possible all diversity.

For the philosophy of Grammar the division of speech into words and letters is a convenient fiction made for pedagogical purposes, to teach words with precision and economy of effort. The basic division of sentences into words and words into bases (nouns and verb roots) with their respective suffixes is seen to be phenomenal and not ultimately real. A clear analysis of a hierarchy of levels of language is offered from overt or *vaikharī* speech to internal or *madhyamā* speech, with all of these levels being preceded logically by a more unitary stage, *paśyantī*, in which there is no sequence of words but just a glimpse of the separation of word and meaning—the intentionality of the primordial urge to express onself. All of these concepts presuppose a unitary ground out of which distinction is manifested. This ground is called Śabda Brahman because the approach to this Absolute (Brahman) and the manifestation of it is through words (*śabda*).

The philosophical analysis of language offered in the Grammarian literature that follows is not just a logical exercise to satisfy intellectual curiosity, but an earnest and sustained spiritual approach to identify onself with the ground of all speech phenomena, Śabda Brahman.

The philosophy of Grammar sees itself finally as a straight pathway to ultimate freedom (*mokṣamāṇamām ajihmā rājapaddhatiḥ*).

PART TWO

SURVEY OF THE LITERATURE OF GRAMMARIAN PHILOSOPHY

1

PHILOSOPHICAL ELEMENTS IN VEDIC LITERATURE

John G. Arapura and K. Kunjunni Raja

Ṛg Veda

The earliest available literature, the *Ṛg Veda,* contains glowing tributes to the power of speech. To the Vedic seers, who were facing the problem of communicating their mystic experiences, language was naturally an object of wonder and reverence. Many of the later philosophical theories on language may be seen in a subtle form in the Vedic literature itself. There are three hymns that deal mainly with divine Speech (*Vāc*): the *Asyavāmīya* hymn (1.164), which is one of the most philosophical hymns of the *Ṛg Veda,* but full of difficult symbols; 10.71 on the origin of language, which has been subjected to a great deal of interpretation by later Grammarians; and 10.125, where the Goddess of Speech, Vāgambhṛṇī, herself describes her power and functions. (These follow paraphrases of these three hymns.)

Asyavāmīya Hymn

The seer Dīrghatamas asks the question: "I ask thee about the ultimate abode of speech," and answers "the ultimate abode of speech is this Brahman."

The place of *Vāc* is at the peak of the universe. "On the top of yonder sky, they say, is *Vāc,* who knows all, but does not enter all" (verse 10).

Vāc has been divided into four parts. Those Brahmins with insight know them. Three parts that are hidden in the cave, the mortals do not activate. They speak only the fourth part (verse 45).[1]

The seer Dīrghatamas tells us that *Vāc,* like a bull, lowed and thus fashioned the tumultuous, chaotic floods (verse 41). But she had also produced the *akṣara*, the permanent syllable with which the chaotic material was to be organized. She taught it to Agni.

Vāc possessed the *akṣara* of the *Ṛg* (verses 39, 42), who possesses a thousand *akṣaras*.

The same *Vāc* is described by the Brahmins by different names: Agni, Yama, and Mātariśvan (verse 46).

Vāc is also identified with the river Sarasvatī. In the Brāhmaṇas the two are equated: "Your inexhaustible breast, Sarasvatī, a source of delight with which you cause all the choicest things to flourish, which grants treasure, bestows wealth, confers good food—present that here to be sucked" (verse 49).

Ṛg Veda 10.71

Bṛhaspati ! When they came forth to establish the first beginning of language, setting up names, what has been hidden in them as their best and purest good became manifest through love. (1)

When the sages fashioned language with their thought, filtering it like parched grain through a sieve, friends recognized their friends. Their beauty is marked on their language. (2)

They traced the course of language through ritual; they found it embodied in the seers. They gained access to it and distributed it widely; the seven chanters cheered them. (3)

Many who look do not see language, many who listen do not hear her. She reveals herself like a loving and well-adorned wife to her husband, only to some. (4)

Although all the friends have eyes and ears, their mental intuitions are uneven. Some are like shallow ponds, which reach up to the mouth or armpit; others are like ponds that are fit for bathing. (7)

Here the contrast between the two types of people is clearly indicated—those who see *Vāc* and understand her and those who see the form but do not understand her. The Vedic seers were not claiming to be composers of the hymns, rather the seers of an eternal, impersonal truth.

Ṛg Veda 10.125

Here *Vāc* is a personal deity.

I travel with the Rudras and the Vasus, the Ādityas and the Viśvedevāḥ. Both Varuṇa and Mitra do I support, Indra, Agni, and the Aśvins. (1)

I am the sustainer and nourisher of Soma, Tvaṣṭṛ, Pūṣan, and Bhaga. I bestow wealth on the zealous patron of the sacrifice who makes the oblation and presses the Soma. (2)

I am the queen, the gatherer of treasures, the one with penetrating perception, the first of those who should be worshipped. The gods have distributed me manifoldly and caused (the chants) to enter many places. (3)

I am the one through whose *māyā* everyone sees, breathes, and hears. (4)

I am the lone speaker of welcoming words for the feast to the gods and men. Whoever is my favorite, him I make powerful, a true knower of the mystic power, a *ṛṣi* and an intelligent man. (5)

I stretch the bow for Rudra so that his arrow may reach the hater of religion and destroy him. I rouse the battle fury for the people. I have penetrated heaven and earth. (6)

I breathe like the wind supporting all the worlds. Beyond the sky, beyond this earth so great have I become by my might. (8)

The Vedic seers believed that metaphysical knowledge can be had through transcendental vision by the exercise of mental concentration. It is a sort of intuition. The source of all true knowledge is *Vāc*, who may communicate it to whomsoever she favors.

Ṛg Veda 1.164.37 deals with the question of man's self-knowledge. "What *This* is I know not (what I am in reality I know not). Shackled in mind, I move about. As the first born of *ṛta* has approached me, then I got a portion of that *Vāc*." This first born of *ṛta* is Agni; Agni possesses a part of *Vāc*, has a function in the cosmos, and is immortal.

Here *Vāc* must be clearly understood as Logos, and its connection with self-knowledge is a seminal thought already exhibited by this text. Furthermore, its connection with *ṛta* is significant, because the latter stands for the regularity, invariability, and consistency of such paramount importance in the Logos insofar as it is the ratio that goes with it. The idea that the imperishable *Vāc* (Word/Logos) is the first born of *ṛta* shows up again in the *Taittirīya Brāhmaṇa* 2.8.8.5 ("Vāg akṣaram prathamajā ṛtasya"). Now the question about *Vāc* and the question about the self are not associated with each other accidentally, for, on the contrary, that they are related at the greatest depth becomes evident in the Brāhmaṇas and the Upaniṣads.

Cows are often used as symbols for *Vāc*. Ancient texts on etymology and interpretation inform us that "cow" stands for speech. The *Bṛhadāraṇyaka Upaniṣad* (5.8.1) says that "one should meditate on speech as a milch-cow."

The deity *Vāc* was identified with Sarasvatī in the *Atharva Veda* (5.7.5) as *Vāc* Sarasvatī; also in the Brāhmaṇas. In the *Ṛg Veda*, Sarasvatī is an earthly river, 1.164; 49 foreshadows the later identification.

One of the most remarkable characteristics of the Vedas is that the two aspects of *Vāc*, which may be distinguished as the revealing word and the word in invocation (or recitation), are at root the same. The integrity of these two is quite significant in the way the Logos functions in the Vedas. And it is because *Vāc* as the Logos is the basis of the ratio that ratiocination has the potential to act as the open door to truth (*satya*), though by itself it can never realize its own potentiality. But this frustrating incapacity of ratiocination teaches a positive lesson too, namely, that as thinking (*manana*) it is dependent on, and follows, the hearing (*śravaṇa*) of the *Vāc* and that it also leads the way to the deeper thinking called *nididhyāsana*. The primary complement to the mystery of self-revelation, indeed to the very concrete possibility of it, is the other mystery, namely, that of the release of truth the invoking word signifies. With both these, man's power to know encounters its own transcendence. The unfolding of all these hidden dimensions takes place in the Upaniṣads.

Atharva Veda

Stanzas 1–47 of *Ṛg Veda* 1.164 are reproduced with some variations, omissions, and additions in *Atharva Veda* as hymns 9.9 (*Ṛg Veda*, 1–22) and 9.10 (*Ṛg Veda* 23–47). Stanzas 48–52 of *Ṛg Veda* 1.164 are omitted. It may mean that *Ṛg Veda* 1.164 is a blend of two hymns originally separate.

Upaniṣads

Equating of Brahman with speech is also found in the Upaniṣadic literature.

"Speech, truly, is Brahman" ("Vāg vai brahmeti", *Bṛhadāraṇyaka Upaniṣad*, 4.1.2). Here *Brahman* is defined as one reality, without a second, which is identical with speech.

The *Māṇḍūkya Upaniṣad* (3.3) tries to link this absolute, which is unspeakable, with the speakable through speech itself "by creating the deeply meaningful symbol of AUM which traversing the phenomenal levels of consciousness, waking, dreaming, and deep, sleep reaches out beyond to the transcendent where the sound itself comes to an end." Brahman, identical with speech, is also identical with AUM. Just as leaves are held together by a stalk, so is all speech held together by AUM (*Chāndogya Upaniṣad* 2.23.3).

The supersensuous vision of *Vāc* is the ultimate experience of the Real. For the Upaniṣadic seers this intuition of the self has an internal, rather than an external, focus in its symbolic expression.

Uddālaka's teaching in the Sadvidyā passage of *Chāndogyopaniṣad* refers to the role of *Vāc* or language in the manifestation of the world ("Vācārambhaṇaṃ vikāro nāmadheyam mṛttiketyeva satyam," 6.1.3). In clay products clay alone is the real (*satya*), while the product such as a pot or a bowl is the creation of *Vāc* in its dual role of name and form (*nāmarūpa*), the appearances. *Vāc* represents Brahman as the powerful and creative word.

There are several ancient statements quoted in Bhartṛhari's *vṛtti* on his *Vākyapadīya* proclaiming the greatness of the goddess of speech. Many of them have not been identified. It is *Vāc* alone that created the entire universe; the immortal and mortal—all came from *Vāc*. It is *Vāc* that sees objects, that talks about them; *Vāc* alone brings objects together; it is through *Vāc* that the world becomes many, that one reality transforms itself into many.

This attitude of high appreciation of language finds its echo in the words of Daṇḍin in the *Kāvyādarśa* (1.3): "The entire world would have been plunged in darkness, if the light in the form of language had not been shining throughout."

It may, however, be noted that Upaniṣadic seers have at times spoken also about the absolute reality as being beyond the range of language and mind, to point out the inadequacy of language to reveal Reality fully and clearly; for example, "From which the words, as well as the mind, return unable to approach it."

Vedāṅgas

There are six *Vedāṅgas* or auxiliary sciences in the study of the Vedas; *śikṣā* (phonetics), *vyākaraṇa* (grammar), *chandas* (meter), *nirukta* (etymology), *kalpa* (rubrics about rites and rituals), and *jyotiṣa* (astronomy/astrology). The first four are linguistic disciplines and the other two are nonlinguistic. Phonetics, grammar, and meter are traditionally assigned the task of safeguarding the sound aspect of the words in the Vedas, keeping the oral tradition intact. *Nirukta* is concerned with the correct interpretation of the words of the Vedic text, and it goes hand in hand with *vyākaraṇa*. Yāska says that a knowledge of grammar is a prerequisite to the study of *nirukta*. The validity of *nirukta* is based on the fact that it follows from a long tradition from the Brāhmaṇas themselves.

Like the *śikṣās*, the *prātiśākhyas* were also devoted to the preservation of the correct pronunciation for the texts of the Vedic *mantras* and did their work with meticulous care, prescribing rules for prosody, phonetics, accentuation, and the rules of euphonic combination. The term indicates that it is a practical handbook for each school of the Vedas. There is a maxim that in case of conflict between the *śikṣā* and the *prātiśākhya*, the *prātiśākhya* is to be followed.

While *vyākaraṇa* deals with linguistic analysis to determine the exact form of words, *nirukta* is concerned with linguistic analysis of the words to get the proper meaning of the words in the context. *Nirukta* emphasizes the derivation of difficult and apparently unanalyzable terms. The *Uṇādisūtras* take an intermediate standpoint and try to analyze irregular terms, using to a great extent Pāṇini's technique.

The earliest attempts at the interpretation of Vedic *mantras* is found in the Brāhmaṇas themselves, though not in a systematic manner. Explaining the ritualistic background and pointing out the esoteric significance underlying the rituals, they led the way for the ritualistic (*adhiyajña*) and metaphysical (*adhyātma*) interpretations of the Vedas, though the emphasis is on the former. In his *Nirukta* Yāska refers to the ancient view that the *mantras* of the *Ṛg Veda* admit of a threefold interpretation—from the point of view of the performance of religious rites (*adhiyajña*), with reference to the deities (*adhidevatā*), and with reference to the soul (*adhyātman*). There was also a fourth way of interpreting the Vedas, the historical or *aitihāsika*, considering that the gods mentioned in the text are individuals figuring in legends and narratives. It is generally accepted that a text need not have an absolute single meaning. The Vedic poets like ellipses, double meanings, and obscurities. The *Śatapatha Brāhmaṇa* (6.1.1.2) says that the gods like subtle ways ("parokṣapriyā hi devatāḥ").

The *Bṛhaddevatā*, another ancient tool of Vedic exegesis, ascribed to Śaunaka, contains some discussions about language. At 11.117, it says that a sentence is a collection of words, a word is a collection of phonemes. And at 11.118, it says that the meaning of Vedic passages has to be understood with the help of contextual factors: the purpose to be served (*artha*), the subject matter under discussion (*prakaraṇa*), an indication from another place (*liṅga*), propriety, the place, and the time. This requirement applies even to ordinary sentences.

2

PHILOSOPHICAL ELEMENTS IN YĀSKA'S NIRUKTA

K. Kunjunni Raja

The *Nirukta*[1] by Yāska (fifth century B.C.) is a commentary on the *Nighaṇṭu* or collection of Vedic words, discussing the etymology in context. *Nirukta* is one of the *Vedāṅgas* or ancillaries to the study of the Vedas. Yāska is generally considered to be earlier than Pāṇini; but Paul Thieme holds that Yāska knew Pāṇini's work.[2] Cardona thinks that it is better to leave open the question of priority of one over the other.[3]

Yāska follows a long tradition in the Brāhmaṇas of giving the etymological explanation of words. Critics who find some of his etymologies fanciful forget this fact. He wanted etymology to work hand in hand with grammar. He stressed the importance of considering the context while explaining the meaning and etymology of words. The same word could be derived and explained in different ways to suit different contexts.

Yāska's Definitions of the Verb and the Noun

"A verb is chiefly concerned with *bhāva*, whereas nouns have *sattva* as the chief element in their meaning."[4] The term *bhāva* is derived from the root *bhū*, meaning "to become," and the term *sattva* is derived from the root *as*, meaning "to be." These two roots, *as* and *bhū*, are almost synonymous and mean "to exist."

Nirukta 1.2 refers with approval to the view of Vārṣāyaṇi that there are six modes for this *bhāva* or "becoming." Vārṣāyaṇi says that there are six modes for *bhāva*: a thing comes into existence, exists, changes, grows, decays, and ceases to exist.[5] One of these modes, "exists" (*asti*) is derived from the same root as *sattva*, hence there is a possibility of confusion.

Bhartṛhari explains that reality (*sattā*), when it appears in a temporal sequence in various particular things, is called *kriyā* or *bhāva* and, when viewed without any such temporal sequence, is called *sattva*. Thus, *sattva* and *bhāva* are two aspects of the same existence seen from the static and the dynamic points of view, respectively.[6] Yāska himself has suggested the same by saying, "The verb indicates the action, which takes place in a temporal sequence."[7] And Patañjali says that even verbal nouns have the static element predominating their meaning.[8]

Audumbarāyaṇa's Theory

"It is the statement as a whole that is regularly present in the perceptive faculty of the hearer."[9] According to the interpretation of this passage, Audumbarāyaṇa and Vārttākṣa held the view that it is only the sentence that is really found in the minds of the speaker and the listener; therefore, the fourfold classification of words into nouns (*nāman*), verbs (*ākhyāta*), prepositions (*upasarga*), and particles (*nipāta*) has no absolute validity. Audumbarāyaṇa's theory is considered the forerunner of Bhartṛhari's *sphoṭa* theory.[10]

Derivation of Nouns from Verbal Roots

The fundamental assumption of the etymologist was that nouns were derived from verbal roots. Yāska generally subscribed to this view, and we find in his *Nirukta* the tendency, often mechanical, to derive words from imaginary roots, as in the case of *pumān* from *puṃs*. Śākaṭāyana, to whom one tradition ascribed the *Uṇādisūtras* and who is mentioned by both Pāṇini and Yāska, seems to have been a staunch advocate of this theory. But Gārgya and some of the Grammarians held a more sober view that it is not possible to trace all nouns to verbal roots.[11]

Following Gārgya, Yāska discussed the pros and cons of this problem. If all nouns are derived from verbal roots that denote action, on the one hand every object will have as many names as the actions with which it is associated, and on the other hand each noun can be applied to as many objects as are associated with an action indicated by that verbal root. Thus the term *aśva*, "a horse," derived from the root *aś*, "to move," would have to be applied to a camel as well, and for a pillar that stands upright fixed to a hole and joins a beam, different names indicating these different aspects would have to be applied. Yāska's explanation of this problem is that the words are used naturally (*svabhāvataḥ*). Language designates things in an incomplete manner; it can choose only one of the many activities associated with an object. Incidentally, this discussion also indicates the explanation for the presence of synonyms and homonyms in language.

Yāska accepts the general rules that all nominal forms are to be derived from verbal roots and that in deriving words proper attention should be paid to accent, grammatical formation, and meaning. The particular rules mentioned are the following:

(1) A nominal form is to be derived from a verbal root that has the sense of that act which solely belongs to the thing denoted by the noun in such a way that its accent and formation are based on rules of grammar, for example, *kāraka* from *kṛ*.

(2) When the current meaning of a word does not agree with the meaning of the root apparent in it and when its nominal form cannot be developed in the ordinary manner from the root by the rules of grammar, one should take one's stand on the general meaning only and explain the word through its resemblance to the verbal or nominal form of a root with the related meaning. For example, *hasta*, "a hand," should be derived not from *has*, "to laugh" apparent in it, but from *han*, "to strike" because the hand is quick at striking.

(3) When there is no resemblance between a word and any form of a root that has its meaning, the resemblance or community of even a single letter (vowel or consonant) should be the basis of etymology.

(4) Even inflected case forms may be adjusted to the meaning.

(5) Similarly, secondary (*taddhita*) derivatives (formed by adding suffixes to nouns) and compounds (whether of two or more members) should be broken down into their component elements and the component elements explained. One should never give up the attempt at derivation ("na tveva na nirbrūyāt").

Secondary Meaning (*Lakṣaṇā*)

Yāska knew that in etymology the semantic aspect is as important as the phonetic aspect; a word may be applied to a thing through similarity of meaning as well, through metaphoric transfer. He was also aware of onomatopoeia (*śabdānukṛti*) as a factor in the naming of some birds, such as *kāka*; also *dundubhi* is derived similarly. But he does not mention secondary meaning (*lakṣaṇā*) explicitly.

Yāska's aim was to explain Vedic words in the contexts of the Vedic passages themselves; hence to suit the contexts he gave different derivations for the same word as it occurred in different contexts. Meaning was the principal element to which other elements were subordinated. Yāska was concerned mainly with the primary sense of words and did not pay much attention to the importance of metaphoric meaning. Thus the term *asura* referring to the gods and the same term referring to the demons are differently derived; he does not consider that the latter sense is through pejorative tendency. It may be noted here that even Pāṇini did not recognize metaphoric transfer as an extension of the primary sense, and he gave separate enumeration of the use of the container for the contained among the meanings of the nominative case.

Classification of Words

Yāska divided Sanskrit words into four parts of speech: noun, verb, preposition, and particle. A verb is concerned with dynamic activity involving the time factor, while nouns represent static things.[12] *Sarvanāman* (pronouns) are also recognized. Regarding prepositions, Yāska says that Śākaṭāyana held the view that a preposition detached from the verb has no meaning, that it is only suggestive (*dyotaka*). Gārgya held the opposite view, that prepositions do have a meaning. Yāska seems to have agreed with Gārgya, for he enumerates twenty prepositions together with their meanings.

3

PHILOSOPHICAL ELEMENTS IN PĀṆINI'S *AṢṬĀDHYĀYĪ*

K. Kunjunni Raja

Pāṇini's *Aṣṭādhyāyī* of the fifth century B.C.[1] is a complete grammar of the Sanskrit language, including the Vedic language. In eight chapters, each subdivided into four *pādas*, it contains about four thousand rules in *sūtra* style, preceded by abbreviation rules grouping the phonemes of Sanskrit. The *sūtras* refer to groups of verbal roots (*dhātu*) and of nominal bases (*gaṇa*), hence the *dhātupāṭha* and the *gaṇapāṭha* form adjuncts to the work. It is believed that meanings were attached to the roots later by Bhīmasena and did not form part of the original. The *Uṇādisūtras* as they survive today are not Pāṇini's.

Pāṇini refers to ten earlier authorities, most of them presumably grammarians. He also refers to differences in the usage of words by people in different parts of India ("northerners," "easterners," and so on). Considerable thought had been devoted before Pāṇini to phonological and grammatical statements. On the basis of all of these and his own observations of the language, Pāṇini composed the *Aṣṭādhyāyī*, which remains a monumental work, even now, as a model of descriptive grammar.

Cultural Usage of Language

Pāṇini uses the term *bhāṣā* (speech) for the Sanskrit spoken by the cultured and educated people (*śiṣṭa*). They are the final authority in the case of language, says Patañjali, who points out the importance of cultivated usage in many places.[2]

Pāṇini (or Kātyāyana) says that the authority of the popular usage of words (*aṃjñā*) must supersede the authority of the meaning dependent on derivation.[3] The meanings of words (the relations between word (*śabda*) and meaning (*artha*)) are also established by popular usage.[4]

Derivation of Nouns from Verbal Roots

Pāṇini generally accepts the view that verbal roots are the basic units to which affixes are added. But he does not accept Śākaṭāyana's view that all nouns are derivable from verbal roots. The *Uṇādisūtras*, explaining the derivation of irregular nouns from verbal roots, are not Pāṇini's, though Pāṇini was aware of such attempts (3.3.1, 3.4.75). Patañjali refers to such irregular nouns as nonderivable nominal bases.[5] Pāṇini seems to accept Gārgya's view that it is not possible to derive all nouns from verbal roots.[6]

Syntax

Pāṇini is mainly concerned with the formation of correct words. But syntax is not completely excluded. His system implies a sentence analysis, and his discussion of compound formations is based on syntactic considerations.

Rule 2.1.1 is *samārthaḥ padavidhiḥ*, "an operation involving two or more words (*padas*) applies only to such words as are syntactically and semantically related." The term *sāmarthya* is explained by Patañjali and Kātyāyana as implying unity of semantic function (*ekārthībhāva*) and mutual syntactic connection (*parasparā vyāpekṣā*).

Thus Pāṇini's concept of a sentence seems to be almost the same as that of Jaimini, whose *Mīmāṃsāsūtra* defines it thus: "A group of words serving a single purpose forms a sentence if on analysis the separate words are found to have mutual expectancy."[7]

Of the three conditions of syntactic unity for a sentence, namely, mutual expectancy (*ākāṅkṣā*), phonetic contiguity (*sannidhi*), and semantic fitness (*yogyatā*), the first two are tacitly accepted by Pāṇini but not the third. Pāṇini does not make any provision for an utterance derived by his rules to be semantically appropriate; even deviant and semantically unacceptable sentences can be grammatically correct.

Pāṇini does not define a sentence (*vākya*). Kātyāyana's definition (*ekatiṅ vākyam*), "a sentence is that collection of words having one finite verb," does not seem to reflect Pāṇini's view. Pāṇini's rule "an item terminating in a verbal ending (*tiṅ*) has no high pitched vowel, after an item that terminates in an ending other than a verbal ending (*tiṅ atiṅaḥ*)" (8.1.28), shows that Pāṇini accepted the possibility of a finite verb preceded by another finite verb in the same sentence.[8]

Lakṣaṇā or Secondary Meaning

Pāṇini sanctions the nominative case ending not only for the nominal stem notion (*prātipādika*) but also for indicating the additional notions of gender, measure and number. The rule reads: "The nominative ending is to be added when there is nothing but the nominal stem notion, nothing but the gender, nothing but the measure, nothing but the number" (2.3.46).

From the discussion of the term "measure" (*parimāṇa*) in this rule by later writers it is clear that Pāṇini wanted to justify the nominative ending in transferred uses such as that of the container for the contained. Jinendrabuddhi explains that the term *parimāṇa* here is an indicator (*upalakṣaṇa*) of other transferred senses, as in "the boy is a lion" (*siṃho māṇavakaḥ*).[9] The term "measure" sanctions use of the nominative in cases like "a measure of grain" (*prastho vrīhiḥ*), in which there is the additional notion of being measured by; hence even in cases like "the Brāhmaṇa is fire," in which the additional notion of "similarity to the fire" is to be indicated, the nominative ending is justified. From the preceding it is clear that Pāṇini did not accept secondary meaning as a separate function of words, for otherwise there was no need to include measure in the *sūtra*.

Explaining the *sūtra* 1.4.42, *sādhakatamaṃ karaṇam* ("*karaṇa* is that instrument which is the most immediate one in accomplishing action"), Patañjali says that the use of the superlative *tama* here is to indicate that the rules relating to the case endings (*kāraka*) may be applied even in extended cases, not only to those expressly stated but also to those implied thereby. Thus instances of implied usages of secondary meaning could also come under the scope of that *sūtra*. For example, proximity can be one of the implied meanings of the locative case, and *gaṅgāyāṃ gāvaḥ*, "cows on the Ganges," can come under the purview of the rule governing the locative.

Reference and Use

The dual function of an expression to refer to both its own form and its meaning is noted by Pāṇini. Rule 1.1.68 ("svaṃ rūpaṃ śabdasyā-śabdasaṃjñā") states that in his grammatical text an expression serves to denote itself unless it is a technical term.

In ordinary language a word normally refers to its meaning unless it is a quotation; and usually to indicate that it is a quotation the word *iti* (thus) is added at the end of the word quoted. But in grammatical metalanguage, a word normally refers to its own form except when it is a technical term. The rule *agner ḍhak* (4.3.23) introduces *ḍhak eya* after the term *agni*; the suffix is applied to the form *agni* and obviously not to its meaning (or synonyms). When *iti* is added to an expression in a rule, the preceding refers to the meaning and not to the form; thus in *na veti vibhāṣā* the sanctioning option applies to the meaning "or not" and not to the form *na vā*.[10]

4

PHILOSOPHICAL ELEMENTS IN PATAÑJALI'S MAHĀBHĀṢYA

K. Kunjunni Raja

Patañjali's *Mahābhāṣya* of the second century B.C. is an extensive discussion of select rules from Pāṇini and Kātyāyana's comments on them given in his *vārttikas*. It is not a full commentary on Pāṇini's *Aṣṭādhyāyī*. It incorporates Kātyāyana's *vārttikas*; it also contains *vārttika*-like statements in verse (called *ślokavārttikas*). It is an elaborate commentary that analyzes each rule into its components, adding items necessary to the understanding of the rule, giving examples and counterexamples illustrating how the rule operates and discussing the need for the *vārttikas* to bring out the full significance of Pāṇini's *sūtra* or to account for usages apparently not covered by the rule or against the rule. Both Kātyāyana and Patañjali wanted to test the validity and consistency of the rules. Some scholars have suggested that historical changes in Sanskrit are responsible for Kātyāyana's comments that modify and correct Pāṇini. Patañjali often presents arguments to support or reject several views, leaving it difficult to know his "finally accepted view" (*siddhānta*).

As far as the philosophical ideas are concerned, Patañjali seems to have been influenced by Vyāḍi's *Saṃgraha*, which is not extant; he quotes many ideas from the *Saṃgraha* with approval. Most of the philosophical ideas are found in the introductory section.

Śabda and *Artha*

Patañjali discusses whether the relation between a linguistic item (*śabda*) and its meaning (*artha*) is permanent or the invention of someone. A linguistic item, according to the grammarian, is not merely the sound but that unit (or symbol) which, when articulated, brings about the notion of the thing meant.[1]

"What is the word 'cow'? It is that by means of which, when uttered, there arises the understanding of creatures with dewlap, tail, hump, hooves, and horns."[2] The commentators have made it clear that the term "uttered" (*uccarita*) is used in the sense of "revealed" or brought to light (*abhivyakta*). Thus Patañjali lays special emphasis on the fact that a linguistic item is a word only when it has a meaning. This concept contradicts the Mīmāṃsā view that an aggregate of letters, when manifested, is a linguistic utterance, even when there is no meaning or when the meaning is not understood.[3]

A linguistic item is considered eternal and not capable of being newly produced. Patañjali says that one goes to a potter requesting him to make a pot so that one may use it; but one does not go to a grammarian with the request to make new words so that one may use them. A distinction is made between absolute eternality (*kūṭastha nityatā*) and the permanence of the items as used through generations by speakers (*pravāhanityatā*). Bhartṛhari distinguishes between normal permanent words in a language (*ājānika*) and modern technical terms coined by writers like Pāṇini (*ādhunika*).

Regarding the meaning of a word, the problem discussed is whether it is the universal (*jāti*) or the individual (*dravya*). According to Patañjali, Pāṇini accepted both as meanings, and in either case "meaning" refers to something permanent.[4]

The relation between linguistic item and meaning is established (*siddha*) and is known from the usage of educated people.[5]

Are Letters Meaningful?

On the one hand, letters may be said to be meaningful, because meaning can be understood from verbal roots, stems, suffixes, or particles that consist of a single letter, and also because the substitution of a different letter can produce a different meaning, while the absence of a letter may make it impossible to understand the meaning of a word. On the other hand, it may also be said that letters are meaningless in themselves, because a meaning is not understood by the hearer from each letter separately.[6] Patañjali does not give any final answer to this question. Unlike Bhartṛhari, Patañjali did not consider the word to be an indivisible and timeless symbol, apart from the letters that are revealed when the word is uttered.

The Primary Meaning of a Word

Patañjali discusses the problem of whether the primary meaning of a nominal word is the particular substantive or the universal essential attribute. Among grammarians Vyāḍi, author of the *Saṃgraha*, held that a word primarily denotes a substance (*dravya*), while Vājapyāyana held the Mīmāṃsaka view that it is the universal (*jāti*) that forms the primary meaning of a word.[7]

Patañjali says that according to Pāṇini the primary meaning of a word is both the universal and the particular, for *sūtra* 1.2.58[8] is based on the view that a word means the universal, while *sūtra* 1.2.64[9] is based on the assumption that a word means a particular.[10] Helārāja says that according to the school of Pāṇini a word means both the universal and the particular.[11]

Bhartṛhari discusses elaborately the various problems involved in these two views and concludes that whether the meaning of a word is the universal or the substance it is something real and permanent. Patañjali has also defined an "individual" (*dravya*) as that which does not lose its essence when different qualities come to inhere in it.[12]

Perception of a Temporal Series

Patañjali and Kātyāyana discuss the problem of how a word can be grasped as a whole, if the different sounds come one after another in the exact order in which they are uttered and there is not a single moment in which all of the sounds are perceived together.[13]

Taking the example of the word for cow, *gauḥ*, he says, "When the speech is in *g*, it cannot be in *au* and *ḥ*; when it is in *au*, it cannot be in *g* and *ḥ*, and when it is in *ḥ*, it cannot be in *g* and *au*. ... Each letter requires a special effort to produce it, and it disappears as the effort is changed to produce the next letter."[14]

Patañjali solves the problem thus: even though the letters cannot coexist at the time of utterance, they can do so in the mind of the speaker as well as in that of the listeners; the sequence of the letters is also to be grasped in the mind on the basis of the meaning.[15] Patañjali does not discuss the problem in detail; but he says that the simultaneous grasping of the word as a whole is somehow effected in the mind, even though the letters that make it up are pronounced separately.

Patañjali's View of the *Sphoṭa*

Patañjali distinguishes between *sphoṭa* and *dhvani*. The former is the permanent element in the word and may be considered the essential word, while the latter is the actualized and ephemeral element and an attribute of the former.[16]

The *sphoṭa* as described by Patañjali may be a single letter or a fixed pattern of letters. It is the norm: it remains constant and is not affected by the peculiarities of the individual speakers. Even when pronounced by different speakers with different tempos its linguistic value is the same. The absolute vowel length and the individual peculiarities of the particular instances are the sounds (*dhvani*) and depend on the individuality of the speaker and on the effort with which the words are uttered. The *sphoṭa* is permanent and unchanging and is manifested by the ephemeral sounds uttered by the speaker and heard by the listener, which are analogous to Bhartṛhari's *prākṛta* sound and *vaikṛta* sound.

This distinction is supposed to have been made by Vyāḍi, author of the *Saṃgraha*. *Vākyapadīya* 1.77,[17] defining the two types of sounds, is ascribed to Vyāḍi by commentators. According to this account, *prākṛta* sound (= Patañjali's *sphoṭa*) causes the perception of letters, and *vaikṛta* sound (= Patañjali's *dhvani*) causes the differences in speed of utterance.

Kātyāyana on 1.1.70 says that the letters are fixed and that the styles of diction depend on the speech habits of the speaker.[18] Explaining this concept, Patañjali illustrates it with the analogy of a drum beat: "When a drum is struck, one drum beat may travel twenty feet, another thirty, another forty; but the *sphoṭa* is precisely such and such a size, the increase in length is caused by the sound."[19] Patañjali uses the term *sphoṭa* even to designate a single letter (*varṇa*):[20] "In both cases (*r* and *l*) it is only the *sphoṭa* that is taught in the *sūtra*."

Gender

The *Mahābhāṣya* on *sūtra* 4.1.3 takes up the question of grammatical gender and first attempts to correlate it with sex: "A female is characterized by breasts and hair, a male by his body hair, and the others by neither."[21] But this concept of gender (*liṅga*) does not apply to Sanskrit grammar. So Patañjali tries to explain grammatical gender in terms of the constituents (*guṇas*). He states clearly that the grammarians cannot take the grammatical gender to be the same as the gender of normal worldly usage (referring to the sex).[22] Every object is characterized by different states of constituent element (*guṇa*), and these states constitute the gender of the thing.[23] Patañjali does not refer to the three Sāṃkhya *guṇas* of *sattva*, *rajas*, and *tamas* here; but later commentators consider that they are implied.

Patañjali also proposed a formal definition of grammatical gender: that which is referred to by the pronoun *ayam* is masculine, that which is referred to by *iyam* is feminine, that which is referred to by *idam* is neuter.

Purpose of Studying Grammar

One who knows the correct formation of words (*śabdasaṃskāra*) can discriminate correct words (*sādhu*) from incorrect words. Although communication may be possible even by using incorrect words, it is only by the use of proper words that one achieves merit (*dharma*).

While discussing the Vedic hymn beginning "catvāri śṛṅgāḥ..." Patañjali does not refer to the later theory of Bhartṛhari according to which the symbolic meaning of the passage refers to the four stages in the evolution of speech from the highest speech principle—*parā*, *paśyantī*, *madhyamā*, and *vaikharī*. The "four horns of the bull" are explained by Patañjali as the four classes of words, noun, verb, prefix, and particle (*nāmākhyātopasarganipātāḥ*).

5

BHARTṚHARI

The central figure of the philosophical development of grammar is Bhartṛhari, whose dates are still in dispute, though recent scholarship has come to general agreement about their likely confines. It has been shown that quotations from Bhartṛhari's works appear in the *Pramāṇasamuccaya* of Dignāga, the great Buddhist logician, who must be dated in the fifth and sixth centuries. Furthermore, Siṃhasūrigaṇi, a sixth-century Jain writer, tells us that Bhartṛhari studied under a Grammarian named Vasurāta, whom he identifies as a brother-in-law of a pupil of another famous Buddhist, Vasubandhu. Erich Frauwallner suggests, on the basis of these considerations, that because Dignāga presumably flourished between A.D. 485 and 540, we may date Bhartṛhari between 450 and 510 and Vasurāta between 430 and 490.[1] These dates are accepted by most recent scholarship as the best we can currently do.

As with many great figures of classical times in India, a large number of works have been attributed to Bhartṛhari, and once again current scholarship has hardly settled all questions concerning the authenticity of some of these claims. By definition, the Bhartṛhari we are speaking of is the author of the work that is regularly referred to as the *Vākyapadīya*, a seminal work on Grammar and grammatical philosophy the influence of which, though difficult to calculate precisely, is certainly considerable in subsequent philosophical developments, both within Grammar and outside it. This work has three chapters, and it was more properly termed *Trikāṇḍī* on that account. Ashok Aklujkar has argued that only the first two chapters constitute the *Vākyapadīya*. It seems likely that Bhartṛhari also composed the commentary called *vṛtti* on at least the first two chapters of the *Trikāṇḍī*.[2] Beside this body of literature—verses and prose commentary—Bhartṛhari apparently also wrote a commentary—or part of one—on Patañjali's *Mahābhāṣya*. Again, the proper title is a matter of discussion: Aklujkar points out that the title *Tripādī* for it has extensive sanction among early commentators in the grammatical tradition, while the title under which it is frequently known nowadays, *Mahābhāṣyadīpikā*, has only one manuscript mention in its favor. No doubt the work is referred to regularly as a *ṭīkā* on the *Mahābhāṣya*. It seems likely that it was a lengthy work, perhaps covering the entire scope of Patañjali's masterpiece, though only a small portion is now available.

There are occasional references to another work, called *Śabdadhātusamīkṣā*, which is attributed to Bhartṛhari by Somānanda and Utpalācārya, two Kashmiri Śaivas of the ninth and tenth centuries. Utpalācārya indicates that in this work Bhartṛhari set forth the kind of awareness he calls *paśyantī*, which is also discussed in the *Trikāṇḍī*. This work has unfortunately not been preserved, as far as we can tell.

Indian tradition identifies Bhartṛhari the Grammarian with the famous poet who wrote the *Subhāṣitatriśatī*, three sets of a hundred stanzas each bearing the titles of *Nīti-*, *Śṛṅgara-*, and *Vairāgya-śataka*. Actually, the number of stanzas is many hundreds more than three hundred, which complicates the arguments on identity of authorship perhaps beyond hope of any definitive solution.

Brief Analysis

Ashok Aklujkar

Language

(1) Language (*vāk*) has four levels or phases: speech (*vaikharī*), mental/intellectual or potential speech (*madhyamā*), latent totality of units (*paśyantī*), and pure, basic language principle (*parā paśyantī-rūpa*).

(2) Viewed as a specific totality or sign system, language consists of three classes of units: phoneme (*varṇa*), word (*pada*), and sentence (*vākya*).

(3) If what is cognized is a meaning having no expectancy for an unused or absent word, then its signifier is a sentence. Such a signifier may consist of only one word.

(4) A single phoneme signifying some fairly well-associated meaning is a word.

(5) The sentence, word, and phoneme are unitary entities (*sphoṭa*). Only while being perceived (due to association with sound, which by nature has a sequence) and when conscious or subconscious grammatical analysis is being carried out do they appear to be made up of parts. Even so, the parts, though accepted commonsensically and on the level of analysis, do not exhaust the wholes.

(6) The linguistic units sentence, word, and phoneme can be regarded either as universals (*śabdākṛti*) or as particulars (*śabdavyakti*).

(7) The linguistic units are permanent (*nitya*).[3]

(8) The sentence is the primary linguistic unit.

(9) Language is infinite. There is no numerical limit to the sentences possible in a language.

(10) Sentence meaning is the direct or indirect basis of meaning at other linguistic levels. It is in the form of an action-oriented cognition or "intuition" (*pratibhā*). It comes into being through the instrumentality of word meanings but is not confined to them. As an event, it is a unitary entity. On the level of analysis, it can be conceived in various ways: as a coalescence (*saṃsarga*) of general word meanings; as a meaning that comes in addition (*ādhikya*) to the word meanings; as differentiation (*bheda, apoha*) from entities that are not intended; as establishment of a relation (*saṃbandha*); as relation that brings words, associated with general (*sāmānya*) meanings, into association with specific or qualified (*viśiṣṭa*) meanings; and as action as cognized from the verb (not the physical action) and as qualified by the meanings of other sentence components (*viśiṣṭa kriyā*).

(11) Word meanings are of the signified (*vācya*, denotatum) or cosignified (*dyotya*, functional/grammatical) variety. The former are meanings that are entirely unsignified prior to the use of words that signify them (consider the meanings of "bull," "white," and "moves"). The latter are meanings that are *possibly* signified but are not definitely known before the use of appropriate signifiers (consider the meaning of "and" as revealed by the pair of phrases "Devadatta Ḍittha" and "Devadatta and Ḍittha").

(12) Signified (*vācya*) meanings have either a reified, accomplished (*siddha*) nature or a sequential, to-be-accomplished (*sādhya*) nature. If a pronoun can stand for what a word signifies, then that signified belongs to the former category.

(13) Meanings of words, whether compound (*vṛtti, samasta*) or non-compound (*asamasta*), are unitary at the level of ordinary communication; they come to be viewed as made of parts on the level of analysis.

(14) Word meanings are primarily mental or intellectual entities (*buddhyartha*), only secondarily and not always physical entities (*vastvartha*). As mental entities, they are not just "images". In fact, in the ultimate analysis, meanings have no existence apart from the linguistic units, which are also mental, that signify them.

(15) Word meanings, entertained as separate entities for the sake of analysis and in deference to the common way of thinking, can be regarded either as particulars or as universals.

(16) The relation between a word and its meaning can be characterized in several ways: as the relation of capability (*yogyatā*), as a cause-and-effect relation (*kāryakāraṇabhāva*), and as one of identification or superimposition (*abhedādhyāropa* or *adhyāsa*). Under any of these charac-

terizations, the relation is permanent (*nitya*), in different senses of the word "permanent."[4] When a convention of the type "X means X_1" is established, "X" is not newly made capable of signifying "X_1"; only its capacity is thereby restricted.

(17) Language is innate and without a beginning. It has been in existence as long as living beings have been in existence.

Epistemology

(1) In the sphere of ordinary experience there is no cognition that is not oriented to some kind of object, nor is there a cognition that is purely of the thing or physical reality. Linguistic expressions and the conceptual scheme they embody invariably figure in cognitions.

(2) No type of cognition (perceptual, inferential, testimonial) points to reality without ever failing. Validity is not a built-in feature of any type. It can be determined only by testing the content of the cognition under consideration against the totality of experience and the principles the totality has developed.

(3). All cognitions are infused with language in one way or another.

(4) Extraordinary cognitions—in other words, cognitions that transcend the limitations of ordinary cognitions in terms of dependence on objects, reflection of preconceptions, validity, and presence of linguistic expressions—are possible in the case of those who have spiritually perfected themselves; but such cognitions are not the basis of worldly communication and conceptualization.

(5) Every cognition is unitary, that is, devoid of divison and sequence. It appears as having parts or distinct elements (*mātrā*) because the diversity of its objects is transferred to it.

(6) The similarity and hence the universal (*sāmānya*) of cognitions are derived from the similarity of objects reflected in them.

(7) A cognition as an event, in its own consciousness form (*saṃvidākāra*), does not ever become an object of cognition; it is self-manifest.

(8) All cognitions enjoy the same period of existence.

(9) The distinctions drawn among sentience (*citi*), cognizer (*buddhi*) proceeding toward cognizing, instrument of cognition, fact of cognition, and the reflected form of the object are only conceptual; the entities spoken of are not physically distinct.

(10) The intellect can unify, juxtapose, differentiate, and identify entities irrespective of what obtains in the realm of perceptible reality. Furthermore, it has a capacity to view its own constituents as external to itself.

Ontology

(1) We can determine the existence or nonexistence of something only if it is reflected in cognition and hence in language.

Ontic decisions differ with difference of perspective. A scaled or tiered ontology is therefore to be preferred. For the grammarian or linguist, who has to work with meanings, it suffices to accept the existence of everything that language reflects as existing. By contrast, one who is out to find out what really exists will realize that ultimately only the physical things and the language principle exist; the rest of the multiplicity of objects is simply a result of the interaction of these two existents. Qualities (*guṇa/dharma*), capacities (*śakti*), relations (*saṃbandha*), universals (*jāti*), numbers (*saṃkhyā*), phases (*avasthā*), grouping (*sāhitya, sāmagrī, samūha*), and absence (*abhāva*) do not have any existence of their own apart from the physical objects. Time (*kāla*) and space (*diś*) are, however, capacities and creations of the language principle. To come to the third tier of ontology, the perspective is of someone who wishes to go beyond worldly experience and existence. For him only the language principle exists; the traces of physical things that exist in the intellect in the form of specific linguistic expressions are necessarily wiped out.

(3) As a thing can be cognized and spoken of in a number of ways, it can be viewed as a collection of capacities.

(4) Actions can first be grouped into six categories: "is born," "exists," "changes," "increases," "decreases," and "is destroyed." These categories can be further reduced to three: "is born," "exists," and "is destroyed." Because birth (or production) and destruction can be proved to be only appearance and disappearance of the specific forms of the thing (the thing is never entirely destroyed to be born or produced again), only "exists" or existence (*sattā*) ultimately remains.

New Contributions to the System

Bhartṛhari's work is chronologically the fourth surviving work in the Pāṇinian grammatical tradition. Much earlier literature that shaped his thinking and much subsequent literature that could have indicated the extent of his original contribution has been lost to us. Consequently, one cannot determine with ease or certainty the contribution he made to his system for the first time. Bhartṛhari does not write in a way that would set apart his views from those of his predecessors or contemporaries. Although one feels the assurance of an original, self-confident thinker in his style, and the tradition speaks of his having held distinct views,[5] Bhartṛhari makes neither a general claim of distinction nor specific statements identifying his own views. The following observations are, therefore, to be read as stating what is *probably* a new contribution.

(1) Grammar (*vyākaraṇa*) becomes a full-scale *darśana*, a purposive view of reality, in Bhartṛhari's work.

(2) Speculation on the nature and role of speech (*vāc*) going back to the earliest Vedic philosophers combines in Bhartṛhari's work with

descriptive grammar, which arose out of concern with Vedic texts. Theories of grammar and theories of language are treated together in a measure far surpassing that of earlier available works.

Trikāṇḍī OR *Vākyapadīya*, WITH *Vṛtti* ON BOOKS 1 AND 2

Ashok Aklujkar, with Karl H. Potter

The summary that follows is the work of Ashok Aklujkar, with occasional adumbrations by Karl H. Potter. *E* references are to the editions by K.A. Subramania Iyer for book 1 (Deccan College Monograph Series 32, Poona, 1966); by K. Raghavan Pillai for book 2 (Motilal Banarsidass, Delhi, 1971); and by K.V. Abhyankar and V.P. Limaye for book 3 (University of Poona Sanskrit and Prakrit Series 2, Poona, 1965). *T* references are to the translation of K.A. Subramania Iyer for book 1 (Deccan College Building Centenary and Silver Jubilee Series 26, Poona, 1965), book 2 (Motilal Banarsidass, Delhi, 1977), book 3, part 1 (Deccan College Building Centenary and Silver Jubilee Series 71, Poona, 1971), and book 3, part 2 (Motilal Banarsidass, Delhi,

BOOK 1

1—4 (*E*1; *T*1). Brahman has neither beginning nor end, either temporarily or spatially. It is the language principle (*śabdatattva*), the permanent syllable (*akṣara*). It turns into (*vivartate*) a temporarily real multiplicity through its capacities of time and space.

Vṛtti (*E*1-14; *T*1-3). Brahman is a principle beyond all conceptual constructions (*vikalpa*). It has all powers (*śakti*) that are neither identical with nor different from it. Its form is a disjunction of *vidyā* and *avidyā*. Even though its manifestations appear as temporally and spatially ordered, Brahman remains unaffected; it is free from spatial or temporal limitations. All of its manifestations, though apparently different from one another, are to be understood as linguistic, because they share their generative source (*prakṛti*). Because we grasp things through language they must be recognized as sharing in the language principle.

Brahman is said to be the permanent syllable because it is the condition (*nimitta*) of the permanent syllable. Its individual manifestation (*vyakti*) takes place for the purpose of making known to others what is inside each person's consciousness (*caitanya*).

"It turns into a temporarily real multiplicity"—that is, manifestation (*vivarta*) is a single thing's taking on unreal (*asatya*) distinctions as belonging to other things and without losing its own unitary nature; it is like the appearances of contents in dream.

(A number of verses follow that may or may not be quoted from elsewhere. These verses develop the idea of an inner controller [*antaryāmin*], Brahman, who while remaining unaffected creates the diversity of the world out of language.)

2 (*E*14; *T*4). This (Brahman), which has been traditionally taught as single and appears to be many through its various powers, though not separate from its powers, appears to be so.

Vṛtti on 2 (*E*14-17; *T*4). "Through its various powers" the language principle, in which Brahman's powers are collected, remains one, just as an awareness that comprehends many contents—earth, people, and so on—remains one. Thus the form (*ākāra*) of the awareness is not different from the form of the contents, for the unity of the one is not opposed to the diversity of the other. "Though not separate from its powers," in other words, it is not that some of Brahman's powers differ from others as, say, particulars and universals differ from each other, but rather, just as in illumination the illuminator appears different from what is illumined, though they are really identical (*tādātmya*), so it is here.

3 (*E*18; *T*5). The six modifications—birth and so on—are the source of the distinctions among states (*bhāva*), depending on the temporal power (*kālaśakti*) of that (Brahman).

Vṛtti on 3 (*E*18-20; *T*5). All (other) powers come to be in dependence on the independent (power of) time. The apparent temporal sequence of things is a function of the limitations of the powers things have to take many forms, limitations operating through obstruction and permission. Thus time is the auxiliary cause (*sahakārikāraṇa*) of all modifications, in virtue of its postponing or effecting their occurrence. Because it thus produces sequential appearances, sequence is attributed to it (time), as the lines of a scale that result from contact with the thing being weighed are attributed to the scale. In this way the six transformations (*pariṇāma*) or modifications—birth and so on—become the source of the modifications in (types of) existence.

4 (*E*21; *T*6). That single seed of all things thus comes to have a state of multiplicity as experiencer (*bhoktṛ*), experienced (*bhokta*), and experience (*bhoga*).

5 (*E*22; *T*7). The Veda is both a means of attaining to and a reflection of That (Brahman). Though single, the Veda has been passed down by tradition in many different ways.

Vṛtti on 5 (*E*22-26; *T*7-8). Attainment of Brahman is merely getting beyond egoity. Others say it is the absorption of the modifications into *prakṛti*, or stopping the organs (*vaikaraṇya*), or contentment not as a means (*asādhana-paritṛpti*), or the Self, or desire for the Self, or not having any adventitious thing as one's purpose, or possession of perfected powers, or escape from functioning in time, or attainment of no-self.

"A reflection" of Brahman means that the Vedas as language reflect Brahman as our dreams reflect or suggest waking things.

6–10 (*E*27-38; *T*9-15). Brief discussion of Vedic branches and of the Veda as a source of rites, *smṛti*, philosophical schools, and traditional lore.

11 (*E*39; *T*16). Grammar is the first among the (six) auxiliary sciences, the one nearest to Brahman, the best austerity.

Vṛtti on 11 (*E*40-41; *T*16-17). It is "first" because most important in gaining the same results as knowledge of the Vedas. It is "nearest to Brahman" because it is that science through which all the others are understood. It is the "best austerity" in contrast to other forms of austerity because it leads to the highest results.

12 (*E*41; *T*17). Grammar is the shortest path to attainment of the highest essence (*rasa*) of speech (*vāc*) that has become differentiated.

13 (*E*44; *T*19). On language depend the principles governing practical purposive activities (*arthapravṛttitattva*), and the understanding of the principles of language cannot occur except through grammar.

Vṛtti on 13 (*E*44-47; *T*19-20). The Sanskrit compound *arthapravṛttitattva* is analyzed in six alternative ways. What depends on language may be the expression of the speaker's intended meaning, the possibility of applying a word to a thing, the ability to combine words into sentences, the connecting of objects with actions, identification of a thing as to be accomplished, or the projection of the content of an awareness as an external object. By "the principles of language" is meant the proper forms of language.

14 (*E*47; *T*21). Grammar is the door to liberation, the remedy of blemishes of speech, the purifier of all branches of knowledge.

Vṛtti on 14 (*E*47-49; *T*21-22). One who knows the correct forms of language understands the nature of language; he then goes beyond temporal sequence and gains union (*yoga*). Through the merit he gets by his correct usage he attains union with the greatest language essence (*mahāntaṃ śabdātmanam*) and is without organs. He thus reaches the stage of undifferentiated speech and appreciates the chief among its modes, namely, intuition (*pratibhā*). Through that intuition and the repetition of the union the highest *prakṛti*, free from all modes, is realized.

15–22 (*E*49-51; *T*22-23). These stanzas dwell on the importance of grammar.

23 (*E*51; *T*24). Words, meanings, and their relations are held to be permanent (*nitya*) in grammar.

Vṛtti on 23 (*E*52-63; *T*24-28). The basis of the science (of grammar) is that linguistic sounds, meanings, and the relation between the two is permanent. Here by "linguistic sound" we intend the general feature (*ākṛti*) of each word, not the differentiating genus of language as such. "Being a linguistic sound" is a property that inheres in a thing along with a set of features (*ākṛti*) that are mutually opposed to other such features and so cannot coinhere with them in the same thing. It is this specific generic feature—for example, the feature of the word "tree"—that we call a "linguistic sound." Just as the universals "substanceness," "earthness," and "potness" can all coinhere in a pot, so in "tree" the universals "being attributive" (*guṇatva*), "being a linguistic sound" (*śabdatva*), and "being the word 'tree'" (*vṛkṣaśabdatva*) coinhere.

Objection: The cases are not alike. The parts of a pot, which are not pots, combine to cause the manifestation of an instance of the universal potness. But the parts of a word do not combine to produce a linguistic sound, for they do not exist at the same time. The universal being a linguistic sound exists in each part of the word "tree," but if the general feature specific to the word "tree" exists in each part of the word "tree" we should think of trees as soon as we hear the first letter of the word.

Answer: No. The analogy intended is with specific actions such as lifting, turning, pouring, and the like, which arise successively and do not manifest a whole as product. And just as one does not recognize, say, lifting until it has gone on a bit, likewise one does not recognize that "tree" is being spoken until that action goes on a bit, so that several elements in the series manifesting that word can be grasped. The initial sounds in the series prepare the hearer's mind so that when the last sound occurs he recognizes the word. Grammarians do not necessarily think of inherence as the medium by which a general feature or universal is suggested to the hearer. There are, indeed, various views among grammarians about the constitution of linguistic sounds and the manner in which such a sound is made known.

24-26 (*E*64; *T*30). Grammar deals directly or indirectly with eight topics: (1) meanings determined through analysis—abstracted meanings (*apoddhārapadārtha*); (2) given or stable meanings (*sthitalakṣaṇa artha*); (3) linguistic forms that are to be analyzed (*anvākhyeya śabda*); (4) linguistic forms that figure in grammatical derivations (*pratipādaka śabda*); (5) the cause-and-effect relation (*kāryakāraṇabhāva saṃbandha*); (6) the relation of capability (*yogyatā saṃbandha*); (7) the relation(s) that lead(s) to merit; and (8) the relation(s) that bring(s) about communication (*pratyayāṅga saṃbandha*). This work takes up some of these topics for consideration.

Vṛtti on 24-26 (*E*65-81; *T*31-37). (1) Abstracted meanings are a matter of theoretical preconceptions, choice and convenience for the purposes of the science of Grammar. (2) Given meanings are those conveyed by sentences, single despite being made known through awareness of the separated word meanings. (3) The linguistic forms that are to be analyzed will differ depending on which of them, words or sentences, are taken to be the limit (*avadhi*) of analysis, and this factor also determines (4) the forms that will figure in grammatical derivations. (The rest are explained in turn.)

Verbal complementation is necessary for sentencehood. Where no specific action is mentioned, an action as existing is understood. Such single words or phrases are in fact sentences.

27–29 (*E*81-84; *T*40-42). While both grammatical and ungrammatical expressions are means of communication, only the grammatical ones are means of merit (*dharma*). Matters of merit are determined by reference to tradition (*āgama*) as maintained by the spiritual elite (*śiṣṭa*).

30–43 (*E*85-99; *T*42-51). Merit cannot be determined by *tarka* alone without the help of the tradition. Even the sages got their awareness of merit through the tradition. The traditions about merit cannot be sublated by *tarka*, because they are accepted by the world (*lokasiddha*). The natures of things are very difficult to establish by inference, because they have different properties in different circumstances, because there are obstructors to the normal powers of a thing, and because what is inferred by a clever thinker can always be explained otherwise by one cleverer. Expertise in jewels or coins comes from practice (*abhyāsa*), not from inference, and the fathers (*pitṛ*), demons (*rakṣas*), and goblins have powers born of their karma that go beyond what perception or inference can explain, as well as the yogi's power to see the past and the future. We must depend on the tradition, which hands down the direct awareness of people with such expertise and powers; one does not set it aside, any more than one sets one's own perception aside, on the basis of mere reasoning. So the elite have explained language on the basis of impersonal scientific treatises (*śāstra*) and tradition (*smṛti*).

Vṛtti on 38 (*E*95–96; *T*48). Examples of things seen directly by those sages responsible for *āgama* include the inner controller (*antaryāmin*), atoms, unmanifest language-Brahman (*anabhivyakta śabdabrahman*), the gods, the tendencies bred by action leading to one result rather than others, the subtle body.

44–48 (*E*100–106; *T*52–55). Expressions that convey meaning, including their own form as meaning[6] (*upādāna śabda*), can be viewed in two ways: as mental (*buddhistha, sphoṭa*), as cause of expressions that are heard; or as audible (*śruti, dhvani/nāda*), as sequential sound that conveys meaning. Just as the fire in the sticks (that are rubbed) is the cause of the fire that springs up, likewise the language in the mind of the speaker is the cause of the audible language expressing it.

Vṛtti on 47–48 (*E*105–107; *T*55 56). When the speaker seeks to superimpose linguistic form onto his intended meaning, the language appears to change its nature into something else (the meaning) and to project it as sounds from the vocal organ. Thus the unchanging (*avivartamāna*) language principle appears to be changing: in other words, it manifests through the imperceptible pervasive *dhvani*-sounds those gross *nāda*-sounds which are articulated by the vocal organs. These gross *nāda*-sounds, though temporarily ordered in a sequence, illuminate the *sphoṭa* or mental language by obstructing it and permitting it (to manifest in the temporal sequence). Thus the *sphoṭa*, though single, appears to have parts sequentially arranged.

49–52 (E107–111; *T*56–58). Other similes illustrating the relationships in question are now offered. The reflection in the water seems to move because the water ripples, just as the *sphoṭa* appears to be protracted or short, fast or slow through being "reflected in" the gross *nāda*-sounds. Or, just as awareness by nature grasps its own form as well as that of its object, likewise in language the forms of both the meaning and the language principle itself are illuminated. Again, a painter paints in stages a figure he sees as a single thing.

53–54 (*E*113–114; *T*59–60). Just as the speaker first thinks of the linguistic forms one by one, so the initial awareness (*vyavasāya*) of the hearer is produced from those (linguistic forms). But people, intent on understanding the meaning, do not attend to the linguistic forms *per se*.

Vṛtti on 53 (*E*113; *T*59 60). Because the hearer is concentrating on understanding the meaning (of the entire utterance), he does not identify a linguistic form as a separate item. So the linguistic forms are first experienced as primary in importance and then become secondary to the production of meaning.

55–60 (*E*115–119; *T*61–64). Just as light has two powers, as grasper and as grasped, so all linguistic forms have those two powers. Linguistic forms by themselves do not convey any meaning; only when they themselves become contents of awareness do they do so. That is why when the nature of a linguistic form is not understood the speaker is asked "what did you say?" It is unlike the case of the sense organs, which are not grasped when they reveal their objects. The action subsequent to the perception of a linguistic form sometimes has the form and sometimes the meaning, depending on the purpose in a particular context. For example, grammatical operations pertain to the forms of expressions covered by rules of grammar.

61–64 (*E*120–122; *T*65–67). In any case, that which is uttered can itself never be the object of the subsequent action; that object must be what it conveys.

65–57 (*E*124–127; *T*68–70). An expression may not convey meanings of other types, but it is never without its own form as meaning.

68–69 (*E*127; *T*70–71). Pāṇini's rule 1.1.68, "svaṃ rūpaṃ śabdasyāśabdasaṃjñā", has been interpreted variously, depending on whether the own form (*svarūpa*) of an expression is viewed as an individual (*vyakti*) or a universal (*jāti*).

Vṛtti on 68–69 (*E*127–132; *T*70–73). Some Grammarians hold that unalloyed perception of and reference to individuals do take place; others are of the view that expressions, having come into existence because of the perception of universals, can refer to individuals only as colored by the universals.

70–74 (*E*133–139; *T*74–77). Some Grammarians say that (a linguistic form) is single, whether it be held to be a product or to be permanent; others say it is many whether it be produced or eternal. Some view realizations of an expression in different phonetic contexts as the presence of the same permanent individual; others as presence of what is felt to be the same but has in fact perished with each occurrence; still others as occurrence of what must be assumed to be the same for the sake of communication. Furthermore, there are thinkers who view all such realizations as different either because one permanent expression cannot become part of another permanent expression (then the latter will have parts and be impermanent) or because expressions are not permanent and hence cannot last long enough to become part of some other expression.

75–77 (*E*140–143; *T*78–80). *Sphoṭa*, though without temporal distinctions, appears to have temporal divisions of two kinds: difference in the form of short vowel or long vowel, and so on;[7] and difference in the form of a quick (*drutā*), medium (*madhyamā*), or slow (*vilambita*) pace of utterance, due to division in the manifesting sound (*dhvani*). A part of the sound is the minimum needed for the manifestation of the linguistic units (*prākṛta dhvani*); the remainder, if any, simply keeps the manifestation in effect for a longer time (*vaikṛta dhvani*). The former is related to the distinction conveyed by "short," and so on, the latter to the distinction conveyed by "fast," and so on.

78–80 (*E*144–146; *T*81–82). How exactly the sound manifests the *sphoṭa* is variously understood. Some think that a dispositional tendency (*saṃskāra*) is produced in the auditory sense organ, others that it is produced in the linguistic form, and still others that it is produced in both. Only the organ is conditioned by applying ointment or by concentration (*samādhāna*), say the first group. But those who believe that the visual organ goes out to reach its object hold that both the content and the organ are conditioned by light, and thus the analogous view about sounds.

Vṛtti on 78–80 (*E*145–146; *T*81–82). That is to say, some think that the sound, when it has arisen, conditions the auditory sense and that the auditory sense, thus conditioned, becomes the means of auditory awareness. The second view mentioned is that it is the linguistic form that, conditioned by relation to the sound, is the content of the auditory experience. The third view is that the sound conditions both the linguistic form and the auditory organ, which, along with other causal factors, produce awareness that has the linguistic form as content. This view is analogous to the view, mentioned in the text, about the way light conditions both sense organ and object in perception by those who think the organ goes out.

81 (*E*147; *T*83). Some Grammarians say that the sound is cognized as being the same as the *sphoṭa*. Others say the sound is not cognized at all. Still others say that it is cognized as an independent thing.

82–92 (*E*148–157; *T*84–90). There is no doubt, however, that the manifestation (of the linguistic form) is gradual. Each succeeding element of the sound continuum serves to make the nature of the intended *sphoṭa* clearer and clearer. There are sometimes interim cognitions of units other than the one intended—of units that could be regarded as parts of the intended unit. They are an unavoidable feature of the medium of manifestation and a consequence of the nature of the hearer's cognitive mechanism. They are instrumental in producing the final cognition, but they are not parts of it.

Vṛtti on 92 (*E*157–158; *T*90–91). The Bhedavādins (believers in the ultimacy of distinctions between phoneme meanings) think that the word "cow" is just the several phonemes *c*, *o*, and *w* and that there is no indivisible linguistic form that they express and that is cognized by the understanding hearer. But according to their view, because the parts are manifested in sequence no single nature (of the linguistic form) could be cognized, and the final cognition in the series would have no content. A second view would be that all the parts, being eternal, are manifested at once, but then there would be no difference between the nature of the sounds "vega" and "gave."

93–94 (*E*159–160; *T*91–92). The *sphoṭa* is held by some to be a universal that is manifested by the individuals, the sounds.[8] Others go beyond the level of specific units, where the distinction of universal versus particular is applicable, and think of one linguistic form (that is, one *sphoṭa*) being manifested in various forms.

Vṛtti on 95 (*E*161; *T*92–93). *Objection*: The linguistic form is noneternal, because it is manifested, like a jar.

95 (*E*161; *T*92). *Answer*: Manifestation does not only occur in that which is noneternal; it is also seen that eternal universals are manifested by their individual (instances).

Vṛtti on 96 (*E*162; *T*93–94). *Objection*: Linguistic forms are not manifested, because the manifester and the manifested are in different places—the linguistic forms are in one place, the vocal organs elsewhere.

96 (*E*162; *T*93). *Answer*: Only embodied things (*kāyavat*) can occupy places. Neither sounds nor linguistic forms are actually located anywhere in space.

Vṛtti on 97 (*E*163; *T*94). *Objection*: Linguistic forms are not manifested, because their so-called "manifesters" are regulated—the sounds that cause the manifestation of a particular phoneme cannot manifest any other phoneme—while manifested things, properly speaking, can always be manifested by several alternative things; a jar can be manifested—in other words, made a content of awareness—by a jewel or a lamp or some other source of illumination.

97 (*E*163; *T*94). *Answer*: Just as the fitness of a certain kind of sense quality to be the manifestation of a certain kind of sense organ is regular, so particular sounds are likewise fit to be manifested only by *sphoṭa*.

Vṛtti on 99 (*E*164–165; *T*95–96) *Objection* : A linguistic form is not manifested, because we find that its manifesters undergo increase and decrease and difference in number depending on the way the vocal organ is used, and in proper cases of manifestation, such as illumination by a lamp, such changes in the manifesters never take place.

99 (*E*164; *T*95). *Answer*: There are many kinds of manifestation; consider a mirror, which manifests everything reflected in it; these reflected things change in various ways, but the mirror remains one.

Vṛtti on 99 (*E*165; *T*96). *Objection*: In the case of the mirror the prototype, for example, the moon, gets into the mirror.

100 (*E*165; *T*97). *Answer*: Big objects like the moon or a mountain cannot get into small objects, like a mirror or a diamond !

101 (*E*166; *T*97). So, phonemes, words, and sentences, which are without temporal distinctions, are taken to have such because of the temporal differences of their manifesting sounds.

102–107 (*E*167–173; *T*97–101). The terms *sphoṭa, dhvani,* and *nāda* have been understood differently by those who do not advocate permanency. The explanation of short vowels, long vowels, and the like given by these thinkers is also different.

Vṛtti on 102–107 (*E*167–177; *T*98–101). They hold the *sphoṭa* to be the first sound produced by the vocal organ. The *dhvanis,* according to them, are the resulting sounds, which spread out from that first sound and by hearing which awareness of the *sphoṭa* or first sound is made possible. Some say that the term *nāda* refers to what is manifested by the *dhvanis* that result from the activity of the vocal organ. Still others think that the *sphoṭa* and the *dhvani* come into existence at the same time; the *sphoṭa* is the meaningful sound, the *dhvani* mere articulated sound. There is no consensus on this matter.

108–119 of *Vṛtti* (*E*177–195; *T*102–106). The process of speech production can be described variously.

112–114 (of *E*183–188), 120–122 (of *T*107–110). Knowers of the tradition say that the world is the transformation of language. All understanding of what is to be done (*itikartavyatā*) depends on language. Even the child understands, because he has dispositional tendencies arising from prior births. Without such dispositional tendencies the child would not attempt to produce linguistic sounds.

Vṛtti on the preceding. What exists is as good as nonexistent unless it is spoken of. And even completely nonexistent things such as a hare's horn or the city of the Gandharvas can be involved in our activities like something real, provided they are brought to mind by hearing language. Because children have speech in them through the traces born of their use of language in previous births, they come to understand how to act purposively through awareness based vaguely on heard language. Children's attempts to speak are not taught them by others but arise by intuition.

115–117 (of *E*188–192), 123–125 (of *T*110–112). Language infuses all cognition. Without this close relationship between awareness and language nothing would become known; it makes identification of things possible. Language is the basis of all branches of knowledge (*vidyā*), or all crafts (*śilpa*) and arts (*kalā*).

Vṛtti on the preceding. When the linguistic *bhāvanā* is restrained, no (practical) effect is produced from the nonconceptual (*avikalpaka*) awareness that arises with regard to objects. For example, when walking quickly over earth and grass one is not aware of them and does nothing to or with them. But when the seed of the linguistic *bhāvanā* is awakened and the powers of words to express meanings are manifested, then the object becomes cognized as having a certain form; thus the object is clearly conceived and can be identified as having a certain form, and we are said to be aware of it. And when this language seed is awakened through certain other causal conditions it produces memory. Some teachers say that sleeping persons have awarenesses just like waking persons; the only difference is that the language-*bhāvanā*-seeds operate subtly in dreams—that is why that state is called "darkness." Finally, it is because of this close relation between language and cognition that we are able to understand the meaning of a sentence from hearing the words.

118–119 (of *E*193–195), 126–127 (of *T*113–114). The consciousness of all transmigrating beings does not go beyond language. The linguistic form that makes possible waking-state activities that are effective also becomes the object of effective activities in dreams.

120–123 (of *E*196–201), 128–131 (of *T*115–118). Some take everything to be merely the self (*svamātra*); others claim that everything is merely the Highest (*paramātra*); in any case, as things are presented by language so they are understood; the object is established by language. Even such a thing as the "circle of fire" (*alātacakra*), which is not an actual object, is brought clearly to mind by language describing it.

Because the Self is that with which one desires union and that Self is the language within us, one attains that highest Self (*paramātman*) through purification (*saṃskāra*) of language, and one who is aware of the principles of language's activity attains immortal Brahman.

Vṛtti on the preceding. The first view (*svamātravāda*) itself has varieties. (a) There are those who think that all modifications are merely the self, existing inside each person but appearing to be external—"internal" and "external" being the results merely of usage. But that is impossible, for that self is single and immaterial. (b) Other *svamātravādins* say that all awareness and all differences are transformations (*pariṇāma*) of a single principle of conscious activity (*citkriyātattva*). Likewise the second view (of *paramātravāda*) has varieties: some say that consciousness (*caitanya*) is the source of beings that differentiate themselves from it as oil from sesame seed, while others hold that it is more like sparks from a fire, or trees from seeds. But actually it does not matter whether an object exists externally; in either case it is always connected with language as the thing expressed by a linguistic form.

Language is of two kinds, eternal and produced. The produced sort is involved in usage and reflects the nature of language (or the self, which is language). The eternal sort of language is the source of all usage, unsequenced, within everyone, the seat of all modifications, the locus of all actions, the basis of satisfaction and frustration, capable of producing any effects anywhere but with its field of enjoyment restrained like a lamp covered by a jar, the limitless generating cause of all beings...the Lord of all (*sarveśvara*), omnipotent (*sarvaśaktir*), the great bull of language (*mahān śabdavṛṣabha*). Those who know linguistic yoga (*vāgyogavida*) break the knot of egoity and are united with language without any distinction from it.

Well-being (*abhyudaya*) regularly follows upon purification of the language principle of all incorrect forms. Then by practice, after union with the language principle, and after having understood the intuition of which the source is that language-pıinciple, attainment of the *summum bonum* (*kṣema*) must follow.

124–133 (of *E*203–212), 132–141 (of *T*119–124). The thesis that expressions sanctioned by the grammar of the elite can lead to merit can be supported in two ways. First of all, the thesis is a matter of tradition. One can always refuse to follow any tradition or to interpret the accepted tradition differently, but the only interpretation of the tradition that is proper is that which does justice to the capacities of words by taking into consideration their context, and so on. That grammatical expressions are meritorious is such an interpretation.[9] In the second place, once a tradition is accepted, it can be supported by appropriate inference. Because pronunciation of certain words (in *mantras* and hymns) produces perceptible results like the removal of poison and is said to produce imperceptible results of a specified sort, one can infer that it is possible that knowledge and use of grammatical expressions lead to merit. Grammar is a *smṛti* preserved or composed by the spiritual elite.

134 (of *E*213), 142 (of *T*125). Grammar is the highest station of the threefold speech (*vāc*) of *vaikharī, madhyamā,* and *paśyantī,* and it appears in a different form in each of its loci.

Vṛtti on the preceding. The "correct/incorrect" (*sādhu/asādhu*) distinction extends only to the first three levels of phases of speech. *Vaikharī* is so called because it is cognized by others, is a content of auditory awareness, and is regulated according to the nature of what is heard. It is produced from a drum or a flute, and its correctness or incorrectness is well established, being mixed up with or manifested in *varṇas*. *Madhyamā*, however, resides within and seems to have sequence. The intellect (*buddhi*) is its only substratum (*upādāna*). Some think that even though sequence in it is suppressed, still it is accompanied by subtle breath. *Paśyantī* is achieved when sequence is suppressed, but it has the power to produce sequence even though it is without distinctions. It is restless and concentrated, hidden and pure. It is without form (*nirākāra*), or the forms of the objects of knowledge have been suppressed within it, but it may or may not appear to support distinctions of different sorts of objects. But the higher form of *parapaśyantī* is beyond ordinary usage and experience. It is not covered by grammar, which can at the most be an indirect instrument in reaching it. In the threefold speech there is innumerable variation. Not more than one-quarter of speech appears in human beings, and even of that one-quarter only a portion figures in communication. The rest remains unrealized potential.

135–137 (of *E*221–225), 144–146 (of *T*129-132). Grammatical treatises are composed from time to time by the spiritual elite in deference to differing capacities of individuals and by taking into consideration the changed capacities of expressions as far as merit and demerit are concerned. It cleanses one's language.

Vṛtti on the preceding. Some hold that scripture is authoritative only about things that have invisible consequences (*adṛṣṭaphala*) and hold human opinion to be doubtful and untrustworthy. They say that both *śruti* and *smṛti* are the product of a continuous tradition; *śruti* (scripture) is preserved in the same versions according to strict rules of expression, while *smṛti* was composed by the elite at different times and places in prose, poetry, or other forms.

Some teachers believe that no action has in itself a visible or an invisible consequence. Rather, by acting contrary to scripture one manifests demerit (*pratyavāya*), and by acting according to scripture one manifests merit (*dharma*). Scripture itself teaches that, for example, killing a brahmin is a sin in some contexts but a cause of exceeding well-being in others. Others think that scripture only makes known the particular power of each object known. Merit and demerit are the results of the natures of substances, not of scripture; scripture merely makes the natures of substances known.

138–147 (of *E*228–234), 147–155 (of *T*132–136). An *apabhraṃśa* or incorrect linguistic form (*asādhu śabda*) is that expression which the speaker employs with the intention of expressing the meaning associated with a specific expression derived by grammar, but which turns out to be different from that specific expression. *Apabhraṃśas* are not to be determined by taking only the form into consideration; with change in the intended meaning, an expression may cease to be *apabhraṃśa*. For those accustomed to grammatical speech, the *apabhraṃśas* convey meaning through the corresponding grammatical expressions. A reverse phenomenon is noticed when those who habitually use *apabhraṃśas* encounter grammatical speech.

BOOK 2

1–2 (*E*36; *T*1). A sentence has been characterized by "logicians" (*nyāyavādins*) in at least eight ways: (1) as verb (*ākhyāta*), (2) as a collection of linguistic forms (*śabda saṃghāta*), (3) as the proper universal (*jāti*) that occurs in the collection (*saṃghātavartinī*), (4) as a single partless linguistic form, (5) as a sequence (of words), (6) as what hangs together in the intellect (*buddhyanusaṃhṛti*), (7) as the first word (*pada ādya*), and (8) as all the words severally possessing expectancy (for each other, *pṛthaksarvapada sākāṃkṣā*).

3–6 (*E*36–37; *T*2–4). The definition of *Kātyāyana*, the author of the *Vārttika* (namely, "a sentence verb along with the indeclinables, case words, and qualifiers") does not agree with the Mīmāṃsā definition, "that in which the words have mutual expectancy and which does not require additional words, has action as its principal element, has other subordinate words, and is a single linguistic form." Some objections to Kātyāyana's definition are met.

7–12 (E37–39; *T*4–5). Just as that single entity which is the awareness of all objects (*sarvārthapratyaya*) is differentiated according to the distinctions among what is perceived, so it is with the awareness of the meaning of the sentence. Just as one picture may be analyzed as having colored parts, so the one sentence, without expectancy, is said to contain linguistic forms that require each other. Just as a word can be analyzed as having stem, suffix, and so on (as parts), so the sentence can be analyzed as having words as parts. The parts of words are meaningless, but they come to be communicative through analysis by agreement and difference (*anvayavyatireka*).

13–14 (*E*39; *T*6). A linguistic form has no disjunction, so its meaning has none either. Only the ignorant thinks it actually does have parts.

Vṛtti on 13–14. The sentence *sphoṭa* is indivisible; its meaning—that is to say, intuition (*pratibhā*)—is likewise indivisible. It would be very difficult to understand the meaning of a sentence without analyzing it; nonetheless, a good student understands that such analysis is only a means to an end and that the linguistic form and meaning are indivisible.

15–16 (*E*39–40; *T*7–8). The general (noncontextual) meaning (of an earlier word in a sentence), having disappeared (after its utterance), cannot remain in the particular meaning (it has in the context of the other words in the sentence). By contrast, if the meaning of the sentence is not a matter of the linguistic forms that express it, the same should be held about the meaning of each word, so the relation between language and meaning would be destroyed.

17–18 (*E*40; *T*8–9). Some[10] hold that the words of a sentence are only apparently similar to words noticed in isolation or in other sentences. The words of each sentence are in fact expressive of the sentence's particular meaning right from the start; the understanding of the sense becomes firmer as the sentence is gradually perceived. Thus, each word bears the meaning of the entire sentence in which it figures.

19 (*E*40–41; *T*9). When sentence and sentence meaning are said to be unitary, the reference is not to language in the form of sound. In addition to its speech form, audible to individuals other than the speaker, language has *upāṃśu* ("audibility only to the speaker"), *paramopāṃśu* ("appearance of an expression only in the intellect"), and *pratisaṃhṛtakrama* ("latent, unthought expression") forms. Beyond these four exists its undifferentiated form, bereft of sequence.[11]

20-21 (*E*41; *T*10). Just as a motion is not grasped as distinct even though it is a particular movement, but when it is repeated its universal property as, say, turning is manifested, so linguistic forms such as phonemes, sentences, and words, even though quite different from each other, appear to be the same.

22-26 (*E*41-42; *T*11-13). How can an eternal thing really be earlier or later than something? It only appears to be so through the power of the one (the sentence *sphoṭa*). And just as, though awarenesses that something is "fast" or "slow" are without temporal extent, they appear to be temporally characterized, so vowels appear to be long or short. Time, which is eternal, cannot be differentiated through *mātrās* belonging to something else. But in the absence of distinct *mātrās*, how can there be any sequence? The awareness produced by them (the *mātrās*) is single and without parts; through its own power it seems to be differentiated and to have sequence.

27 (*E*43; *T*13). This sequenceless (sentence) (seemingly) has the

power of having sequence when analyzed. So its meaning, though not differentiated, is experienced as having distinctions.

Vṛtti on 27. It is like space (*diś*), which has no division but which we speak of as if it had them when we speak of "east", "west", and so on.

28-29 (*E*43; *T*14). If these words are in the sentence, and those phonemes are in the word, then in the phonemes there would be distinctions of parts, such as atoms. As these parts cannot combine there would be neither phoneme nor word—and then what could a word be?

Vṛtti on 28-29. If it is held (as in view [2] of *kārikās* 1-2) that a sentence is a collection of linguistic forms, then words and phonemes also in turn should be analyzed into components, say, atoms. But these ultimate atoms—by analogy with the process of analysis in question—would not be simultaneous and could not contact each other, so no phoneme, word, or sentence could result, for nothing could express any meaning.

30 (*E*43; *T*15). Others (who espouse view [6] of *kārikās* 1-2) say that the single inner language principle is illuminated by the sounds (*nāda*) uttered, and that unity is in the sentence.

Vṛtti on 30. They think that language is an inner consciousness that becomes the sentence when manifested by the sounds considered (wrongly) to be its parts. It is like the written symbols that are mistaken for the word.

31 (*E*44; *T*15). According to them the inner meaning is illuminated by its parts. Linguistic form and meaning are inseparable divisions of a single nature.

Vṛtti on 31. There are two versions of this opinion. On the assumption that external things are noneternal, the meanings reflected in the intellect are taken to be identical with the external objects. On the contrary assumption, that external object is eternal, it manifests itself according to the power of sequence in the intellect. So, both word and object meant are in the intellect. Another variation of this second assumption is that the object is reflected in the intellect, which inheres in the self that is pure consciousness but which assumes the form of the intellect, so that the power of being what is experienced and of being the experiencer, though actually belonging to different things, become indistinguishable in the intellect. In any case, on all such views the single intellect, in which the different powers of being meant and conveying meaning are not separated, is the locus of language—that is, of the sentence.

32 (*E*44; *T*17). The language principle (*śabdatattva*), the nature of which is essentially internal (*antarmātrātman*), is cause and effect, illuminator as well as illumined.

Vṛtti on 32. The linguistic principle, being identical with consciousness, is beyond the distinctions of presence and absence.

33 (*E*44; *T*18). That linguistic principle has the powers of existing or not existing; without sequence, it appears to have sequence and thus provides the basis for communication (*vyavahāra*).

34–40 (*E*44–46; *T*18–21). Several possible objections to the thesis of unitariness can be refuted. The thesis can also be supported with positive arguments. Any view that admits actual presence of words in a sentence at the time of sentence cognition can be shown to end up in an absurd conclusion. Compound words serve as an analogy in that they are also made up of words. In their case too logic demands that unitariness be accepted.

41–43 (*E*46; *T*22–23). Some think of sentence meaning as that additional element which comes about when words with their ordinary, lexical meanings are joined by a relation. The substratum of this additional meaning is given differently as each word constituting the sentence and as the string of words taken as a whole.

44–46 (*E*46–47; *T*23–24). Some think of sentencehood as consisting in the delimiting or qualification, through being related, of a generality. Capabilities of words are only circumscribed when they join to form a sentence.

47-48 (*E*47; *T*24–25). Some think of words in a sentence as circumscribed or qulified right from the start. The adjaçent fellow words simply make the qualification manifest.

49-53 (*E*48; *T*25-26). Some think of sequence as the crucial element of a sentence. It is sequence that reveals the unrevealed distinctions, already existent, of word meanings.

54–55 (*E*49; *T*26–27). Restatement of the preceding views.

56–57 (*E*49–50; *T*27). The sentence is the primary unit of language. Words and word meanings are derivative.

58–59 (*E*50; *T*27–28). Vedic statements and Patañjali's *Mahābhāṣya* are cited in favor of the view that the sentence is an indivisible unit (*akhaṇḍapakṣa*).

60 (*E*50; *T*29). Just as the meaning of the word is not understood from hearing any single phoneme, so the meaning of the sentence is not understood from hearing any single word.

Vṛtti on 60. Awareness of sentence meaning is self-illuminating, as well as illuminating its content. Being self-illuminating, that awareness is its own authority.

61–87 (*E*51–57; *T*29–42). *Objection* (by a *Padavādin*, Mīmāṃsaka, or upholder of the thesis that it is words that are the primary units of meaning): Just as sentence meaning is understood when the words are gathered together, so word meaning is understood when all of the phonemes are together. We only see a small object when it is together with others. So it is here. (1) If words did not have meaning, then it would be impossible to understand as we do (for example) "sacrifice with rice" as meaning "sacrifice with a substance—rice if possible, if not some other substance"; for if "rice" excluded all alternatives it would exclude the meaning of substance as well. (2) If words had no meanings of their own, then one could not inquire about the meaning of an unfamiliar word. (3) The method proposed by Jaimini, which requires distinguishing primary from secondary meanings, becomes hopeless to apply, for one cannot distinguish between what is directly meant by a word and what is secondarily meant. (4) A compound (or complex) sentence is one in which the component clauses, through their expectancy for one another, combine to convey the meaning of the whole, which cannot happen according to the indivisible meaning thesis. (5) Jaimini's exegetical rules require the recognition of the meanings of iniividual words for their application. Because such meanings are denied the rules cannot be applied.

88–94 (*E*57–59; *T*42–44). *Answer*: These arguments do not contradict our position, for we hold that a sentence, even though its meaning is indivisible, can be analyzed into smaller sentences (which can in turn be analyzed along the lines proposed in the objections). It is like the scent that appears different when found in distinct flowers, or like the "cowness" that is (erroneously) ascribed to a *gayal* because we have not previously seen a *gayal*; in the same way, when two sentences differ in only one word, they appear to be similar, even though the two sentences have entirely distinct unitary meanings. Just as light (*prakāśa*) and consciousness (*cetas*), though each without parts, seem to be similar to each other in one part and different in another, so the two sentence meanings appear to resemble each other in one part and to differ in another, though they are really without parts.

95-111 (*E*59–63; *T*45–49). There are several instances in which a meaning is cognized, but its usual signifier is either not explicitly present (because of extended meaning [*tantra*], or some other factor) or is present in an altered form (due to word-connection [*saṃdhi*], a different pronunciation, or the like). One who thinks that a sentence is made up of distinct words even at the time it delivers its meaning will not be able to account for this phenomenon.

112 (*E*63; *T*50). *Answer* to item (4) of the objections in 61-87 above: In the case of one-word sentences (*padasarūpa vākya*) one can say that what is ordinarily a constituent of a sentence has acquired an independent meaning. Similarly, if a sentence embedded in a larger sentence appears in separation, it will have an independent meaning.

113–115 (*E*63–64; *T*50–51). Those who maintain that a sentence has only purpose (*prayojana*) as its meaning, who say that it does not have a lexical (*abhidheya*) meaning as words do, cannot account for the relations between (such) sentences. But if it is (qualified) word meaning that is held to be revealed (by each succeeding word), the process will be one of recurrence (*āvṛtti*) or restatement (*anuvāda*). The (sentence) meaning that is (said to be) complete with each (word, it should be noted), comes about when those (words) are together.[12]

116–118 (*E*64–65; *T*51–52). Various views are held regarding meaning. Despite the sentence's having a single meaning, different opinions (*vikalpa*) with respect to the topic are derived based on the (different) experiences (*bhāvanā*) (of their proponents). Some say that every linguistic form causes an intuition (*pratibhā*) through practice (*abhyāsa*), as is seen in the understanding of meanings by children and animals. This practice is not a matter of tradition. Some say it is conventional. It is of the form "this is to be done after that."

119–124 (*E*65–66; *T*53–54). There are twelve views of meaning that take sentence meaning to be constituted from word meanings: (1) Each linguistic form marks a notion that the form has a meaning, so that a word like "cow's" meaning is like the meaning of words like *apūrva*, *devatā*, or *svarga* (in other words, each one means merely that something exists that corresponds to that form). The association of a linguistic item with a specific feature comes through usage, perception, and practice; it is not the content of the linguistic form, but is based on a distinct effort.

(2) According to a second view, some distinctive features (*bheda*) are revealed by the linguistic units that designate them. Some things that are only subsequently (or incidentally) understood are then taken to be the meanings of linguistic forms as well.

Critique of (2): But a linguistic form, when it evokes the notion of the generic property (*jāti*), does not evoke the idea of the individual distinguishing features that are characterized by that generic property.

125-142 (*E*66-70; *T*55-60). (3) Others say that the designation of a linguistic form is regular both as to usage (*prayoga*) (in other words, what is implied) and means (*sādhana*) (that is to say, instrumentality to a resulting action).

(4) The designation is a collection (*samudaya*), but without choice or combination (*avikalpasamuccaya*).

(5) Meaning is a nonexistent (*asatya*) relation (between the word and the property designated).

(6) Meaning is the relation with a linguistic form of something existent as obstructed (or conditioned, *upādhi*) by what is nonexistent.

(7) Linguistic form and its meaning are the same thing. In ordinary affairs the meaning is the more important aspect, but in grammar either may be relevant according to the speaker's intention.

(8) Linguistic forms are invented so as to present in a manner regulated by a single meaning a thing having in itself no power, (9) or all powers.

(10) The meaning is an intellectual content (*buddhiviṣaya*) that is related to an external object (*bāhyavastu*) and is cognized as such.

(11) Some (meanings) are based on manifested memories that have distinct features. Others present themselves as bare awareness (*saṃvinmātra*).

(12) Just as a sense organ indicates its content in various ways, so the meaning is conveyed through language in many ways. A linguistic form intended by the speaker to mean one thing is heard as having various meanings by different hearers. And even the same hearer, at different times or different places, may understand a particular linguistic form in different ways. Everyone but those who have seen the natures of things are subject to this unreliability of language, and their visions, though based on reality, cannot be made relevant to practical affairs because those visions are not related to language. Language is no more reliable than perception—both are subject to illusions. The wise man should examine through reasoning (*yukti*) even what has been directly presented by perception, and in speaking he should follow the conventions of ordinary usage concerning objects, for they are difficult to explain correctly.

143–152 (*E*70–72; *T*60–63). Sentence meaning is produced by word meanings but is not constituted by them. Its form is that intuition, that innate "know-how" awareness (*pratibhā*) possessed by all beings. It is a cognitive state evident to the hearer. It is not describable or definable, but all practical activities depend on it directly or through recollection of it. It comes to a person through maturing, just as animals and birds know innately how to act. Intuition is said to have six varieties: (1) natural (*svabhāva*), (2) Vedic (*caraṇa*), (3) through practice (*abhyāsa*), (4) yogic (*yoga*), (5) through invisible factors (*adṛṣṭa*), and (6) through instruction or intervention (*upapādita*).

Vṛtti on 143–152. Examples of (1), the tendency of *prakṛti* to evolve into *buddhi*, and the like, or our natural tendency to wake up after sleeping. Of (2), Vasiṣṭha's knowledge. Of (3), water divination. Of (4), awareness of the contents of other people's minds. Of (5), the power of Rakṣaokas to enter others' bodies. Of (6), Sañjaya's knowledge of the progress of the Mahābhārata wars through Kṛṣṇadvaipāyana's specially qualified reports.

153–163 (*E*72–74; *T*63–68) Just as the word "cow" designates things that are associated with certain substances but does not itself designate those substances, so the linguistic form used to designate cows associated with a certain shape, color, and parts does not designate those portions. But language fails to function in usage if it is separated from its designation, as opposed to separation from the associated features, which does not preclude the functioning of language. Thus even though "cow" can be used of something where hair, hoof, and so on, are missing, it cannot be used where cowness is missing.

164–169 (*E*75–76; *T*68–71). There are different views regarding the way that number and other factors are conveyed by the combination of suffix and stem or root. Some see no difference between the mode of conveying meaning seen in the case of stems or roots and the mode of conveying meaning seen in the case of suffixes. Others characterize the former as "designating" (*abhidhāyaka* or *vācaka*) and the suffixes as "indicative" (*dyotaka*). Their criterion is that of positive and negative concomitance (*anvayavyatireka*).

170–179 (*E*76–78; *T*70–76). Synchronic derivation of words (*nirvacana, śabdavyutpatti*) is an area in which there is considerable scope for difference of perception and choice of elements. In such a derivation, the precise meanings of elements are frequently ignored in favor of their general, approximate meanings.

180–191 (*E*78–81; *T*76–82). Regarding the stage in which a prefix or preposition is joined to a root, there are two views. Some see this stage as preceding the semantic connection of the root, through the action it denotes, with action bearers (*sādhana*); others see it as succeeding this semantic connection. The prefix can be said to be denotative (*vācaka*), indicative (*dyotaka*), or jointly signifying (*sahābhidhāyin*).

191–196 (*E*81–82; *T*82–84; *T*81–82). The indeclinable particles (*nipāta*) can be said to be either indicative or capable of conveying a meaning only in conjunction with other words (*pada*) that constitute the sentence.

197–204 (*E*82–84; *T*84–89). A fifth category of linguistic forms (in addition to nouns, verbs, prepositions, and particles) is that of the postpositions (*karmapravacanīya*). Linguistic forms in this category serve to delimit in a unique way the action implicit in the relationship of the two words they connect. The other justification for their separate grouping is formal. Once the postpositions are separated from the prepositions the phenomenon of change of *su* to *ṣu* can be better described in a grammar.

205–212 (*E*84–86; *T*90–93). Of words that have an identifiable designation several types can be specified from the point of view of their constitution. In some words the constituents have no meaning of their own; only the collection is a meaning bearer. In others, the constituents too bear meanings. Among the latter, in some the constituents contribute their meanings to make the meaning of the collection, while in some there is no recognizable or definite relationship between the meanings of the constituents and the meaning of the collection. There are also words in which a part is a meaning bearer and the remainder is not. One can also divide words into phonemes that have no meanings of their own; unless one chooses to identify some single-phoneme words with similar phonemes constituting a word. Some constituents of words (such as a root) have only abstracted meaning, based on grammatical analysis.

213–215 (*E*86; *T*93–94). Phonemes do not express any meaning by themselves. This fact is evident from the fact that word *x*, which is distorted due to loss, addition, or reversal of a phoneme, does not fail to convey its usual meaning by reminding the hearer of the undistorted form, provided that the distortion is not such as to turn *x* into another word *y*.

216–228 (*E*87–89; *T*95–100). A compound word conveys a specific undivided meaning. It should be viewed as made up of parts only in the context of analysis.

229–234 (*E*90–91; *T*101–102). The elements set up in grammar and the meanings associated with them are a matter of practicality. It is ignorance (*avidyā*) that is described in the science (*śāstra*) of Grammar in different ways. Understanding (*vidyā*) arises spontaneously, free from the alternative opinions (conceptual constructions?) (*vikalpa*) conveyed through tradition. Just as the result is not related on its occasion (*nimitta*) and is thus indescribable (*nirupākhya*), so understanding, though inexpressible (*anākhyeya*), is regarded as having the science of Grammar as its means (*upāya*).

235–238 (*E*91; *T*103). Understanding of linguistic meaning comes from repetition, which is beginningless and false and appears to be natural. For example, an uneducated person (*apaṇḍita*) takes an atom to have parts, and takes a whole made of parts to be joined with the parts (of other things). Because of our experience of pots and other things (as spatially divided), we take the world to be so divided, and because objects have a beginning, even the eternal Brahman is thought to have a beginning. Means that are intended for students can be misleading for children. One understands the truth by remaining on the path of untruth.

239–249 (*E*91–94; *T*104–108). (So), incompatibility of various sorts is noticed between the final meaning of a sentence and the meaning constructed by putting together the meanings of its components. Even the explanation of a simple negative sentence is fraught with logical difficulties as long as the explanation proceeds on the assumption that each succeeding sentence constituent modifies the meaning of the preceding constituent—that sentence meaning is perceived in parts and pieces. This point goes to prove the validity of unitariness.

250–257 (*E*94–96; *T*108–112). In the case of homophonous concatenations that figure as sentence constituents and are associated with more than one meaning (mutually related or unrelated), there are two views. Some theoreticians think of each such concatenation as one and the same word. Others prefer to look on such a concatenation as different words in reality.

Vṛtti on 250–257. When identity of the word is presupposed, the process of its association with a meaning other than its regular meaning is explained in various ways: first, the word, potentially capable of expressing any meaning, is restricted to one meaning by context. Second, the word is directly associated with only its regular meaning, but that meaning is changed through superimposition of another meaning. Third, the word has its own form as its invariable, immediate, and unique meaning. That meaning, in the form of form, is superimposed on each contextual meaning as the case may be.

258–262 (*E*96–97; *T*113–115). Considerations analogous to the ones in the preceding paragraph are applied by some thinkers to sentence and to Vedic *mantras*.

263–297 (*E*97–104; *T*115–129). Those who think that one linguistic form has many meanings base the distinction between its primary and secondary meanings on its being well known or not well known. Others trace the distinction to context. Again, it is taken to be a matter of the relative fullness or deficiency of features. Others think the meaning conveyed is a universal property. Still others say that the meaning conveyed results from deviation or distortion (*viparyāsa*) of some sort, as with the snake and the rope. Other such examples are cited.

298–313 (*E*104–107; *T*129–135). A word form conveys a cluster of (grammatical) meanings such as number, tense, and person. Not all of them are intended when the action expressed by the sentence is to be carried out. One must distinguish between possible and intended meaning, usual and contextually appropriate meaning, meaning element that prompts the use of a word (*prayojaka artha*) and meaning element that is unavoidable (*nāntarīyaka*) because the word must appear with a certain suffix, or meaning that simply serves to indicate the participant in an action (*upalakṣaṇa artha*) and that means the participant itself (*pradhāna artha*).

314–317 (*E*108–109; *T*135–138). The factors that determine the meaning to be assigned to a linguistic form in a particular sentence are, among others:[13] sentence (*vākya*), especially the action expressed in the sentence; context (*prakaraṇa*), in terms of the general activity going on at the time of utterance; meaning (*artha*) of co-occurring words, or textual context; propriety or suitability (*aucitya* or *auciti*); spatial context (*deśa*); temporal context (*kāla*); relation (*saṃsarga* or *saṃyoga*), accompaniment by an entity that would serve to distinguish; absence of an entity that would serve to distinguish (*viprayoga* or *viyoga*); mention of an entity that regularly accompanies (*sāhacarya*); opposition (*virodha*); indication (*liṅga*) available in a related sentence; presence of a specifying word (*anyaśabdasaṃnidhi* or *śabdāntarasaṃnidhāna*); probability (*sāmarthya*); gender (*vyakti*); accent (*svara*).

In the *bhedapakṣa* or *nānātvapakṣa*, which holds that a homophonous expression is in reality many words, these factors serve only to reveal the already existent distinction—to remove the obscuration caused by the identity of form. According to the proponents of *ekatvapakṣa*, they make known the then-operative capacities of the word—they delimit its potentiality.

318–324 (*E*109–110; *T*138–139). There are instances in which the meanings of the constituent words do not add up to the import or message of the sentence.

325–327 (*E*110–111; *T*140–141). Whether something is a word or a sentence does not depend on the number of constituents; the matter is to be decided on the basis of the meaning conveyed. Single words, whether noun or verb, that convey a self-sufficient meaning or one free of expectancy are sentences.

328–345 (*E*111–116; *T*141–148). Some hold that "deficient sentences" (elliptical sentences) or sentences in which one of the expected or ordinary constituents is missing convey their meaning by first reminding the hearer of their full form. This view is unacceptable; the so-called full sentence and the deficient sentence are in fact different expressions that are viewed as related in analysis and because of their similar outcomes. Categorization of words as nouns and so on is a product of analysis and a matter of convenience. It should not be viewed as primary truth to be retained at any price.

346–351 (*E*116–117; *T*148–151). In the case of a science like Grammar, a sentence is to be interpreted by taking into consideration what the related sentences state. The meaning to be assigned to a linguistic form in a sentence is held to be qualified by exceptions, specifications, and the like, right from the outset. The talk of a sentence (an exception (*apavāda*)), specification (*viśeṣavidhi*), or prohibition (*pratiṣedha*) qualifying, obstructing, or canceling sentence p (a statement of a general rule, *utsargavākya*, *sāmānyavidhi*) is to be understood as an inference that p does not reach the area of q and q does not reach the area of p (*aprāptyanumāna*). The cases in which acceptance of such demarcated areas is not possible are cases of option.

352–361 (*E*117–119; *T*152–155). There are instances in which an entity is referred to by an identifying expression (*saṃjñā*) and also by an expression that could be considered to be a part of that identifying expression (for example, *datta* is a part of *devadatta*). Some thinkers postulate the process of understanding the meaning here to be as follows: perception of the part (*datta*), recollection of the (full) expression (*devadatta*), cognition of the named, that is, the person Devadatta. It is better, however, to hold that the name and what seems to be a part of it are in fact two names associated with each other in genesis and analysis, but not in the act of signification. Grammar derives, through devices such as elision (*lopa*) and the like, parts that can designate, as not all parts are acceptable substitutes for the full name.

362–370 (*E*120–122; *T*156–159). Some forms are acceptable only as identifying expressions, others almost identical with them are only acceptable in a role other than that of identifying. A name can occasionally be employed with the intention of designating the conditioning factor (*nimitta*) that led to its coining; it can also apply appropriately (in keeping with its meaning in nonidentifying use) to an entity (for example, *kṛṣṇa*, "black," employed as name of a person of dark skin). When a word is said to be a designator of some entity, its capacity (to designate) is only restricted; a new capacity for designation is not created (for its designative capacity is natural to it). In science (principally Pāṇini's Grammar), a longer identifying expression (*mahatī saṃjñā*) indicates that the conditioning factor is intended or that a special consideration (such as assumption of recurrence) is involved. It is also noticed that the technical sense and the ordinary sense of an identifying expression are acceptable simultaneously in some instances and exclusively in others.

371–383 (*E*122–125; *T*160–164). How the action expressed in a sentence takes place with respect to the entities mentioned in it depends on the nature of the action and the intention in a particular context. An action like eating applies in its completeness to each of the individuals designated in the sentence. A fine imposed on a community, by contrast, applies collectively, unless it is specified that each member of the community must pay a specific amount. A dramatic performance is realized only when each individual involved contributes his expected share of subactions. Seeing, to illustrate another variety, can be brought about either way: collectively or with respect to each member of the collectivity. Similar variation is noticed when identifying expressions in Pāṇini's Grammar are applied to their nominate or when rules describing changes, such as that from *ṇ* to *n*, are interpreted.

384–388 (*E*125-126; *T*164-166). There are two views regarding the unity of an action involving many entities. Some think of it as becoming different with each change in the factors (agent, object, and the like) that are involved. It is expressed as one because the entities concerned are regarded as forming a collectivity. Others think of it as essentially single, but expressed with an indication of differentiation (such as plural number) because the factors involved are many and different.

389–393 (*E*126–127; *T*166–168). *Objection*: Each constituent sentence (or clause) applies to each individual item to which the major sentence applies. These constituents are not what is meant by the major sentence, but when the major sentence is uttered the hearer understands the distinct meanings of the constituent sentences.

Answer: If the whole meaning of a linguistic form is contained in the meanings of its constituents, then what is the need for the existence of separate word meanings? If the meaning of a linguistic form exists in each constituent, then either it contradicts that constituent's own meaning, or it accords with it. And if the latter, then linguistic forms do not have eternal meanings (as the opponent believes).

394–398 (*E*127–128; *T*168–170). The single generic meaning is established with respect to each component expression as well as to the whole collection of constituents and to each segment of the sentence. Analogously, even though phonemes have meanings, the case ending is added to the stem and not to each phoneme. Just as everyone sees the same property by means of the same lamp, so grammatical number is understood from one case ending. Thus meaningfulness does not belong exclusively to word, phoneme, or sentence. Such a view, found in tradition, only appears to conflict (with ours).

399–404 (*E*128–129; *T*171–174). A linguistic form does not illuminate its objective unless it is used (that is to say uttered). Just as the visual organ sees (an object) only when it has access to it, so language expresses its meaning (or objective) only when intentionally applied to it. Just as the relation between an instrument (*karaṇa*) and its object (*karman*) is brought about through action (*kriyā*), so the relation between designating (*abhidhāna*) and its designatum (*abhidheya*) is brought about through designation (*abhidhā*). And when several (distinct) things might be designated by a certain designating expression, the linguistic form is established in a particular case through its intentional application (*abhisaṃdhāna*). So, some say that Vedic linguistic elements are meaningless when they are repeated and that when taught to others they merely stand for their own forms, but that these same Vedic expressions, which each have a single meaning, when in use have different meanings depending on the different intentions of their speakers.

405–407 (*E*129–130; *T*174–175). Others, however, take each difference in usage to signify complete difference (between the meanings of the linguistic forms used), saying that a word such as *akṣa* (which can mean a fruit, or dice, or an axle) is indeed many linguistic forms being considered as having a single common property (in virtue of all the words having the same ordered set of phonemes). So each linguistic form has its own fixed meaning, and there is no speaker's intention other than just using the expression, which must have its meaning. The fact that an expression means different things in different contexts just shows that it is not one expression but several.

408–410 (*E*130; *T*176). For the advocates of the unitary sentence meaning, the question broached (between the advocates of fixed meaning and speaker's intention) is a pseudoquestion because it rests on the incorrect assumption that the speaker begins with unrelated words and goes on to relate them.

411–418 (*E*131–132; *T*176–180). Among those who view the speaker as proceeding forth with related words, there are two views. Some think of the action expressed in the sentence as related to its bearers only generally at the initial moment, while others think of the action as specifically related to its bearers right from the first moment. Others think that it is not language that establishes the meaning, but that language only produces a memory (*smṛti*), which is like the meaning in appearance. Thus, a burned man understands burning from his contact with fire; it is otherwise when one learns the meaning of burning from the word "burning."

419–430 (*E*132–134; *T*180–185). Just as the sense organs—which differ by nature from one another and have each their specific sphere of operation—cannot function except through the body, so words—which are individually related to their meanings—do not have meaning disjoined from a sentence. The relational form (of the sentence) is grasped when the actual objects that are meant are connected to it, but its essential nature is not indicated thereby, as the meanings of the words are not seen. Awareness likewise remains in its true, formless state but appears to be colored by relations to actual things. Again, a meaning can only be designated as related to existence or nonoccurrence; so it is the sentence that is fit (to designate). The meaning of a word, whether existent or the opposite, is not understood in communication without some connection to an action. So it does not exist. Even the one-word sentence "(it) exists" cannot be thought without some relation (assumed) with an action in the form "it was" or "it was not." It is the action (part of the meaning of the sentence) that is first analyzed, because of its primacy. The other means is used to effect that action. Its result is its motivation. But it is just the speaker, the intender, who forms the conception of the thing to be effected, its means, and the relation between them. A meaning (in other words, an objective that can be meant), because it has all powers (to play any role needed), is established as assisting in whatever the speaker wants to say.

431–440 (*E*135–136; *T*185–189). (Through language) things far apart can be presented as together, or vice versa; and one may be presented as many, or vice versa. This fact can be explained through supposing either that an object's nature is everything or that it has no nature at all. It is language that has extremely fixed power, that relates (the things meant). A linguistic form is only an indicator (*upalakṣaṇa*) of an actual object (*vastu*); it does not express the powers (if any) of an object. The meanings of words are established through marks (*lakṣaṇa*), but not as they actually are (*vastutas*); such an object is understood in different manners through its uses. The relationship that is the nature of a sentence's meaning does not reside in the individual word meanings or in their aggregate. In communication we speak of it that way, but that is a product of analysis, which is needed to explain and thus understand it. In such analysis parts are distinguished that require each other. So the unity of sentence meaning must be understood from small indications.

441 (*E*137; *T*189–190). The external meaning (or object), whether existent or not, is to be distinguished from that meaning which is notional (*sampratyaya*). That distinction consists in analyzing the powers (of the words to signify external objects).

442–446 (*E*137–138; *T*191–194). A sentence is considered to be one by some if it has one finite verb; others thinks of it as one even if it has more than one finite verb, provided the verbs are expectant of (*sākāṃkṣa*) each other. Whether a sentence is complete should be determined by examining whether it is wanting in a word. Nonspecification of the way that the action expressed is carried out does not make a sentence incomplete.

447–450 (*E*138–139; *T*194–195). Action, while physically the same, appears different if the point of emphasis in the sentence is changed. Conversely, individual actions may be physically different due to difference of agent, means, and the like and yet may be expressed without an expression of the difference.

451–456 (*E*139–140; *T*195–197). Action expressed generally for a group takes place recurrently with respect to each individual agent in the group. Some explain this fact by pointing out that there is no one-to-one correspondence between linguistic utterance (*uccāraṇa*) and comprehension (*pratipatti*) in any case. Others theorize that the one initial sentence gives rise to many sentences, which then apply individually to the agents. The latter seek support for their view in Pāṇini's practice of employing general and specific sentences.

457–458 (*E*140; *T*197–198). According to some thinkers the distinction between universal and particular is inapplicable to action. Others view action as containing a particular element (*vyaktibhāga*) and a common or universal element (*sāmānyabhāga*). The latter, they say, explains expressions in which distinctions of time, agent, or object are not reflected.

459–475 (*E*141–145; *T*198–203). Sentences in which a single word performs a role in more than one part of the sentence—for example, having a different sense in combination with each of several verbs in the sentence—are explained in a variety of ways, based on (a) assumption of difference between utterance and comprehension; (b) recognition of sequence and simultaneity as possible processes in the employment of expressions; (c) division of words as aggregates of phonemes into those in which the distinction of parts is manifest, those in which that distinction is not explicit, and those in which there are no parts to begin with; (d) postulation of the arising of individual-oriented sentences in the period between utterance and comprehension; (e) ascription of more than one capacity to an expression depending on the expectation (*arthitva*) of the hearer; and (f) acceptance of recurrence (*āvṛtti*).

476–485 (*E*145–146; *T*203–205). These epilogue verses make a few remarks about the passing of the Pāṇinian tradition, starting with the *Saṃgraha* (referred to also by Patañjali), proceeding through Patañjali himself, Candra, and Bhartṛhari's teacher, and having suffered at the hands of "dry logicians" (*śuṣkatarkānusāra*) such as Baiji, Saubhava, and Haryakṣa. All the traditions discussed heretofore, and many more, were mastered by Bhartṛhari's teacher; a fuller discussion will be found in the third book, to follow. It is important to become familiar with other traditions than one's own and to understand the older teachers, in order that one's understanding be clear.

BOOK 3

1. On Universal Property (*Jātisamuddeśa*)

1-5 (*E*58; *T*1-9). Words abstracted from sentences have been regarded as falling into two (noun, verb), four (with the addition of prepositions and particles) or five (with the addition of postpositions) categories. In the analysis into word meanings there are said to be two eternal word meanings for all language (or linguistic forms), namely universal and particular. Sometimes the particular as characterized by the universal of its class is intended, and sometimes without such a characterization.

6–13 (*E*58–59; *T*10–16). Every linguistic form first designates its own universal property, which is then identified by conceptual construction superimposed (*adhyāropakalpanā*) as having the form of the universal of a meaning (or thing meant, *artha*). This identification happens just as the principle in the quality "red color" is attributed to lac and is then, because of the lac's being in contact with a piece of clothing, say, apprehended as residing in that piece of clothing; likewise, the universal property residing in language, because of the relation between language and meanings, is imagined to do the job of the universal property when there is attribution of properties to things meant. The universal property common to all universal properties is the linguistic form "universal property"; it is arrived at by elimination; the universal property common to linguistic universals is also "linguistic universal." This linguistic universal is in linguistic forms but is different from linguistic forms; it includes as well the universal property "being a linguistic universal" (*śabdajātitva*). Even if universals can actually designate objects meant (and not only as an appearance, a superimposition), every linguistic form designates a universal, for the meanings of words are determined according to their (the words') operations (*vyāpāra*).

So, even according to the view (not accepted by the author) that words designate substances (that is, particulars) they do so by virtue of having the properties of substances; so it is the property that should be held to be the meaning (of linguistic forms).

14–24 (*E*59; *T*17–21). A universal property is that property common to all members of a class which distinguishes the particular members of that class from nonmembers. Or, some say, the "general feature" (*ākṛti*) is that which is spoken of as common, and it is again spoken of as "particular substance" (*dravya*) to indicate differentiation. But difference or identity requires limitation (*upādhi*) by something other (than the things differentiated or identified). Only if things are connected (somehow) can they be thought to be different from or the same as each other. In fact, it is the one Self that has all powers; to suppose that things differ in their natures is unnecessary. So substance and the like are distinctly marked powers in tandem that assist men in gaining their purposes, but not separately. This connection among them is not, however, something above and beyond the powers, any more than the causal collocation (*sāmagrī*) of sense organs is something above and beyond those organs.

25-40 (*E*60–61; *T*22–30). It is the universal that is the prompter (*prayojaka*) of the coming to be of the particular, being present antecedently in its causal conditions. Just as a face reflected in water is called merely a "face," so it is only the universal manifested by the individuals that is designated (by language). And just as the differences among the sense organs, even though they be not perceived, lead us to postulate differences among the sense objects grasped by those organs, so in the same way the individuals, though not perceived, lead us to accept differences in our awareness of (their) universal properties. But it is the universal that is the existent (*satya*), the individual being nonexistent (*asatya*). Indeed, it is existence (*sattā*) alone that differentiated through its relata is said to be the "universal"; and all language is based on that ("existence"). This existence is the meaning of the stem and of the root; it is the great Self, and it is designated "action" (*kriyā*) when there is sequence among individuals. This existence universal takes on six states (*avasthā*) when there is modification of becoming (*bhāvavikāra*) in apparent sequence; that sequence is likewise the nature of that Self in which time is seen as if it were divided into stages of before and after. The nonexistence of a thing is its being taken to be hidden (*tirobhāva*); its origination (*janma*) occurs when that existence universal has left a previous stage and has not yet arrived at the next one. The causes of our finding distinctions in this existence universal arise from its own powers.

41–48 (*E*61; *T*30–35). A universal does not need to have any shape of its own in order to manifest itself as earth or something else, and it persists when its locus is destroyed. Some say that it is not the case that everything is simultaneously dissolved at the time of *pralaya*; others say that when the various objects are merged in *prakṛti* their universals have a single locus, the *dravyasattva* (pure Substance?). Still another view is that each universal resides in every being, but only comes to be known in its particular manifestations. Yogīs, however, are aware of universals through all their senses sharpened by practice.

Some universals—for example, the one expressed by the phrase "man-lion" (in other words, a heroic person)—have no linguistic forms that designate them but are established through expressions designating their parts that appear similar (to other words, namely, "man," "lion").

49–91 (*E*61–65; *T*35–56). That words have endings expressing number—despite their designating a single universal property each—can be explained in various ways in different cases. Sometimes the number serves other purposes; sometimes it is not even significant. Cases are adduced of these sorts.

In general, activity with respect to a particular thing (or substance) depends on our understanding its relevant qualities. Indeed, substance and quality are mutually dependent (*sāmarthya*). A sentence that indicates the relations of both quality and substance to an action should not be viewed as a compound sentence; both are conveyed together. Because it is the universal, and not the substance or quality, that is designated by the words, and because it is therefore the universal that is most closely connected with the action rather than the substance or quality, we find that one can maintain the action meant while substituting another quality for the one first indicated (for example, one can perform a sacrifice with a black goat if a white one is not available). And even though substance and quality are mutually dependent, the fact that one is allowed to find a substitute for a quality (in such a context as above) but not for the substance can be explained by noting that the universal property is closely associated with the kind of substance (goat) but not so closely with the quality (say, its color).

92–102 (*E*65–66; *T*57–61). Synonyms for "universal" are "lack of difference in form among things (of the same class)," "similarity," "the powers involved in the very nature of things." But even though one may get the idea of a stick from being aware that someone desires a stick, one does not thereby get the idea that he is actually a stickholder. For that one requires something else (namely, the universal). Otherwise the natural powers of things would remain indeterminate (*avyapadeśya*) and communication could not occur. But when, abandoning distinctions, the nature of individuals is apprehended as single, then a single awareness occurs. When unity is considered to be among many, the idea of a "collection" (*samūha*) is born. And when the individual members of the collection are considered first as different and then in terms of their unity, there arises the idea of their similarity. And just as an awareness, though different from the next one, is considered to be the same, so an object, though it has the nature of excluding others, is apprehended (as being the same in nature).

We do not have language to express the differences among things that are similar to one another; neither is that difference cognized. Thus, because of the difficulty of establishing the different specific contents of our awarenesses and of the meanings of linguistic expressions, we come to see them as identical. Or, according to the view of those who believe in relations, just as there are universal characters of (in) our awarenesses, so there are universals of (in) all objects, and the awareness universals prove the object universals.

103–106 (*E*66; *T*61–63). (Or, according to another view) the universals in the objects of our awareness help distinguish the awarenesses as well. An awareness does not require another awareness to cognize it, any more than a lamp requires another lamp to illuminate it. The awareness "this is an awareness of jar" is different from the awareness "this is a jar"; the form of being an awareness is not cognized as a content; we do not grasp its nature as distinct from the nature of the object meant.

2. On Substance (*Dravyasamuddeśa*)

1–6 (*E*66–67; *T*64–68). Synonyms of *dravya* (substance) are "self" (*ātman*), "actual entity" (*vastu*), "(thing having its) own nature" (*svabhāva*), "body" (*śarīra*), "thatness" (*tattva*).[14] This eternal existent is made known to us through nonexistent forms (*ākāra*); likewise, it is this existent alone that is designated by linguistic forms that designate nonexistent limitations (*upādhi*). In the same way, though the word "house" designates a bare house, Devadatta's house is designated by the word through temporary indications (*nimitta*) of it; or the word "gold" is used to refer to particular impermanent golden ornaments, even though really it refers to gold in its purity alone. And just as the power of the visual organ is limited when one looks through a tube, so the power of language to express all meanings is limited by the (particular) forms. But because those forms are essentially identical with the substance (whose forms they are supposed to be), language that designates them designates the eternal substance.[15]

7–18 (*E*67–68; *T*68–74). The tradition of old is that there is no distinction between substance (*tattva*) and what is not substance (*atattva*). Rather, substance when not properly understood (*avicārita*) is thought to be something other than substance. That (real substance), the form of which is not subject to conceptual construction (*avikalpita*), appears as if subject to constructions. For example, though not subject to temporal distinctions it appears as if it is. Just as the properties of contents cannot characterize awarenesses, yet appear to be characterizing them, so forms of the modifications, which cannot characterize substance, appear to do just that.

What is existent is that which remains at the end when forms disappear. It is eternal, expressed by language and not different from the language principle. It is neither existent nor nonexistent; neither single nor separate; neither connected nor disjoined; neither modified nor unmodified. This single (substance) is seen as language, meaning, and the relation between them. It is what is seen, seeing, the seer, and the result of seeing.

3. On Relation (*Saṃbandhaparikṣā*)

1–2 (*E*68; *T*76–77). From linguistic forms that are uttered three entities can be known: the speaker's awareness (what he is thinking of), the external object, and the linguistic form's own nature. A hearer may fail to cognize the first two, but not the third.

3–28 (*E*68–70; *T*79–92). The relation between word and meaning is indicated by the use of the genitive case ("*y* is the meaning of *x*"). There is no expression that designates this relation as a relation, for expressions reify—turn dependent entities like relation into independent, apparently substantive entities. This problem can be seen in the case of contact (*saṃyoga*) and inherence (*samavāya*), though neither of those two relations is the relation that connects linguistic forms and their meanings. Some say that relation is not among things meant by words (*padārtha*); others say that relations such as contact and inherence fall among the things meant. But they cannot comprehend the meaning relation in their system, for language can designate substances, qualities, and universals, and the relations between language and meaning differ in different cases. Anyway, there can be no word expressing inherence. Some words (such as *ākāśa*) designate their own substrata, or their own universal properties, to which they are related by inherence. Other words designate a quality that coinheres in the same substratum as they do. A word such as "jar" designates an item that is related to it by the relation of *being in contact with what it* (*the word*) *inheres in* (*samavetasaṃyoga*). An expression such as "the jar's black color" designates an item that is related to it by the relation of *inhering in what is in contact with its* (*the word's*) *inherence locus* (*svāśrayasaṃyuktasamavāya*). An expression such as "colorness" designates an item that *inheres in what inheres in what is in contact with its* (*the word's*) *inherence locus*. A word such as "time" designates an item that is related to it by the relation of *being in contact with what is in contact with its* (*the word's*) *locus*. (So the items belonging to the other five categories of the Vaiśeṣika six are accounted for, but) no other relation is found to relate the word "inherence" to its alleged designatum. But that word, "inherence," cannot be meaningless, nor can any word mean any old object. So the (Vaiśeṣika) analysis of linguistic meaning in terms of contact and inherence will not work.

Objection: You say that inherence is inexpressible; but because you have just expressed it, it has become expressible ! Or if you say even the word "inexpressible" does not express it, we could not understand what your claim means.

Prima facie reply: What we mean is that inherence's dependent nature cannot be expressed.

Objector's reply: Then inherence itself cannot be expressed, and your words do not convey anything.

Siddhāntin's answer: A doubt cannot be itself doubted. Again, a belief cannot itself come to be the thing it itself believes. To take another case: in saying "all that I am saying is false" (*sarvaṃ mithyā bravīmi*) one does not intend to include that very sentence in the scope of its meaning, for then, as what one is saying would be implicitly false, the intended meaning would not be conveyed. Generally, what is expressive cannot at the same time be what it expresses, and if something x is conveyed by y then y cannot itself be expressed by something other than y. Another example: "the thesis (*pratijñā*) is not probative (*sādhaka*)" does not apply to itself.

29–38 (*E*70–71; *T*92–97). The meaning relation is just the beginningless fitness (*yogyatā*) between linguistic forms and their meanings, analogous to the fitness sense organs possess for their contents. It is the correct (*sādhu*) linguistic form that expresses the fit meaning; incorrect forms are expressive only by inference. The word "relation" designates relations, and "fitness" designates fitness, because they are fit to do so (so that the analogous difficulty to the one about "inherence" does not arise). Awareness of this capacity comes through convention. Language is the cause of meaning, so from the meaning that is a content of (the speaker's) awareness language (for it) is understood (by the hearer). There was never a time that this fitness between language and meaning did not exist (as a general phenomenon); neither does it cease to exist when the thing a word refers to ceases to exist, for the thing is permanent as designatable (*abhidheyātmanā*).

39–51 (*E*71–72; *T*98–104). What words convey or imply can be called existence of a secondary nature (*upacārasattā*). This existence differs from actual existence in that it can be reconciled with any property—even with properties ordinarily thought to be contrary to existence.[16] It is in this way that negative particles are meaningful, that we can talk of things not yet in existence, and so on.

52-60 (*E*72; *T*105-109). Coverage of only a part, grasping something as limited by something else (such as a universal), reversal (or error, *viparyaya*), and absence or negation are inherent in linguistic communication. In this aspect it reflects features and limitations of cognition. There is, therefore, no ordinary way in which external things are cognized or expressed purely as they are. The child and the pandit, insofar as they are communicators, both express only partial views of things. Pure awareness (*śuddhajñāna*) (beyond the level of communication) embraces all objects and is not based (on sensory perception). An even purer stage, some say, occurs in awareness without form (*arūpika*). When awareness exhibits the forms of external objects it is, as it were, impure through getting mixed up with those forms. And a meaning becomes impure in the same way, falling away from its true nature through being limited. And because the meaning, the linguistic form, and the awareness are all thus in error, there is no essential difference in the manner in which positive things (*bhāva*) and negative ones (*abhāva*) appear in communication; both are mutually dependent in that respect.

61–71 (*E*72–73; *T*109–113). Positive and negative being are two conceptual constructions and are not different from the one self. Theories that seek to derive an existent from a nonexistent, or one existent from another existent, or a nonexistent from (the destruction of) an existent are logically problematic. They lead their proponents to advocate either something existent or something nonexistent as the ultimate source, but the derivation of the opposites from such sources is logically questionable. One must, therefore, accept as ultimate source an entity (*ātman*, *artha*) that unites in itself both existence and nonexistence—which is indifferent to the distinction, which can be thought of either way. Linguistic usage does not proceed with this transcending reality as its basis. Its basis is rather what is *thought* to exist, what is conceptually constructed.

72–77 (*E*73–74; *T*114–115). Those who know the Upaniṣads (*trayyantavedinaḥ*) have declared that what really exists is that on which is constructed seer, seen, and seeing. Language expresses the universal as well as the particular as differentiated. Therefore it operates with distinctions that do not really exist, and among such distinctions is that between positive being and negative being.

78–88 (*E*74–75; *T*116–119). Furthermore, language is incapable of expressing the cause-and-effect relationship without problematic implications. That an entity called effect comes into existence when another entity called cause is present is a matter of experience; it cannot be denied, it is like a miracle (*atyadbhuta*) in that words fail to convey it with precision.[17] The sequence (*krama*) presupposed in the transition of cause to effect is not something physically different from the existent that undergoes the change, just as simultaneity is not physically over and above the entities involved. The philosophers who accept a permanent existent have, therefore, thought of sequence as a capacity of the (one) existent. An entity does not actually exist merely because an expression for it exists. In the science of Grammar, however, all entities presupposed by expressions are thought to exist, and meanings of expressions are analyzed irrespective of actual existence or nonexistence.

4. More on Substance (*Bhūyodravyasamuddeśa*)

1–3 (*E*75; *T*121–123). The subject matter of the following chapters concerns certain word meanings (*padārtha*) abstracted in traditional ways from their forms in coalescence (*saṃsarga*, that is, the sentence) and from awareness (*saṃvid*). The nature of these word meanings is inferred from the rules of grammar. They are a basis of grammaticality (*sādhutva*).

A substance (individual, particular, *dravya*) is any entity that can be referred to by a demonstrative pronoun and that is viewed in the utterance as capable of differentiation.[18]

5. On Quality (*Guṇasamuddeśa*)

1-9 (*E*75–76; *T*126–132). A quality (*guṇa*) is that entity which accompanies the substance, which is active in the role of differentiating it, and which is viewed as dependent on the substance for its existence. A substance cannot be referred to purely in itself; it needs qualities in order to be expressed. It is the excellence (or superiority, *prakarṣa*)[19] of a quality, not of the substance, that is expressed in comparison and similar constructions. Because such expressions are particularistic (only relatively more specific, *viśeṣaśabda*, than some other expression), they cannot exhaust all elements of a substance that can be used for differentiating it. Thus there is always the possibility of being able to specify in a finer way, of turning the dependent element or *guṇa* of an earlier stage into the principal element (*pradhāna*) or substance of the next stage. (Compare the sentences "*x* has a form," "*x* has a white form," "*x* has a whiter form," "The whiteness of *x* has a shine to it," and so on.)

6. On Spatial Direction (*Diksamuddeśa*)

1 (*E*76; *T*133). Words refer to spatial direction (*dik*), action bearers (or means, *sādhana*),[20] action (*kriyā*), and time (*kāla*) as if they were actual entities. That they are in reality powers (*śakti*) arising from things is obliterated in usage.

2–5 (*E*76; *T*133–135). Spatial direction is that power which is behind such cognitions and usages as "*x* is before *y*," "this thing is straight (without bends)," and "this action is one of going upward." It is single, but is divided into many (for example, the ten directions) on account of adjuncts (*upādhi*, such as contact with the sun at a particular time). Direction differentiates material things (*mūrta*) in terms of nearness and remoteness, while time distinguishes them in terms of sequence of actions. Direction is the basis of the talk of contact and disjunction through the perception of occupied and unoccupied regions of the sky or *ākāśa*.[21]

6–11 (*E*76–77; *T*136–139). There is no fixed arrangement of spatial direction. The various compass directions, which seem to divide systematically, are mere names when they are divested of reference to the things (for example, the sun at a particular time) with which they are associated. Names of regions of space contain in some cases references to the directions used conventionally without regard to the actual position of the speaker or hearer.

12–22 (*E*77–78; *T*139–144). Based on distinctions such as "this," "that," "eastern," "western," and the like, which are introduced by spatial direction, are the divisions seen in things from mountains to atoms. These divisions are characterized in terms of the accompanying entity (for example, presence or absence of light) or configuration, but the concept or capacity called "spatial direction" is their ultimate foundation. Things per se are beyond division, sequence, and fixation by region. Division with which the adjuncts invest them has no end and cannot be something inherent to them. Yet division cannot be avoided. Spatial direction is operational everywhere. Along with time, it is part of the very nature of living beings. There would be confusion in communication and action if entities such as spatial direction were to be abandoned, if they could at all be abandoned. Sometimes they are explicitly present (with extent or limit mentioned), sometimes implicitly.

23–28 (*E*78; *T*144–146). It is also possible to view space as a property or power of consciousness (so far it has been viewed as a power of things). Under either alternative, there is no gain in trying to prove either that it is ultimately one or that it is ultimately many (in other words, that it is a set of several powers). Spatial direction is not an actual entity. Its existence rests on convention. Besides, singularity and plurality are mutually relative concepts; one presupposes the other. They cannot, therefore, be exclusively applied. If spatial direction is declared to be single, the sense of "single" cannot be the usual sense, which contains an implicit reference to plurality.

7. On the Means to Action (*Sādhanasamuddeśa*)

1–8 (*E*78–79; *T*147–152). Means (*sādhana*) is the power to bring about the action (or actions) expressed in the sentence. This power is located in what are viewed as the loci (agent, object) of the action as well as in other entities mentioned in the sentence that are not so viewed (such as the instrument, *karaṇa*). It need not always be physically or really present in the entities in which it is supposed to reside. It is what the intellect assumes to be present there. Entities are bundles of powers. The intellect enjoys autonomy in investing them with powers and in activating only some powers at the time of sentence formation. Thus it is possible, for example, to say "he is making a sound." Although the sound has evidently not become a physical reality at the time of uttering this sentence, it is viewed as an existent acting as the power of an object with respect to the action of making.

9–13 (*E*79; *T*153–156). The "relationalists" (*saṃsargavādinaḥ*, that is, the Vaiśeṣikas)[22] view powers as ontically subsumed under the categories that they admit. A means for them is what should be viewed in the context of their ontology as instrumental in bringing about the action expressed. Thus, in "he sees a pitcher" the qualities of the pitcher such as its medium dimension are the means, but in "he sees a form (or color)" the universal called "formness" (or "colorness") is the means. Such means are not specifically expressed in the words of the sentences concerned; they are implied by endings (*vibhakti*) and are logically reconstructed.

14–17 (*E*79–80; *T*156–157). Things that have come to exist are taken as means when they, as it were, oblige the action by being instrumental in bringing the object about. The power of being instrumental has been claimed by some to be an entity identical with the thing, or over and beyond the thing, which is instrumental in this manner. It does not matter (to the Grammarian) which is the case. As long as it is seen to be different it can be held to be the means. In the same fashion an action can be a means with respect to a succeeding action it might generate.

18–27 (*E*80; *T*158–166). These passages discuss the range of application of the terms *kāraka* and *hetu*.

28–31 (*E*80–81; *T*167-168). Powers are latent in substances that will become means of actions. These powers are revealed at the time the action takes place.

32-42 (*E*81-82; *T*168-172). Some thinkers view means as existing prior to the action, some as simultaneous with the action, and some as subsequent to the action. There is also a difference of views concerning what it is that brings about the action and bestows the status of means on entities—some of the candidates include karmic force (*apūrva*), time (*kāla*), the power of time, and action itself. The division of means into six *kārakas* has also been viewed by some as natural, by others as derivative. Some have defended the identity with, as well as the distinctness from, the entity involved of the power that is means to action. It is not realized that an assertion of identity has an implicit reference to difference and vice versa, and that reality transcends both concepts.

43–44 (*E*81; *T*173-174). By comparing and contrasting (*anvayavyatireka*) pairs such as *vṛkṣas*/*vṛkṣam*, one is led to hold that case endings (*vibhakti*) are themselves meaningful. The category to which their meaning belongs is called *kāraka*. It has seven varieties: *karman*, *karaṇa*, *kartṛ*, *sampradāna*, *apādāna*, *adhikaraṇa*, and *śeṣa*.

45–53 (*E*82–83; *T*174–178). *Karman*, the object of action, which is of the kind that is what the agent wishes most to reach with his action, has three varieties: (a) a kind of object that is to be brought into existence (*nirvartya*) and is not a transformation of its material cause; (b) a kind of object that is a modification (*vikārya*) of its material cause; and (c) a kind of object that is to be reached or obtained (*prāpya*), in which no change is seen to take place when the action succeeds. There are alternative ways of explaining (a) and (b), (a) as that kind of object which did not exist before its production, and (b) as either the result of the destruction of material or the result of modification of substance. As for those objects of action which are other than the kind most desired to be obtained, they are of four kinds: (d) that regarding which the agent is indifferent (*audāsīnya*); (e) that which the agent (ordinarily) avoids (*anīpsita*); (f) that which is not covered by the other designations of kinds of *kārakas*; and (g) that which, though logically another kind of *kāraka*, is to be viewed as object (*karman*) in the process of sentence derivation on the Grammarian's instruction.

54–58 (*E*83; *T*179–181). The objects of types (a), (b), and (c) are involved as elements that bring about the action of which they are the objects. To that extent they are agents (*kartṛ*). But the logical, first-level agenthood is replaced by objecthood in linguistic expression once another entity appears on the scene as instigating or causing the action—an agent marked by *preṣaṇā*, that is to say directing, commissioning, impelling, or setting in motion.

59-66 (*E*83-84; *T*183-187). These passages discuss *Mahābhāṣya* on Pāṇini 1.3.67 and 3.2.60, concerning certain complications about expressions that indicate objecthood and agency.

67–80 (*E*84–85; *T*188–197). Discussion of other *sūtras* relating to object. Time and the like are objects with a different status, having become a kind of substratum for the substance objects. They are secondary (*apradhāna*) or external (*bahiraṅga*) objects. By contrast, the principal (*pradhāna*) object is the one that is the prompter (*prayojaka*) of the action.

81–86 (*E*85; *T*198–200 These *kārikās* discuss constructions in which the object does not appear in the accusative case.

87–89 (*E*85–86; *T*200–203). An action does not appear in a sentence as *akarmaka*—not requiring an object—simply because the object it requires already exists or is supposed to exist before it is related to the object or because its relating to the object leaves no traces. It appears as *akarmaka* either (a) because the root used to express it has a different meaning elsewhere, or (b) because it already includes as a concept that which would be object in a construction with similar meaning, or (c) because its object is too well known to be specified, or (d) because the intention is merely to state it without specifying the object.

90–100 (*E*86; *T*203–208). The second category of case ending, instrument (*karaṇa*), is now discussed. The instrument is that entity after the activity or operation (*vyāpāra*) of which the action being expressed takes place in the speaker's view at the time of sentence formation. Whether a specific instrument's activity is actually or invariably necessary for the realization of the action concerned, or whether that activity in fact immediately precedes the realization of the action, or whether the instrument physically exists does not matter. Similarly, there need not be only one instrument for an action. All entities that are viewed as more instrumental in bringing about the action than the rest of the *kāraka* entities of the sentence can be instruments. Such an understanding of "instrument" does not conflict with the eminence enjoyed by the agent (*kartṛ*) with respect to the action on account of his freedom to initiate or not to initiate it.

101–105 (*E*87; *T*209–211) The third category of case endings, the agent (*kartṛ*), is next treated. An agent is defined as independent (*svatantra*) by Pāṇini (1.4.54) in the sense that it takes precedence over other *kārakas* in the speaker's perspective and is viewed as bestowing particular roles on the other *kārakas*. It need not necessarily be sentient and capable of willful action. Whatever the speaker chooses to present as independent becomes the agent. This dependence on the speaker's intention (*vivakṣā*) and the fact of *kārakas* such as agent being primarily linguistic (as opposed to actual) are evident from the following: what is physically single can be assumed to be different even in the course of one sentence. Usages such as "he kills himself with his own hands" (*hanty ātmānam ātmanā*) are possible because the (physically) same "he" is cognized from the perspective of three possible capacities: the capacity to be the agent, the capacity to be the object (*ātmānam*), and the capacity to be the instrument (*ātmanā*).

Realization of this phenomenon, namely, that different cognitive stances toward the same thing are reflected in linguistic usage, provides a key to the understanding, for example, of sentences speaking of the birth or creation of something. A sentence such as "a sprout comes into being" (*aṅkuro jāyate*) would have to be declared illogical, marred by internal contradiction, if the reference of "sprout" in it is held to be primarily to a sprout actually existent or nonexistent at the time of utterance (if the sprout already exists, how can one assert that it [newly] comes into being? If the sprout does not exist at the time of utterance, how can one assert its coming into being?). But if the sentence is understood as implicitly containing two views of the sprout—as an entity in the mind of intellect and as a physical entity—then there is no incongruence. The natural understanding of the expression "sprout" is an existent sprout. As soon as the expression "comes into being" is connected with "sprout," it is implied that the sprout cannot be an existent in the usual sense—that it must have an assumed existence; then only can it be the agent of "comes into being."

106–113 (*E*87–88; *T*211–215). Other possible ways of accounting for a usage like "a sprout comes into being" follow:

(a) An effect is nothing but a specific form taken by the cause. The real meaning of a sentence such as "a sprout comes into being" is that the seed becomes a sprout. As the cause—the seed—becomes the effect, it is referred to by the word, "sprout," which denotes the effect. Actually, there is no creation of something that did not exist before.[23]

(b) If the cause and the effect are not viewed as a continuum and the effect is thought to be something previously nonexistent that came into being, then also a usage such as "a sprout comes into being" can be understood in such a way as to be free from internal contradiction; it can be understood as meaning that the sprout, which existed as a universal, appeared in the form of an individual. As a universal it already exists and hence can become the agent of the action of coming into being.[24] At the same time, as an individual the sprout is an entity to be produced, hence its coming into being can be asserted.

(c) In all linguistic indication whatever entity is perceived is perceived as a positive existent (*bhāva*). Even in sentences such as "*X* does not exist," the word *X* denotes *X* as existing, as having some form (*ākāra*) or individuality (although the precise manner of existence, whether actual or imagined, permanent or temporary, may be stated later). Thus the existents as well as the nonexistents of the physical world are on a par as far as language goes; language can proceed without knowing which entity truly exists and which does not. As it is thus indifferent to external reality, the kind of problem that is seen in the case of "a sprout comes into being" is not a properly posed problem to begin with. The problem assumes that words of language are there to reflect external reality, when in fact the words are not intended to carry any such assurance.[25]

(d) The very concepts of "coming into being" and "going out of existence" are due to one's thinking being misled by mere appearances. In reality there is only one undifferentiated, changeless entity. Hence, just as other usage in which existence or nonexistence is explicit or implicit is accepted as valid in ordinary life, "a sprout comes into being" should be accepted.

(e) The real meaning of "a sprout comes into being" is that the cause of the sprout (say, the seed) takes the form of the sprout. Here, although the cause is the real agent, it is referred to by "sprout", the word standing for the effect, just as subactions that lead to the action of cooking are referred to by a word like "cooks," as in "he cooks rice."[26]

114–121 (*E*88; *T*215–219). Sometimes, as in "the seed becomes the sprout" the cause (specifically, the material cause, *prakṛti*) is presented as the agent; sometimes, as in "a sprout comes into being," the effect (the product, *vikāra*) is presented as agent.[27] This twofold possibility of expression is due to the very nature of coming into being, namely, birth or creation. The entity that is coming into being straddles both the earlier (causal) phase and the phase to come. Consequently, it can be expressed through either.

122–128 (*E*88–89; *T*219–222). In causal constructions such as "Yajñadatta makes Devadatta cook rice," the agent of the (apparently) incorporated sentence "Devadatta cooks rice" does not lose his independence (*svātantrya*) with respect to the *kārakas* of that sentence. It continues as prompted agent, while Yajñadatta becomes the causal or prompting agent.

The instigation of action that is seen in a causal construction is different from the instigation seen in an imperative or optative mood construction. The former applies to agents that are presumed to be already engaged in action and is a property of the expressed content. By contrast, the instigation in an imperative or optative mood construction belongs to one who expresses the content; in other words, in that instance instigation is a disposition and presupposes absence of engagement in action up to that point on the part of the one receiving the command or request (allusions to Pāṇini 1.4.52-55 and 3.1.26, and *Mahābhāṣya* thereon).

129–135 (*E*89; *T*223–226). The *kāraka* called *saṃpradāna* (indicated by the dative) is now discussed. *Saṃpradāna* is that *kāraka* which prompts or participates in the action of giving/parting with as recipient or destination of the object of the giving or parting.

136–147 (*E*89–90; *T*226–232). Next, the *kāraka* called *apādāna* (the ablative) is discussed. (That is *apādāna* which is uninvolved [*udāsina*] in the action of moving away. Whether it be itself actually in motion or not, it is considered to be fixed [*dhruva*] with respect to that which is expressed as moving away from it.)[28]

Apādāna has three varieties: first, one in whose case the action of moving away is explicitly stated (*nirdiṣṭaviṣaya*), for example, "village" in "he comes from the village"; second, one in whose case the explicitly stated action contains the element of moving away from it (*upāttaviṣaya*), for example, "cloud" in "the lightning shines from the cloud"; and, third, one in whose case no action (implicitly or explicitly) containing movement is mentioned, but is nevertheless expected (*apekṣitakriyā*), for example, "residents of Pāṭaliputra" in "the residents of Mathurā are richer than the residents of Pāṭaliputra.[29]

Which item is taken to be the fixed thing, the starting point, depends entirely on the context—in relation to the horse's trotting, Devadatta is fixed, while in regard to Devadatta's falling, the horse is fixed. If, as in the case of two rams separating, both are moving, there are two starting points, one for each act of separation. A speaker does not want to predicate simultaneously such contrary properties as difference and identity, or being the separating element and being the element separated from. A single item can be, for example, both an instrument (*karaṇa*) and a starting point (*apādāna*) at the same time, but either there is a rule specifying which suffix takes priority, or else one assumes that the two capacities are in fact one.

148–155 (*E*91; *T*232–236). Next comes a discussion of the locative case relation (*adhikaraṇa*). It indicates that which helps accomplish the action by holding (*dhārayan*) the agent or the object. Such service may include nondestruction (of the cause, which will be the effect), independently supporting the weight of the agent or the object, or their connection with portions of space. Some say the locus of everything in contact with others is *ākāśa*, which allows us to say "this thing is here." Likewise, the locus of all processes is time.

156–162 (*E*91–92; *T*237–240). The remaining type of meaning of case endings (namely, of the genitive case ending) is called "the rest" (*śeṣa*). It indicates secondary or subordinate relationships, not an added kind of accessory to the action.

163–167 (*E*92; *T*241–243). The nature of the vocative case (*sambodhana*) is to call the attention of the hearer to somebody already there. The vocative is not part of the sentence meaning.

These meanings of the case endings are analyzed from the sentence meaning.

8. On Action (*Kriyāsamuddeśa*)

1–10 (*E*92–93; *T*1–11). Whenever something, whether completed (*siddha*) or uncompleted (*asiddha*), is designated as something to be completed (*sādhya*), it is to be designated as an action (*kriyā*), because it has the nature of sequence (*krama*) inherent in it. For example "it sounds," "it whites" indicate actions (namely, of sounding, of shining as white) in contrast with merely "sound" or "white." An action is a collection (*samūha*) of parts that originate in sequence and is conceived to be identical with those parts. Then each part comes to be called by the name of the action, so that differences between the parts in the process can be apprehended, along with different tenses indicating the different times in the process. The whole action cannot be perceived, but is grasped from its perceptible parts, like the fire wheel (*alātacakra*).

11-19 (*E*93-94; *T*11-16). That action, which is expressed through verbs, has a form that, following temporal flow, is said to be existing (*asti*), until it has completely finished, when it is said to have become (*bhāva*). Each part of the action, which actually has no sequence, appears to have sequence because the powers of the subsequent parts are attributed to it. The primary meaning of "action" is that moment (in the sequence) immediately after which the result occurs. The other moments (prior to that one) are also called (parts of the) action because they have the same outcome as their purpose. As long as a thing exists in the form of a cause, before it is born, being something to be accomplished, it is indicated (by a verb). Once it is accomplished it does not require any more accessories, for its purpose is fulfilled. Thus, the verb is not used then.

21–25 (of *E*94), 20–24 (of *T*16–18). Others say an action is a universal that inheres in many particulars. It is not to be accomplished (being a universal and so eternal), but in its form as particular it is perceived as if it were something to be accomplished. Alternatively, it is that universal which inheres in the last (portion of the series of moments). Or, action is existence inhering in the agent and the object, or inhering in the specific operation. Still others say that action is something mental that is superimposed on objects.

26–35 (of *E*94–95), 25–34 (of *T*19–23). Among (Yāska's) six modifications of becoming (*bhāvavikāra*), two, manifestation and being hidden—or birth and destruction—are postulated of action for the purposes of practical affairs. All six are ultimately not different from existence. Birth is the stage of existence just prior to its accomplishment, and its (the action's) destruction is the stage following that—namely, the accomplishment itself. We use a verb to express the former, a noun for the latter. (Other versions of Yāska's account are considered.)

37–39 (of *E*95–96), 36–40 (of *T*23-25). Others think that action is activity (*pravṛtti*), not resident in anything particular, which together with accessories produces the result. At first, it is general (*sāmānya*), then it becomes disjoined into parts. Still later, in the form of the operation (*vyāpāra*) it is established in the thing to be accomplished. This activity is the material (*prakṛti*) of all the accessories, the first among them. Others say that the operations are different from the activity.

40–53 (of *E*95–97), 41–52 (of *T*25–30). Because the (other) accessories are all completed things, the verb primarily designates action.

Question: What about a word like "cooking" (*pāka*), which, having case endings, functions as a noun but designates an action? How can the same word have two contrary attributes, of naming both an accomplished thing and something to be accomplished?

Answer: Just as in grammar we artificially divide a verb into two parts (root and suffix), one indicating the action, the other the accessories (such as number, tense, and so on), so the same analysis holds good for a noun (like *pāka*): its root designates the action, its ending the accessories. Thus the same word expresses both things, just as in a sentence such as "See! The deer runs" the same word, "runs," expresses both the object of the seeing and the action of the deer.

54–64 (of *E*97), 53–63 (of *T*30–35). Because the meaning of verbs is an uncompleted process, there can be no identification of two actions except through using the expression "as it were" (*iva*), and no comparison or similarity (*upamāna*) between actions. Every action is completely present in its locus; so, because comparison (similarity) requires a standard having more or less of the relevant property, no comparison can obtain between actions of the same kind; and because actions of different kinds have no points of similarity at all, they cannot be compared either.

9. On Time (*Kālasamuddeśa*)

1–12 (*E*98–99; *T*36–39). Some say that time is a substance, single, omnipresent, permanent, without operation, the measure or dimension of things possessing motion. They say it is the cause of the origin, maintenance, and destruction of objects. Time is said to be the thread holder (*sūtradhāra*) of the world *yantra* (puppet show?), who by holding some back and allowing others to go on differentiates the universe. Time, though single, has many forms because of its being the locus of differences among the things residing in it. Nothing is one or many, white or nonwhite, in itself; a substance appears in one way or another due to its relations to other things. Because of the distinctions among those relata time is thought to be differentiated, so it provides the basis for the stages of processes. Again, actualization of a power is caused by time, so that the regulation of birth, maintenance, and destruction of a thing depends on time. Every stage of the world requires time, so time is the very self (*ātman*) of everything; it is operation itself.

13–26 (*E*99–100; *T*39–43). Time is the creator of the cycles. It holds back the various functionings of everything and then releases them, so that the potentialities come to mature at the appropriate time as particular manifestations of eternal activity. Then that power called inherence sublates differences and gives rise to an identity, as it were, between effects and their causes. This identity is prompted by universals, which come to be reflected in the particular effects. Then the qualities (*guṇa*), conditioned by their (own) causes, come to be perceived in those effects and in turn lead to the manifestation of their own universals. Because the loci of the particulars are eternal they persist over periods of time, dependent on relevant causes of that maintenance, and continue to perform their functions with the help of other existing things. Eventually time, through its power called "old age" (*jarā*), which is opposed to its other powers, prevents things from performing their functions by developing propensities that are contrary to those functions, which in turn results in the cooperating objects disappearing. So the thing perishes.

27–45 (*E*100–101; *T*43–48). Time is that with reference to which processes can be distinguished as fast or slow. It is the measure of the great ages differing in the moral qualities of the agents inhabiting them; it is the measure of the turning of the seasons. Though single, it comes to go by myriad names because of the divisions and distinctions among those things measured by it. When limited (*upādhi*) by motions it becomes differentiated into eleven forms of past, present, and future, specifically, five kinds of past, two kinds of present, and four kinds of future.

46–56 (*E*102; *T*49–52). It is time that makes the universe (*viśva*), which actually has no sequence, appear as if it had sequence. Past, present, and future are three powers of time; past and future cover over things while present illuminates them. The power called "future" allows birth to take place; the power called "past" suppresses birth. These three powers or "paths" (*adhvan*) have no sequence, but objects get sequence from them. Two of them are like darkness, and one is like light. An object is present while its causes are active and functioning; when they have stopped functioning it is said to be "past."

Some say, however, that time has only two powers, one that brings about the appearance, the other the disappearance of things.

57-58 (*E*102-103; *T*52-53). There are those who say that time is only a mental construction. But whether it be dependent on awareness or existent outside of awareness, it is not possible to speak except in a temporal context.

59–62 (*E*103; *T*53–54). There are those who say that every object has three powers; through these powers every object either exists or does not. They say that sequence is just these powers. The same thing is seen or not seen depending on these powers; nothing is really destroyed.

Whatever be the various views about time, whether it be a power, the self, or a god, it is in any case the first form of ignorance to arise, and it is not known in correct understanding.

63–84 (*E*103–105; *T*55–62). *Objection*: If temporal differences are only apparent, how can one explain the fact that there is actually more water flowing out of the measuring instrument while pronouncing a long vowel than there is while pronouncing a short one?

Answer: There actually are differences in the objects by reference to which temporal differences are measured. The flow of water through the measuring tube is itself the result of time's prevention or permission, though not solely; other factors enter in. For that matter, everything is differentiated only through other things. Temporal differences result from the dissimilarity between the parts of an action that are themselves constitutive actions.

85–90 (*E*105; *T*63–64). *Objection*: An actual entity either exists or does not; there is no third way. Thus there is no further possibility (for an action) beyond being past or future. A single thing without distinctions cannot have sequence, and if an action could be single everything would be unified, consisting of partly existent and partly nonexistent elements.

Answer: The present time of an action is when it is perceived in its own form, when it is reflected in a single act of awareness.

91–114 (*E*105–107; *T*65–73). *Objection*: The nonaccomplishment of an action is its complete nonarising; it can be neither past nor future.

Answer: But the opposite action (namely, the one that happens because its opposite does not) has a limit either in the past or in the future, so the unaccomplished action is temporally located by reference to that.

The remainder of this section takes up further points relating to tense.

10. On Person (*Puruṣasamuddeśa*)

1–3 (*E*107; *T*75–76). Certain suffixes indicate limitations (on the action) according to whether the action is by the speaker or by someone else. Even when consciousness is not existent in these, it is understood through use of these personal suffixes. But the third-person suffix cannot express consciousness in the agent, even when the verb is such as *budh*, *jña*, or *cit* (which indicate mental acts); these verbs themselves indicate consciousness, not the suffixes.

4–9 (*E*108; *T*77–78). Some say that wherever the second-person suffix is used the vocative meaning is to be understood as stemming from that suffix, not from the rest of the sentence.

11. On Number (*Saṃkhyāsamuddeśa*)

1–14 (*E*108–109; *T*79–84). Any existent has number. It is on number that identity and difference are based in the world. Whether number is a property different from or the same as its locus, in any case it is that on which differentiation is based. It distinguishes that in which it inheres (namely, substance), though it is sometimes imagined in other things (such as quality) and enables us to speak of their differences as well (as, for example, "twenty-four qualities"). Actually, the separation of quality from substance is a result of abstraction;

language and thought cannot deal with things except in terms of their properties. Thus we can think of, and speak of, the universal resident in universals, the individuator of individuators, the number of numbers, or the gender of genders. The different categories of things, though distinguished in theory and each having its own function, actually are found mixed up together, and their identification with one another depends on the occasion.

15–32 (*E*109–111; *T*84–92). Unity is the source of duality, and so on, for unity is prior to all other distinctions, which depend on a thing's being single. Some think the two unities require a mediating enumerative cognition (*apekṣābuddhi*) to create duality; others do not think so. Still others say that duality and the like are a collection of two or more unities, and that the number of a collection is due to the differences among its constituents.

The remainder of this section treats the grammar of expressions indicating number.

12. On Aspect (*Upagrahasamuddeśa*)

1–27 (*E*111–113; *T*93–104). Ways of indicating in the verb the different sorts of purposes with which an action is done are discussed.

13. On Gender (*Liṅgasamuddeśa*)

1–31 (*E*113–116; *T*105–119). There are seven views about what gender is: it is the thing qualified by its relation to signs of gender such as breasts or hair; it is those signs themselves so related; it is the universal residing in those signs; it is (three) stages of the constituents (*guṇa*); it is the three constituents themselves in these stages; it is a meaning attributed to things by language; it is a property of language itself. The author appears to lean toward the latter two views.

14. On Linguistic Formations (*Vṛttisamuddeśa*)

1–627 (*E*116–135; *T*121–411). Five sorts of complex formations are treated in this section: primary derivatives (*kṛdanta*), secondary derivatives (*taddhitānta*), compounds (*samāsa*), reduction of two verbs to one (*ekaśeṣa*), and nominal verbs (*nāmadhātu*). As the discussion concerns technical grammar it will not be summarized here.

Ṭikā on Patañjali's *Mahābhāṣya*

K. Kunjunni Raja

Bhartṛhari's philosophical ideas are found in their fully developed form in the *Vākyapadīya*, which is his magnum opus; but the germs of his theories may be found in his commentary on the *Mahābhāṣya,* of which a fragmentary manuscript alone is now available. It has been established that this fragmentary manuscript forms a genuine part of Bhartṛhari's *Mahābhāṣyaṭīkā.* This work was mentioned by Itsing in the seventh century and by Kaiyaṭa as a source book for his *Pradīpa* commentary on the *Mahābhāṣya.*

The *Ṭīkā* is not a regular word-for-word commentary on the *Mahābhāṣya.* It contains observations and comments on select words and points raised in them. Some of the ideas that were developed later into a cogent system are found scattered here and there in the commentary on the *Mahābhāṣya.* In some cases Bhartṛhari's comments in the *Ṭīkā* help us to understand his basic standpoint in the *Vākyapadīya.*

Survey of Philosophical Topics

1. *Sphoṭa* Theory

The *sphoṭa* theory of the Grammarians considers the expressive word or sentence to be an integral, indivisible unit. The word *sphoṭa* occurs in the *Mahābhāṣya* twice, without any reference to its meaning-bearing function but in the sense of a phoneme, shorn of all variations owing to the special circumstance. But Patañjali uses the term *śabda* in the sense of the meaning-bearing unit. Later commentators like Kaiyaṭa explain that by *śabda* Patañjali meant *sphoṭa.* S. D. Joshi says that even in Bhartṛhari's *Vākyapadīya* there is no clear statement that *sphoṭa* is a meaning-bearing unit of language.[30]

In the *Bhāṣyaṭīkā* Bhartṛhari says that there are different views on the problem. The one he seems to prefer is that *sphoṭa* is the permanent essence ("etac cārthasvarūpaṃ sphoṭo' yam eva śabdātmā nityaḥ").[31] And Kaiyaṭa says in the *Pradīpa* that this definition has been established by Bhartṛhari in the *Vākyapadīya.*

Patañjali says that *śabda* is of two kinds, the eternal one (*nitya*) and the transitory one (*kārya*). Bhartṛhari's commentary gives the following clarification. The eternal one could be understood as either the universal or the *sphoṭa* and the transitory one as either the particular or the sound (*dhvani*).[32] It is clear that Bhartṛhari does identify *śabda* with *sphoṭa,* the meaning-bearing unit. Kaiyaṭa is only following him.

Bhartṛhari distinguishes *prākṛtadhvani* and *vaikṛtadhvani* in his *Ṭīkā* thus: "Among the sounds which manifest the eternal word, some are primary and some secondary. That sound which is produced by the contacts of the vocal organs and that which is produced by such a sound, these two are primary. Through these two, distinction in vowels can be perceived. That sound which comes from another sound is called secondary, because no distinction is perceived through it."[33]

2. Meaning of the Term *Nitya*

While explaining the term *siddha* as *nitya*, Patañjali discusses its implications. Here Bhartṛhari explains two kinds of *nityatva* (eternality); *kūṭastha nityatā*, absolute eternality, and *pravāhanityatā* or continuity, which is free from three kinds of *anityatā*: *saṃsargānityatā* (disappearance due to contact, as in the case of the color of a crystal in the presence of a colored flower); *vipariṇāmānityatā* (disappearance through transformation, as in the case of the color of a fruit changing when it becomes ripe); and *vastuvināśānityatā* (disappearance due to destruction'[34]

3. Instruments of Knowledge (*Pramāṇa*)

Bhartṛhari accepts perception (*pratyakṣa*), inference (*anumāna*), and scriptures (*āgama*) as means of valid cognition. Perception is liable to be erroneous, and sometimes inference may be superior to perception.[35] Thus the perception of a circle of fire (*alātacakra*) is erroneous. *Āgama* or *śabda*, which consists of *śruti* and *smṛti*, is a strong instrument of knowledge and is stronger than inference.

Scriptures form the basis for *dharma*. *Dharma* is the course of knowledge (*jñāna*). All the scriptures have their source in the three Vedas (*trayī*). Grammar is a *smṛti* revealed by sages who possess superhuman powers of vision.

4. Contextual Meaning and Etymological Meaning

The meaning of a word depends on the words with which it is collocated syntactically by association or contrast. In the phrase "Rāma and Lakṣmaṇa," "Rāma" means the son of Daśaratha; in "Rāma and Keśava" "Rāma" means Balarāma; and in "Rāma and Arjuna" Rāma means Paraśurāma (Arjuna means Kārttavīryārjuna).

The derivation of a word also has to be made to suit the context. "Vāsudeva" in the sense of "the son of Vāsudeva" has to be derived according to the rule applicable to the *kṣatriyas*. If it is in the sense of "God," the term "Vāsudeva" has to be derived as "vasanty asmin devāḥ." (It is in this sense that the word is used in the *sūtra* "Vāsudevārjunābhyām vun.")

5. Language and the External World

Grammar is not directly concerned with the nature of the external world. For grammar meaning is what the words present. Just as the existence of words like "heaven" (*svarga*), *apūrva*, and "god" (*devatā*) leads to the inference about the existence of things meant by them, the existence of words can also be inferred on the basis of the object available.

6

DURVINĪTA OR AVINĪTA

This writer has been identified as a seventh-century king of the western Gangetic area. He was traditionally held to be a patron of Bhāravi, author of the *Kirātārjunīya*, and of Dāmodara, ancestor of Daṇḍin. The title of his lost work on grammar is *Śabdāvatāra*.

7

DHARMAPĀLA

Dharmapāla (530–561, or 625?), the Yogācāra teacher, is held to have composed a *vṛtti* on the *Prakīrṇa* (third) book of Bhartṛhari's *Trikāṇḍī*, according to the Chinese tradition and I-tsing. The title of this commentary is given as *Prakīrṇavṛtti* by Durveka Miśra in his *Dharmottarapradīpa*.

8

HARI VṚṢABHA OR VṚṢABHADEVA

Ashok Aklujkar

An author whom scholars date about A.D. 650, the son of Devayaśas and a protégé of King Viṣṇugupta, this author provides the first extant commentary on the *Vākyapadīya* or *Trikāṇḍī* composed by someone other than Bhartṛhari. The title of the work is *Vākyapadīyapaddhati*.

9

MAṆḌANA MIŚRA

For historical details on this author, see *Advaita Vedānta up to Śaṃkara and His Pupils*, volume III of this encyclopedia, pp. 346-347. Originally a Pūrvamīmāṃsaka, he is said to have been converted to Advaita, and is in any case the author of an Advaita work, the *Brahmasiddhi*, as well as of several Bhāṭṭa Mīmāṃsā works. The *Sphoṭasiddhi* is, as far as we know, his only work written from the Grammarian standpoint.

Although Bhartṛhari provided the basic insights into the *sphoṭa* theory, it remained for Maṇḍana Miśra to systematize Bhartṛhari's thinking for purposes of philosophic debate. This goal was brilliantly accomplished by Maṇḍana in his *Sphoṭasiddhi*. The main opponents of Bhartṛhari's *sphoṭa* theory were the Mīmāṃsakas. Kumārila Bhaṭṭa, in his *Ślokavārttika*, skillfully argues against Bhartṛhari's ideas. Maṇḍana had this full debate before him as he wrote the *Sphoṭasiddhi*; his method is to summarize Kumārila's position and to attack effectively from the strong base of his logical reordering of Bhartṛhari's position. A good example of this method is found in *kārikās* 2–15, where he debates the question of how language conveys meaning. Maṇḍana paraphrases the main arguments of Kumārila with supporting quotations from the *Ślokavārttika* and then rephrases Bhartṛhari's position in the form of a counterargument.[1]

Maṇḍana made an important contribution in first stating that the *sphoṭa* is an empirical entity that can be directly perceived by the sense organs. This claim at once raised the *sphoṭa* from being merely a theoretical postulate (as stated by Kumārila) to the status of a verifiable fact; though what exactly the contents of the final cognition are, if not phonemes themselves, still remains vague, because Maṇḍana merely says that ultimately the cognitions of phonemes are sublated by that of the word. Maṇḍana's insistence that every letter sound or phoneme can manifest the whole of the *sphoṭa*, his graphic description of the process of perceiving the *sphoṭa*, and his polemical sharpness made him the greatest supporter of Bhartṛhari's *sphoṭa* theory.

Maṇḍana also clarifies some aspects that were not very clear in Bhartṛhari's treatment and had tended to veil the theory in some sort of mysticism. Maṇḍana made it crystal clear that the *sphoṭa* is not any entity over and above the word and sentence, but is the word and sentence themselves, which gave the *sphoṭa* a much-needed earthly character.

Sphoṭasiddhi

G. B. Palsule, Harold G. Coward,
and Karl H. Potter

References labelled *ET* are to the edition and translation by K. A. Subramania Iyer (Poona: Deccan College, 1966). References are by *kārikās*.

3 (*ET* 2–7). What is this "word" (whose doctrine is being defended here)? It is the linguistic element (*śabda*). What is meant by "linguistic element"? Not the phonemes. Rather, a linguistic element is that which is the occasion for the arising of awareness of a thing (*arthāvasāyapraś-vanimitta*).

Objection: If that were so, smoke, which is the occasion for the arising of the awareness of fire, would be a linguistic element. Furthermore, an item of speech would not be a linguistic element before understanding of its meaning arises, and would be one after that—so that "cow," for example, would be both a linguistic element and not a linguistic element. The definition offered above is not right. The correct definition is rather that a linguistic element is anything that can be heard. It is the phonemes that satisfy this definition, and this fact accords with common usage, which also finds the phonemes to be linguistic elements.

Answer: Our definition fits what the author of the *Mahābhāṣya* has said. In an experience involving the utterance of, say, "cow" many items figure, such as universal, substance, quality, phoneme, *sphoṭa*. Among them, asks the author of the *Mahābhāṣya*, which is the linguistic element? Just so one might ask, which one among those in the hall is Devadatta? Now if one should answer the latter question by saying "(Devadatta is) the one wearing earrings," we will not understand him to be speaking of someone outside the hall, nor will we require that Devadatta has to wear earrings all the time to continue to be Devadatta. Likewise, when we say that a linguistic element is the occasion for the arising of awareness of a thing, the context assures that we are speaking of heard sounds (and not of something like smoke), and furthermore, a linguistic element continues to be one even during those times in which it is not occasioning the arising of awareness. Occasioning of the arising of awareness is an accidental indicator (*upalakṣaṇa*), and it is language qua meaningful expressions that is indicated as the subject matter of Grammar at the beginning of the *Mahābhāṣya.*

Merely being audible cannot be the correct definition of a linguistic element, for all sorts of things are audible, including universals—like existence, soundness, linguistic-elementness, phonemeness, all of which reside in sounds and are grasped by the auditory organ.

Objection: We mean that a linguistic element is *only* graspable by audition (universals are graspable by other means).

Answer: No, for phonemes (which are according to you the linguistic elements) can also be grasped by the internal organ.

Objection: We do not admit the existence of universals such as existence or phonemeness.

Answer: Then you should not admit any universals, because the basis for cognizing these two is as good as for any others. The only reason for postulating universals is our experience of kinds. We cognize cowness upon seeing Bāhuleya, having seen Śābaleya previously, and with no other information; likewise having heard *ka, ca, ta, pa* we cognize phonemeness.

4 (*ET*9–13). *Objection*: The phonemes are the occasions for understanding designation; when grouped they are called words.

Answer: No, a phoneme cannot singly produce an awareness. Furthermore, because phonemes occur one after another, they cannot coexist and so cannot collectively occasion cognition, and when uttered by different speakers or in different order they do not occasion understanding of a meaning.

Objection: Even so, the phonemes should be viewed as occasioning awareness of objects when in certain kinds of conditions—such as having an appropriate sequence—even though they are not causative by themselves, just as the seed is taken to be the cause of the sprout when accompanied by soil, moisture, and so on, even though by itself in the granary it does not produce a sprout.

Answer: But because each phoneme disappears immediately after it arises, at a certain moment the only thing present to occasion awareness is a single phoneme.

5 (*ET*13–15). *Mīmāṃsaka*: Ritual actions—sacrifices and the like—do not occur simultaneously, and yet they produce their result together. Likewise repetition of the Vedas, or for that matter the various subordinate acts in the activity of moving, have a collective result provided they are performed in the appropriate order and by the same agent, and so on. It is the same with the phonemes producing awareness.

Answer: The cases are not alike. In the case of the sacrifices the actions produce *apūrvas* that last and eventually produce the final result; no result is produced from an act in isolation. As for the repetition of Vedic passages, the result—learning the passages by heart—is actually produced through the dispositional tendencies left by each repetition aided by those produced by previous recitations. As for the case of movement through space, the intermediary is the reaching of a point of space; this reaching becomes the cause of reaching the next point, and so on. But no such intermediary operates for the phonemes.

6 (*ET*16–17). *Mīmāṃsaka*: Yes. In the case of the *varṇas*, the earlier ones leave latent dispositions, which then cooperate in producing the result once the last one has been uttered.

Answer: No. A latent disposition produces the awareness of the thing that occasioned it, and not anything else. Therefore it is still unexplained how a phoneme can occasion awareness of an object.

7 (*ET*17–20). *Objection*: Because the result does not come from the phonemes individually and they cannot coexist, some other cause for occasioning awareness must be supposed. It cannot be *sphoṭa*, for that would involve unnecessary complexity of supposition. After all, everyone admits latent dispositions to be present, so it is simpler to postulate the ability of the latent dispositions to produce awareness of objects other than the objects that caused them.

Answer: That would be to ascribe to a power—latent disposition—another power, or disposition, namely, expressive power, which would lead to infinite regress. Anyway, if the latent dispositions are cognized in a different order they too do not occasion awareness, so they cannot be the cause of the awareness in any case.

8 (*ET*20–24). *Objector*: Our view is that, though the latent dispositions do not directly produce understanding of the meaning, because they continue and thus all come to exist simultaneously they then produce a single awareness in which all the phonemes figure. So the *sphoṭa* doctrine is unnecessary.

Objection to the objector: But the simultaneity is then a matter of memory, not of perception.

Objector: Fine. Construe the single awareness either as a memory pure and simple, or as a complex involving both perception and memory.

Objection to the objector: Things perceived in a sequence cannot be remembered all at the same time.

Objector: Surely they can. Everyone recognizes, for example, that having perceived twenty things one remembers that there were twenty.

Maṇḍana's answer: The later phonemes reveal all the previous ones simultaneously, and the previous awarenesses of previous *varṇas*, having ceased, do not affect this revelation.

Objection: The simultaneity is of the awareness, not of the things cognized in it. The phonemes are sequential, but they are cognized in a single memory.

Answer: No, for the phonemes qua phonemes have no sequence, being eternal and all-pervasive. When we remember the entire word, we do not remember a sequence of phonemes. And furthermore, if the objector's position were correct we should understand the meaning of the word from the phonemes perceived in any order as long as they now figured in the final cognition produced by them all together. But we do not. Therefore we should conclude that it is something else (the *sphoṭa*) that is responsible for production of understanding of the meaning.

9 (*ET*25–29). It is generally said that we understand the meaning from the linguistic elements (expressing that meaning) (*śabdādarthaṃ pratipadyāmahe*). Here the linguistic elements in question cannot be the phonemes (as *per* above). They cannot be the universals of those linguistic elements (*śabdajāti*), either, for linguistic elements *qua* universals cannot signify a collection (*samudaya*). Thus, for example, the words "cow" and "horse," both being words, should indicate the same thing if all that counted were their wordness. A linguistic element indicates either the universal (for example, "cow" signifies cowness) or the individuals in which the universal inheres (the cows), but not a collection of individuals.

Objection: An utterance such as "the mango trees are a forest" (*sahakārāḥ vanam*) shows that the expression "mango tree," which signifies a universal, also expresses a collection (the forest).

Answer: Not really. Otherwise the expression for "mango trees" (*sahakārāḥ*) would not be in the plural. Here the apposition proceeds through ignoring the distinction between the collection and the things that belong to it. This kind of apposition is not pertinent in the present case—the word "cow" (*gauḥ*) is not plural and not a collective compound of *varṇas*. So, the popular saying (that we understand the meaning from the linguistic elements) is inexplicable without postulating a linguistic essence (*śabdātmā*, that is *sphoṭa*).

Objection: So let it be inexplicable ! Popular sayings are sometimes intelligible, sometimes not. One cannot draw any conclusion from inability to construe one.

Answer: But we understand the popular saying in question, so we must assume that it has an intelligible meaning. And in any case there is proof for a linguistic essence, because people do make this (popular) statement without doubting it or debating it.

10 (*ET*29–33). *Objection*: Then let the earlier view, according to which the last phoneme accompanied by the latent dispositions laid down by the previous phonemes expresses the meaning, stand, but let us understand by "latent disposition" something that operates analogo-

usly to the *apūrva* that explains how ritual acts can have results much later than their occurrence. The phonemes must have been produced in a certain order and by the same person. This view does not violate the (*Mīmāṃsā*) view about the eternality of the relation between word and meaning, nor does it imply that the previous phonemes are meaningless, for they assist the final phoneme in producing understanding. As such latent dispositions must in any case be admitted, the postulation of *sphoṭa* in addition is unnecessary and cumbrous.

Answer: The believer in the phonemes as expressing meaning has to postulate something unseen (*adṛṣṭa*), namely *apūrva*, while we, the believers in *sphoṭa* as expressing meaning, need only presume that kind of latent disposition (namely, *vāsanā*) which is evidently the cause of memories.

11 (*ET*33). Indeed, the believer in phonemes as expressing meaning has to postulate much more on the basis of scripture—the restriction of the results of a linguistic (or ritual) act to the same agent, the proper sequence, and the like—none of which we are required to postulate.

12 (*ET*35–36). The phonemes could only produce an additional result (in other words, express a meaning) if they were peculiarly suited to do so by their own nature or if they did so through association with others. They are not suited to do so by their own nature (because by themselves they do not produce understanding of word meaning). And because they are not simultaneous they cannot produce meaningfulness in association.

13 (*ET*37). Even the final phoneme is in itself without meaning.

Objection: Does this objection not equally apply to *sphoṭa*?

Answer: No, for we shall show that (the *sphoṭa*) is cognizable by sensory awareness.

Question: Why all this effort to produce inferential reasoning to support it?

Answer: To convince someone who, perversely, does not trust even perception.

15 (*ET*39–40). Is identity of the speaker of the phonemes constituting a meaningful expression a constituent (*aṅga*) of understanding or not? Because we sometimes understand meaning when we do not know (or wrongly assume) whether one or more speakers has spoken (for example, in a crowd) it cannot be a causal constituent, but at best an indicator (*jñāpaka*).

17 (*ET*41–42). Therefore, as singleness of speaker is not a causal condition, and as the latent dispositions produced by the phonemes are the same whether one or more speakers produced them, and yet we do not generally understand sounds randomly collected as significant of meaning, something else must be the cause of significance.

Objection: How does the postulation of *sphoṭa* help avoid the difficulty?

Answer: Because when there is more than one speaker the *sphoṭa* is not perceived.

18 (*ET*43–45). Our view is as follows. In the case of every significant utterance an effort, depending on specific desires of the utterer and perceptible in his mental activity, produces a distinction in the sound uttered. Each sound produced with such an effort (but not sounds not so produced) reveals the entire *sphoṭa*. The earlier sounds figuring in the utterance of a word, when heard by a hearer without any particular dispositions already conditioning his understanding, sows the seed of the cognition of the meaning by producing a vague conception of the *sphoṭa*, which lays down a disposition capable of helping produce a later clear understanding of the meaning. When the final sound involved in the word is heard, the clear understanding of the *sphoṭa* ensues, caused by the dispositions left by the vague cognitions seeded by the previous sounds.

19 (*ET*46–50). *Objection*: This theory, as much as that of the believer in phonemes as expressing meaning, has to maintain that one kind of thing, a phoneme, when heard produces something entirely different, a cognition of word meaning, *qua sphoṭa*. But if one kind of thing can produce awareness of something else entirely, then any awareness might have anything whatever as its content. If latent dispositions are adduced to connect the hearing of the *varṇas* with the resultant understanding of meaning, then the theory attributes to the dispositions an ability they do not have, namely, to produce cognition of something other than what produced them. The theory is that hearing the phonemes, through the latent dispositions produced, produces an erroneous awareness of those phonemes appearing as a significant word. But an erroneous awareness must have a cause—and the theory does not explain what that cause could be. The cause cannot be the phonemes or the latent dispositions, for they serve to produce *correct* apprehension (of the word itself). The theory also assumes that hearing the phonemes under appropriate circumstances will always and necessarily produce cognition of meaning, the erroneous awareness in question. But other errors are not so necessitated—for example, if one mistakenly cognizes a rope, one need not cognize it as a snake; one might see it as a stream, or something else. In any case, to call this awareness erroneous is to imply there is a later sublation—and there is not.

Answer: We do find that a thing when first cognized vaguely sometimes appears different from what it really is. It would be wrong to suppose that, for example, the vague perception of a rope cognized as a snake is not produced by the rope. Now contact of the senses with one thing cannot cause cognition of something else. So it must be the progressively clearer latent dispositions, which arise as our perceptions become clearer, that eventually are responsible for the clear awareness that, for example, it is a rope. Otherwise we would have had to have a clear cognition at the first glance.

Objection: Surely it is because we got closer and inspected the rope more carefully?

Answer: No, for it also arises for one who stays where he is and attends more carefully. And even those whose sense organs are quite normal sometimes misperceive at the outset and later get it right in this way. So the initial erroneous awareness is not due to a defect in the organs.

Objection: What happens is that first the bare essence (*svarūpamātra*) is perceived but is interpreted through its similarity as remembered from previous experiences.

Answer: One could say the same thing about the linguistic case as well—the bare essence of the *sphoṭa* is first perceived but interpreted as constituted of phonemes and so on because of previous experience.

20 (*ET*51-52). In any case it is the sounds, which resemble one another, that are the cause of the erroneous awareness, as well as what causes eventual clarification. But because sounds are produced by different intentions, efforts, articulations, which nevertheless resemble one another, one naturally mistakes one thing (the *sphoṭa*) for something else (the phoneme), as well as eventually getting it right on further consideration.

21 (*ET*53-56). The misinterpretation of *sphoṭa* as phoneme is inevitable, as it always occurs through the same procedure. It is analogous to the case of cognition of a new (large) number—the cognition of the previous (nonexistent) numbers is the cause of its cognition in a fixed series leading to it. Here cognition of (nonexistent) phonemes is the cause of cognition of word meaning. Likewise, when a word is taught by one person to another there is inevitable misinterpretation of the word as phonemes, for there is no other way of teaching it. It has been said that the great sages, who did not learn language from others, apprehended the word essence without misconception and taught it directly as *mantras*; the rest of us, by learning the text of the Vedas and Vedāṅgas as we were incapable of receiving the *mantras*, at least understand the means of arriving at correct understanding.

22 (*ET*57-59). It has been remarked that to call something an erroneous awareness is to imply that there is a later sublation, which there is not in the case of the awareness of phonemes. But indeed there is a later sublation, that sublation being the clear realization of the *śphoṭa*.

Objection: There is no incompatibility between a word's being a single *sphoṭa* and its being composed of phonemes, for indeed we see that the idea of the word is cognized as mixed up with that of the phonemes. So the later realization is not a sublation of the earlier cognition.

Answer: Of course it is. Just as the face comes eventually to be known as single, though initially confusedly thought to be in the mirror, so the *sphoṭa* is eventually known as single, though initially confusedly thought to be subject to distinctions of the phonemes.

23 (*ET*59-61). Only the sense organs are capable of apprehending an object more or less clearly or confusedly. The other instruments of knowledge either apprehend the object or not at all. Now the *sphoṭa* is cognized through perception. We know that it is perceptually cognized because the clear cognition of the *sphoṭa*, which is different from that of the phonemes, must have some supporting object (*ālambana*).

24 (*ET*61-64). *Objection*: There is such a clear cognition, but it does not have a different supporting object from the phonemes; they alone are the supporting object. In the final cognition they are cognized collectively, while in the preceding erroneous awarenesses they are cognized distributively.

Answer: Even though a cognition concerns one thing it does not follow that it may not have something else as its supporting object. For example, the awareness of a universal property, though it is mixed up with the form of the individual, still has the universal, not the individual, as its supporting object; likewise, the idea of a picture, despite its connection with the colors of its parts, is about the picture, not the parts.

25 (*ET*65). *Objection*: The unity of the phonemes is caused by their being cognized in a single mental act or by their serving collectively a single purpose.

Answer: Then there is no unity anywhere, for the same account can be invoked to question any case of supposed unity.

26 (*ET*66-67). Unless the nature of a word is known, its meaning cannot be understood; if that in turn depends on its cognition (as the previous objection would imply), there will be mutual dependence.

27 (*ET*68-77). That which appears to be different even though the phonemes are the same, and that which appears to be one even though the phonemes are different, is the word; it is that which is perceived (the *sphoṭa*).

Objection (Kumārila, *Sphoṭa* section, verse 131): "Phonemes and sounds do not manifest the *sphoṭa* in words or sentences because they are revealers, like lamplight."

Answer: Depending on precisely how this argument is interpreted, it either proves what is already established (because words and sentences are *sphoṭa* according to the believer in *sphoṭa*) or it commits fallacies of unknown qualificandness in its *pakṣa* and unestablished locus (*āśrayāsiddha*) in its *hetu*, as well as suffering from other faults.

Kumārila (*Sphoṭa* section, verse 133): "Phonemes and sounds do not manifest the *sphoṭa* of words or sentences, because they are manifesters (directly), like the light of a lamp." Or (according to a different reading), "Phonemes and sounds belonging to words or sentences do not manifest *sphoṭa,* because they are manifesters, like the light of a lamp."

Answer: According to the second reading, the argument commits the fault of proving what is already accepted, for words and sentences are themselves *sphoṭas*. The first formulation involves the fallacy of unestablished locus, for the auditory sense and the internal organ manifest *sphoṭas* but do not manifest meanings directly.

Kumārila (*Sphoṭa* section, verse 134): "Phonemes and sounds do not manifest the *sphoṭa* of words or sentences, because they exist, like the jar, and so on."

Answer: This *hetu* is inconclusive (*anaikāntika*), for it has been shown that *sphoṭas* are directly perceptible by the auditory sense. Further, a word that consists of just one phoneme is admitted by even the Mīmāṃsakas to be manifested by the sound that it consists of, so the thesis contradicts their own tenet.

Kumārila (*Sphoṭa* section, verse 135): "The *sphoṭa* is not expressive of meaning, because it is other than the phoneme, like a jar, and so on."

Answer: Because the Mīmāṃsaka does not accept *sphoṭa,* his reason is unestablished (*svato'siddha*). (Other reasons are also given.)

Kumārila (*Sphoṭa* section, verse 136): "Whoever denies that phonemes are expressive of meaning denies what is perceived, just as one who denies that 'moon' denotes the thing having the hare on it."

Answer: What is perceived is that *words* are expressive of meaning, not the correct analysis of words.

Kumārila (*Sphoṭa* section, verses 137-138): "Awareness of objects arises from phonemes, because it arises immediately following awareness of them, just as awareness of fire arises from awareness of smoke."

Answer: The Mīmāṃsaka admits that the awareness of the word arises from the phonemes before the comprehension of meaning, so he cannot appeal to this argument.

(*ET*77–83). *Buddhist objection*: There is no sentence apart from the phonemes, for no such thing is perceived.

Counterobjection: We can infer some such different thing, because understanding requires a cause.

Buddhist: Just the phonemes are the cause.

Counterobjector: The same meaning does not arise from hearing *jarā* as from hearing *rāja,* so the meaning cannot come just from the phonemes.

Buddhist: It has to be shown that the phonemes (in the two words) are not different.

Counterobjector: That is shown through recognition.

Buddhist: Recognition may be in error. Anyway, all objects are momentary and so different from one another.

Counterobjector: Because we know that the sentences (one with *jarā* in it, the other with *rāja* in it) are different we know that they mean different things.

Buddhist: It is wrong to attribute the difference to an imporceptible difference (among sentences) when there is a perceptible difference among the phonemes. Furthermore, the notion of a single sentence is problematic: does it have parts or not? If it has parts, are those parts meaningful or not? If meaningless, how can they constitute a sentence? If meaningful, do they have parts? If so, they are sentences, and the argument repeats indefinitely. If a sentence has no parts, it would be impossible to explain why one does not grasp the meaning of a sentence until its utterance is completed. (Other arguments are offered as well.)

28 (*ET*84–85). *Answer*: Just because phonemes figure in awareness of meaning, it does not follow that nothing else does.

29 (*ET*85). The believer in *sphoṭa* holds that neither the sentence nor the word has parts. And we have already explained how grasping the meaning of a word or sentence is a gradual process.

30 (*ET*86). Even if phonemes are different each time they are produced, it is by virtue of their generic features, not of their newborn individuality, that they figure in the expression of meaning.

31 (*ET*87). What is "sequence" (*krama*, that is, the gradual understanding of the meaning)? Not merely the causal relation between the experiences of sounds or phonemes, for then understanding should arise even when the speakers of the sounds are known to be different.

32 (*ET*88–89). Indeed, the causal relation between the experiences of sounds cannot be what is called sequence; only when that causal relation is itself *known* can it produce understanding.

33 (*ET*89). A word is a unit. Analogously, scholars admit that an action, like raising a hand, is a unit manifested by different moments of activity.

34 (*ET*90–91). That the *sphoṭa* is eternal follows from its unity.

35 (*ET*91–92). *Objection*: Because awareness of a word depends on something else (namely, the phonemes) it is a mere construction (*kalpanā*).

Answer: Awareness of a universal property depends on awareness of the individual instances of it.

36–37 (*ET*92–93). Thus *sphoṭa* is established.

10

HELĀRĀJA

This important commentator on Bhartṛhari tells us that he is the son of Bhūtirāja and a descendant of a minister named Lakṣaṇa, or King Muktāpīḍa of Kashmir. Abhinavagupta, who flourished in 1014, appears to have studied with Bhūtirāja as well as with a son of Bhūtirāja whom Abhinavagupta calls "Indurāja." It is clear that Abhinavagupta is referring to Helārāja in some passages, as he is credited with having written a grammatical work called *Prakīrṇakavivaraṇa*, which may have been a commentary on Helārāja's *Prakīrṇakaprakāśa*—at least the title strongly suggests Abhinavagupta's awareness of Helārāja's work.[1] Thus we may place Helārāja's date about A.D. 980.

Regarding his commentary on Bhartṛhari's *Trikāṇḍī*, it seems clear that such a work was written covering the entire three chapters. There is some doubt about which portions of the work are available to us now. The commentary on book 3 is available in print.[2] Aklujkar argues that its proper title is *Prakīrṇakaprakāśa*, and that Helārāja's commentary on book 1 was called *Śabdaprabhā*, while that on book 2 was *Vākyakāṇḍaṭīkā* or *Vākyapradīpa*.[3] Aklujkar further argues that the *Ṭīkā* on book 2, which is available in print and credited to Puṇyarāja, is in fact Helārāja's work instead.[4]

Helārāja tells us that he wrote at least three other works, none of which is now available. One was an explanation of Kātyāyana's *vārttikas* on Pāṇini, titled *Vārttikonmeṣa*. Another work, called *Kriyāviveka*, is intended to establish that action (*kriyā*) is the main idea expressed by a sentence. A third, named *Advayasiddhi*, seems to have been a work on *śabdādvaita* or linguistic monism; Helārāja remarks that in it he "has shown that the ultimate manifests itself as the experiencer and the experienced and that all that is experienced rests in consciousness."[5]

Commentary on Bhartṛhari's *Trikāṇḍī*

Survey of Philosophical Topics

1. On Universal Property

In the case of words abstracted from sentences Bhartṛhari tries to reconcile the universalist view of Vājapyāyana and the substantialist view of Vyāḍi. The meaning of a word is permanent, whether a universal or a substance. All words—nouns, verbs, prefixes, and postpositions—can be reduced to the category of universals. Every word primarily refers to the universal of its form—the word universal—which is then identified with the meaning universal through superimposition. According to Pāṇini both the universal and the particular are primarily signified by words; and both are understood simultaneously, because they are so intrinsically interconnected that one cannot exist without the other. According to those who consider the primary meaning as the universal, its connection with action may be direct or indirect. In the sentence "one should not kill a Brāhmaṇa" the whole class is meant, but in "fetch a Brāhmaṇa" only the individual is meant.

Although Vaiśeṣikas do not accept a universal within a universal, the Grammarians accept a hierarchy of universals, like classes and subclasses: for example, the animal universal entails the universals of cowness and horseness.

All nominal stems signify Being, which is eternal. Just as treeness is contained in the *śiṃśapā-ness*, Being is found in everything. It is the all-comprehending universal. The status of the phenomenal universal depending on convention (*saṃketa*) is not affected by the great universal, *mahāsāmānya*. Being itself becomes action when viewed as having a sequence of time.

Helārāja favored the metaphorical model of language rather than the crystal model. According to his model an object in the external world is given a name when the universal located in the name is superimposed upon a universal belonging to a particular bearer in the external world. The thing universals have an ontological separate existence. But language is independent of the world.

2. On Substance

Another view is that all words denote substance (*dravya*), the individual, the concrete, the particular. Substance is of two kinds, the real (*pāramārthika*) and the expressional (*saṃvyavahārika*). It is the second kind of substance that is dealt with in the supplementary section and is declared to be the meaning of all words by Vyāḍi. Through all these things with different forms, it is the same Ultimate Reality Brahman that is cognized. Words express these forms directly, and through them the Ultimate Reality also. The many forms that we cognize as the meanings of words are unreal, but the real runs through them all. Although there are different gold ornaments, actually everything is gold. Looking at a Jandscape through a tube, we are able to perceive only a limited portion; similarly, every word expresses an aspect of Reality.

3. On Relations

A word expresses the speaker's idea, the external object and the word form. The word form is understood by all even without understanding the conventional meaning. The relation between a linguistic form and its meaning is neither conjunction (*saṃyoga*) nor inherence (*samavāya*). The meaning relation is the beginningless fitness (*yogyatā*), like the fitness of sense organs for their contents. A word expresses only its correct meaning; incorrect words convey meaning only by inference the correct form.

What words convey can be called existence of a secondary nature (*upacārasattā*). External objects are conveyed only in parts by words.

4. On Quality

A substance requires qualities for being expressed. Qualities help to specify a substance in a finer way.

5. On Direction

Direction (*dik*) is a power of Brahman, inferred from its effects. Those who believe that the whole manifestation of the external world exists within the Supreme Consciousness hold that the manifestation is not external, though it seems to be so. Everything is an inner manifestation of Brahman. Strictly there is no distinction between inner and outer; there is only one Reality.

6. On the Means to Action (*Sādhana*)

The powers to produce various kinds of effects constitute the essential nature of the objects in the world. A normal sentence expresses a complex meaning of which the central meaning is some action, to which the other elements contribute. The verb expresses the central element and the nouns express the other elements. *Sādhana*, means to action, is the name given to the concrete objects that help to accomplish the action.

In the use of words the power of a thing is more important than the thing itself, and the speaker's intention plays an important role in deciding what type of *kāraka* is to be taken. "He cooks in the pot," "he cooks with the pot," and "the pot cooks" are all correct. The *sādhana* can be purely mental, as when a storyteller narrates the story of Kṛṣṇa killing Kaṃsa. The means depends on the intention. In "he sees a pot" it is the dimension of the pot that is seen, but in "he sees the form," it is the color. The Grammarian is interested in what the expression says.

7. On Action

The root is defined as something that expresses action (*kriyā*)—a particular behavior on the part of the accessories. *Kriyā* is different from the accessories that play a part, direct or indirect, in its accomplishment. It is not *pratyakṣa* (perceptible) but has to be inferred, and even in the case of "to exit" it is an action, the continued existence of *sattā* in time. Helārāja makes it clear that what is being discussed in grammar is not what action really is, but what action as presented by words is. There were conflicting views among early writers—whether it is a definite of action or the nature of the meaning conveyed by the verbal roots, and so on. The idea that action is a process is found in Yāska. Helārāja says that a process is something that has parts arranged in a temporal sequence. How can the idea of a single action be conveyed, if the series of actions constituting it be not simultaneous? Unity is ascribed to the series of actions on the basis of the ultimate result. The unity is mental.

8. On Gender

The grammatical gender does not always correspond to the sex. Several attempts have been made to explain this inconsistency. Does gender depend on the form of words or on the meaning? Helārāja merely elucidates the views of Bhatṛhari and tries to correlate them with the views found in the *Mahābhāṣya.*

9. On Time

Helārāja summarizes Bhartṛhari's view of time as follows. Time is an independent power of Brahman. On the basis of this power, differentiation as the six transformations (birth and so on elaborated by Vārṣyāyaṇi) take place. The apparent sequence in the appearances of being is based on this time factor. Time is a creative power, not an eternal substance as the Vaiśeṣikas hold. It is the *svātantryaśakti* (power of complete freedom) of Brahman. As the creative power time is responsible for the birth, continuity, and destruction of everything. The other special causes, such as the material cause, depend on time, which is the auxiliary cause. Time is compared to the stage manager (*sūtradhāra*) of a puppet show, who pulls the strings and makes the puppets move according to his wish. The appearance and the disappearance of things are based on the permissive power and the preventive power of time, respectively; the continuity of things is also based on the permissive power of time.

Time is measured by action, and action is determined or measured by time. Statements about an action being "slow" or "quick" are based on time. Although time is really one, it appears to be differentiated and in sequence. It is because of actions that distinctions such as past, present, and future are attributed to time. Action that is complete is given the name of past. The fact that things are remembered is a proof of the existence of time. All divisions of time into parts are artificial and based on actions that are brought about by it.

If external movements are not available for measuring time, one can use one's own breathing movement for the purpose. The yogins actually use the movement of their breath to determine time.

Helārāja says that Bhartṛhari devoted a whole section on time not to discussing its philosophical aspects, but to explaining adequately the tenses in the language.

Brahman is true knowledge without any sequence, but under the influence of time (which is a power of Brahman) it is presented in a temporal sequence. Nescience (*avidyā*) is the cause of the phenomenal world, consisting of differentiation both temporal and spatial. Of the two, temporal differentiation comes first. Consciousness in the form of *paśyantī* is without any sequence, but in association with the *prāṇa* principle, it shines as though it had sequence. When true knowledge dawns, the division of sequence also disappears. The main function of time is to present phenomena in a temporal sequence.

11

PRAMEYASAṂGRAHA

The unknown author of a lost commentary on the *Vākyapadīya* called *Prameyasaṃgraha* must have flourished about A.D. 1000.

12

PUṆYARĀJA

Two different commentaries on the *Trikāṇḍī* have been credited to this author, but in both cases the authorship has been questioned. For a long while the *ṭīkā* on Book 1, which had been published in the Benares Sanskrit Series in 1887, was credited to Puṇyarāja, though the colophon clearly mentions the author's name as Hari Vṛṣabha. The mistake was pointed out by Haraprasad Shastri and again later by C. Kunhan Raja, as well as by K.A. Subramania Iyer.[1] In addition, as mentioned previously, Ashok Aklujkar has offered reasons to doubt Puṇyarāja's authorship of the commentary on Book 2.

13

KAIYAṬA

Kaiyaṭa, author of the *Pradīpa* ("light") commentary on Patañjali's *Mahābhāṣya*, occupies a high position in the history of the Pāṇinian school of Grammar, along with Bhartṛhari and Nāgeśa Bhaṭṭa. He was the son of Jaiyaṭa Upādhyāya and pupil of Maheśvara, and probably belonged to Kashmir. He generally followed the views of Bhartṛhari, as stated in the beginning of the commentary, and was influenced by the *Kāśikā* of Vāmana and Jayāditya. He is assigned to the later half of the eleventh century.

A verse from Kaiyaṭa's work (*bhāṣyābdhiḥ kvātigambhīraḥ*) is quoted in Ruyyaka's *Alaṃkārasarvasva*, composed between 1135 and 1150; another verse is quoted by Maheśvarasūri in the commentary on the *Anekārtha-saṃgraha* of his teacher Hemacandra (1088–1172). Puruṣottamadeva refers directly to Kaiyaṭa in his *Bhāṣāvṛtti* (about 1150). Kaiyaṭa's work contains indirect references to Helārāja's commentary on the *Vākyapadīya*.[1] The generally accepted posteriority of Haradatta to Kaiyaṭa is rejected by Peri, because Haradatta is mentioned by name in Dharmakīrti's *Rūpāvakāra* (before the tenth century). There is a tradition that Kaiyaṭa was a younger brother of Mammaṭa.

The *Pradīpa* is an elaborate and complete commentary on the *Mahābhāṣya*, elucidating the meanings of words and expressions in that work and discussing the different views held by scholars in the interpretation of particular passages. There is little scope for giving his own views about problems on the philosophy of Grammar; still, the importance of the *Pradīpa* in elucidating the views of Patañjali and Bhartṛhari is considerable.

Pradīpa on Patañjali's *Mahābhāṣya*

S. R. Bannerjee and K. Kunjunni Raja

(1) *Śivasūtras*. About the arrangement of the alphabets of Sanskrit in

the *Śivasūtras*, Kaiyaṭa says that they are essential for *pratyāhāra* or selecting groups of them as used by Pāṇini, and the enunciation of the *sūtras* is not for explaining the proper pronunciation of the alphabets (*svarūpakathana*).

(2) Kaiyaṭa enunciates the principle that among the three great authorities on Sanskrit grammar—Pāṇini, Kātyāyana, and Patañjali—the later the sage, the greater the authoritativeness.[2] Elsewhere he states that the authority rests with the three sages.[3]

(3) On Patañjali's statement regarding scripture as a *prayojana* for the study of Grammar, Kaiyaṭa says that the term *prayojana* should be taken in the sense of motivating force (*pravartaka*). "A Brahman shall learn and understand the Veda with its six ancillaries without any motive of gain."[4]

14

JYEṢṬHAKALĀŚA

Another Kashmiri author of a commentary on the *Mahābhāṣya*, now lost, was Jyeṣṭhakalāśa of Kauṣika *gotra* (lineage), son of Rājakalāśa, grandson of Muktikalāśa, of the Konmukha village in Kashmir. One of his sons was Bilhaṇa, author of a *kāvya* work titled *Vikramāṅkadeva-carita*. From Bilhaṇa's date Yudhisthira Mimamsaka has calculated that Jyeṣṭhakalāśa must have lived between 1005 and 1082.

15

MAITREYA RAKṢITA

This Buddhist Grammarian in eastern India lived between 1092 and 1122, according to Yudhisthira Mimamsaka, who thinks he may have been a Bengali. In addition to works on Buddhist Grammar, including *Dhātupradīpa*, *Durghaṭavṛtti*, and a *Tantrapradīpa* on Jinendrabuddhi's *Kāśikānyāsa* (a fragmentary manuscript, which is listed as residing at the Asiatic Society Library in Calcutta), he appears to have written a *ṭīkā* on the *Mahābhāṣya*, which has been lost.

16

PURUṢOTTAMADEVA

During the later half of the twelfth century in Bengal, during the reign of Lakṣmaṇasena, a number of grammatical works were composed by this writer, who may have been a Buddhist. One of his works was a *Prāṇāpana* or *Laghuvṛtti* on the *Mahābhāṣya,* of which a fragment is available. Other works are *Bhāṣāvṛtti, Paribhāṣāvṛtti, Gaṇavṛtti, Jñāpakasamuccaya,* and a commentary on the *Uṇādisūtras,* as well as a number of lexicographical treatises.

17

DHĀNEŚVARA

Yudhisthira Mimamsaka places this writer at the beginning of the thirteenth century. In addition to a *Prakriyāratnamaṇi*, preserved in a single manuscript at Adyar, he also wrote a *Cintāmaṇi* on the *Mahābhāṣya*. He was apparently the teacher of Vopadeva, the famous Bengali Grammarian.

18

(ṚṢIPUTRA) PARAMEŚVARA II

This well-known Pūrvamīmāṃsā writer flourished about 1410. He was a member of the important Payyur family of Bhāṭṭas and composed a commentary on Maṇḍana Miśra's *Sphoṭasiddhi,* called *Gopālikā.* In K. A. Subramania Iyer's translation of *Sphoṭasiddhi* use has been made of the *Gopālikā,* and a number of readings and explanations in his footnotes are based on Parameśvara's commentary. A few of the most important are repeated in the following set of notes. References are by *kārikās.*

Sphoṭasiddhigopālikā
K. A. Subramania Iyer

2. It is the *Gopālikā* that identifies the opponents in question as Kumārila. Specifically *Ślokavārttika, sphoṭa* section 119, is cited.
7. Parameśvara says that the first sentence of Maṇḍana's answer in this section summarizes an explanation of "dispositional tendency" provided by Kumārila in the *Tantravārttika* on *Mīmāṃsāsūtra* 2.1.5., where Kumārila is specifically speaking about *apūrva.*
13. Although Maṇḍana's text, in explaining why the final *varṇa* is without meaning, confines itself to showing how the latent disposition laid down by the previous phonemes is beyond the range of perception and inference, Parameśvara goes farther and shows that it is beyond the range of comparison and presumption as well.
10. The *Gopalikā* points out that all erroneous awarenesses are caused by things that are the causes of veridical awarenesses as well.
21. Parameśvara explains that the analogy of our cognition of a new large number is here predicated on the theory about number, that it is neither a separate category nor a quality (*guṇa*), a view different from the more commonly held Vaiśeṣika view that number is a quality.

22. The *Gopālikā* points out that sublation may be by either a positive or a negative cognition. For example, when one discovers that "this is not silver," it is negative, but if the discovery is "this is shell," it is positive.
23. The sense organs referred to here include both external and internal ones.
27. Last sentence. The *Gopālikā* explains why one does not grasp the meaning of a sentence until its utterance is completed. It is because the following stages take time: (1) understanding each phoneme; (2) recognition of each one as a stem or a suffix and thus the construction of a word; (3) understanding each word's meaning; (4) satisfying the requirements of mutual expectancy, fitness, and contiguity; (5) connecting the several word meanings; (6) understanding the sentence.

19

ŚEṢA KṚṢṆA

The Śeṣa family of Banaras is celebrated, and frequent attempts have been made to reconstruct its genealogy. According to *New Catalogus Catalogorum*, volume 4, p. 365b, this author was the grandson of Śeṣa Rāmacandra and the son of Śeṣa Nṛsiṃha, who was the author of the work on *dharma* entitled *Govindārṇava*. This Kṛṣṇa was also the elder brother of Śeṣa Cintāmaṇi, author of *Rasamañjarīvyākhyā*. His sons were Śeṣa Vīreśvara, who was the guru of Jagannātha Paṇḍitarāja, a very famous figure of those days, and (Śeṣa) Nārāyaṇa (Bhaṭṭa), author of the *Sūktiratnākara* (see below, author 23). The *New Catalogus Catalogorum* places Śeṣa Kṛṣṇa in the latter half of the sixteenth century, but if the preceding set of relationships is to be worked out consistently with the secure facts that are known, it would seem this date should be pushed back a bit—we suggest 1510 as the time in which he must have flourished.

He is said to have composed a work entitled *Śabdāharaṇa* or *Śabdālaṅkāra*, which is lost. The *New Catalogus* also ascribes to him a small work on *sphoṭa* theory, entitled *Sphoṭatattvanirūpaṇa*. A work with this title is available, though manuscripts do not identify its author.

Sphoṭatattvanirūpaṇa
G. B. Palsule

This work is small, consisting of nineteen stanzas with the author's own commentary. The text has no pretensions to either original ideas or an exhaustive treatment of the topic, its aim apparently being to present the doctrine and the accompanying arguments in succinctly worded stanzas. It is worth mentioning that, though one of the late works, it is content with presenting the doctrine in its classical form and is free from such innovations as we find in the *Sphoṭacandrikā*.

Its Vedāntic bias is discernible when it speaks of the *sphoṭa* (=*śabda-brahman*) as a basis (*adhiṣṭhāna*), with the phoneme, word, and sentence as its illusory manifestation (*vivarta*), which are wrongly imposed (*adhyasta*) on it.

The work is edited by M. G. Bakre in *Vadarthasamgraha* (Bombay, 1913), vol. 1, pp. 1–15. Numbered references are to stanzas.

1. The first stanza salutes the *śabdabrahman*, the basis (*adhiṣṭhāna*) for the manifestations of phoneme, word, and sentence.

2. Previous authorities are named.

3. This stanza declares the inability of the phonemes in any way to convey meaning. *Sphoṭa* alone can do it. There are two kinds of *sphoṭa* (word and sentence). According to the view that *sphoṭa* is partless, sounds directly manifest *sphoṭa*. But if *sphoṭa* is accepted as having parts, then the sounds manifest phonemes, which in turn manifest *sphoṭa*. The author refutes the view that *sphoṭa* has parts.

4. Recognition of identity does not necessarily guarantee eternality for phonemes. Cognitions like "*g* is produced" can show the opposite.

5. Even if one accepts the eternality of phonemes, there cannot be a cognition of a simultaneous whole when they are screened by winds (that manifest them) or by sounds.

6. There cannot be any conveying of meaning by the accumulated dispositions in company with the final phoneme, because meaning-conveying is against the nature (*svabhāvasya viparyayāt*) of the dispositions. Assumption of such an *ad hoc* power involves unnecessary assumption (*gaurava*).

7. No actual sequence is possible in the case of eternal and all-pervasive phonemes. Even in the final cognition sequence is impossible, because cognition is one.

8. The phonemes in the final memory cannot retain the sequence of their cognitions because they (previous cognitions) are not a subject of the final memory.

9. A single *sphoṭa* is clearly experienced in the cognitions "this is a word," "this is a sentence," "this is a phoneme." So the *sphoṭa* is a fact of experience, it is not just a postulate, the commentary adds. The commentary also adds that because no change of meaning is there, even when the order of words in a sentence is changed, an indivisible sentence has to be accepted.

10. Neither as perishable nor as imperishable can phonemes be the parts of the sentence (=*sphoṭa*). They are only its illusory manifestations as the world of the Brahman.

11. The variety of appearance of a single *sphoṭa* is due to different sounds, like the variety of reflections of a single face in different reflections. This fact also explains the differences in meaning from utterance to utterance, the commentary adds.

12. Though different from the phonemes, the *sphoṭa* appears to be tinged by them, because of imposed identity.

13. This stanza describes the gradual perception of the *sphoṭa*, with the help of previous impressions, and provides the usual illustration of the inspection of a gem.

14. The cognition of the superimposed entity (here phonemes) is the cognition of the substratum (here *sphoṭa*) itself.

15. Erroneous cognitions can be a means of correct cognition. The usual illustration, a tree mistaken as an elephant, is offered.

16. In section 19 of Maṇḍana's text the progressive clarity must be taken as referring to the perception of *sphoṭa*, not to the understanding of meaning (from phonemes), because this feature is peculiar to knowledge by direct perception (and the understanding of meaning is not an act of direct perception, adds the commentary).

17. In spite of the sameness of phonemes the *sphoṭa* differs in cases like *nādī/dinā*. So it must be different from the phonemes.

18–19. The unity of a word cannot be explained away as a secondary one (for example, because it conveys a single meaning), because the boundaries of a word are to be first understood before any meaning can be known. Moreover, such reasoning will amount to banishing all unity (and also the diversity based on it) from the face of the Earth.

20

SATYĀNANDA OR RĀMACANDRA SARASVATĪ

Author of a *Laghuvivaraṇa* on Kaiyaṭa's *Mahābhāṣyapradipa*, this writer appears to have been the father of Īśvarānanda, who wrote a corresponding "*Bṛhad*" *Vivaraṇa* on Kaiyaṭa. As a manuscript of Īśvarānanda's work dated 1603 (=1551?) is extant, we must date his father to the first half of the sixteenth century.

21

ŚEṢA CINTĀMAṆI

A brother of Śeṣa Kṛṣṇa, so presumably contemporaneous (thus, early sixteenth century), he may have been the author of a commentary, *Prakāśa*, on Kaiyaṭa's *Mahābhāṣyapradipa*.[1]

22

ŚESA VĪREŚVARA OṘ RĀMEŚVARA

One of Śeṣa Kṛṣṇa's sons, he is mentioned in one or two grammatical works of later times and may be identical with a Vāṭeśvara also named. We know of no works authored by him. Annambhaṭṭa was a pupil of his.

23

ŚEṢA NĀRĀYAṆA BHAṬṬA

Younger brother of Śeṣa Vīreśvara, this writer must have flourished about 1540 (though Yudhisthira Mimamsaka gives a date half a century easlier). He is the author of a commentary on the *Mahābhāṣya* titled *Sūktiratnākara,* which appears to have been written at the instigation of a King Pirinda or Phirinda. A manuscript of this work exists in the India Office Library, London.

24

VIṢṆUMITRA

This writer's *Kṣīrodara* on the *Mahābhāṣya* appears to be lost. It is referred to by Śivarāmendra Sarasvatī and by Bhaṭṭoji Dīkṣita. Because the latter's date must be the late sixteenth century, Viṣṇumitra must have lived at least a few decades earlier, say about the middle of the sixteenth century at the latest.

25

ĪŚVARĀNANDA or ĪŚVARĪDATTA SARASVATĪ

The son of Satyānanda (Rāmacandra Sarasvatī, see above, author 20) and datable to about the middle of the sixteenth century on the basis of evidence in a manuscript of his work, Īśvarānanda wrote a *Bṛhat* (large) *Vivaraṇa* on Kaiyaṭa's *Mahābhāṣyapradīpa.* One manuscript list cites another work by him, *Śabdabodhataraṅgiṇī.*

26

BHARATA MIŚRA

(The date of this writer is unknown. His work presumably precedes the anonymous *Sphoṭasiddhinyāyavicāra* [next entry], which depends on it.)

SPHOṬASIDDHI

G. B. Palsule

Whereas Bharata Miśra makes a clear-cut statement (not found in Bhartṛhari or Maṇḍana) that it is the sounds (*dhvani*) and not the phonemes (*varṇa*) (though he does not say how he differentiates the two) that manifest the *sphoṭa*, his most original contributions are in reconciling the theories of *sphoṭa* as universal (*jāti*) and of *sphoṭa* as individual (*vyakti*), and of *sphoṭa* as inner mental word (*antaḥśabda*). The universal theory takes division to be real and belonging to the individuals, the individual theory regards it as superimposed, really belonging to the manifesters. According to Bharata Miśra the different views are meant for students at different levels. The whole idea seems to have been tacitly accepted by the later authors.

Maṇḍana's influence on Bharata Miśra is evident not only in the title of the work but also in many an argument. But Bharata Miśra is by no means without originality. The progress in methodology can be seen in the three clear-cut sections that offer three independent proofs in support of the *sphoṭa*. While the idea is not wholly new, Bharata Miśra seems to have been the first to have developed Vedic authority as a full-fledged argument in favor of the *sphoṭa* theory; the first section, however, carries forward Maṇḍana's concept that *sphoṭa* is auditorily perceptible.

The salutation to Bharata Miśra in the anonymous *Sphoṭasiddhinyāyavicāra* and adoption there of many of Bharata Miśra's arguments and methodological features (like the three sections) would indicate his position among the writers on *sphoṭa*.

The work is divided into three sections: perception, pp. 1–16; meaning, pp. 16–27; and Vedic authority, pp. 27–42 in the edition by K. Sambasiva Sastri (Trivandrum Sanskrit Series 89, Trivandrum, 1927). It is a prose work, but when each argument is over, it is summarized in a stanza (there are ten in all). *E* references are to Sastri's edition. The summary here is by G. B. Palsule.

Survey of Philosophical Topics

1. Perception

(*E*1–9). An expression like "cow" (*gauḥ*), when heard, is directly perceived to be a single word-entity (*padatattva*). But this cognition of unity is sought to be explained with four alternative possibilities (*anyathāsiddhi*) by the opponents so as to do away with the concept of a single word-entity. These possibilities are that the feeling of unity is due (1) to the phonemes appearing in a single cognition, (2) to their conveying a single meaning, (3) to the quickness of pronunciation, or (4) to a single power of the phonemes. They are contradicted as follows. (1) There being no sequence in a single cognition, there will be nothing to distinguish between the meanings of *pika* "a cuckoo" and *kapi* "a monkey," which contain the same phonemes but in different sequences. (2) No meaning can be conveyed before a word is first grasped, because the word is the cause and the meaning its result. (3) Even in the case of long words like *titau*, there is a single perception. (4) Apart from other objections to this suggestion, the objection contained in (1) remains, that the phonemes cannot appear in a single cognition.

(*E*9–11). Bharata Miśra confirms this unitary word-entity in the context of the sentence "gośabdād artham pratipadyāmahe" ("we understand the meaning from the word "cow"). The opponent's arguments, seeking to explain the unity of the word "cow" (*go*) on grounds other than the positing of *sphoṭa*, are refuted practically on the same lines as in Maṇḍana's *Sphoṭasiddhi*.

Bharata Miśra further points out that the statement concerned is not just figurative, nor erroneous, and that by the word *go* the final sound alone is not meant.

(*E*11–14). The perception of parts in a word is explained. According to the theory of *sphoṭa* as universal, the division into parts belongs to the individuals; according to the theory of *sphoṭa* as individual, the division into parts belongs to the manifesters (*vyañjaka*) that are superimposed on the word. The universal theory takes the division into phonemes to be real; the individual theory, by contrast, takes it to be erroneously imposed.

A parallel given for the unitariness of a word (and a sentence) despite apparent differentiation is that of the special vowel *ai*, technically called *vṛddhatālavya*, believed to be unitary by the opponent (*Mīmāṃsaka*) himself (cf. *Mīmāṃsāsūtras* 9.2.32–33). If he questions the unitariness of a word, he cannot logically hold the unitariness of this vowel.

2. Meaning

(*E*16–21). In this section, which is meant to support the proof of direct perception in favor of the *sphoṭa* by showing that otherwise the understanding of meaning cannot be accounted for (*anyathānupapatti*), Bharata Miśra makes the following points.

(1) Phonemes in no way have the meaning-conveying capacity. (The arguments are much the same as in Maṇḍana's *Sphoṭasiddhi.*)

(2) The case is similar for the dispositions. (Incidentally, Bharata Miśra defines power [*śakti*, a disposition is a power] as "extrasensory form restricted to bringing about a specific effect of an object" ["kāryaviṣayaniyatam antīndriyam rūpam"].

(3) The first phoneme is without the benefit of a preceding dispositional trace. So the progressive imparting of excellence to phoneme cognitions is impossible, and, consequently, the dispositional trace cannot have the ad hoc power of conveying meaning.

(4) There is no compelling reason to assume a trace of the type of *apūrva*.

(5) The singleness of the speaker cannot be a cause of conveying the meaning.

(6) *An important statement*: according to the Grammarians it is the sounds, and not phonemes, that manifest the *sphoṭa*. The sounds in the word *vṛṣa* are different from the first four in the word *vṛṣabha*.

(*E*22). The indistinctness (*avyaktatā*) of the *sphoṭa* is not of the nature of cognition-cum-noncognition (*upalabdhatānupalabdhatātmikā*) but of that of relative distinctness (*tāratamyena*).

(*E*23). The initial cognitions of phonemes constitute an *anyathākhyāti* of the *sphoṭa*. (Maṇḍana had used the word *viparyāsa.*) (1) The sounds bringing about the error (of part perception) are different from, but similar to, the sounds that bring about the correct cognition of the word. (Maṇḍana, *kārikā* 2, simply says that the same sounds are responsible for both of these results.)

(*E*23–24). (2) Bharata Miśra shows how the sounds cause the erroneous cognition of parts in a sentence.

(*E*24–25). (3) The threefold uniformity of error is justified. (These three kinds of *niyatatā* are already in Maṇḍana.)

(*E*25). (4) The *ṛṣis* perceive the partless *sphoṭa* directly (cf. Maṇḍana,

p. 33). Only direct perception is capable of progressive clarity (see Maṇḍana, section 23).

(*E*25–26). This section states an important point. There is no conflict in the three theories about the *sphoṭa*, as universal (*jāti*), as an individual (*vyakti*), and as inner mental word (*śabdatattva*). They are meant for different levels of students.

3. Vedic Authority

(*E*27–36). This section purports to establish the *sphoṭa* (actually the words used are *varṇātiriktaṃ vāktattvam*, "superphonemic speech-principle") on the basis of scripture, by showing that this doctrine is tacitly admitted in certain Vedic texts.

(1) The first line of the celebrated Vedic stanza "uta tvaḥ paśyan" (*Ṛg Veda* 10.71.4) is interpreted to mean that the common man, seeing with his eyes the physical world, does not recognize it as an effect (manifestation) of the language principle. Similarly, the second line is interpreted to mean that, being deluded by the physical speech sounds, he does not grasp the language principle that controls them.

(2) Bharata Miśra also quotes some passages from the Brāhmaṇas like "saitam mantram apaśyat" (*Aitareya Brāhmaṇa* 5.23) in which, he maintains, the clairvoyant perception of a *mantra* or other passage is possible only if a superphonemic word principle is accepted.

(3) It is also claimed that in the celebrated *Nirukta* passage (1.20) beginning "sākṣātkṛtadharmāṇa..." the direct perception of *dharma* is meant to indicate that direct perception of word has preceded the perception of phonemes.

(*E*36–40). The reality at the basis of the whole word is *sphoṭa*, which can also be perceived directly. In a lengthy argument Bharata Miśra tries to show that the ultimate reality is existence, with its indescribable power and form, which descends to the level of the phenomenal world ("advitīya sattaivānirvācyasvaśaktirūpavargadvayavati vyavahārapatham avatarati").

Two additional noteworthy points are made. First, like Maṇḍana, Bharata Miśra uses expressions such as "word above and beyond the phonemes" (*varṇātiriktaṃ padam*) or "speech principle" (*vāk tattvam*) or "language principle" (*śabdatattvam*) along with *sphoṭa*. Second, Bharata Miśra mentions (*E*1) Audumbarāyaṇa as the advocate of the *sphoṭa* theory and Upavarṣa as its opponent, but adds that there is no real difference of opinion between the two, because Uapavarṣa's purpose is only practical (*E*28).

27

SPHOṬASIDDHINYĀYAVICĀRA

G. B. Palsule

This anonymous work is a good epitome of the usual arguments for and against the *sphoṭa*, but otherwise there is little originality in it. It is considerably influenced by the *Sphoṭasiddhi* of Bharata Miśra (to whom, along with others, an obeisance is made in the initial stanza); indeed, in a limited sense, the present work could be called a metrical recast of Bharata's work.

One may in passing note that the author practically identifies, without expressly saying so, the individual *sphoṭa* (*vyaktisphoṭa*) with the language principle (*śabdatattva*). Another interesting item is the scathing criticism of the notion of sequence (*krama*).

The edition (*E*) is by T. Ganapati Sastri (Trivandrum Sanskrit Series 54, Trivandrum, n.d.). References are by stanza.

1 (*E*1). Apart from the three Munis and Hari, the author mentions Bharata (and, of course, Maṇḍana) in the initial stanza.

2 (*E*2). The object of the work is to establish the superphonemic language principle (*varṇebhyo vyatirekeṇa śabdatattvam*) on the strength of direct perception, presumption (*arthāpatti*, the difficulty of explaining otherwise how we understand meaning), and scripture (*āgama*).

3 (*E*3–10). The distinct cognition of the word as a single entity apart from the phonemes is explained.

4 (*E*11–16). (a) This section elaborates the usual difficulties in the way of attributing meaningfulness to phonemes.

(*E*17–116). (b) Various suggestions are put forth by the opponent to show meaningfulness of phonemes and are refuted by the author: (1) excellence (*viśeṣa*) imparted by phonemes to one another (17–29); (2) assigning a special power of conveying meaning, in the form of dispositions, to phonemes (30–49); (3) direct perception of the final phoneme combined with the memory of the preceding phonemes (49–53); (4) a simultaneous whole of the phonemes reflected in the final memory (53–116). The arguments for rejecting these suggestions are the same as those in the *Sphoṭasiddhis* of Maṇḍana and Bharata. Stanzas 84–115 contain a long-drawn-out argument challenging the concept of sequence and its usefulness in assigning meaningfulness to the phonemes. So the author concludes that if *sphoṭa* be not accepted, we cannot account for the difference of meaning in words like *saraḥ* and *rasaḥ*.

5 (*E*117–121). The popular saying "We understand meaning from word" (*śabdād arthaṃ vijānīmaḥ*) is explicable only by the *sphoṭa* theory, not by the phoneme theory.

6 (*E*121–131). *Objections*: There is no perception of any entity different from phonemes (as that of the thumb from other fingers); also, if such an entity existed, what would be its relation to the phonemes?

(*E*131–174). *Answer*: By the relationship of the manifester and the manifested, the sounds manifest either the words (as individuals manifest a universal)—*sphoṭa* as universal (136–144)—or a single word-principle, with illusion of parts (word, phoneme, sentence)—*sphoṭa* as individual (*vyaktisphoṭa*) (145–174). There are two kinds of sound, *prākṛta* and *vaikṛta*, and their functions are described (151–155). Sounds have a deceptive nature and hence produce an illusion (156–164). The final cognition of unity sublates the initial cognitions of plurality (165–174).

7 (*E*175–202). *Sphoṭa* manifests itself gradually.

8 (*E*203–205). Indistinct cognition is possible only in sense perception (which grasps *sphoṭa*), not in the understanding of meaning from word.

9 (*E*206–209). The three theories about *sphoṭa* (as universal, as individual, as inner mental word) are reconciled.

10 (*E*210–242). *Sphoṭa* is established as the authority of scripture (on the same lines as in Bharata's *Sphoṭasiddhi*).

11 (*E*243–245). Conclusion.

28

ANNAMBHAṬṬA

This author, who flourished about 1560, is well known to students of Nyāya as the author of the most commonly studied introduction to the Nyāya system, the *Tarkasaṃgraha*, as well as of a commentary, *Dīpikā*, thereon. A native of the Telugu-speaking country, he identifies his father as "Tirumala Ācārya" of the family of Advaitavidyācārya Rāghava Somayāji.[1] P.P.S. Sastri says the family of Rāghava Somayāji resided in Garikapada, which was formerly in the possession of Nizam Ali.[2]

In addition to the *Tarkasaṃgraha* and several Nyāya commentaries, Annambhaṭṭa wrote a *Mitākṣara* on the *Brahmasūtras*, an Advaita commentary on Nṛsiṃhāśrama's *Tattvaviveka*, and Pūrvamīmāṃsā commentaries on Kumārila's *Tantravārttika* and Someśvara Bhaṭṭa's *Nyāyasudhā*. His works on grammar were a *Mitākṣara* on Pāṇini's *Aṣṭādhyāyī*, and an *Uddyotana* on Kaiyaṭa's *Mahābhāṣyapradīpa*, which has been edited several times

Annambhaṭṭa studied grammar with Śeṣa Vīreśvara (see above, author 22), the son of Śeṣa Kṛṣṇa, while in Kāśī. In his *Uddyotana* commentary on Kaiyaṭa's *Pradīpa*, Annambhaṭṭa says, "There is no reason to believe that only Sanskrit was created by God at the time of creation. When the Yāvaṇas, and so on, were created their language was also created. We do not have any evidence to show that the Yāvaṇas also first used Sanskrit and only later shifted to their own language."

29

APPAYYA DĪKṢITAI

The first and most famous of a number of members of the Bhāradvāja lineage that bear this name, this writer is responsible for a large number of treatises that range over topics in Vedānta, Mīmāṃsā, Dharma, and Alaṃkāra *śāstras*, as well as a handful of grammatical works. He was the son of Raṅgarājādhvarīndra, a southern Brahmin, a grandson of Ācārya Dīkṣita, and an elder brother of Accān Dīkṣita, who in turn was the father of Nīlakaṇṭha Dīkṣita, a famous *kāvya* author of more than one hundred works.

A good deal is known about Appayya's life and times. Y. Mahalinga Sastri gives Appayya's dates as 1520–1593. That he died in his seventy-second year is declared by Nīlakaṇṭha Dīkṣita. He is known to have had several royal patrons, of whom the first was Chinna Timma of the Vijayanagara empire, who ruled until around 1550, and whom Appayya himself credits with having commissioned Appayya's commentary on Vedānta Deśika's *Yādavābhyudaya*. A second patron, Chinna Bomma, ruled at Vellore from 1549 to 1578, and Appayya mentions him more than once. Finally, Veṅkaṭapati of Pennugonda, whose rule began in 1585, is mentioned in Appayya Dīkṣita's *Vidhirasāyana* and *Kuvalayānanda*. There is an inscription at Adayapalam dated 1582 that refers to him as an author of a hundred works, as well as having been bathed in gold by Chinna Bomma. He is associated most closely with the town of Chidambara, where he is held to have passed away.

Appayya Dīkṣita engaged in controversies with other Vedāntins, through whose relative chronology Appayya's date can be further confirmed. Notable among them is Śrī Tātācārya (1508–1583), author of *Pañcamatabhañjana*, a critique of Appayya, who was influential at the Vijayanagara court in the middle of the sixteenth century between 1545 and 1585, during which time Appayya had apparently nothing to do with the Vijayanagara court. Mahācārya, another famous Viśiṣṭādvaitin, wrote *Chandamaruta* in response to Appayya's polemics. Another important personality of the same period was Vijayīndra Bhikṣu, the Dvaitin, who died in 1595 and is said to have written 104 works to rival the same number of Appayya's. Still another Dvaitin who responded to Appayya's arguments was Vādirāja, head of one of the Udipi maths (ashrams), who lived in this same period.

One of Appayya Dīkṣita's important pupils was Bhaṭṭoji Dīkṣita, the author of *Siddhāntakaumudī*, who came from the north to study Vedānta and Mīmāṃsā and wrote *Śabdakaustubha* as a commemoration of his discipleship under Appayya. A story is told that Bhaṭṭoji found Appayya living unostentatiously in a village, belying widespread fame and royal patronage.

After Vācaspati Miśra I in the tenth century, Appayya Dīkṣita is the most outstanding instance of a writer who transcended the scholastic boundaries to write treatises that were and still are revered and read by followers of a variety of systems and indeed of a variety of *śāstras*. His works on Viśiṣṭādvaita and Dvaita, as well as, of course, on Advaita and Mīmāṃsā, are studied by proponents of those systems. He is the author of poetry, learned treatises on *Alaṃkāraśāstra*, literary criticism, and word derivations, as well as popular works on prayer and didactic works counseling how to live a fruitful life.

His works on Grammar are not in print. He wrote a commentary on Pāṇini, a manuscript of which lies in the Adyar Library, according to the *New Catalogus Catalogorum*. Other grammatical treatises ascribed to him include the *Tiṅantaśeṣasaṃgraha* and *Kaumudīprakāśa*.

30

BHAṬṬOJI DĪKṢITA

This famous Grammarian flourished toward the end of the sixteenth century. He was a Brahmin of Maharashtra or Telugu country (uncertain), a member of an important family that comprises several other famous names among Grammar specialists. His father was Lakṣmīdhara; his brother Raṅgoji Bhaṭṭa, author of several Advaita works, who was himself the father of Kauṇḍa Bhaṭṭa (see below, author 37). Bhaṭṭoji's own sons were Bhānuji Dīkṣita and Vīreśvara, the father of Hari Dīkṣita (see below author 43). His teachers are also well known: they included the Mīmāṃsaka Śaṃkara Bhaṭṭa, the polymath Appayya Dīkṣita (see above, author 29), and Śeṣa Kṛṣṇa (see above, author 19). Yudhisthira Mimamsaka dates him from 1513 to 1593. He is held to have made his home in Varanasi, where he founded a school of Grammarians. He was roundly attacked by Jagannātha Paṇḍitarāja, a controversial figure.

Śabdakaustubha

E references in the following summary refer to the edition published by the Asiatic Society of Bengal, no date given.

(*E*1–5). The correctness of a word depends on the meaning also; *asva*, instead of *aśva*, in the sense of a horse, is incorrect, but the term is correct if the intended meaning is "poor."

(*E*6–7). Division into stem and suffix in the study of words is only a means, it has no reality. Alternative division is also possible. Although grammar gives *laṭ* and the like as indicators of the tense, actually it is the form *ti* and so on that are used (in, for example, *pacati*) to convey the meaning, for meaning is known through the usage of elders, and they use only the full words, never artificial symbols such as *laṭ*,

Although grammar gives the meaning of the artificial suffixes such as *laṭ* and then prescribes the actual form, such as *ti*, as substitutes for them, it is the substitutes that actually bear the meaning, for they are the forms used in the world.

(*E*8–11). Strictly speaking, meaningfulness is based on *sphoṭa* alone. There are several views: *varṇasphoṭa*; *padasphoṭa*; *vākyasphoṭa*; *akhaṇḍapadasphoṭa*; and *akhaṇḍavākyasphoṭa* are individual *sphoṭas*; there are three *sphoṭa* universals, *varṇasphoṭa* and *vākyasphoṭa*. (The arguments are the same as in the *Sphoṭavāda* of *Nāgeśa*.) Bhaṭṭoji says that all of the views have been suggested in *Mahābhāṣya* passages here and there; and also in Bhartṛhari's *Vākyapadīya*. The experience as one word or one sentence is the basis for assuming *padasphoṭa* and *vākyasphoṭa*. The phonemes (*varṇas*) suggest the *sphoṭa*, which is the meaning bearer. Because the primary source for understanding the language is the elders' statements, which are in the form of sentences, the sentence has to be taken as the primary unit of meaning.

(*E*12). The question of whether indeclinables are denotative or suggestive of meaning is valid only at the analytical level.

31

ŚEṢA VIṢṆU

A great-grandson of Śeṣa Nārāyaṇa, Śeṣa Viṣṇu composed a *Prakāśikā* on Patañjali's *Mahābhāṣya,* a manuscript of which is held at a library in Bikaner. He must have flourished about 1605.

32

ŚIVARĀMENDRA SARASVATĪ

This author's *Mahābhāṣyaratnaprakāśa* is published. Theodor Aufrecht cites him as having written a *ṭikā* called *Ratnākara* on the *Siddhānta-kaumudī*. There is also a reference to a commentary on Pāṇini.[1]

33

(ŚEṢA) CAKRAPĀṆI (DATTA)

Cakrapāṇi was the grandson of Śeṣa Kṛṣṇa, the younger son and pupil of Vīreśvara, and the younger brother of Śeṣa Puruṣottama, as well as the father of Śeṣa Gopīnātha. This important scion of the great Śeṣa family of Varanasi wrote a critique of Bhaṭṭoji Dīkṣita's *Prauḍhamanoramā*, aptly named *Khaṇḍana*. It is apparently the same work that is called *Paramatakhaṇḍana*, though Yudhisthira Mimamsaka believes then to be distinct works.[1] He is also credited with a *Kārakatattva* or *Kārakavicāra*.[2]

34

MALLAYA YAJVAN

The author of a *Ṭippaṇi* on Kaiyaṭa's *Mahābhāṣyapradīpa,* Mallaya was the father of Tirumala Yajvan (see below, author 40), the author of *Darśapaurṇamāsamantrabhāṣya.* Yudhisthira Mimamsaka speculates that Tirumala was the father of Annambhaṭṭa, which would, of course, place Mallaya in the fifteenth century. There is no evidence to support this view, however, and it seems more likely that this author belongs to the seventeenth century, say, about 1630.

35

NĪLAKAṆṬHA ŚUKLA

This Nīlakaṇṭha flourished between 1610 and 1670. A pupil of Bhaṭṭoji Dīkṣita, he wrote in 1637 a grammatical work titled *Śabdaśobhā*, as well as various works on rhetoric.[1]

36

NĀRĀYAṆA (ŚĀSTRIN)

In his *Vyākhyā* on Kaiyaṭa's *Mahābhāṣyapradīpa,* Nārāyaṇa Śāstrin pays his respect to his guru, the famous Dharmarājādhvarīndra, author of *Vedāntaparibhāṣā* and other works. He is the father of Rāmakṛṣṇa Yavjan. His date must be about 1640.

37

KOṆḌA (or KAUṆḌA) BHAṬṬA

The famous author of the *Vaiyākaraṇabhūṣaṇa* was the son of Raṅgoji Bhaṭṭa, the author of several Advaita manuals,[1] and the nephew of Bhaṭṭoji Dīkṣita (see above, author 30). Thus he must have flourished about 1650. He was a resident of Varanasi.

Vaiyākaraṇabhūṣaṇa AND *Vaiyākaraṇabhūṣaṇasāra*

S.D. Joshi

The *Vaiyākaraṇabhūṣaṇa* is a commentary on the verses of his uncle Bhaṭṭoji Dīkṣita, which are known as *Vaiyākaraṇamatonmajjana*.[2] On this commentary, which defends Grammarian views and refutes the theories of meaning found in Nyāya and Mīmāṃsā, Koṇḍa Bhaṭṭa also composed an abridgment known as *Vaiyākaraṇabhūṣaṇasāra*. He is also credited with a *Vaiyākaraṇasiddhāntadīpikā*. In the *New Catalogus Catalogorum*, volume 5, p. 92, he is also cited as having written works in the Bhāṭṭa tradition (*Bhāṭṭamatapradīpikā*), as well as in Nyāya (*Padārthadīpikā*, *Tarkapradīpa*, *Tarkaratna*).[3]

The *Vaiyākaraṇabhūṣaṇa* has been edited many times. Most of these editions also contain the text of the *sāra*. *B* references to the *Bhūṣaṇa* edition are to the Bombay Sanskrit and Prakrit Series edition of 1915, while *S* references are to the edition of the *-sāra* in the same volume. "Verse" indicates Bhaṭṭoji's verses.

Section 1

(*B*2) verse 2. A verbal root denotes a result (*phala*) and an operation (*vyāpāra*). The personal endings of finite verbs denote either the agent of activity or the object in which the result appears. That is to say, in the active the personal endings denote the agent (*kartṛ*), and in the passive, the object (*karman*). The operation is syntactically predominant with respect to the result. The meanings "agent" and "object" are qualifiers of the operation and the result denoted by the verbal root, respectively.

The relation between the operation and the result is that of an accomplisher and the accomplished, for the activity produces the result.

(*B*3). The word "result" (*phala*) means a single effect of an action (*kriyā*), produced by various operations conveyed by the root. For example, the root *pac* denotes any of the operations that go to make up the action of cooking, such as setting fire under the pot, fanning the fire, putting rice in the pot, and so on. Here, we see that all activities result in a single effect.

An action is a specific sort of activity, another name for which is productive operation (*bhāvanā*, "bringing into being"), which is also called *sādhya*, "to be effected."

(*B*3–4). It is by these terms—*sādhya*, "to be effected," and *siddha*, "effected,"—that verbs are distinguished from nouns. *Pacati*, "he cooks," gives us the notion that the action of cooking is in progress, while *pāka* refers to an effected, completed action. The distinction between *pacati*, "he cooks," and *pākaḥ*, "cooking," is that the first expression is complete in itself while the second is in expectation of some other action.

(*B*4–5). The root *pac* denotes in general any operation that leads to the result, namely, the softening of the food. In different instances the root *pac* refers to specific operations such as blowing, setting the fire under the pot, fanning it, putting the rice in the pot, and so on. These specific operations are limited by various properties such as "operation limited by blowing" (*phūtkāratvāvacchinna-vyāpāra*) and "operation limited by setting the fire below (the pot)" (*saṃtāpanatvāvacchinna-vyāpāra*). In one instance, the root *pac* means blowing on the fire, while in another instance, it denotes the activity of setting the fire, because that is what is intended in these particular instances by the speaker. The singleness of denotation is determined by the speaker's intention.

(*S*271). When one uses the pronoun *tad*, "it," one may be referring to anything in the world. But this fact does not mean that *tad* has an infinite number of denotations. It has only one denotation, which may be limited by the speaker's intention.

(*B*5). In a majority of the cases *pacati* refers to the action of the main agent. But in *kāṣṭhaṃ pacati*, "the sticks of the firewood cook," *pacati* refers to the action of the firewood. In *sthālī pacati*, "the pot cooks" (that is, contains a particular quantity), it refers to the action of containing or holding. In this way *pacati* may refer to the action of other *kārakas* also.

The Mīmāṃsakas propose that the personal endings denote only the productive operation. But because an operation is inconceivable without an operator, we may say that agent is implied. Finally, the Mīmāṃsakas suggest that the notion of the agent can be furnished in the sentence not by the verb at all but by the word in the nominative case.

(*B*6). To this objection the Grammarians reply as follows: Pāṇini 3-4-69 prescribes *l*-suffixes (finite verb endings) to denote the sense of object and agent.

Mīmāṃsaka's objection: Pāṇini's rule 3.4.69 means that *l*-suffixes denote *kartṛtva* (agentness, volition, or productive operation) and *karmatva* (objectness, result). The number denoted by the personal endings is to be construed with the implied notion of the agent and the object.

Answer: The Mīmāṃsakas maintain that the primary suffixes (*kṛt*) such as *-āna*, *-at* (the present and future participle endings), which are also substitutes of *-l*, denote the sense of agent, while the personal endings in *pacati*, *pacataḥ*, and so on which are also substitutes of *-l*, denote the sense of *kartṛtva* (volition) and *karmatva* (result). This claim involves contradiction. The personal endings must denote the sense agent (or object) because we see syntactic agreement between the noun "Devadatta" and the verb "cooks" in *devadattaḥ pacati*. Unless the meaning "agent" (or object) is denoted by the personal endings in verbs like *pacati*, no syntactic agreement (coreferentiality) would be possible between the nouns and verbs.

(*B*6–7). Moreover, the meaning "number" denoted by the personal endings cannot be connected with the implied meanings "agent" or "object," because the rule, according to the Mīmāṃsakas, is that two meanings ("number" and "productive operation") denoted by the same word unit must be connected with each other. But it would be wrong to connect "number" with "productive operation." Therefore, we must admit that the meaning "number" denoted by a personal ending should be connected with "agent" or "object". Consequently, "agent" or "object" must also be the denoted meanings of the personal endings.

(*B*21–22). The personal endings denote agent or (grammatical) object, number, and time. Of them the agent is the qualifier of the activity and the (grammatical) object is the qualifier of the result. Number is a qualifier of the agent if the personal endings of the active voice are used, and it is a qualifier of the (grammatical) object if the passive endings are used. Time is a qualifier of an operation (action). If a time is construed with the agent or object then the idea of past, present, and future will depend on the state of the agent or object. As long as the agent or object exists, the usage will be "he cooks" or "it has been cooked" even if the action of cooking has ceased or not yet begun.

The semantic analysis of "caitraḥ taṇḍulam pacati" ("Caitra cooks rice") is as follows: an operation (action) of the present time, of which the agent is limited by singularity and is identical with (Caitra), which operation is favorable to (a result, namely) softening, residing in (an object) rice grains limited by singularity (generic singular). And the analysis of "taṇḍulaḥ pacyate caitreṇa" ("rice is cooked by Caitra") is essentially the same: an operation of the present time favorable to (a result, namely) softening residing in (an object) which is identical with rice grain limited by singularity (generic singular), of which (operation) the agent is limited by singularity and is identical with Caitra.

(*B*23). Although elsewhere it is accepted that of the meanings denoted by a base form and a suffix the meaning denoted by a suffix is syntactically predominant, it is accepted here that meanings denoted by a verbal base are syntactically predominant over the meanings "agent" and "object" denoted by the personal endings. This claim is made on the authority of the *Nirukta*, which states that a root presents the meaning "substance" as predominant.

(*B*24) verse 9. The finite endings of the passive voice, the passive *vikaraṇa* suffix *ya* and the like, reveal the sense of object, and the present stem formants reveal the sense of agent.

(*B*25). In the case of the reflexive passive (*karmakartari*), "pacyate odanaḥ svayam eve" ("the rice boils itself"), the personal endings designate an object as an agent. Therefore, the personal endings have an active sense in the reflexive passive. An operation (*vyāpāra*) is a producing (*bhāvanā*), which is the same as bringing into being (*utpādana*) and as an action (*kriyā*). Roots cannot denote action only, without any result, because in that case there would be no difference in denotation of the roots *kṛ* and *yat*. Both denote the action of exertion only. Consequently the root *kṛ*, like the root *yat*, would be intransitive.

(*B*24–27). Naiyāyikas argue that effort (volition) is the denotation of personal endings on the basis of the fact that *pacati*, "cooks", is explained as *pākaṃ karoti*, "he makes a cooking"; *karoti*, according to Nyāya, can be applied only to sentient agent. When the root *kṛñ* is used with reference to a nonsentient thing, it is used metaphorically, for instance, *ratho gacchati*, "the chariot moves." According to Nyāya, the agent is not simply a substratum of activity, as the grammarians would have it. If we accept the Grammarians' view then every *kāraka* can be an agent. Nyāya distinguishes (the sentient) agent from the other *kārakas* by its independence. The Naiyāyikas say that the meanings of the personal endings fall within the area of exertion (*kṛtitva*, a universal property).

According to Grammarians the personal endings denote agent and object. The limiting property of these meanings will be *kartṛtva* (agentness) and *karmatva* (objectness). The *kartṛtva* or *karmatva* are properties that are present in all agents and objects and present in no other entity. These properties are nothing more than the actions and results residing in agents and objects, respectively; and there will be many different actions and results, depending on differences in agents and objects. This situation involves complexity; but such complexity is no defect if it accords with the fact.

(*B*28–29). The result should be included in the denotation of the root. If it is not included in the root meaning, then the roots *gam* (to go) and *tyaj* (to leave) should be synonymous. The distinction between *gam* and *tyaj* lies only in their denoted result. *Gam* means an activity in the form of motion favorable to conjunction with a consequent point, while *tyaj* means an activity in the form of motion favorable to disjunction from a preceding point. The denoted activity in the form of motion is the same in both instances.

The ancient Naiyāyikas, who denied to verbal roots the denotation of result, said that the general idea of result is indicated by the accusative case ending, which contains the meaning of the roots *gam* and *tyaj*. One can say that the meaning of *gam*, when it is juxtaposition with an accusative, implies a result different from the result implied by *tyaj*, when it is connected with an accusative case ending. The Grammarians' point is that without an accusative also, *gacchati* and *tyajati* indicate difference in meaning, therefore result should be included in the denotation of root.

(*B*31–32) verse 6. According to Grammarians, a root is transitive when the operation and result denoted by it have different loci. Thus, in *pacati*, "he cooks," the operation resides in the cook, the result in rice. But such definitions are impossible unless the root denotes both operation and result.

According to Naiyāyikas, the result is not part of the denoted meaning of the root. But the general idea of result is denoted by the accusative case endings. Thus a verb is transitive when it denotes activity conditioned by result; the root's denotation includes result in the broadest sense. In its specific form it is understood from an accusative.

Therefore, the roots *kṛñ* and the like denote effect (and so on) connected with a result in the form of coming into being, and not an operation or result alone. So the reflexive passive construction (*karmavadbhāva*), as in "kriyate odanaḥ svayam eva" ("the rice comes into being itself"), is allowed. This construction is permitted only with roots of which the denoted results are visible in their objects. If we deny to the root *kṛñ* the denotation of result, it will be impossible to use it in such a reflexive construction.

(*B*32–33) verse 7. The reflexive passive construction is permitted when the object is producible or modifiable by the action of agent but not when the object is simply attainable.

The grammatical object is of three sorts: producible, modifiable, and attainable. An example of the first one is *ghaṭaṃ karoti*, "he makes a jar"; of the second one, *somaṃ sunoti*, "he extracts the soma juice"; of the third one, *rūpaṃ paśyati*, "he sees color." Attainability of an object means nonapprehensibility of a change brought about in the object by the action of the agent. By looking at an object (a village or pot) one cannot apprehend that this pot is cognized by someone or that this village has been visited by some. In the case of attainable objects the reflexive passive construction is not permitted.

(*B*42) verse 8. Therefore, the root *kṛ* explains the sense of the root (for example, *pac*) and not of the personal endings. The phrase *pakvavān*, "he has cooked," is explained as *pākaṃ kṛtavān*, "he has done the cooking," and the phrase *kiṃ kṛtam*, "what has been done?" is answered by *pakvam*, "it has been cooked."

(*B*45). The Mīmāṃsakas and the Grammarians agree that *pacati* may be explained as *pākaṃ karoti*. The Mīmāṃsakas claim, however, that the word *pākam* in the explanation denoting result explains the meaning of the root *pac*, while the word *karoti*, denoting activity, explains the meaning of the personal ending. The Grammarians oppose this claim by showing that the root *kṛ* is also used in explaining other forms that contain no personal endings. *Pakvavān* is explained as *pākaṃ kṛtavān*. The Grammarians' assignment of meanings "result" and "activity" to a verbal root is based on the following analysis:

FORMS	MEANING
(1) *pacatai* (*pac+personal ending*)	result, activity, agent
(2) *pakvavan* (*pac+tavat*)	result, activity, agent
(3) *pakvam* (*pac+vam*)	result, activity, object

One morpheme and two meanings are common in these examples. Here the root morpheme denotes two meanings, "result" and "activity."

(*S*308). If the root denotes the result alone, then we should have the notion that the village is possessed of going (*gramo gamanavān*) because the village is the substratum of the result of conjunction (reaching). Likewise, when the result (namely), the softening of the rice, has not yet occurred even though the activity (favorable to softening) is in progress, we could not say *pāko bhavati*, "cooking comes into being." When, by contrast, the operation (favorable to softening) has ceased and the result is present, we would say *pāko vidyate*, "the cooking continues."

(*B*45). The denotation of the agent by the primary endings is necessary in order to establish the connection of the agent with number. Furthermore, in words like *pakvavān*, the denotation of action is just necessary in order to establish the connection (of the action) with the notion of *kāraka*. The meaning "number" can be construed only with the meaning "agent." The meaning "time" can be construed only with the meaning "operation."

If the Mīmāṃsakas claim that the root *kṛ* explains the sense of action denoted by the personal endings because *kiṃ karoti*, "what does he do?" is answered by *pacati*, "he cooks" (*pākaṃ karoti*), then they will have to accept also that the root *kṛ* explains the sense of nouns derived from the primary (*kṛt*) suffix. For instance, *kiṃ kāryam*, "what is to be done?" is answered by *pakvavān*, "cooking should be done." But the Mīmāṃsakas say that the root morpheme denotes the result, the personal ending denotes the productive operation, and the primary suffixes denote the agent and object and imply productive operation. Thus the Mīmāṃsakas' analysis violates the principle that the common meaning should correspond to the common element.

(*B*45). verse 9. Furthermore, there can be no such thing as a root without denotation of activity. That verbal roots denote actions (*kriyā*) has been accepted by Pāṇini, Kātyāyana, and Patañjali.

In the word *kāryam*, the primary suffix is used in the sense of *karman* (in the passive sense). In *jyotiṣṭomayājī*, "who has sacrificed with *jyotiṣṭoma* sacrifice," the primary suffix *in* denotes the sense of agent. The meaning of these suffixes must be connected with action, which proves that the operation must be denoted by the root. It is impossible to call something a *kāraka* if it is not related to the notion of action. It is, accordingly, impossible to use a suffix denoting a *kāraka* in the absence of a connection with the notion of action.

(*B*50–51). *Objection*: If verbal roots are supposed to denote action then the roots *as* (to be) and the like, which are not denotative of action, would not be termed roots, for when we say *asti*, "he is," the meaning "action" is not cognized.

Answer: Roots such as *as* also denote action. In the case of intransitive roots, because agent and object of action are the same, the action is not subservient to any other entity than the agent. Therefore, the distinction between the actor and the one acted on is lost. Consequently, the notion of action in the case of *as* is not immediately apparent. Further, we do cognize an action favorable to the result "existence" from *as* (to be) and similar roots. Suppose a man is on the verge of death and with reference to him someone asks "what is he doing?" the answer "he is," in other words, "he exists" is approved as meaningful by everyone. Here the answer refers to a particular activity (existing with great effort) on the part of the agent.

(*B*50–51) verse 12. And further, if actions were not denoted by roots like *as*, actions would not be specified as past, present, and future, which they are.

(*B*56) verse 13. When the operation and the result reside in the same substratum a root is intransitive; and when they reside in different substrata the root is called transitive.

(*B*57). In "ātmā ātmānaṃ jānāti" ("the self knows the self"), the self limited by the adjunct body is the object, and it is the substratum of the result, knowledge, while the self limited by the adjunct mind is the agent, and it is the substratum of activity. Thus the activity and the result have different substrata.

(*B*59) verse 14. In the verb the root morpheme denotes *sādhya* (action), namely, action in progress or durative, and the finite verb ending denotes the *sādhana* (operator), which is capable of bringing the action into being. In a word like *pāka,* which ends in the primary suffix *ghañ* (*a*), the root morpheme denotes action in the process and the primary suffix denotes *siddha* (accomplished) action that has the characteristics of an operator (*sādhana*). An accomplished action behaves like a substance and is thus always capable of being used as an instrument of action in progress. *Bhūṣaṇa* explains this sense quite differently.

(*B*60) verse 15. In a noun ending in a suffix such as *ghañ* (*a*), a root portion denotes action in progress, while its frozen (accomplished) aspect is associated with suffix *ghañ* (*a*).

For this reason we have a distinction between the constructions *stokaḥ pākaḥ,* "a small amount of cooking", and *stokaṃ pākaḥ,* "cooking to a small extent." In the first case *stoka* is syntactically connected with the primary suffix *ghañ* (*a*), which denotes activity frozen (substantivated), and in the second case *stoka* is syntactically connected with the root *pac,* which denotes the action in process. Durative activity is void of gender and number (*asattvabhūta*).

(*B*64–68) verses 16–17. A word ending in the vocative case suffixes having the sense of *kṛtvas* (counting of recurrences), the *kārakas* (instrumental in bringing about the action), the first suffix *vat* (Pāṇini 5.1.115: prescribed in the sense of what is similar is an activity), the suffixes, infinitives, and so on, prescribed under the governing section (Pāṇini 3.4.1), verbal particle of negation (that is, other than nominally bound negative), the locative absolute (Pāṇini 2.3.37) form proper construction only with durative action.

(*B*69). In *stokaṃ pākaḥ* the ending *aṃ* is a formal constructional appendage because a substantive cannot be used without a case ending. Substantivated activity does possess, however, number and gender. Therefore, when *stoka* is construed with the suffix *ghañ* it takes masculine gender and whatever number is appropriate.

(*B*69) verse 19. Just as the inseparable action (denoted by the root *gam*) in the word *gata,* "has gone," is constructed with the object *grāma* in the phrase *grāmaṃ gataḥ,* so the activity (denoted by the root *kṛ*) in the phrase *kṛtapūrvī kaṭam,* "one who has made a mat before" is connected with the object *kaṭam.*

Even when the activity denoted by a root is subordinate to the agent or object denoted by a suffix, a *kāraka* denoted by a separate word with oblique case ending is still construed with the action and not with the denotatum of suffix. This fact holds true in cases like *grāmaṃ gataḥ*, "he has gone to the village," where the *kāraka*, *grāmaṃ* is construed with *gam* rather than with the suffix *-ta*. In *kṛtapūrvī kaṭam*, "he who has made a mat before," and *bhuktapūrvī odanam*, "he who has already eaten rice," *kaṭa* and *odana* are construed with *kṛ* and *bhuj* rather than with the suffix *-in*. In these cases, outside words *grāmam*, *kaṭam*, and *odanam* are indeed construed with the subordinate members *gam*, *kṛ*, and *bhuj*, respectively. Such constructions are allowable.

(*B*70) verse 21. Correctness has no invariable connection with communication. Even in the absence of correct forms, verbal knowledge is not denied by the Grammarians.

(*B*70–71). The Naiyāyikas and the Mīmāṃsakas hold the view that whatever is denotative is correct. Corrupt words are not denotative, so they are incorrect. The corrupt words like *gāvī* appear to be denotative of the meaning "cow" because they remind us of the correct words like *go*. The Grammarians refute this view. If the corrupt words had no denotative function they would convey no meaning. It does not help us to say that the corrupt words remind us of correct words and through them they are denotative, because ignorant persons who do not know the correct words understand the meaning from incorrect ones. According to the Grammarians, the correct word *go* and the corrupt word *gāvī* are both denotative of the cow. The only difference is that the use of corrupt words leads to religious demerit, while the use of correct words leads to merit.

Section 2: The Meanings of Tenses and Moods (*Lakārārthanirṇaya*)

(*B*73) verse 22. *Laṭ* and so on (the phrase stands for ten markers *laṭ*, *liṭ*, and so on, which do not occur in actual utterances; they represent the personal endings, *ti*, *tas*, and so on, that come in place of *l-* the common symbol for all the finite suffixes of tenses and moods) are to be understood in the following meanings: present, past not witnessed (by the speaker), what is going to happen tomorrow, future (simple), injunction, request, and so on.

(*B*73). *Laṭ* denotes the present. Presentness is defined as being (a time) that is characterized by an action that is begun but not ended or as the property of being a time other than the past or future.

(*B*73–75). The question is raised whether "time" is the denoted (*vācya*) or the cosignified (*dyotya*) meaning of *l*-suffixes (personal endings). According to the first view, time is the denoted meaning of the *l*-suffixes. A verbal root cannot denote all the specific aspects of action, including specific time. In that case the denotative area of verbal roots will be too wide. It is simpler to say that a root denotes operation and result, and *l*-suffixes (personal endings) denote specific aspects of action, including time. Moreover, Pāṇini's rules (Pāṇini 3.2.123 and elsewhere) lay down that *l*-suffixes denote time and aspects (injunction and so on).

According to the second view, the *l*-suffixes are time-indicative suffixes and not independently denotative of *time*. These *l*-suffixes only single out the particular meaning that is to be adopted in a particular context. The verbal root already denotes all aspects of action, including time in general.

In this connection, the final view of the *Bhūṣaṇa* is that time is considered to be the measurer of an action. But in reality time is measured by action, for time cannot be divided without being associated with action. According to Grammarians, time and action are identical because time has no reference to anything outside the domain of an action. Thus the general notion of time is denoted by verbal roots, when it denotes action. But the specific aspect of time, such as presentness, is indicated by *l*- suffixes. Therefore, the second view appears to be correct.

(*B*75). Then a question is raised: how to account for the use of the present tense in such sentences as *ātmā asti*, "the self exists," and *parvatāḥ santi*, "the mountains stand," because existence and standing go on continuously without stopping? Therefore, continuous actions "existing" and "standing" cannot be associated with the three divisions of time.

The *Bhūṣaṇa*, following the *Mahābhāṣya*, answers that the existence of the self and the standing of the mountains are also differentiated as present or past with the aid of the contemporary actions of the kings belonging to different periods of time.

Liṭ (perfect tense) expresses past action that happened at a definite time in the past, not witnessed by the speaker. *Parokṣatva*, imperceptibility (being not witnessed by the speaker) means the property of not being the object of the knowledge that can be described as "I perceive," which resides in the speaker. Imperceptibility either means imperceptibility of action or imperceptibility of *kārakas* engaged in an action. Although the action as a whole is always imperceptible, yet its parts are clearly perceptible. Thus the perfect is not to be used when some parts of the action as a whole are perceived by the narrator. The perfect in the first person is allowed when even one's activity is not perceived by oneself due to one's being absorbed in something or for some other reason.

(*B*76). *Luṭ* (periphrastic future) expresses only future action, exclusive of today, that is, action that is going to take place at a definite time to come. *Lṛṭ* denotes any future action.

Leṭ (Vedic subjuntive) denotes permission, injunction, command (Pāṇini 3.4.7), inquiry, and the like.

Loṭ (imperative) denotes command, permission, and the like. There is no sharp line of distinction between the imperative (*Loṭ*), the subjunctive (*Leṭ*), and the optative (*Liṅ*).

Laṅ (imperfect) denotes a completed action that happened at a definite time in the past (*anadyatane*).

Liṅ (optative) expresses *vidhi*, injunction (including command); *nimantraṇa*, summoning to do something; *āmantraṇa*, invitation; *adhiṣṭa*, respectful request; *saṃpraśna*, inquiry; and *prārthanā*, request. The first four of these meanings can be reduced to one, namely, prompting or instigation (*pravartanā*). *Pravartanā* is defined as an activity on the part of the prompter that leads the prompted person to do something. The definition cannot be applicable to Vedic injunctions because the Vedas are not composed by any human being. Therefore, in connection with Vedic injunctions we assume that the optative forms in the Veda itself prompt someone to do the thing stated in the Veda.

(*B*77–79). But what is the precise nature of *pravartanā*? The *Bhūṣaṇa* mentions several views on this subject, as put forward by the Naiyāyikas, by the Prabhākara Mīmāṃsakas, and by Koṇḍa Bhaṭṭa himself.

According to the Naiyāyikas, the person to be prompted does not become inclined to act unless he knows the following three factors of action:

(1) Feasibility (*kṛtisādhyatva*): the prompted person does not proceed to perform impossible tasks such as bringing down the peak of Mount Meru, bringing down the moon, and the like. Therefore, feasibility is the meaning of *liṅ*-suffixes.

(2) Knowledge that this (act) leads to the desired result (*iṣṭasādhanatājñāna*): a person does not act unless he ascertains that this (act) will achieve something he desires. The person desiring satisfaction of his thirst does not thrash the water because he knows that this action will not bring him the desired result. Therefore, *iṣṭasādhanatva* is the meaning of the *liṅ*-suffixes.

(3) The cognition of not entailing a greatly undesired result (*balavadaniṣṭānanubandhitva*). No one eats a food mixed with honey and poison. There is no inclination toward the eating of such a food because it leads to a greatly undersired result, namely, death.

Unless the person to be prompted knows these things beforehand he does not proceed to perform any act.

(*B*79–82). According to the Prābhākaras, something new to be achieved (*apūrva*) is the meaning of the injunctive sentence containing-*liṅ* (optative suffix). *Apūrva* is the same as *kārya*, the thing to be brought about by exertion (*kṛti*) or that toward which the activity is directed (*kṛtyuddeśya*). *Apūrva* has been called prompting (*niyoga*) because it acts as an incentive to the prompted person to perform the act prescribed. The sacrifice does not directly precede heaven. Because *apūrva* is the immediately preceding cause of heaven, it is cognized as the thing to be done (*kārya*) and it is the meaning of -*liṅ*.

The Prābhākaras deny the property of being the means to a desired result (*iṣṭasādhanatva*) as the meaning of the *liṅ*-suffixes (optative). The reason is that there are certain obligatory rites, the performance of which does not lead to any desired result. Thus in the obligatory rites the inclination to act is due to *apūrva*.

It is also not correct to say that a *liṅ*-suffix denotes the state of being an indirect cause of the desired result, if no operation (*vyāpāra*, that is, *apūrva*) be known. Therefore, it is better to suppose that *apūrva* is the direct cause that immediately precedes the result, heaven. Therefore, *apūrva* (the thing to be done) is the meaning of -*liṅ*. It is also our common experience that the knowledge "this act is to be done" acts as an instigator (prompter).

(*B*82–96). According to Koṇḍa Bhaṭṭa, the *liṅ*-suffixes express *iṣṭasādhanatva* or *hitasādhanatva*, the property of being the means to a desired result. Here Koṇḍa Bhaṭṭa follows the view of Maṇḍana Miśra, the author of the *Vidhiviveka*. The person to be prompted requires some incentive. There can be no inclination to activity unless one knows that it leads to a desired result. Thus it is a means to a desired result and the cause of the performance of the act in general.

Koṇḍa Bhaṭṭa, following Madhva (1197–1273), rejects feasibility as the meaning of -*liṅ*. If we accept that feasibility leads to an action, there will be inclination for prohibited things such as killing a brahmin, because killing is feasible. Further, the general rule is that only that meaning which cannot be obtained by any other means is accepted as verbal knowledge. There will be no inclination to act when the action involved is not feasible. Our common experience shows that the efforts toward nonfeasible acts are wasted, as they produce nothing. Then aversion is created in the mind of a prompted person, and accordingly he does not proceed to perform nonfeasible acts.

According to Koṇḍa Bhaṭṭa, the property of not entailing a greatly undesired result (*balavadaniṣṭānanubandhitva*) is also not the meaning of *liṅ*-suffixes. Noninclination toward disastrous acts can be caused by aversion, which prevents the agent from undertaking any activity. Moreover, there is no way to determine how much frustration will be a deterrent factor in the case of different acts and in the case of different individuals. For some persons, even a little trouble will be enough to remove the inclination to act. Therefore, it is aversion that should be accepted as the deterrent. Once it is accepted, the separate factor, *balavadaniṣṭānanubandhitva*, for inclination to act is not necessary.

Koṇḍa Bhaṭṭa also rejects the view of the Prābhākara Mīmāṃsakas

According to him, there is no evidence for saying that the immediately preceding cause of a result (namely, the *apūrva* accepted by the Prābhākaras) is a prompter or instigator. Moreover, what immediately precedes may not be necessarily the main cause of the effect. Further, *apūrva* means something to be produced by effort (*kārya*). This property of being something to be effected (*kāryatā*) in fact belongs to the action denoted by the verbal root. So what is to be produced is sacrificing (*yāga*) and not *apūrva*, as accepted by the Prābhākaras. According to Prābhākaras, *apūrva* is considered to be the denoted meaning of *-liṅ*. But it is hard to grasp the relation of *apūrva* and *-liṅ*. Without first knowing *apūrva* independently, how can one grasp the significatory association of *apūrva* and *-liṅ*? Koṇḍa Bhaṭṭa states that *apūrva* cannot be a goal at all. The object of desire alone can be the goal of action. Therefore, *apūrva* can be an intermediate link (as in, sacrifice-*apūrva*-heaven), and *apūrva* cannot be the object of desire.

Luṅ (aorist) denotes the past in general.

Lṛṅ (conditional) is used in the past or future value to indicate that something is going to happen without any effect.[4]

Section 3: Meanings of the Case Endings
(*Subarthanirṇaya*)

(*B*99) verse 24. The substratum, the limit (of separation), the recipient, relation, or capacities (of these things) are considered to be the denotation of case endings on the authority of the *Mahābhāṣya*.

The accusative, the instrumental, and the locative denote the meaning substratum. The accusative denotes the substratum of the result (*phalāśraya*). The instrumental denotes the substratum of the operation, and the locative denotes the substratum of either operation or result through the medium of agent or object. The ablative case denotes the sense of limit from which the separation is to be effected. The dative case denotes the sense of recipient of the fruit of action (*uddeśya*). The genitive case denotes the relation *śeṣa* between the meanings denoted by two nouns.

(*S*367). The term *karman* is defined (Pāṇini 1.4.49) as that which is the most desired to be obtained (by the agent). The word *karman* means the object that is the substratum of the result produced by the activity. It is only through the possession of the result produced by the activity that the object becomes the most desired to the agent.

In the sentence *odanaṃ pacati*, "he cooks the rice," *odana* is the object, because it is the substratum of the result softening (of the rice grains). In the sentence *ghaṭaṃ karoti*, "he makes a jar," the jar is the substratum of the result production. In the sentence *ghaṭaṃ jānāti*, "he knows a jar," the jar is the object because it is the substratum of the result breaking of the veil (of ignorance) denoted by the root *jñā*.

(*S*369–370). *Objection*: While going to a village, the usage "caitraḥ caitraṃ gacchati" ("Caitra goes to Caitra") would be correct, because Caitra is also the substratum of the result conjunction produced by the activity in the form of motion, like the object village, because conjunction is a property that resides in two things. Here it resides in the object *grāma* as well as in the agent Caitra. Similarly, in the sentence "prayāgāt kāśīṃ gacchati" ("he goes to Kāśī from Prayāga") the *apādāna-kāraka*, namely, *prayāga*, would also be *karman* because it is the substratum of the result disjunction produced by the activity of motion. The action of motion produces invariably two results: conjunction and disjunction.

(*S*372). *Answer*: Although Caitra, like the village, is the substratum of the result, still the designation agent belonging to Caitra sets aside the designation object, following Pāṇini 1.4.1. Therefore, the usage "caitraḥ caitraṃ gacchati" is not allowed. The designation "object" to the word *prayāga* in the sentence "prayāgāt kāśīṃ gacchati" is ruled out because the word *phala* in *phalāśraya* is qualified by the phrase *dhātvartha*. The phrase *dhātvartha* debars the designation because the result disjunction is not denoted by the root *gam*. The root *gam* denotes the action of moving, producing invariably two results: conjunction with a consequent point and disjunction with a subsequent point. Out of these two results, the root *gam* denotes only the former one.

(*B*102–105). The Naiyāyikas claim, however, that the word *kriyā* in the definition "kriyājanyaphalāśrayaṃ karma" is qualified by the phrase *parasamavetatva*, which serves to distinguish the object from the agent. The definition "parasamavetakriyājanyaphalāśrayaṃ karma" means that *X* is the *karmakāraka*, if *X* is possessed of the result produced by the action that appears in anything other than *X*. If *X* stands for Caitra in the definition "caitro grāmaṃ gacchati," the definition of the *karmakāraka* does not apply to Caitra because the action of going does not inhere in anything other than *X*. If *X* stands for a village (*grāma*) that is the substratum of the result conjunction, the definition applies to the village because the action of going inheres in Caitra, who is other than the village.

Koṇḍa Bhaṭṭa does not agree with this definition given by the Naiyāyikas. The meaning *parasamaveta*, inherent in the other, and so on, is not the denoted meaning of the accusative because this assumption involves complexity. Moreover, this definition does not exclude the prompter agent (*prayojaka*) and reflexive agent (*karmakartṛ*) from the province of the *karmakāraka*. Therefore, the simple answer to exclude the agent from the province of the *karmakāraka* is to assume that the designation agent (*kartṛ*) prevails over the designation *karman*.

(*B*105–106). The *karmakāraka* is divided into seven categories. The *ipsitatamakarman*, the object most desired by the agent, is of three kinds:

(1) *Nirvartya,* the object to be produced, for instance, *ghaṭaṃ karoti,* "he makes a jar."

(2) *Vikārya,* the object to be modified. One kind of *vikāryakarman* is that which arises on account of the destruction of the material, as ashes from the firewood: *kāṣṭham bhasma karoti,* "he reduces firewood to ashes"; another kind is that which arises on account of the origination of new qualities, as a modification of gold: *suvarṇam kuṇḍalaṃ karoti,* "he fashions an earring out of gold."

(3) *Prāpya,* attainable. *Prāpyakarman* is that in which the effectuation of particular features due to action cannot be understood from perception of the object or from inference, for instance, *ghaṭaṃ paśyati,* "he sees a jar."

The object not positively desired to be reached by the agent (*anīpsita-karman*) is categorized into four types:

(1) *Udāsīna,* indifferent, for instance, grass *tṛṇam* in "grāmaṃ gacchan tṛṇaṃ spṛśati" ("while going to the village he happens to touch the grass".

(2) *Dveṣya,* odious, for instance, *viṣam bhuṇkte,* "he eats poison."

(3) *Anākhyāta,* unexpressed object. That is an unexpressed object (*akathita*) which is not intended to be otherwise expressed as *apādāna, adhikaraṇa,* and so on. In other words, that is a *kāraka* which can be expressed otherwise, but not expressed by way of any other *kāraka* relation. But if the speaker intends to express it as *apādāna, adhikaraṇa,* and so on, he is free to do so, for example, "gāṃ payo dogdhi" or "goḥ payo dogdhi," ("he milks the cow" or "he milks from the cow").

(4) *Anyapūrvaka,* an object that has been declared to be the *karmakāraka* by the special rule in place of *sampradāna,* and the like, for example, "krūram abhikrudhyati," ("he is angry with a cruel person").

(*B*107–108). The third case representing agent denotes substratum. A *kāraka* is invariably considered to be an agent provided that the action belonging to it be denoted by the verbal root. In the sentence "devadattaḥ kāṣṭhaiḥ sthālyām odanaṃ pacati" ("Devadatta cooks the rice in a pot with the help of firewood"), Devadatta functions as the agent who independently initiates the action and sets the other *kāraka* in motion. Normally, *pacati* refers to the action of the main agent; still, it may also refer to the activities of the other *kārakas.* For instance, if the speaker wants to convey the idea that firewood considerably facilitates the action of cooking, he will say *kāṣṭhāni pacanti,* "firewood cooks." Here *pacanti* refers to the action of the firewood. In *sthālī pacati,* "the vessel cooks," the verb *pacati* refers to the action of containing or holding.

(*B*108). The *kartṛ-kāraka* is divided into three types:

(1) *Śuddhakartā,* simple agent, for instance *devadattena* in "devadattena hariḥ sevyate" ("Hari is worshiped by Devadatta").

(2) *Prayojakakartā,* prompter or causal agent, for instance *kāryate hariṇā,* "someone is made to do by Hari."

(3) Reflexive agent: when the object is transferred to the states of the agent it is called reflexive agent. For instance, "odanaḥ pacyate svayam eva," "the rice cooks itself."

(*B*109). The instrumental case denotes the sense operation also. The most effective means of operation is called *karaṇa*. The most effective means is nothing but possession of the most important operation that produces the (desired) result immediately.

The feature of being the most effective means for the accomplishment of an action is not fixed with regard to any specific *kāraka*. Whether a particular *kāraka* plays the role of *karaṇa* is determined by the speaker's intention. One can say *sthālyāṃ pacati*, "he cooks in the vessel," *sthālyā pacyate*, "(it) is cooked by means of the vessel," *kāṣṭhaiḥ pacati*, "he cooks by means of firewood," "or *kāṣṭhāni pacanti*, "the firewood cooks."

The locative case also denotes the substratum of action through the medium of the agent or the object. The following are the varieties of the locative case:

(1) *Abhivyāpaka*, coextensive or location of pervasion. For instance, *tileṣu tailam*, "oil in sesame seeds."

(2) *Aupaśleṣika*, location of contact. When the superstratum (*ādheya*) forms its connection with only a part of substratum, the *adhikaraṇa* is called *aupaśleṣika*; for example, *kaṭe āste*, "he sits on the mat."

(3) *Vaiṣayika*, nonphysical location, as in *mokṣe icchāsti*, "he desires liberation." The ablative case denotes the sense limit or fixed point (in connection with separation), which is called *apādāna*.

(*B*110–112). Following Bhartṛhari's *Vākyapadīya*, Koṇḍa Bhaṭṭa gives three varieties of the *apādānakāraka*:

(1) *Nirdiṣṭaviṣaya*, in which *apāya* "separation" has been directly stated by the verbal base, for instance *aśvāt patati*, "he falls down from the horse."

(2) *Upāttaviṣaya*, in which the verbal base denotes its own meaning, which indirectly includes the notion of separation; for instance, *balāhakād vidyotate*, "(it) is lightning from the cloud."

(3) *Apekṣitakriyā*, in which the word denoting the action of separation is not stated at all, for instance, *pāṭaliputrāt*, "(I came) from Pāṭaliputra."

Following Pāṇini (1.4.32), Koṇḍa Bhaṭṭa says that the dative case denotes the *sampradāna kāraka*. It is defined as that which is aimed at by the agent through the instrumentality of the object of action, for instance, "viprāya gāṃ dadāti" ("he gives a cow to the brahmin"). Here the brahmin is called *saṃpradāna* because brahmin is connected with the action of giving through the direct object cow.

According to Koṇḍa Bhaṭṭa, the dative denotes the sense *uddeśya*, the object for which the action is intended. Here Koṇḍa Bhaṭṭa considers that the *saṃpradāna kāraka* is positionally predominant (although a brahmin does not syntactically predominate over the cows that are given to him). Therefore, the *saṃpradāna* is called by the Mīmāṃsakas *śeṣin*, positionally predominant, to which something is *śeṣa*, subservient.

Then Koṇḍa Bhaṭṭa makes two points: first, the designation *saṃpradāna* is not restricted in connection with the verbs having the sense of giving. Further, the root *dā* does not imply transference of ownership. To prove this point he quotes usages from the *Mahābhāṣya*: "na śūdrāya matiṃ dadyāt" ("one should not impart instruction to a *śūdra*"), "khaṇḍikopādhyāyaḥ tasmai capeṭāṃ dadāti" ("the *khaṇḍika* teacher gives him a slap"). In these usages the dative is used in connection with the root *dā* when there is no question of ownership. But, according to the *Kāśikāvṛtti*, the genitive is used when the thing is not denoted. For instance, "rajakasya vastraṃ dadāti" ("he gives his clothes to the washerman") is the correct usage, not "rajakāya vastraṃ dadāti."

Following the *Vākyapadīya*, Koṇḍa Bhaṭṭa divides *saṃpradāna* into three types:

(1) *Saṃpradāna* by not denying the offer (*anirakartṛ*): "Sūryāya arghyam dadāti" ("he offers the water to the Sun god").

(2) *Saṃpradāna* by making a request (*preraka*): "Viprāya gāṃ dadāti" ("he gives a cow to the brahman"). Hence the receiver incites the giver to give something to him.

(3) *Saṃpradāna* by giving one's consent (*anumantṛ*): "Upādhyāyāya gāṃ dadāti" ("he gives a cow to his teacher"). Here the teacher permits a donor to present a cow to him, though he does not request the donor to do so.

(*B*113). The genitive case denotes a very general relationship. The relation denoted by the genitive (*śeṣa*) is not regarded as a *kāraka*. The *kārakavibhaktis* denote the relation between the noun and the verb, while *śeṣa* is the relation between two nouns.

(*B*114; *S*393). Then Koṇḍa Bhaṭṭa says that the relation between the stem meaning and the case meaning is one of syntactic identity The case endings stand for the possessors of properties (*dharmin*) rather than for properties alone (*dharma*). For instance, the word *taṇḍulam*, ending in the accusative, denotes the sense *taṇḍulābhinnāśrayaka*, substratum (of the result, softening) not different from the (objects) rice grains. The primary (*kṛt*) and secondary (*taddhita*) endings also denote the sense *dharmin* instead of *dharma*, for instance, *devadattaḥ paktā*, "Devadatta a cook." The syntactic agreement between Devadatta and a cook cannot be maintained unless it is assumed that the suffix stands for the concrete objects rather than for abstract properties. Therefore, the accusative and so on denote the locus (*āśraya*) rather than locusness (*āśrayatva*).

Finally, Koṇḍa Bhaṭṭa maintains that the direct denotation of the case endings is *dharma* (in other words, the abstract property). Koṇḍa

Bhaṭṭa furnishes us with the support of the Mīmāṃsakas' *ākṛtyadhikaraṇa*: a word always denotes primarily the meaning attribute (that is, the qualifier or *viśeṣaṇa* or property or generic notion), while the meaning qualificand (*viśeṣya* or *vyakti* or *dharmin*) is indicated by the secondary function of the words. Thus, the case terminations primarily denote the abstract property locusness (*āśrayatva*), and the concrete idea of locus (*āśraya*) can be obtained from nominal stems or it can be inferred from the fact that there is no *dharma* without *dharmin*.

(*B*115–116). Following Patañjali, Koṇḍa Bhaṭṭa states two alternative views with regard to the restriction of case endings and their meanings. These two views are restriction imposed on case endings (*śabdaniyama* or *vibhaktiniyama*) and restriction imposed on meanings conveyed by the case endings (*arthaniyama*). Pāṇini 4.1.2 introduces the case endings without specifying the meanings to be conveyed by them. Thus the accusative prescribed by Pāṇini 2.3.2 is available to convey *karman* and other syntactic meanings. Because the accusative is already available to convey the meaning *karman* from Pāṇini 4.1.2, the rule *karmaṇi dvitiyā* (Pāṇini 3.4.2) does not add anything new to our knowledge. Therefore, it becomes restricted. The restriction can be imposed in two ways. The first is *karmaṇi eva dvitīyā* (*vibhaktiniyama* or *śabdaniyama*): the accusative case ending is used to convey the sense of *karman* only. From this restriction it does not follow that the sense of *karman* is not bound to any specific case ending. The second is *karmaṇi dvitīyā eva* (*arthaniyama*): to convey the sense of *karman*, the second (case ending) only is used. Here the sense of *karman* becomes bound to the accusative case ending only. But it does not follow that *karman* is the only sense conveyed by the accusative case ending. The accusative case ending may also convey the other syntactic meaning. Koṇḍa Bhaṭṭa does not show any preference for either of these alternatives; he simply says that both are useful.

Finally Koṇḍa Bhaṭṭa says that according to the modern Naiyāyikas the relation between the verbal activity and the *kārakas* cannot be determined by the logical definition of the different *kārakas*, but is decided according to the nature of verbal activity and the context. Therefore, in some cases the secondary function comes into play to convey the accurate sense of the case terminations when the general sense of the case termination is abstracted. By contrast, the Grammarians and the ancient Naiyāyikas think that the *kārakas* are rational and syntactic categories, and they have somewhat precise and consistent meanings in the majority of the cases.

Section 4: Nominal Meanings (*Nāmārthanirṇaya*)[5]

(*B*117) verse 25. First Koṇḍa Bhaṭṭa enumerates five different views concerning nominal meanings. They can refer to (1) a generic property (alone) or an individual alone; (2) a generic property and an individual; (3) a generic property, an individual, and gender; (4) a generic property, an individual, gender, and number; or (5) a generic property, an individual, gender, number, and a *kāraka*. The following passages elaborate these views.

(*B*117–120). The first view (*jātivāda*) claims that a generic property alone is the primary meaning of nominal stems. This view was first propagated by the pre-Kātyāyana Grammarian Vājapyāyana and was later upheld by the Bhāṭṭa Mīmāṃsakas.

According to the Bhāṭṭa Mīmāṃsakas, a generic property is cognized first, before an individual is cognized. Therefore, in the *jātivāda* the generic property alone is the primary meaning, and all the individuals possessing that generic property are regarded as secondary meanings. The individuals are infinite, and it would be practically impossible to grasp the relation of a word with each individual (*ānantya*). If a word denotes a specific individual (*X*) it would fail to convey many other individuals (other than *X*, that is, *vyabhicāra*). But in communication the individual object implied by the generic property is construed with an action in sentences such as "bring a bull." Thus the primary meaning of a word is only a generic property, and the individual object is conveyed by implication (*ākṣepa*), secondary function (*lakṣaṇā*), inference (*anumāna*), or presumption (*arthāpatti*).

(*B*118–120). Next Koṇḍa Bhaṭṭa discusses the view that the primary meaning of a nominal stem is only an individual (*vyaktivāda*). This view is first proposed by Vyāḍi, a pre-Kātyāyana Grammarian, and followed later by some of the Navya-Nyāya school. According to this view, the specific individual is the primary meaning, and other individuals are indirect meanings through generic property. The undenoted generic property as an indicator (*upalakṣaṇa*) is accepted as the limiter of primary meaning, which explains the cognition of all individuals. The generic properties do not belong to the denotative area, yet their ontological existence helps us in cognizing all individuals belonging to a class. Koṇḍa Bhaṭṭa (following Gaṅgeśa) criticizes the Prābhākara Mīmāṃsakas' view that the primary function conveys reference to the individual objects. His argument is that the simultaneous operation of both of the functions, namely, primary and secondary, to convey the sense of generic property and the individual is regarded as a fault. The argument of infinity (*ānantya*) and deviation (*vyabhicāra*) launched against *vyaktivāda* can equally be launched against *jātivāda*. The reason is that, according to *jātivāda*, the individual is cognized through the secondary function of words, and consequently we are forced to accept an infinite number of secondary functions corresponding to the infinite number of individuals. Usage shows that the individual objects are primary denotations of words because actions are not seen to be related to generic properties.

(*B*120–121). The second view is *jātiviśiṣṭavyaktivāda*. According to this view an individual qualified by the generic property is the meaning of a word, and both of these meanings figure in the meaning cognition. This view is presented in two versions. First, according to the Naiyāyikas' version, a cognition of a word's primary function produces the cognition of an individual qualified by the generic property. Therefore, it is necessary that the primary function of a word be grasped with respect to an individual qualified by a generic property, not just with respect to a generic property alone. The primary function bound with respect to a generic property will never cause a cognition of an individual qualified by a generic property.

Second, according to the Prābhākaras' version, the primary function of a word is grasped with respect to a generic property alone. The cognition of the primary meaning with respect to the generic property produces the verbal cognition of an individual qualified by the generic property. According to this view, the generic property is cognized from a word at first, but it can in turn produce the verbal cognition of an individual qualified by a generic property. The Prābhākara Mīmāṃsakas do not accept that the denotative function of words causes the cognition in respect of the individual. The individual is cognized just by its inseparable existence (*svarūpasat*). The denotative function is the direct cause of cognition of the universal. The individual is grasped by its inseparable relation with the generic property.

(*B*121–122). The third view proposes that the primary meaning of a nominal stem includes gender as well as a generic property and an individual. Koṇḍa Bhaṭṭa also offers a number of views on the nature of gender.

(1) *Arthadharma*: the gender is a property of objects signified by words. According to this, the naturalist view, the linguistic gender is an expression of physical sex (*laukikaliṅga*). One who has breasts and long hair is a woman. One who has hair on the body is a man. That which has neither is neuter. The primary function of words is grasped with respect to physical sex distinctions. The primary function of words like *kumāra*, "boy,", *chāga* "goat," *brāhmaṇa*, "brahmin," is grasped with respect to the technical masculine gender qualified by the physical sex. Here the physical sex is also the primary meaning of words. While actually inanimate objects do not have any sex genders, this naturalist view assumes superimposition of physical sex on inanimate objects to explain gender distinctions in the words that stand for inanimate objects. The masculine gender of the word *dārāḥ*, which signifies the female sex, is explained by superimposing the masculine nature on the

object. This explanation, in reality, amounts to saying that words have no relation to physical sex.

(*B*122–123). (2) *Śabdadharma*: this view maintains that the gender is a property of words and not of objects signified by word. This view can be further divided into two views: that gender as a property of words is of metaphysical nature; and that the gender of words is of purely formal linguistic nature.

Koṇḍa Bhaṭṭa states Patañjali's philosophical conception of gender. Objects are composed of three elements: *sattva*, *rajas*, and *tamas*. The masculine object represents an increase of these elements, the feminine objects a decrease of these elements, the neuter gender merely represents the existence of these elements. But the proportion of these elements is constantly changing. Therefore, the objects of the world are never stable. The activities of increase and decrease of constituent elements are common to all objects, so the gender of the objects depends on the intention of the speaker. If the speaker intends to represent increase then he uses the word in masculine gender; decrease, in feminine gender; neither decrease nor increase, in neuter gender. The speaker decides the gender, and gender is considered to be located in words (*śabdadharma*).

Finally, Koṇḍa Bhaṭṭa says that there is nothing wrong in holding that the gender of words has no necessary connection with physical sex. Masculine and feminine words are used to signify members of the opposite sex or objects with no physical sex. For instance, the masculine gender signified by the word *dārāḥ* does not necessarily imply the physical sex of the object.

(*B*125). According to the fourth and fifth views, gender, number, and *kārakas* are also signified by the case suffixes on the basis of agreement (*anvaya*) and difference (*vyatireka*). For instance, when the case suffix is dropped, the nominal stem itself signifies *kāraka*, gender, and number. In *dadhi paśya*, "look at the curds," where the accusative singular suffix *-am* is deleted, the nominal stem *dadhi* itself denotes all of the nominal meanings, including the *karma kāraka*. The neuter gender is also the meaning of the *prātipadika* because lexical (*liṅgānuśāsana*) texts ascribe the meaning gender also to the nominal stem.

(*B*125–128). In certain cases the nominal stem signifies the sixth element, namely, the phonetic form of the word (*svarūpa*). The word *iti* in Sanskrit indicates that a word stands for its own form. Without the use of the word *iti*, sometimes words also stand for their own form. In normal usage, a word signifies its meaning as qualified by its own word form, while normally in grammar a word signifies its own form as qualified by its meaning. In normal usage a word with *iti* signifies the word form as qualified by its meaning, while in grammar a word with *iti* signifies its meaning as qualified by its word form.

(*B*130–132). With regard to a word form signified, Sanskrit Grammarians employ two terms: *anukārya*, "imitated word," and *anukaraṇa*, "imitation word." Again *anukaraṇa* is of two types: it may be of inarticulate sounds (*avyakta*) or of articulate sound (*vyakta*). The imitation word *paṭat* is an onomatopoetic imitation of inarticulate physical sound. By contrast, in the sentence "gauḥ iti ayam āha" ("he said the word gauḥ"), the expression gauḥ is imitation of the word *gauḥ* that occurs in such sentences as *gauḥ tiṣṭhati*, "a bull stands." The imitated word *gauḥ* signifies a bull, while the imitation word signifies a word form.

Then Koṇḍa Bhaṭṭa discusses the question of identity and difference between the imitation word and the imitated word. He states that according to Grammarians the imitation word and the imitated word are identical because their phonetic shapes are not different. Difference in signification does not differentiate words.

As a general rule, imitation words are not meaningful words, and they are not nominal stems (*prātipadika*). But Pāṇini uses inflectional suffixes after meaningless imitation words for metalinguistic purposes. The phonetic form of a word may form part of verbal cognition, but it is not considered to be the meaning of a word. Thus a word signifies its phonetic form, and yet it is not regarded as a meaningful item. According to the Grammarians the imitated word and the imitation words are identical as far as the phonetic forms are concerned.

Section 5: The Meaning of Compounds (*Samāsārthanirṇaya*)

(*B*134) verse 28. Koṇḍa Bhaṭṭa gives a sixfold classification of compounds on the basis of the morphological structure of constituents without involving the primary and subordinate status of their meanings:

(1) *Supāṃ supā*, "combination of case-inflected words before entering into compounding," for instance *rājapuruṣa*, "a king man," which is derived from two case-inflected words, *rājñaḥ puruṣaḥ*.

(2) *Supāṃ tiṅā*, "combination of case-inflected words with a verb form," for instance, *paryabhūṣat*, "he attended to," *anuvyacalat*, "he moved subsequently." This combination consists of the preverb as the first member and the verb as the second member. These forms become single finished words by compounding.

(3) *Supāṃ nāmnā*, "combination of case-inflected word with a nominal stem (*kṛdanta*)," for instance, *kumbhakāra*, "pot maker." Here the case-inflected word *kumbham* is compounded with the *kṛdanta* noun *kāra* before the case ending has been added to it. This compound is called the *upapadasamāsa*.

(4) *Supāṃ dhātunā*, "combination of case-inflected word with a verbal base," for instance, *āyatastūḥ*, "a panegyrist." Here the case-inflected word *āyatam* is compounded with a verbal base *stu*.

(5) *Tiṅān tiṅā*, "a combination of two finite forms," for instance, *khādatamodatā*, "eat and rejoice" (continual eating and rejoicing). Here two finite verb forms *khādata* and *modata* are compounded.

(6) *Tiṅāṃ supā*, "a combination of a finite verb form with a case-inflected word," which consists of the verb as the first member and the case inflected word as the second member, for instance, *jahistambaḥ*, constantly striking against the post."

(*B*134–135) verses 29–30. According to Pāṇini, four broad categories of compounds are *avyayībhāva*, *tatpuruṣa* (with subdivisions *vibhaktitatpuruṣa*, *karmadhāraya*, and *dvigu*), *dvandva* (with subdivisions *samāhāradvandva* and *itaretarayogadvandva*), and *bahuvrīhi*. This fourfold classification cannot cover all cases of compounds. For instance, *bhūtapūrva*, *iva*-compounds, *ayatastū*, and more do not come under any one of these categories.

Patañjali has defined these terms semantically. The *avyayībhāva* is a compound in which the meaning of the first member is predominant. The *tatpuruṣa* is a compound in which the last member is predominant. The *bahuvrīhi* is a compound in which the meaning of another word is predominant. Koṇḍa Bhaṭṭa says that these semantic definitions work in the majority of cases, but not everywhere. For instance, in an *avyayībhāva* compound such as *sūpaprati*, "a small quantity of soup," the meaning of the second member is predominant. In the *avyayībhāva* compound *unmattagaṅgam*, "the country where the Ganges flows impetuously," the additional meaning stands predominant. In the *tatpuruṣa* compound *ardhapippali*, "the half of a pepper," the first member stands predominant.

(*B*135–140). First Koṇḍa Bhaṭṭa states Patañjali's views on compound formation. Kātyāyana and Patañjali maintain that compound forms denote a single (integrated) meaning (*ekārthībhāva*). That is to say, meanings of the compound's constituents are not presented separately, but they present their meanings as inseparably fused together.

Then Kātyāyana and Patañjali state another view, namely, *parasparavyapekṣā*, mutual dependency, according to which the constituents of compounds present their meaning separately. This view maintains that the constituents of a compound present their meaning the same way that the constituents of the uncompounded word group present their meaning. So *rājapuruṣaḥ* and *rajñaḥ puruṣaḥ* are syntactically equivalents.

(*B*140–142). Patañjali (under *vārttika* 11 on Pāṇini 2.1.1) mentions the *nityapakṣa* view: there is no need to formulate grammatical rules to explain the meaning of compounds, for compounds are not generated by grammatical rules. In this view a compound is a single word standing for a single meaning (*ekārthībhāva*). There cannot be mutual dependency (*vyapekṣā*) because the constituents of a compound do not present their meanings separately.

The *kāryaśabdavāda* differs from the *nityapakṣavāda* in the explanation of the *ekārthībhāvapakṣa* view. According to this view the compounds and the corresponding word groups are derived according to the rules of grammar, and the underlying syntactic structures of a compound and the corresponding word group are identical. The unified sense of a compound is not intrinsic (*svābhāvika*), rather it is the result of applying grammatical rules. The *kāryaśabdavāda* uses the term *vṛtti*, "complex formation," to explain how the compound is formed from the corresponding word group. *Vṛtti* means integration, which gives rise to the additional meaning.

(*B*135–142). But when the constituents are connected, what happens to the meaning of constituents? Patañjali mentions two theories: *jahatsvārtha vṛtti*, integration with loss of meanings of constituents, and *ajahatsvārtha vṛtti*, integration without abandoning the meaning of constituents.

According to the first view the constituents of a compound give up their own meaning. A compound as a whole conveys an integrated meaning, and in conveying that meaning the constituents have no separate function from the whole. It does not mean that constituents lose their meaning completely. Still, in a compounding, the meanings of the constituents are either related to each other (*saṃsarga*) or differentiated from each other (*bheda*) or both related and differentiated (*ubhaya*). For instance, in the compound *rājapuruṣa* the meanings, king and servant, are related to each other (*saṃsarga*), excluding the servant, which is not related to a king (*bheda*). *Bheda* and *saṃsarga*, which are responsible for the syntax in the sentence, are also responsible for compounds.

According to the second view the first constituent retains its meaning as a qualificant to the meaning of the main member but does not independently denote its meaning.

These two views have a place in the *nityapakṣa* and the *kāryapakṣa* too to explain the role of the constituent meaning in the meaning of a compound. Koṇḍa Bhaṭṭa refers to the several opinions stated in the *Mahābhāṣya* and then makes his own comments on their outcomes.

(*B*142–145). Koṇḍa Bhaṭṭa states first Kaiyaṭa's view. Kaiyaṭa summarizes the whole discussion of the *Mahābhāṣya* into three different views. First, the compound as a whole denotes a single indivisible meaning. The compound and the corresponding word group belong to two different domains. In the uncompounded word group, meanings are separately presented. This view of *ekārthībhāva* has been propagated by the *nityapakṣavādin*, who says that we do not require the grammatical rules to explain the specialized compound meaning. A compound is not to be derived; it is a natural element of language.

The second view says that a compound is derived from the corresponding uncompounded word group. For the formation of a compound, mutual dependence of the constituents is required. But the derived compound conveys a single integrated meaning. The generation of compounds from the uncompounded word group is the view propagated by the *kāryaśabdavādin*. In the *kāryapakṣa* there are two theories, namely, *iahatsvārtha* and *ajahatsvārtha*, which decide the meaning of compounds. According to this second view the compound constituents give up their own meaning and assume one undivided meaning (*jahatsvārtha*).

The third view is that the compound and the corresponding uncompounded word group are syntactically and semantically equivalent. In both compound and uncompounded word group the constituents are mutually dependent. This view has been adopted by the *kāryaśabdavādin*, and it adopts the *ajahatsvārthapakṣa*.

Next Koṇḍa Bhaṭṭa refers to Haradatta's theory. According to him *ekārthībhāva* implies that the principal member denotes its meaning as qualified by the meaning of the subordinate member, and the subordinate member denotes its meaning in a qualifying function, not as an independently signifying something. If the constituents of the compound are independently denotative of their meaning, the subordinate member could form a connection with the word lying outside of the compound.

Haradatta says that for compound formation mutual dependence is also equally necessary. Otherwise the compound could have been formed out of constituents semantically unrelated. He also makes the point that the *jahatsvārtha vṛtti* has no place in compound formation, because the constituents are related to each other without abandoning their meaning. If we assume that the constituents lose their meaning completely we will have to assign a special denotative function to the compound as a whole, which becomes a separate lexical item. But the assumption of such a denotative function is unnecessary because the compound's meaning can be derived from the constituent's meaning itself. Thus, Koṇḍa Bhaṭṭa remarks, according to Haradatta *ekārthībhāva*, *vyapekṣā*, and *ajahatsvārtha vṛtti* are all necessary conditions for forming a compound.

Koṇḍa Bhaṭṭa disagrees with Kaiyaṭa and Haradatta and maintains that the whole discussion of Patañjali can be reduced to two points, namely, *jahatsvārtha* and *ajahatsvārtha*, which correspond to *ekārthībhāva* and *vyapekṣā*, respectively. According to the *jahatsvārtha* view, when integration takes place the members of the compound do not express their meaning separately. Therefore, a compound as a whole denotes its meaning; for the denotation of single integrated meaning we have to assign an aggregate denotative function (*samudayaśakti*) to the compound form as a whole. According to the *vyapekṣā* view the meaning of the constituents are presented separately, and syntactic connection between them is denoted by the morphemic elements. So the *vyapekṣā* view is reduced to the *ajahatsvārtha* view, according to which constituents retain their meaning.

Koṇḍa Bhaṭṭa criticizes Kaiyaṭa's claim that according to Kaiyaṭa, in the *nityapakṣa* view *ekārthībhāva* amounts to indivisibility of the meaning of compound. But to Koṇḍa Bhaṭṭa this goes against the logical interpretation of the *Bhāṣya*. According to Patañjali, *samartha* means emergence of a single integrated meaning of constituents that present their meaning separately in the uncompounded word group. Kaiyaṭa's interpretation of the *nityaśabdavāda*, which totally denies the relation between the constituent meanings and the compound as a whole, is not correct. If the *ekārthībhāva* claims that the compound is indivisible and the constituents in a compound do not have any meaning at all, then one could also extend this theory to the sentence and deny meaning to the constituents of the sentence, which would mean that the undivided sentence conveys undivided meaning. But this extended theory goes against the intention of Patañjali, who maintains the mutual dependence (*vyapekṣā*) of the constituents in a sentence.

(*B*145–156). Similarly, Haradatta's statement is also subject to criticism. Haradatta says that both *vyapekṣā* and *ekārthībhāva* are the necessary conditions for the formation of compounds. But this claim also goes against the intention of Patañjali, who, according to Kaiyaṭa, maintains that single integrated meaning (*ekārthībhāva*) exists in a compound and that mutual dependence (*vyapekṣā*) exists in a sentence. It is also incorrect to consider that the *jahatsvārtha* view has no place in a compound formation. Patañjali himself shows at length that in the *jahatsvārtha* view the subordinate member of the compound does not lose its meaning completely. The *jahatsvārtha* view is also necessary to explain the relation between the constituent meanings and the meaning of the compound as a whole.

Of these two views, *ekārthībhāva* and *vyapekṣā*, the first one implies according to Koṇḍa Bhaṭṭa that a compound, as a whole, denotes one single meaning and has a separate denotative function (*samudayaśakti*) through which it gives rise to the single meaning. The second view, however, states that each word in a compound has a separate denotative function, and a compound as a whole has no separate denotative function. Of these two views Bhaṭṭoji, the author of the verse text, and Koṇḍa Bhaṭṭa maintain that the *ekārthībhāva* is the only correct view. Just as in the case of the word *paṅkaja* its etymological meaning (growing in the mud) cannot explain the conventional meaning *lotus*, so it is assumed that a word as a whole denotes the conventional meaning. Similarly, the compound as a whole has the separate denotative function.

(*B*153). Moreover, the *ekārthībhāva* view has been adopted because the other view involves complexities (*gaurava*). It is necessary to formulate rules to account for the following special features of a compound: absence of inflectional suffixes after the constituent members of a compound; inseparability of the members of a compound by other words; the fixed order of the constituents; possession of a single accent; ambiguity as regards the number of the subordinate member; ambiguity as regards the syntactic relation between the compound members; inability to construe the subordinate word with a word outside the compound; absence of words such as *ca*, "and," to indicate conjunction and other connections; the statement of option between compound and uncompounded word group.

(*B*153–157). In the following compounds—*niṣkauśāmbiḥ*, "departed from Kauśāmbi (departed from)," *gorathaḥ*," a chariot to which oxen have been yoked (to which have been yoked)," *ghṛtaghaṭaḥ*," a pot filled with *ghee* (*pūrṇa*, 'filled with')," *guḍadhānāḥ*, "crisps made of barley mixed with brown sugar (mixed with)," *suvarṇālaṃkāraḥ*, "gold produced ornament (produced)," *dvidaśa* "two times ten (times)," and *saptaparṇaḥ*, "a tree having clusters of seven leaves"—(at each point), we understand the additional meanings not conveyed by constituents, namely, *krānta* (departed from), *yukta* (yoked), *pūrṇa* (filled), *miśra* (mixed), *vikāra* (product), *saṃkhyā* (counting), *vīpsā* (distribution). In the *vyapekṣā* view every meaning element should occur in the analytical paraphrase. Therefore, the lexical items such as *krānta*, *pūrṇa*, and so on, should be supplied in the constituent analysis, which are subsequently to be deleted. For the deletion of these elements we will have to phrase new rules. But according to the *ekārthībhāva* view as explained by Koṇḍa Bhaṭṭa there is no question of deriving compounds from the uncompounded word groups to account for these meanings, for the compounds and the corresponding uncompounded word groups may differ a great deal as far as meaning is concerned. The compound as a whole conveys the specialized meaning, and we do not require special rules. Thus there is an advantage in adopting the *ekārthībhāva* view.

In other words, Koṇḍa Bhaṭṭa recognizes a separate denotative function for the compounds that is called *samudayaśakti*, aggregate denotative function, apart from that of constituents. He argues that the compound should be assigned a distinct function because it conveys a meaning that supersedes the meaning denoted by constituents. For instance, the *bahuvrīhi* compound *citragu* does not mean a brindle cow, which is the meaning of the constituents, but refers to a person who owns brindled cows. Similarly the compound *pāṇipādam* does not mean "hands, feet" but rather an aggregation of hands and feet. Many meanings like *krānta* (departed from), *pūrṇa* (filled with), and others are denoted by the compound as a whole but not by its constituents. Further, in the case of unanalyzed compounds (*nityasamāsa*) a formally corresponding compounded word group is lacking. In such cases the meaning of a compound is determined by the compound form as a whole and not by the constituents themselves.

(*B*157, 168–170). The Naiyāyikas and the Mīmāṃsakas hold that a compound is formed of its constituents, and the meanings of the constituents give rise to the qualified meaning denoted by the compound. They do not accept that there is a necessity to assign a separate denotative function (*samudayaśakti*) to a compound as a whole. Both the Naiyāyikas and the Mīmāṃsakas accept only mutual dependence (*vyapekṣā*), not any *vṛtti* or *ekārthībhāva*, in a compound. Both the Naiyāyikas and the Mīmāṃsakas resort to secondary meaning (*lakṣaṇā*) to explain any additional meaning that is denoted by the compound over and above the constituent meanings. For instance, in *rājapuruṣaḥ* the constituent *rājan* signifies the sense of relation by the secondary function along with its lexical meaning. In the case of *karmadhāraya*, *lakṣaṇā* need not be resorted to; rather, the constituents themselves can convey qualified sense. In the case of *bahuvrīhi*, the Naiyāyikas adopt the *padalakṣaṇā* while the Mīmāṃsakas adopt the *vākyalakṣaṇā*. So all these differences between a compound and corresponding uncompounded word groups, which are due to *ekārthībhāva* according to the Grammarians, are explained as caused by the *nirūḍha lakṣaṇā* or "conventional function."

(*B*182–183). Kumārila observes that denotative function assigned to the *bahuvrīhi* as a whole conveys *anyapadārtha*, denotation of the meaning of another word. In a *bahuvrīhi* the constituents express their own meaning but not *anyapadārtha*. The sense *anyapadārtha* cannot be brought out by the primary or secondary function of words because the primary meanings of the constituents are not given up at all. The reason is that the reference to a meaning other than what is denoted by the compound's constituents is understood only when the outside word is used along with the *bahuvrīhi* compound. Therefore, the *anyapadārtha* is the denoted meaning of a compound. The Mīmāṃsakas observe that the *anyapadārtha* is conveyed by the *nirūḍha lakṣaṇā* through the primary meanings of the compound's constituents. In *bahuvrīhi* the Mīmāṃsakas postulate the *vākyalakṣaṇā*, where the *vākya* means a phrase as a whole. The semantic connection exists between *citraguḥ* (and) *devadattaḥ*, "brindled cow (owner) Devadatta." The question is how this meaning "owner" is arrived at; the answer, according to the later Mīmāṃsakas, is that this meaning "owner" is conveyed by the secondary function belonging to a sentence.

(*B*176–177). But, according to the Naiyāyikas, either the word *citra* or the word *go* conveys the additional meaning, in other words, reference to the *anyapadārtha*. But this view is untenable because the first member, *citra*, cannot be indicative of the meaning "the owner of the brindled cows." Consequently, *go* cannot be connected with *citra*. The reason is that *citra* does not refer to the meaning "brindled" any longer. Similarly, it is wrong to say that the word *go* indicates the sense of *gosvāmin*, owner of the cows, because in that case *citra* no longer forms connection with *go*. We cannot say either that both of the *padas* together convey the sense "owner of the brindled cows," for even then it will be impossible to bring out the proper sense of the *bahuvrīhis* like *prāptodako grāmaḥ*, "water-reached village." In the analysis "prāptam udakaṃ yam," *udaka*, "water" is the agent and the village is the object of the action of reaching. In *prāpta* the suffix *kta* has been added in the sense of agent. The sentence denotes primarily the agent of the action of reaching, while the compound denotes primarily the object of the action of reaching. Here reference to the object (the village) by a compound form cannot be explained by the secondary function (*lakṣaṇā*) because the constituents in the sentence stand in the syntactic agreement water, the agent of the action of reaching. If the secondary function indicates the sense of object (village), then the compound would mean the water, identical with the object of reaching. But this meaning is not the one intended by the compound. The other word, *udaka*, also cannot imply the sense of *karman* because the compound's meaning cannot be judged without the proper understanding of the first member. To avoid all of these difficulties, Koṇḍa Bhaṭṭa advocates the aggregate denotative function on the basis of practical experience that a compound is one word. He puts forth the view that the compound meaning is understood even by children without knowing the grammatical or constitutional analysis of compounds.

(*B*157–158). The Naiyāyikas also advocate that the indeclinables in compounds are secondarily indicative (*lakṣaṇā*) of the sense of proximity and so on, as in *upakumbham*, "in the vicinity of a jar." The sense of nearness is not included in the meaning of the second member of the compound. Therefore, it is held to be implied by the second member. Koṇḍa Bhaṭṭa argues that the indeclinables are suggestive (*dyotaka*) of the sense "nearness," or whatever, but the sense of the compound as a whole, namely, "near a jar," is denoted by the aggregate power of the compound.

(*B*137, 151). Kātyāyana proposes the view *yugapadadhikaraṇavacanatā* for the formation of *dvandva* compounds. According to this view, each item in a *dvandva* compound, just as in the case of *ekaśeṣa*, represents the meaning of the other item simultaneously. The *ekaśeṣa* and *dvandva* items are not singly represented but always together with another item or other items. In the case of *dvandva* and *ekaśeṣa*, we find joint representation of items.

But Patañjali rejects the view of joint representation and states that in a *dvandva* the items are separately presented and that meaning of conjunction comes from integration only. The joint representation of items in a *dvandva* or *ekaśeṣa* is a result of *ekārthībhāva* (integration) only.

Koṇḍa Bhaṭṭa remarks that this view of simultaneous representation is formulated by the *vyapekṣāvādins*, who maintain that constituent meanings are separately represented. This view (*yugapadadhikaraṇavacanatā*) is especially necessary to maintain the joint representation of the two items in the constituent analysis. But this simultaneous representation, according to Koṇḍa Bhaṭṭa, cannot exist in the constituent analysis, because dual or plural is not added to each constituent in the analytical paraphrase. We have instances like *dyāvāpṛthivī* in which items are separately represented in the dual. But these instances are Vedic usages, which are exceptions to the general rules. According to the theory of *samudayaśakti* or *ekārthībhāva*, a *dvandva* compound is a single word denoting an aggregate of several individuals.

(*B*158). In the case of *dvandva* the Naiyāyikas accept *yugapadadhikaraṇavacanatā* in a different sense. They argue that there is a syntactic relation between the primary sense of the constituents and the dual number added to a compound. If each constituent is related to a dual, then the compound *dhavakhadirau* would mean two *dhavas* and two *khadiras*. Therefore, to justify the dual number we must assume that the first constituent denotes association (*sāhitya*). Because this sense of association is not conveyed by the primary function of the constituents, the Naiyāyikas resort to secondary meaning to convey *sāhitya*, which indicates the joint representation of two objects, while number, dual or plural, represents the objects that have been associated. The sense association indicated by the first member in compounds like *dhavakhadirau* does not mean two *dhavas*. It (*dhava*) does not mean *dhava* and *khadira* either, because *dhava* cannot mean *khadira*. The sense association or simultaneous representation is only through secondary meaning.

According to Koṇḍa Bhaṭṭa, the aggregate denotative function expresses the meaning of *dvandva* as in the case of other compounds. In the *itaretarayoga*, the aggregate denotative function expresses the items that are grouped together, which justifies reference to two or more items. In the case of *samāhāra* (group of items), the *samudayaśakti* (aggregate denotative function) denotes the aggregation or group, which justifies the singular number.

(*B*161). The Naiyāyikas and the Mīmāṃsakas do not accept a separate denotative function with regard to a compound as a whole. The Grammarians argue that if an aggregate denotative function is not assigned to a compound as a whole, the compound form cannot be called a nominal stem (*prātipadika*) by Pāṇini 1.2.45, because the basic condition for the designation *prātipadika* is meaningfulness. We cannot apply the designation *prātipadika* by the next rule, Pāṇini 1.2.46, because the word *samāsa* in that rule is restrictive. The *sūtra* means that if the designation *prātipadika* is to be applied to a collection of words having a sense it must be restricted to a compound. It is not to be applied to a sentence.

Moreover, if the compound as a whole has no denotative function it cannot have a secondary meaning, which is based on the denotative function (*abhidhā* or *śakti*) of words.

(*B*174–175, 177). The Mīmāṃsakas hold that a genitive compound like *rājapuruṣa* must be analyzed as "rājā cāsau puruṣaś ca" and not as "rājñaḥ puruṣaḥ." The first analysis indicates that the relation of qualified and qualifier is dependent on the mutual expectancy of constituents and not on the case endings added to them. In the case of the genitive *tatpuruṣa* compounds, the sense of relation, namely, "servant and master," is to be conveyed by the genitive suffix. But the compound *rājapuruṣaḥ* does not refer to the relation between the two related; rather, *rājan* in *rājapuruṣaḥ* denotes the meaning of *puruṣa* in the sense that *rājan* becomes a qualifier to *puruṣa*. The constituent analysis must convey the meaning of the compound. The constituent analysis "rājā cāsau puruṣaś ca" can convey the qualifier and qualified relation (*abheda*), but the analysis "rājñaḥ puruṣaḥ" fails to point it out. Therefore, "rājā cāsau puruṣaś ca" is a proper analysis. Similarly, the *bahuvrīhi* compound *citraguḥ* must be analyzed as "citrāṇāṃ gavām ayam" ("he, the owner of the brindled cows") and not as "citrā gāvo yasya" ("possessed of brindled cows"). In the case of *bahuvrīhi* compounds, the constituent analysis must be such as can convey reference to the *anyapadārtha*. If we assume the analysis "citrānāṃ gavām ayam," it can point out reference to the *anyapadārtha*. But the constituent analysis "citrā gavo yasya" primarily refers to the *svapadārtha* "constituents' own meaning."

(*B*180–181, 186). Later Mīmāṃsakas do not accept the aggregate denotative function of the whole compound or secondary meaning in the case of a *karmadhāraya* compound. In *nīlaghaṭa*, "a blue jar," the words *nīla* and "*ghaṭa*" are in apposition, and their coreferentiality is brought out by merely joining the stems *nīla* and *ghaṭa*. But in a *tatpuruṣa* compound like *rājapuruṣaḥ*, "king's man," the servant-master relationship cannot be brought about by mere constituents. The syntactic relationship is dependent on the case ending: in the compound the case ending is not there. Therefore, this relationship is indicated by the secondary function. So in case of doubts, the *karmadhāraya* compound, which does not involve the secondary function, is preferred to the *ṣaṣṭhītatpuruṣa*, which does. Consequently, the word *niṣādasthapati* is taken to mean *niṣādaḥ sthapatiḥ*, a chief who himself is a *niṣāda*, rather than *niṣādānām sthapatiḥ*, a chief of the Niṣāda tribe. But Koṇḍa Bhaṭṭa's standpoint is that the aggregate denotative function belongs to all compounds, and there would be no difference between a *tatpuruṣa* and a *karmadhāraya* compound. Then it would go against the Mīmāṃsā doctrine, which proves that *niṣādasthapatiḥ* must be taken as a *karmadhāraya* compound and not as *ṣaṣṭhītatpuruṣa* for the sake of economy. To avoid this difficulty, Koṇḍa Bhaṭṭa answers that when a compound word denotes various meanings, the speaker's intention (*tātparya*) must be taken to decide the sense of the compound. If we took the compound *niṣādasthapati* in the context of ritual as a genitive *tatpuruṣa* compound, it would go against the interest of the author's statement. Moreover, the true meaning of the compound is determined by its accent.

(*B*183–186). Koṇḍa Bhaṭṭa replies that the constituent analysis and the compound need not be semantically and syntactically equivalents. Therefore, we may find the reversion of the principal and subordinate relation in the meaning indicated by the constituent analysis and compound. Therefore, the analysis "citrā gāvo yasya" for the compound *citraguḥ* and "rājñaḥ puruṣaḥ" for the compound *rājapuruṣaḥ* may not be objectionable.

Even the Mīmāṃsakas assume that productive operation (*bhāvanā*) stands as predominant with respect to the *kārakas* in the case of verbal forms, while in the case of *kṛdanta* words the *kārakas* stand predominant with respect to *bhāvanā*. Therefore, the constituent analysis may not be exactly equivalent to the compound meaning.

Section 6: The Relation Between a Word and Its Meaning (*Śaktinirṇaya*)

(*B*188). The relation of a word with its meaning, according to Koṇḍa Bhaṭṭa, is power (*śakti*) or intrinsic fitness (*yogyatā*). Following Bhartṛhari, Koṇḍa Bhaṭṭa states that semantic fitness (*yogyatā*) is the relation between a word and its meaning. The natural or intrinsic capacity of words to convey any meaning is called *yogyatā*. Just as the organs of perception (*indriya*) have a natural power to perceive objects, so words also have an innate capacity for conveying any meaning. The Grammarians and the Mīmāṃsakas consider this power to be a separate category, while the Naiyāyikas assume that it is based on convention.

(*S*496–497). According to the Naiyāyikas the connection between the words and their meanings is not natural but rather based on convention (*saṃketa*), which is established by God's desire. According to this view language is created by God. The words are capable of conveying a sense because God has so desired. In the case of proper names like Devadatta, however, the desire is that of Devadatta's father. The later Naiyāyikas, however, maintain that this relation need not always be established by the will of God.

(*B*189–190). According to the Mīmāṃsakas the relation between words and their meanings is natural and eternal, not something brought about by convention of human beings. This relation between words and their meanings is without beginning. The Mīmāṃsakas and the Grammarians agree that the natural relationship is understood from the use of the elderly persons. This relation between the words and their meanings cannot be the desire of God because the Mīmāṃsakas and the Buddhists, who do not believe in the existence of God, also understand the meanings of words.

(*B*191). Koṇḍa Bhaṭṭa concludes that the nature of the power (*śakti*) of words is to convey meaning, the signifierness (*bodhakatva*) of the words. The primary function of the word *ghaṭa* ("pot") is its power or capacity to cause a cognition. This power of words is comparable to the power of the organs of sense to cause the cognition of objects. Koṇḍa Bhaṭṭa presents the view of the *Pañcapādikāvivaraṇa* (an Advaita Vedānta text) to support his position.

In addition to power, the Mīmāṃsakas and the Naiyāyikas assume a secondary function of words to convey their extended meaning. Koṇḍa Bhaṭṭa refuses to accept the secondary meaning even though he accepts suggestion (*vyañjanā*) as a separate function to convey emotional overtones attached to words in literary writings. The argument for not accepting secondary meaning is that the power that is *bodhakatva*, the capacity of words to cause cognition of meaning is also the same in the case of extended meanings.

(*B*195–198). The Naiyāyikas maintain that the corrupt forms of words that are current express their meaning indirectly by recalling the correct forms. Kumārila, the Mīmāṃsaka, states that the corrupt words (*mlecchaśabda*) equally convey meaning. But the corrupt forms convey their meaning only through the original correct words, having brought them to our mind, whenever corresponding correct usage is available. The corrupt words that may convey their meaning indirectly cannot be regarded as synonyms for the original correct words. Thus, for instance, when the corrupt word *gāvi* is pronounced, it brings to our mind the correct Sanskrit word *gauḥ*.

The Grammarians do not accept the view of the Naiyāyikas and the Mīmāṃsakas that corrupt words have no denotative power. If corrupt words have no denotative power, they can convey no meaning. It will not be correct to say that incorrect words remind us of correct words and we therefore know the meanings from the incorrect words, because ignorant persons who do not know correct words know the meaning from corrupt words. As far as conveying of meaning is concerned, there is no difference between the correct and corrupt forms. But the main difference is that the use of correct forms leads to spiritual merit, while the use of incorrect forms leads to spiritual demerit. And grammar teaches us the correct forms of words. The words that are derived according to grammatical rules are considered to be correct.

(*B*197). The Grammarians insist that the corrupt forms derived from Sanskrit equally convey meaning. Thus in the case of languages like Marathi derived from Sanskrit, the meaning of words is understood not indirectly through the correct Sanskrit forms.

Following Bhartṛhari, Koṇḍa Bhaṭṭa says that semantic fitness is understood from the usage of elderly persons (*vṛddhavyavahāra*). The denotative potency of words to convey any meaning is intrinsic and beginningless, but the use of elderly persons makes us acquainted with the natural capacity.

Section 7: The Meaning of
the Negative Particle Nañ (*Nañarthanirṇaya*)

(*B*201). According to the first view proposed by Koṇḍa Bhaṭṭa (in connection with the negative *tatpuruṣa* compound), the reference of the compound is determined by the second member. The negative particle *nañ* (*na* or *a* or *an*) suggests the sense of superimposition (*āropitatva*). The function of *nañ* in *abrāhmaṇa* is to convey the secondary sense that the word *abrāhmaṇa* is used with reference to a *kṣatriya*. One superimposes brahminhood on a *kṣatriya*, on account of the fact that the *kṣatriya* shares a number of characteristics with a brahmin. To convey that the word *brāhmaṇa* is used in the sense of *kṣatriya*, the speaker uses *nañ* along with the word *brāhmaṇa*.

If the negative particle stands for absence (*abhāva*), then *abrāhmaṇa* would mean a person not existing as a brahmin, according to which the first member would represent the main meaning. But this view is not correct because it involves various difficulties. In the negative *tatpuruṣa* compound *asaḥ*, "other than he," the second member, *saḥ* (*tat*), will be subordinate. Therefore, it will not be called *sarvanāman*. So we cannot apply the operations prescribed for pronominal stems. The result is that the compound form will be *atad* instead of *asaḥ*. Therefore, this view should be discarded.

(*S*515). There are six meanings in which the negative particle *nañ* (*na* or *a*) is used in compounds: similarity (*sādṛśya*), as in *abrāhmaṇaḥ*, "like a brahmin"; absence (*abhāva*), as in *apāpam*, "absence of sin"; being other than something (*tadanyatvam*, mutual absence), as in *anaśvaḥ*, "other than a horse"; smallness of something (*tadalpatā*), as in *anudarā kanyā*, "a girl with a thin belly"; impropriety or unfitness (*aprāśastya*), as in *apaśavaḥ*, "unfit animals (for sacrifice)"; and contrariety (*virodha*), as in *adharma*, "contrary to *dharma*." Of these six meanings only one is primarily denoted by *nañ*, namely, absence. The rest are secondary to this primary meaning.

(*B*201–202). According to the Naiyāyikas there are two primary meanings of *nañ*, namely, absence, as in *apāpam*, "absence of sin," and mutual absence (*anyonyābhāva*), as in *asaḥ*, "other than he." But according to Koṇḍa Bhaṭṭa the basic meaning of *nañ* is only absence.

(*B*203-204). Patañjali explains that the function of *nañ* is to convey the sense *nivṛttapadārthaka*, namely, bringing the absence of something to our notice. In other words, the function of *nañ* is to convey the absence of something in physical reality. Kaiyaṭa interprets this *Bhāṣya* to mean that a word like *brāhmaṇa* in *abrāhmaṇa* is used in a secondary sense, namely, that of *kṣatriya*, upon whom brahminhood has been superimposed. The function of *nañ* in *abrāhmaṇa* is only to bring to our notice that *brāhmaṇa* is used in the secondary sense.

Koṇḍa Bhaṭṭa criticizes Kaiyaṭa's view. In instances like *ghaṭo nāsti*, "there is no jar," and *abrāhmaṇa*, "(he is) not a brahmin," the particle (*nañ*) does not have two different meanings of absence and superimposition (*āropitatva*). Rather, in both of these cases *nañ* denotes the sense *nivṛttapadārthaka*, which implies that *nañ* brings to our notice the fact that something is absent. In other words, according to Patañjali *nañ* denotes absence. He further argues that if superimposition were the meaning of *nañ*, as Kaiyaṭa thinks, then *nañ* would also denote the sense of similarity (*sādṛśya*). In that case there would be six different denotations, as stated earlier. This position involves complexity.

The negative particle *nañ* expressing absence may be sometimes subject or qualificand (*viśeṣya*) and sometimes adjunct or qualifier (*viśeṣaṇa*). In the forms *asaḥ*, "other than he," *atvam bhavasi*, "(somebody) other than you become," or *anekam*, "more than one," the second member is principal. That explains the pronominal operations, the number, and the person, which are determined by the predominance of the second member. Thus the view of the meaning predominance of the second member (*uttarapadārthaprādhānya*) explains these examples. But according to the other view, the particle *nañ* denotes "absence," which stands as a qualificand, so the meaning of *nañ* is the main meaning. In the aforementioned special cases the predominance of the second member is retained by resorting to secondary meaning, which conveys the sense of difference or mutual absence. In such cases the negative particle denies the relation of identity in the form of denying reference to the meaning of the second member.

Section 8: The Meanings of Preverbs and Particles (*Nipātārthanirṇaya*)

(*B*205). Grammarians and Naiyāyikas do not agree with each other about the nature of particles (*nipāta*). According to the Naiyāyikas the particles are directly denotative (*vācaka*). Particles belong to the category of independently significant words, but preverbs (*upasarga*) do not. The Grammarians disagree with this view.

(*B*205) verse 41. Koṇḍa Bhaṭṭa following Patañjali and Bhartṛhari, maintains that both preverbs and particles are suggestive (*dyotaka*) and not independently denotative (*vācaka*). Preverbs and particles acquire meaning only in combination with other words. We find contrast in the meaning denoted by *āste*, "he sits," and *upāste*, "he worships," which does not spring from the meaning inherent in the preverb. The presence and absence of *upa* signal this contrast, which is actually inherent in the root meaning. The root *as-* does not convey by itself the transitive meaning "to worship." The passive endings are added only to the transitive roots. Therefore, to explain the passive construction *upāsyete hariharau*, "Hari and Hara are worshiped," we have to assume that the root *as-* stands for the meaning "to worship."

(*B*205–206). In some cases the preverbs only enlarge the meaning of roots. For instance, when we say *prajayati*, "he wins well," the meaning of the preverb does not alter the meaning of the root *ji*. Sometimes preverbs determine the specific meaning of the following root. For instance, the root *sthā* denotes the sense to stop the movement. But when it is joined with the preverb *pra* it denotes altogether a different meaning, "to move forward."

For the proper application of a grammatical operation such as augmentation, it is necessary to separate a verbal root from a preverb. For instance, the augment *at* (that is, *a* in forms like *anvabhavat*) is inserted between a verbal root and a preverb. The finite verb form (*abhavat*) is formed first. Subsequently, the preverb is united with the verb to reveal its meaning. In such cases the preverbs are suggestive rather than denotative.

(*B*206) verse 42. Particles (*cādi*), like preverbs (*prādi*), are also suggestive of the meanings of forms to which they are attached. Unless we assume the suggestiveness of particles we cannot explain the passive voice *sākṣātkriyate*, "it is perceived," *alaṃkriyate*, "it is adorned," or *namaskriyate*, "he is saluted." These passive voices could be explained if we assume that the root *kṛ-* denotes the sense of perceiving, adorning, and saluting that make the root *kṛ-* transitive.

(*B*207). The Naiyāyikas make a specific distinction between particles and preverbs. According to them, the particles are directly denotative, but the preverbs are suggestive. Preverbs such as *pra* have independently distinctive meanings of their own when they are disjoined from verbs. The preverbs suggest different meanings in connection with different verbs. Preverbs only disclose one of the several meanings of the verbal root that is to be adopted in a particular case. But particles like *sākṣāt*, "directly," and *namas*, "salutation," denote fixed meaning.

(*B*215) verse 46. The Naiyāyikas maintain that the meaningfulness of particles is established on the basis of agreement (*anvaya*) and difference (*vyatireka*). If we examine the pair *vṛkṣaḥ ca*, "also tree," and *vṛkṣaḥ*, "tree," we find that the particle *ca* reveals the contrast in meaning and expression. When we say *vṛkṣaḥ*, "tree," we do not understand the sense of conjunction (namely, also). Therefore, by the process of agreement and difference it is clear that the particles are denotative.

The Grammarians criticize the view of the Naiyāyikas. According to the Grammarians neither preverbs nor particles are capable of being used independently of other words. For instance, we do not use the phrase *bhūyān pra*, "greater excellence," the way we use the phrase *bhūyān prakarṣaḥ*, "greater excellence." Similarly, we do not use the phrase *śobhanaś ca*, "beautiful collection," the way we use the phrase *śobhanaḥ samuccayaḥ*, "beautiful collection."

(*B*08–209) verse 43. Koṇḍa Bhaṭṭa further points out that the meaning of particles never stands in appositional relation with another nominal stem meaning. Take the instance *ghaṭaś ca*, "and jar." The meaning conjunction (namely, and) does not stand in appositional relation with the meaning "jar." But the semantic rule is that two nominal stem meanings are related to each other appositionally. No one understands, however, that the meaning "conjunction" stands in appositional relation with the meaning "jar." To remove this difficulty the Naiyāyikas have to make a special provision that the aforementioned semantic rule does not apply to the particles. The Grammarians do not have this difficulty. The particle *ca*, according to the Grammarians, does not convey the sense of conjunction independently. It only functions as the suggester of meaning. Therefore, "conjunction" is not regarded as nominal-stem-meaning (*nāmārtha*).

(*B*209–210) verse 44. In addition, Koṇḍa Bhaṭṭa points out that if the particles are directly denotative of meaning we will have to assume the discontinuousness of meaningful elements. To illustrate this point he presents the phrase "usraiḥ iva śaraiḥ," ("by rays, similar, by arrows"). The phrase actually means: by rays (that are) like arrows. The phrase consists of the following meaningful elements: *usra* (ray), *-ais* (by), *iva* (similar), *śara* (arrows), *-ais* (by). The instrumental ending *ais* added to the word *usra* does not convey the instrumentality of *usra* alone, rather that of *usra*+*iva* (by rays like). This sense is, however, not allowed by the grammatical theory, which insists that the case termination *ais* must be construed with the stem *usra*. One should not disturb the inseparable relation that exists between the stem and the suffix. Therefore, the analysis *usra*+*iva*+*bhis* (rays like by) goes against the principle of word formation. To avoid this difficulty, the Grammarians maintain that the base *usra* denotes the sense *usrasadṛśa* (rays like). The following particle *iva* does not denote independently the meaning "similar," it only discloses the meaning of *usra*, "rays like," which is to be adopted in this particular context. Because in the phrase *usraiḥ iva*, the stem *usra* denotes the sense *usrasadṛśa*, "rays like," the meaning of the instrumental case ending "by" can be easily connected with it.

But according to the Naiyāyikas, the particle *iva* denotes the sense "similar." Therefore, to maintain the meaningful relation between the constituents of the phrase *usraiḥ iva* the Naiyāyikas will have to assume the construction *usra* (rays), *iva* (similar), *ais* (by). This construction violates the principle that the case endings must be construed with the stems.

(*B*210–211) verse 45. An objection is raised by the Naiyāyikas. If particles are not independently denotative of meaning, then in the *tatpuruṣa* compound formed with the negative particle *nañ*, the first member, *nañ* (that is, *a* in the compounds like *abrāhmaṇa*, "other than a brahmin"), will be meaningless. If the first member is meaningless, the question of the second member's predominance does not arise at all. Consequently, the definition of the *tatpuruṣa* compound (*tatpuruṣa* is a compound in which the meaning of the second member is predominant) will not be applicable. Similarly, particles and preverbs that are not independently meaningful will not be called nominal stems (*prātipadikas*) because the basic condition for the designation *prātipadika* (Pāṇini 1.2.45) is meaningfulness.

The Grammarians answer that particles and preverbs are suggestive of meaning, so they are not totally meaningless. If one takes into account the suggestive nature of particles and preverbs, the designations *tatpuruṣa* and *prātipadika* are applied.

(*B*215–216). Finally, Koṇḍa Bhaṭṭa points out that one should not insist on any one of the two alternatives, suggestiveness or denotativeness. Some preverbs and particles are suggestive and some are denotative. Nonetheless, he disagrees with the Naiyāyikas and the Mīmāṃsakas, who insist that particles are directly expressive, while preverbs are always suggestive of meaning.

Section 9: The Meaning of Suffixes Forming Abstract Nouns (*Bhāvapratyayārthanirṇaya*)

(*B*217). In the case of a compound, a primary derivative (*kṛt*), or a secondary derivative (*taddhita*), the suffixes prescribed in the sense of *bhāva*, or abstract notion, convey a relation excluding the words that have a conventional sense (*rūḍhi*), adjectives (*abhinnarūpa*), and words expressing a relation that is inseparable. (The source of this statement quoted by Koṇḍa Bhaṭṭa is not known. Helārāja also quotes it in his commentary on the *Vākyapadīya*, *kāṇḍa* 3, chapter 5, verse 1.)

(*B*217–218). The addition of abstract suffixes to such compounds as *rājapuruṣa*, "king's servant," denotes the sense of king's relation to a servant, and the expression *aupagavatva*, "cowherd-sonness," expresses the son's relation to the father cowherd. The abstract noun *pācakatva*, "cookness," stands for the actor–action relation.

This rule has three exceptions. The *rūḍha* word *kṛṣṇasarpa* conventionally refers to a poisonous snake. The word *śukla*, when it is adjectivally used, refers to a white thing, a substance. When we formulate the expression *śuklatva*, "white-thingness," it means the quality "white color." *Sattā* is an instance of the third type, inseparable relation. The word *sat* refers to an existing thing, and *sattā* denotes invariable relation to an existing thing. In other words, *sattā* cannot be separated from *sat*. As opposed to this claim, the Mīmāṃsakas maintain that in words like *daṇḍī*, "a person carrying a stick," the passive suffix *-in* denotes only a substance and not a relation of owner–owned. The idea of the relation between *daṇḍa* (a stick) and *-in* (that is, a person referred to by the possessive suffix) arises after the relation of qualifier (*daṇḍa*) and the qualified (in other words, a person qualified by *daṇḍa*) is comprehended. Therefore, *daṇḍī* does not denote a relation between *daṇḍa* (stick) and the person referred to by the *taddhita* suffix *-in*. Similarly, *pācaka* does not denote a relation between the stem meaning (action) and the suffix meaning (agent). The relation between *pāka*, the action of cooking, and *kartṛ*, agent (the meaning of the suffix) is neither the sense of the root nor that of the suffix. Thus the primary (*kṛt*) and the secondary (*taddhita*) derivatives do not denote any relation. But the abstract-noun-forming suffixes *tva* and *tal* in *pācakatva* and *daṇḍitva* denote the sense of relation. Koṇḍa Bhaṭṭa criticizes this Mīmāṃsaka view by pointing out that if the relation is not expressed by the words *daṇḍin* and *pācaka*, it will not be expressed by the words *daṇḍitva* and *pācakatva*. The Mīmāṃsakas accept the principle halfway but not in its entirety.

(*B*219). Koṇḍa Bhaṭṭa refers to Kātyāyana's *vārttika* 5 on Pāṇini 5.1.119. Kātyāyana says that the suffixes *tva* and *tal* denote the quality due to the presence of which a word is applied to an object. The quality denoted by an abstract suffix is any characteristic that is dependent on the thing meant as its substratum. This characteristic (*prakāra*) or quality, which determines the meaning expressed by the stem, is denoted by the suffixes *tva* and *tal*. For instance, when the word *śukla* denotes a substance (white thing), the expression *śuklatva* denotes a white quality. But when the word *śukla* denotes white color, then the expression *śuklatva* stands for the universal common to white colors. Words like *aṇu*, "atomic," *mahat*, "big," or *dīrgha*, "long," always stand for the objects that have these qualities. The expressions *aṇutva*, *mahattva*, or *dīrghatva* stand for the qualities (such as size or length) that distinguish these objects from others. The expression *pācakatva* stands for the relation between the agent and the action (cooking). The expression *ghaṭatva* stands for the notion of a universal jar. Koṇḍa Bhaṭṭa, following Bhartṛhari, states that from the point of ultimate reality the different universals like *ghaṭatva* are nothing more than the *mahāsattā*, the highest universal. All words express the *mahāsattā* as it exists in all different things.

(*B*220–221). Koṇḍa Bhaṭṭa quotes another *vārttika* on Pāṇini 5.1.119. Each word is employed to express a thing (*artha*) on some ground (*pravṛttinimitta*), and it is this ground that is expressed by the addition of the abstract suffixes *tva* and *tal*.

Kaiyaṭa explains this view as follows. The expressions *gotva*, *pācakatva*, *śuklatva*, and the like point to the thing (that is, the referent) through some property known as its ground for application (*pravṛttinimitta*). In the case of the word *go* the expressed sense is a substance, while the ground for the term's application is *gotva*, the universal feature. In the case of the word *pācaka*, the expressed sense is the agent of the action of cooking, and the ground for the term's application is the action of cooking. In the compounds *rājapuruṣaḥ*, "king's servant," and so on, the referent is the king's servant and the ground for the term's application is the relation between a king and a servant. "Ḍittha" refers to a person, *ḍitthatva* refers to the ground for application, in other words, the name that identifies the person called Ḍittha. Thus, according to Kaiyaṭa, the meaning of the suffix *tva* is *pravṛttinimitta*, the ground for the application of the term, which may be either a universal or action or relation or name.

Koṇḍa Bhaṭṭa explains the real implication of the *vārttika* as follows: all words express their meaning on account of their ground for the term's application (*pravṛttinimitta*). This *pravṛttinimitta* in the case of proper nouns is nothing but the word form. When we first learn to use proper nouns like "Hari," "Hara," or "Nala" we know that someone is expressed by these words. Here we do not have any property that can be considered as ground for application of the term. The same thing is true in case of medicinal herbs growing in a forest, which do not convey any specific sense to persons living in cities. These names of medicinal herbs refer to a substance, and the ground for application of these terms is the name (word form) of these herbs. Then the abstract expression like *haratva* refers to the word form or to the name.

Section 10: The Meaning of Suffixes Added to the Names of Deities (*Devatāpratyayārthanirṇaya*)

(*B*224). In *aindram haviḥ*, "an oblation presented to the god Indra," the *taddhita* suffix *-aṇ* is added to the stem *indra-* in the sense of *sā*; for example, *sya devatā* (Pāṇini 4.2.24): "this is its deity." Therefore the sense of the *taddhita* suffix *-aṇ* and others like it is an oblation presented to a particular deity. The meaning of the stem is construed with the meaning "deity in relation of apposition (*abhedasaṃbandha*)," which is a part of the suffix's meaning. The meaning *devatā* stands syntactically subordinate (that is, as the qualifier) with respect to the meaning *deya*, an oblation. The meaning *deya* stands syntactically predominant (that is, qualified) with respect to the meaning *devatā*. Thus the meaning of the suffix is *devatoddeśyakaṃ deyam*, an oblation to be presented that is subservient to a deity.

Koṇḍa Bhaṭṭa mentions the second view that the meaning *devatā*, deity (of the rites), and *deya*, an oblation to be presented, are two separate denotations of the *taddhita* suffix. According to the first view, however, these meanings are always presented together and not the one separately without the other.

(*B*225). The third view stated by Koṇḍa Bhaṭṭa is that the sense "deity" comes from the stem itself. The word *indra*, in the context of the sacrificial rite, stands for the deity Indra, and it is an accepted popular usage (*nirūḍhā lakṣaṇa*). Because the sense "deity" is already expressed by the stem it need not be expressed again by the *taddhita* suffix.

Section 11: The Nondenotation of Number (by the Subordinate Constituent of *Vṛtti* or Complex Formation) (*Abhedaikatvasaṃkhyā-nirṇaya*)

(*B*226) verse 54. In the case of a complex formation the question is whether the subordinate member of the formation conveys the idea of a particular number or of no number at all. In compounds like *rājapuruṣaḥ*, "king servant," we do not know whether the man belongs to one king, two kings, or more than two kings. Following Bhartṛhari, Koṇḍa Bhaṭṭa answers that we apprehend *abhedaikatvasaṃkhyā*, singular number without differentiation, from the subordinate member of the complex formation.

The term *abhedaikatvasaṃkhyā* is interpreted in two ways. According to the first interpretation, from a subordinate member of a complex formation we apprehend singular number, which includes other numbers too. The notion of other numbers co-exists in the singular. From the singular one can understand any required number according to the fact of communication. In this view, the subordinate member expresses singular number, which is noncommittal and may represent any number. Just as the honey elixir represents an undifferentiated combination of the flavors of many medical herbs, so all three numbers have merged in the singular and become one.

The second interpretation is that *abhedaikatvasaṃkhyā* means the notion of numbers in general, without specification being made. In the same way, from a distance a person who cannot see the exact color of a thing tells us that it has some indistinct color without knowing any specific color, like white. The same is true of number conveyed by the subordinate member of the complex formation: it conveys some number without committing any specific one.

In some cases of compounds a particular number is clearly indicated, for instance, *dviputraḥ*, "having two sons," *triputraḥ*, "having three sons," and so on, where the meaning of the nominal item itself is a particular number. In the word formation *tāvakīnaḥ*, "belonging to you," *māmakīnaḥ*, "belonging to me," the substitutes *tāvaka* and *māmaka* indicate singular number (Pāṇini 4.3.3).

(*B*227) verse 54. Koṇḍa Bhaṭṭa refers to the example *kapiñjalān ālabheta*, "one should kill (three partridges by immolating)" from the *Pūrvamīmāṃsā*. Here from the plural *kapiñjalān* only three partridges are understood because the idea of three comes first. The idea of four and more includes the idea of three, but the idea of three can exclude the idea of four or more. There is no reason to abandon the idea of three. Therefore, the Mīmāṃsakas conclude that the scripture prescribes killing of three partridges only and not of more than three. Similarly, in complex formation, when there is nothing that gives us an idea of a particular number we understand the idea of singularity, which comes first (verse 54, *Bhūṣaṇa*, p. 227).

Section 12: Intended and Unintended Denotation of Number (*Saṃkhyāvivakṣārthanirṇayaḥ*)

(*B*229). Koṇḍa Bhaṭṭa refers to the Mīmāṃsā principle *grahaikatva*, singularity of cups (unintended). In the sentence *grahaṃ saṃmārṣṭi*, "he cleans a cup" the singular number of the cup is not intended. By this sentence, cleaning with reference to a cup is prescribed. Here "cup" functions as the subject (*uddeśya*, in other words, that with reference to which something is prescribed) and "cleaning" functions as the predicate (*vidheya*, in other words, that which is prescribed with reference to something). The subject is *guṇa*, subsidiary, with regard to the predicate, and the predicate is *pradhāna*, principal, with regard to the subject. A subject phrase that figures as qualifier to a subject is *avivakṣita* (not intentionally used). Therefore the number of the subject is not intentionally used, that is to say, no special significance is attached to it. So "cup" stands for any cup and not for one particular cup.

Again, the Mīmāṃsakas hold that whatever figures as a qualifier in the predicate phrase is *vivakṣita*, intentionally used, for instance, *paśunā yajeta*, "one should bring about a sacrifice by means of an animal." The sentence is interpreted to mean "yāgam uddiśya paśur vidhīyate" ("with reference to a sacrifice an animal is enjoined"). In the predicate the qualifying number is intentionally used. Therefore, in *paśunā*, singular number is intentionally used. Accordingly, the sacrifice should be performed with one animal.

The Grammarians do not accept this view. Whether number is intentionally used or not intentionally used in subject and predicate words depends on particular instances. We cannot make it a rule just because the Mīmāṃsakas have done it. The Grammarians do not accept the view that a word that figures as the qualifier in the subject phrase is not significant or intentionally used. For instance, *valādi*, beginning with a consonant other than *y*, which figures as a qualifying condition with reference to the qualified *ārdhadhātukasya* in the subject phrase "valādeḥ ārdhadhātukasya" (Pāṇini 7.2.35), is significant and intentionally used.

(*B*229–230). Similarly, the view of the Mīmāṃsakas that a work that figures as the qualifier in the predicate phrase is significant and intentionally used is also not acceptable to the Grammarians. For instance, the singular number conveyed by the phrase *naḥ* (replaced by the phoneme *n*), which figures as the qualifier in the predicate phrase (Pāṇini 8.4.1), is not significant. That is why *nn* has been substituted in *bhinna* for *d* and *t* in *bhid+ta*. Finally, Koṇḍa Bhaṭṭa accepts that whatever figures as a qualifier in the predicate phrase should be taken to be intentionally used.

Section 13: The Meaning of the Primary Suffixes Such as *Ktvā* (*Ktvāpratyayādīnām arthanirṇayaḥ*)

(*B*232). According to the *Vārttikakāra* (*vārttika* 3 on Pāṇini 3.4.26), the suffixes *ktvā* (that is, *tvā*) and *tumun* (that is, *tum*) have the same meaning (namely, agent/object) as the finite verb. But according to Patañjali, *tva* or *tum* (gerunds or continuatives) denote only *bhāva* (action).

Appayya Dīkṣita in his *Parimala* maintains the view that in "paktvā odano bhujyate devadattena" ("the rice is eaten by Devadatta after having cooked it"), the verb *bhujyate* along with the suffix *tvā* expresses the sense *karman*. Similarly, therefore, Pāṇini 2.3.1 stops it from adding the accusative *-am* to the word *odana* by Pāṇini 2.3.2. In "paktvā odanam bhuṅkte devadattaḥ" ("Devadatta eats rice after having cooked it"), the fact that Devadatta functions as the agent is *abhihita*, already expressed, by the verb ending *-ti* as well as by suffix *-tvā*. As the sense "agent" is *abhihita* we are not allowed to add the instrumental ending after the stem Devadatta, according to Pāṇini 2.3.18.

(*B*232-235). Koṇḍa Bhaṭṭa disagrees with this view. According to him the suffix *-tvā* does not express the sense "agent." Pāṇini's rule 3.4.21 means: (the suffix *-tvā* is added to a verbal root, which expresses) the prior action of two (verbal actions) that have the same agent. The rule only says that both actions have the same agent; it does not say that the suffixes *-tvā* and *-tum* denote the sense "agent." Following Patañjali, Koṇḍa Bhaṭṭa maintains that the suffixes *-tvā* and *-tum* denote only *bhāva*, action. But this view does not mean that the object/agent of the action expressed by *-tvā*/*-tum* will be used in the accusative/instrumental. Following Bhartṛhari, he maintains that in the examples "paktvā odano bhujyate" and "paktvā odanaṃ bhuṅkte devadattaḥ," *odana* is the object of both actions (the action of eating, which is the principal one, and the action of cooking, which is the subordinate one), and Devadatta is the agent of both actions. In the first example the sense "object" (*karman*) is expressed by the finite verb but not by the suffix *tvā*. Similarly, in the second example the sense "agent" (*kartṛ*) is expressed by the finite verb but not by the gerund-forming suffix *-tvā*. When the sense "agent/object" is expressed by the main verb, the agent/object word is used in the nominative. The object/agent of the subordinate action is always in consonance with those of the principal action. The fact is that the *abhihita/anabhihita* by the main verb determines which case endings are to be added to a nominal stem.

The expression *bhuktvā vrajati*, "he goes away after eating," is regarded as one single sentence. *Bhuktvā* and *vrajati* are not to be read in isolation but as connected with each other by the qualifier–qualified relation. The action denoted by the finite verb is the qualified one, and the action denoted by the gerund is the qualifier one.

This qualifier qualified relation may be of four types: *janyajanakabhāva*, the producer–produced relation, as in, for instance, *bhoktuṃ pacati*, "he cooks for eating," because eating cannot be undertaken without cooking; *pūrvottarabhāva*, the relation of preceding and succeeding, as in, for instance, *bhuktvā vrajati*, "he goes after eating," where we find that the action of going follows the action of eating; *sāmānādhikaraṇya*, coreferentiality, as in, for instance, *bhuktvā vrajati*, where both of the actions have the same agent, because we understand that the eater and the goer are the same person; and *vyāpyatva*, the relation of pervasion, as in, for instance, *adhītya tiṣṭhati*, "while studying he stands," "or *mukhaṃ vyādāya svapiti*, "while keeping his mouth open he sleeps." Here the action of studying is coextensive with the action of standing, and the action of keeping the mouth open is coextensive with the action of sleeping. The main actions, studying and sleeping, are regarded as coinciding with the actions of standing and keeping the mouth open.

Section 14: The Doctrine of *Sphoṭa* (*Sphoṭanirṇaya*)

(*B*236–239). Koṇḍa Bhaṭṭa classifies the *sphoṭa* into eight different varieties: *varṇavyaktisphoṭa*, the phoneme event is the conveyer of meaning; *padavyaktisphoṭa*, the word event is the conveyer of meaning; *vākyavyaktisphoṭa*, the sentence event is the conveyer of meaning; *akhaṇḍapadasphoṭa*, the finished word as an undivided linguistic unit is the conveyer of the meaning; *akhaṇḍavākyasphoṭa*, the sentence as an undivided linguistic unit is the conveyer of meaning; *varṇajātisphoṭa*, the phoneme type is the conveyer of meaning; *padajātisphoṭa*, the word type is the conveyer of meaning; and *vākyajātisphoṭa*, the sentence type is the conveyer of meaning. The term *varṇasphoṭa* does not mean that each single phoneme is regarded as *sphoṭa*, but the phoneme or phonemes constituting either a stem or a suffix are regarded as such.

(*B*257) verses 60–69. Although the eight varieties of *sphoṭa* are accepted by the Grammarians, it is the sentence *sphoṭa* alone that represents the essential nature of the *sphoṭa* doctrine.

(*B*236–237) verse 59. According to the Naiyāyikas fictional constituents, namely, *sthānin*, prototype, like the symbol -l "el" and the like, are the conveyers of meaning. In opposition, the Grammarians maintain that the constituents that belong to the usable form of the language, like *-ti* (in *bhavati*) or *ḥ* (in *rāmaḥ*) are conveyers of meaning, not the fictional units such as -l "el" or *-su*.

The Naiyāyikas argue that it is more reasonable to maintain that the prototypes are denotative of meaning than to assign the denotative function to the suffixes that are actually used. The reason is that compared to the prototype "el" -l, which stands for all verb endings, the substitutes *-ti*, *-tas*, *-anti*, and so on are numerous. If the denotative functions were assigned to the substitutes it would lead to assumptions of endless denotative functions.

As an answer to the objection raised by the Naiyāyikas, Koṇḍa Bhaṭṭa argues that if the prototypes were denotative of meaning there would be some ambiguity, because different grammatical schools have chosen different prototypes. We find that the prototypes are variable, while the substitutes are of fixed character. Further, the Grammarians maintain that the substitutes that are actually heard by listeners are meaning-bearing units but that the prototypes, which are not actually used in the language, are not.

(*S*579). Some exponents of the phoneme *sphoṭa* theory formulate a different point of view. According to them, the meaning is conveyed by the last phoneme only, and the impressions of the individual phonemes constituting a word are helpful to produce only the simultaneous recollection of the phonemes heard. The last sound, helped by impressions left behind by the previous perceptions of sounds, reveals the meaning.

Koṇḍa Bhaṭṭa criticizes this claim on the ground that it becomes difficult to answer why the meaning is not understood, even if the phonemes are uttered in different periods of time.

Padasphoṭa

(*B*239) verse 63. In such forms as *ghaṭena*, "by a jar," it is very difficult to determine precisely which part of the word represents the stem and which, the suffix. There is no fixed criterion that would enable us to determine that *ghaṭa* is the base and *na* is the suffix or that *ghaṭ* is the base and *ena* is the suffix. Similarly, it is very difficult to point out the division between the stem portion and the suffix in the accusative optional plural *vaḥ*, *naḥ* of the personal pronouns *yuṣmad* and *asmad*. Therefore, the *padasphoṭa* (word *sphoṭa*) maintains that the finished word as a unique entity conveys the meaning.

Vākyasphoṭa

(*B*240–241) verse 64. The *padasphoṭa* theory also presents a difficulty in analyzing a sentence such as *hare'va*, "Hari protect me," because the listener grasps the meaning even if he fails to recognize exactly the isolated constituents *hare* and *ava*, due to ignorance of the laws of euphonic combination. Because the listener grasps the meaning without understanding the division of the sentence, the Grammarians contend that the sentence should be considered as a single unit for the purpose of communication.

The Grammarians' *vākyaśakti* theory assumes that the entire sentence is endowed with denotative function, and the sentence as a whole conveys one single meaning.

The Naiyāyikas claim that the meaning of a word is first remembered, and the relational meaning is cognized at the time of verbal knowledge. Thus according to the Naiyāyikas the sentence conveys some new meaning (*apūrva*). This additional meaning, over and above the word meaning, is the distinctive feature of the sentence meaning (*vākyārtha*), and it is conveyed by factors like syntactic expectancy (*ākāṅkṣā*), or relational seam, or the particular juxtaposition of words (*saṃsarga-maryādā*), or speaker's intention (*tātparya*). The Naiyāyikas raise the objection to the *vākyaśakti* that according to the Grammarians the distinction between the meaning cognized through the denotative function and the meaning cognized through the verbal cognition (*śābdabodha*) can no longer remain because, according to the *vākyaśakti* theory, the entire meaning of a sentence is known before the verbal cognition has taken place in the mind.

The Grammarians answer that the objection can be raised against the theory of denotation of meaning as related to the meanings of other words (*anvitābhidhānavāda*) maintained by the Prabhākara school of Mīmāṃsā. The Prābhākaras contend that the relational meaning is also the denoted meaning of a word. According to this school, the relational meaning of words is also known in a general way, and the definite relationship between the meanings of words in their precise form is clearly brought out at the time of verbal knowledge. The Grammarians, arguing on the same lines maintain that the denotative function of a sentence denotes the meaning of the individual words distinctly and their relation along with the other word meanings in a general way. That is to say, the precise relation among the various word meanings is cognized at the time of verbal knowledge alone.

To prove that the sentence meaning is known through the sentence function, Koṇḍa Bhaṭṭa cites the example "haridrāyāṃ nadyām ghoṣaḥ" ("a hamlet [is situated] on [the bank of] the river Haridrā".) When a person who has not heard the name of Haridrā previously hears this sentence, he understands the meaning of the word *haridrā*. He can guess the meaning of the word *haridrā* because he understands the meaning of the rest of the sentence, and then he is able to identify the meaning of the isolated words. The Prābhākaras claim that meaning exists in words that are fragments of a sentence. The procedure for understanding the meaning is to set side by side the sentences in which only one word is different. The child understands the meaning of words by the method of *āvāpodvāpa*, agreement and contrast. According to the Prābhākaras, words first convey the meaning related to one another, and later on we comprehend the meaning from isolated words. This analytical approach claims that an individual word is endowed with meaning, not the sentence as a whole.

The Grammarians who are exponents of the *vākyaśaktivāda* maintain that although a child in a later stage identifies and isolates the word in a sentence, still it understands first the meaning from a sentence. The division of a sentence into words is an analytical method. When one hears a sentence it is not taken into account in terms of a series of meaningful units but as a whole.

(*B*240–241) verse 65. Koṇḍa Bhaṭṭa points out that the Grammarians agree partially with the Bhāṭṭa school, for they maintain that a unified sentence meaning is verbal. According to the Bhāṭṭa school, the cognition of unified meaning becomes verbal (*śābda*) as it is conveyed by secondary meaning. According to the Grammarians, primary designation or denotative function (*abhidhā*) assigned to a sentence conveys a unified sentence meaning. But according to the Bhāṭṭas, the secondary function conveys syntactically unified meaning.

(*B*54–62). Koṇḍa Bhaṭṭa states that just as we comprehend the meaning of words from the words, so also do we comprehend the meaning of a sentence from the sentence. Consequently, just as the denotative function conveying the sense of words is assigned to the words, so the denotative function conveying the sense of a sentence should be assigned to the sentence. Thus the word *sphoṭa* and the sentence *sphoṭa* are established.

(*B*241–244). The Naiyāyikas hold that words primarily denote isolated meanings and the relational or syntactic meaning is communicated by the speaker's intention or specific juxtaposition of the words. Thus, according to the Naiyāyikas, the denotative function resides in isolated words. Now the Grammarians argue that if the denotative function resides in isolated words and not in the sentence, the layman might understand the meaning from the unconnected words: *ghaṭa*, "jar," *karmatva*, "objecthood," *ānayanam*, "bringing," and *kṛtiḥ*, "effort," as he understands the meaning from the sentence *ghaṭam ānaya*, "bring a jar," because the amount of information furnished by the unconnected words is practically the same as that furnished by the parts of the sentence *ghaṭa*+*am*, *ā*+*nay*+*a*. But it is experienced that a layman cannot grasp the meaning from unconnected words that do not form an organized sentence. Yet if it is held that the sentence as a whole is denotative of meaning, the difficulty does not arise, for the unconnected words mentioned above do not form an organized sentence. If the Naiyāyikas assume that the words convey the meaning only when they are organized in a sentence form such as *ghaṭam ānaya*, then nothing but the theory of the *vākyasphoṭa* is established.

(*B*249) verse 66, taken from *Vākyapadīya*. There are no phonemes in the words, and (there are) no parts in the phonemes. There is no absolute and clear-cut separation of words from sentence. Koṇḍa Bhaṭṭa, on the basis of this statement, lays emphasis on the indivisible nature of the *sphoṭa*. The verse implies that the word is without any sequence of phonemes and that the sentence is bereft of the sequence of words, even if they are cognized as having the sequence of phonemes and words. Koṇḍa Bhaṭṭa argues that, as in the phonemes *e*, *o*, *l*, *r*, though the parts *a*, *i*, *l*, *r* are separately cognized, they are not regarded as separate parts of the phonemes, so in the same manner a word should not be considered to be divisible into stems and suffixes.

The diversity in knowledge such as "this is the phoneme *k*," "this is the phoneme *j*," can be justified simply by assuming a diversity in the delimiting property of production (*utpatti*) or revelation (*abhivyakti*) of various phonemes, residing in the conjunction of the wind (generally), accepted as giving rise to the various sounds. It is clearly stated in the section dealing with the deities (*devatā*) in the *Bhāmatī* (Vācaspati Miśra's commentary on the *Śaṃkarabhāṣya*) that the shrillness (and other qualities) residing in the wind are superimposed upon the phonemes. Koṇḍa Bhaṭṭa points out that breath wind comes into contact with the different vocal organs, and it assumes the form of different phonemes. The diversity belonging to the airwaves (*vāyusaṃyoga*) that come into contact with the different articulatory points is superimposed upon sounds that are modifications of airy substances.

Thus the *pūrvapakṣin* raises the following objection: instead of assuming that the phonemes are denotative, why do we not consider the sound-producing movements themselves to be denotative? Koṇḍa Bhaṭṭa answers by reasoning that the auditory perception of phonemes experienced by people cannot be ascribed to the sound-producing movements, which are beyond the sense organs. The speaker makes the sound-producing movements, and from them, the listener perceives the phonemes. The listener identifies the outer phonemes and not the inner sound-producing movements, which are beyond the reach of sense organs.

(*B*249–250). Koṇḍa Bhaṭṭa furnishes instances of recognition: it is the same phoneme *g*, it is the same word, it is the same sentence. The first instance points out that the phoneme *sphoṭa* remains the same, though it is distinctively revealed by the peculiarities of the individual speakers. The experience shows that the phonemic *g* is a single entity and gives a unitary character to the phoneme *g*. Similarly the experiences of one word and of one sentence cannot be attributed to the phonemes, or stems or suffixes or words, because the notion of unitariness cannot present different objects as its contents. Koṇḍa Bhaṭṭa suggests that we cannot attribute this unitary perception to the collective notions of the phonemes in a single memory. The perceptive experience shows that the word *gauḥ* is a single entity, and it corresponds to the unity of meaning. It is not possible to argue that this unitary experience is based on the single memory of all phonemes combined together, because meaningless phonemes cannot give rise to a meaning even when they are put together in a single memory.

(*B*250–251). Koṇḍa Bhaṭṭa maintains the view that sounds perceived by the listeners are not different from the *sphoṭa*. The *sphoṭa* is cognized in the form of the distinctive sounds *g-h-a-ṭ-a*. Koṇḍa Bhaṭṭa holds the view that the object of cognition is the indivisible word-*sphoṭa*, but its form is nothing else than the phonemes auditorily perceived. The phoneme *g* manifested by sound is identified with the phoneme *g*, which appears to be the part of indivisible *sphoṭa* word. Owing to this confusion, the *sphoṭa*, which is partless, appears to have parts. In reality, the individual phonemes are not conceived to be different from the partless *sphoṭa* progressively revealed by sounds.

(*B*252). The *pūrvapakṣin* raises the question. Do the sound-producing airwaves reveal *sphoṭa* individually or collectively? It cannot be held that the sound-producing airwaves reveal *sphoṭa* individually, because if it were so, any particular sound-producing airwave would be enough to reveal *sphoṭa*, and the remaining airwaves would be redundant. It cannot be argued that the sound-producing airwaves reveal the *sphoṭa* collectively, because they are momentary, and each airwave perishes as soon as the succeeding one comes into existence.

Koṇḍa Bhaṭṭa meets this argument by saying that the sound-producing movements reveal *sphoṭa* individually. A single airwave, for instance, in the word *gauḥ* reveals *sphoṭa* through the medium of the sound *g*, another reveals *sphoṭa* through the medium of the sound *au*; and the third one reveals *sphoṭa* through the medium of *visarga* (*ḥ*). Thus the *sphoṭa* is more and more clearly revealed with each succeeding airwave. In this manner, Koṇḍa Bhaṭṭa says, the *sphoṭa* word *gauḥ* is revealed by each individual wave through the medium of the order of sounds, *g*, *au*, *ḥ*. The different sounds are considered to be nondifferent from the *sphoṭa* word *gauḥ*.

(*B*262). The Naiyāyikas object that the relation of immediate sequence cannot be maintained between the two sounds, because the first has died out by the time the second has come into existence. The relation of priority and posteriority arises only when two things exist simultaneously. There cannot be any combination of what is nonexistent with what exists.

Koṇḍa Bhaṭṭa answers this objection by assuming that the combination of nonexisting things is possible in cognition. The combination can be maintained between two sounds, because at the time of the knowledge of the *utpatti* (production), the knowledge of *sthiti* (duration) of the first sound has not died out.

(*B*248, 252). Kaiyaṭa contends that the unity of word or sentence cannot be attributed to phonemes because one cannot account for the simultaneity of phonemes. The combination of phonemes itself is impossible, because each phoneme perishes as soon as it is uttered. There cannot be a combination of what exists with what has ceased to exist. Neither can the unity of the word be explained with reference to the collective recollection of the phonemes. In the collective recollection also, the phonemes do not figure in any sequence because the sequence of phonemes is an impossible task. Further, it would lead to the cognition of the same meaning from words that contain the same phonemes in a different order. The difference between the words *nadī* and *dīna* and their meanings ("river" and "poor") would be unaccountable by the collective recollection of phonemes that constitute the words *nadī* (river) and *dīna* (poor), because the constituent phonemes of the said words are the same. The impressions left by the phonemes will be the same even when the order is reversed. There is no sequence in the recollection because we cannot remember the objects in the same order as we have perceived them. Because the unitary experience "this is one word" cannot be explained with reference to the series of phonemes, and because the difference between the words *nadī* and *dīna* and the like is otherwise unaccountable, the grammarians establish the existence of the *sphoṭa* as an indivisible meaning-bearing unit.

Koṇḍa Bhaṭṭa disagrees with the Grammarians' view that the main justification of the *sphoṭa* entity stems from the fact that the combination of the sequence of phonemes that constitute the word cannot be explained. Following the theory of association, he maintains that each succeeding phoneme progressively reveals the substructure of a word in the form of a certain sequence, and all of these substructures directly or indirectly reveal the word, which is an aggregate of phonemes *p, a, ṭ, a*. Now at the time of perceiving the second phoneme, not only is the phoneme *a* cognized, but the substructure *pa* is also cognized through the impression of phonemes that is left on the mind of listener. In this manner, the whole structure *paṭa* is cognized at the time of perceiving the last phoneme *a*. Each subsequent sound reveals the substructure of the preceding and the succeeding sounds, and thus we can establish the coexistence of phonemes. Therefore, Koṇḍa Bhaṭṭa argues, the main reason for accepting the *sphoṭa* theory is not unaccountability of the idea of sequence, but the experience that the word is single and unitary.

(*B*251). (The question is raised in the *Parimala* commentary whether the *sphoṭa* revealed by synonyms *ghaṭa* and *kalaśa* [both mean "pot"] are identical or different.) According to the Grammarian the *sphoṭa* word is indivisible, and it is something over and above the phonemes. Accordingly, the *sphoṭa* words cannot be said to have phonetic shapes. Thus the *sphoṭa* character of the word cannot be rendered different through the differences in the phonetic shape of words. The *sphoṭa* character of synonyms like *ghaṭa* and *kalaśa* cannot be distinguished semantically either, because the meaning conveyed by these words is identical. If the *sphoṭa* character of the synonyms *ghaṭa* and *kalaśa* is assumed to be identical, a man who is aware of the convention of the word *ghaṭa* but is ignorant of the convention of the word *kalaśa* will understand the meaning from the *sphoṭa* word *kalaśa*, which is identical with the *sphoṭa* word *ghaṭa*.

To get rid of this difficulty, the Grammarians maintain that the difference in the phonetic shape (in other words in the revealing sound of the *sphoṭa*) causes the difference in the revealed *sphoṭa*. The knowledge of the convention must be separately grasped in the case of the different *sphoṭa*, though they may convey the same meaning. When this separation is maintained, the *sphoṭa* word revealed by the phonetic shape *gh-a-ṭ-a* becomes different from the *sphoṭa* word revealed by the phonetic shape *k-a-l-a-ś-a*. There remains no possibility of verbal cognition from the *sphoṭa*-word *kalaśa* when one knows the convention of the word *ghaṭa* alone, because the two words are different.

Sphoṭa words are different, and the knowledge of the denotative function must be grasped separately, with reference to each *sphoṭa* word. The Grammarians do not maintain a difference between two things: the difference in the *sphoṭa* word and the difference in the phonetic shape.

(*B*253–254) verse 67. It is argued by the *pūrvapakṣin* that if the Grammarians maintain that the *vākyasphoṭa* alone is real, how can they be justified in analyzing the sentence into different words, and words into stems and suffixes? The Grammarians answer that acceptance of the *padasphoṭa* and the *varṇasphoṭa* is undoubtedly a fiction, inasmuch as there is no separate existence of words apart from the sentence of which they are parts. This device, though unreal, is still helpful from the point of unreal reality to describe our mind. The study of the grammatical science enables us to realize the ultimate reality through the unreal or illusory analysis of words. Just as the knowledge of the five sheaths (*pañcakośa*) in the Vedānta is a means to attaining the knowledge of the ultimate reality, Brahman, so also the teaching of eight divisions of *sphoṭa* is a practical device for comprehending the ultimate knowledge of the real, partless sentence-*sphoṭa* (*akhaṇḍa-vākya-sphoṭa*).

(*B*257) verse 69. The Mīmāṃsakas maintain that the different attributes (*upādhi*) such as shortness (*hrasvatva*), longness (*dīrghatva*), lowness (*anudāttatva*), and the like, belong in reality to the sound-producing airwaves, though they are superimposed on the phonemes.

These superimposed qualities serve to distinguish one phoneme from the others. Arguing on the same lines, the Grammarians maintain that the *k*-ness (*katva*) and so on, which belong to the airwaves, appear to be superimposed on the phonemes revealed by the airwaves. Similarly, the production and destruction are properties of airwaves, but they are felt to be associated with the phonemes. In this manner the cognition "the phoneme *k* is produced" is justified.

(*B*255). The Grammarians maintain that the phoneme *g* in *gaṇa* and *gati* is the same and permanent, because we have the recognition *so'yaṃ gakāraḥ*, "this is the same phoneme *g*." The recognition referring to the sameness of individual phoneme *g* forces one to accept the permanency of phonemes. The Naiyāyikas disagree with the Grammarians, however, and maintain that the cognition *so'yaṃ gakāraḥ*, "this is the same phoneme *g*," does not follow from the identity of the individuals but from the sameness of the individuals' universal character. The two phonemes g_1 and g_2 are different from each other, still they are considered to be the same and can be grouped under the universal character "g-ness."

The Grammarians say that the recognition "this is the same phoneme *g*" does not follow from the knowledge of the two individuals as related to the same class, but it refers to the sameness of the individual phoneme *g* pronounced at different times and by different individuals. The Naiyāyikas controvert the Grammarians' theory by pointing out the fact that, if the phonemes are permanent, it cannot be justified to make a statement like *gakāra utpannaḥ* because the phonemes are not subjected to the origination. The Grammarians respond that the cognition *gakāra utpannaḥ*, "*g* is produced," refers to internal air issued forth from speaker's mouth. This internal air, which appears and vanishes, is identified with the auditory image of the phoneme *g*.

By contrast, the Naiyāyikas maintain that the cognition *so'yaṃ gakāraḥ*, which points out the sameness of the phonemes g_1 and g_2 is, considered erroneous as far as it refers to the sameness of individuals. According to the Naiyāyikas the cognition of appearance and disappearance is valid, while the cognition of identity between the two individuals is invalid or erroneous. Thus the controversial point between the Grammarians and the Naiyāyikas is whether the vocal organs produce a sound or make it manifest.

Jātisphoṭa and *Vyaktisphoṭa*

(*B*255) verse 69. The word *gauḥ* is a class that comprises varied utterances by different individuals. If the individual utterance *gauḥ* is regarded as denotative of meaning it would lead to the assumption of multiplicity of the denotative functions corresponding to the differences in the utterance of words. Therefore, it is assumed that the universal word (*jātisphoṭa*), into which all the different spoken words with varied accents and tones are assembled, is denotative of meaning. This concept is called the class-character of the *sphoṭa* word.

The *vyaktisphoṭa* view maintains that there are no different individual words that might be grouped into a single class. The *vyaktisphoṭa* denies the plurality of individual words. The loudness, length, lowness, and so on are the properties of the articulate sound but not of the *sphoṭa* word. It is the articulate sound that usually appears to be long or short, but the *sphoṭa* word or manifested sound remains entirely unchanged. The *varṇavyakti* or *padavyakti* is one, but it appears divergent due to the variation in the articulated sound of different individuals.

The Phonemes and *Sphoṭa*

(*B*256–257). The phonemes and *sphoṭa* are intimately related to each other. In the cognition of the *sphoṭa* the phonemes are not irrelevant because they are not different from the *sphoṭa*. One cannot remain indifferent to the differences of phonemes when we think of the cognition of the word. We undoubtedly cognize the individual phonemes when we perceive or cognize the indivisible single *sphoṭa*. The phonemic entity (*varṇavyakti*) isolated from the other members of the class is distinct from the *sphoṭa*. The perception *gatvavān sphoṭa*, "the *sphoṭa* word contains the phoneme *g*," is an illusory perception because the *sphoṭa* word as a whole is indivisible. When the indivisible word is manifested by the sounds, the phonemes appear to be cognized as a part of the word owing to the hearer's incapacity to perceive the word without perceiving the sequence of phonemes. We undoubtedly cognize the individual phonemes, but they are not identical with *sphoṭa* word. The *sphoṭa* word is unitary, and it is taken as a single and indivisible meaning-bearing unit of the language. While phonemes are many they are not considered to be the meaning-bearing units. They only progressively reveal the *sphoṭa* word.

Revelation of the *sphoṭa* by the same phonemes but in a different order does not convey the same meaning. For instance, the words *saraḥ* and *rasaḥ*, which contain the same phonemes, do not convey the same idea. The sequence of phonemes, which is the character of articulate sound, is left to be associated with the revealed *sphoṭa*. The difference in the *sphoṭa* words *saraḥ* and *rasaḥ*, which have the same constituent sound units, is justified because the cognition of the sequence of phonemes appears in the *sphoṭa* word as its associative feature.

(*B*258–260) verse 70, taken from Bhartṛhari's *Vākyapadīya* 1.93. This verse supports the class *sphoṭa* (*jātisphoṭa*) theory. Koṇḍa Bhaṭṭa interprets it to mean that phonetic entities such as *p*, *a*, *t*, *a* reveal the *sphoṭa* word *paṭa*. The word *paṭa* represents a class that comprises varied utterances made by different people. The universal *sphoṭa* is the conveyer of meaning because an expression uttered by different people does not convey different meaning to the listeners. There is only one class of all the particular events of the spoken word *ghaṭa*.

The idea of the *varṇasphoṭa* is not concerned with the meaning. The *varṇajātisphoṭa* means that the phoneme *p* represents a class sound that comprises varied utterances made by different people.

The second half of the verse 70, according to Koṇḍa Bhaṭṭa, denies the distinction between *varṇavyakti* and *dhvani* as pointed out by other Grammarians who maintain that the term *varṇavyakti* stands for the individual auditory perception of the articulated sound, while the term *dhvani* stands for the varied individual articulated sounds.

(*B*258–260) verse 71. There are two elements, real and unreal, in every object. The unreal elements are regarded as particulars (*vyakti*). The real element is known as the universal. The term *jāti* ultimately refers to Brahman which essentially underlies all objects (verse 71). *Jāti*, which is the essence of things, is equated with *mahāsattā*, the highest universal.

(*B*258–260) verse 72. The Grammarians equate the term *śabda* with the *sphoṭa*, which is again identical with Brahman. It is also called the *śabdatattva* by the Grammarians. The word *sphoṭa* etymologically means "from which meaning bursts forth" or "that which is revealed by sounds."

38

TĀRAKA BRAHMĀNANDA SARASVATĪ

A disciple of Gopālānanda Yati, and thus presumed to have flourished about 1650, this writer composed some notes on Grammar called *Vyākaraṇakroḍapattra.*

39

COKKANĀTHA OR ŚOKANĀTHA DĪKṢITA

The *New Catalogus Catalogorum* dates this writer to the middle of the seventeenth century and indentifies him as the "son of Nārāyaṇa, alias Dvādaśāhayājin of Kauśikagotra and preceptor and father-in-law of Rāmabhadra Dīkṣita (author of *Jānakīpariṇayanāṭaka*); preceptor of Sadāśiva Dīkṣita (a. of *Gītāsundara*) and father of Nalla Perumal Dīkṣita (a. of C. on *Śabdakaumudī*" (vol. 7, p. 85a). He is held to have composed at least two works, the *Śabdakaumudī* and a *Mahābhāṣyaratnāvalī*. At the foregoing location in the *New Catalogus*, Cokkanātha is also said to have written a commentary on *Śabdakaumudī* entitled *Śābdikarakṣā*, but at vol. 10, p. 62b, the *Śābdikarakṣā* is ascribed to (Bālapatañjali) Dvādaśāhayājin, grandson of Nārāyaṇa.

40

TIRUMALA YAJVAN

The son of Veṅkaṭeśa and grandson of Sarasvatī Makhin of the Ṣaḍdarśana family, this writer composed a *Sumanoramā* on the *Siddhāntakaumudī* (Adyar D, vol. 6, no. 355). He may also have been responsible for a commentary on the *Mahābhāṣya* titled *Anupāṭa*. He appears to have lived around 1660. Yudhisthira Mimamsaka[1] thinks he is the father of Annambhaṭṭa, but he would seem to have been a different Tirumala.

41

(RĀMA) NĀRĀYAṆA (ŚARMAN) (VANDYOPĀDHYĀYA)

The *New Catalogus Catalogorum* (vol. 10, p. 85a) lists this writer, "of the Vandyaghāṭīya family" and flourishing in 1664, as author of *Śuddhi* (*tattva*) *kārikā*, *Sārāvali* (and *vṛtti* in seven *pādas*), and possibly a *Dhāturatnākara*.

42

SADĀŚIVA

This Sadāśiva, the author of a commentary, *Gūḍhārthadipani*, on the *Mahābhāṣya*, was a son of Nīlakaṇṭha Dīkṣita and a pupil of Kamalākara Dīkṣita, who was in turn a pupil of Dattātreya.[1]

43

HARI DĪKṢITA

Hari Dīkṣita was the grandson of Bhaṭṭoji Dīkṣita and the son of Vīreśvara, alias Bhānuji, also called Rāmāśrama. He taught Nāgeśa Bhaṭṭa. He is considered to have written two commentaries on Bhaṭṭoji's *Prauḍhamanoramā* called *Śabdaratna*, a larger (*Bṛhat*) and a shorter (*Laghu*) one. Some scholars hold the opinion that Nāgeśa actually wrote the *Bṛhatśabdaratna* and ascribed it to his teacher Hari.

Students of Grammar regularly study the *Laghuśabdaratna* up to the end of the *kāraka* chapter along with the *Prauḍhamanoramā* after they have mastered the *Siddhāntakaumudī*.

44

RĀMABHADRA DĪKṢITA

Rāmabhadra Dīkṣita was the son of Yajñarāma Dīkṣita, student and son-in-law of Cokkanātha Dīkṣita (author of the *Śabdakaumudī* on Sanskrit grammar, protégé of King Śāhaji of Tanjore who ruled from 1684 to 1712 and belonged to Kaṇḍaramāṇikkam in Tamil Nadu. He was also a student and protégé of the great poet Nīlakaṇṭha Dīkṣita. Among his works are the *Jānakīpariṇaya Nāṭaka*; several *stotras* on Rāma, *Patañjalicarita*, which is a *Mahākāvya* on the life of Patañjali; and the following technical works: *Uṇādimaṇidīpikā* an elaborate commentary on the Pāñcapādi version of the *Uṇādisūtras*; *Ṣaḍdarśinīsiddhāntasaṃgraha*; with a section on Grammar; and *Śabdabhedanirūpaṇa*.

Ṣaḍdarśinīsiddhāntasaṃgraha (*Vyākaraṇa Section*)

K. Kunjunni Raja

Sanskrit words may be classified into Vedic and classical (*laukika*). The former class consists of those occurring in the four Vedas, while the latter comprises words found in Sanskrit literature from the Vedāṅgas and Smṛtis to contemporary works.

Rejecting the view that correct or incorrect usage makes little difference as long as the intended meaning is understood by the listeners, because the purpose of language is communication, Rāmabhadra points out that one has to be choosy and use only what is correct. The analogies of selecting proper food and of taking an eligible woman as wife are also mentioned.

Laukika or common words are classified into four: *jāti*, *guṇa*, *kriyā*, and *saṃjñā*.

Regarding wrong usages (*apaśabda*), Rāmabhadra points out that the term applies not only to words but also to sentences and expressions.

Not using the proper *kārakas* and case endings and not observing the rules of concordance between adjective and the noun qualified are also instances of *apaśabda*; for example, "bhavān gām ānaya" is wrong because the term *bhavān* requires the third person singular *ānatyatu.* The correctness also depends on the intention or the context. *Aśvam ānaya,* "bring the poor man," may be correct in itself, but is an *apaśabda* when the context requires *aśvam ānaya,* "bring a horse."

Rāmabhadra Dīkṣita accepts the view that among the three great sages, Pāṇini, Kātyāyana, and Patañjali, each preceding author is more authoritative than the next.

A brief analysis of the contents of the *Aṣṭādhyayī* is also given in the text.

Śabdabhedanirūpaṇa

K. Kunjunni Raja

Use of words in literature is divided into primary, secondary, and suggestive. *Abhidhā* is the primary meaning. *Lakṣaṇā,* secondary meaning, is resorted to when it is impossible to take the literal sense in the context (*anvayānupapatti*), but there is no incongruity with the speaker's intention (*tātparyānupapatti*). Secondary meaning may be based on different relations between the primary and the actual referents. One is *dhāryadhārakabhāva,* relation of the possessor and the possessed, for example, "the *pāñcajanya* was heard." Here *pāñcajanya,* a conch, is used for the sound produced by it (hearing the bell for hearing the sound of the bell), The second relation is *ādhārādheyabhāva,* the locus for what is on it, for example, *Laṅkātaṅka,* "anxiety of Laṅkā." Here "Laṅkā" stands for the people of Laṅkā, for anxiety is for the people. The third is *sādṛśya,* similarity, as in *nagotsaṅga,* "the lap of the mountain." Here "lap" is used for the slope, through similarity. This third variety is also called *gauṇī.*

45

NĀGEŚA (OR NĀGOJI) BHAṬṬA

Of all the great Grammarians of the sixteenth to eighteenth centuries—indeed, of all those after Bhartṛhari himself—perhaps none is more important for philosophical contributions than Nāgeśa Bhaṭṭa. He came from the family of Bhaṭṭoji Dīkṣita, who was his great-grandfather. Nāgeśa's father was named Śiva Bhaṭṭa; his mother was Satī, of the Kale family of Maharashtra Brahmins. He was patronized by Rāmavarman of Śṛṅgaverapura near Allahabad. He taught such illustrious followers as Gaṅgārāma, Vaidyanātha Payaguṇḍa, and his own son, Bālaśarman. His literary activity extended between 1670 and 1750.[1]

Nāgeśa's output was extensive and ranged widely. He wrote *Padārthadīpikā* and *Tarkabhāṣātyuktimuktāvalī* on Nyāya, a commentary (*Laghuvṛtti*) on the *Sāṃkhyasūtras*, another *vṛtti* on the *Yogasūtras*, and a work on Vedānta titled *Vedāntabhāṣyapradīpoddyota*. In Sanskrit grammar he is accepted as the final authority. Some fourteen works on Grammar are known to exist by his hand, and others are mentioned in the literature. In addition to the works that focus on philosophical grammatical theories, summarized below, Nāgeśa wrote a commentary, *Śabdenduśekhara*, as well as a briefer version of the same (*Laghuśabdenduśekhara*) on the *Siddhāntakaumudī*, and a number of independent treatises on various aspects of Grammar. The latter include the *Paribhāṣenduśekhara*, the definitive treatise on that subject, works on particular grammatical forms (*Śabdānantasāgarasamuccaya*, *Suptiṅantasāgarasamuccaya*, *Śaṅkāsamādhāna*), and commentaries on other grammatical works (*Viṣampaḍī* on *Śabdakaustubha*, *Prabhākaracandra* on *Tattvadīpikā*, and perhaps a *Laghuśabdaratna* based on his teacher Hari Dīkṣita's larger *Śabdaratna*, though this ascription is controversial.

Nāgeśa wrote three works on the philosophy of Grammar titled *Mañjūṣā*, *Laghusiddhāntamañjūṣā*, and *Paramalaghumañjūṣā*. The last is an abridgment of the second, which is in turn an abridgment of the first. Like Koṇḍa Bhaṭṭa's *Vaiyākaraṇabhūṣaṇa* and *-sāra,* these works are comprehensive, establishing the view of the Grammarians after discussing and refuting the views of other schools, mainly the Nyāya and Mīmāṃsā. Nāgeśa has been influenced by Koṇḍa Bhaṭṭa, but in many cases he takes independent positions. As far as the *sphoṭa* theory is concerned, he differs from Bhartṛhari, though he does not say so, and he was influenced by Kashmir Śaivism and by Tantric works.

Paramalaghumañjūṣā

K. Kunjunni Raja

E references are to the edition by Kalika Prasad Sukla (with the editor's *Jyotsnā* commentary), published at Baroda in 1961.

Significative Power (*Śakti*)

(*E*1–13). *Sphoṭa* can be classified into eight varieties: *varṇasphoṭa, padasphoṭa, vākyasphoṭa* (each divided into the universal or the particular), *akhaṇḍa padasphoṭa*, and *akhaṇḍa vākyasphoṭa.* Of these types the *vākyasphoṭa* is the most important, for the sentence is the unit of speech in worldly usage. The division of the sentence into words, and further into the stems and suffixes, is only a grammatical device for analysis and has no reality.

(*E*15–32). Verbal testimony is accepted as a means of valid cognition; but it is defined as the statement of a reliable person. For understanding the statement a knowledge of the meanings of the words spoken is essential. One who does not know the meaning of a word in the utterance, or who has forgotten it, cannot understand the statement.

(*E*37). Meaning (*vṛtti*) is of three kinds, primary significative power (*śakti*), secondary meaning (*lakṣaṇā*), and suggestion (*vyañjanā*). The Naiyāyikas consider the significative power to be conventional, having been established by the will of God; but according to the Grammarians it is a relation between a word and its meaning, the signifier-signified relationship. On the basis of the superimposition of one over the other, there is a sort of identity and one evokes the other.

(*E*40). This relationship exists both in words and in sentences. It is known through recollection (*smṛti*). Even though the relationship is there permanently, it becomes effective only when it is known.

(*E*41). The Naiyāyika view that the significative power is based on the convention set by the will of God is not acceptable. Meaning is known from words directly, without the intervention of God's will.

(*E*43). The identity and the superimposition of word and meaning are in the mind. Strictly speaking, the existence of the meaning, as well as that of the word, is only in the mind. The word is the integral *sphoṭa*. The meaning is a *vikalpa*, a mental construct that comes along with the knowledge of the word and has nothing to do with the actual existence. Empty words like "the son of a barren woman" (*vandhyāsuta*) are meaningful, though there may not be any corresponding external object. But for meaningfulness, the nominal suffixes ordained for meaningful stems (*prātipadika*) cannot be applied to such empty words.

(*E*44). The Naiyāyika's view that in "the hare's horn" (*śaśaśṛṅga* there is only error in the horn's belonging to the hare is not acceptable; for in the sentence "there is no hare's horn," there is no need to see such an animal, and the suffixes are possible if the stem is meaningful.

On the basis of the identity of a word and its meaning, it is accepted that when the meaning changes, the word also changes (in the case of homophones); the usage "the word has many meanings" is in the sense that the words are similar.

(*E*46–48). This significative power exists in correct words and corrupt words equally, for usage by the people, which is the best means of learning the meaning of words, works in the same way in both. On observing the behavior of elderly people, one may remember the meaning known in one's previous birth. That is how children and animals understand the connected sense (of utterances).

Objection: The Naiyāyikas say that the meaning of corrupt words is known by recollecting the correct words.

Answer: This claim is false, for meaning is known (from corrupt words) even without recollecting the corresponding correct words. Otherwise one who does not know the corresponding correct word will not be able to understand the meaning.

One cannot say that meaning is got from corrupt words through an erroneous notion of the meaningfulness. Meaning is known without any doubt (from corrupt words), hence no confusion is to be assumed. That is why women, uneducated people, and children have to be told the corrupt words, when they have doubts on hearing the correct words. The *Mahābhāṣya* passage, "although meaning is known from correct as well as corrupt words, grammar gives the rules about meritorious usage," and Bhartṛhari's line, "Although there is no difference in meaningfulness, the grammatical rules are for metrit and demerit in usage," are in favor of this view. The discussion regarding the Āryan and Mleccha usages in Mīmāṃsā also shows this view. This discussion itself shows that both the Āryan and the Mleccha usages are valid; the Āryan usage is preferred as far as the Vedic terms are concerned.

(*E*49–50). This significative power is of three kinds: conventional (*rūḍhi*), derivative (*yoga*), and conventional derivative (*yogarūḍhi*). When the whole word gives the meaning, which cannot be analyzed into its components through grammatical rules, it is conventional, as in the case of words like *maṇi* and *nūpura*. If the meaning is analyzable into its components according to the rules of grammar, it is derivative, as in the case of words like *pācaka*, "cook" (from *pac*, "to cook," and agent suffix *aka*). Conventional derivation is that significative power in which, along with the meaning determined through grammatical analysis, some special restriction is also present, as in *paṅkaja* (literally "mud-born," but restricted to the lotus). Sometimes on the basis of the intention (*tātparya*), the word can be used in the pure (*yoga*) derivational sense also, a usage called *yaugikarūḍha* (derivative-cum-conventional). Examples are *aśvagandhā* ("a kind of herb" and "having the smell of horses").

(*E*51–53). In case of ambiguous expressions, the meaning is restricted by contextual factors. They are given by Bhartṛhari (*Vākyapadīya* 2.315–17): *saṃyoga*, mention of the accompaniment of an entity; *viprayoga*, mention of the absence of it; *sāhacarya*, mention of something that usually goes with it; *virodhita*, mention of its well-known adversary; *artha*, the purpose served; *prakaraṇa*, the situational context; *liṅga*, indication available (in a related sentence); *anyaśabdasannidhi*, the presence of another word in collocation; *sāmarthya*, "probability"; *aucitya*, propriety, the time, the place, the gender, and accent.

Secondary Meaning (*Lakṣaṇā*)

(*E*54–57). According to the Naiyāyikas, secondary meaning is a relation to the primary meaning. It is of two types: *gauṇī*, based on common quality, and *śuddhā* or pure, in which the relation is something other than similarity. It can be divided into two classes in another way: *ajahatsvārthā*, in which the primary meaning is not abandoned, and *jahatsvārthā*, in which the primary meaning is abandoned. The former takes some additional meaning along with its own; for instance, *chatriṇo yānti*, "people with umbrellas are going" (used for some people with umbrellas and some without), *kākebhyo dadhi rakṣyatām*, "protect the curd from crows" (used for protecting from crows and also non-crows, such as dogs). The latter abandons its primary meaning. "Teach the Bāhīka bull"; here the bull cannot be taught, so the term gives up its meaning and is applied to the man who is dull (like the bull). The relation between the primary meaning and the actual meaning is given as the substratum, common quality, proximity, association, and purpose (for example, "the cats are crying," "he is a lion," "the village is on the Ganges," "bring the sticks" [for stick bearers], and "Indra" [used for the pole intended for Indra].

The actual basis of secondary meaning is the incompatibility of the primary meaning with the meaning intended in the context; the incompatibility could be removed in different ways by assuming secondary meanings for different words.

(*E*59). According to early authorities, there is also a variety of *lakṣaṇā* called *jahadajahallakṣaṇā*, in which part of the primary meaning of a term is abandoned and part retained, as in *paṭo dagdhaḥ*, "the cloth is burned" (when only part is burned). In *tattvam asi*, "That thou art," both *tat* and *tvam* have to give up some of their primary sense to permit identification.

(*E*60). Some say that secondary meaning is the relation to what is conveyed by the expression, for instance, "the village is on the *deep* river." Here the term "deep" cannot refer to the bank of the river; hence the connected meaning "deep river" is to be understood first and then the sense of *bank* is determined through secondary meaning. In *dvirepha* ("two *rs*"), referring first to the word *bhramara* and then to a bee, the term *lakṣitalakṣaṇā* is used by some.

(*E*63). Again, secondary meaning can be of two types, intentional—used with a purpose in view—(*prayojanavatī*) and conventional (*rūḍhā*). In "the village is on the Ganges," the purpose is to indicate the sanctity and coolness of the place.

The Grammarians reject secondary meaning per se. The *Mahābhāṣya* says that "every word has the capacity to express any meaning if there is the intention." The significative power is of two kinds, well known and less known. The first is called primary and the second secondary. The *tātparya* (intention) can be that of God or the tradition of elders.

Suggestion (*Vyañjanā*)

(*E*63). Suggestion is a kind of impression in the mind produced by a flash of insight (*pratibhā*) or similar event, on the basis of the contextual factors, which is independent of any incompatibility to the literal meaning and which may or may not be associated with the literal meaning.

(*E*64). Suggestion is acceptable to the Grammarians, for they consider *nipātas* as suggestors (*dyotakas*); the *nipātas* suggest the power existing in the words that are uttered along with them. The *sphoṭa* is also accepted as suggested by the phonemes. This suggestive power is experienced in the phoneme, the literal meaning, the word, part of a word, the texture of the expression, and so on. Contextual factors are only helpful in revealing the suggestive power.

(*E*65). The Naiyāyikas reject suggestion, saying that it can be included in secondary meaning. This view is not acceptable, for secondary meaning requires incompatibility of the primary meaning and leads to a meaning somehow connected to it. Suggestion does not meet these criteria and cannot be included in secondary meaning.

Sphoṭa

(*E*66). Now, what is the meaning-bearing element in an expression?

The Mīmāṃsaka view that it is the individual phonemes is not correct, for then the utterance of later phonemes (other than the first) will be superfluous and unnecessary. It cannot be the collection of phonemes, for simultaneity of the phonemes is impossible, as each phoneme disappears as soon as it is uttered. Revelation or production is an instantaneous one, and there is no time available for the phonemes or their group to be perceptible.

(*E*67). The Naiyāyikas say that even though the phonemes are impermanent, the word can be perceived on the basis of the last phoneme, together with the impressions of the experience of the previous phonemes in their specific order. Or it can be assumed that each earlier phoneme produces its own subtle echo, extending till the last phoneme is revealed, and hence the word can be considered perceptible. Or the meaning is understood from the last phoneme together with the impressions of the earlier phonemes.

None of these explanations is possible. In the first view sequence cannot be perceived, because one phoneme is lost and the next alone remains. In the second, meaning cannot be assigned to the word, because the word does not exist. In the third, the order of sequence cannot be retained, because in recollection of impressions there is no need for such sequence.

Then what is the meaningful element? It is *sphoṭa*.

(*E*68–69). There are four levels of speech (*vāc*): *parā*, *paśyantī*, *madhyamā*, and *vaikharī*. Of the, *parā vāc* is *śabdabrahman* without any activity (*spanda*) of the form of *bindu*, originating (from *Kuṇḍalinī*) in the *mūlādhāracakra*, the spot inside the body between the anus and the sex organ. When it is raised by the internal air to the *nābhicakra* (or *svādhiṣṭhānacakra* in the navel region) and becomes perceptible to the mind, it is called *paśyantī*. These two are said to be realized by yogins in their *nirvikalpaka* and *savikalpaka* types of *samādhi*. Raised farther up by the same air to the *anāhatacakra* in the region of the heart, it is called *madhyamā*, still too subtle to be comprehended by the sense organs, but in the form of *sphoṭa*, bearing the meaning, and comprehensible by the mind at the time of *japa* (concentrated, silent utterance). Then, coming to the vocal organs in the mouth and articulated, it becomes the *vaikharī* and is capable of being heard by others also.

(*E*71–72). For *madhyamā* and *vaikharī* the sound is produced simultaneously; the former reveals the *sphoṭa*, the meaning bearer; the latter is just meaningless sound. The *madhyamā* is subtle, can be realized internally at the time of *japa*, and so on. It reveals the permanent *śabda sphoṭa* identical with Brahman, the speech principle according to Bhartṛhari. Though integral and indivisible, the *padasphoṭa* or *vākyasphoṭa* appears as phonemes and the like on the basis of the adjuncts through which it is revealed. Strictly speaking, it has no parts.

(*E*72). The phonemes, which are factors of the sound (*dhvani*) that reveal the *sphoṭa*, seem to be part of the *sphoṭa*. The apparent multiplicity in the *sphoṭa* is due to that of the *dhvani* that reveals it. According to the view that *sphoṭa* can be analyzed, it is revealed by the last phoneme, the previous phonemes being helpful to indicate the intention.

(*E*73–75). *Dhvani* is of two kinds, *prākṛta* and *vaikṛta*. The former is the revealer of the *sphoṭa*, the latter is produced from the former and keeps it (to be heard by the listener), and is responsible for such modifications of the sound as the speed of utterance (*vṛtti*).

(*E*76–77). When a man utters a sentence like "bring the pot", the speech at the *vaikharī*-level is heard by the listener, reaches his mind through the sense organ, and reveals the meaning. The term *sphoṭa* can be derived as that from which the meaning bursts forth. As far as the speaker is concerned, the sound is produced simultaneously by the *madhyamā* and the *vaikharī*. To the listener, the *vaikharī* helps in revealing the *madhyamā* that gives the *sphoṭa*, the meaning bearer.

All eight varieties of *sphoṭa* are based on their meaningfulness. Strictly, only the *vākyasphoṭa* is meaningful, for in the word it is the complete utterance that reveals the meaning.

Accessory Conditions for Understanding Sentence Meaning

(*E*77–80). Expectancy (*ākāṅkṣā*), consistency (*yogyatā*), contiguity (*āsatti*), and intention (*tātparya*) are the accessory conditions for understanding the sentence's meaning. Expectancy is responsible for giving the unity of the sentence. It is the desire on the part of the listener on hearing a word in a sentence to know the idea that can be related to its meaning, in order to get a complete sense; though expectancy is on the listener's part, it is figuratively attributed to the words and their meanings. It can be called incompleteness of the expression. Patañjali says (in 2.1.1) that *sāmarthya* is *vyapekṣā*, or interdependence, which is not between words but between their meanings. In a sentence such as "See, the deer is running," the word "see" requires an object, and hence the whole utterance becomes a complete sentence; in "Devadatta cooks rice," the verb "cooks" requires the agent and object for completion of meaning, and thus there is unity of sentence. "The pot is the object, bringing is the action" is not a single sentence like "bring the pot," for expectancy requires the relevant *kārakas* in the proper case endings.

(*E*81–82). Semantic fitness (*yogyatā*) is the competence for mutual connection. "He wets it with water" has fitness, because wetting requires a liquid and water is a liquid; but "he wets it with fire" has no fitness, because fire is not a liquid and has no competence for wetting, which can be done only with a liquid. The Naiyāyikas say that in such cases (of incongruity) the words give their individual meanings, but there is no knowledge of the syntactic connection; this claim is wrong. The meaning being mental, there is no obstruction for a connected idea. Hence empty words like "the son of a barren woman" are meaningful. Bhartṛhari has said that worlds convey meanings, even if they are nonexistent in the world. The knowledge of incongruity itself is based on the knowledge of the sentence meaning.

(*E*82–83). Contiguity (*āsatti*) is the absence of words unconducive to understanding the syntactical connection. It exists to help dull people to get the sentence meaning; intelligent persons can easily get it with the help of expectancy, even if there is no contiguity. Intervention of irrelevant words may stand in the way of understanding the meaning.

(*E*84–85). Intention (*tātparya*) is God's desire that a word or a sentence must be uttered to indicate its particular meaning. Although the Grammarians accept that any word can be capable of conveying a meaning, it only does so when there is *tātparya*; the word "pot" does not convey the meaning of a cloth, because there is no intention. In the case of ambiguous expressions the disambiguating intention is that of the speaker, and the intention is to be ascertained on the basis of contextual factors. In the case of Vedic sentences, God's intention is to be assumed.

If the significative power (*śakti*) can be regulated through contextual factors, what is the need for assuming intention? Our experience is that in ambiguous expressions we get both meanings through the power of the expressions themselves, and we feel uncertain regarding the intention.

Meaning of Verbal Roots (*Dhātvartha*)

(*E*85–87). The meaning of the verbal root is an operation (*vyāpāra*) conducive to the production of a result (*phala*) and accompanied by a volition or effort (*yatna*). The term "result" means the effect of the action indicated by the verbal root. And "*operation*" means the operation indicated by the root for producing the result. "Conducive" (*anukūla*) means the association (*saṃsarga*) of the action and the result.

(*E*88). The *Nirukta* statement "The verb has an operation as its predominant element, and the nouns have existence (*sattva*) as their predominant element" shows that the operation is the most important element in a verb. The verbal suffix indicates the number and the *kāraka* relationship; the time (tense) qualifies the activity.

(*E*89–90). Others say that a verbal root denotes both the result and the operation, and that the relation between the two is one of the accomplisher (*uddeśya*) and the accomplished (*vidheya*). The two meanings arise separately and are connected with difficulty. And it is cumbersome to assume two separate explanations for the same word. So they say that the significative power of the verbal root is the operation delimited by the effect or the effect delimited by the operation.

(*E*92). The Mīmāṃsakas (Maṇḍana Miśra) say that the meaning of the verbal root is the effect, and the meaning of the personal suffix is the operation. This view is against such a rule as Pāṇini's "*La* is added in the sense of *karman*" and so on (3.4.69), where the personal suffix is not assigned the meaning of operation. Moreover, for words in different tenses—*pacati*, "cooks," *pakṣyati*, "will cook," and so on—the meaning of the operations of blowing the fire and the rest will have to be assigned to different suffixes, which is more cumbersome than assigning it to the single verbal root.

Again, if the suffix indicates the operations of blowing and so on, even in words like *gacchati*, "he goes," the same operation will be meant, and to avoid that problem one will have to say that the suffix indicates the operations of blowing and so on, when used along with the root *pac*.

(*E*94). Moreover, the distinction between transitive and intransitive verbs will be affected, if such a view is taken.

(*E*95–96). Bhartṛhari has stated that what is accomplished (*siddha*) or what is not accomplished (*asiddha*) is described as a durative process of bringing into being (*sādhya*). It is called a verb (*kriyā*). The various minor operations, subordinate to the main operation, taking place in an order of sequence, considered in the mind as integral are called a verb (*kriyā*). The various operations that form parts of the overall operation take place in a sequence, but together, considered as a single operation, they form the verb (*kriyā*). The unity of the various operations is only in the mind. Thus the term *pacati*, "he cooks," can be applied for any one of the various operations involved in cooking.

(*E*98). *Objection*: In *ghaṭaṃ karoti*, "he makes a pot," the noun *ghaṭa*, "pot," seems to be *sādhya* or "to be accomplished", hence seems to come under the classification of verb.

Answer: From the word *ghaṭa* it is the accomplished pot that is understood, along with the word *karoti*, "he makes." The word may convey the idea that the pot is yet to be made.

Existence (*sattā*) is the meaning of the roots *as*, *bhū*, *vṛt*, and *vid*. They come under *kriyā* or activity because existence continues to operate in time, as a durative activity. "Existence" here means continuously having its own nature.

(*E*99). When the operation and the effect take place in different substrata, the verb is called transitive; and when the operation and the effect take place in the same substratum, the verb is called intransitive. It is intransitive when there is no question of effect, as in the case of the root *as*, "to be," for which the meaning is only existence, and no effect is discernible. The *Nirukta* explains it while interpreting the term *asti* in the six *bhāva vikāras*.

(*E*100). Strictly speaking, transitiveness is to be taken as the possibility of association with the meaning of what is *karman* (object) according to the rules of grammar. In the case of *adhyāsitā bhūmayaḥ*, "the grounds have been occupied," *adhyās* is transitive, for *bhūmi*, "ground," though semantically a substratum (*adhikaraṇa*), is *karman* according to a special rule of Pāṇini, *adhiśiṅsthāsāṃ karma*. In the verb *jīvati*, "lives," the idea of bearing life may be implied, still grammatically it is intransitive. In the verb *jānāti*, "he knows," knowledge is the effect, and the operation is the contact of the *ātman* and the mind; hence usages like *mano jānāti*, "the mind knows," *ātmā ātmānaṃ jānāti*, "one knows oneself," and the like are acceptable, for the operation and the effect have different substrata, one self limited by the body and the other self limited by mind.

(*E*103). Naiyāyikas say that the effect and the operation form the meaning of the verbal root, and the personal endings indicate the effort or volition (*kṛti*). The meaning of the verbal root is subordinate to the meaning of the suffix, which is predominant, and the meaning of the personal endings is subordinate to that of the noun in the nominative case.

(*E*104). Naiyāyikas distinguish sentient agent from insentient beings; effort (*yatna*) can be applied only to a sentient agent. *Caitraḥ pacati*, "Caitra cooks," means Caitra whose effort is conducive to the operation favorable to the softening of food. In *ratho gacchati*, "the chariot goes," because the chariot is insentient and cannot have a volition, the usage is explained as secondary.

(*E*104–105). This view is not acceptable to the Grammarian; Pāṇini's rule "yuṣmady upapade samānādhikaraṇe...says that the second-person suffix in the present tense is to be used when the *kāraka* indicated by the suffix and the second person (you) have the same substratum. This rule is not possible according to the Naiyāyika view. Even in the case of present participles, which are also substitutes of *la* just like the personal endings, only the meaning of volition will be obtained. You cannot say that the participles have significative power toward the agent, for according to the Nyāya view the prototype *la* has expressive power, not its many substitutes such as the participles and personal endings.

(*E*107). Assumption of secondary meaning for explaining usages like "the chariot moves" is cumbersome.

Pāṇini's rule *kartṛkaraṇayostṛtīyā* (2.3.12) comes under the general rule *anabhihite* (2.3.1); if the personal endings express only the volition (*kṛti*), as the Naiyāyika believes, the agent and the object (*karman*) being unexpressed, a sentence like *Caitraḥ pacati*, "Caitra cooks" will be impossible, because the word for the agent, Caitra, will have to be in the instrumental case.

(*E*108–109). The view that the meaning of the verbal root qualifies the meaning of the personal endings is also not correct. The general rule is that in a word the meaning of the stem and the meaning of the suffix go together to give the full meaning, and that the suffix meaning is predominant. Thus in *pācaka*, "cook", the meaning "agent" is predominant. Yāska's statement that the *ākhyāta* (verbal ending) has activity as the predominant meaning is an exception to that rule. Here *bhāvapradhānam* has to be taken as a *bahuvrīhi* compound.

(*E*110–111). The Naiyāyikas believe that in a sentence the principal qualificand is what is denoted by a nominative form. According to this view, a sentence like "paśya mṛgo dhāvati" ("see the deer is running") could be "paśya mṛgaṃ dhāvati" (which is wrong). But according to the Grammarians the activity of seeing (indicated by *paśya*) is the predominant sense. The running of the deer would be its object. Through mutual association (*saṃsarga*), the idea of *karman* is achieved. Even a verb can qualify another verb, the main verb.

Meaning of Particles (*Nipāta*)

(*E*113–114). In an expression like *sukham anubhūyate*, "happiness is being experienced," happiness being the object of experience, the verb is transitive. But that meaning of experiencing cannot be in the root, for without the preverb it is not known; and it cannot be in the preverb, because the meaning of personal ending associates only with the meaning of the verbal root. Hence suggestive power has to be assigned to the preverb.

This suggestiveness (*dyotakatva*) is the capacity to reveal the meaning potentially present in the word along with which it is used. Sometimes the suggestiveness may modify the action; sometimes it may indicate a relationship, as in the case of *karmapravacanīya*.

(*E*115). Naiyāyikas consider preverbs to be suggestive and the other indeclinables to be expressive, because lexicons give the meaning of indeclinables such as *sākṣāt* and *namaḥ*. This view is improper because in both cases the understanding of the meaning is similar.

(*E*118–120). Even the meaningfulness of particles is based on their suggestive power. Verbal roots have several meanings; in *pratiṣṭhate* the less-known sense ("to move") of the root *sthā*, "to stand," is made clear by the preverb *pra*. The accepted position is that the root is first associated with its *kārakas* and then only with the preverb.

In *candra iva mukham*, "moonlike face," the word *candra*, "moon," gets the meaning "something like the moon" figuratively, and the word *iva*, "like", acts only to suggest that intended meaning.

(*E*122–128). Some say that the word *iva* has the meaning of similarity, so there is no need for secondary meaning here. This notion is not correct, for according to this view the words *candra* and *mukha* cannot have the same substratum (and the genitive case ending may come for the word *candra*).

Some others consider the word *iva* to be suggesting the standard of comparison, indicating that both have the same qualities.

Negation is of two types, *paryudāsa* and *prasajyapratiṣedha* (the former is nominally bound and the latter is verbally bound). The negation in *paryudāsa* suggests some positive entity, for instance, *abrāhmaṇa* (non-Brahmin) indicates a *kṣatriya*. The compound is *tatpuruṣa*, which normally requires predominance for the meaning of the second member. The suggestive nature of the negation is quite in keeping with it. Normally this *paryudāsa* negation applies to someone similar to the one negated. Bhartṛhari says that the negative particle *nañ* indicates five meanings: similarity ("nonhorse," referring to a donkey), absence ("bring a nonhuman being"), littleness ("a girl without waistline," *anudarā kanyā*), pejoration ("non-Brahmin" applied to a Brahmin), and opposition (*adharma*, "demerit"). Cases of mutual exclusion (as in "the pot is not a piece of cloth") also come under this type; but normally examples of *paryudāsa* are compound words (of *nañ-tatpuruṣa* type). *Prasajyapratiṣedha* (verbally bound negative) can be either in a compound or in an uncompounded expression: "There is no pot in the house"; *asūryaṃpaśyā rājadārāḥ*, "the king's wives do not see the sun." Examples like "no doubt" (*na sandehaḥ*) come under this heading. *Prāgabhāva* (prior absence) and *pradhvaṃsābhāva* (posterior absence or destruction) are not suggested by the negative particle. *Atyantābhāva* (nonexistence) is syntactically connected with the verb, for instance, "There is no pot".

(*E*130–131). *Objection*: Anything that exists cannot be negated; negation does not apply to a nonexistent thing; thus negation becomes meaningless.

Answer: Both the expression and the meaning exist in the mind; what exists in the mind can be negated outside in real life. The word "pot" gives the idea of the existence of the pot, while the negation is to remove it—this view of the Naiyāyikas (who do not consider the meaning of words to be purely mental) has no stand, for existence or negation cannot apply to the mind. According to the *Mahābhāṣya*, secondary meaning is not accepted, and particles are not considered to be meaningful.

(*E*132–138). The word *eva*, "only," suggests the meanings of restriction and negation. Even without the use of the word, the meaning may be obtained. So they say that every word in a sentence has a restrictive sense. The restriction is of three kinds: when applied to a qualificand, it negates it in other places (for example, "Arjuna *alone* is a bowman"); when applied to an adjective, it emphasizes it ("the conch is white *alone*"); and when applied to a verb, it indicates absence of nonassociation *nīlaṃ sarojaṃ bhavaty eva*, "the blue lotus *does* exist").

Sometimes *eva* is understood. What Mīmāṃsakas call *parisaṃkhyā* (for instance, *pañca pañcanakhā bhakṣyāḥ*, "among five-nailed animals, five may be eaten") is included by the *Mahābhāṣya* as *niyama* or restriction.

Meaning of Verbal Endings (Tenses and Moods)

(*E*138–140). Although the Naiyāyikas discuss the meaning of the ten *L*-signs, the Grammarians accept meaningfulness only for what is actually spoken and therefore discuss the meaning of the substitutes, the actual verbal suffixes used in the world. Pāṇini gives meaning to *laṭ* and so on as a simpler means for description.

The meanings of the *L*-substitutes are number, time (present, past, and future tenses), *kārakas*, and the action noun (*bhāva*). Thus *laṭ*-substitutes express the present tense; along with class suffixes such as *śap*, the agent; and along with the suffixes *yak* and *ciṇ*, the action and the object.

Bhaṭṭoji Dīkṣita says that the verbal root denotes both the result and the activity and that the verbal suffixes denote the substratum (*āśraya*). In the active voice the activity is more important, and in the passive voice the result is more important. Together with the verbal suffixes, the verbal roots also indicate the number and the *kāraka* relationship.

(*E*141–143). The present tense is indicated by an activity that is started but not completed. *Liṭ* indicates the past tense earlier than today and also indirect information (in other words, information not directly perceived). In the case of auxiliary verbs *kṛ*, *as*, and *bhū* used along with other roots and the affix *-ām*, they indicate only action in general (as in *edhāṃ cakre*).

(*E*143–145). *Luṭ* indicates future, other than today, in addition. *Lṛṭ* is used in simple future. *Leṭ* is used only in Vedic language and has the same sense as *liṅ* (injunction and so on). *Loṭ* has the same sense of injunction and so on. *Laṅ* indicates the past tense, other than today. *Liṅ* has various meanings: injunction (*vidhi*), a summoning to do something (*nimantraṇa*), an invitation to do something (*āmantraṇa*), respectful command (*adhiṣṭa*), permission (*saṃpraśna*), and request (*prārthanā*). The first four meanings are different shades of prompting (*pravartana*) to action; this prompting is through the knowledge that the action will lead to a desired object, that the action is capable of performances, and that it is not associated with a strong undesirable result.

Luṅ indicates past tense in general, with past meaning prior to the present. *Lṛṅ* indicates the conditional sense, suggesting that the action is over, that if something had happened (which did not happen) another action (which also did not take place) would have taken place, for instance, "if fuel had been available, food would have been cooked."

(*E*146–149). The Naiyāyika view is that there are ten *L*-suffixes. *L*-suffixes indicate the agent, time (tense and mood), and the number.

The Grammarians think that agent is inferred from the term *ca*, "and" in Pāṇini's rule *laḥ karmaṇi ca-*. Bhāṭṭa Mīmāṃsakas consider that operation (*vyāpāra*) is meant instead. The Naiyāyikas take volition or effort to be the meaning, as it is simpler; they consider that *L*-suffixes indicate the meaning, not *L*-substitutes, which are many. In the passive sentence "maitreṇa gamyate grāmaḥ" ("the village is reached by Maitra"), the *L*-suffixes indicate volition (given in the instrumental case) and the *ātmanepada* indicates the result (the village). The main idea in the comprehension of the sentence meaning is the noun in the nominative case.

(*E*149–151). *Laṭ* indicates the present tense; *laṅ*, *luṅ*, and *liṭ* indicate the past tense; and *luṭ* and *lṛṭ* indicate the future. *Liṅ*, *loṭ*, and *leṭ* indicate injunction. The number is also indicated by the suffixes. *Leṭ* is used only in the Veda. The tenses, such as the present, are for the activity. *Laṭ* directly expresses the present tense and through secondary meaning indicates the substratum (*āśraya*). Time (past or future) that is very near the present may also be indicated by *laṭ*.

(*E*152–154). According to the Grammarians and the Bhāṭṭa Mīmāṃsakas the meaning obtained from the verbal suffixes has an operation as its main factor; according to the former an operation is the meaning of the verbal root, and according to the latter it is the mental activity (*bhāvanā*) and is conveyed by the verbal suffixes. "Caitraḥ taṇḍulaṃ pacati" ("Caitra cooks rice") means to the Grammarians "the activity of cooking that has Caitra as the agent and rice as the object." To the Mīmāṃsakas it means "the mental activity toward the action of cooking that has Caitra as its agent and rice as its object." The Naiyāyika insists that the meaning of the sentence has the noun in the nominative case as the main element, "Caitra who has a volition conducive to the action of cooking that has rice as the object."

(*E*157–158). *Liṅ* has the meanings injunction and benediction. *Loṭ* can mean injunction or permission. The Bhāṭṭa Mīmāṃsakas explain *vidhi* (injunction) as *pravartana* or prompting. On hearing a *liṅ* from the teacher the student has the knowledge that the teacher wants him to do something; this view is not correct. There is no authority to consider such knowledge as the cause for action on the student's part. It is the knowledge that the action will lead to some desired result that prompts action.

(*E*159–164). The Prābhākara Mīmāṃsakas say that the injunction means something should be done. *Svargakāmo yajeta*, "one desirous of heaven should perform the sacrifice" means (1) something should be done regarding sacrifice by heaven seeker; (2) something should be done, which is the means for heaven, and which is about sacrifice by one who is qualified; (3) sacrifice should be performed by heaven seeker, who is the person qualified to do it; (4) the performer of sacrifice is the heaven seeker; (5) I am a heaven seeker, therefore the sacrifice can be performed by my effort.

Naiyāyikas consider three powers for *liṅ*, meaning the knowledge of prompting. First, it is capable of being performed by effort; second, it will lead to a desirable result; and third, it will not be associated with a very bad effect. The power is not in all three together, but separately.

In the case of *lṛṅ* there is an argument based on the influence involved, as in "if there had been no fire, there would have been no smoke."

Kārakas

(*E*164–168). The six *kārakas* are *kartṛ*, agent; *karma*, object; *karaṇa*, instrument; *saṃpradāna*, recipient; *apādāna*, the fixed point from which splitting takes place; and *adhikaraṇa*, substratum. *Kārakas* such as the agent bring about the action. *Kartṛ*, agent, is the substratum of the operation indicated by the verbal root in the context. Thus in the example "he cooks with fire," burning may be an operation of fire but not of the contextual action, cooking, so fire is not the agent. When this operation is expressed by the verbal root, the agent will be in the nominative case; according to Pāṇini's view the nominative case indicates the *prātipadika* stem, and the *kārakas* are expressed by specific suffixes. In *Caitro bhavati*, "Caitra exists," Caitra is the agent (*kartṛ*); although that *kāraka* (*kartṛ*) is already expressed by the verbal suffix, the nominative case also indicates the same. In "Caitreṇa grāmaṃ gamyate" ("the village is reached by Caitra"), the meaning understood is "the contact with the village is a result of the action whose agent is Caitra."

The vocative (*saṃbodhana*) is also a *kāraka* because it is syntactically connected with "you" (understood from the context) and thereby with the action to be performed.

(*E*169–170). The definition of *kāraka* as the cause of action (*kriyānimittam*) is not correct, for it will apply even to the genitive case in "Caitrasya taṇḍulaṃ pacati" ("he cooks Caitra's food"), because Caitra is indirectly responsible for the cooking. The definition "those bringing about the action" is better; direct connection with the operation indicated by the verb is necessary. That is why the meaning of the genitive case, as well as of the nouns directly connected with other words (*upapada*), is not considered by the Grammarians to be *kāraka*. If the expectancy is not resolved, necessary words have to be taken as understood to explain the elliptical sentence.

(*E*169–170). The Naiyāyika view that the agent (*kartṛ*) is the *kāraka* that prompts all the other *kārakas* (to bring about the action) is not correct, for in cases like *sthālī pacati*, "the vessel cooks," and *asiḥ chinatti*, "the sword cuts," there is no prompting on the part of the vessel or the sword.

(*E*171–178). *Karma*, object, is that (*kāraka*) which is intended to have the same substratum as the effect of the action meant by the relevant verbal root and prompted by its main activity. It is the meaning of *īpsitatama*, "intended most" in Pāṇini's rule on *karma*. In "kāśīṃ gacchan pathi mṛtaḥ" ("going to Kāśī, he died on the way"), though he does not reach Kāśī, the intention was there, hence Kāśī is *karma kāraka*.

(*E*178–179). *Karaṇa*, instrument, is that *kāraka* the activity of which immediately brings about the action (meant by the verb). In "Rāmeṇa bāṇena hato bālī" ("Bālī was killed by Rāma with an arrow"), the activity of the arrow is the immediate cause for the death, though Rāma's activity may have begun earlier. Hence *bāṇa* is the instrument and Rāma the agent (*kartṛ*).

(*E*180–183). *Saṃpradāna*, recipient, is that *kāraka* for whom the operation meant by the verb is taking place. In "brāhmaṇāya gāṃ dadāti" ("he gives the Brahmin a cow"), the Brahmin is the recipient. The view that the gift meant is not to be returned is not valid. For giving clothes to the laundry man *saṃpradāna* is also possible: "rajakāya vastraṃ dadāti" and "rajakasya vastraṃ dadāti" are both correct. Patañjali gives the example "the teacher gave the student a thrashing." *Saṃpradāna*, used in the dative case, means the person to whom the action is intended. "Maitrāya vārttāṃ kathayati" ("he tells the news to Maitra") means the operation of telling that has the news as object and Maitra as the person for whom the operation is intended. In an intransitive verb also, as in *patye śete*, "she lies down for her husband," it is similar, it means she is lying down for the sake of her husband.

(*E*183–187). *Apādāna* is the substratum of the point of departure indicated by the contextual verb, and it is the same as the limit. The departure can be real or mentally conceived. In "vṛkṣaṃ tyajati khagaḥ" ("the bird abandons the tree"), separation is not the meaning of the root *tyaj*, hence *vṛkṣa* does not become *apādāna*. By limit is meant only the relatively fixed point as far as the relevant action is concerned. Hence we get "dhāvataḥ aśvāt patati" ("falls from the running horse"), for as far as falling is concerned, the horse is the fixed point, though it is also running. The meaning of the ablative case is the limit. "Vṛkṣāt parṇam patati" ("the leaf falls from the tree") means the falling that has the leaf as the agent and the limit (or the fixed point from which the separation takes place) as the tree.

(*E*187–189). *Adhikaraṇa*, substratum, is where the activity takes place, either through the agent or through the object. In "sthālyām odanaṃ gṛhe pacati" ("he cooks food in a vessel in the house"), the vessel is the place in which the object is affected by the action, and the house is the place of the agent's activity.

This *adhikaraṇa* is of three types. The first is *abhivyāpaka*, all-comprehensive, as in "tileṣu tailam asti" ("there is oil in the sesame"). The second is *aupaśleṣika*, proximity, as in Pāṇini's *sūtra* "iko yaṇ aci" ("*i*, *u*, *r*, *l* change to *y*, *v*, *r*, and *l*, respectively in the proximity of [when followed by] a vowel"). Kaiyaṭa's example *kaṭe āste*, "he sits on the mat," is not happy. (It means he sits on a part of the mat.) The third type is "vaiṣayika kaṭe āste."

(*E*190). Relations, like that of master and servant, which are different from the *kāraka* relations are indicated by the genitive case, as in *rājñaḥ puruṣaḥ*, "the king's servant."

Meaning of Nouns

(*E*192–196). The Mīmāṃsakas say that words denote the universal; the particulars are innumerable and it is cumbersome to assign the meaning to the particulars. Even though the word directly means the universal, the particulars are known through secondary meaning. If one particular is given as the meaning of a word (like "cow"), it will not be possible to associate the word with another particular.

Answer: Although particulars are innumerable, a particular can be an indication (*upalakṣaṇa*) of the universal, and there is no need to assume innumerable powers to refer to the individuals. Among the means of understanding the meaning of words, the most important—namely, the usage of elders—will give the meaning as applied to the particular. As Patañjali has said, even to one who takes the universal to be the meaning of a word, the particular does not cease to be the meaning.

(*E*197). The gender is also the meaning of a noun; the suffixes only suggest. The gender of many Sanskrit words, such as *khaṭvā*, "a cot" (feminine), has nothing to do with sex. One formal way of distinguishing the genders is the following: whatever can be put in apposition with "he" is masculine, with "she" is feminine, and with "it" is neuter.

(*E*198–203). The number is also the meaning of a noun. The nominal suffixes only suggest number; it is the stem that actually expresses it. The *kāraka* is also the meaning of nominal stem. Thus the nominal stem indicates five things—the universal, the particular, gender, number, and *kārakas*. Sometimes the expression itself can be the meaning of the word, as in referring to a name, in imitating sounds, and similar instances.

Meaning of Compound Words

(*E*203–204). The meaning of compounds is of two kinds: *jahatsvārtha*, giving up their own meaning, and *ajahatsvārtha*, without giving up their original meaning. The word *śuśrūṣā*, "serving," has given up the derivative meaning, "desire to hear". In *rājapuruṣa*, "the king's servant," the parts do not give up their meaning completely. In all five *vṛttis* accepted by the Grammarians—*kṛt*, *taddhita*, *samāsa*, *ekaśeṣa*, and *vākya*—the meaningfulness is in the whole, not in parts, because something more than the sum of the meanings of the parts is conveyed by them.

(*E*211–212). Naiyāyikas and Mīmāṃsakas, who accept *vyapekṣā* (mutual expectancy or association) in compound words and the like, say that there is no special power for the compound word. In a compound like *rājapuruṣa*, "the king's servant," the word *rāja* can mean related to *rājan* through secondary meaning. In an example like *ghanaśyāma*, "cloud-black," the meaning of similarity (black like the cloud) can be obtained through secondary meaning. Understanding the meaning of the components is essential for determining the meaning of the compound.

Answer: If a special meaning is not accepted for the compound word as a whole, the stem will not be a *prātipadika*, so nominal suffixes cannot be applied. The rule *kṛttaddhitasamāsaśca* is not to make the compound a *prātipadika*, but to restrict the term *prātipadika* to compounds alone (and not to a sentence).

Objection: If unity of meaning (*ekārthībhāva*) is accepted for compounds, the components will be meaningless, and syntactic connection will be difficult.

Answer: The special meaning comes only after the componential meanings have been understood and connected.

(*E*213–216). When the componential meaning is against the accepted popular usage, the individual meanings are rejected, and the component will be *jahatsvārtha*.

MAHĀBHĀṢYAPRADĪPODDYOTA

V. K. S. N. Raghavan

This work is a commentary by Nāgeśa Bhaṭṭa on Kaiyaṭa's *Pradipa*. In it Nāgeśa explains the views of Patañjali following Kaiyaṭa for the most part though sometimes he differs from him. *E* references are to the edition of the work in five volumes by Vedavrata, published by the Haryana Sahitya Samsthana, Gurukula Jhajjhar, Rohtak, 1969. A small section (2.1.2–2.1.49) has been translated by Shivaram Dattatrey Joshi (Centre for Advanced Study in Sanskrit, University of Poona, Poona, 1969: G627), and references labeled *ET* are to this publication. The numbers refer to philosophical points made in the text.

Summary of Philosophical Topics

1 (*ET*16–17). Explaining the *Mahābhāṣya* passage "catvāri padajātāni, nāmākhyātopasarganipātāśca" ("there are four types of words, noun, verb, preverb, and indeclinables also"), Nāgeśa says that the

word *ca*, "also", suggests the fourfold classification of speech (*vāc*): *parā*, *paśyantī*, *madhyamā*, and *vaikharī*.

2 Referring to the two heads of the bull (of *vāc*) mentioned in the Vedic stanza, Patañjali's explanation that they were the permanent (*nitya*) and the produced (*kārya*) was interpreted by Kaiyaṭa to mean the suggested (*vyaṅgya*) and the suggestor (*vyañjaka*). Nāgeśa elucidates this interpretation by saying that the suggested is the *madhyamā* type and the suggestor the *vaikharī* type of speech.

3 (*ET*18). *Ṛg Veda* 1.164.45, quoted by Patañjali, says: *Vāc* has been divided into four levels, which the learned Brahmins know; the first three are kept (hidden) in the cave; people speak only the fourth. Nāgeśa gives two explanations: first, each of the four parts of speech—noun, verb, preverb, and indeclinable—has only one-fourth in the speech of common people; and, second, the first three parts of speech (namely, *parā*, *paśyantī*, and *madhyamā*) are hidden.

4 He quotes *Vākyapadīya* 1.143 "(Vaikharyā madhyamāyāśca... tryayya vācaḥ param padam) and explains: *vaikharī* is the audible speech; *madhyamā* is the speech in the mind of the speaker, and cannot be perceived (by the listener), but is the cause of the speech utterance. *Paśyantī* is beyond the scope of worldly parlance (being undifferentiated), but the yogins are able to visualize it and even analyze it. At the *parā* stage, speech is beyond the reach even of yogic perception.

Nāgeśa gives another quotation in support of his view. "Svarūpajyotir evāntaḥ parā vāg anapāyinī tasyāṃ dṛṣṭasvarūpāyām adhikāro nivatate" ("The supreme speech [*parā vāk*] is imperishable and is of intrinsic brilliance; if one realizes the exact nature of the eternal resplendent luster, the (*karmic*) bondage or *avidyā-karman* retracts from one").

Just as Vedāntins hold the supreme being to be Absolute, Nāgeśa considers the supreme speech (*parā vāk*) to be Absolute, the realization of which leads one to release from karmic bonds.

5 (*E*19). While commenting on the *Ṛg Vedic* stanza "saktum iva" (10.71.2), quoted in the *Mahābhāṣya*, Nāgeśa identifies *vāc* with Supreme Brahman. Those persons who have an adequate knowledge and capacity to think deeply with regard to Vedic grammar achieve union (*sāyujya*) with Śabda Brahman. First they acquire deep knowledge by correctly understanding the unique import of words.

In the case of word conveying the meaning of Brahman, there is the knowledge of the identity between the word and its meaning. Persons of extraordinary wisdom achieve *sāyujya* or identity with the Supreme Speech because the blessed goddess Laksmī, with self-brilliance and Brahman's form, resides in every articulated speech of those well-versed Grammarians.

6 (*E*8). Explaining Patañjali's explanation of *śabda* (word) as "the sound that conventionally conveys a particular sense," Nāgeśa says:

"The term *pratītapadārthaka* refers to a word that is well known among the people as capable of indicating precisely a certain object." It is the word that is made up of sounds (in the form of articulated sound syllables) that are audible to the sense of hearing. It is also necessary that a word must have a precise meaning well known in the world. The grammatical text analyzes such words into their components and explains them.

7 Explaining the terms *dhvani* and *sphoṭa* used in the *Mahābhāṣya*, Nāgeśa says that *sphoṭa* refers to the *madhyamā* type of *vāk*, while *dhvani* refers to the *vaikharī* type.

8 Among the uses of Grammar, Patañjali gives the first place to the protection of the Vedas; Kaiyaṭa explains it as gaining the *puruṣārthas*. Elaborating this notion, Nāgeśa says that *puruṣārtha* means *dharma* and *mokṣa* here. Grammar is useful for obtaining a correct understanding of the forms and meanings of Vedic texts, so it forms part of the means for the achievement of *dharma* and *mokṣa*. The study of Grammar results in understanding the correct sense of Vedic passages, enabling one thereby to perform the ordained rituals, hence causing the enjoyment of heavenly bliss (*svarga*). Grammar is also useful for correctly understanding the meaning of Upaniṣadic passages, thereby causing the attainment of supreme bliss (*mokṣa*). A study of Grammar is essential for understanding the Vedic and Upaniṣadic texts correctly, enabling one to perform one's duties properly and to have a correct knowledge of reality.

SPHOṬAVĀDA

K. Kunjunni Raja

Sphoṭavāda is an independent work by Nāgeśa Bhaṭṭa on the *sphoṭa* theory. According to Nāgeśa, the founder of the theory was the sage Sphoṭāyana, mentioned by Pāṇini in formulating one of his rules. This tradition is unknown to Bhartṛhari, who considers Audumbarāyana (mentioned by Yāska) as having held a view similar to the *sphoṭa* theory. Nāgeśa differs considerably from Bhartṛhari and shows the influence of Kashmir Śaivism and the Tantric tradition. Minor differences can be seen between the views given in this work and those offered in the *sphoṭa* section of the *Paramalaghumañjūṣā* (see above).

The edition (*E*) referred to is that by V. Krishnamacharya (Adyar Library and Research Centre, Madras, 1946). Numbers refer to philosophical points made in the text.

Summary

(*E*1). According to the Grammarians there are eight kinds of *sphoṭa*: phoneme (*varṇa*) *sphoṭa* (particular and universal forms), indivisible-word (*akhaṇḍapada*) *sphoṭa*, word (*pada*) *sphoṭa* (particular and universal forms), indivisible-sentence (*akhaṇḍavākya*) *sphoṭa*, and sentence (*vākya*) *sphoṭa* (particular and universal forms).

(*E*5–6). The term *sphoṭa* means that from which the meaning bursts out, that is, the signifier. The eight types of *sphoṭa* are all designating (*vācaka*) linguistic signs. The letters actually heard, along with the order of sequence, bear the meaning, not the prototype (*sthānin*), the grammatical technical term (like *la* in *bhavati*). It may seem simpler to assume that the meaning-bearing capacity belongs to the single technical term *la*, instead of to its substitutes like *ti*; but the common man (who is not a Grammarian) will not understand the meaning from *la* and the like. Even though Pāṇini's Grammar may be an accessory to the Vedas (*Vedāṅga*), terms like *la* (for verbal endings) have no meaning bearing power. Even secondary meaning cannot apply to them.

Objection: One who has learned the various substitutes for different technical terms may get confused and have difficulty understanding the meaning.

Answer: As in the case of the scripts reminding the phonemes, here also it is possible. All of the items are needed to help the recollection.

(*E*7). Moreover, worldly usage, the most important among the means of understanding the meaning of words, applies only to the words used, not to the artificial technical term, such as l-suffixes.

(*E*9). It may be noted that the meaning-bearing capacity is only for the phonemes when they are together (in a particular sequence), not for them individually. Otherwise, each phoneme will be a nominal (*prātipadika*) stem and get nominal suffixes.

(*E*10). Thus meaningfulness is only for the actual expressions used in language, not for the artificially assumed prototype. The word *ghaṭena* has *ghaṭa* as the stem and *-ena* as the instrumental singular suffix; only the grammarian knows it, not the ordinary man who uses the language, to whom the splitting is artificial. Hence the whole word *ghaṭena* must be assumed to convey the full meaning.

Similarly in the sentences *hare'va*, "Oh Hari! protect (us)" and *viṣṇo'va*, "O Visnu! protect (us)," the same argument shows that the whole sentence has to be taken as the meaning-bearing unit. Thus word *sphoṭa* and sentence *sphoṭa* have to be accepted.

(*E*11). The sentence meaning, which is of the form of the association (of word meanings), is something new, and therefore here the significative power is the relationship.

Objection: The primary meaning of words is understood from the behavior of elderly people. Still, after the individual meanings of words have been understood from the words, the mind with the knowledge of their mutual expectancy understands the sentence meaning; there is no need for a special power.

Answer: The understanding of the word meanings from the words is impossible if the words are not understood clearly; mutual expectancy (*ākāṅkṣā*) is the same as the sentence power (*vākyaśakti*).

Objection by a Mīmāṃsaka: The mutual association of the word meanings is known as the object of intention (*tātparya*). Intention is desire to convey the particular meanings; in the absence of such an intention or in the presence of another intention, the proper meaning will not be understood. Instead of taking these last two cases as obstructions to the knowledge of the sentence meaning, it is simpler to take the knowledge of intention as one of the positive conditions for understanding the sentence meaning.

(*E*12–13). *Answer*: The novelty (*apūrvatva*) of the sentence meaning cannot be the object of intention, and even from the primary meanings of the words the sentence meaning can be obtained (without the help of intention). In the case of words uttered by a parrot, the meaning of the utterance is understood, even though it is certain that there is no intention on the part of the parrot. Hence intention is not essential for understanding the sentence meaning. God's intention also cannot be assumed, for it can be known only through the effect. Mīmāṃsakas who do not accept the existence of God understand the meaning (without the help of intention); and Vedic sentences will be meaningless if intention is necessary (for there is no intention of the speaker or God there). Even the intention of the teacher cannot be assumed for the Veda, for the teacher may be a fool or a wise man. "Two meanings appear from the sentence, we do not know which one will suit the context—such general experience is also against assuming intention as a cause for the understanding of the sentence's meaning.

(*E*15–17). In ambiguous cases it is the context that helps in deciding the meaning, not the intention. Thus in a sentence like "bring the pot" the sentence meaning, which is of the nature of the mutual association of the word meanings, is determined from the sentence itself. From worldly experience it is known that the sentence gives the connected sentence meaning; but through the method of substitution the words are also assumed to have their individual meanings. Hence the sentence meaning can be considered to be mutual association (*saṃsarga*) of word meanings, which is obtained from the sentence as a whole (*vākyaśakti*).

(*E*17–18). *Naiyāyika objection*: What is the need for assuming a significative power for the sentence, if the mutual association (*saṃsarga*) can be obtained from the word meanings themselves with the help of mutual expectancy and so on? Mutual expectancy (*ākāṅkṣā*) is the desire to understand the word syntactically related to the other words in the sentence in order to bring out the intended connected meaning. The sentence "bring the pot" will be understood by the ordinary man, but not the statement "bringing is the activity and the pot is the object"; the latter may be understood by the Nyāya scholar, to whom the morphemes *ghaṭa* (pot), *-am* (the accusative singular suffix indicative of the object), and so on are separate words (*pada*).

(*E*18–21). *Answer*: You cannot say that because the intention of God is fixed (this word must give this particular meaning), a special new sense in the sentence meaning cannot be obtained, for I can accept God's intention for the sentence meaning as well (Let this sentence give this particular meaning). You cannot say that a special power should be assumed to convey the special added meaning in the sentence, for assumption of a special power involves complexity. The view that a *pada* is a meaningful item is not affected, for it is not the *pada* but its knowledge that leads to the sentence meaning. Thus what the Grammarians call the significative power of the sentence (*vākyaśakti*) is the same as what the Naiyāyikas call mutual expectancy (*ākāṅkṣā*). Hence it is said that the sentence meaning is the mutual association of the word meanings (*saṃsargo vākyārthaḥ*). And that is why the *Mahābhāṣya* says that Pāṇini's rule *kṛttaddhitasamāsaśca* uses the term *samāsa* to exclude the sentence.

(*E*24–27). Some others say that meaningfulness is located only in the sentence and not in its parts, the words. People understand the meaning only from the behavior of elders, and that is with reference to sentences. The meaning of words is understood separately through the substitution method; but that does not make the sentence meaning unreal. And in cases like *hare'va,* "O Hari! protect," it is necessary to take the sentence as a whole. With the help of the knowledge of word meanings one can get the sentence meaning; but then without the help of word meanings also the sentence meaning can be understood directly (through observing the behavior of elders).

(*E*28–29). This view is not accepted by some others. The word *ghaṭam* indicates the meaning of the pot and its being the object; hence there is no need to accept a collective power for the sentence. Knowledge of meaning is based on the way it is learned.

(*E*29–30). Even among those who accept significative power for the sentence, some may get the knowledge of sentence meaning directly, others after understanding the *kārakas,* and some by other means. But the sentence meaning is based on the mutual association of the individual word meanings.

(*E*30–31). *Objection*: Knowledge of word meaning is the cause for the knowledge of the connected sentence meaning, for on hearing a new sentence one who knows the word meanings does have the knowledge of the sentence's meaning.

Answer: Without knowing the significative power of the sentence, one does not know the sentence's meaning. People who are able to understand the meaning from a sentence sometimes find it difficult to identify the words and other parts, if they have no grammatical knowledge. And acceptance of significative power for words does not involve complexity, because it is valid in worldly usage.

(*E*31–53). *Question*: Just as words convey word meanings, why should the sentence not also convey the sentence meaning? And just as the word meanings are remembered, why should the sentence meaning not also be remembered? The sentence meaning itself is the *śabdabodha*, the meaning arrived at for the sentence.

Answer: The sentence meaning is not directly experienced. The words produce their individual meanings through recollection, but the sentence does not. The words convey their meaning to the listener through recollection; then with the help of the sentence's significative power, the knowledge of the sentence meaning is determined, consisting of the word meanings and their mutual association.

(*E*54–55). The Mīmāṃsakas say that it is not proper to assume a special power for the sentence, because secondary meaning is sufficient. The sentence meaning is not something new. On hearing the sentence "the village is on the river Haridrā," even a person who does not know such a river will know that it is the name of a river because of the use of the word "river" accompanying it in the sentence; similarly, when the words have conveyed their individual meanings, it is possible to understand the sentence meaning with the help of the knowledge of mutual expectancy. To make it a verbal knowledge, secondary meaning is assumed. The secondary meaning gives the meaning related to what is conveyed by the primary meaning. It does not affect the authoritativeness of the Vedas, even though the sentence meaning is conveyed, not directly, but by secondary meaning from the word meanings on the basis of expectancy and so on.

Answer: This view is not acceptable. Secondary meaning operates when there is some incompatibility with the literal sense. We cannot say that the condition for secondary meaning is the incompatibility with the speaker's intention, for that does not work everywhere; and we have to assume an intention. It is simpler to assume a power to the sentence than to assume an intention.

In fact, secondary meaning is the relation to the literal meaning, not the relation to what is understood; according to the Vedas it is not possible to assume secondary meaning here.

(*E*56–58). *Objection*: by Prābhākara Mīmāṃsakas: The sentence has no special power to convey the sentence meaning. By contrast, the words have the power to convey the connected meaning. When it can be explained by the significative power of words, there is no valid reason for assuming a power to the sentence. The understanding of the sentence meaning is not possible unless it becomes the object of the significative power. It is simpler to assume it for the words instead of assuming a separate power (to the sentence). So each word gives the syntactic connection also (along with its own meaning) on the basis of mutual expectancy and so on and the fact that the words have been uttered together (as one group). Moreover, on hearing a word there is always a desire to know its syntactic position, and that desire can be satisfied only from words. It is not something new, for the syntactic relation of each word is known in a general way. The view that the power of a word is to give its meaning as syntactically connected with that of other words is not correct. The meaning of the other words can be obtained only from those words. The impression that a word like *ghaṭa*, "a pot," gives only its isolated meaning is erroneous.

(*E*59). *Answer*: This view is not acceptable, for even though you assume that the words have a power to indicate the syntactic relationship, its exact nature is known only by the other words uttered, and the utterance together (*samabhivyāhāra*) of the words has to be assumed as a cause for knowing it, which is more complex.

(*E*60–61). You have to assume that the words give the syntactic relation in a general way and that the specific relation is understood through inference. Then that inference itself can give the syntactic relation (*saṃsarga*). The experience is that the sentence's meaning is determined from the sentence itself, not that it is determined from inference or perception.

(*E*66–68). *Objection*: The cause of understanding the sentence meaning is the word meanings or their recollection, not the knowledge of words. On seeing a vague white form and hearing the sound of hooves and neighing, one gets the idea that a white horse is running. Here there is no syntactic relation between the seeing of the white form and the hearing of the neighing.

Answer: Such a knowledge can be obtained even from inference. If the knowledge is to be verbal, it must be from words.

(*E*68–69). *Objection*: Knowledge of a word or a sentence is impossible, because sequence is part of the utterance, and the phonemes are never together.

Answer: Each phoneme is received as associated with the previous ones; that is why there is difference between *sara* and *rasa*, where the same phonemes appear in different sequence. The view that the word is grasped through the perception of the last phoneme and the recollection of the earlier phonemes is not acceptable, because there is no rule regarding the sequence between what is heard and what is recollected. There is no rule that recollection of past experience is always in the same order.

(*E*69–70). The three types of *sphoṭa* discussed (phoneme, word, and sentence) are differentiated on the basis of the listener. Some understand the distinct meanings of the stem and the suffix, some get the meaning from the words, and some others from the sentence as a whole. The meaning is understood from the whole.

Akhaṇḍasphoṭa

(*E*71–74). On the basis of the experience "it is a single word" and "it is a single sentence," it is necessary to assume an indivisible word (*sphoṭa*) and an indivisible sentence (*sphoṭa*) free from the distinctions of phonemes, stems, and suffixes. It is not like the idea of "forest" for a collection of trees. Otherwise even a phoneme could be divided like *ṛ*, split into *r* and vowel bits.

(*E*74–75). *Objection*: There is no evidence for the existence of the phonemes. It is the articulated sounds that are heard, and the *sphoṭa* can directly be suggested by these sounds, even without the assumption of a phoneme between them.

Answer: Let the articulated sounds be identical with the phonemes. But mere sounds may not be able to reveal the *sphoṭa*. The phonemes are the revealers of *sphoṭa*.

This *sphoṭa* is the designator (*vācaka*), because we have the experience "This meaning is obtained from this word or sentence." According to some, the *sphoṭas* are innumerable (each word or sentence having a separate *sphoṭa*). Others say that it is simpler to assume that there is only one *sphoṭa* and that it appears to be many on the basis of the differences in the phonemes that suggest it.

(*E*76). It is to be noted that the meaning is understood from the *sphoṭa* revealed by the phonemes in a specific sequential order. In the case of synonyms, the *sphoṭas* are to be taken as different (the synonyms *ghaṭa* and *kalaśa*, both meaning a pot, are different *sphoṭas*).

(*E*80–83). Others say that there is only one phoneme. It appears to be many on the basis of the differences in the place of articulation, in the effort taken, and so on. Recognition of the same phoneme or word is on the basis of the differences in the revealing medium. This view is not acceptable.

(*E*92–94). The *sphoṭa* theory that claims the word or the sentence as indivisible does not take away the validity of the science of Grammar, which is concerned with the linguistic analysis of words into stem and suffixes. Just as the discussion of the five sheaths (*pañcakośa*) in the Upaniṣads is to lead the seeker after truth step by step to the knowledge of Brahman, so linguistic analysis of words is a step in the right direction. Even if the division into stem and suffixes may be artificial, it is useful as a means for arriving at the ultimate truth.

(*E*95–96). Some say that "phoneme *sphoṭa*" means those monophonemic words found in lexicons: "*sakhaṇḍa* word *sphoṭa*" means that a word indicates its meaning when its derivation is also known; so also the sentence *sphoṭa* is the sentence understood along with its further analysis. The indivisible word and the indivisible sentence are not understood in a way that involves knowledge of their derivations.

Sphoṭa-Universal (*Jātisphoṭa*)

(*E*96–101). Some say it is reasonable to assume meaningfulness of the universal word or sentence rather than of the individuals. This universal is revealed by the phonemes in the specific order of sequence. Although *sphoṭa*, being a universal, is eternal, the meaning is understood only when it is known. The universal is identical with existence (*sattā*), identical with Brahman. Thus both the signifier *sphoṭa* and the signified meaning (*sattā* existence) are identical with Brahman.

(*E*102). The Grammarian Nāgeśa has revised and explained the *sphoṭa* theory of the ancient seer Sphoṭāyana.

46

JÑĀNENDRA SARASVATĪ

This writer appears to have flourished about 1730. He was the teacher of Nīlakaṇṭha Dīkṣita and himself a pupil of Vāmanendrasvāmin. He composed a *Tattvabodhinī* on the *Siddhāntakaumudī*, which he was apparently unable to complete; it was completed by Jayakṛṣṇa Maunin as *Subodhinī* (see below, summary 51).

47

GOPĀLAKṚṢṆA ŚĀSTRIN

Gopālakṛṣṇa is the author of *Śābdikacintāmaṇi*, on the *Mahābhāṣya*. His father's name was Vaidyanātha, and he identifies his guru as Rāmabhadra Adhvarin. The *New Catalogus Catalogorum* tells us that Gopālakṛṣṇa was a classmate of Sadāśivendra Brahmendra (who flourished about 1720) and the spiritual teacher of King Vijaya Raghunātha Tondaiian I of Pudukottah (1730–1769), as well as the teacher of the Appayya Dīkṣita who composed *Pāṇiniyasūtraprakāśa*. Yudhisthira Mimamsaka infers from all this information that his dates fall between 1597 and 1647,[1] but he is probably about a century early, and a date approximating 1725 would be preferable. Gopālakṛṣṇa also composed a commentary on the *Uṇādisūtras*.

48

DHARAṆĪDHARA

The *New Catalogus Catalogorum*, vol. 9, p. 237b, cites a work on Grammar called *Bodhapaddhati*, composed in 1730 by Dharaṇīdhara, son of Jvalānanda of Tīkṣṇajñatīya.

49

VAIDYANĀTHA PAYAGUṆḌA

Vaidyanātha, the son of Veṇī and Mahādeva, was a direct disciple of Nāgeśa Bhaṭṭa, so he should have flourished about 1735. He hailed from Kāśī, that is, Varanasi, where he prepared a line of pupils. The name Bālaṃbhaṭṭa is given as the author of some of his works, such as the *Kalā* on Nāgeśa's *Laghumañjūṣā*, but his son, who wrote a *Mitākṣara-vṛtti*, was known as Bālaṃbhaṭṭa.

Vaidyanātha wrote a number of commentaries, including *Prabhā* on Bhaṭṭoji's *Śabdakaustubha*, *Bhāvaprakāśikā* on Hari Dīkṣita's *Śabdaratna*, a *Chāyā* on Nāgeśa's *Pradīpoddyota*, *Kalā* on Nāgeśa's *Laghumañjūṣā*, and *Bhāvaprakāśa* on Bhaṭṭoji's *Prauḍhamanoramā*. The last two works have been edited. He also wrote a *Bhāvaprakāśikā* on the *Bṛhatśabdendu-śekhara*, a *Cidasthimala* on the *Laghuśabdenduśekhara* (which has been edited), and a *Kāśikā* or *Gadā* on *Paribhāṣenduśekhara*, in addition to a short independent treatise called *Rapratyāhārakhaṇḍana*. He seems to have been the most important of Nāgeśa's commentators, and probably the premier Grammarian after Nāgeśa.

50

SATYAPRIYA TĪRTHA SVĀMIN

This writer composed a *Vivaraṇa* on Patañjali's *Mahābhāṣya*. Yudhisthira Mimamsaka gives *saṃvat* 1764–1801 (1711–1748) as his dates.

51

JAYAKṚṢṆA MAUNIN

Jayakṛṣṇa was the elder brother of Śrī Kṛṣṇa Maunin, the son of Raghunātha Bhaṭṭa and Jānakī, and grandson of Govardhana Bhaṭṭa. He wrote a number of independent works in the grammatical tradition, including (*Śabdārtha*) *Sāramañjarī*, *Śabdārthatarkāmṛta*, *Śuddhicandrikā*, *Vibhaktyarthanirṇaya*, *Vṛttidīpikā*, and an *Arthanirṇaya* on Raghunātha Śiromaṇi's *Ākhyātavāda*. He also completed Jñānendra Sarasvatī's *Tattvabodhinī* on Bhaṭṭoji's *Siddhāntakaumudī* (see above, number 46). He is sometimes credited with authorship of the *Sphoṭacandrikā* (see introduction to the section on Śrīkṛṣṇa Maunin, below, number 54).

52

HARIVALLABHA

According to V. Krsnamacarya, this writer was the son of Vallabha Utprabaṭiya, author of a Vedānta work called *Vinodamañjarī* (cf. volume 1 of this encyclopedia [2d ed.], p. 585). Harivallabha flourished in 1747. He is the author of a *Darpaṇa* on Koṇḍa Bhaṭṭa's *Vaiyākaraṇabhūṣaṇasāra* (Adyar D, vol. 6, no. 574), which has been edited.

53

VĀSUDEVA DĪKṢITA

Vāsudeva is known to Mīmāṃsakas as the author of the *Kutūhalavṛtti* on Jaimini's *Mīmāṃsāsūtras*, edited several times (cf. volume 1 of this encyclopedia [2d ed.], p. 466). He was the son of Annapūrṇāmbā and Mahādeva Dīkṣita and the younger brother of Viśveśvara Dīkṣita. He seems to have lived about the middle of the eighteenth century. His *Bālamanoramā* on *Siddhāntakaumudī* has been published.

54

ŚRĪKṚṢṆA BHAṬṬA MAUNIN

Śrīkṛṣṇa was apparently Jayakṛṣṇa's younger brother, though there is a suspicion that the two may be the same person. He wrote a series of works on grammatical topics, the most important of which is perhaps the *Sphoṭacandrikā*, summarized below. In addition, he produced the *Tarkacandrikā*, "a set of *Kroḍapatras* on grammatical works of recent times" (Adyar D, vol. 6, no. 457), such as Kaiyaṭa's *Pradīpa*, the *Siddhāntakaumudī*, *Prauḍhamanoramā*, *Laghuśabdaratna*, and *Laghuśabdenduśekhara*. His *Vṛttidīpikā* has been twice published; it deals with the powers of words. In addition, he is credited in the *New Catalogus Catalogorum* with a commentary on Raghunātha's *Ākhyāta* called *Arthacandrikā* (*nirṇaya*), and a *Lakārārthanirṇaya*.

SPHOṬACANDRIKĀ

G.B. Palsule

The *Sphoṭacandrikā* is one of those late works on *sphoṭa* doctrine which gives it something of a final form and which betrays considerable influence of standard texts such as the *Vaiyākaraṇabhūṣaṇa*. While on the one hand this text shows a certain staunchness and a penchant for hair-splitting polemics, on the other hand it also shows a spirit of accommodation and realism. The form of the *sphoṭa* doctrine here is considerably different from its classical form—indeed, there is a revolutionary change in some respects. The transitoriness of the phonemes or their incapacity to form a simultaneous whole is no longer the reason for accepting the *sphoṭa* theory: phonemes can be permanent, or, alternatively, even transient phonemes can form a simultaneous whole in memory. The reason is only tactical: it achieves simplicity of procedure (*lāghava*). Similarly, *sphoṭa* need not now be necessarily over and above the phonemes; it can consist of the phonemes themselves. Altogether, one is not quite sure that, while successful in preserving the name *sphoṭa* in their grim fight against the Naiyāyikas, these texts have not lost some of the old soul of *sphoṭa*. But at the same time, in optionally equating an indivisible (*akhaṇḍa*) word *sphoṭa* with an unanalyzable (*rūḍha*) word, or a divisible (*sakhaṇḍa*) word *sphoṭa* with a partly (*yogarūḍha*) or wholly analyzable (*yaugika*) word, the author displays a robust realism that serves to bring down the *sphoṭa* theory from its mystic heights to a solid earthly footing.

E references are to the edition by M. G. Bakre in *Vādārthasaṃgraha* (Bombay, 1913), vol. 1, pp. 1–16. The references are to philosophical points made in the text.

Summary

1 (*E*1). *Sphoṭa* is a *yogarūḍha* (conveying a partly etymological and partly conventional meaning) word, so called because the meaning bursts out (*sphuṭati*) from it. The name *sphoṭa* attaches either to the individual words or to the universals inhering in them.

2 In all, eight kinds of *sphoṭa* are recognized: the five individual (*vyakta*) *sphoṭas*, namely, phoneme (*varṇa*), word (*pada*), sentence (*vākya*), indivisible word (*akhaṇḍapada*), and indivisible sentence (*akhaṇḍavākya*) *sphoṭas*; and the three universal (*jāti*) *sphoṭas*, namely, phoneme, word, and sentence *sphoṭas*, all three of which, by the very nature of the universal, are indivisible (*akhaṇḍa*). By implication, *padasphoṭa* and *vākyasphoṭa* are divisible (*sakhaṇḍa*).

3 Only the indivisible sentence is the real *sphoṭa*. The designation *sphoṭa* for the others (phonemes, and the like) is a fiction resorted to as a convenient means of analysis. It is like the designation "Brahman" given to sheaths like the *annamaya* (1.13–19).

Phoneme *Sphoṭa*

4 (*E*1–6). This term refers to single phonemes or phoneme complexes that form grammatically significant elements, such as stems and suffixes (like *pac*-, *ti* (P), and the like). It is clear that in the cases of suffixes the term applies to those actually used, and not to their prototypes (like -*l*), which appear only in the system.

Śrīkṛṣṇa refutes the Naiyāyikas' definition of a word, *śaktaṃ padam*, and of the four varieties of words, conventional (*rūḍha*), derivative (or etymological, *yaugika*), derivative and conventional (*yogarūḍha*), and derivative or conventional (*yaugikarūḍha*).

Another view of phoneme *sphoṭa* is that it consists of all single letters to which meaning has been assigned by the lexicons of words consisting of single letters (*ekākṣarakośa*).

Śrīkṛṣṇa criticizes Koṇḍa Bhaṭṭa's *Bhūṣaṇa*, which regards the word *sphoṭa* as purely etymological (*kevala yaugika*).

There follows a lengthy discussion of what constitutes denotative power (*śakti*), whether it be one or many, whether it resides in incorrect words also, and so on. The author's view is that despite their meaningfulness, incorrect words do not get the designation *sphoṭa* because such words are not accepted by Grammar.

Word *Sphoṭa*

5 (*E*6–9). More internal (*antaraṅga*) to the sentence because it directly forms a constituent of the sentence in the word *sphoṭa*. A phoneme is only an indirect constituent in that it builds the direct constituents of the sentence, namely, the words (*pada*).

What is called a divisible word *sphoṭa* (*sakhaṇḍapadasphoṭa*) by the Grammarians (*pac* + *ati*; *rāmaḥ*) is the *vākyasphoṭa* of the Naiyāyikas.

The indivisible word *sphoṭa* (*akhaṇḍapadasphoṭa*) is the one in which the whole word is manifested by all the phonemes.

Śrīkṛṣṇa refutes the objections against *sphoṭa* by the Naiyāyikas and Vedāntins, taking a remarkable position (partly following the *Bhūṣaṇa*), in contrast to the classical *sphoṭa* doctrine, that phonemes are not transitory and that even if they were they could form a whole in memory.

Still the *sphoṭa* (as an entity over and above phonemes) is accepted for the sake of economy of process, in that here the physical speech sounds (*dhvani*) are regarded as directly revealing the *sphoṭa* (thus doing away with the phonemes). This *sphoṭa* is identified with the *śabdabrahman*.

Next he presents a variation of the indivisible word *sphoṭa*. Here the *sphoṭa* is not regarded as over and above the phonemes. The idea is that what the Naiyāyikas call derivative (*yaugika*) and derivative-conventional (*yogarūḍha*, wholly or partly analyzable) words are regarded here as divisible word *sphoṭas*, while conventional (*rūḍha*) words are regarded here as indivisible word *sphoṭas*. (A grammatically ignorant person accepts the individual word *sphoṭa* even in the case of derivative words.)

According to this view of the indivisible and divisible word *sphoṭas*, the difference between the Grammarians and the Naiyāyikas boils down to a quarrel over the name, as the author remarks.

He closes this part with an incidental refutation of some doctrines of the Tārkikas (which have nothing to do with linguistic theory).

Sentence *Sphoṭa*

6 (*E*9–11). The basis of the sentence *sphoṭa* is the actual communication, which consists of sentences and from which later one learns a language.

Sentence *sphoṭas* are of two kinds: divisible and indivisible. The latter is revealed by the indivisible words and is distinct from them. It alone is meaningful. It is accepted for the purpose of economy of process.

The indivisible sentence *sphoṭa,* further, is of two kinds, either over and above the phonemes, or not (where the physical speech sounds directly reveal the sentence).

A variation of the indivisible sentence *sphoṭa* is accepted only in cases like *Hare'va,* "Save me, O Hari," where word boundaries cannot be distinguished. In those cases in which word boundaries are clear (such as *ghaṭam ānaya,* "bring a jar"), one accepts the divisible word *sphoṭa.*

7 (*E*11–12). This section discusses whether the import of a sentence is predominantly nominal (*prathamāntaviśeṣyakaḥ śābdabodhaḥ*) and similar topics (such as whether the sentence meaning is the grammatical object in such sentences as "paśya, mṛgo dhāvati" ["See, a deer is running"]. Śrīkṛṣṇa also refutes the *Vyutpattivāda.*

8 (*E*12–13). This section treats the application of divisibility and indivisibility in certain other types of sentences. A proposal is considered for a secondary sentence *sphoṭa* in the case of the statement "tat tvam asi" ("that thou art"). Ultimately it is rejected, and the designative sentence *sphoṭa* (*vācakavākyasphoṭa*) is accepted. The type of secondary meaning posited by Advaitins, *jahadajahallakṣaṇa,* is refuted.

9 (*E*13–14). So far the discussion has concerned a sentence that is not poetic (*kāvyātmaka*). Now the poetic sentence is considered. Mammaṭa's definition is justified against the attacks of Jagannātha.

10 (*E*14–15). Śrīkṛṣṇa discusses some figurative sentences (such as *vahninā siñcati,* "sprinkles with fire") and establishes sentence *sphoṭa* in such cases.

11 (*E*15–16). What is the indivisible sentence *sphoṭa*? It is a single phoneme (*eko varṇaḥ*), auditorially perceived (*śravaṇa*). It is like the *citra rūpa* of the Nyāya or the composite vowels accepted by Grammarians. It is this indivisible sentence *sphoṭa,* consisting of a single phoneme, that is designative (*vācaka*). It is identical with *śabdabrahman.*

55

UMĀMAHEŚVARA or ABHINAVA KĀLIDĀSA

This author was responsible for several Advaita works (cf. volume 1 of this encyclopedia [2d ed.], p. 465) as well as a work on Grammar, *Pāṇinīyavādanakṣatramālā*. Of a Vellala family, he was the son of Veṅkaṭārya of the Mokṣaguṇḍa family; a pupil of Akṣayasūri; and himself the guru of Kavikuñjara, author of *Śabharañjanaśataka*. He flourished about 1750.

56

NĪLAKAṆṬHA DĪKṢITA

The grandson of Rāmabhadra Dīkṣita and a pupil of Jñānendra Sarasvatī, Nīlakaṇṭha was patronized by Puratam Tirumal Devanarayana of Ambalappuzha. His father was Varadeśvara Dīkṣita, who studied with the son of some Appayya Dīkṣita and died at Varanasi as an ascetic. He had an elder brother called Sundareśvara Yajvan, who composed a work titled *Pāṇinipradīpa.* Although Yudhisthira Mīmamsaka attributes his works to Nīlakaṇṭha Vājapeyin of the sixteenth century, it seems more likely this author flourished about the middle of the eighteenth century.

This Nīlakaṇṭha's works include a *Paribhāṣāvṛtti*, a *Tattvaviveka* on the *Mahābhāṣya*, *Gūḍhārthadīpikā* on his teacher Jñānendra's *Tattvabodhinī*, and a *Laghuśabdakaustubha.*

57

ĀŚĀDHARA BHAṬṬA

Āśādhara was a pupil of Dharaṇīdhara and should be dated to about 1770. U. P. Shah has published a note on his life and works.[1] His (*Śabda*) *Triveṇikā*, a short treatise on the three powers of a word, has been edited twice. In addition, he wrote a *Padasaṃjñavicāra*, as well as work known under various titles, such as *Pūrvapakṣapraśnottarī* or *mañjūṣā* or *mañjarī*. He also seems to have composed an Advaita work, *Advaitaviveka* (cf. volume 1 of this encyclopedia [2d ed.], p. 471).

58

RĀMASEVAKA

This writer is the author of a *Vyākhyā* on Kaiyaṭa's *Mahābhāṣyapradīpa*. He was the father of Kṛṣṇamitrācārya (or Durbalācārya), a prolific grammatical writer of various commentaries (cf. below, number 60).

59

INDRADATTA UPĀDHYĀYA

The *New Catalogus Catalogorum* tells us that Indradatta of the Garga *gotra* (lineage) was the son of Lālamaṇi Upādhyāya and Kṣemavatī Devī, the grandson of Mohana Lāla, and the great-grandson of Muralīdhara. A manuscript of Indradatta's *Śabdatattvaprakāśa* exists that was copied in 1820. The work is based on Nāgeśa.

60

KṚṢṆAMITRĀCĀRYA or DURBALĀCĀRYA

One of the most prolific writers on Indian philosophy that ever lived, Kṛṣṇamitrācārya contributed extensively to the literature on Nyāya, Sāṃkhya, and Grammar. His father was Rāmasevaka of Lakṣmapura (see above, number 58), his grandfather Devīdatta. Only two of his works to my knowledge have been published so far, the *Tattvamīmāṃsā*, a Sāṃkhya treatise, and a *Kuñcikā* on Nāgeśa Bhaṭṭa's *Vaiyākaraṇalaghu-mañjūṣā*. In Grammar he also wrote a commentary on the *Paribhāṣendu-śekhara*, *Bhāvapradīpa* on Bhaṭṭoji's *Śabdakaustubha*, *Kalpalatā* on the *Prauḍhamanoramā*, *Ratnārṇava* on *Siddhāntakaumudī*, and a commentary on the *Vaiyākaraṇabhūṣaṇa*. He must have flourished at the beginning of the nineteenth century.

61

HARIBHAṬṬA

Haribhaṭṭa flourished in 1801, and was the author of *Darbana* on the *Vaiyākaraṇabhūṣaṇasāra.*

62

DHARAṆĪDHARA (II)

This Dharaṇīdhara was patronized by Thomas Henry of Calcutta, and he wrote his *Vaiyākaraṇasarvasva* in 1809.

63

MANNUDEVA or MANYUDEVA or GOPĀLADEVA

Mannudeva was the son of Durgā and Śambhu, the younger brother of Kṛṣṇadeva, and a pupil of Pāyaguṇḍa Bālakṛṣṇa, who was in turn the son of Vaidyanātha Pāyaguṇḍa (see above, summary 49), a direct disciple of Nāgeśa Bhaṭṭa. He wrote *Laghubhūṣaṇasārakānti* on the *Vaiyākaraṇabhūṣaṇasāra*, *Doṣoddhāra* on the *Laghuśabdenduśekhara*. The *New Catalogus Catalogorum* also attributes to him an *Arthavatsūtravāda*.

64

BHAIRAVA MIŚRA

Bhairava was the son of Bhavadeva Miśra of the Agastya family, who wrote a commentary on Hari Dīkṣita's *Śabdaratna*. M.S. Bhat dates Bhairava "circa 1780–1840."[1] He wrote the following works, all of which are in print: *Sphoṭaparīkṣā*, *Vaiyākaraṇabhūṣaṇasāra-Parīkṣā*, *Candrakalā* on the *Laghuśabdenduśekhara*, *a* commentary on *Paribhāṣenduśekhara*, and a commentary on the *Śabdaratna* (which appears not to be the same as his father's).

65

KUMĀRA TĀTAYA

This writer composed a *Pārijātaṃ Nāṭakam* on the *Mahābhāṣya*. He appears to have lived in the early nineteenth century, about 1825.

66

SATĀRĀ RĀGHAVENDRĀCĀRYA (GAJENDRAGADKAR)

Author of several grammatical works, this Maharashtrian was the pupil of Nīlakaṇṭha Vyāsa, who died in 1853, according to B.N.K. Sharma, following Theodor Aufrecht.[1] His works are *Candrikā* on Nāgeśa's *Laghuśabdenduśekhara*, *Tripathagā* on Nāgeśa's *Paribhāṣenduśekhara*, *Prabhā* on Bhaṭṭoji's *Śabdakaustubha*, *Śabdaratnaprabhā*, and *Tipāṭhaga* on Patañjali's *Mahābhāṣya* (uncertain attribution).

67

GAṄGĀDHARA KAVIRĀJA

Gaṅgādhara was a Vaidya of Bengal, born at Jessore. His life covered the period from 1798 to 1885. Some of his works are partly published in *Gaṅgādharamaniṣā* (Calcutta, 1911). Two works are on Grammar: *Trikāṇḍaśabdaśāsana* and *Trisūtravyākaraṇa*, both in verse.

68

TĀRĀNĀTHA TARKAVĀCASPATI

A well-known master pandit, whose expertise led him to contribute works in Nyāya, Sāṃkhya, and Advaita as well as in grammar (listed in volume 1 of this encyclopedia, 2d ed.). He lived from about 1840 to 1900. His works on Grammar included *Tarkaratnamālā* and a *Saralā* on the *Siddhāntakaumudī*.

69

KHUDDI JHĀ (ŚARMAN)

A widely celebrated paṅdit who flourished at the beginning of the twentieth century. He was a Maithila of Varanasi. His notes on the *Laghuśabdenduśekhara*, titled *Nāgeśoktiprakāśa*, were published at Varanasi in 1899. He also wrote a *Tiṅarthavādasāra* on the *Vaiyākaraṇabhūṣaṇasāra*.

70

NITYĀNANDA PANTA PARVATĪYA

Nityānanda flourished about 1925. Two works of his are published, a commentary on the *Paramalaghumañjūṣā*, and *Dīpikā* on *Laghuśabdenduśekhara.*

71

DRAVYEŚA JHĀ

This writer's *Pratyekārthaprakāśikā* on the first book of Bhartṛhari's *Vākyapadīya* or *Trikāṇḍī* was published at Vrindavan in 1926.

72

SŪRYANĀRĀYAṆA ŚUKLA

Another commentary on book 1 of the *Vākyapadīya*, entitled *Bhavapradīpa*, was composed by this author and published initially in 1937. He also wrote on other systems.

73

GOPĀLA ŚĀSTRĪ NENE

This scholar was active during the first half of the twentieth century. He has written a *Saralā* on the *Vaiyākaraṇabhūṣaṇasāra*.

74

P.S. ANANTANĀRĀYAṆA ŚĀSTRĪ

A recognized scholar who wrote a work on Grammar titled *Vākyatattva*. His dates are 1885–1947.

75

BRAHMADEVA

Brahmadeva wrote his *Vaiyākaraṇasiddhāntamañjūṣā* in 1943

76

V. KṚṢṆAMĀCĀRYA

Master savant, leader in many scholarly activities in and around Madras, Kṛṣṇamācārya composed a *Sphoṭavāda-Upodghāta*, which was published as Adyar Library Series 55 in 1946.

77

SADĀŚIVA ŚĀSTRĪ (ŚARMAN)

Sadāśiva Śāstrī wrote an *Arthadīpikā* on the *Paramalaghumañjūṣā*, published in 1946.

78

BĀLA KṚṢṆA PAÑCOLĪ

His *Prabhā* on *Vaiyākaraṇabhūṣaṇasāra* was printed in 1947.

79

RĀMA PRASĀDA TRIPAṬHĪ

A *Subodhinī* on the *Vaiyākaraṇabhūṣaṇasāra* was published in 1952.

80

RUDRADHARA JHĀ ŚARMAN

Rudradhara Jhā Śarman published a *Tattvāloka* on Patañjali's *Mahābhāsya* in 1954.

81

KĀLIKĀ PRASĀDA ŚUKLA

He published a *Jyotsnā* on the *Paralaghumañjūṣā* (1961).

82

ŚABHĀPATI ŚARMAN UPĀDHYĀYA

Śabhāpati Śarman Upādhyāya wrote a *Ratnaprabhā* on *Paramalaghumañjūṣā*, published in 1963.

83

RAGHUNĀTHA ŚARMAN

His extensive commentary, *Ambākartrī*, on the *Vākyapadīya*, was published at Varanasi between 1963 and 1974. He also published *Vyākaraṇadarśanabindu*, Varanasi, 1971.

84

SATYAKĀMA VARMĀ

He published a commentary on the first book of the *Vākyapadīya* in 1970.

85

RĀMĀJÑĀ PĀṆḌEYA

His *Vyākaraṇadarśanapratimā* was published at Varanasi in 1979.

BIBLIOGRAPHY ON GRAMMAR (*VYĀKARAṆA*)

No bibliography is entirely exhaustive. In the present case it is important to understand what the list is intended to cover and what it is not. Nyāya, Mimāṃsā, Vedānta and the writings of other *darśanas* on grammatical philosophy are listed in volume 1 of this encyclopedia, *Bibliography of Indian Philosophies,* and are not to be found here. The present bibliography is an effort to list publications that deal with the Indian science of *vyākaraṇa,* but not in all languages. While the primary sources, Sanskrit texts, are covered, secondary materials in Indian languages, including Sanskrit, are not. Secondary materials in European languages that pertain to *vyākaraṇa* should be listed here, but closely related sciences, such as *nirukta,* are not covered. Furthermore, papers and monographs on Indian linguistics that concentrate on specific words or syllables have not been listed here. The primary literature in Sanskrit is exclusively dealt with; Pali writers are omitted.

The general plan followed resembles that utilized in volume 1 of the encyclopedia. Part 1 deals in chronological order with the Sanskrit authors whose dates are roughly known. Part 2 lists classical writers on *vyākaraṇa* (grammar) and others whose dates are not known. Part 3 lists secondary materials that are not specifically related to a particular work or author. This bibliography was prepared by the general editor of the encyclopedia, Karl H. Potter.

Abbreviations for Grammar Bibliography

ABORI—*Annals of the Bhandarkar Oriental Research Institute* (Poona)
ACIL—see PICL
Acta Asiatica—*Acta Asiatica* (Tokyo)
ActOD—*Acta Orientalia* (Copenhagen)
ActOP—*Acta Orientalia* (Bucharest)
ACUT—*Acta et Communicationes Universitatis Taruensis* (Finland)
Adyar D—*A Descriptive Catalogue of Sanskrit Manuscripts in the Adyar Library,* compiled by V. Krishnamacharya, Adyar, Madras
AG—*Acyuta Granthamala* (Varanasi)
AIK—*Aus Indiens Kultur* : *Festschrift Richard von Garbe,* Erlangen, 1927
AIONSL—*Annali, Istituto Orientale di Napoli,* sezione linguistica
AIPHOS—*Annuaire de l' Institut de Philologie et d'Histoire Orientales et Slaves* (Brussels)
AJP—*American Journal of Philology* (Baltimore)
AKM—Abhandlungen für die Kunde des Morgenlandes
ALB — *Adyar Library Bulletin* (— *Brahmavidya*)
ALS — Adyar Library Series
AMGG — Abhandlungen der Marburger Gelehrten Gesellschaft

Anvīkṣā — *Anvīkṣā: Research Journal of the Department of Sanskrit, Jadavpur University*
AO — *Archiv Orientalni* (Prague)
AOR — *Annals of Oriental Research* (Madras)
AOSE — *American Oriental Series Essay*
AP — *Aryan Path* (Bombay)
AsP — *Asian Profile* (Hong Kong)
ASS — Ānandāśrama Sanskrit Series (Poona)
ASVOI — *Annals of the Śrī Veṅkateśwara Oriental Institute* (Tirupati)
AUJ — *Annamalai University Journal* (Annamalainagar)
AUSS — Allahabad University Sanskrit Series
AUSt — *Allahabad University Studies*
BB — *(Bezzenbergers) Beitrage zur Kunde der indogermanischen Sprachen* (Göttingen)
BCLV — D. R. Bhandarkar et al., eds., *B. C. Law Volume*, 2 volumes, Calcutta, 1945
BDCRI — *Bulletin of the Deccan College Research Institute* (Poona)
BEFEO — *Bulletin de l'École Française d'Extréme-Orient* (Paris)
Belvalkar — Shripad Krishna Belvalkar, *An Account of the Different Existing Systems of Sanskrit Grammar, being the Vishwanath Narayan Mandlik Gold Medal Prize Essay for* 1909, (Poona, 1915)
BEPHE — *Bulletin de l'École Pratique des Hautes Études* (Paris)
BenSS — Benares Sanskrit Series
BGWL — *Berichte über die Verhandlungen der königlichen sächsischen Gesellschaft der Wissenschaften zu Leipzig*
Bh — *Bhāratī : Bulletin of the College of Indology, Banaras Hindu University*
BhaKau — *Bhārata-Kaumudi: Studies in Indology in Honor of Dr. Radhakamal Mookerji*, Allahabad, 1945
BHUSS — Benares Hindu University Sanskrit Series
BhV — *Bhāratīya Vidyā* (Bombay)
BI — Bibliotheca Indica (Calcutta)
BNKSarma — B. N. Krishnamurti Sharma, *A History of the Dvaita School of Vedānta and Its Literatutre*, revised edition, Delhi, 1981
BonnOS — *Bonner Orientalischen Studien*
BORIS — Bhandarkar Oriental Research Institute Post-graduate and Research Series
BPSC — *Bulletin of the Philological Society of Calcutta*
BSOAS — *Bulletin of the School of Oriental and African Studies, University of London*
BSPS — Bombay Sanskrit and Prakrit Series
Budruss — Georg Budruss, ed., *Paul Thieme; Kleine Schriften*, 2 volumes, Wiesbaden, 1971
Cardona — George Cardona, *Pāṇini: A Survey of Research*, Delhi, 1976
CASS-St — *Center of Advanced Study in Sanskrit* (Poona), *Studies*
CDSFV — *Charudeva Shastri Felicitation Volume*, volume I, Delhi, 1974
CHI — *The Cultural Heritage of India*, 4 volumes, Calcutta, 1937; revised edition 1952–1953; second edition 1958
ChSS — Chowkhamba Sanskrit Series
ChSSt — Chowkhamba Sanskrit Series Studies
CIDO — *Proceedings of the International Congress of Orientalists*
CLTA — *Cahiers de linguistique théorique et appliquée* (Bucharest)
COJ — *Calcutta Oriental Journal*
CR — *Calcutta Review*
CSCRS — Calcutta Sanskrit College Research Series
CWRGB — *Collected Works of Sri R. G. Bhandarkar*, 4 volumes, GOSBORI, Class B, 1–4, Poona, 1933
DAWIO — *Deutsche Akademie der Wissenschaften zu Berlin, Institut für Orient forschung*
DCBCSJS — Deccan College Building Centenary and Silver Jubilee Series

DCBS — Deccan College Building Centenary Series
DCDS — Deccan College Dissertation Series
DCMS — Deccan College Monograph Series
DKRPV — *D. C. Kunhan Raja Presentation Volume*, Madras, 1946
DNSFV — *Dr. D. N. Shastri Felicitation Volume*, Keshav Ram Pal, ed., Ghaziabad, 1982
DRBCV — *D. R. Bhandarkar Volume*, ed. B. C. Law, Calcutta, 1940
EOI — Satya Vrat Sastri, *Essays on Indology*, Delhi, 1963
ERE — Hastings, *Encyclopedia of Religion and Ethics*
EW — *East and West* (Rome)
Festschrift Aditya Natha Jha — *Saṃskṛti : dāktar Āditya Nātha Jhā abhinandana-grantha*, Gopinath Kaviraj, ed., 3 volumes, Delhi, 1969
Festschrift Bochenski — *Contributions to Logic and Methodology in Honor of J. M. Bochenski*, Anna-Teresa Tymieniecka, ed., with Charles Parsons, Amsterdam, 1965
Festschrift Bohtlingk — *Festgrüss an Otto von Böhtlingk zum Doktor-Jubilaum* 3 *Februar* 1888 von seinen Freunden, Stuttgart, 1888
Festschrift Charudeva Shastri — *Charudeva Shastri Felicitation Volume : Presented to Prof. Charudeva Shastri on the Occasion of His Seventy-fifth Anniversary by his Friends and Admirers*, S. K. Chatterji et al., eds., Delhi, 1974
Festschrift Emeneau — *Studies in Indian Linguistics* (*Professor M. B. Emeneau Ṣaṣṭipūrti Volume*, B. Krishnamurti, ed., Poona, Annamalainagar, 1968
Festschrift F.B.J. Kuiper — *Pratidānam*: *Indian, Iranian and Indo-European Studies Presented to Franciscus Bernardus Jacobus Kuiper on His Sixtieth Birthday*, J. C. Heesterman et al., eds., The Hague, 1968
Festschrift Kahane — *Issues in Linguistics : Papers in Honor of Henry and Renee Kahane*, B. B. Kachru et al., eds., Urbana, 1973
Festschrift Morgenstierne — *Indo-iranica*; *mèlanges presentés a Georg Morgenstierne à l'occasion de son soixante-dixième anniversaire*, G. Redard, ed., Wiesbaden, 1964
Festschrift Rajeswar Sastri Dravid — *Ṛṣikalpanyāsaḥ*, Devadatta Sastri, ed., Allahabad, 1971
Festschrift Roth — *Festgrüss an Rudolf von Roth zum Doktor-Jubilaum*, Stuttgart, 1893
Festschrift Siddeshwar Varma — *Siddha-bhāratī*, 2 volumes, Hoshiarpur, 1950
Festschrift Turner — *Sir R. L. Turner Jubilee Volume Presented on the Occasion of His Seventieth Birthday* (*5th October*, 1958), Sukumar Sen, ed., 1958–1959
Festschrift Weber — *Gurupūjakaumudī*; *Festgabe zum fünfzigjahrigen Doctor-Jubilaum Albrecht Weber von seinen Freunden und Schülern dargebracht*, Leipzig, 1896
Festschrift Whatmough — *Studies Presented to Joshua Whatmough on His Sixtieth Birthday*, E. Pulgram, ed., The Hague, 1957
Festschrift Ernst Windisch — *Festschrift für Ernst Windisch zum siebzigsten Geburtstag am* 4. *September* 1914 *dargebracht von Freunden und Schülern*, Leipzig, 1914
FL — *Foundations of Language*
FLSS — *Foundations of Language*, supplementary series
FRSD — see *Festschrift Rajeswar Sastri Dravid*
FVSKB — *Felicitation Volume Presented to Professor Sripad Krishna Belvalkar*, Varanasi, 1957
Gaurinath Sastri Festschrift — *A Corpus of Indian Studies*: *Essays in Honor of Professor Gaurinath Sastri*, G. M. Bhattacharya et al., eds., Calcutta, 1980
GBS — Govind Book Series
GOS — Gaekwad's Oriental Series
GOSBORI — Government Oriental Series, Bhandarkar Oriental Research Institute, classes A to C
GSAIF — *Giornale della Società Asiatica Italiana* (Florence)
GSPM — Grantha -saṃśodhana-prakāśana-maṇḍala
GSS — Gurukula Sanskrit Series

HDVCV — *H. D. Velankar Commemoration Volume,* S. N. Gajendragadkar and S. A. Upadhyaya, eds., Bombay, 1965
HKNMM — Ḥari-kṛṣṇa-nibandha-maṇi-māla
Hockett — Charles Francis Hockett, ed., *A Leonard Bloomfield Anthology,* Bloomington, 1970
HSS — Haridas Sanskrit Series (Varanasi)
HTCMR — Edward Byles Cowell, ed., *Miscellaneous Essays of H. T. Colebrooke,* 2 volumes, London, 1873
HTR — Jose Pereira, ed., *Hindu Theology: A Reader,* New York, 1976
HVNRSS — Hindi-Visvavidyalayiya-Nepalarajya-Samskrita-Granthalayah Kusumar
IA — *Indian Antiquary*
IC — *Indian Culture*
IF — *Indogermanische Forschungen* (Berlin)
IHQ — *Indian Historical Quarterly*
IIJ — *Indo-Iranian Journal*
IJDL — *International Journal of Dravidian Linguistics* (Trivandrum)
IL — *Indian Linguistics: Journal of the Linguistics Society of India*
IndF — Indische Forschungen (Breslau)
IndPQ — *Indian Philosophical Quarterly*
IPR — *Indian Philosophical Review* (Bombay)
IS — *Indische Studien* (Berlin)
ITaur — *Indologica Taurinensia* (Torino)
IZAS — *International Zeitschrift für allgemeine Sprachwissenschaft* (Heilbronn)
JA — *Journal Asiatique*
JAHRS — *Journal of the Andhra Historical Research Society* (Hyderabad)
JainJ — *Jain Journal*
JAOS — *Journal of the American Oriental Society*
JASBe — *Journal of the Asiatic Society of Bengal* (Calcutta)
JASL — *Journal of the Asiatic Society of Bengal* (Calcutta), *Letters*
JASP — *Journal of the Asiatic Society of Pakistan*
JAU — *Journal of the Annamalai University* (Annamalainagar)
JBBRAS — *Journal of the Bombay Branch of the Royal Asiatic Society*
JBRS — *Journal of the Bihar and Orissa Research Society* (Patna)
JDL — *Journal of the Department of Letters, University of Calcutta*
JDSUD — *Journal of the Deprtment of Sanskrit, University of Delhi*
JGJKSV — *Journal of the Gaṅganātha Jhā Kendriya Sanskrit Vidyāpīṭh* (Allahabad)
JGJRI — *Journal of the Gaṅganātha Jhā Research Institute* (Allahabad)
JIBSt — *Journal of Indian and Buddhist Studies* (— *Indobukkyogakyu Kenkyu*) (Tokyo)
JIH — *Journal of Indian History*
JIP — *Journal of Indian Philosophy* (Dordrecht)
JKU — *Journal of the Karnatak University*
JLSP — *Janua Linguarum,* series practica
JMU — *Journal of the Madras University*
JMysoreU — *The Half-Yearly Journal of the Mysore University*
JOI — *Journal of the Oriental Institute* (Baroda)
JOR — *Journal of Oriental Research* (Madras)
JPMJG — Jñānapīṭha Mūrtidevī Jaina Grantha-mālā
JRAS — *Journal of the Royal Asiatic Society* (London)
JSVOI — *Journal of the Śrī Veṅkatesvara Oriental Institute*
JSML — *Journal of the Tanjore Sarasvatī Mahal Library*
JUB — *Journal of the University of Baroda*
JUP — *Journal of the University of Poona* (Humanities)

KAG — Kaviraja-abhinandana-grantha (Lucknow)
KSS — Kashi Sanskrit Series (Varanasi)
KSVS — Kendriya Sanskrit Vidyapeetha Series (Allahabad)
KUDSP — Kerala University Department of Sanskrit Publications (Trivandrum)
KUJ — *Kurukshetra University Journal* (Arts and Humanities)
KVRACV — *Prof. K. V. Rangaswami Aiyangar Commemoration Volume*, Madras, 1940
KZ — (*Kuhns*) *Zeitschrift für vergleichende Sprachforschung auf dem Gebiete der indogermanischen Sprachen* (Göttingen)
LDS — Lalbhai Dalpatbhai Series (Ahmedabad)
Lg — *Language* (Baltimore)
LIPR — Harold G. Coward, ed., *Language in Indian Philosophy and Religion*, Calgary, 1978
LM — *Le Muséon* (Paris)
MAPS — *Memoirs of the American Philosophical Society*
MGOML — Madras Government Oriental Manuscripts Library
MGOMS — Madras Government Oriental Manuscripts Series
MIK — *Miscellanea Indologica Kiotensia* (Kyoto)
MO — *The Mysore Orientalist*
MSL — *Memoires de la Sociètè Linguistique de Paris*
MSS — *Münchener Studien zur Sprachwissenschaft* (Munich)
MSUOS — Maharaja Sayajirao University Oriental Series
MSURS — M. S. University of Baroda Research Series
MT — *A Triennial Catalogue of Manuscripts Collected for the Government Oriental Manuscripts Library, Madras*, M. Rangacarya, S. Kuppuswami Sastri, and Z. A. Sankaran, eds., 9 volumes, Madras, 1913–1943
MUSS — Madras University Sanskrit Series
NCat — *New Catalogus Catalogorum*, V. Raghaven, K. Kunjunni Raja, et al., eds., Madras, 1949 to present.
NGGW — *Nachrichten von der königlichen Gesellschaft der Wissenschaften zu Göttingen*
NIA — *New Indian Antiquary* (Bombay)
NTS — *Norsk Tidsskrift for Sprogvidenskap* (Oslo)
NUJ — *Nagpur University Journal*
OH — *Our Heritage* (Calcutta)
OLZ — *Orientalistische Literaturzeitung* (Leipzig)
Oriens — *Oriens*; *Journal of the International Society for Oriental Research* (Leiden)
OS — *Orientalia Suecara* (Uppsala)
OT — *Oriental Thought* (Nasik)
OU — *Occident und Orient* (Göttingen)
PAICL — *Proceedings of the All-India Conference of Linguists*
PAIOC — *Proceedings and Transactions of the.. All-India Oriental Conference*
Pan — *The Pandit* (Varanasi)
Paribhāṣāsaṃgraha — Kashinath Vasudev Abhyankar, ed., *Paribhāṣāsaṃgraha*, BORIS 7, Poona, 1967
PB — *Prabuddha Bhārata* (Calcutta)
PBS — Prachya Bharati Series
PCASS — *Publications of the Centre of Advanced Study in Sanskrit, University of Poona*
PEFEO — *Publications de l'Ecole Francaise d'Extrême-Orient* (Hanoi, Paris)
PEW — *Philosophy East and West* (Honolulu)
PICI — *Publications de l'Institut de Civilisation Indienne*, (Paris)
PICL — *Proceedings of the...International Congress of Linguists*
PICP — *Proceedings of the International Congress of Philosophy*
PIFI — *Publications de l'Institut francais d'Indologie* (Pondicherry)
PISC — *Proceedings of the...International Sanskrit Conference*

PO — *Poona Orientalist*
POWSBST — Princess of Wales Saraswati Bhavana Studies (Varanasi)
POWSBT — Princess of Wales Saraswati Bhavana Texts (Varanasi)
PQ — *Philosophical Quarterly* (amalner)
PVKF — *A Volume of Studies in Indology Presented to P. V. Kane*, Poona, 1941
QJMS — *Quarterly Journal of the Mythic Society* (Bangalore)
Rau — Wilhelm Rau; ed., *Franz Kielhorn: Kleine Schriften, mit einer Asswahl der epigraphischen Aufsätze*, 2 volumes, Wiesbaden, 1969
RDSO — *Rivista degli studi orientali* (Rome)
Renou and Filliozat — Louis Renou and Jean Filliozat, *L'Inde classique; manuel des études indiennes*, volume 2, with Paul Demiéville, Olivier Lacombe, and Peirre Meile, Paris, 1953
RPG — Rajasthan Puratan Granthamala (Jodhpur)
RSCG — Shri Rajasthan Sanskrit College Granthamala
Rtam — *Ṛtam; Akhila Bhāratīya Sanskrit Parishad* (Lucknow)
RUB — *Revue de l'Universite de Bruxelles*
Sambodhi — *Sambodhi* (Ahmedabad)
SAMV — *Sir Asutosh Memorial Volume*, Patna, 1926
SAS — Sanskrit Academy Series
SB — *Siddha Bhāratī*, Hoshiarpur, 1950
SBAW — Sitzungsberichte der Berliner Akademie der Wissenschaften
SBGM — Sarasvatī Bhavana Granthamālā
SHAW — Sitzungsberichte der Heidelberger Akademie der Wissenschaften
SIAL — Sources of Indo-Aryan Lexicography
SIBSY — *Studies in Indology and Buddhology Presented in Honour of Susumu Yamaguchi*, Kyoto, 1955
SII — *Studien zur Indologie und Iranistik* (Germany)
SIL — *Studies in Linguistics*
SILH — P. K. Gode, *Studies in Indian Literary History*, volume 1, SJS 37, Bombay 1953
Silverstein — Michael Silverstein, ed., *Whitney on Language: Selected Writings of William Dwight Whitney*, Cambridge, Mass., 1971
SJS — Singhi Jain Series
SKACV — *Dr. S. Krishnaswami Aiyangar Commemoration Volume*, Madras, 1936
SPAIOC — *Summaries of Papers of the...the All-India Oriental Conference*
SPISC — *Summaries of Papers of the...International Sanskrit Conference*
SPP — *Śāradā Pīṭha Pradīpa* (Dwarka)
SSGM — Savitarāya-smṛti-rakṣaṇa-grantha-mālā
SSPS — Sanskrit Sahitya Parishad Series (Calcutta)
Staal — *A Reader on the Sanskrit Grammarians*, J. F. Staal, ed., Studies in Linguistics 1, Cambridge, Mass., 1972
SVOS — Sri Venkatesvara Oriental Series (Tirupati)
SVSI — Satyakam Varma, *Studies in Indology*, New Delhi, 1976
SVUOJ — *Sri Venkatesvara University Oriental Journal* (Tirupati)
SWAW — *Sitzungsberichte der kaiserlichen Akademie der Wissenschaften zu Wien*
SWSC — *World Sanskrit Conference; Summaries of Papers*
TAPA — *Transactions of the American Philological Association* (Hartford/Cleveland)
TD — P.P.S. Sastri, *Descriptive Catalogue of the Sanskrit Manuscripts in the Sarasvati Mahal Library, Tanjore*, Srirangam, 1943
TPS — *Transactions of the Philological Society* (London)
TSS — Trivandrum Sanskrit Series
UCR — *University of Ceylon Review*
ULBTFPL — *Université Libtre de Bruxelles, Travaux de la faculté de philosophie et lettres*

UMS — Usha Memorial Series
UPHSJ — *Uttar Pradesh Historical Society Journal*
UPSPS — University of Poona Sanskrit and Prakrit Series
Vāk — *Vāk* (Poona)
VBGSM — Vidyābhavana Sanskrit Granthamālā
VGPCV — *V. G. Paranjpe Commemoration Volume: Some Aspects of Indo-Iranian Cultural Traditions*, Delhi, 1977
VIDK — *Verhandlungen de...international en Dialektologenkongresses*
VIJ — *Vishveshvarananda Indological Journal* (Hoshiarpur)
VJPSG — V. S. Joshi, *Papers on Sanskrit Grammar.* 1980
VKAWA — *Verhandelingen der koninklijke Akademie van Wetenschappen te Amsterdam*, Nieuwe Reeks
VRFV — *Sanskrit and Indological Studies: Dr. V. Raghavan Felicitation Volume,* R. N. Dandekar, ed., Delhi 1975
VSMV — *Vidarbha Saṃśodhana Maṇḍala Vārṣika* (Nagpur)
Wackernagel — J. Wackernagel, *Kleine Schriften*, 2 volumes, Göttingen, 1953
WoolCV — *Woolner Commemoration Volume*, Lahore, 1940
WZKM — *Wiener Zeitschrift für die Kunde des Morgenlandes* (Bombay/Vienna)
WZMLUH — *Wissenschaftliche Zeitschrift der Martin-Luther-Universität* (Halle/Wittenberg)
WZKSOA — *Wiener Zeitschrift für die Kunde Süd-und Ostasiens*
YJG — Yásovijaya Jaina Granthamālā (Bombay)
YM — Yudhisthira Mimamsaka, *Saṃskṛta Vyākaraṇaśāstra kā Itihāsa*, 3 volumes, Ajmer, 1950–1966
ZDMG — *Zeitschrift der deutschen morgenlandischen Gesellschaft* (Wiesbaden)
ZII — *Zeitschrift für Indologie und Iranistik*

In cross — references :
a — article
b — book
d — dissertation
e — edition
t — translation

PART 1 : AUTHORS WHOSE DATES ARE (MORE OR LESS) KNOWN

INDRA (GOMIN) (*pre-Pāṇini?*)
(Cardona, p. 150; Belvalkar, p. 9; NCat 3. 90)

?*Indravyākaraṇa*

G1 : A. C. Burnell, *On the Aindra School of Sanskrit Grammarians, Their Place in the Sanskrit and Subordinate Literatures.* Bangalore, 1875; reprinted Varanasi, 1976.

G2 : Franz Kielhorn, "Indragomin and Other Grammarians," IA 15, 1886, 181–183. Reprinted in Rau, pp. 244–246.

G3 : Edited by E. Sieg. SBAW 1907–1908.

G4 : B. N. Krishnamurti Sharma, "Indra and Pāṇini," IHQ 8, 1932, 380.

G5 : Varadaraja Umarji, "The Aindra School of Sanskrit Grammar," PO 19, 1954, 47–54.

G6 : ———, "The Aindra School of Sanskrit Grammar (Part — Two)," PO 20, 1955, 31–40.
G7 : ———, "Aindra School of Sanskrit Grammar (Its History and Geographic Extent)," SVUOJ 1, 1958, 5–11.
ŚĀKALYA (pre-Pāṇini)
AUDUMBARĀYAṆA (pre-Pāṇini?)
G8 : John Brough, "Audumbarāyaṇa's Theory of Language," TPS 1952, 73–77.
G9 : Nils Simonsson, "Audumbarāyaṇa's Theory of Sound," OS 10, 1961, 22–30.
ĀPIŚĀLI (pre-Pāṇini?)
?*Āpiśāliśikṣā*
G10 : Raghu Vira, "*Apiśāliśikṣā*," *Journal of Vedic Studies* 1, 1934, 225–248.
G11 : Vittore Pisani, "A Note on Apiśāli," JOI 5, 1956, 272.
G12 : Edited and translated in B. A. Van Nooten, "The Structure of a Sanskrit Phonetic Treatise," ACUT (1973), 408–436.
G13 : George Cardona, "On *Āpiśalaśikṣā*," *Gaurinath Sastri Festschrift*, pp. 245–256.
KĀŚYAPA (pre-Pāṇini?)
(NCat 4. 144; G1624, p. 84)
?*Dhātuvṛtti*
(NCat 4. 144)
GĀRGYA (pre-Pāṇini?)
(NCat 6. 17; G1624, p. 80)
GĀLAVA (pre-Pāṇini?)
(NCat 6. 19; G1624, P. 67; YM 1. 150)
CAKRAVARMAN (pre-Pāṇini?)
(G1624, p. 99)
BHARADVĀJA (pre-Pāṇini?)
(G1624, p. 95)
ŚAKAṬĀYANA (pre-Pāṇini?)
(the traditional author of the *Uṇādisūtras*; Cardona, p. 149; Belvalkar, P. 21; G1624, pp. 69. 254)
G14 : F. Kielhorn, "On the Grammar of Śakaṭāyana," IA 16, 1888, 24ff.
G15 : Satyakam Varma, "Contribution of Śakaṭāyana to Sanskrit Grammar," SPAIOC 27, 1974, 229–230.
G16 : Mrityunjay Acharya, "The Uṇādisūtras and Śakaṭāyana," SPAIOC 27, 1974, 226–227.
G17 : Satyakam Varma, "Śakaṭāyana: The Great Gaammarian," SVSI pp. 133–143.
SENAKA (pre-Pāñini?) (GI624, p. 101)
SPHOṬĀYANA (pre-Pāṇini?) (G1624, p. 100)
PAUṢKARASĀDI (pre-Pāṇini?) (Belvalkar, p. 26; G1624, p. 135)
G18 : M.S. Bhat, "Ācārya Pauṣkarasādi and the Date of Pāṇini," JOI 8 1959, 385–388.
AUDAVRAJI (pre-Pāṇini?)
(NCat 3. 98)
KĀŚAKṚTSNA (pre-Pāṇini?)
(Belvalkar, p. 8; Cardona, p. 151; G1624, p. 135; YM 1.106, 504, NCat 4.115)
?*Kāsakṛtsnaśabdakalāpadadhātupāṭha*
G19 : Kshitish Chandra Chatterji, "Kāśakṛtsna," IHQ 8, 1932, 224–227.
G20 : Edited in Kannada script, with Cannavirakavi's Kannada commentary. Sources of Indo-Aryan Lexicography 5. Poona, 1952. Roman transliteration in BDCRI 19, 1958–1959, 154–235, 330–414. Sanskrit translation by Yudhisthira Mimamsaka. Ajmer, 1965.

G21 : Gajanan Balakrishna Palsule, *A Concordance of Sanskrit Dhātupāṭhas*. DCDS 14. Poona, 1955.
G22 : G. B. Palsule, "A Glimpse into the Kāśakṛtsna School of Sanskrit Grammar," PAIOC 17, 1953, 349–355.
G23 : Edited, with editor's commentary, by Yudhisthira Mimamsaka. Ajmer, 1965.

KAUTSA (pre-Pāṇini?)
(NCat 5.106)
G24 : Sadashiv Lakshmidhar Katre, "Kautsavyākaraṇa: A Detailed Notice," NIA 1, 1938, 383–396.
G25 : Madhav Deshpande, "New Material on the Kautsa-Vyākaraṇa," JOI 26, 1976–1977, 131–144.

PĀṆINI (350 B.C.?)
(Belvalkar, p. 10; Cardona, p. 260; G1624, p. 104)
Aṣṭādhyāyī
(NCat 1.468) (includes *Dhātupāṭha, Gaṇapāṭha*)
G26 : Edited, with Dharaṇīdhara's and Kāśinātha's commentaries. Calcutta, 1809.
G27 : Edited in Otto Böhtlingk, *Pāṇini's acht Bücher grammatischer Regeln*. 2 volumes. Bonn, 1839–1840.
G28 : Edited Varanasi, 1852, 1869.
G29 : Theodor Aufrecht, "Zwei Pāṇini zugeteilte Strophen," ZDMG 14, 1860, 581-583.
G30 : Edited, with Bhaṭṭoji Dīkṣita's *Siddhāntakaumudī*, by Taranatha Tarkavacaspati. Calcutta, 1863–1864. Without *Siddhāntakaumudī*, Calcutta, 1871.
G31 : Edited, with Jayāditya and Vāmana's *Kāśikā*, by Bala Sastri, *Pan* 8 (1873–1874)–n.s. 3 (1878-1879). Reprinted, 2 volumes, Varanasi, 1876–1878.
G32 : R. G. Bhandarkar, "Dr. Goldstücker's Theory About Pāṇini's Technical Terms," IA 6, 1877, 107–113. Reprinted CWRGB 1.496–510.
G33 : Edited in Telugu script. Madras, 1881, 1894.
G34 : Chapter 1. 1–5 edited and translated in W. Goonatilleke, *Pāṇini's Eight Books of Grammatical Sūtras*. Bombay, 1882.
G35 : *Dhātupāṭha* edited, with Mādhava's *Vṛtti*, by Damodara Sastri and Gangadhara Sastri. *Pan* n.s. 4 (1882)–19 (1897). Reprinted Varanasi, 1897.
G36 : Edited Bombay, 1883, 1886, 1888.
G37 : Edited, with Bhaṭṭoji Diksita's *Siddhāntakaumudī*, and Hemacandra's *Liṅgānuśāsana*, by Sivarama Sarman. Bombay, 1887.
G38 : Edited and translated into German by Otto Böhtlingk. Leipzig, 1887. Reprinted Hildesheim, 1964.
G39 : F. Max Müller, "On the *dhātupāṭha*," IZAS, 3, 1887, 1–26.
G40 : Edited, with Jayāditya's and Vāmana's *Kāśikā*, by Bhagwatprasada Tripathi. 2 volumes. Varanasi, 1890.
G41 : Edited and translated, with translation of Jayāditya and Vāmana's *Kāśikā*, by Srisa Chandra Vasu. 2 volumes. Allahabad, 1891. Reprinted Delhi, 1962.
G42 : Otto Franke, "Pāli *maññe* (skr. *manye*, Pāṇini I.4.106)," ZDMG 46, 1892, 311-312.
G43 : *Pāṇini's Grammatical Aphorisms* Allahabad, 1892.
G44 : Georg Bühler, "The Roots of the *Dhātupāṭha* Not Found in Literature," WZKM 8, 1894: 17–42, 122–136.
G45 : Otto Franke, "Miscellen; 1. *a-pacasi*, etc. 2. Pāṇ. 6.3.57 (*uda* für *udaka*), 3. *pakṣa* — *rājakuñjara*, 4. *iti* — 'etc.,' " ZDMG 48, 1894, 84–88.

G46 : F. Kielhorn "Pāṇini i' 3, 11 *svaritenādhikāraḥ*," in *Festschrift Weber*, pp. 29–32 Reprinted in Rau, pp. 290–293.

G47 : O. Böhtlingk, "Neue Miscellen: 4. Pāṇini's *adhikāra*," BGWL 1897, 46–48.

G48 : Sylvain Lévi, "Des Préverbes chez Pāṇini (*sūtra* I, 4, 80–82)," MSL 14, 1906–1908, 276–278.

G49 : Edited, with Jayāditya and Vāmana's *Kāśikā*, by Gangadhara Sastri. KSS 37. Varanasi, 1908.

G50 : George Abraham Grierson, "Vāsudeva of Pāṇini IV, iii, 98," JRAS 1909, 1–22.

G50A : Selections from *Aṣṭādhyāyī* and *Kāśikā* translated into German by Richard Garbe in O. Böhtlingk, ed., *Sanskrit Chrestomathie*, 3d part, Leipzig, 1909, 251–278.

G51 : Edited in grantha script. Cidambaram, 1910.

G52 : B. C. Mazumdar, "Vāsudeva of Pāṇini," JRAS 1910, 170–171.

G53 : R. G. Bhandarkar, "Vāsudeva of Pāṇini IV. 3.98," JRAS 1910, 168–170. Reprinted in CWRGB 1.214–216.

G54 : Edited, with Bhaṭṭoji Dīkśita's *Siddhāntakaumudī*, Trichinopoly, 1911–1912. Published separately as Balamanorama Series 2, 1912.

G55 : Edited Arsagranthavali Series 8.6–7. Lahore, 1912.

G56 : Edited with *Pāṇinīyaśikṣā* and Bhaṭṭoji Dīkṣita's *Siddhāntakaumudī*. Bombay, 1913.

G57 : Bruno Liebich, *Zur Einführung in die indische einheimische Sprachwissenschaft*, volume 2, *Historische Einführung und Dhātupāṭha*. SHAW 15. Heidelberg, 1919.

G58 : *Dhātupāṭha* edited by Bruno Liebich, vol. 3 of G57. Heidelberg, 1920.

G59 : Bruno Liebich, *Materialen zum Dhātupāṭha*. SHAW 7. Heidelberg, 1921.

G60 : Umesh Chandra Bhattacharjee, "The Evidence of Pāṇini on Vāsudeva-worship," IHQ 1, 1925, 483–489; 2, 1926, 409–410, 865.

G61 : K. G. Subrahmanyam, "A Note on the Evidence of Pāṇinian Vāsudeva-worship," IHQ 2, 1926, 186–188, 864–865.

G62 : R. M. Bhusari, "A Short Note on the Term *bhakti* in Pāṇini's Sūtras," ABORI 8, 1926–1927, 198–199.

G63 : Edited, with editor's commentary, by Dayananda Sarasvati, 2 volumes. Ajmer, 1927–1961.

G64 : Leonard Bloomfield, "On Some Rules of Pāṇini," JAOS 47, 1927, 61–70. Reprinted in Hockett, pp. 157–165; Staal, pp. 266–272.

G65 : K. A. Subramania Iyer, "On the Fourteen *maheśvara sūtras*," PAIOC 4, 1927, 133–143.

G66 : Barend Faddegon, "The Mnemotechnics of Pāṇini's Grammar," PICL 1, Leiden, 1928. Also ActOD 7, 1929, 48–65. Reprinted G1625, pp. 275–285.

G67 : Bruno Liebich, *Konkordanz Pāṇini-Candra*. IndF 6. Breslau, 1928.

G68 : Edited, with *Pāṇinīyaśikṣā* and Kātyāyana's *Vārttikas*, by S. Chandrasekhara, Sastrigal. Madras, 1928.

G69 : W. Caland, "A Rhythmic Law in Language," ActOD 9, 1931, 59–68.

G70 : Raghu Vira, "Discovery of the Lost Phonetic Sutras of Pāṇini," JRAS 1931, 653–670.

G71 : Vidhusekhar Bhattacharya, "Pāṇini's Grammar and the Influence of Prakrit on Sanskrit," IL 2, 1932, 439–441.

G72 : K. C. Chatterji, The *anubandhas* of Pāṇini," COJ 1, 1933, 100–116.

G73 : Hermann Buiskool, *Pūrvatrasiddham: Analytisch onderzoek aangaande het systeem der Tripādī van Pāṇini's Aṣṭādhyāyī*. Amsterdam, Paris, 1934. Translated into English, Leiden, 1939.

G74 : K. C. Chatterji, "The *śiva sūtras*," JDL 24, 1934, 1–10.

G75 : Vittore Pisani, "Pāṇini 1, 2, 23," RDSO 14, 1934, 84.
G76 : B. Breloer, "Die 14 *pratyāhāra-sūtras* des Pāṇini", ZII 10, 1935–1936, 133–191.
G77 : K. C. Chatterji, "A Rule of Pāṇini," COJ 3, 1935, 17–28.
G78 : ———, "The Aṣṭādhyāyī and the Siddhāntakaumudī," COJ 3, 1935, 1–2.
G79 : S. P. Chaturvedi, "Homogeneity of Letters in the Pāṇinian System," PAIOC 7, 1935, 165–174.
G80 : Saraswati Prasad Chaturvedi, "Need for Rewriting Pāṇini's Grammar," NUJ 1, 1935, 5–10.
G81 : Prabodh Chandra Lahiri, *Concordance Pāṇini-Patañjali* (*Mahābhāṣya*). IndF 10. Breslau, 1935.
G82 : Shridhar Shastri Pathak and Siddheshvar Shastri Chitrao, *Word Index* to *Pāṇini-sūtrapāṭha and Pariśiṣṭas*. GOSBORI, Series C-2. Poona, 1935.
G83 : I. S. Pawte, *The Structure of the Aṣṭādhyāyī*. Hubli, 1935.
G84 : Paul Thieme, "*Bhāṣya* zu *vārttika* 5 zu Pāṇini 1.1.9 und seine einheimischen Erklärer; ein Beitrag zur Geschichte und Würdigung der indischen grammatischen Scholastik," NGGW 1935, 171–216. Reprinted Staal, 299–332.
G85 : Barend Faddegon, *Studies on Pāṇini's Grammar*. VKAWA 38.1, 1936.
G86 : Mangala Deva Shastri, Appendix III (A Comparison of the *Ṛgvedaprātiśākhya* with the Pāṇinian Grammar), pp. 329–344 of his edition and translation of the *Ṛgveda-prātiśākhya* with the commentary of Uvaṭa. Lahore, 1937.
G87 : Krishnadeva Upadhyaya, "New Verses of Pāṇini," IHQ 13, 1937, 167–171.
G88 : Edited with Kātyāyana's *Vārttikas* and *Pāṇinīyaśikṣā* by Sankara Rama Sastri. Sri Balamanorama Series 2. Madras, 1937.
G89 : S. P. Chaturvedi, "On the Original Text of the *Aṣṭādhyāyī*," NIA 1, 1938, 562–569.
G90 : Pierre Boudon, "Une Application du raisonnement per l'absurde dans l'interpretation de Pāṇini (les *jñāpakasiddhaparibhāṣā*)," JA 230, 1938, 65–121. Reprinted G1625, pp. 358–391.
G91 : Edited by Harisankara Pandeya. Patna, 1938.
G92 : P. E. Pavolini, "La Grammatica di Pāṇini," *Asiatica* (Rome) 3.1, 1938, 1–9.
G93 : Jakob Wackernagel, "Eine Wortstellungsregel des Pāṇini and Winkers Aleph-Beth-Regel," IF 56, 1938, 161–170. Reprinted Wackernagel, pp. 434–443.
G94 : V. N. Gokhale, "Studies in Pāṇini," PO 4, 1939, 97–120; 5, 1940, 109–122.
G95 : V. S. Agrawala, "Pūrvācārya *saṃjñās* for *lakāras*," NIA 3, 1940–1941, 39–40.
G96 : S. P. Chaturvedi, "Technical Terms of the *Aṣṭādhyāyī*," PAIOC 9, 1940, 1191–1208.
G97 : ———, "Scholastic Disquisitions in the Pāṇinian System of Grammar," BhV 2, 1940, 59–63.
G98 : ———, "Pāṇini's Vocabulary—Its Bearing on His Date," WoolCV, pp. 46–50.
G99 : K. Madhava Krishna Sharma, "Technical Terms in the *Aṣṭādhyāyī*," JOR 14, 1940, 259–267. Reprinted in G485, pp. 15–23.
G100 : ———, "The Text of the *Aṣṭādhyāyī*," UPHSJ 13, 1940.
G101 : ———, "Some Problems in Pāṇini," JMU 13, 1941, 203–225.
G102 : B. K. Ghosh, "*Pūrvācāryas* in Pāṇini," DRBCV. pp.
G103 : S. P. Chaturvedi, "On References to Earlier Grammarians in the *Aṣṭādhyāyī* and the Forms Sanctioned by Them," NUJ 7, 1941, 46–53.
G104 : ———, "On Pāṇini's *sūtra* VI.1.90—Wrong Wording or Corrupt Reading?" ABORI 23, 1942, 77–79.

G105 : ———, "Significance of Pāṇini's *sūtra* VI.1.92," NUJ 9, 1943, 68–69.
G106 : Sten Konow, "The Authorship of the Śivasūtras," ActOD 19, 1943, 291–328.
G107 : K. M. Shembavnekar, "*Saṅghas* in Pāṇini," ABORI 25, 1944, 137–140.
G108 : S. P. Chaturvedi, "On the Arrangement of the *taddhita sūtras* in the *Aṣṭādhyāyī*," BharKau 1945, 209–214.
G109 : B. K. Ghosh, "Aspect of pre-Pāṇinian Sanskrit Grammar," BCLV 1, 334–345.
G110 : A. B. Keith, "Pāṇini's Vocabulary," BharKau 1945, 343–345.
G111 : K. C. Chatterji, "Technical Terms of Sanskrit Grammar," NIA 8, 1946, 51–53.
G112 : Vasudev Sharan Agrawala, "Current Proper Names (*manuṣyanāma*) in Pāṇini," BharKau 1947, 1049–1063.
G113 : Translated into French by Louis Renou, *La Grammaire de Pāṇini*. 2 volumes Paris, 1948–1954. Revised edition, including Sanskrit text, Paris, 1966.
G114 : S. P. Chaturvedi, "On the Technique of Anticipation in the Application of the Pāṇinian Sutras," SPAIOC 15, 1949, 189.
G115 : P. C. Divanji, "*Bhagavadgītā* and *Aṣṭādhyāyī*," ABORI 30, 1949, 263–276.
G116 : Gajanan Balakrishna Palsule, "An Interpolated Passage in the *Aṣṭādhyāyī*," ABORI 30, 1949, 135–144.
G117 : Siddhesvar Varma, "The Vedic Accent and the Interpretations of Pāṇini," SPAIOC 15, 1949, 17.
G118 : Ram Shankar Bhattacharya, "Pāṇinian Principles of Determining the Desired Import of Words," JAHRS 21, 1950–52, 133–141.
G119 : Edited, with editor's *Tattvaprakāśikā*, by Gangadatta Sastri, 2 volumes. GSS 8. Hardwar, 1950–1962.
G120 : S. P. Chaturvedi, "Some Aspects of the Technique of the *anuvṛtti* Procedure in the *Aṣṭādhyāyī*," PAIOC 13.2, 1951, 109–112.
G121 : Suddhir Kumar Gupta, "Authorship of the Phonetic *sūtras* edited by Dayānanda," SPAIOC 16, 1951, 174–176 (summary); PO 16, 1952, 66–69.
G122 : Ram Shankar Bhattacharya, "Kinds of Agents (*kartā*) as depicted by Pāṇini," *Vāk* 3, 1953, 129–133.
G123 : Shrisrshna Sakharam Bhawe, "Pāṇinı's Rules and Vedic Interpretation," PAIOC 17, 1953, 231–240. Also IL 16, 1955, 237–249.
G124 : S. P. Chaturvedi, "A Study into the Principles of Preference ın the Application of Pāṇinian *sūtras* and Their Working," SPAIOC 17, 1953, 91–92.
G125 : S. K. Gupta, "Nature and Authorship of the Grammatical Works Attributed to Maharṣi Dayānanda Sarasvatī," SPAIOC 17, 1953, 93–94.
G126 : G. B. Palsule, "A Concordance of the Sanskrit *dhātupāṭhas*," BDCRI 15.1–2, 1953, 1–203. Reprinted as DCDS 14, Poona, 1955.
G127 : Louis Renou, "Études pāṇinéennes, I : Les Transitions dans la grammaire de Pāṇinı," JA 241, 1953, 412–427.
G128 : Subhadra Jha, "Unjustıfiability of the Principle of *jñāpana* on the Basis of the *Aṣṭādhyāyī* of Pāṇini," PAIOC 17, 1953, 240.
G129 : Ram Shankar Bhattacharya, "Importance of the First Words of the *gaṇapāṭha-s*," BhV 15, 1954, 29–34.
G130 : ———, "Some Unknown Senses of the Plural Number as Shown by Pāṇini," JUB 23.2, 1954, 45–48.
G131 : ———, "On the Original Reading of a Pāṇinian *sūtra*," JOI 4, 1954–1955, 268–269.
G132 : William Sidney Allen, "Zero and Pāṇini," IL 16, 1955, 106–113.
G133 : Priyatosh Banerji, "Some Observations on the Interpretation of the Pāṇini

sūtra Vāsudevārjunābhyāṃ vun and the antiquity of the Bhāgavatas," JBRS 40.1, 1955, 74–79.
G134 : Ram Shankar Bhattacharya, "Some Characteristics of the Ancient *vṛttis* on the *Aṣṭādhyāyī*," IHQ 31, 1955, 168–174.
G135 : Robert Birwé, "Interpolations in Pāṇini's *Aṣṭādhyāyī*," BonnOS 3, 1955, 27–52.
G136 : S. K. Chatterji, "On the Interpretation of a Rule of Pāṇini," IL 16, 1955, 194–195.
G137 : Edited with editor's Malayalam commentary by I. C. Chacko. Ernakulam, 1955.
G138 : Louis Renou, "Les *nipātana-sūtra* de Pāṇini et questions diverses," PICI 1, 1955, 103–130.
G139 : Ram Shankar Bhattacharya, "Some Objections on the Textual Order of the *Aṣṭādhyāyī* and Their Refutation," JGJRI 13, 1956, 119–129.
G140 : ———, "Some Anomalies in the *Aṣṭādhyāyī* and Their Justifications," BhV 15, 1956, 110–119.
G141 : Rajendra Chandra Hazra, "Some Observations on the Repetition (*anuvṛtti*) of 'śeṣa' from Pāṇini's Rules *ṣaṣṭhi śeṣe*," JASL 22, 1956, 99–131.
G142 : Sergiu Al-George, "Le Sujet grammatical chez Pāṇini," ActOP 1, 1957, 39–47.
G143 : G. B. Palsule, "The Sanskrit *Dhātupāṭhas*: A Critical Study." Ph.D. diss., Poona University, 1957. Published Poona, 1961.
G144 : Vinayak W. Paranjpe, "Analysis of Case Suffixes with Special Reference to Pāṇini's Grammar," CIDO 24, 1957, 574–577.
G145 : C. Kunhan Raja, "The *śiva sūtras* of Pāṇini (an Analysis)," AOR 13, 1957, 65–81.
G146 : Th. Simenscly, *Grammatica lui Pāṇini*. Bucharest, 1957.
G147 : Robert Birwe, "Variae Lectiones in Adhyāya IV and V der Aṣṭādhyāyī," ZDMG 108, 1958, 133–154.
G148 : Yutaka Ojihara, "Causeries vyākaraṇique (I): 1.1.62 vis-à-vis de 1.1.56," JIBSt 6, 1958, 302–305; 8, 1960, 369–370.
G149 : G. B. Palsule, "Groupings, *anubandhas* and Other Technical Devices Used in the *dhātupāṭhas*," BDCRI 19.1–2, 1958, 1–30. Reprinted in G143, pp. 59–88.
G150 : ———, "A Brief Account of the Different *dhātupāṭhas*," *Festschrift Turner*, pp. 103–133. Reprinted in G143, pp. 27–56.
G151 : S. M. Ayachit, "*Gaṇapāṭha*—A Critical Study." Ph.D. diss., Poona University, 1959.
G152 : Kapil Deo, "A Critical Edition of *Gaṇapāṭha* of Pāṇini." Ph.D. diss., Banaras Hindu University, 1959.
G153 : G. T. Deshpande, "Extended Application of Some Pāṇini-*sūtras*," SPAIOC 21, 1959, 144. Full paper in one of the annual numbers of the Vidarbha Samsodham Mandal, Nagpur.
G154 : Yutaka Ojihara, "Causeries vyākaraṇique (II): Anteriorité du *gaṇapāṭha* par rapport au *sūtrapāṭha*", JIBSt 7, 1959, 785–797.
G155 : G. M. Patil, "The *visarga-sandhi* in Pāṇini's Grammar," SPAIOC 21, 1959, 143.
G156 : S. M. Ayachit, "*Gaṇapāṭha*: A Critical Study," IL 22, 1961, 1–63.
G157 : Robert Birwé, *Der Gaṇapāṭha zu den Adhyāya IV und V der Grammatik Pāṇini: Versuch einer Rekonstruktion*. Wiesbaden, 1961.
G158 : Yutaka Ojihara, "Causeries vyākaraṇique (II): Addenda et corrigenda: La Necessité ultime de *su*. 1.1.34–36," JIBSt 9, 1961–62, 749–753.

G159 : *Kāraka* section edited, with related section of Bhaṭṭoji Dīkṣita's *Siddhāntakaumudī*, by Umesh Chandra Pandeya. Vidyabhavana Samskrta Granthamala 60. Varanasi, 1961.

G160 : Ludo Rocher, "Geschiedenis en achtergrond van de Pāṇini-interpretatie," in *Handelingen can het xxive Vlaams Filologen-congres* (*Leuven*, 6–8 *April* 1961), pp. 112–119.

G161 : S. Sengupta, "Contribution Towards a Critical Edition of the *Gaṇapāṭha*," JASBe 3.3–4, 1961, 89–186.

G162 : Betty Shefts, *Grammatical Method in Pāṇini: His Treatment of Sanskrit Present Stems*. AOSE 1. New Haven, 1961.

G163 : M. D. Balasubrahmanyam, "The Accentuation of *arya-* in Pāṇini and in the Veda," BDCRI 23, 1962–1963, 94–100. Reprinted in G1596.

G164 : *Vaidikaprakrīya* section edited, with related section of Bhaṭṭoji Dīkṣita's *Siddhāntakaumudī*, by Uma Shankara Sharma. Vidyabhavana Samskrta Granthamala 80. Varanasi, 1962.

G165 ; M. D. Pandit, "Zero in Pāṇini," JOI 11.1, 1962, 53–66.

G166 : Sukumar Sen, "The Names of the *samāsas* in Pāṇini's Grammar," BPSC 3, 1962, 90–92.

G167 : Johan Frederick Staal, "A Method of Linguistic Description: The Order of Consonants According to Pāṇini," Lg 38, 1962, 1–10.

G168 : Edited, with *Pāṇinīyaśikṣā*, Śāntanava's (?) *Phitsūtras*, Bhattojı Diksita's *Siddhantakaumudi* and editor's *Sugandha*, by Acyutananda Sastri, Kasi, 1963.

G169 : E. A. Grantovskij, "Plemennoe ob edinenie *parŠu-parŠava* u Panini," in W. Ruben et al., eds., *Istorija i kul'tura drevnej Indii* (*k xxvi Mazdunarodnomu kongressu vostokovedov*). Moscow, 1963, pp. 68–100.

G170 : A. N. Jani, "An Emendation of a *sūtra* of Pāṇini," JOI 12, 1963, 71–73.

G171 : Kapil Deva, "Significance of the Word *prakāra* in the *sūtras* of the *Aṣṭādhyāyī*," VIJ 1, 1963, 239–246.

G172 : S. D. Joshi, "The Two Methods of Pāṇini's Interpretations," summarized in SPAIOC 22, 1963, 40–41. PCASS-A 5, 1965 (JUP 23), 53–61.

G173 : Chandra Kant Pandey, *Pāṇini and His Aṣṭādhyāyī*. Patna, 1963.

G174 : M. D. Pandit, "Some Linguistic Principles in Pāṇini's Grammar," IL 24, 1963, 50–69.

G175 : ———, "Pāṇini—A Study in Noncompounded Word Structures," VIJ 1, 1963, 224–238.

G176 : Bommakanti Ramalinga Sastri, "Pāṇini's Method of Morphemic Analysis," SPAIOC 22, 1963, 128.

G177 : Edited with analysis and translated into Hindi by Brahmadatta Jijnasu (vols. 1–2) and Prajna Devi (vol. 3) as *Aṣṭādhyāyībhāṣyaprathamavṛtti*. Ram Lal Kapur Trust Series 32, 1964–1968.

G178 : George Cardona, "On Translatıng and Formalizing Pāṇinian Rules," JOI 14, 1964–1965, 306–314.

G179 : ———, "The Formulation of Pāṇini 7.3.73," JOI 14, 1964, 38–41.

G180 : Sureshachandra Dhyaneshwar Laddu, "Pāṇini and the 'akalakaṃ vyākaraṇam,'" IL 25, 1964, 187–199. Reprinted CIDO 26.3, 1969, 99–104.

G181 : Vidya Niwas Misra, "Pāṇini's Grammar as a Mathematical Model," IL 25, 1964, 157–178. Reprinted in G206.

G182 : ———, "The Structural Framework of Pāṇini's Linguistic Analysis of Sanskrit," PICL 9 (Janua Linguarum, series main 12), 1964, 743–747.

G183 : Rosane Rocher, " 'Agent' et 'objet' chez Pāṇini," JAOS 84, 1964, 44–54.

G184 : ———, "The Technical Term *hetu* in Pāṇini's *Aṣṭādhyāyī*, VIJ 2, 1964, 31–40.

G185 : M. D. Balasubrahmanyam, "An Accentual Note on *vikata*-in Pāṇini and the Veda", IL 26, 1965, 18–26.
G186 : Saroja Sadashiv Chitari, "Pāṇini and the Pāṇiniyas on the Concept of *guṇa*," PAIOC 22.2, 1965, 88–92.
G187 : G. T. Deshpande, "Pāṇinian Concept of *pada*," NUJ 16.1, 1965, 62–69.
G188 : George Cardona, "On Pāṇini's Morphophonemic Principles," Lg 41, 1965, 225–238.
G189 : do, "On Translating and Formalizing Pāṇinian Rules," JOI 14, 1965, 306–314.
G190 : Murray Fowler, "How Ordered are Pāṇini's Rules?" JAOS 85, 1965, 44–47.
G191 : K. Kunjunni Raja, "Pāṇini's Attitude Towards *lakṣaṇā*," ALB 29, 1965, 177–187. Summarized in SPAIOC 22, 1963, 247.
G192 : Y. Ojihara, "Ā la Recherche de la motivation ultérieure du Pāṇini-*sūtra* 1.1.62," MIK 6–7, 1967, 69–85.
G193 : Edited by D. P. S. Patanjal as *Aṣṭādhyāyīprakāśikā*. New Delhi, 1965.
G194 : Rosane Rocher, "La Formation due futur périphrastique sanskrit selon Pāṇini: Un Example de déscription linguistique," AIONSL 6, 1965, 15–22.
G195 : J. Frits Staal, "Context-sensitive Rules in Pāṇini," FL 1, 1965, 63–72. Reprinted in *Festschrift Emeneau*, pp. 332–339.
G196 : ———, "Euclid and Pāṇini," PEW 15, 1965, 99–116.
G197 : Bhagiratha Prasada Tripathi, *Pāṇinīyadhātupāṭhasamīkṣā*. POWSBST 14. Varanasi, 1965.
G198 : M. D. Balasubrahmanyam, "The Three Pāṇinian Suffixes *Ṇac*, *inUṆ*, and *Ktri*," PCASS-A 6, 1966. Also JUP 23, 1966, 133–138.
G199 : ———, "An Accentual Problem in Pāṇini and the Veda à Propos of the Word *hāyana*-," BDCRI 25, 1966, 43–58. Also *Vedasamīkṣā* (Proceedings of the Vedic Seminar). Tirupati, 1967.
G200 : M. S. Bhat, "The Vedic Stem *rātrī*- and Pāṇini," JBBRAS 41–42, 1966–1967, 8–11.
G201 : Robert Birwé, *Studien zu Adhyāya III der Aṣṭādhyāyī Pāṇinis*. Wiesbaden, 1966.
G202 : G. T. Deshpande, "Pāṇinian Treatment of *krama-samādhi*," SPAIOC 23.1, 1966, 136.
G203 : A. N. Jani, "The *śivasūtras* and Music," JOI 15, 1966, 400–402.
G204 : Bimal Krishna Matilal, "Indian Theorist on the Nature of the Sentence," FL 2, 1966, 377–393.
G205 : V. P. Limaye, "Necessity for New *vārttikas* to Pāṇini 1.1.27 and 5.2.39," VIJ 4, 1966, 228–229.
G206 : Vidya Niwas Mishra, *The Descriptive Technique of Pāṇini: An Introduction*. JLSP 18. The Hague, 1966.
G207 : G. B. Palsule, " '*Saṃjñāyam*' in Pāṇini," PCASS-A 10, 1966. Also JUP 25, 1967, 31–75.
G208 : M. D. Pandit, "Mathematical Representation of Some Pāṇinian *sūtras*," PCASS-A 7, 1966. Also JUP 23, 1966, 139–152.
G209 : ———, "Pāṇinian IT-*saṃjñā*—a Symbolic Zero," BDCRI 25, 1966, 77–94.
G210 : Sailendranath Sengupta, "Contribution Towards a Critical Edition of the *dhātupāṭha*," JASBe 8, 1966, 191–217.
G211 : J. Frits Staal, "Pāṇini Tested by Fowler's Automaton," JAOS 86, 1966, 206–209.
G212 : Sergiu Al-George, "The Semiosis of Zero According to Pāṇini," EW 17, 1967, 115–124.
G213 : M. D. Balasubrahmanyam, "The System of *Kṛt*-Accentuation in Pāṇini and Veda." Ph.D. diss., Poona University, 1967.

G214 : George Cardona, "Negations in Pāṇinian Rules," Lg 43, 1967, 34–56.

G215 : ———, "Pāṇini's Syntactic Categories," JOI 16, 1967, 201–215.

G216 : G. T. Deshpande, "Pāṇini : *sūtras* VII.1.9 and 10," NUJ 18, 1967, 192–200.

G217 : G. V. Devasthali, *Anubandhas of Pāṇini*. PCASS-B 2. Poona, 1967.

G218 : Kapil Deva, *The Gaṇapāṭha Ascribed to Pāṇini*. Kurukshetra, 1967.

G219 : S. M. Katre, *Pāṇinian Studies I*. DCBCSJS 52. Poona, 1967.

G220 : S. D. Laddu, Evolution of the Sanskrit Language from Pāṇini to Patanjali with Reference to the Primary Formations. Ph.D. diss., Poona University, 1967.

G221 : V. P. Limaye, "Pāṇini 6.1.121: *avapathāsi ca* or *apavathāsi ca*?" VIJ 5, 1967, 193–195.

G222 : ———, "The Basis of Pāṇini (8.1.59 and 65) in Ṛgveda," KAG 1967, 282–288.

G223 : B. A. Van Nooten, "Pāṇini's Replacement Technique and the Active Finite Verb," Lg 43, 1967, 883–902.

G224 : Buddha Prakash, "On Pāṇini's *sūtra* IV. 3.98, *vāsudevārjunābhyaṃ vun*," KUJ 1, 1967, 1–19.

G225 : M. S. Narayana Murti, "*Ekasaṃjñādhikāra* in the *Aṣṭādhyāyī*," SVUOJ 10, 1967, 11–22.

G226 : Y. Ojihara, "Causeries vyākaraṇique (IV): *jāti* 'genus' et deu definitions pré-patañjaliennes," JIBSt 16, 1967, 451–459. Reprinted G1625, pp. 425-431.

G227 : ———, "Sur l'Énoncé pāṇiniéen *astrīviṣaya* (IV.1.63): Deux Interprétations et leur rapport avec le *gaṇapāṭha*," ALB 31–32 (*Festschrift V. Raghavan*) 1967–1968, 125–143.

G228 : Sergiu Al-George, "The Extra-linguistic Origin of Pāṇini's Syntactic Categories and Their Linguistic Accuracy," JOI 18, 1968, 1–7.

G229 : George Cardona, "Pāṇini's Definition, Description and Uses of *svarita*," *Festschrift F.B.J. Kuiper*, pp. 448–461.

G230 : Amrit Madhav Ghatge, "Pāṇini I.4.32," IL 29,9, 1968, 150–154.

G231 : S.M. Katre, *Pāṇinian Studies II–IV: Dictionary of Pāṇini*. 3 volumes. DCBCSJS 53, 62, 63. Poona, 1968–1969.

G232 : G.B. Palsule, "Some Primary Nominal Formations Missing in Pāṇini," PCASS-A 18. Poona, 1968. Also JUP 27, 1968, 145–151.

G233 : ———, "The Role of *kṛ* in the Sanskrit Grammatical Terms," PCASS-A 24. Poona, 1968. Also JUP 29, 1969, 11–29.

G234 : C. Ramachari, "Taksan and Similar Artisans in the *Aṣṭādhyāyī*," MO 1, 1968, 105–114.

G235 : Rosane Rocher, *La Théorie des voix du verbe dans l'école Pāṇinéenne* (*le* 14e *āhnikā*). ULBTFPL 35. Brussels, 1968.

G236 : ———, "*Dhātupāṭha* et dialectologie indienne," VIDK 2.II, 1968, 699–707.

G237 : Kapil Muni Tiwari, "Pāṇini's Description of Nominal Compounds." Ph.D. diss., University of Pennsylvania, 1968.

G238 : H.S. Ananthanarayana, "The Feminine Formation in Pāṇini's Grammar," IL 30.2, 1969, 1–12.

G239 : *Dhātupāṭha* edited by Kanakalala Sarma. HSS 281. Varanasi, 1969.

G240 : *Dhātupāṭha* edited Amritsar, 1969.

G241 : Part 2, including *Liṅgānuśāsana*, edited by Dayananda Sarasvati with editor's commentary. Ajmer, 1969–1970.

G242 : K. V. Abhyankar, "A Brief Note on the Chronological Order of the Phiṭsūtras, the Uṇādisūtras and the Aṣṭādhyāyī," JOI 19, 1969–1970, 331–332,

G243 : Sergiu Al-George, "Sign (*lakṣaṇā*) and Propositional Logic in Pāṇini," EW 19, 1969, 176–193.

G244 : George Cardona, *Studies in Indian Grammarians*, volume 1, *The Method of Description Reflected in the Śivasūtras*. Transactions of the American Philological Society 59.1. Philadelphia, 1969.

G245 : Dayashankar Madhusudan Joshi, Pāṇini's *Taddhita* Affixation Rules. Ph.D. diss., University of Pennsylvania, 1969.

G246 : S. D. Joshi, "Sentence Structure According to Pāṇini," IA 3d series 3, 1969, 14–26.

G247 : Paul Kiparsky and J. Frits Staal, "Syntactic and Semantic Relations in Pāṇini," FL 5, 1969, 83–117.

G248 : B. A. Van Nooten, "Pāṇini's Theory of Verbal Meaning," FL 5, 1969, 242–255.

G249 : M. S. Narayana Murti, "Two Versions of the *ekasaṃjñādhikāra*," SVUOJ 12, 1969, 75–84.

G250 : Edited, with Jayāditya's and Vāmana's *Kāśikā*, by Sri Narayana Misra. 2 volumes. KSS 37. Varanasi, 1969–1972.

G251 : Narendra Chandra Nath, *Pāṇinian Interpretation of the Sanskrit Language*. BHUSS 2. Varanasi, 1969.

G252 : M. D. Pandit, "Pāṇini: A Statistical Picture of Sanskrit Sounds," IA 3d series 3, 1969, 128–138.

G253 : Buddha Prakash, "On Pāṇini's *sūtra* V.3.99," *Festschrift Aditya Natha Jha* 3, 394–404.

G254 : Rosane Rocher, "The Concept of Verbal Root in Indian Grammar (à Propos of Pāṇini 1.3.1)," FL 5, 1969, 73–82.

G255 : David Ellis Rogers, "A Study on the Context of Pāṇini's *Kārakas*," Ph.D. diss., University of Michigan, 1969.

G256 : Albercht Wezler, *Paribhāṣā IV, V and SV*; *Untersuchungen zur Geschichte der einheimischen indischen grammatischen Scholastik*. Berlin, Zurich, 1969.

G257 : Laidslav Zgusta, "Pāṇini—Descriptivist or Transformationalist?" AO 37, 1969, 404–415.

G258 : Saroja V. Bhate, 'Pre-Pāṇinian Grammatical Elements in Pāṇini's *Aṣṭādhyāyī*.' Ph.D. diss., University of Poona, 1970.

G259 : George Cardona, "The Pāṇinian View Regarding Agency and Animation," *Ṛtam* 2-6, 1970-1975, 135–146.

G260 : ———, "Some Principles of Pāṇini's Grammar," JIP 1, 1970, 40–74.

G261 : ———, "A Note on Pāṇini's Technical Vocabulary," JOI 19, 1970, 195–212.

G262 : Sadashıv Ambadas Dange, "Some Peculiarities of the Eastern Dialect According to Pāṇini," VSMV 1970, 173–198.

G263 : Madhav Deshpande, "Pāṇini and Pāṇinīyas on Dialectical Variation in Sanskrit," JOR 40–41, 1970-1972, 49–74.

G264 : S. D. Laddu, "A Linguistic Phenomenon from the Mahābhārata," *Ṛtam* 2-6, 1970-1975, 69–72.

G265 : Narendra Chandra Nath, "Are Feminine Bases *prātipadikās* According to Pāṇini?" VIJ 8, 1970, 82–85.

G266 : G. B. Palsule, "Some Views of Pāṇini and His Followers on Object-language and Metalanguage," PCASS-A 36. Poona, 1970. Also JUP 33, 1971, 1–7. Reprinted in ACUT 2.2, 1973, 310–320.

G267 : Sukumar Sen, *Pāṇinica*, CSCRS 74. Calcutta, 1970.

G268 : B. A. Van Nooten, "The Vocalic Declensions in Pāṇini's Grammar," Lg 46, 1970, 13–32.

G269 : Edited, with Puruṣottamadeva's *Bhāṣāvṛtti.* PBS 9. Varanasi, 1971.

G270 : M. D. Balasubrahmanyam, "Vedic *starya-* and Pāṇini 3.1.123," JGJKSV 27–28, 1971–1972, 21–28.

G271 : G. T. Deshpande, "Import of the Term *deva-vani*" in his *Indological Papers I.* Nagpur 1971, pp. 29–48.

G272 : ———, "Pāṇinian Concept of *pada*" in his *Indological Papers I.* Nagpur, 1971, pp. 49–57.

G273 : ———, "Pāṇinian Concept of *pragṛhya*" in his *Indological Papers I.* Nagpur, 1971, pp. 58–65.

G274 : ———,"Pāṇinian Treatment of *krama-sandhi*" in his *Indological Papers I.* Nagpur, 1971, pp. 66–77.

G275 : ———, "*Ārṣa prayogas* and Pāṇinian Rules" in his *Indological Papers I.* Nagpur, 1971, pp. 78–89.

G276 : A. N. Jani, "Fresh Light on Pāṇini's *sūtra* 'tasyādita udāttam ardhahrasvam' (I.2.32)," JGJKSV 27–28, 1971–1972, 261–264. Also PAIOC 24, 1972, 257–259.

G277 : D. M. Joshi, "On Expressing *kārakas,* à Propos of Pāṇini 2.3.1," IL 32, 1971, 107–112.

G278 : S. M. Katre, *Pāṇinian Studies V–VII: Dictionary of Pāṇini: Gaṇapāṭha.* DCBCSJS 72–74. Poona, 1971.

G279 : S. C. Laddu, "Vedic Forms and Pāṇini—a Glance," *Festschrift Rajeshwar Shastri Dravid,* English section, pp. 54–68.

G280 : George Cardona, "Cause and Causal Agent: The Pāṇinian View," JOI 21, 1971, 22–40. Reprinted in ACUT 2.2, 1973, 354–381.

G281 : Y. Ojihara, "Un Chapitre de la Saddaniti compare aux données pāṇineennes," JA 259, 1971, 83–97.

G282 : Rama Nath Sharma, "*Padavidhi* in Pāṇini." Ph.D. diss., University of Rochester, 1971.

G283 : M. D. Pandit, "Pāṇini : Statistical Study of Sanskrit Formations," ABORI 52, 1971, 175–209.

G284 : G. M. Patil "Pāṇinian Formation of Sanskrit and English Sandhis" (abstract), PAICL 1, 1971, 212.

G285 : Yudhisthira Mimamsaka, *Saṃskṛtadhātukośa.* Delhi, 1971.

G286 : Hartmut Scharfe, *Pāṇini's Metalanguage.* MAPS 89. Philadelphia, 1971.

G287 : Jag Dev Singh, "Pāṇini's Theory of Language," KUJ 5, 1971, 73–86. Also PAICL 1, 1971, 257–270. Also IJDL 1, 1972, 80–96.

G288 : K. M. Tiwari, "*Asiddham bahiraṅgam antaraṅge*: A Metarule of Ruleordering in Pāṇini," IL 32, 1971, 241–257.

G289 : M. D. Balasubrahmanyam, "Pāṇini 5.2.28–29," JGJKSV 28.3–4, 1972, 79–100.

G290 : H. S. Ananthanarayana, "A Syntactic Classification of Verbs in Pāṇini's Grammar," AICL 3, 1972, 30.

G291 : M. D. Balasubrahmanyam, "Vedic *sriyase* and Pāṇini 3.4.9," VIJ 10, 1972, 7–10.

G292 : ———, "Paninian System of *kṛt*-suffixation and Accentuation," in *Pāṇini Seminar.* Kurukshetra, 1972, 10 pp.

G293 : Saudamini Bahulikar, 'Some Criteria for Determining the Insertions in the *Aṣṭādhyāyī.*' Ph.D. diss., Harvard University, 1972.

G294 : S. L. Athalekar, "Pāṇini's Way of Mentioning Roots," in *Pāṇini Seminar,* Kurukshetra, 1972, 6 pp.

G295 : George Cardona, "Pāṇini's Use of the Term *upadeśa* and the *ekānta* and *anekānta* Views Regarding *anubandhas,*" SPISC 4, 1972, 23–25,

G296 : Karunasindhu Das, "On Indicatory Letters and Symbols (*anubandhas*) in Pāṇinian Pronouncements (*upadeśas*)," SPAIOC 26, 1972, 101–102.

G297 : Madhav Murlidhar Deshpande, "Pāṇinian Procedure of *taparakaraṇa*: A Historical Investigation," KZ 86, 1972, 207–254.

G298 : Sukheswar Jha, "A Study of the Pāṇinian System of Accent." Ph.D. diss., Darbhanga University, 1972.

G299 : S. D. Laddu, "The Device of Contiguity as a Key to Interpreting Pāṇini's Rules," CASS-St 1, 1972, 157–171.

G300 : P. D. Nawathe, "Ritualistic Prolation and Its Treatment in Pāṇini's Grammar," CASS-St 1, 1972, 55–64.

G301 : G. B. Palsule, "Pāṇini 3.4.87–88 vis-à-vis Vedic Imperatives in *-si*," JGJKSV 27–28, 1971–1972, 443–453.

G302 : ———, "Pāṇini's Treatment of Tense and Mood Formations," CASS-St 1, 1972, 173–183.

G303 : M. D. Pandit, "Pāṇini—a Study in Abbreviations," *Vimarsa* (Delhi) 1 (English section), 1972, 21–30.

G304 : J. D. Singh, "Pāṇini's Technique of Description," KUJ 6, 1972, 137–150. Also *Festschrift Charudeva Shastri*, pp 279–293.

G305 : ———and K. Doraswamy, "The Case: Tolkappiyam and Pāṇini, a Comparative Study," KUJ 4, 1972, 119–129.

G306 : P. S. Subrahmanyam, "Deep Structure and Surface Structure in Pāṇini," (abstract), AICL 3, 1972, 20–21. Full paper IL 36, 1975, 346–366.

G307 : Ram Nath Sharma, "Referential Indices in Pāṇini," AICL 3, 1972, 19–20.

G308 : Vishva Bandhu, *New Vārttikas to Pāṇini's Grammar*. Hoshiarpur, 1972.

G309 : Albrecht Wezler, "Marginalien zu Pāṇini's *Aṣṭādhyāyī*. I: *sthānin*," KZ 86, 1972, 7–20.

G310 : Saudamini Bahulikar, "Concerning the Structure of Pāṇini's *Aṣṭādhyāyī*," IL 34, 1973, 75–99.

G311 : George Cardona, "On the Interpretation of Pāṇini 1.4.105–8," ALB 37, 1973, 1–47.

G312 : Murray Fowler, "Pāṇini's Primary Accent-rules," ACUT 2.2, 1973, 322–335.

G313 : B. S. Godse, "Concept of *vipratiṣedha* in Pāṇinian Grammar," ABORI 54, 1973, 250–256.

G314 : Jan Gonda, "Pāṇini and Modern Linguistics," ACUT 2.2, 1973, 335–352.

G315 : Edited by Yudhisthira Mimamsaka. Bahalgarh, Haryana, 1973.

G316 : T. S. Paik, "Pāṇini's Treatment of the Augment *i* in Sanskrit." Ph. D. diss., University of California, 1973.

G317 : M. D. Pandit, "Formal and Non-formal in Pāṇini," ABORI 54, 1973, 179–192.

G318 : Anil C. Sinha, "Generative Semantics and Pāṇini's *kārakas*," JOI 23, 1973, 27–39.

G319 : S. Bahulikar, "Use of the Particle *ca* in the *Aṣṭādhyāyī*," CASS-St 2, 1974, 67–82.

G320 : M. D. Balasubrahmanyam, "Pāṇini 6.1 209–210," CDSFV 1974, 189–193.

G321 : *Kāraka* section edited, with related section of Bhaṭṭoji Dīkṣita's *Siddhānta-kaumudī* and English explanation, by Bishnupada Bhattacharya, Calcutta, 1974.

G322 : K. V. Abhyankar, "*Upalekhasūtram*," ABORI 54, 1974, 45–76.

G323 : George Cardona, "On Pāṇini's Metalinguistic Use of Cases," in *Festschrift Charudeva Sastri*, 305–326.

G324 : ———, "Pāṇini's *Kārakas*: Agency, Animation and Identity," JIP 2, 1974, 231–306.

G325 : K. C. Chattopadhyaya, "Did Pāṇini Envisage 'A' as a Close (*samvṛta*) Vowel?" in *Festschrift Charudeva Sastri*, pp. 194–205.
G326 : G. V. Devasthali, "Á propos *ardhamātralāghava paribhāṣā*," VIJ 12, 1974, 96–102.
G327 : ———, "*Vākya* According to the *munitraya* of Sanskrit Grammar," in *Festschrift Charudeva Shastri*, pp. 206–215.
G328 : Karl Hoffman, "Pāṇini VII.2.69 *saniṃ sasanivaṃsam*," MSS 32, 1974, 73–80.
G329 : ———, "Pāṇini V.4, 61 *ativyathane*," MSS 33, 1975, 45–50.
G330 : S. D. Joshi, "Pāṇini's Rules 1.4.49–51," SPAIOC 27, 1974, 442–443.
G331 : ———, "Pāṇini's Treatment of *kāraka*-relations," in *Festschrift Charudeva Sastri*, pp. 258–270.
G332 : Sudesh Kumari, "A Study of *Anubandhas* in Pāṇinian Grammar," Ph. D. diss., University of Delhi, 1974.
G333 : Mahavir, "Some Anomalies Regarding *Aṣṭādhyāyī*," SPAIOC 27, 1974, 392.
G334 : N. V. Rajagopalan, "*Kāraka* in Paninian Grammar" (abstract). PAICL 2, 1974, 173.
G335 : Aleka Chandra Sarangi, "An Enquiry into Pāṇini's Placement of the *tacchilika* Suffixes Within the Present Suffixes Section," SPAIOC 27, 1974, 239. Full paper in PCASS-E 4 (CASS-St 3), 1976, 121–129.
G336 : Krishna Kumar Sharma, "Pāṇinian Concepts of Morphophonemics," SPAIOC 27, 1974, 392.
G337 : J. D. Singh, "Phonologic Component in Pāṇini," PAICL 2, 1974, 7–46.
G338 : ———, "Pāṇini's Theory of *kārakas*," IJDL 3, 1974 287–320.
G339 : Kailas Pati Tripathi, "Presupposition of Pāṇini," SPAIOC 27, 1974, 232–233.
G340 : Satyakam Varma, "Technical Terms of Pāṇini," SPAIOC 27, 1974, 230.
G341 : ———, "Importance of *Maheśvara-sūtras*," SPAIOC 27, 1974, 229.
G342 : George Cardona, "On Rules of Pāṇini's Grammar Said to Expatiate on Other Rules," JOI 25, 1975–76, 241–251.
G343 : George Cardona, "A Note on the Formulation of Pāṇini 6-1-67," AOR Silver Jubilee Volume, 1975, 11–20.
G344 : Madhav Deshpande, "The Scope of Homogeneous Representation in Pāṇini," AOR Silver Jubilee Volume, 1975, 271–291.
G345 : ———, "Phonetics of *V* in Pāṇini," ABORI 56, 1975, 45–65.
G346 : Venkatesha Shastri Joshi, "The Significance of the Word 'Bhāṣā' in the *Aṣṭādhyāyī*," ABORI 56, 1975, 212–218.
G347 : H. P. Dvivedi, "The *svārthika* Secondary Affixes in Sanskrit According to Pāṇini," IL 36, 1975, 152–156.
G348 : Ram Nath Sharma, "Referential Indices in Pāṇini," IIJ 17.1–2, 1975, 31–39.
G349 : Albrecht Wezler, *Bestimmung und Angabe der Funktion von Sekundar-Suffixen durch Pāṇini*. Wiesbaden, 1975.
G350 : H. S. Ananthanarayana, *Four Lectures of Pāṇini's Aṣṭādhyāyī*. Annamalainagar, 1976.
G351 : M. D. Balasubrahmanyam, "Pāṇini III.iv.10 and the Vedic Facts," SVUOJ 19, 1976, 5–10.
G352 : Pratibha P. Gokhale, "A Note on the *paribhāṣā* 'stipa sapanubandhana," PAIOC 27, 1976, 377–378.
G353 : ———, "Various Ways of Naming a Verbal Root in the *Aṣṭādhyāyī*," PCASS-E 4 (CASS-St 3), 1976, 101–111.
G354 : S. D. Joshi, "Pāṇini's Rules: 1.4.49, 1.4.50 and 1.4.51," PCASS-E 4 (CASS-St 3), 1976, 59–71.
G355 : K. Kunjunni Raja, "Pāṇini's Concept of a Sentence," ALB 40, 1976, 165–171.

G356 : J. L. Shaw, "Subject and Predicate," JIP 4, 1976, 155-180.

G357 : K. A. Sivaramakrishna Sastri, "Some Anomalous Sūtras in the *Aṣṭādhyāyī*," BDCRI 35.3-4, 1976, 132-136.

G358 : Satyakam Varma, "Technical Terms of Pāṇini," SVSI 1976, 8-102.

G359 : ———, "Phonetic Arrangement of Pāṇini," SVSI 1976, 62-79.

G360 : Indu Bala, "A Study of Phonetic Theories in the Light of Ancient Indian Grammarians (with special reference to Pāṇini)." Ph.D. diss., Kurukshetra University, 1977.

G361 : G. V. Devasthali, "Vedic Hiatus Nasalization and Pāṇini," VGPCV 1977, 38-46.

G362 : R. B. Diksitulu, "A Study of *Pratyayas* in Pāṇini's Aṣṭādhyāy" Ph.D. diss., Andhra University, 1977.

G363 : H. P. Dvivedi, *Studies in Pāṇini: Technical Terms of the Aṣṭādhyāyī*. Delhi, 1977.

G364 : P. B. Junnankar, *An Introduction to Pāṇini*. Baroda, 1977.

G365 : Edited, with *Liṅgānuśāsana* and Śāntanava's (?) *Phiṭsūtras*, by Virajananda Daivakarana. Haryana Sahitya Samsthan, 1977.

G366 : K. C. Acharya, "The Etymology of Rāvaṇa à Propos Pāṇini IV.1.112" (abstract), PAICL 4, 1978, 299.

G367 : Sergiu Al-George, "Are Pāṇini's *sūtras* Descriptive or Prescriptive Sentences?" ABORI 58-59, 1978, 27-36.

G368 : Biswanath Bhattacharya, "A Proposed Emendation on the Tibetan Translation of Pāṇini's *Aṣṭādhyāyī* 1/1/7," ABORI 58-59, 1978, 511-512.

G369 : R. S. Bhattacharya, "Import of the Word 'śiśukrandaya' in *Aṣṭādhyāyī* IV.3.88," *Ṛtam* 10, 1978-79, 21-22.

G370 : S. D. Joshi, "The Ordering of the Rules in Pāṇini's Grammar," ABORI 58-59, 1978, 667-674.

G371 : V. K. Kshirsagar, "Pāṇini Explained and Defended." Ph.D. diss., University of Bombay, 1978.

G372 : V. P. Limaye, "*Akumāram yaśaḥ Pāṅineḥ* Corrupt for *akumāri yaśaḥ Pāṇineḥ*?" ABORI 58-59, 1978, 727-732.

G373 : Mahavir, *Pāṇini as a Grammarian (with Special Reference to Compound Formations)*. Delhi, 1978.

G374 : Siddhesvara Varma, *Pāṇini and Elision*. Panjab University Indological Series 12. Hoshiarpur, 1978.

G375 : M. D. Balasubrahmanyam, "*Ase*-words in Pāṇini and the Veda," ITaur 7, 1979, 65-74.

G376 : J. Bronkhorst, "The Role of Meanings in Pāṇini's Grammar," IL 40, 1979, 146-157.

G377 : Paul Kiparsky, *Pāṇini as a Variationist*. PCASS-B 6. Poona, Cambridge, Mass, London, 1979.

G378 : Uma C. Vaidya, "Aphorisms Indicative of Option in the *Aṣṭādhyāyī*." Ph. D. diss., University of Bombay, 1979.

G379 : M. D. Balasubrahmanyam, "Accent *It*-s in the *kṛt* Suffixes," ALB 44-45, 1980-1981, 543-555.

G380 : George Cardona, "On the Domain of Pāṇini's Metarule 1.3.10: *yathāsaṃkhyam anudeśaḥ samānam*," ALB 44-45, 1980-1981, 394-409.

G381 : Johannes Bronkhorst, "*Asiddha* in the *Aṣṭādhyāyī*: A Misunderstanding Among the Traditional Commentators?" JIP 8, 1980, 69-86.

G382 : Alaka Hejib and Aravind Sharma, "A Note on Pāṇini 6.1.87," ALB 44-45, 1980-1981, 635-638.

G383 : V. S. Joshi, "Pāṇini and the Pāṇinīyas on *Saṃhitā*," VJSPC 1980, 20-26.

G384 : ———, "Pāṇini and the Pāṇiniyas on *parasavarṇa*," VJSPG 1980, 27-28.

G385 : ———, "Some Historical Observations in the Descriptive Grammar of Pāṇini," VJSPG 1980, 49–59.

G386 : ———, "The Ten Predecessors Mentioned in the *Aṣṭādhyāyī*," VJSPG 1980, 60–65.

G387 : ———, "Reduplicated Forms Treated as Basic Roots (*dhātu*) in the *Aṣṭādhyāyī*," VJSPG 1980, 66–69.

G388 : ———, " 'Even Homer Nods': The Fault of 'anyonyāśraya' in the *Aṣṭādhyāyī* and a New Suggestion to Avoid It," VJSPG 1980, 70–78.

G389 : ———, "The Word *saṅghatitha* and Pāṇini," VJSPG 1980, 102–106.

G390 : Vir Bhadra Misra, "Meaning of *īpsita* in Pāṇini's *kārakas*," PAIOC 29, 1980, 422–423.

G391 : Hartmut Scharfe, "Overinterpretation Versus Redundancy," ALB 44–45, 1980–1981, 352–357.

G392 : Johannes Bronkhorst, "Meaning Entries in Pāṇini's *Dhātupāṭha*," JIP 9, 1981, 335–358.

G393 : ———, "Nirukta and *Aṣṭādhyāyī*: Their Shared Presuppositions," IIJ 23, 1981, 1–14.

G394 : George Cardona, "On the *paribhāṣā anirdiṣṭārthaḥ pratyayaḥ svārthe*" (Summary). SWSC 5. Delhi, 1981, pp. 14–15.

G395 : Karuna Sindhu Das, "On Concept of Loss as a Grammatical Phenomenon in Pāṇini" (summary). SWSC 5, Delhi, 1981, p. 21.

G396 : H. P. Dvivedi, "A Rethinking into the Meaning-character of Some of the Secondary Affixes of the *Aṣṭādhyāyī*" (summary). SWSC 5. Delhi, 1981, p. 29.

G397 . S. Venkatasubramania Iyer, "Variants in Pāṇini-*sūtras* Affecting accent" (summary). SWSC 5, Delhi, 1981, p. 115.

G398 : S. D. Joshi, "The *siddha* Theory and Its Implications in Interpreting the *Aṣṭādhyāyī* (summary). SWSC 5, Delhi, 1981, p. 42.

G399 : Avanindra Kumar (Satya Vrat Shastri?), *Archaic Words in Pāṇini's Aṣṭādhyāyī*. Delhi, 1981.

G400 : Mahavir, "Definition of *apasargas* in Pāṇini," PISC 4, 1981, 45–48.

G401 : ———, "Concept of 'Śabda' in Pāṇini" (summary). SWSC, 5, Delhi, 1981, pp. 48–49.

G402 : Hari Mohan Mishra, "Non-Aryan Words in the *Aṣṭādhyāyī*" (summary), SWSC 5. Delhi, 1981, p. 54.

G403 : Dipti Sharma, "Pāṇini's Grammar and Contemporary Language," PISC 4, 1981, 35–42.

G404 : Mahesh Dutt Sharma, "*Siṃhāvalokitanyāya* in Explaining Pāṇini" (summary). SWSC 5, Delhi, 1981, pp. 92–93.

G405 : Yajan Veer, "A Tale of 3 Terms (*vā*, *vibhāṣā*, and *anyatarasyam*)" (summary). SWSC 5, Delhi, 1981, pp. 116–118.

G406 : Mahavir, "Concept of *śabda* in Pāṇini," VIJ 20, 1982, 58–62.

G407 : Saroja Bhate, "The Place of P. I.2.22 and P. 7.2.51 in the *Aṣṭādhyāyī*", ABORI 63, 1983, 227–232.

G408 : M. A. Mehendale, "On Pāṇini I.3.41," ABORI 63, 1983, 225–226.

G409 : Paul Thieme, "Missverstandenen Pāṇini," ZDMG Supplement 5, 1983, 280–289.

Uṇādisūtras

G410 : Edited by Otto Böhtlingk. St. Petersburg, 1844.

G411 : K. B. Pathak, "Pāṇini and the Authorship of the *Uṇādisūtras*," ABORI 4, 1922–1923, 111–136.

G412 : K. G. Subrahmanyam, "The Authorship of the *Uṇādisūtras*," JOR 1, 1927, 53–66.

G413 : T. R. Chintamani, "A Note on the Authorship of the *Uṇādisūtras*," JOR 1, 1927, 181–183.

G414 : K. B. Pathak, "Further Remarks on the Unādi Sūtras of Pāṇini," ABORI 11, 1930, 90–93.

See b 82.

G415 : K. Madhava Krishna Sarma, "Authorship of the *Uṇādisūtras*," PVKF, pp. 395–404.

G416 : Edited with editor's commentary by Dayananda Sarasvati. Ajmer, 1949–1950.

G417 : Louis Renou, "Études paninéennes, III: Les Unādisūtra," JA 244, 1956, 155–165.

G418 : Ram Awadh Pandey, "A Comparative Study of *Uṇādisūtras*." Ph.D. diss., Banaras Hindu University, 1963.

G419 : Kanshi Ram, "A Study of Sanskrit *Uṇādisūtras*." Ph.D. diss., University of Delhi, 1971.

See a242.

G420 : Edited, with Dayananda Sarasvati's *Vaidikalaukikakośa* as *Uṇādikośa*, by Yudhisthira Mimamsaka. Bahalgarh, Haryana, 1974.

G421 : S. Venkitasubromania Iyer, "On the *Uṇādisūtra* 'mithune maṇiḥ,' " SVUOJ 18, 1975, 45–50.

G422 : Nomita Dutt, "Yāska's Nirukta and *Uṇādisūtras*," SVUOJ 19, 1976, 1–4.

Liṅgānuśāsana

See b82.

G423 : D. G. Koparkar, "The Pāṇinīya-liṅgānuśāsana: Its Date and Authorship," SPAIOC 15, 1949, 49–50.

See e241; e365.

?Pāṇinīyaśikṣā

G424 : Edited and translated into German. IS 4, 1858, 345–371.

G425 : F. Kielhorn, "Remarks on the *śikshās*," IA 5, 1867, 141–144. Reprinted Rau, pp. 158–169.

See e56; e68.

G426 : Edited and translated by Raghu Vīra. JRAS 1931, 653–670.

See b82.

G427 : Edited and translated, with edition and translation of Candragomin's *varṇasūtras*, editions of the (anonymous) *Vedāṅgaśikṣāpañjikā* and a *Śikṣāprakāśa*, by Manomohan Ghosh. Calcutta, 1938.

G428 : Edited with editor's *Pradīpa*, by Rudra Prasada Sarma. HSS 59, Varanasi, 1947–1948.

G429 : Edited with editor's commentary by Dayananda Sarasvati. Ajmer, 1950–1951.

See e168.

General

G430 : Theodor Goldstücker, *Pāṇini*. London, 1861; Allahabad, 1914; Osnabrück, 1966. Abridged version ChSSt 48, 1965.

G431 : Albrecht Weber, "Zur Frage über das Zeitalter Pāṇinis, mit specieller Beziehung auf Th. Goldstückers 'preface' zum 'Mānavakalpasūtra' ", IS 5, 1862, 1–176.

G432 : T. Aufrecht, "Pāṇini," IA 4, 1875, 281.

G433 : Leopold von Schroeder, "Ueber die Maitrāyanī Saṃhitā," ZDMG 33, 1879, 177–207.

G434 : T. Aufrecht, "Beiträge zur Kenntnis indischer Dichter," ZDMG 36, 1882, 361–383.

G435 : F. Kielhorn, "Der Grammatiker Pāṇini," NGGW 1885,185–199. Reprinted in Rau, pp. 188–202. Partially reprinted in Staal, pp. 103–105.

G436 : Otto Böhtlingk, "Versuch, eine jungst angefochtene Lehre Pāṇini's in Schutz zu nehmen," BGWL 42, 1890, 79–82.

G437 : Otto Franke, "Die Kasuslehre des Pāṇini vergleichen mit dem Gebrauch der Kasus im Pali und in den Aśoka-inschriften," BB 16, 1890, 64–120.

G438 : Bruno Liebich, *Pāṇini: Ein Beitrag zur Kenntnis der Indischen Literature und Grammatik*. Leipzig, 1891. Chapter 5 reprinted in G1625, pp. 159–165.

G439 : P. Peterson, "Pāṇini, Poet and Grammarian," JRAS 1891, 311–335.

G440 : William Dwight Whitney, "The Veda in Pāṇini," GSAIF 7, 1893, 243–254.

G441 : Otto Böhtlingk, "Neue Miscellen : 4. Pāṇini's *adhikāra*," BGWL 1897, 46–48.

G442 : A. Foucher, "Pāṇini," *La Grande Encyclopedie*. Paris, 1900, pp. 945–946.

G443 : Johannes Hertel "Von Pāṇini zu Phaedrus " ZDMG 62, 1908, 113–118.

G444 : Kashi Prasad Jayaswal, "Dates of Pāṇini and Kātyāyana," IA 47, 1918, 138.

G445 : K. V. Lakshmana Rao, "Did Pāṇini Know Buddhist Nuns?" IA 50, 1921, 82–84.

G446 : Radhakumud Mookerji, "Ancient Hindu Education as Revealed in the Works of Pāṇini, Kātyāyana and Patañjali," QJMS 12, 1921–1922, 156–170.

G447 : ———, "History of Sanskrit Literature from the Works of Pāṇini, Kātyāyana and Patañjali," IA 52, 1923, 21–24.

G448 : Hannes Sköld, *Papers on Pāṇini and Indian Grammar in General*. Lund, 1926.

G449 : ———, "The Relative Chronology of Pāṇini and the Prātiśākhyas," IA 55, 1926, 181–185.

G450 : K. G. Subrahmanyam, "Pāṇini and Yāska—a Rejoinder," JOR 1, 1927, 380–384.

G451 : K. B. Pathak, "The Age of Pāṇini and Sanskrit as a Spoken Language," ABORI 11, 1930, 59–83.

G452 : ———, "Were the Vājasaneyī Saṃhitā and Śatapaṭha Brāhmaṇa Unknown to Pāṇini?" ABROI 11, 1930, 84–89.

G453 : Raghu Vīra, "The Author of the Śiva-sūtras," JRAS 1930, 400–402.
See a4.

G454 : K. C. Chatterji, "Pānini as a Poet," COJ 1, 1933, 1–24, 135.

G455 : Bata Krishna Ghosh, "Pāṇini and the Ṛkprātiśākhya," IHQ 10, 1934, 665–670.

G456 : Nali Nath Das Gupta, "Pāṇini and the Yāvanas," IC 2, 1935, 356–358.

G457 : Paul Thieme, *Pāṇini and the Veda*. Allahabad, 1935.

G458 : ———, "Zur Datierung des Pāṇini," ZDMG 89, 1935, 21–24. Reprinted Budruss, pp. 528–531.

G459 : A. Berriedale Keith, "Pāṇini and the Veda," IC 2, 1936, 735–748.

G460 : S. P. Chaturvedi, "History of an Important Historical Word in the Pāṇinian School of Grammar," PAIOC 8, 1937, 739–744.

G461 : Kshetresh Chandra Chattopadhyaya, "Pāṇini and the Ṛkprātiśākhya II," IHQ 13, 1937, 343–349.

G462 : Paul Thieme, "Pāṇini and the Ṛkprātiśākhya, I," IHQ 13, 1937, 329–343. Reprinted Budruss, pp. 537–571.

G463 : S. P. Chaturvedi, "Pāṇini and the Ṛkprātiśākhya," NIA 1, 1938, 450–459; 2, 1940–1942, 723–726.

G464 : Mangal Deva Shastri, "A Comparison of the Ṛgvedaprātiśākhya with the Pāṇinian Grammar," POWSBSt 10, 1938, 143–161.

G465 : K. C. Chattopadhyaya, "Thieme and Pāṇini," IC 5, 1938, 95–98.

G466 : Bata Krishna Ghosh, "Mr. Chaturvedi on Pāṇini and the Ṛkprātiśākhya," NIA 2, 1939, 59–61.

G467 : K. Madhava Krishna Sharma, "The Pāṇinian School and the Prātiśākhyas: Post-Pāṇinian Reciprocity of Influence," BhV 2, 1941, 230–238; 4, 1942, 46–53.

G468 : V. S. Agrawala, "Pāṇini, His Life and Works," JGJRI 2, 1945, 81–144.

G469 : ———, "Pāṇini," JOR 19, 1949, 124–134.

G470 : Ram Shankar Bhattacharya, "Some Principles of Tracing pre-Pāṇinian Portions in Pāṇinian Works," JGJRI 8, 1951, 407–418.

G471 : S. P. Chaturvedi, "Pāṇini's Vocabulary and His Date," in *Festschrift Siddheshwar Varma* 2. 144–147.

G472 : V. S. Agrawala, "Some Chronological Considerations About Pāṇini's Date," IHQ 27, 1951, 269–286.

G473 : R. S. Bhattacharya, "Pāṇini's Notion of the Authoritativeness of the Views of his Predecessors," JGJRI 9, 1952, 163–182.

G474 : ———, "Some Chief Characteristics of Pāṇini in Comparison to His Predecessors," JOI 2, 1952, 165–173; 5, 1955, 10–18.

G475 : Carlo Della Casa, "Uddhya e bhidya in Pāṇini e Kālidāsa," RDSO 26, 1952, 67–70.

G476 : Vasudeva Sharana Agrawala, *India as Known to Pāṇini*. Lucknow, 1953; 2d edition, Varanasi, 1963.

G477 : K. C. Chatterji, "Pāṇini and Whitney," CR 125, 1952, 55–58; 126, 1953, 49–52.

G478 : Siddheshwar Varma, "A Plan for the Evaluation of Pāṇini on the Vedic Languages," SPAIOC 17, 1953, 104–105.

G479 : Paul Thieme, "Pāṇini and the Pāṇinīyas," JAOS 76, 1956, 1–23. Reprinted Budruss, pp. 573–595

G480 : ———, "Pāṇini and the Pronunciation of Sanskrit," in *Festschrift* Whatmough, 1957, pp. 263–270. Reprinted Budruss, pp. 612–618.

G481 : Parasaram Gopalakrishna Murty, "Pāṇini and the Earlier Grammarians," SPAIOC 20, 1957, 71.

G482 : S. K. Ramachandra Rao, "Specimens of Pāṇini's Poetry," QJMS 50, 1959, 115–127.

See a17.

G483 : Hartmut Scharfe, "Pāṇini's Kunstsprache" (summary), WZMLUH 10.6, 1961, 1396.

G484 : S. Bhattacharya, "A Note on Pāṇini," Bh 6.2, 1962–1963, 76–80.

G485 : V. S. Agrawala, *Gotras in Pāṇini*. Varanasi, 1963.

G486 : Deo Prakas Shastri Patanjal, *A Critical Study of Ṛgveda* (1. 137–163), *Particularly from the Point of View of Pāṇinian Grammar*. New Delhi, 1963.

G487 : G. V. Devasthali, "Śāyaṇa Utilising Pāṇini in His Ṛg-Veda-Bhāṣya," JBBRAS 38, 1963, 165–173.

G488 : ———, "Pāṇini as an Aid to Ṛgvedic Interpretation," HDVCV, pp. 20–26.

G489 : Venkatesh Laxman Joshi, "Pāṇini and the Pāṇinīyas on *samhita*," IL 26, 1965, 66–71.

G490 : Paul Thieme, "Die Kobra bei Pāṇini," KZ 79, 1965, 55–68. Reprinted Budruss, pp. 239–246.

G481a : G. V. Devasthali, "Pāṇini and Ṛgvedic exegesis," IA 3d series 2.3, 1967, 1–8. Also ABORI 48–49, 1968, 75–81. Also PCASS-A 22, 1968, 1–8. Also JOR 40–41, 1970-1972, 41–48. Also VRFV, pp. 97–104.

G482a : S. D. Laddu, "Pāṇini and the Veda." Ph.D. diss., University of Poona, 1967.

G483a : Sumitra Mangesh Katre, *Pāṇinian Studies*. Poona, 1967.
G484a : D. N. Shastri, "A Reappraisal of Pāṇini," KAG 1967, 296–301.
G485a : K. Madhava Krishna Sarma, *Pāṇini, Kātyāyana and Patañjali*. Delhi, 1968.
G486a : Louis Renou, "Pāṇini," *Current Trends in Linguistics*, volume 5, *Linguistics in South Asia*, ed. T. A. Sebeok. The Hague, 1969, pp. 481–498.
G487a : S. D. Laddu, "The *laukika*, *vaidika* and *yājñika* Accentuation with the *munitraya* of Sanskrit Grammar," IA 3d series 3, 1969, 93–111.
G488a : M. D. Pandit, "Pāṇini and the Vedic Interpretation," in *Festschrift Rajeshwar Shastri Dravid*, English section, pp. 49–53.
G489a : Peter H. Salus, *Pāṇini to Postal: A Bibliography in the History of Linguistics*. Edmonton, 1971.
G490 : Hari Mohan Mishra, "A Reappraisal of Pāṇini," ITaur 3–4, 1975–1976, 317–320.
G491 : Sergiu Al-George, "Pāṇini and Modern Thought," PISC 2.2, 1976, 82.
G492 : S. D. Laddu, *Evolution of the Sanskrit Language from Pāṇini to Patañjali*. Poona, 1974.
G493 : Mavelikara Achyathan, *Educational Practices in Manu, Pāṇini and Kauṭilya*. Trivandrum, 1974–1975.
G494 : Bishnupada Bhattacharya, "The Impress of Pāṇinian Grammar on Sanskrit Poetics," OH 27.2, 1979, 35–50.
G495 : Johannes Bronkhorst, "The Orthoepic Diaskeuasis of the Ṛgveda and the Date of Pāṇini," IIJ 23, 1981, 83–95.
G496 : K. C. Varma, "Date of Pāṇini," VIJ 20, 1982, 29–57.

VADAVA (pre-Patañjali)

KUNI (pre-Patañjali) NCat 4. 176)

KUNARABADAVA (pre-Patañjali)

GOṆIKAPUTRA (pre-Patañjali)

G497 : Rajendralal Mitra, "On Goṇikaputra and Goṇārdiya as Names of Patañjali," JASBe 52, 1883, 261-269.

GOṆĀRDIYA (pre-Patañjali)

See 497.

G498 : Sylvain Lévi, "Goṇārda, le berceau du Goṇārdiya," SAMV 3.2, 1925, 197–205.

VYĀḌI (pre-Kātyāyana)

(G1624, pp. 130, 216; Belvalkar, p. 9)

Saṃgraha

G499 : Ram Shankar Bhattacharya, "A New Verse of the *Saṃgraha* (by Vyāḍi)," PO 19, 1954, 4–5.

Paribhāṣā

G500 : Edited in *Paribhāṣāsaṃgraha*, 31–43.

General

G501 : Mysore Hiriyanna, "Vyāḍi and Vajapyāyana," IHQ 14, 1938, 261–266.

VĀJAPYĀYANA (pre-Kātyāyana)

(G1624, pp. 134–135)

See a501.

KĀTYA or BHĀVAN (pre-Kātyāyana)

Mahāvārttika (lost)

KĀTYĀYANA or VARARŪCI (250 B.C.)

(Cardona, pp. 247, 250, 267; Belvalkar, pp. 9, 23; G1624, p. 136)

Vārttika(s) on Pāṇini's *Aṣṭādhyāyī*

G502 : Otto Böhtlingk, "Kātyāyana oder Patañjali im Mahābhāṣya," ZDMG 29, 1875, 183–190.

G503 : F. Kielhorn, *Kātyāyana and Patañjali: Their Relation to Each Other and to Pāṇini*. Bombay, 1876. Reprinted Varanasi, 1963; Osnabruck, 1965, Rau, pp. 1–64.

See e871.

G504 : Sylvain Lévi, "Notes de chronologie indienne: *devānāṃpriya*, Aśoka et Kātyāyana," JA 1891, 549–553.

G505 : Edited (?) with Nārāyaṇa's *Dīpaprabhā* by T. Ganapati Sastri. TSS 33. Trivandrum, 1913.

G506 : Kashi Prasad Jayaswal, "Kātyāyana and Pārthiva," IA 48, 1919, 12.

See a444; a446

G507 : Vasudeva Gopala Paranjpe, *Le vārtika de Kātyāyana: Une étude du style, du vocabularie et des postulats philosophiques*. Heidelberg, 1922.

See a447; e68.

G508 : K. G. Subrahmanyam, "The Vārttikas," JOR 2, 1928, 25–33.

See a84.

G509 : V. R. Ramachandra Dikshitar, "Kātyāyana—the grammarian," IHQ 11, 1935, 316–320.

G510 : Vasudeva S. Agrawala, "Pūrvācārya *saṃjñās* for *lakāras*," NIA 3, 1940, 39–40.

G511 : K. Madhava Krishna Sarma, "Kātyāyana," PO 5.2–3, 1941, 126–132; 6.1–2, 1942, 74–92.

G512 : G. V. Devasthali, "The Aim of the Vārtika of Kātyāyana," BhV 20–21, 1960–1961, 52–63.

G513 : S. D. Laddu, "The Sphere of Reference of the Technical Term Tṛjādi according to Kātyāyana and Patañjali," PCASS-A 23, 1968 (— JUP 29), 1–10.

See b485.

G514 : B. A. Van Nooten, "The Grammarian Kātyāyana and the White Yājurveda School," IL 29.1, 1968, 43–46.

G515 : S. D. Laddu, "Authorship of a Vārttika from the *Mahābhāṣya*," PCASS-A 38, 1970 (- JUP 33), 13–22.

G516 : A. M. Ghatage, "Kātyāyana and the Transformational Approach," PAICL 1, 1971, 31–35.

G517 : G. V. Devasthali, "Kātyāyana's Use of *yogavibhāga*," BDCRI 35, 1975, 42–48.

G518 : Y. Ojihara, "Qu'on ne confonde pas un vārttika avec un sūtra!" ITaur 7, 1979, 333–338.

AUTHOR UNKNOWN (100 B.C.)

Laghubhāṣya on Pāṇini's *Aṣṭādhyāyī*

G519 : K. V. Abhyankar, "Laghubhāṣya and Its Author," SPAIOC 14.1, 1948, 23.

PATAÑJALI (150 B.C.)

(Cardona, pp. 243, 256; Belvalkar, p. 26)

Mahābhāṣya on Pāṇini's *Aṣṭādhāyī*

(Cardona, p. 256; NCat 11.89)

G520 : Friedrich Max Müller, "Das *Mahābhāṣya*," ZDMG 7, 1853, 162–171.

G521 : Volume 1 edited, with Kaiyaṭa's *Pradīpa* and Nāgeśa's *Uddyota*, by J. R. Ballantyne and the pandits of the Benares college. Mirzapore, 1855; with translation of text, 1856.

G522 . Edited, with Kaiyaṭa's *Pradīpa*, Nāgeśa Bhaṭṭa's *Uddyota*, and editor's *Tippanī*, by Bala Sastrin. Varanasi, 1870, 1886, 1906.

G523 : R. G. Bhandarkar, "On the Date of Patañjali and the King in Whose Reign He Lived," IA 1, 1872, 299–302; 2, 1873, 59–61. Reprinted CWRGB 2. 108–114; G1625, pp. 78–81.

G524 : ———, "On the Interpretation of Patañjali," IA 2, 1873, 94–96.
G525 : ———, "Patañjali's *Mahābhāṣya*," IA 2, 1873, 69–71. Reprinted CWRGB 1, 121–124.
G526 : Albrecht Weber, "On the Date of Patañjali" (trans. D. C. Boyd), IA 2, 1873, 61–64.
G527 : ———, "On Patañjali, etc.," IA 2, 1873, 206–221.
G528 : ———, "Das *Mahābhāṣya* des Patañjali, Benares 1872," IS 13, 1873, 293–496. Portion translated in IA 6, 1877, 301–307.
G529 : Photolithographed, with Kaiyaṭa's *Pradīpa* and Nāgeśa Bhaṭṭa's *Uddyota*, by T. Goldstücker. 6 volumes. London, 1874.
G530 : Edited, with Kaiyaṭa's *Pradīpa*, by T. Goldstücker. London, 1874.
G531 : Kashinath Trimbak Telang, "The Rāmāyaṇa Older than Patañjali," IA 3, 1874, 124.
G532 : R. G. Bhandarkar, "Allusions to Kṛṣṇa in Patañjali's *Mahābhāṣya*," IA 3, 1874, 14–16. Reprinted CWRGB 1.209–213.
See a502.
G533 : Albrecht Weber, "On the Yāvanas, Mahābhāṣya, Rāmāyaṇa, and Krishnajanmāṣṭamī," IA 4, 1875, 244–251.
See b503.
G534 : F. Kielhorn, "On the *Mahābhāṣya*," IA 5, 1876, 241–251. Reprinted in Rau, pp. 169–179.
G535 : J. G. Buhler, "Mss. of the *Mahābhāṣya* from Kashmir," IA 7, 1878, 54ff.
G536 : Edited by F. Kielhorn. 3 volumes. BSPS 18–22, 28–30. Bombay, 1878–1885, 1892, 1906, 1909, 3d revised edition by K. V. Abhyankar, Poona, 1962-1972.
G537 : Partly edited, with editor's *Maṇiratnaprabhā*, by Viprarajendra, 1880.
G538 : Peter Peterson, "Note on the Date of Patañjali," JBBRAS 16, 1883–1885, 181–189. Reprinted in his *The Auchityalaṃkara of Kshemendra*. Bombay, 1885.
G539 : R. G. Bhandarkar, "The Date of Patañjali : A Reply to Professor Peterson," JBBRAS 16, 1883–1885, 199–222. Reprinted in CWRBGB 1.157–185.
G540 : P. A. Danielsson, "Die Einleitung des *Mahābhāṣya*, übersetzt," ZDMG 37, 1883, 20–53.
G541 : R. G. Bhandarkar, "Date of Patañjali, no. 2: Being a Second Reply to Professor Peterson," CWRGB 1.186–207.
G542 : F. Kielhorn, "Quotations in the *Mahābhāṣya* and the *Kāśikāvṛtti*," IA 14, 1885, 326–327.
G543 : ———, "Prākṛtwörte im *Mahābhāṣya*," ZDMG 39, 1885, 327.
G544 : Edited, with Kaiyaṭa's *Pradīpa*, Nāgeśa'a *Uddyota*, and Guruwara Bāla Śāstri's *Ṭippanī*, by Dāmodara Śāstri Bharadvaja, Gangadhara Sastri Manavalli and Tatya Sastri Pattavardhana. 3 volumes. Varanasi, 1886.
G545 : F. Kielhorn, "Notes on the *Mahābhāṣya*," IA 15, 1886, 80–81, 203–211; 16, 1887, 101–106, 178–184, 228–233. 244–252, Reprinted Rau, pp. 202–206, 220–241. Partially reprinted in Staal, pp. 150–151, 107–114, 115–123.
G546 : R. G. Bhandarkar, "The Maurya-passage in the *Mahābhāṣya*," IA 16, 1887, 156–158, 172–173. Reprinted CWRGB 1.148–156.
G547 : Edited, with Kaiyaṭa's *Pradīpa* and Bāla Śāstrin's *Ṭippanī*. Poona, 1887.
G548 : Otto Böhtlingk, "Noch ein Wort zur Maurya-Frage im *Mahābhāṣya*," ZDMG 41, 1887, 175–178.
G549 : Govinda Das, "Prof. Kielhorn's edition of the *Mahābhāṣya*," IA 18, 1889, 128.
G550 : Edited, with Kaiyaṭa's *Pradīpa* and Nāgeśa Bhaṭṭa's *Uddyota*, by Bahuvallabha Sastri. BI 142. Calcutta, 1899ff.

G551 : Bernhard Geiger, "*Mahābhāṣya* zu P. VI.4.22 und 132 nebst Kaiyaṭa's Kommentar, ubersetzt, erläutert und mit einem Anhang," SWAW 160.8. Vienna, 1908, pp. 1-76. Reprinted Staal, pp. 209–259.

G552 : Adhyāyas 1.2 through 2 edited, with Kaiyaṭa's *Pradīpa* and Nāgeśas *Uddyota*, by S. D. Kudala. Bombay, 1908, 1912.

G553 : K. B. Pathak, "The Divine Vāsudeva Different from the kshātriya Vāsudeva in Patañjali's Opinion," JBBRAS 23, 1909-1914, 96–103.

G554 : Chandradhar Guleri, "On 'Śiva-bhāgavata' in Patañjali's *Mahābhāṣya*," IA 41, 1912, 272.

G555 : Edited, with Bhaṭṭoji Dīkṣita's *Sūtravṛtti*, by Syamacarana Kaviratna. Calcutta, 1914.

G556 : Edited Bombay, 1917.

See a446; a447.

G557 : K. G. Subrahmanyam, "Patañjali and kāvya Literature Presumed by Him," PAIOC 3, 1924, 96-99.

G558 : 1.1.1 translated by Prabhat Chandra Chakravarti. IHQ 1, 1925, 703–739.

G559 : K. G. Subrahmanyam, "Some Notes on Mr. Keith's Interpretation of a *Mahābhāṣya* Passage," JRAS 1925, 502–505.

G560 : ———, "A Short Note on Mr. Jayaswal's Interpretation of a *Mahābhāṣya* Passage in His 'Hindu Polity' (p. 122)," IHQ 2, 1926, 416–418.

G561 : Prabhat Chandra Chakravarti, "Patañjali as He Reveals Himself in the *Mahābhāṣya*," IHQ 2, 1926, 67-76, 262–289, 464–494, 738–760.

G562 : Kshetresh Chandra Chattopadhyaya, "Patañjali and His Knowledge of Science," IHQ 3, 1927, 181–182.

G563 : Otto Strauss, "*Mahābhāṣya* ad Pāṇini 4.1.3 und seine Bedeutung für die Geschichte der indischen Logik," AIK 1927, 84–94.

G564 : Shridhar Shastri Pathak and Siddheshvar Sastri Chitrao, *Word Index to Patañjali's Vyākaraṇa-mahābhāṣya* (*Mahābhāṣya-śabdakośaḥ*). GOSBORI series C. Poona, 1927.

G565 : *Āhnikas* 1-2 edited by Madhava Sastri Bhandari. Lahore, 1929.

G566 : Edited with editor's *Kuñcikā*, by Harisamkara Jha. Bareilly, 1929.

G567 : Edited Calcutta, 1930.

G568 : K. B. Pathak, "On the Text and Interpretation of Some Passages in the *Mahābhāṣya* of Patañjali," ABORI 13, 1932, 17–24.

G569 : Āhnikas 1-5 translated into German by Valentin Trapp. Leipzig, 1933, 352–380.

See a84; b81.

G570 : Amalananda Ghosh, "A Study of the *smṛti* Passages in the *Mahābhāṣya*," IHQ 11, 1935, 70–90.

G571 : K. C. Chatterji, "Some Technical Terms of Sanskrit Grammar," COJ 3, 1936, 105–132.

G572 : V. S. Agrawala, "Patañjali on the *kṣudraka-mālavas*," PO 1.4, 1937, 1–7.

G573 : Edited with Marathi translation by V. S. Abhyankar and K. V. Abhyankar. 7 volumes. Poona, 1938–1954.

G574 : Edited, with Kaiyaṭa's *Pradīpa* and Nāgeśa's *Uddyota*, by Samkara Sastri Marulkar. 2 volumes. ASS 108. Poona, 1938.

G575 : Edited, with Kaiyaṭa's *Pradīpa* and Nāgeśa's *Uddyota*, by Guruprasada Sastri. 9 volumes. RSCG. Varanasi, 1938.

G576 : Dinesh Chandra Sircar, "Date of Patañjali's *Mahābhāṣya*," IHQ 15, 1939, 633–638.

G577 : V. S. Agrawala, "Patañjali and the *vāhika-grāmas*," IC 6, 1939, 129–136.

G578 : Louis Renou, "On the Identity of the Two Patañjalis," IHQ 16, 1940, 586–591.

G579 : D. G. Bhave, "A Note on the 'Abhiras' in Patañjali," BDCRI 2, 1940, 137–138.

G580 : K. Madhava Krishna Sarma, "Patañjali, a *lakṣyaikacakṣus*: His Lofty Realism," JOR 14, 1940, 204–209.

G581 : S. P. Chaturvedi, "Notes on a *vārtika* (?) and Its Misplaced Occurrence in the *Mahābhāṣya*," PVKF 1941, 82-83.

G582 : 1.1, 4.4-5, and 5.6 edited, with Kaiyaṭa's *Pradīpa* and Nāgeśa's *Uddyota*, by Bhargavasastri Bhikaji Josi. Bombay, 1942, 1945, 1951.

G583 : K. Madhava Kirshna Sarma, "Patañjali and His Relations to Some Authors and Works," IC 11.2, 1944.

G584 : P. V. Kane, "The *Mahābhāṣya* and the *Bhāṣya* of Śabara," BhV 6, 1945, 43–45.

G585 : S. Vaiyapuri Pillai, "Tolkappiyar and Patañjali," in *C. K. Raja Commemoration Volume*. Madras, 1946, pp. 134–138.

G586 : Mangal Deva Sharma, "The Traditional Basis of the *udāharaṇas* in the *Kāśikā* and the *Mahābhāṣya* and the Mutual Relation of the Two Works Regarding the Same," PAIOC 12, 1947, 333–339.

G587 : 1.1.4 edited, with Kaiyaṭa's *Pradīpa* and Annambhaṭṭa's *Uddyotana* thereon, by P.P.S. Sastri and A. Sankaran. MGOMS 7, 1948.

G588 : G. V. Devasthali, "Śabara and Patañjali," JUB 20.2, 1951, 101–106.

G589 : P. S. Subrahmanya Sastri, *Lectures on the Mahābhāṣya*. 6 volumes. AUSS 11. Annamalainagar, 1951–1962.

G590 : 2.5-9 edited, with Kaiyaṭa's *Pradīpa* and Annambhaṭṭa's *Uddyotana* thereon, by T. Chandrasekharan. MGOMS 13, 1952.

G591 : R. S. Bhattacharya, "Significance of the Examples in the *Mahābhāṣya*," JGJRI 10, 1952–1953, 39–48.

G592 : Sukumar Sen, "The Story of Devadatta in the *Mahābhāṣya*," IL 12, 1952 1953, 189–196. Also PAIOC 16, 1953, 268–275.

G593 : M. G. Gaidhani, "The Attitude of Patañjali Towards Kātyāyana," PAIOC 16.2, 1953, 95–104.

G594 : Louis Renou, "Études paninéennes, II: Le Veda chez Patañjali," JA 241, 1953, 427–464.

G595 : R. S. Bhattacharya, "One Corrupt Reading of the *Mahābhāṣya*, PO 19, 1954, 2–3.

G596 : ———, "The Mahābhāṣya vs. the Kāśikā," JSVOI 15, 1954, 61–70.

G597 : ———, "Some Characteristic Expressions of Patañjali," JSVOI 15, 1954, 139–146.

G598 : 1.1 edited, with Kaiyaṭa's *Pradīpa*, Nāgeśa's *Uddyota* and editor's *Tattvāloka*, by Rudradatta Jha Sarman. KSS 153. Varanasi, 1954.

G599 : Bishnupada Bhattacarya, "Philosophical Data in Patañjali's *Mahābhāṣya*," OH 4, 1956, 51–65.

G600 : K. C. Chatterji, "How Patañjali Has Been Misunderstood," IL 17, 1956, 100–102.

G601 : Introductory chapter edited and translated by K. C. Chatterji. UMS 7, 1957.

G602 : E. R. Sreekrishna Sarma, "The Words *ākṛti* and *jāti* in the *Mahābhāṣya*," ALB 21, 1957, 54–65.

G603 : Adoft Janacek, "Two Texts of Patañjali and Statistical Comparison of Their Vocabularies," AO 26, 1958, 88–100.

G604 : C. K. Pandey, "Patañjali," JBRS 44.3–4, 1959, 220ff.

G605 : V. Swaminathan, "Patañjali and the Nirukta" (summary), SPAIOC 21, 1959, 143. Full paper PAIOC 21, 1966, 185–209.

G606 : Ram Suresh Tripathi, "Conception of *jāti* in the *Mahābhāṣya* of Patañjali," SPAIOC 21, 1959, 196.

G607 : Erich Frauwallner, "Sprachtheorie und Philosophie im *Mahābhāṣya* des Patañjali," WZKSOA 4, 1960, 92–118.

G608 : Hari Deo Mishra, "A Critical Study of Some Aspects of Sanskrit Grammar with special reference to the Mahābhāṣya of Patañjali," Ph.D. diss., University of Poona, 1961.

G609 : Y. Ojihara, "Le *Mahābhāṣya, adhyāya* I, *āhnika* 8: Un Essai de Traduction," MIK 2, 1961, 9–22.

G610 : Hartmut Scharfe, *Die Logik im Mahābhāṣya*. DAWIO 50. Berlin, 1961.

G611 : Partially edited, with Kaiyaṭa's *Pradīpa* and Nāgeśa Bhaṭṭa's *Uddyota*, by Vedavrata. 4 volumes. Rohtak, 1961–1963.

G612 : First *adhyāya* edited, with editor's Hindi commentary, by Charudeva Sastri. Varanasi, 1962.

G613 : Stanley Insler, "Verbal Paradigms in Patañjali: 250 Roots and Their Paradigmatic Derivations as Used and Discussed by Patañjali in the *Mahābhāsya*." Ph. D. diss., Yale University, 1963.

G614 : S. D. Joshi, "Patañjali on Two Methods of Interpreting the *Aṣṭādhyāyī*," SPAIOC 22, 1963, 120.

G615 : Y. Ojihara, "*Mahābhāṣya* ad Pāṇini 1.1.56: Un Essai de traduction," *Acta Asiatica* 4, 1963, 43–69.

G616 : Siddheshwar Varma, "Scientific and Technical Presentation of Patañjali as Reflected in the *Mahābhāṣya*," VIJ 1, 1963, 1–36.

G617 : Paul Thieme, "Patañjali über Varuṇa und die sieben Ströme," in *Festschrift Morgenstierne* pp. 168–173. Reprinted Budruss, pp. 620–625.

G618 : Sudarshan Arora, "Patañjali's Criticism of Kātyāyana," SPAIOC 23.1, 1966, 151.

G619 : M. D. Balasubrahmanyam, "Patañjali and the pre-Pāṇinian *anubandhas ṅ* and *c*," PCASS-A 11. Poona, 1966. Also JUP 25, 1967, 77–82.

G620 : S. D. Joshi, "Patañjali's Definition of a Word—a Reinterpretation," BDCRI 25, 1966, 65–70. Reprinted CIDO 27.3., 94–95.

G621 : S. D. Laddu, A Possible Light on the Relative Age of Yāska and Patañjali," SPAIOC 23.1, 1966, 156.

G622 : *Adhyāyas* 1–3 edited, with Kaiyaṭa's *Pradīpa*, Nāgeśa's *Uddyota* and Vaidyanātha's *Chāyā*. 3 volumes. Delhi, 1967.

See d220.

G623 : E. de Guzman Orara, "An Account of Ancient Grammatical Studies down to Patañjali's *Mahābhāṣya*: Two Traditions," *Asian Studies* (Quezon City, Philippines) 5, 1967, 369–376.

G624 : Satya Vrat, "Conception of Time in the *Mahābhāṣya*," MO 1, 1967–1968, 19–21, 88–91.

See b485; a513.

G625 : 2.1.1 edited and translated by S. D. Joshi. PCASS-C 3. Poona, 1968.

G626 : Baij Nath Puri, *India in the Time of Patañjali*. Bombay, 1968.

See a487.

G627 : 2.1.2–49 edited and translated, with Kaiyaṭa's *Pradīpa* and Nāgeśa's *Uddyota*, by S. D. Joshi and J. A. F. Roodbergen. PCASS-C 5. Poona, 1969.

G628 : G. B. Palsule, "Patañjali's Interpretation of RV 10.71.2," IA 3d series 3, 1969, 27–29,

G629 : Sudarshan Kumari Arora, "Patañjali as a Critic of Kātyāyana and Pāṇini." Ph. D. diss., Delhi University, 1969.

G630 : Y. Ojihara, "Les Discussions patañjaliennes afferntes au remaniement du Gaṇapātha," IIJ 12, 1969–1970. 81–115.

See a515.

G631 : J. A. F. Roodbergen, 'Patañjali's Vyākaraṇa-Mahābhāṣya-Bahuvrīhi-dvandvāhnika.' Ph. D. diss., University of Poona, 1971.

G632 : 2.1.51–72 edited and translated, with Kaiyaṭa's *Pradīpa*, by S. D. Joshi and J. A. F. Roodbergen. PCASS-C 6. Poona, 1971.

G633 : 2.2.2–23 edited, with Kaiyaṭa's *Pradīpa*, by S. D. Joshi and J.A.F. Roodbergen. PCASS-C 7. Poona, 1973.

See a327; b492.

G634 : 2.2.23–38 edited and translated by J.A.F. Roodbergen and S. D. Joshi. PCASS-C 9. Poona, 1974.

G635 : V. P. Limaye, *Critical Studies on the Mahābhāṣya*. Hoshiarpur, 1974.

G636 : Alekhacandra Sarangi, "Authorship of a Line from the *Mahābhāṣya*," BhV 35, 1975, 13–17.

G637 : George Cardona, "Still Again on the History of the *Mahābhāṣya*," ABORI 58–59, 1977–1978, 79–99.

G638 : Y. Ojihara, "Sur une Formule patanjalienne: *na cedānīm ācāryāḥ sūtrāṇi kṛtvā nivartayanti*," ITaur 6, 1978, 219–234.

G639 : 1.2 edited, with Madhava Sastri Bhandari's *Sphoṭavimarśinī*, by Veda Prakasa Vidyavacaspati. New Delhi, 1979.

G640 : S. D. Laddu, "A Reconsideration of the History of the *Mahābhāṣya*" (summary), SWSC 5. Delhi, 1981, pp. 46–47.

ŚARVAVARMAN (1st century A.D.)

(NCat 3. 306; Belvalkar, p. 69)

Kātantrasūtras

(NCat 3. 307, 9. 288)

G641 : Edited, with Durgāsiṃha's *Vṛtti*, by Navakumara Tarkapancanana. Calcutta, 1870.

G642 : Edited, with Durgāsiṃha's *Vṛtti*, by Julius Eggeling. BI 81. Calcutta, 1874–1878.

G643 : Edited, with Trilocanadāsa's *Vṛttipañjikā*, by Madhavacandra Tarkacudamani Bhattacarya. Calcutta, 1878.

G644 : Edited, with editor's *Pañjikāṭīkā*, by Candrakanta Tarkalamkara. Barasol, 1880.

G645 : Edited, with Durgāsiṃha's *Vṛtti*, by Jivananda Vidyasagara. Calcutta, 1884.

G646 : Edited Calcutta, 1885.

G647 : Edited, with Śivarāma Śarman's *Kṛṅmañjarī*, by Candrakanta Nyayalamkara. Dacca, 1886.

G648 : Otto Böhtlingk, "Über die Grammatik Kātantra," ZDMG 41, 1886, 657–666.

G649 : Edited with Śripatidatta's *Pariśiṣṭa*. Dacca, 1886; Calcutta, 1910.

G650 : Edited, with Bhavasena Traividyadeva's *Rūpamālā*, by Lallurama Jivarama Sastrin. Bombay, 1895.

G651 : Edited, with Candrakānta Tarkālaṃkāra's *Chandaḥprakrīyā*, by Gurunatha Vidyanidhi Bhattacarya. Calcutta, 1896.

G652 : Edited, with editor's *Ṭīkā*, by Mahendranatha Bhattacarya. Dacca, 1900.

G653 : Edited, with Durgāsiṃha's *Vṛtti*, Śripatidatta's *Pariśiṣṭa*, Vidyāsāgara's *Ākhyātaṭīkā*, Trilocanadāsa's *Pañjikā*, Rāmakisora Śarman's *Aṣṭamaṅgala*,

Bilveśvara's *Kalāpacandra*, Raghunandana Ācārya's *Tattvārṇava*, and Harirāma Bhaṭṭācārya's *Sāra*, by Gurunatha Vidyanidhi Bhattacarya. Calcutta, 1905.

G654 : *Dhātupāṭha* edited with Rāmanātha's *Manoramā*. Calcutta, 1905.

G655 : *Dhātupāṭha* edited with Śrinātha Śiromaṇi's *Manorāma*. Calcutta, 1905.

G656 : Edited, with Durgāsiṃha's *Vṛtti*, Trilocanadāsa's *Pañjikā*, Piṭāmbara Vidyābhūṣaṇa's *Dhātusūtrīya*, Susena Kavirāja Miśra's *Kalāpacandra*, Puṇḍarīka Vidyāsāgara's *Pradīpa*, and Kulacandra's *Durgāvākyaprabodha*, by Gurunatha Vidyanidhi Bhattacarya. Calcutta, 1908, 1910.

G657 : Edited, with Durgāsiṃha's *Vṛtti*, Trilocanadāsa's *Pañjikā*, Bilveśvara's *Ṭīkā*, and Kulacandra's *Prabodha*, by Prasannakumara Bhattacarya. Calcutta, 1910.

G658 : *Ākhyāta* section edited, with Durgāsiṃha's *Vṛtti*, Trilocanadāsa's *Pañjika*, Bilveśvara's *Ṭīkā*, and Sitānātha Śastrin's *Saṃjīvanī*, by Sitanatha Siddhantavagisa Bhattacarya. Calcutta, 1910, 1912.

G659 : Edited in L. Finot, "Fragmente du Kātantra, provenant de Koutche." LM 1911.

G660 : Edited and translated into German in Bruno Liebich, *Zur Einführung in die indische einheimische Sprachwissenschaft*: *Das Kātantra*. SHAW 10. Heidelberg, 1919.

G661 : Edited by Narada Bhiksu. Calcutta, 1927.

G662 : A. Venkatasubbiah, "On the Grammatical Work Si-T'An-Chang," JOR 10, 1936, 11-26.

G663 : Edited, with Saṃgrāmasiṃha's *Bālaśikṣā*, by Maniraja Jinavijaya. RPG 3. Jodhpur, 1968.

KUMĀRALABDHA or KUMĀRALĀTA (2d-3d century?)

Commentary on the Kashmiri recension of the Kātantra.

G664 : Fragments edited in H. Lüders, *Kātantra und Kaumāralāta*. SBAW 25. Berlin 1930, pp. 483-538.

ŚĀNTANAVA ĀCĀRYA (350?)

(Cardona, p. 22; Belvalkar, p. 22)

?*Phiṭsūtras*

G665 : Edited and translated into German by F. Kielhorn. AKM 4.2. Leipzig, 1866. Reprinted 1966.

G666 : A. N. Choudhari, "Notes on the Phiṭsūtra Śāntanava," PAIOC 11. Hyderabad, 1941.

See e168.

G667 : Edited and translated by Govind Vinayak Devasthali. PCASS-C 1. Poona, 1967.

See a242.

G668 : Edited, with Sudarśanadeva's *Pradīpa*, by Vedananda Vedavagisa. Jhajjar, Haryana, 1969.

See e365.

SAUBHAVA (350?)

(G1624, p. 165)

HARYAKṢA (350?)

(G1624, p. 165)

DHYĀNAKĀRA (pre-Bhartṛhari)

G669 : V. P. Limaye, "Dhyānagrāha-Kāra or Dhyāna-kāra: A pre-Bhartṛhari Grammarian," VIJ 4, 1966, 228-229.

G670 : K. A. Subramania Iyer, "Some Lost Works on *Vyākaraṇa*," VRFV 1975, 137-144.

PŪJYAPĀDA or DEVANANDIN (500?)
(Belvalkar, p. 53)
Jainendravyākaraṇa (there are two versions)
G671 : F. Kielhorn, "On the Jainendra-Vyākaraṇa," IA 10, 1882, 75ff.
G672 : K. B. Pathak, "Pūjyapāda and the Authorship of the *Jainendra-Vyākaraṇa*," IA 12, 1884, 19ff.
G673 : Edited, with Abhayanandin's *Mahāvṛtti*, by V. P. Dvivedin. *Pan* n.s. 31ff., 1909–1922.
G674 : Edited, with Guṇanandin's commentary. SJS 5, 1914.
G675 : K. B. Pathak, "The Text of the *Jainendra-Vyākaraṇa* and the Priority of Candra to Pūjyapāda," ABORI 13, 1931–1932, 25–36.
G676 : Edited, with Abhayanandin's *Mahāvṛtti*. JPMJG 17, 1956.

BHARTṚHARI (450? 530?)
(G1624, p. 167)
Vākyapadīya or *Trikāṇḍī*, and *Vṛtti* thereon
G677 : F. Kielhorn, "The Concluding Verses of the Second or Vākyakāṇḍa of Bhartṛhari's *Vākyapadīya*," IA 3, 1874, 285–287. Reprinted in Rau, pp. 156–157.
G678 : G. Bühler, "Über die Erlklärung des Wörtes *āgama* in *Vākyapadīya* III.6," ZDMG 36, 1882, 653–654.
G679 : F. Kielhorn, "On the Grammarian Bhartṛhari," IA 12, 1883, 226–227. Reprinted in Rau, pp. 185–186.
G680 : Edited, with Helārāja's *Prakīrṇaprakāśa* on book 3 and Puṇyarāja's *Prakāśa* on books 1 and 2, by Ramakrishna Sastri Patavardhana, Gangadhara Sastri Manavalli, Ramachandra Sastri Kotbhaskara and Gosavami Damodara Sastri. BenSS 5, 6, 11, 19, 24, 95, 102, 103, 160, 161, 162, 163, 164. Varanasi, 1884–1937.
G681 : Ermenegildo La Tersa, "Su Bhartṛhari," CIDO 12. Rome, 1899. Volume 1, *Section Inde et Iran*, pp. 201–206.
G682 : K. B. Pathak, "Bhartṛhari and Kumārila," JBBRAS 18, 1890–1894, 213–238.
G683 : Edited, with Dravyeśa Jhā Śarmā's *Pratyekārthaprakāśikā*, by Sitaramacari Sastri. Vrndavana 1926–1927.
G684 : K. G. Subrahmanyam, "A Note on the *Vākyapadīya Ṭīkā*," JOR 1, 1927, 185–187.
G685 : Charudeva Shastri, "Bhartṛhari: A Critical Study with Special Reference to the *Vākyapadīya* and Its Commentaries," PAIOC 5, 1930, 630–655.
G686 : M. Ramakrishna Kavi, "The Discovery of the Author's *Vṛtti* on the *Vākyapadīya*," JAHRS 4, 1930, 235–241.
G687 : *Brahmakāṇḍa* edited, with the *Vṛtti* and Vṛṣabhadeva's commentary thereon, by Charudeva Sastri. Lahore, 1934.
G688 : Third *kāṇḍa* edited, with Helārāja's *Prakīrṇakaprakāśa*, by K. Sambasiva Sastri and L. A. Ravi Varma. TSS 116, 148. Trivandrum, 1935, 1942.
G689 : C. Kunhan Raja, "I-tsing and Bhartṛhari's *Vākyapadīya*," SKACV 1936, 282–298.
G690 : *Brahmakāṇḍa* edited, with Narain Datta Tripathi's *Prakāśa*, by Avadh Bihari Mishra. GBS 1. Varanasi, 1937.
G691 : *Brahmakāṇḍa* edited by S. Suryanarayana with editor's commentary. KSS 124. Varanasi, 1937, 1961.
G692 : Book 2, part 2, section 1 edited, with the *Vṛtti* and Puṇyarāja's *Ṭīkā*, by Charudeva Sastri. Lahore, 1939–1940.
G693 : K. A. Subramania Iyer, "*Pratibhā* as the Meaning of a Sentence," PAIOC 10, 1941, 326–332.

G694 : N. Gopala Pillai, "The Conception of Time According to Bhartṛhari," *Sri Citra* (The Sanskrit College Magazine: Trivandrum) 2.2, 1942, 1–6.

G695 : K. Madhava Krishna Sarma, "Gleanings from the Commentaries on the *Vākyapadīya*," ABORI 23, 1942, 405–412.

G696 : K. Kunjunni Raja, "Yāska's Definition of the Verb and the Noun in the Light of Bhartṛhari's Explanations" (summary), SPAIOC 18, 1953, 97. Full article at AOR 13, 1957, 86–88.

G697 : Hajime Nakamura, "Tibetan Citations of Bhartṛhari's Verses and the Problem of His Date," SIBSY, pp. 122–136.

G698 : V. A. Ramaswami Sastri, "Bhartṛhari's Interpretation of 'grāhaṃ sammārṣṭi' and 'paśunā yājeta,'" JOR 25, 1955-1956, 74–78. Also PAIOC 18, 1958, 185–188.

G699 : Gaurinath Sastri "Absolute Consciousness as Bhartṛhari Views It," SPAIOC 19, 1955, 144–145.

G700 : C. T. Kenghe "Bhartṛhari's Commentary on the *Vākyapadīyakārikās*: Its Nature and Extent," SPAIOC 19, 1955, 47–48.

G701 : Gaurinath Sastri, "Philosophy of Bhartṛhari," JASBe 22, 1956, 71–74.

G702 : Sadhu Ram, "Authorship of Some *kārikās* and Fragments Ascribed to Bhartṛhari," JGJRI 13, 1956, 51–80.

G703 : Satya Vrat, "Conception of Space (*dik*) in the *Vākyapadīya*," JASBe 23, 1957, 21–26. Revised version in EOI pp. 205–215.

G704 : ———, "The Conception of Time According to Bhartṛhari," ABORI 39, 1958, 68–78. Revised EOI, pp. 165–190.

G705 : C. Ramachari, "Renunciation, the Final Import of the *Śatakatraya* of Bhartṛhari," JMysoreU 18, 1958–1959, 13–20.

G706 : Gaurinath Sastri, *The Philosophy of Word and Meaning*. Calcutta, 1959.

G707 : Wilhelm Rau, "Über sechs Handschriften des *Vākyapadīya*," *Oriens* 15, 1962, 374–398.

G708 : E. R. Sreekrishna Sarma, "Some Aspects of Bhartṛhari's Philosophy," SVUOJ 5, 1962, 37–42.

G709 : Book 3, part 1 edited, with Helārāja's commentary, by K. A. Subramania Iyer. DCMS 21. Poona, 1963.

G710 : *Brahmakāṇḍa* edited, with *Vṛtti* and editor's commentary, by K. A. Subramania Iyer. Varanasi, 1963.

G711 : Edited, with editor's *Ambākartrī*, by Raghunatha Sarma. 3 volumes. SBGM 91. Varanasi, 1963, 1968, 1974.

G712 : E. R. Sreekrishna Sarma, "The Philosophy of Sanskrit Gender," SPAIOC 22, 1963, 127.

G713 : Hemanta Kumar Ganguli, *Philosophy of Logical Construction*. Calcutta, 1963.

G714 : Santi Bhiksu Sastri, "Āgamasamuccaya Alias Vākyapadiya-brahmakāṇḍa of Bhartṛhari, translated and annotated," WZKM 12.1, 1963, 191–228.

G715 : K. Kunjunni Raja, "Bhartṛhari's List of Sentence-definitions," ALB 28, 1964, 206–210. Summarized in SPAIOC 21, 1959, 197–198.

G716 : Wilhelm Rau, "Handschriften des *Vākyapadīya*. Zweiter Teil," *Oriens* 17, 1964, 182–198.

G717 : Kapil Deva Shastri, "Bhartṛhari's Discussion on *sāmānādhikaraṇya*," ALB 28, 1964, 41–54.

G718 : ———, "Bhartṛhari's Discussion on the Relation Between the *upamāna* and the *upameya* in His *Vākyapadīya*." IL 25, 1964, 229–233. Also VIJ 2, 1964, 87–92.

G719 : K. A. Subramania Iyer, "Bhartṛhari on *vyākaraṇa* as a Means of Attaining mokṣa," ALB 28, 1964, 112–131. Summary in CIDO 26, summaries 1964, 129.

G720 : Madeleine Biardeau, *Théorie de la conaissance et philosophie de la parole dans le brahmanisme classique*. Paris, La Haye, 1964.

G721 : *Brahmakāṇḍa* translated, with the *Vṛtti*, by K. A. Subramania Iyer. DCBCSJS 26. Poona, 1965.

G722 : *Brahmakāṇḍa* edited and translated into French, with the *Vṛtti*, by Madeleine Biardeau. Paris, 1965.

G723 : Kapil Deva, "*Upamāna*, *upameya* and *sāmānyavacana* According to the *Vākyapadīya* of Bhartṛhari," VIJ 3, 1965, 19–28.

G724 : V. Anjaneya Sarman, "The *śabdabrahman* and the *prasthānatrayī*," SVUOJ 8, 1965, 31–36.

G725 : Edited and translated into Marathi by Vamana Balakrishna Bhagavat. GSPM. Poona, 1965.

G726 : Edited by K. V. Abhyankar and V. P. Limaye. UPSPS 2. Poona, 1965.

G727 : Edited, with *Vṛtti* and Vṛṣabhadeva's *Paddhati*, by K. A. Subramania Iyer. DCMS 32. Poona, 1966.

G728 : K. A. Subramania Iyer, "Bhartṛhari on *dhvani*," ABORI 46, 1966, 49–65.

G729 : Hemanta Kumar Ganguly, "Metaphysics of Meaning," *Anviksa* 2.1, 1967, 38–48; 2.2., 1967, 13–24; 3.1, 1968, 61–72; 3.2, 1969, 71–84.

G730 : Gaurinath Sastri, "Monism of Bhartṛhari," WZKSOA 12–13, 1968–1969, 319–323.

G731 : Ashok Aklujkar, "Two Textual Studies of Bhartṛhari," JAOS 89, 1969, 547–562.

See a487

G732 : K. A. Subramania Iyer, "Bhartṛhari on the Primary and Secondary Meanings of Words," IL 29.1, 1968, 97–112.

See a487.

G733 : Ashok Aklujkar, "Two Textual Studies of Bhartṛhari," JAOS 89, 1969, 547–562.

G734 : K. A. Subramania Iyer, *Bhartṛhari: A Study of the Vākyapadīya*. DCBCSJS 68. Poona, 1969.

G735 : Ashok Aklujkar, "The Philosophy of Bhartṛhari's Trikāṇḍī." Ph. D. diss., Harvard University, 1970.

G736 : ———, "Ancient Indian Semantics," ABORI 51, 1970, 11–29.

G737 : *Brahmakāṇḍa* edited by Satyakama Varma. New Delhi, 1970.

G738 : *Kālasamuddeśa* section of book 3, translated, with Helārāja's commentary, by Peri Sarveswara Sharma. Delhi, 1970.

G739 : Books 1 and 2 edited and translated by K. Raghavan Pillai. Delhi, 1971.

G740 : Wilhelm Rau, *Die handschriftliche Überlieferung des Vākyapadīya und seiner Kommentare*. AMGG 1971. 1. Munich, 1971.

G741 : Ashok Aklujkar, "The Number of *kārikās* in *Trikāṇḍī*, Bk. I," JAOS 9, 1971, 510–513.

G742 : Book 3, part 1 translated by K. A. Subramania Iyer. DCBCSJS 71. Poona, 1971.

G743 : Ashok Aklujkar, "The Authorship of the *Vākyapadīya-Vṛtti*," WZKSOA 16, 1972, 181–198.

G744 : M. S. Bhat, "Two Passages from the *Vākyapadīya*," JUB 42, 1973, 45–58.

G745 : Hajime Nakamura, "Buddhist Influence upon the *Vākyapadīya*," JGJRI 29, 1973, 367–388.

G746 : Mithilesh Chaturvedi, "Notes on a *kārikā* Ascribed to Bhartṛhari," JGJRI 29, 1973, 203–210.

G747 : Book 3, part 2 edited, with Helārāja's *Prakīrṇaprakāśa*, by K. A. Subramania Iyer. Poona, 1973.

See 327.

G748 : Peri Sarveswar Sharma, "What Is the *atyadbhutavṛtti* (Miraculous Course of Action) in the *Vākyapadīya*?" VIJ 12, 1974, 351–360.

G748A: Book 3, part 2 translated, with Helārāja's *Prakīrṇaprakāśa*, by K. A. Subramania Iyer. Delhi, 1974.

G749 : Albrecht Wezler, "Ein bisher missverstandener Vers in der *Vākyapadīyavṛtti*," MSS 32, 1974, 159–164.

G750 : Ashok Aklujkar, "The Authorship of the *Vākya-kāṇḍa-ṭīkā*," CDSFV 165–188.

G751 : K. A. Subramania Iyer, "Bhartṛhari on *taddhita* Formations Involving Comparison," CDSFV, 241–257.

G752 : Virendra Shastri, "Critical Study of *Sambandha Samuddeśa* of Vākyapadiya in the Light of Helārāja's Commentary." Ph. D. diss., Kurukshetra University, 1975.

G753 : Virendra Sharma, "Is the Eternal Verbum of Bhartṛhari a Dynamic Principle?" VIJ 13, 1975, 337–350.

G754 : Selections translated in HTR, pp. 224–237.

G755 : Satyakam Varma, "*Śabdapūrva yoga*," SVSI 1976, 238–247.

G756 : ———, "Linguistic Contents in *Vākyapadīya*," SVSI 1976, 224–237.

G757 : Harold G. Coward, "Language as Revelation," IndPQ 3, 1976, 447–472.

G758 : Book 2 translated by K. A. Subramania Iyer. Delhi, 1977.

G759 : Edited, with word index, by Wilhelm Rau. AKM 42.4, 1977.

G760 : Wilhelm Rau, "Zwei neue *Vākyapadīya*-Handschriften," SII 3, 1977, 114–123.

G761 : ———, "Metrical Peculiarities in Bhartṛhari's *Vākyapadīya*," ABORI 58–59, 1977–1978, 263–269.

G762 : Ashok Aklujkar, "The Concluding Verses of Bhartṛhari's *Vākya-Kāṇḍa*," ABORI 58–59, 1977–1978, 9–26.

G763 : S. D. Joshi, "Bhartṛhari's Concept of *pratibhā*: A Theory on the Nature of Language Acquisition," VGPCV 1977, 71–76.

G764 : Ashok Aklujkar, "The Number of Verses in *Trikāṇḍī*, Bk. II," ALB 42, 1978, 142–167.

G765 : ———, "Emendation of Some Verses in Bhartṛhari's *Trikāṇḍī*", WZKSOA 23, 1979, 63–74.

G766 : Mithilesh Chaturvedi, "*Upamāsamuddeśa*—a Part of *Vṛttisamuddeśa* of *Vākyapadīya*," JOI 31, 1980–1981, 195–197.

G767 : K. A. Subramania Iyer, "Bhartṛhari on Grammatical Analysis (*apoddhāra*)," VIJ 18, 1980, 69–79.

G768 : K. A. Subramania Iyer, "Bhartṛhari on the Sentence," ALB 44–45, 1980–1981, 15–49.

G769 : Ashok Aklujkar, "Interpreting *Vākyapadīya* 2.486 Historically (Part I)," ALB 44–45, 1980–1981, 581–601.

G770 : M. Srimannarayana Murty, "Bhartṛhari on *svaṃ rūpaṃ śabdasyaśabdasaṃjñā*," ALB 44–45, 1980–1981, 602–613.

G771 : P. Sriramamurti, "Grammarians and Literary Critics on *pratibhā* in Sanskrit," PAIOC 29, 1980, 301–305.

G772 : M. Srimannarayana Murti, "Time According to Bhartṛhari," VIJ 19, 1981, 140–146.

G773 : Hans G. Herzberger and Radhika Herzberger, "Bhartṛhari's Paradox," JIP 9, 1981, 1–18.

G774 : Ashok Aklujkar, "Interpreting *Vākyapadīya* 2.486 Historically (Part 2)," in *Indological and Buddhist Studies: Festschrift J. W. de Jong*. Canberra, 1982, pp. 1–10.

G775 : Alex Wayman, "The Citations of Bhartṛhari's *Vākyapadīya* in the *Tattvasaṃgraha* of Śāntarakṣita and Kamalaśīla" (summary), SWSC 5. Delhi, 1981, 185–186.

G776 : Giovanni Bandini, "Die Erörterung der Person. Bhartṛhari's *Puruṣasamuddeśa* und Helārājas *Prakāśa* zum ersten Male übersetzt mit einem Kommentar versehen" ZDMG 132, 1982, 150–173.

G777 : Harold Coward, "Time (*Kāla*) in Bhartṛhari's *Vākyapadīya*," JIP 10, 1982, 277–288.

Dīpikā on Patañjali's *Mahābhāṣya*

G778 : Mysore Hiriyanna, "The First Commentary on the *Mahābhāṣya*," IHQ 2, 1926, 415–416.

G779 : V. Swaminathan, "Bhartṛhari's Authorship of the Commentary on the *Mahābhāṣya*," ALB 27, 1963, 59–70.

G780 : *Āhnikas* 1–4 edited by V. Swaminathan. HVNRSS 11. Varanasi, 1965.

G781 : *Āhnikas* 1–7 edited by K. V. Abhyankar and V. P. Limaye. 2 volumes. Supplements to ABORI 43–47, 50. BORIS 8. Poona, 1967, 1969. Reprinted Poona, 1970.

G782 : Ashok Aklujkar, "*Mahābhāṣya-Dīpikā* or *Tripādī*," ALB 35, 1971, 159–171.

G783 : M. S. Narayanamurti, "Bhartṛhari on '*viśeṣaṇānāṃcājāteḥ*' of Pāṇini," SVUOJ 15, 1972, 49–62.

Śabdadhātusamīkṣā

G784 : K. Madhava Sarma, "*Śabdadhātusamīkṣā*: A Lost Work of Bhartṛhari," ASVOI 1.3, 1940, 65–70.

General

G785 : F. Kielhorn, "On the Grammarian Bhartṛhari," IA 12, 1884, 226ff.

G786 : K. B. Pathak, "Bhartṛhari and Kumārila," JBBRAS 18, 1890–1894, 213–238.

G787 : ———, "Was Bhartṛhari a Buddhist?" JBBRAS 18, 1890–1894, 341–349.

G788 : Ermenegildo La Terza, "Su Bhartṛhari," CIDO 12. Rome, 1899. Volume 1, Section Inde at Iran, pp. 201–206.

G789 : V. A. Ramaswami Sastri, "Bhartṛhari a Bauddha?" JAU 6, 1936–1937, 65–69. Also PAIOC 7, 1937, 254–257.

G790 : ———, "Bhartṛhari, a pre-Śaṃkara Advaitin," JAU 8, 1938, 42–53. Also PAIOC 9, 1937, 548–562.

G791 : O. P. Rangaswami, "Bhartṛhari and Bhāgavṛtti," JOR 11, 1937, 45–50.

G792 : K. Madhava Krishna Sharma, "Bhartṛhari: A Great post-Upanishadic Intuitionist," AP 11, 1940, 538–539.

G793 : ———, "Bhartṛhari Not a Buddhist: Evidence from Nearer Home," PO 5, 1940, 1–5.

G794 : Jambuvijaya Muni, "On the Date of Bhartṛhari, the Author of the *Vākyapadīya*," SPAIOC 14, 1948, 50–51.

G795 : H. R. Rangaswami Iyengar, "Bhartṛhari and Diṅnāga," JBBRAS 26, 1951, 147–149.

G796 : Sadhu Ram, "Bhartṛhari's Date," JGJRI 9, 1952, 135–152.

G797 : V. A. Ramaswami Sastri, "Bhartṛhari as a Mīmāṃsaka," BDCRI 14, 1952, 1–16.

G798 : J. M. Shukla, "The Concept of Time According to Bhartṛhari," SPAIOC 17, 1953, 379–384.

G799 : Satya Vrat Shastri, "Bhartṛhari's Conception of Time," SPAIOC 17, 1953, 244. ABORI 39, 1958, 68–78. Revised version in EOI, pp. 165–190.

G800 : Jean Filliozat, "Á Propos de la Religion der Bhartṛhari," in *Silver Jubilee Volume of the Zinbun-Kagaku-Kenkyusyo, Kyoto University*. Kyoto, 1954, pp. 116–120.

G801 : P. S. Rao, "Bhartṛhari," PB 62, 1957, 347–352.
G802 : V. Swaminathan, "Bhartṛhari and Mīmāṃsā," PAIOC 20, 1961, 309–317.
G803 : Hajime Nakamura, "Bhartṛhari the Scholar," IIJ 4, 1960, 282–305.
G804 : K. A. Subramania Iyer, "Bhartṛhari on *apabhraṃśa*," WZKM 2, 1964, 242–246.
G805 : Kapil Dev, "Bhartṛhari on *samanādhikaraṇa taddhitavṛtti*," SPAIOC 23.1, 1966, 62–65.
G806 : Ashok Aklujkar, "Nakamura on Bhartṛhari," IIJ 13, 1971, 161–175.
G807 : Hajime Nakamura, "Bhartṛhari and Buddhism," JGJRI 22, 1972, 395–406.
G808 : John Brough, "I-Ching on the Sanskrit Grammarians," BSOAS 36, 1973, 248–260.
G809 : Karunesha Shukla, "Bhartṛhari and Advaitism," SPAIOC 27, 1974, 319.
G810 : Mithilesh Chaturvedi, "Bhartṛhari on the Number of Words to be compounded Simultaneously," JDSUD 3, 1974, 31–38. Also JGJRI 35.1–2, 1979, 115–130.
G811 : ———, "*Kakaṭaliya*—a Grammatical Analysis by Bhartṛhari," SVUOJ 17, 1974, 93–100.
G812 : ———, "On Some Formations Involving *luk*-elision," VIJ 13, 1975, 42–49. Also JGJRI 33.4, 1977, 19–30.
G813 : Harold G. Coward, *Bhartṛhari*. Boston, 1976.
G814 : Mithilesh Chaturvedi, "*Yugapadadhikaraṇavacana* in *dvandva*—a Critical Appraisal," VIJ 14, 1976, 82–92.
G815 : ———, "The Negative Compound in Sanskrit—a Semantic Analysis by Bhartṛhari," ALB 40, 1976, 1–40.
G816 : Satyakam Varma, "Tradition and Bhartṛhari," SVSI 1976, 185–200.
G817 : ———, "Bhartṛhari: Works and Achievements," SVSI 1976, 201–223.
G818 : Johannes Bronkhorst, "On Some Vedic Quotations in Bhartṛhari's Works," SII 7, 1981, 173–175.
G819 : Whilhelm Rau, "Bhartṛhari und der Veda," SII 7, 1981, 167–180.

DURVINĪTA or AVINĪTA (Western Gaṅgā king of 6th century)
(NCat 1.427)
Śabdāvatāra (lost)
(cf. JRAS 1883, 298; 1911, 187; 1913, 389)

CANDRA (GOMIN) (470)
(Belvalkar, pp. 29, 48; G1624, p. 165; NCat 6.349)
Candravyākaraṇa or *Candrasūtrāṇi* and *Vṛtti* (incl. *Uṇādi* and *Liṅgānuśāsana*)
G820 : *Sūtras* edited, with Kāśyapa's *Bālāvabodhana*, by William Goonetilleke, *The Orientalist* 1 (1884) 2 (1885). Incomplete.
G821 : F. Kielhorn, "The *Chandra-vyākaraṇa* and the *Kāśikā-vṛtti*," IA 15, 1886, 183–185. Reprinted in Rau, pp. 244–246.
G822 : Bruno Liebich, *Das Candravyākaraṇa*. Gottingen, 1895.
G823 : ———, "The *Chandra-Vyākaraṇa*," IA 25, 1896, 103ff.
G824 : ———, "Das Datum des Candragomin," WZKM 13, 1899, 308–315.
G825 : Edited by Bruno Liebich. AKM 11.4. Leipzig, 1902.
G826 : Sylvain Lévi, "Notes chinoises sur l'Inde: III. La Date de Candragomin," BEFEO 3, 1903, 38–53.
G827 : Edited with *Vṛtti* by Bruno Liebich. AKM 14. Leipzig, 1918.
G828 : Bruno Liebich, *Zur Einführung in die indische einheimische Sprachwissenschaft*, volume 4. *Analyse der Candra-Vṛtti*. SHAW 13. Heidelberg, 1920.
See b67.
G829 : S. K. De, "Candragomin," IHQ 14, 1938, 256–260.
G830 : Edited by K. C. Chatterji. 2 volumes. SISL 13. Poona, 1953–1961.

G831 : Louis Renou, "Remarkable Words in the Candra-*Vyākaraṇa*," *Vāk* 3, 1953, 84–101.
G832 : Edited by Bechardas Joshi. RPG 39. Jodhpur, 1967.
G833 : Robert Birwe, "Ist Candragomin der Verfasser der Candra-Vṛtti?" PICI 28, 1968, 127–142.
G834 : M. Hahn, "Der Autor Candragomin und sein Werk," ZDMG Supplement 2, 1974, 331–355.
G835 : ———, "Strophen des Candragomin in der indischen Sprachliteratur," IIJ 19, 1977, 21–30.
G836 : Madhav Deshpande, "Candragomin's Syntactic Rules," IL 40, 1979, 133–145.
G837 : Anna Radicchi, "On Candravyākaraṇa" (summary). SWSC 5. Delhi, 1981, pp. 72–73.
G838 : Prafulla Chandra Dash, "Chandra and the '*asaṃjñakaṃ vyākaraṇa*,'" DNSFV, Ghaziabad 1982, pp. 43–52.

BHĪMASENA (550)

G839 : P. K. Gode, "Date of the Grammarian Bhīmasena—Before A. D. 600" NIA 2, 1939, 108–110.

DHARMAPĀLA (625)

Vṛtti on book 3 of Bhartṛhari's *Vākyapadīya* (lost)

HARṢAVARDHANA (630?)

(Belvalkar, pp. 44; YM 2.263)

Commentary on Pāṇini's (?) *Liṅgānuśāsana*

G840 : Edited, with Śabarasvāmin's commentary and the *Liṅgānuśāsanas* of Śākaṭāyana and Vararuci and Yakṣavarman's commentary on Śākaṭāyana, by R. Otto Franke. Kiel, 1890.
G841 : Edited, with Pṛthiviśvara's *Sarvalakṣaṇa*, by V. Venkatarama Sharma Vidyabhusana. MUSS 4. Madras, 1931.

VIMALAMATI (648)

(Cardona, p. 284)

Bhāgavṛtti on Patañjali's *Mahābhāṣya* (lost)

G842 : Kshitish Chandra Chatterji, "The Bhāgavṛtti," IHQ 7, 1931, 413–418.
See a791.
G843 : S. P. Bhattacharya, "The Bhāgavṛtti and Its Author," PAIOC 12, 1947, 273–287.
G844 : Citations collected by Yudhisthira Mimamsaka. 3 parts. The first appeared in the *Panjab University Oriental Magazine*. Part 2, in SS 8.1, 1953–1954, 1–16; 8.2, 1953–1954, 83–106. Part 3, in Ajmer, 1964–1965.

(HARI) VṚṢABHADEVA (650)

Paddhati on Bhartṛhari's *Vākyapadīya*

See e683; e727.

KṢAPAṆAKA of Kashmir (7th century?)

(NCat 5.146)

Commentary on *Uṇādisūtras* (lost?)

(NCat 2.295)

JAYĀDITYA and VĀMANA (ĀCĀRYA) (650?)

(NCat 4.116; Cardona, p. 278; G1624, p. 172; Belvalkar, p. 29; YM 1.423, 462)

Kāsikā (*vṛtti*) on Pāṇini's *Aṣṭādhyāyī*

See e31.
G845 : F. Max Müller, "The *Kāśikā*," IA 9, 1880, 305–308.
See a542; a821; e40; et41.
G846 : Edited, with editor's *Ṭippaṇī*, by Bhagavatprasada Sarman. Varanasi, 1890.

G847 : 2.1–2 translated into German by Bruno Liebich. Breslau, 1892.

G848 : F. Kielhorn, "*Pausha Saṁvatsara* in the *Kāśikā Vṛtti* on P. 4.2.21," IA 22, 1893, 83ff.

G849 : Edited, with Haradatta's *Padamañjarī*, by Bharadvaja Damodara Sastri. Varanasi, 1895.

See e49; t50A.

G850 : Surendra Nath Mazumdar, "A Note on *Kāśikā*," JASBe 8, 1912, 57.

G851 : Edited, with Jinendrabuddhi's *Nyāsa*, by S. C. Chakravarti in *Gauḍagranthamālā*. 3 volumes. Rajshahi, 1913, 1919–1924, 1925.

G852 : Malati Sen, "The *Kāśikā* and the *Kāvyālaṇkārasūtravṛtti*," COJ 1, 1934, 229–240.

See a586.

G853 : Edited by Sobhita Misra. 2 parts. KSS 37. Varanasi, 1952.

See a596.

G854 : 1.1 translated into French by Y. Ojihara and L. Renou. 3 volumes. PEFO 48. Paris, 1960–1967.

G855 : Yutaka Ojihara, "Causerie vyākaraṇique (III): Incoherence interne chez la *Kāśikā*," JIBSt 9, 1961, 749–753; 10, 1962, 766–776; 12, 1964, 847–855.

G856 : Vinayak Wasudeo Paranjpe, "A discrepancy in *Kāśikā*," SPAIOC 22, 1963, 55.

G857 : Edited, with Jinendrabuddhi's *Nyāsa* and Haradatta's *Padamañjarī*, by Dwarikadas Shastri and Kalika Prasad Shukla. 4 volumes. Prachya Bharati Series 2. Varanasi, 1965.

G858 : K. V. Abhyankar, "A Dissertation on a Doubtful Passage in the *Kāśikāvṛtti* on P.1.1.4 and Two Passages in the *Taittirīya Āraṇyaka prapāṭhaka* 4," ABORI 47, 1967, 101–103.

G859 : Y. Ojihara, "Read '*parṇam na veḥ*' : *Kāśikā* ad. P. 1.1.4: A Notice," ABORI 48–49, 1968, 403–409.

G860 : Ram Gopal, "Vedic Quotations in the *Kāśikā* and *Siddhāntakaumudī*," ABORI 48–49, 1968, 227–230.

G861 : Edited by Aryendra Sharma, Handerao Deshpande, and D. G. Padhye. 2 volumes. SAS 17, 20. Hyderabad, 1969–1970.

G862 : Edited with editor's Hindi commentary by Narayana Misra. 2 volumes. KSS 37. Varanasi, 1969–1972.

G863 : M. D. Sharma, "The *Kāśikāvṛtti* and *Vaiyākaraṇa Siddhāntakaumudī*: A Comparative Study." Ph.D. diss., University of Poona. 1971.

G864 : Mahesadatta Sharma, *A Comparative Study of Kāśikā Vṛtti and Siddhāntakaumudī*. Poona, 1974.

G865 : Krishna Deo Jha, "A Critical Analysis of the Examples Used in the *Kāśikā*." Ph.D. diss., University of Bihar, 1976.

G866 : Govinda Jha, "A Comparative Study of the *Kāśikā* and *Siddhānta Kaumudī*." Ph.D. diss., University of Bihar, 1976.

G867 : P. Visalakshy, "The Influence of Candra and Kātantra Grammars on *Kāśikāvṛtti*," VIJ 19, 1981, 45–49.

?*Liṅgānuśāsana* and commentary thereon (attributed to VĀMANA)

G868 : Edited by Chimanlal D. Dalal. GOS 6. Baroda, 1918.

G869 : Edited by Vyakaranopadhyaya Vedavati. Ajmer, 1964–1965.

MAṆḌANA MIŚRA (690)

Sphoṭasiddhi

G870 : Edited, with Ṛṣiputra Parameśvara's *Gopālikā*, by S. K. Ramanatha Sastri. MUSS 6. Madras, 1931.

G871 : Edited and translated into French by Madeleine Biardeau. PIFI 13. Pondicherry, 1958.

G872 : Edited and translated by K. A. Subramania Iyer. DCBS 25. Poona, 1966.

JINENDRABUDDHI (725?)

(Cardona, p. 281; G1624, p. 181; Belvalkar, p. 32)

Nyāsa or *Pañjikā* or *Vṛtti* on Jayāditya and Vāmana's *Kāśikā*

(NCat 4.118)

G873 : Pandurang Vaman Kane, "Bhāmaha, the Nyāsa and Māgha," JBBRAS 23, 1909–1914, 91–95.

G874 : K. B. Pathak, "Bhāmaha's Attack on the Buddhist Grammarian Jinendrabuddhi," JBBRAS 23, 1909–1914, 18–31.

G875 : ———, "Daṇḍin, Nyāsakāra and Bhāmaha," IA 41, 1912, 232–236.

See e851.

G876 : K. B. Pathak, "The Nyāsakāra and the Jaina Śākaṭāyana," IA 43, 1914, 205; 15, 1915, 275–279.

G877 : ———, "Jinendrabuddhi, Kaiyaṭa and Haradatta," ABORI 12, 1931, 246–251.

See e831.

G878 : Bhim Sen Shastri, *A Study of Nyāsa*. Delhi, 1979.

ABHAYANANDIN (750?)

(Belvalkar, p. 55; NCat 1.278)

Mahāvṛtti on Pūjyapāda's *Jainendravyākaraṇa*

(NCat 7.307)

See e673; e676.

(ABHINAVA) ŚĀKAṬĀYANA (850?)

(Cardona, p. 149; Belvalkar, p. 57; NCat 1.307)

Śabdānuśāsana and *Amoghavṛtti* thereon

G879 : Georg Bühler, "Notiz über die Grammatik des Śākaṭāyana," OU 2, 1864, 691–706.

G880 : F. Kielhorn, "On the Grammar of Śākaṭāyana," IA 16, 1887, 24–28. Reprinted in Rau, pp. 246–250.

See e840.

G881 : Edited, with Abhayacandra Sūri's *Prakrīyāsaṃgraha*, by Gustav Oppert. Madras, 1893.

G882 : F. Kielhorn, "Die Śākaṭāyana-Grammatik," NGGW 1894, 1–14.

See a876.

G883 : K. B. Pathak, "Jain Śākaṭāyana Contemporary with Amoghavarsha I," IA 43, 1914, 205ff.

G884 : ———, "Śākaṭāyana and the Authorship of the Amoghavṛtti," ABORI 1, 1918–1919, 7–12.

G885 : Edited, with Yakṣavarman's commentary, by Ramasakala Mishra. *Pan* 34, 1912–1942, 1920.

G886 : Edited, with Yakṣavarman's *Cintāmaṇi*, and translated by Vishnu S. Sukhthankar. Leipzig, 1921.

See e882.

G887 : K. B. Pathak, "On the Date of Śākaṭāyana Cintāmaṇi," JBBRAS n.s. 6, 1930, 239–240.

G888 : ———, "On the Unādi Sutras of Jain Śākaṭāyana," ABORI 13, 1931–1932, 154–156.

G889 : Sailendranath Sengupta, "Uṇādi Suffixes and Words Derived with Such Suffixes (a Concordance Based on the Works of Śākaṭāyana, Bhoja and Hemacandra)," JASP 6, 1964, 123–206.

G890 : Edited with *Amoghavṛtti* by Shambhu Nath Tripathi. JPMJG 39. Delhi, 1971.

G891 : J. M. Shukla, "Grammatical *paribhāṣā* of the Jaina Grammarians," JOI 24, 1974–1975, 128–138.

JAYANTA BHAṬṬA (870?)

Vṛtti on Pāṇini's *Aṣṭādhyāyī* (lost)

(NCat 7.180)

GUṆANANDIN (890)

(YM 1.588)

Commentary on Pūjyapāda's *Jainendravyākaraṇa*

(NCat 7.307)

See e650, e674.

PŪRṆACANDRA (950)

(NCat 9.290)

Pañjikā on Candragomin's *Candravyākaraṇa*

(cf. JBRS 22.1, 1936, 43)

RABHASANANDIN or VALLABHĀCĀRYA (950?)

(*Ṣaṭ*) *Kāraka* (*vāda*) or *Kārakasambandhoddyota*

(NCat 3.377)

G892 : Edited by H. P. Shastri. RPG 6. Jodhpur.

DURGĀ (SIṂHA) or DURGĀDĀSA (950?)

(Belvalkar, p. 73)

Vṛtti on (Śarvavarman's?) Kātantra

(NCat 2.295; 3.224, 309; 9.76)

See e641; e642; e645.

G893 : *Uṇādipāṭha* edited Dacca, 1886.

See e653; e656; e657; e658.

G894 : *Uṇādipāṭha* edited MUSS 7.6, 2. Madras, 1934.

G895 : *Liṅgānuśāsana* edited by D. G. Koparkar. SIAL 10. Poona, 1952.

G896 : *Paribhāṣā* section edited in *Paribhāṣāsaṃgraha*, pp. 49–66.

HELĀRĀJA (980?)

Prakīrṇaprakāśa on book 3 of Bhartṛhari's *Vākyapadīya*

See e679; e688; e709; t738; e747; t748A; d752.

Śabdaprabhā on book 1 of Bhartṛhari's *Vākyapadīya* (lost)

(Adyar D, vol. 6, p. 208)

See a670.

Vārttikonmeṣa on Kātyāyana's *Aṣṭādhyāyī-Vārttikas* (lost)

(YM 1.328)

See a670.

Advayasiddhi (lost)

See a670.

Kriyāviveka (lost)

See a670.

General

G897 : K. Madhava Krishna Sarma, "Helārāja, Not a Disciple of Bhartṛhari," IHQ 19, 1943, 79–82.

G898 : V. Swaminathan, "On the Date of Helārāja," SVUOJ 10, 1967, 23–36.

G899 : V. Raghavan, "The Dates of Helārāja and Kaiyaṭa," *Ṛtam* 2–6, 1970–1975, 105–110.

AUTHOR UNKNOWN (1000?)

Prameyasaṃgraha on book 2 of Bhartṛhari's *Vākyapadīya*

G900 : Edited by Wilhelm Rau. Munich, 1981.

TRILOCANADĀSA (1000?)

Pañjikā on Durgā's *Kātantravṛtti*

See e643; e653; e656; e657; e658.

UGRABHŪTI (1000)

(NCat 3.317)

Śiṣyahitanyāsa in five hundred verses in Āryā metre; known in Tibet

PUṆYARĀJA (1000?)

Ṭīkā on book 2 of Bhartṛhari's *Vākyapadīya*

See e679; e692; a750.

DHARMAKĪRTI (1000?)

(Cardona, p. 285; G1624, pp. 186, 262; NCat 9.241)

Rūpāvatāra on Pāṇini's *Aṣṭādhyāyī*

(NCat 3.374)

G901 : Edited by M. Rangacharya and M. B. Varadarajiengar. 2 volumes. Bangalore, 1916–1917, 1927.

G902 : K. A. Nilakantha Sastri, "A Note on the *Rūpāvatāra*," JOR 8, 1934, 277–280.

Commentary on Vararuci's *Kārakacakra* or *Prayogamukha*

G903 : Edited by M. Rangacarya. Madras, 1927.

ABHINAVAGUPTA (1014)

Prakīrṇakavivaraṇa on Bhartṛhari's *Vākyapadīya* (lost)

BUDDHISĀGARA SŪRI (1024)

Pañcagranthī or *Śabdalakṣaṇa*

(NCat 11.12)

G904 : N. M. Kansara, "The Lingānuśāsana of Buddhisāgarasūri," JGJRI 35. 1-2, 1979, 97–100.

DAYAPĀLA (MUNI) (1025)

Rūpasiddhi (an abridgment of Śākaṭāyana's *Śabdānuśāsana*)

(Belvalkar, p. 60; GOS 134, 1961, 196; YM 1.603)

KAIYAṬA (1030)

(Belvalkar, p. 34; G1624, p. 181)

Pradīpa on Patañjali's *Mahābhāṣya*

See e521; e522; e529; e530; e544; e547; e550; et551; e552; a877; e575; e582; e587.

G905 : V. Raghavan, "Chronological Notes: Kaiyaṭa and Dhanañjaya," JOR 19, 1949, 223–224.

See e590; e598; e611; e622.

G906 : Edited by M. P. Misra. Varanasi, 1967.

See a899; e632.

G907 : Peri Sarveswara Sharma, "Kaiyaṭa and His Works," BhV 39, 1979, 5–13.

PRABHĀCANDRA (ĀCĀRYA) (1040)

(Belvalkar, p. 60; GOS 134, 1961, 269)

Nyāsa on Śākaṭāyana's *Amoghavṛtti*

YAKṢAVARMAN (1050?)

(Belvalkar, p. 60; YM 1.603)

Cintāmaṇi on Śakaṭāyana's *Śabdānuśāsana*

See e840; e885; e886; e887.

KṢĪRASVĀMIN (1050?)

(Belvalkar, p. 43; Cardona, p. 288; NCat 5.152)

Kṣīrataraṅgiṇī on Pāṇini's *Aṣṭādhyāyī-Dhātupāṭha*

G908 : Edited, with Śarvavarman's and Śākaṭāyana's *Dhātupāṭhas*, by Bruno Liebich. IndF 8/9. Breslau, 1930.

G909 : Edited by Yudhisthira Mimamsaka. BLKTS 25. Amritsar, 1957–1958.

(*Karmayoga*) *Amṛtataraṅgiṇī* (lost)

(NCat 1.347; 3.205)

Nipātāvyayopasargavṛtti
G910 : Edited svos 28. Tirupati, 1951.
DURGĀSIṂHA (1050?)
(Belvalkar, p. 75; YM 1.564)
Ṭīkā on Durgā's *Kātantravṛtti*
(NCat 3.310)
G911 : Edited Bhowanipore, 1881.
KRAMADĪŚVARA (1050?)
Saṃkṣiptasāra (revised by Jumaranandin)
G912 : Edited with *Rasavatī* and Goyicandra's and Jumaranandin's commentary. Calcutta, 1886, 1888, 1901, 1904, 1911.
G913 : Edited with Nyāyapañcānana's *Dīpikā*. Calcutta, 1920.
G914 : *Prākṛta* chapter edited by Satya Ranjan Benaraji. Ahmedabad, 1980.
Uṇādipariśiṣṭa
(NCat 2.296)
BHOJA (DEVA) or BHOJARĀJA (1055)
(G1624, p. 187)
Sarasvatīkaṇṭhābharaṇa
G915 : Edited by Anandaram Barua. Calcutta, London, 1883, 1884; Gauhati, 1969.
G916 : Partly edited, Varanasi, 1888.
G917 : Edited, with Ratneśvara's commentary and editor's commentary, by Jivananda Vidyasagara. Calcutta, 1894.
G918 : Edited, with Rāmasiṃha's commentary on chapters 1–3, Jagaddhāra's commentary on chapter 4, and Ratneśvara's commentary on chapter 5, by Kedarnath Durgaprasad and V. L. S. Pansikar. in Kavyamala 94. Bombay, 1925.
G919 : *Uṇādisūtras* edited MUSS 7.6, 1. Madras, 1934.
See a889.
G920 : *Paribhāṣās* edited in *Paribhāṣāsaṃgraha*, pp. 105–107.
G921 : Edited, with Jagaddhara's *Ṭīkā*, by Visvanatha Bhattacarya. Kasi, 1979.
HARADATTA (1059)
(Belvalkar, p. 32; Cardona, p. 281; G1624, p. 196; NCat 4.119)
Padamañjarī on Jayāditya/Vāmana's *Kāśikā*
G922 : Edited by Damodara Sastri in *Pan* 10 (1888)–21 (1899).
G923 : Book 2, chapters 1–2 translated into German by Bruno Liebich. Breslau, 1892.
See e849.
G924 : S. S. Suryanarayana Sastri, "Haradatta Miśra and Haradatta Śivācārya," PAIOC 6, 1930, 607–612.
See a877; e857.
G925 : D. K. Kharwandikar, "Haradatta: A Critical Study." Ph.D. diss., University of Poona, 1973.
G926 : ———, "Mnemonic Verses in the Padamañjarī of Haradattamiśra," JGJRI 29, 1973, 285–294.
G927 : ———, "Date of Haradatta: the Author of the Padamañjarī," SPAIOC 27, 1974, 234–235.
JYEṢṬHAKALĀŚA (1060?)
(YM 1.367)
Ṭīkā on Patañjali's *Mahābhāṣya* (lost)
INDU (MITRA) (1070?)
(YM 1.479; NCat 1.203, 2.248)

Anunyāsa on Jinendrabuddhi's *Pañjikā*
G928 : Kshitish Chandra Chatterji, "The Authorship of the *Anunyāsa*," IHQ 7, 1931, 418–419.
G929 : K. Madhava Krishna Sarma, "Author of the *Anunyāsa*," JOR 15, 1941, 25–27.
G930 : V. Raghavan, "Indu, the author of the *Anunyāsa*," JOR 15, 1941, 78.

VARDHAMĀNA (1088)
(Belvalkar, p. 74)
Kātantravistara
(NCat 3.313)

GOVARDHANA (1100?)
(YM 2.204)
Commentary on Pāṇini's *Aṣṭādhyāyī*
(NCat 6.182)

DHANAPĀLA (1100?)
G931 : Neelanjana S. Shah, "About a Forgotten Grammarian Dhanapāla," *Sambodhi* 4.3–4, 1975–1976, 63–78.

NĀRĀYAṆA DANDANĀTHA (1100)
Hṛdayahariṇī on Bhoja's *Sarasvatīkaṇṭhābharaṇa*
G932 : Robert Birwe, "Nārāyaṇa Dandanātha's Commentary on Rules III.2. 106–121 of Bhoja's Sarasvatīkaṇṭhābharaṇa," JAOS 84, 1964, 150–162.

MAITREYA RAKṢITA (1109)
(G1624, pp. 206, 221; YM 1.398)
Ṭīkā on Patañjali's *Mahābhāṣya* (lost)
Tantrapradīpa on Jinendrabuddhi's *Nyāsa*
(NCat 9.291)
Dhātupradīpa
G933 : Edited by Madhavacandra Tarkacudamani. Dacca, 1886.
G934 : Edited by Srish Chandra Chakravarti. SSGM 2. Rajshahi, 1919.
Durghatavṛtti
General
G935 : Kali Charan Shastri, "Maitreya-rakṣita (a Bengali Grammarian of the Pāṇinian System)", BharKau 1947, 887–903.
G936 : ———, "Maitreyarakṣita," OH 4, 1956, 89–98.

TRIVIKRAMA (1118)
Uddyota on Trilocanadāsa's *Kātantravṛttipañjikā*
(NCat 3.311)

VIJAYĀNANDA or VIDYĀNANDA (1140)
Kātantrottara (*siddhānanda*)
(NCat 3.313, 5.130)
G937 : Edited in Rupamala 3. Bombay, 1871.

VARDHAMĀNA (1140)
(Cardona, p. 361; G1624, pp. 80, 191)
Gaṇaratnamahodadhi and *Vṛtti* thereon
(NCat 5.257)
G938 : Edited by Julius Eggeling. London, 1879–1881. Reprinted Delhi, 1963.
G939 : Edited Allahabad, 1894.

HARIYOGIN ŚAILĀVĀCĀRYA, alias PROLANĀCĀRYA (1150?)
(YM 2.98; NCat 9.291)
Śābdikābharaṇa or *Dhātupratyayapañjikā* on Pāṇini's *Aṣṭādhyāyī-Dhātupāṭha*
(NCat 9.291)

HEMACANDRA (1150)
(Belvalkar, p. 60)
Śabdānuśāsana and *Bṛhadvṛtti* thereon, with (abridgment) *Laghuvṛtti*
(NCat 9.289)
G940 : *Liṅgānuśāsana* and *Vṛtti* edited and translated by R. Otto Franke. Göttingen, 1886.
See e37.
G941 : F. Kielhorn, "A Brief Account of Hemachandra's Sanskrit Grammar," WZKM 2, 1888, 18–24.
G942 : *Uṇādisūtras* and *Vṛtti* edited in J. Kirste, *Sources of Sanskrit Lexicography*. Vienna, Bombay, 1895, volume 2.
G943 : *Liṅgānuśāsana* edited by Sivadatta and K. P. Parab. Bombay, 1896.
G944 : *Dhātupāṭha* and *Vṛtti* edited by J. Kirste, *Sources of Sanskrit Lexicography*. Vienna, Bombay, 1901, volume 4.
G945 : *Liṅgānuśāsana* edited YJG 2. Varanasi, 1905.
G946 : Edited, with *Laghuvṛtti* YJG 3. Varanasi, 1905.
G947 : *Sūtras* only edited YJG 6. Varanasi, 1906.
G948 : *Sūtras* only edited in alphabetical order. YJG 11. Varanasi, 1909.
G949 : Edited Varanasi, 1910. Index Varanasi, 1909.
G950 : Vinaya Vijaya Gani, *Haimalaghuprakrīya*. Bombay, 1918, 1949.
G951 : Edited with *Bṛhadvṛtti*. First *pāda* only. Ahmedabad, 1921.
G952 : Edited with Meghavijaya Gani's *Candraprabhā*. Bombay, 1928.
G953 : Edited by Chandra Sagara Suri. Ujjain, 1950.
G954 : *Kṛtpratyaya* section edited by Vijayalvanyasuri. Botad, Saurashtra, 1963.
G955 : Edited by Ratnalal Sanghvi. 2 volumes. Vyavar, Rajasthan, 1963.
G956 : *Paribhāṣās* edited in *Paribhāṣāsaṃgraha* pp. 108–111.
G957 : *Uṇādi* and *Gaṇa sūtras* edited by Manohara Vijaya. Botad, Saurashtra, 1967.
G958 : S. Sengupta, "Hemacandra and Siddha Hema-Śabdānuśāsana," JainJ 2, 1968, 200–206.
G959 : *Dhātuparāyaṇa* edited by Muni Yasovijaya and Municandravijaya. Ahmedabad, 1973.
G960 : J. M. Shukla, "*Dhātupārāyaṇam*—a Review Note," *Sambodhi* 4.3–4, 1975–1976, 40–43.
General
G961 : Hermann Jacobi, "Hemachandra," ERE 6.684–686.
G962 : G. Bühler, "Über das Leben des Jaina Mönches Hemachandra, as Schülers des Devachandra aus der Vajraśākhā," *Denkschriften der phil.-hist. Klasse der Kaiserliche Akademie der Wissenschaften, Vienna* 37, 1889, 171-258. Translated into English by Manilal Patel as *The Life of Hemachandra*. SJS 11. Bombay, 1936.
G963 : Jagdish P. Sharma, "Hemacandra: The Life and Scholarship of a Jaina Monk," AsP 3, 1975, 195–216.
G964 : C. N. Basavaraju, "Hemcandra," MO 11, 1978, 60–64.
SĀRIPUTTA or SĀGARAMATI of Polonnaruva (12th century)
Commentary on Ratnamati's *Ṭīkā* on Candragomin's *Sūtras*
(NCat 7.19)
UTPĀLA (1170?)
(Belvalkar, p. 64; GOS 134, 1961, 80; NCat 2.316)
?*Liṅgānuśāsanavṛttī*
(NCat 2.316)
(MUNI) PRADYUMNA SŪRI (1170?)

Daurgāsiṃhakātantravṛttiṭīkā
(NCat 9.76)
ŚARAṆADEVA (1172)
(Cardona, p. 282; G1624, p. 209)
Durghaṭavṛtti on Pāṇini's *Aṣṭādhyāyī* (revised by Sarvarakṣita)
G965 : Edited by T. Ganapati Sastri. TSS 6. Trivandrum, 1909.
G966 : Edited and translated into French by Louis Renou. 3 volumes. Paris, 1940, 1941, 1956.
G967 : Louis Renou, "Index of Remarkable Words and Forms in the *Durghaṭavṛtti* of Śaraṇadeva," *Vāk* 1, 1951, 19–37.
PURUṢOTTAMADEVA (1175)
(Cardona, p. 282; G1624, p. 209)
Prāṇāpana or *Laghuvṛtti* on Patañjali's *Mahābhāṣya*
G968 : Dinesh Chandra Bhattacharya, "Puruṣottamadeva's Commentary on the *Mahābhāṣya*," IHQ 19, 1943, 201–213.
Bhāṣāvṛtti on Pāṇini's *Aṣṭādhyāyī*
G969 : Edited, with Sṛṣṭidharācārya's Commentary, by Girisacandra Vedantatirtha. BI 209. Calcutta, 1912.
G970 : Edited by Srish Chandra Chakravarti. SSGM 1. Rajshahi, 1918.
G971 : *Paribhāṣā* section edited by D. C. Bhattacharya. Rajshahi, 1946.
G972 : Louis Renou, "List of Remarkable Words (or Meanings) from Paribhāṣenduśekhara, Paribhāśāvṛtti of Puruṣottamadeva, and Paribhāṣāvṛtti of Siradeva," *Vāk* 2, 1952, 117–129.
G973 : ———, "Words from the *Bhāṣāvṛtti* of Puruṣottamadeva," *Vāk* 3, 1953, 1–36.
G974 : *Paribhāṣā* section edited in *Paribhāṣāsaṃgraha*, pp. 112–160. See e269.
G975 : V. S. Joshi, "Some Words from the *Bhāṣāvṛtti* of Puruṣottama Deva translated by Prof. L. Renou," VJSPG 1980, 91–94.
Jñāpakasamuccayabhāṣya
(NCat 7.350)
UDAYACANDRA (1180)
(Belvalkar, p. 66)
Nyāsa on Hemacandra's *Bṛhadvṛtti*
(NCat 2.326)
KUŚALA (1200?)
(Belvalkar, p. 74)
Pradīpa on Trilocanadāsa's *Pañjikā*
(NCat 3.311, 4.256)
KĀŚYAPA (1200)
(a Cāndra writer)
Bālāvabodha
DEVA (1200?)
(NCat 9.100, 169)
Daiva (on Sanskrit roots)
G976 : Edited with Kṛṣṇalīlāśukamuni's *Puruṣakāra*, by T. Ganapati Sastri. TSS 1. Trivandrum, 1905.
G977 : Edited, with Kṛṣṇalīlāśukā's *Puruṣakāra*, by Yudhisthira Mimaṃsaka. Ajmer, 1962–1963.
G978 : Satya Pal Narang, "A Critique of the Grammatical Work *Daiva* by Deva," SPAIOC 27, 1974, 228–229.

DEVENDRASŪRI (1210)
(Belvalkar, p. 66)
Laghunyāsa on Hemacandra's *Śabdānuśāsana*
(NCat 9.160)
GUṆACANDRA (1210)
(NCat 3.318)
Tattvaprakāśikā on the *Kātantravibhrama* (*sūtras*)
G979 : Edited by Shravak Pandit Hargovinddas and Shravak Pandit Bechardas. YJG 34. Varanasi, 1913.
KAṆAKAPRABHĀ (1240)
Nyāsasāra on Hemacandra's *Śabdānuśāsana*
(NCat 3.142)
AMARACANDRA (1250)
(Belvalkar, p. 67)
Syādisamuccaya
G980 : Edited, Varanasi, 1915.
?*Ṣaṭkārakalakṣaṇa* or *Kārakanirūpaṇa*
(NCat 1.332, 3.375)
BHAVASENA TRAIVIDYEŚA (1250)
Kātantrarūpamālā
See e650.
Laghuvṛtti on *Kātantrasūtras*
(NCat 3.313–314)
DHANEŚVARA (1250)
Cintāmaṇi on Patañjali's *Mahābhāṣya*
Prakriyāratnamaṇi
(MS at Adyar)
SĪRADEVA (1250)
(G1624, p. 226; NCat 11.223)
Paribhāṣāvṛtti
G981 : Edited by Harinatha Dube. BenSS 8. Varanasi, 1885–1887.
See a972.
G982 : Louis Renou, "Études paninéennes: La Liste des *paribhāṣā* chez Sīradeva," PICI 2, 1956, 132–136.
G983 : Kali Charan Shastri, "Sīradeva," OH 5, 1957, 103–117.
G984 : Edited in *Paribhāṣāsaṃgraha*, pp. 161–272.
SOMADEVA (1250)
(Belvalkar, p. 55; NCat 8.307)
Śabdārṇavacandrikā on Pūjyapāda's *Jainendravyākaraṇa*
G985 : Edited *Pan* n.s. 31–34, 1908–1911.
VAṆGASENA (1250)
(NCat 2.10)
Ākhyātavyākaraṇa or *Dhāturūpa*
ANUBHŪTI SVARŪPĀCĀRYA (1270)
(Belvalkar, p. 80; NCat 1.208)
Sārasvataprakriyā
G986 : Edited Varanasi, 1852.
G987 : Edited in MS form by Bapu Hara Set Devalekara. Bombay, 1861.
G988 : Edited, with Rāmacandrāśrama's *Siddhāntacandrikā* and Sadānanda's *Subodhinī*. Varanasi, 1864, 1885; Lahore, 1869; Bombay, 1881, 1885, 1888.
G989 : Edited, with Vāsudeva Bhaṭṭa's *Sārasvataprasāda*. Meerut, 1867, 1874, 1876; Calcutta, 1882.

G990 : Edited Amritsar, 1867.
G991 : Edited with Vāsudeva Bhaṭṭa's *Sārasvataprasāda* by Jivananda Vidyasagara. Calcutta, 1874.
G992 : Edited with Rāmacandrāśrama's *Siddhāntacandrikā*. Lucknow, 1875; Bombay, 1884, 1888, 1914.
G993 : Edited Calcutta, 1882.
G994 : Edited Patna, 1882.
G995 : Edited Bombay, 1883, 1885, 1886, 1887, 1888, 1889, 1890, 1891, 1898.
G996 : Edited with Mādhava Bhaṭṭa's *Siddhāntaratnāvalī* and editor's *Mādhavī*, by Madhava. Varanasi, 1887, 1911.
G997 : Edited with editor's *Ṭippaṇī* by Govinda Parasurama Bhatta. Bombay, 1888.
G998 : Edited with Lokeśvara Śarman Śukla's *Siddhāntaratnāvalī*. Lucknow, 1890, 1894.
G999 : Edited with Candrakīrti's *Subodhikā*. Bombay, 1890.
G1000 : Edited by Sagaracandra Kaviratna. Calcutta, 1905–1915.
G1001 : Edited, with Candrakīrti's *Subodhikā*, by Vasudev Laxman Shastri Pansikar. Bombay, 1907.
G1002 : Partly edited, with editor's *Ṭippaṇī*, by Visnuprasada Sarman. Varanasi, 1910, 1920.
G1003 : Edited by Sulavatanka Kalyana Sunvambasamkara Sastri. Bombay, 1914.
G1004 : Edited, with Rāmanārāyaṇa Śarman's *Bhāṣya*, by Vipinacandra Vidyanidhi. Calcutta, 1915.
G1005 : Edited Varanasi, 1925, 1928.
G1006 : Edited by Narahari Shastri Pendse. HSS 4. Varanasi, 1927.
G1007 : R. O. Meisezahl, "Über *jñim* in der Tibetischen Version der Regel *ṃ chandasi* der Śārasvata- Grammatik," IIJ 9, 1965, 139–146.

MAHĀDEVA (1270)
(Belvalkar, p. 74) (a Kātantra author)
Śabdasiddhi
(NCat 3.312)

VOPADEVA GOSVĀMIN (1275)
(Belvalkar, p. 87)
Mugdhabodha (of which the *Dhātupāṭha* is called *Kavikalpadruma*)
G1008 : Edited Shrirampore, 1807.
G1009 : Edited Calcutta, 1826, 1845, 1866, 1868, 1876, 1884.
G1010 : *Kavikalpadruma* edited in Bengali characters, with Durgādāsa's *Dhātudīpikā*. Calcutta, 1831, 1904.
G1011 : Edited Kashipur, 1841, 1853.
G1012 : Edited with Nandakiśora's *Pariśiṣṭa* and Gaṅgādhara's *Setusaṃgraha*. Calcutta, 1843.
G1013 : Edited by Otto Böhtlingk. St. Petersburg, 1847.
G1014 : *Kavikalpadruma* edited, with Durgādāsa's *Paribhāṣāṭīkā*, by Madana Mohana Tarkalamkara. Calcutta, 1848.
G1015 : Edited with Durgādāsa Vidyāvāgīśa Bhaṭṭācārya's *Subodhā*. Shrirampore, 1857.
G1016 : Edited by Govindacandra Vidyaratna. Calcutta, 1861–1862, 1880.
G1017 : Edited with Durgādāsa's *Subodhā* and Rāma Tarkavāgīśa's *Kāraka, Samāsa*, and *Taddhita* sections of his *Pramodajananī*. Calcutta, 1861.
G1018 : Selections edited by Loharam Shiroratna. Calcutta, 1868.
G1019 : Edited with Girīśacandra Vidyāratna's *Ṭippaṇī*. Calcutta, 1871.

G1020 : *Kavikalpadruma* edited, with Durgādāsa's *Paribhāṣāṭīkā*, by Jaranatha Tarkavacaspati. Calcutta, 1872.

G1021 : *Kavikalpadruma* edited, with Durgādāsa's *Paribhāṣāṭīkā*, by Baradaprasada Majumdra. Calcutta, 1876, 1879.

G1022 : Edited, with Durgādāsa's *Subodhā* and Rāma Tarkavāgīśa's *Pramodajananī*, by Rajanikanta Gupta. Calcutta, 1888.

G1023 : *Kavikalpadruma* edited, with Durgādāsa's *Paribhāṣāṭīkā*, by Jivananda Vidyasagara. Calcutta, 1888.

G1024 : Edited, with Durgādāsa's *Subodhā*, Nandakiśora Bhaṭṭācārya Cakravartin's *Pariśiṣṭa*, and editor's *Ṭīkā*, by Durgadasa Vidyavagisa Srirama Tarkavagisa. Calcutta, 1908.

G1025 : Edited, with editor's *Ṭippaṇī*, by Syamacarana Kaviratna. Calcutta, 1910.

G1026 : Edited, with Rāma Tarkavāgīśa's *Pramodajananī*, by Siva Narayana Siromani. BI 201. Calcutta, 1911–1913.

G1027 : *Kavikalpadruma* edited, with Durgādāsa's *Dhātudīpikā*, by Gurunatha Vidyanidhi Bhattacarya. Calcutta, 1912.

G1028 : Edited, with Rāma Tarkavāgīśa's *Pramodajananī* and editor's *Parimala*, by Harendranarayana Devasarman. Berhampur, 1912.

G1029 : *Kṛdanta* section edited with Rāma Tarkavāgīśa's *Pramodajananī* thereon. Varanasi, 1914.

G1030 : Edited with Durgādāsa's *Subodhā* and Rāma Tarkavāgīśa's *Pramodajananī*. Calcutta, 1914.

G1031 : Edited, with Durgādāsa's *Subodhā*, Rāma Tarkavāgīsa's *Pramodajananī*, and Śivanārāyaṇa Śiromaṇi's *Ṭippaṇī*, by Devendranatha Sengupta and Upendranatha Sengupta. Calcutta, 1916.

G1032 : Edited by Syamacarana Kaviratna Vidyavaridhi. Calcutta, 1927.

G1033 : *Kavikalpadruma* edited by G. B. Palsule. SIAL 15. Poona, 1954.

SAṂGRĀMASIṂHA (1279)

Bālaśikṣā on Sarvavarman's *Kātantrasūtras*

See e663.

JINAPRABHĀ (SŪRI) or LEŚAPRABODHA (1280)

(NCat 7.259)

Durga(pada)prabodhā on Trilocana's *Kātantravṛttipañjikā*

(NCat 3.311, 7.259)

KṚṢṆALĪLĀŚUKA (1280)

(NCat 9.100, 169)

Puruṣakāra on Deva's *Daiva*

See e976; e977.

MALAYAGIRI (1280)

(Belvalkar, p. 67)

Vṛtti on Hemacandra's *Śabdānuśāsana*

(NCat 9.290)

G1034 : Edited with autocommentary by Bechardas Jivaraj Doshi. LDS 13. Ahmedabad, 1967.

VIMALA SARASVATĪ (1300)

(Belvalkar, pp. 22, 36; G1624, p. 267)

Rūpamālā

G1035 : Edited with Hindi paraphrase by Kesava Deva Pandeya. 4 volumes. Delhi, 1973.

NARENDRAPURI or PRAJÑĀNASVARŪPA (1300)

Dhātupāṭha, a Sārasvata work

(NCat 9.370)

ABHAYACANDRA (ĀCĀRYA) (1329)
(Belvalkar, p. 60; NCat 1.273) (a Śākaṭāyana author)
Prakriyāsaṃgraha
See e881.
MAṆḌANA, pupil of Narendrapuri (1330)
(Belvalkar, p. 82)
Saṃdhiprakaraṇa on Anubhūti's *Sārasvataprakrīyā*
(NCat 2.374)
ĀNANDAPŪRṆA VIDYĀSĀGARA (1350)
(NCat 3.118)
Prakrīyāmañjarī on Vāmana/Jayāditya's *Kāśikā*
(NCat 2.108, 3.118)
BHĪMASENA (ĀCĀRYA) (14th century)
(G1624, p. 255)
Commentary on a *Dhātupāṭha*
(NCat 9.288)
JAGADDHARA of Kashmir (last half of 14th century)
(NCat 7.317)
Bālabodhinī on the Kashmiri recension of the *Kātantrasūtras*
(NCat 3.317)
Apaśabdanirākaraṇa
(NCat 7.131)
Ṭīkā on Bhojadeva's *Sarasvatīkaṇṭhābharaṇa*
See e918; e921.
ŚĀYAṆA or MĀDHAVA (?) (14th century)
(Cardona, p. 288; Belvalkar, p. 43; G1624; pp. 240, 255)
Mādhavīyadhātuvṛtti on Pāṇini's *Aṣṭādhyāyī-Dhātupāṭha*
See e35.
G1036 : Edited by A. Mahadeva Sastri and K. Rangacaryal. 2 volumes. Government Oriental Series, Bibliotheca Sanskritica. Mysore, 1894-1903.
G1037 : *Nāmadhātuvṛtti* (an appendix) edited by Damodara Sastri. *Pan* n. s. 19, 1897.
G1038 : Edited by Ananta Sastri Phadke and Sadasiva Sarma Sastri Joshi. KSS 103. Varanasi, 1934.
G1039 : Edited by Dwarikadas Shastri. PBS 1. Varanasi, 1964.
MOKṢEŚVARA (1350?)
Commentary on Durgasiṃha's *Kātantravṛtti*
(NCat 3.313, 4.281)
JUMARANANDIN (1350?)
(Belvalkar, p. 91; GOS 134, 1961, 162; YM 1.625)
(Revision of Kramadiśvara's) *Saṃkṣiptasāra* and *Rasāvatī* thereon
See e912.
UJJVALADATTA, alias JĀJALI (14th century? but NCat 2.257 says 1250)
(G1624, p. 233)
Uṇādisūtravṛtti
(NCat 2.294)
G1040 : Edited by T. Aufrecht. Bonn, London, 1859.
G1041 : Edited by Jivananda Vidyasagara. Calcutta, 18.
PADMANĀBHADATTA (1375)
(Belvalkar, p. 93; NCat 11.128)
Supadma
G1042 : *Uṇādi* section published in *Vidyodaya* (Calcutta) 26–27 (1874, etc.),

G1043 : Edited, with Viṣṇumiśra's *Makaranda*, by Trailokyanatha Bhattacarya. Calcutta, 1887.

G1044 : Edited, with Viṣṇumiśra's *Makaranda*, by Upendranatha Bhattacarya. Calcutta, 1900.

G1045 : Edited with a *Vivaraṇapañcikā*. Calcutta, 1903.

G1046 : Edited with editor's *Ṭippaṇī* by Trailokyanatha Bhattacarya. Calcutta, 1910.

KAVIDARPANA RĀGHAVA (1375?)

Pāṇinīyamatadarpaṇa

G1047 : V. Swaminathan, "Pāṇiniyamatadarpaṇa—a Forgotten Work on Grammar," SVUOJ 14, 1971, 61–76.

MERUTUṄGA (1388)

Bālāvabodha on Durgasiṃha's *Kātantravṛtti*

(NCat 3.31)

KULAMAṆḌANA SŪRI (1394)

(NCat 4.238)

Auktika or *Mugdhabālāvabodha*

(NCat 3.97, 4.238)

DHARAṆĪDHARA (1397)

(NCat 9.237)

Pañjikā on Pāṇini's (?) *Pāṇinīyaśikṣā*

G1048 : Edited by Gopala Sastri Nene and Sudama Sarman Misra. HSS 10. Varanasi, 1929.

NANDAKIŚORA ŚARMAN BHAṬṬĀCĀRYA CAKRAVARTIN (1398)

(Belvalkar, p. 90; NCat 9.326)

Pariśiṣṭa to Vopadeva's *Mugdhabodha*

See e1012; e1024.

MAṆḌANA KAVI (1400?)

Kavikalpadrumaskandha Upasargamaṇḍana

(NCat 2.374, 3.270)

MEGHARATNA (1400?)

(Belvalkar, p. 83)

Sārasvata-Vyākaraṇadhuṇḍhikā or *Dīpikā*

GOYĪCANDRA or GOPICAṆḌA (1400?)

(Belvalkar, p. 92; GOS 134, 1961, 145)

Vivaraṇa on Kramadīśvara's *Saṃkṣiptasāra*

(NCat 6.158, 159)

G1049 : Edited in two parts. Calcutta, 1888.

Commentary on Jumaranandin's *Taddhitapariśiṣṭa*

(NCat 6.158)

RĀMACANDRA (1400)

(Cardona, p. 286; Belvalkar, p. 37; G1624, p. 268)

Prakriyākaumudī on Pāṇini's *Aṣṭādhyāyī*

G1050 : Edited, with Viṭṭhala's *Prasāda*, by Kamalasankara Pranasankara Trivedi. BSPS 78, 82. Poona, 1925–1931.

G1051 : Surjit Kumar Mukhopadhyaya, "Tibetan Translations of *Prakrīyākaumudī* and the mention of *Siddhānta-kaumudī* Therein," IHQ 20, 1944, 63–69.

G1052 : Adya Prasada Misra, *Prakriyākaumudīvimarśaḥ*. SBS 15. Varanasi, 1966.

G1053 : Edited, with Śrīkṛṣṇa's *Prakāśa* and editor's *Raśmi*, by Muralidhara Misra. SBGM 111–112. 1977–1980.

(ṚṢIPUTRA) PARAMEŚVARA II (1410)

(NCat 11.191)

Gopālikā on Maṇḍana Miśra's *Sphoṭasiddhi*
See e870.
GUṆARATNA SŪRI (1411)
(Belvalkar, p. 67; NCat 6.51) (Hemacandra writer)
Kriyāratnasamuccaya
G1054 : Edited YJG 10. Varanasi, 1908.
NARAPATI MAHĀMIŚRA (1425)
(YM 1.510)
(*Vyākaraṇa*) *Prakāśa* on Jinendrabuddhi's *Nyāsa*
(NCat 4.119)
ŚUBHAŚĪLA GAṆI (1425)
Uṇādināmamālā
(NCat 2.293)
KṚṢṆĀCĀRYA II (1430)
Upasargārthasaṃgraha and autocommentary
(NCat 2.376)
(ARRA or ERRA) MĀDHAVA BHAṬṬA (1450)
Tripādoddyotinī
(NCat 1.393, 8.235)
ŚRĪPATIDATTA (1450?)
(Belvalkar, p. 75; Abhyankar, p. 396)
Pariśiṣṭa to the *Kātantrasūtras*
See e649; e653.
JONARĀJA or JOGARĀJA (1450)
Padaprakaraṇasaṃgati, topical analysis of the *Kātantrasūtras*
G1055 : Edited in Belvalkar, pp. 99–101.
ŚITIKAṆṬHA (15th century)
Nyāsa on Jagaddhara's *Kātantrabālabodhinī*
(NCat 3.317)
UDAYADHARMA or DHARMASŪRI (1451)
(NCat 3.97)
Auktika or *Vākyaprakāśa*
(NCat 2.326, 3.97, 9.274)
HEMAHAṂSAVIJAYAGAṆI (1457)
(Belvalkar, p. 67)
Nyāyasaṃgraha with *Nyāyārthamañjūṣā* thereon (Hemacandra work)
G1056 : Edited Varanasi, 1911.
JINASĀGARA (1460?)
(Belvalkar, p. 65)
Dīpikā (or *Dhuṇḍhikā*?) on Hemacandra's *Śabdānuśāsana*
(NCat 7.272)
VIṬṬHALA (1460)
(Cardona, p. 285; Belvalkar, p. 37; G1624, p. 270)
Prakrīyāprasāda on Rāmacandra's *Prakriyākaumudī*
See e1050.
KUMĀRAPĀLA (1461)
Gaṇadarpaṇa
(cf. YM 2.404)
PUÑJARĀJA (1485)
(Belvalkar, p. 81)
Commentary on Anubhūti's *Sārasvataprakriyā*

G1057 : P. K. Gode, "Oldest Dated ms. of Puñjarāja's Commentary on the *Sārasvataprakriyā*," ALB 5, 1941, 120–124.

RĀMAKĀNTA or RĀMACANDRA or KAVICANDRA (1489)

Dhātusādhanā

(NCat 9.295)

AMṚTABHĀRATĪ (1490)

(Belvalkar, p. 81; NCat 1.350)

Subodhikā on Anubhūti's *Sārasvataprakriyā*

(NCat 1.350)

ABHIRĀMA VIDYĀLAṂKĀRA (1500?)

(GOS 134, 1961, 37)

Kaumudī on Goyīcandra's *Saṃkṣiptasāraṭīkā-Kārakapada*

(NCat 1.310, 5.110)

AUTHOR UNKNOWN (1500)

Mukhabhūṣaṇa

G1058 : Edited by K. Kunjunni Raja. ALB 37, 1973, 89–172.

KĀŚĪNĀTHA BHAṬṬA (1500?)

(Belvalkar, p. 83; YM 1.633)

Bhāṣya on Anubhūti's *Sārasvataprakriyā*

(NCat 4.127)

SATYĀNANDA or RĀMACANDRA SARASVATĪ (1500)

(YM 1.420)

Laghuvivaraṇa on Kaiyaṭa's *Mahābhāṣyapradīpa*

G1059 : 1.1.8–1.2 edited, with Īśvarānanda's *Bṛhadvivaraṇa*, Śivarāmendra Sarasvatī Yogīndra's *Ratnaprakāśa*, Nārāyaṇa Śāstri's *Nārāyaṇīya*, and Annambhaṭṭa's *Uddyotana*, by M. S. Narasimhacarya. PIFI 51–55. Pondicherry 1973–1980.

DHANEŚVARA BHAṬṬA (1510)

(Belvalkar, p. 83)

Pradīpa on Anubhūti's *Sārasvataprakriyā*

(NCat 9.226)

G1060 : P. K. Gode, "Date of *Sārasvataprakriyā* of Bhaṭṭa Dhaneśvara," PO 1.4, 1936, 30–33.

APPAN NAINĀRYA (1510)

(YM 1.485)

Prakriyādīpikā

(NCat 1.258)

KARMADHARA (1510)

Prakāśa on Durgasiṃha's *Kātantravṛtti*

(NCat 3.310)

MĀDHAVA BHAṬṬA (1520?)

(Belvalkar, p. 82)

Siddhāntaratnāvalī on Anubhūti's *Sārasvataprakriyā*

See e996.

PUṆḌARĪKĀKṢA VIDYĀSĀGARA BHAṬṬĀCĀRYA (1520)

Pradīpa on Durgasiṃha's *Kātantravṛtti*

See e656.

Vaktavyaviveka on a *Kātantrapariśiṣṭa*

(NCat 3.316)

Ṭīkā on Jayāditya/Vāmana's *Kāśikā* (lost)

KṢEMENDRA (1525)

(Belvalkar, p. 81; NCat 5.169)
Commentary on Rāmacandra's *Sārasvataprakriyā*
Commentary on Narendrapuri's (Sārasvata) *Dhātupāṭha*
(NCat 5.169, 9.289)

DHANACANDRA or JINASĀGARA or NANDASUNDARA and UDAYASAUBHĀGYA (1533)
(Belvalkar, p. 65)
Dhuṇḍhikā on Hemacandra's *Bṛhadvṛtti*
Avacūrikā on Hemacandra's *Laghuvṛtti*
(NCat 9.216)

ŚEṢA KṚṢṆA (1540)
(NCat 4.365)
Sphoṭatattvanirūpaṇa
G1061 : Edited in Mahadeva Sarma Gangadhara, ed., *Vadarthasaṃgraha*. Bombay, 1913–1914.
Śabdāharaṇa or *Śabdālaṅkāra* (lost)
Padacandrikā with *Kṛṣṇakautūhula* thereon
(NCat 4.365)
Gūḍhabhāvavivṛti or *Prakāśa* on Rāmacandra's *Prakriyākaumudī*
(NCat 4.365)

(ŚEṢA) NĀRĀYAṆA (BHAṬṬA) (1546)
(YM 1.405)
Sūktiratnākara on Patañjali's *Mahābhāṣya*
(NCat 10.89)

RĀMANĀTHA ŚARMAN (RĀYI) (1546)
(NCat 3.315)
Manoramā on *Kātantra-Dhātupāṭha*
See e654.

VIṢṆUMITRA (1547)
(YM 1.410)
Kṣīrodara on Patañjali's *Mahābhāṣya* (lost)

BHARATA MIŚRA (16th century)
Sphoṭasiddhi
G1062 : Edited by K. Sambasiva Sastri. TSS 89. Trivandrum, 1927.

VIMALAKĪRTI (1550?)
(GOS 134, 1961, 359)
Padavyavasthā(sūtra)kārikā
(NCat 11.102)

GOPINĀTHA TARKĀCĀRYA (1550)
(Belvalkar, p. 75; NCat 3.316)
Prabodha on a *Kātantrapariśiṣṭa*
G1063 : Edited Calcutta, 1890.
Paribhāṣāvṛtti
(NCat 6.163)

IŚVARANANDA or ĪŚVARĪDATTA (1550)
(NCat 2.280)
Vivaraṇa on Kaiyaṭa's *Mahābhāṣyapradīpa*
See e1059.
Śābdabodhataraṅgiṇī
(NCat 2.280)

NĀRĀYAṆA NYĀYAPAÑCĀNANA (1550)
(NCat 10.74)

Commentary on *Kṛdanta* section of Goyīcandra's commentary on *Saṃkṣiptasāra*
(NCat 4.281, 10.74)
Gaṇaprakāśa on *Saṃkṣiptasāra-Gaṇapāṭha*
(NCat 5.256, 10.74)
See e913.
RĀMA TARKAVĀGĪŚA (1550?)
(Belvalkar, p. 90; GOS 134, 1961, 324)
Pramodajananī on Vopadeva's *Mugdhabodha*
(NCat 2.203)
See e1017; e1022; e1026; e1028; e1029; e1030; e1031.
Commentary on the *Kātantrasūtras*
(NCat 3.314)
KULACANDRA (1550?)
(Belvalkar, p. 75)
Durgavākyaprabodha on Durgasiṃha's *Kātantravṛtti*
See e656; e657.
KĀŚĪŚVARA BHAṬṬĀCĀRYA (1550?)
(Belvalkar, p. 90; YM 1.637–638)
Commentary on Vopadeva's *Mugdhabodha*
(NCat 4.141)
Mugdhabodhapariśiṣṭa
(NCat 4.141)
Śabdaratnākara
(NCat 4.141)
MĀDHAVA SARASVATĪ (1550?)
Prakriyāsudhā on Rāmacandra's *Prakriyākaumudī*
G1064 : M. S. Bhat, "An Incomplete Manuscript of Mādhavasarasvatī's *Prakriyāsudhā*, a Commentary on *Prakriyākaumudī*," JIH 37, 1959, 153–155.
AUTHOR UNKNOWN (16th century?)
Sphoṭasiddhinyāyavicāra
G1065 : Edited by T. Ganapati Sastri. TSS 54. Trivandrum, 1917.
SARVEŚVARA or SOMAYĀJIN DĪKṢITA (1555)
(YM 2.416)
Sphūrti on Kaiyaṭa's *Mahābhāṣyapradīpa*
(MS listed in Adyar D, vol. 6, nos. 107–109)
CINTĀMAṆI (1557)
(NCat 7.58; YM 2.418)
Prakāśa on Kaiyaṭa's *Mahābhāṣyapradīpa*
(NCat 7.58)
HARṢAKULAGAṆI (1557)
(NCat 3.97)
Commentary on Udayadharma's *Auktika*
(NCat 3.97)
Versification of Hemacandra's *Kavikalpadruma-Dhātupāṭha*
G1066 : Edited YJG 12. Bombay, 1909.
ANNAMBHAṬṬA (1540? 1560?)
(NCat 1.237)
Uddyotana on Kaiyaṭa's *Mahābhāṣyapradīpa*
See e587; e590; e1059.
Mitākṣara on Pāṇini's *Aṣṭādhyāyī*
G1067 : Edited by S. P. S. Jagannathaswamy Aryavaraguru and Acharya Bhattanathaswamy. BenSS 20. Varanasi, 1903–1906.

VĀSUDEVA BHAṬṬA (1567)
(Belvalkar, p. 82)
Sārasvataprasāda on Anubhūti's *Sārasvataprakriyā*
See e989; e991.

PURUṢOTTAMA VIDYĀVĀGĪŚA BHAṬṬĀCĀRYA or NARA NĀRĀYAṆA (1568)
Prayoga(uttama)ratnamālā
(NCat 6.94)
G1068 : Edited Kuch Bihar, 1890–1903.
G1069 : *Padamañjarī* section edited by Taranatha Gosvami Smrtiratna. Calcutta, 1907.
G1070 : Biswanarayana Shastri, "The Kāmarūpa School of Sanskrit Grammar," in *Gaurinath Shastri Festschrift*, pp. 236–244.

CARITRASIṂHA (GAṆI) (1569)
Avacūrī on *Kātantra (vibhrama) sūtras*
(NCat 3.318; 7.23)

APPAYYA DĪKṢITA I (1580)
Vādanakṣatramālā on Pāṇini's *Aṣṭādhyāyī*
(NCat 1.265)
G1071 : Edited by V. Krishnamachariar. Kumbhakonam, 1910.

GUṆARATNA (1585)
Commentary on Narendrapuri's *Sārasvataprakriyā-Dhātupāṭha*

HARṢAKĪRTI (1586)
(Belvalkar, pp. 82, 86; NCat 1.197)
Dhātupāṭha and *Tārāṅgiṇī* thereon
(NCat 9.289)

CIDRŪPĀŚRAMA or CIDRŪPĀŚRAMIN (1587)
Vyākaraṇadīpa or *Dīpavyākaraṇa*
(NCat 7.55, 9.66)
?*Viṣamī* on a *Paribhāṣenduśekhara*
(NCat 7.55, 11.226)

GOPĀLA BHAṬṬA (1590)
(GOS 134, 1961)
Viṣamapadārthadīpikā or *Gopālabhaṭṭī* on Anubhūti's *Sārasvataprakriyā*
(NCat 6.146)

BHAṬṬOJI DĪKṢITA (1590)
(G1624, p. 273; Cardona, p. 283)
Siddhāntakaumudī on Pāṇini's *Aṣṭādhyāyī*
G1072 : Edited by Babu Rama in MS form. Kidderpur, 1811.
G1073 : Edited Madras, 1858, 1866, 1882, 1886, 1887.
G1074 : Edited with Jñānendra Sarasvatī's *Tattvabodhinī*. Varanasi, 1862, 1885, 1887, 1888.
G1075 : Edited with editor's *Saralā* by Taranatha Tarkavacaspati. 2 volumes. Calcutta, 1863–1864.
See e30.
G1076 : *Liṅgānuśāsana* section edited Calcutta; 1868.
G1077 : Edited with editor's commentary by Taranatha Tarkavacaspati. Calcutta, 1870–1871.
G1078 : Edited Varanasi, 1873, 1880.
G1079 : First *stabaka* edited by Rāmacandra Śarman Guñjikāra. Bombay, 1880.
G1080 : Edited with Vāsudeva Dīkṣita's *Bālamanoramā*. Tiruvadi, 1885; Nandukaveri, 1901.
See e37.

G1081 : Edited with Nāgeśa Bhaṭṭa's *Laghuśabdenduśekhara*. Varanasi, 1888.

G1082 : Edited, with Jñānendra Sarasvatī's *Tattvabodhinī*, by Patavardhana Narayana Sastri. Varanasi, 1897.

G1083 : Edited, with Jñānendra Sarasvatī's *Tattvabodhinī* and Jayakṛṣṇa's *Subodhinī*, by Dinkar Keshava Shastri Gadgil and Vasudev Lakshmana Shastri Pansikar. Bombay, 1899, 1915.

G1084 : Edited, with Nāgeśa Bhaṭṭa's *Laghuśabdenduśekhara*, by Karnataka Kṛṣṇa Sastri. Varanasi, 1903.

G1085 : Edited and translated by Srisa Chandra Vasu and Vaman Das Vasu. 3 volumes. Allahabad, 1905–1907. Reprinted Delhi, 1962.

G1086 : Edited with editor's *Bālacandrī*, by Balacandra Sastri. Meerut, 1908.

G1087 : Edited, with Vāsudeva Dīkṣita's *Bālamanoramā*, by S. Chandrasekhara Sastrigal. Trichinopoly, 1910–1911; Madras, 1927.

G1088 : Edited with Bhairava Miśra's *Ratnaprakāśikā*. Varanasi, 1910.

See e54; e56.

G1089 : Partly edited, with editor's *Paṅkticandrikā*, by Gangaprasada Sastrin. Bṛndāban, 1914; Bharatpur, 1931.

G1090 : Edited with editor's *Sāradarśinī*, by Sivadatta. Bombay, 1914.

G1091 : 1.1 edited, with editor's *Mitabhāṣiṇī*, and translated by Saradaranjan Ray Vidyavinod. Calcutta, 1920.

G1092 : Edited, with editor's *Paṅktipradīpa*, by Nanakarama Sastri. Varanasi, 1924–1925.

G1093 : Edited, with editor's *Bhāvabodhinī*, by Karaputugala Dharma Sri. Part 1. Varanasi, 1925.

G1094 : Edited by Gopal Sastri Nene. HSS 11. Varanasi, 1929.

G1095 : Edited, with Vāsudeva Dīkṣita's *Bālamanoramā*, by C. Sankara Rama Sastrin and R. V. Krishnamachariar. 2d edition. Madras, 1929.

See a78.

G1096 : Edited, with editor's *Viśeṣavivṛti*, by Somanatha Sarman. Varanasi, 1952.

G1097 : Bhadanta Shanti Bhikshu, "An Incorrect Reading Existing from a Long Time in *Siddhāntakaumudī*," SPAIOC 17, 1953, 100–101. Full paper IL 14, 1954, 553–556.

G1098 : Siddheshwar Varma, "The Vedic Limitations of the *Siddhāntakaumudī*," SPAIOC 17, 1953, 105–106.

G1099 : G. B. Palsule, "Discussion of a Reading in the *Siddhāntakaumudī*," SPAIOC 20, 1957, 72.

G1100 : Edited, with Vāsudeva Dīkṣita's *Bālamanoramā* and Jñānendra Sarasvatī's *Tattvabodhinī*, by Giridhara Sarma Caturveda and Paramesvarananda Sarma Bhaskara. 4 volumes. Varanasi, 1958–1961.

G1101 : Edited, with Vāsudeva Dīkṣita's *Bālamanoramā*, by Gopala Shastri Nene. 2 parts. KSS 136, Varanasi, 1958–1961.

G1102 : Edited by Somanatha Sarma. Kasthamandapa, Nepal, 1959.

See e159; e168.

G1103 : *Vibhaktyartha* (*Kāraka*) section edited, with editor's commentary, by Sridharananda Sharma Ghildiyal. Delhi, 1962.

G1104 : Partially edited, with Śabhāpati Śarma Upādhyāya's *Lakṣmī*, by Bala Krishna Pancholi. 2 volumes. Delhi, 1966.

See a860 (1968).

G1105 : Edited with Hindi commentary by Bala Krishna Pancholi. 3 volumes. KSS 191. Varanasi, 1969–1971.

G1106 : *Kāraka* section edited by Dinesh Chandra Guha. Varanasi, 1970.

G1107 : S. Venkitasubramonia Iyer, "The Difference Between Bhaṭṭoji Dīkṣita and

Nārāyaṇa Bhaṭṭa with Regard to Certain Phonetic Observations," VIJ 8, 1970, 86–102.

See d863 (1971).

G1108 : Mahesh Dutt Sharma, "A Note on the *Siddhāntakaumudī* 2882 and 2940," MO 4, 1971, 35–37. Also PAIOC 25, 1972, 317–319.

G1109 : M. S. Narayana Murti, "Bhaṭṭoji Dīkṣita and Koṇḍubhaṭṭa on the Primary Denotation," SVUOJ 15, 1972, 87–98.

See e321; b864.

G1110 : P. C. Naganatha Sastry, *Śrī Bhaṭṭoji Dīkshita's Vaiyākaraṇa Siddhāntakaumudī. The Standard Sanskrit Grammar. An Analysis in English.* 2 volumes. Delhi, 1974, 1983.

G1111 : Pratibha P. Gokhale, "A Note on the *paribhāṣā 'stipa sapanubandhana,'*" SPAIOC 27, 1974, 246–247.

See d866

G1112 : K. Kunjunni Raja, "A So-called Vārttika: *maturmatac putrārthamarhate,*" PAIOC 27, 1976, 383–384.

Prauḍhamanoramā on his own *Siddhāntakaumudī*

G1113 : Edited Varanasi, 1868, 1886, 1888.

G1114 : Edited with Hari Dīkṣita's (?) *Laghuśabdaratna*, by Rama Sastri Manavalli and Gangadhara Sastri. Varanasi, 1874–1888.

G1115 : Edited, with Hari Dīkṣita's (?) *Laghuśabdaratna*, by Ratnagopala Bhatta. Varanasi, 1906–1910.

G1116 : Edited, with Hari Dīkṣita's (?) *Laghuśabdaratna*, by Balakrsna Sastri. Varanasi, 1910.

G1117 : Edited, with Hari Dīksita's (?) *Laghuśabdaratna* and editor's *Prabhā*, by Madhava Sastri Bhandarin. Varanasi, 1920.

G1118 : Partially edited, with Hari Dīkṣita's *Laghuśabdaratna* and Bhairava Miśra's *Śabdaratna Bhairavī*, by Sadasiva Sarma Sastri. KSS 58. Varanasi, 1928.

G1119 : Partially edited, with Hari Dīkṣita's *Laghuśabdaratna*, by Sadasiva Sastri Joshi. HSS 23. Varanasi, 1933.

G1120 : Edited, with Hari Dīkṣita's *Laghuśabdaratna*, Bhairava Miśra's *Bhairavī*, Vaidyanātha Payaguṇde's *Bhāvaprakāśa*, and editor's *Saralā*, by Gopala Sastri Nene. KSS 125, Varanasi, 1939.

G1121 : Edited, with Hari Dīkṣita's *Śabdaratna*, by Narayana Dadaji Wadegaongkar. 7 volumes. Nagpur, 1945–1964.

G1122 : Edited, with Hari Dīkṣita's *Śabdaratna*, by Venkatesh Laxman Joshi. Volume 1: DCMS 31, Poona, 1966. Appendixes published as DCMS 31A, Poona, 1964.

G1123 : Edited, with Hari Dīkṣita's *Bṛhatśabdaratna* and Nāgeśa Bhaṭṭa's *Laghuśabdaratna*, by Sitaram Sastri. Volume 1. HVNRSS 8. Varansi, 1964.

Śabdakaustubha

G1124 : Edited Varanasi, 1876.

G1125 : Edited, with Jayakṛṣṇa's *Sphoṭacandrikā*, by Vindhyesvari Prasada Dvivedin and Ganapati Sastri Mokate. ChSS 2. Varanasi, 1898–1917. 2.5–10 reprinted with *Sphoṭacandrikā*, Varanasi, 1929. 1.1 reprinted Varanasi, 1933.

?*Kriyānighaṇṭu*

G1126 : Edited in Telugu script. Mysore, 1905.

Vaiyākaraṇamatonmajjana or *Vaiyākaraṇasiddhāntakārikās* Printed in many editions of Koṇḍabhaṭṭa's *Vaiyākaraṇabhūṣaṇa* and *sāra*.

See e555.

General

G1127 : K. C. Chatterji, "Jagannātha and Bhaṭṭoji," COJ 3, 1935, 41–51.

G1128 : P. K. Gode, "A New Approach to the Date of Bhaṭṭoji Dīkshita," ASVOI 1.2, 1940, 117–127.

G1129 : Surya Kant Bali, "Contribution of Bhaṭṭoji Dīkṣita to Sanskrit Grammar". Ph.D. diss., University of Delhi, 1971.

G1130 : ———, *Bhaṭṭoji Dīkṣita: His Contribution to Sanskrit Grammar*. Delhi, 1976.

(ŚEṢA) CAKRAPAṆI (1595)

(NCat 6.255)

(*Paramata*)*Khaṇḍana* on Bhaṭṭoji's *Prauḍhamanoramā*

G1131 : Edited by V. P. Dvivedin. *Pan* 32, 1910; 2, 1–60; 33, 1911, 61–76; 34, 1912, 77–120; 35, 1913, 121–134; 36, 1914, title page.

Kārakatattva or *Kārakavicāra*

(NCat 3.375)

Prakriyāpradīpa (lost)

TRILOCANA (1600?)

(Belvalkar, p. 75)

Uttarapariśiṣṭa on *Kātantrasūtras*

(NCat 3.316, 8.262)

BHĀRATA MALLIKA (1600?)

Ekavarṇārthasaṃgraha

G1132 : Edited by Suresh Chandra Banerji, IHQ 36, 1960, 29–34.

ŚIVARĀMA CAKRAVARTIN (1600?)

(Belvalkar, p. 75)

Siddhāntaratnākara on *Kātantrapariśiṣṭa*

(NCat 3.316)

RĀMADĀSA CAKRAVARTIN (1600?)

Vyākhyāsāra or *Candrikā* on *Kātantra*

(NCat 3.314)

Candrikā on a *Kātantrapariśiṣṭa*

(NCat 3.316) (see e632 for extracts)

RĀMACANDRĀŚRAMA (1600?)

(Belvalkar, p. 85; YM 2.249)

(*Vaiyākaraṇa*) *Siddhāntacandrikā* on *Sārasvatasūtras*

(NCat 6.379)

See e988; e992.

G1133 : Edited, with editor's commentary, by Sadasiva Sastri Joshi. HSS 17. Varanasi, 1931.

G1134 : Edited, with Sadānanda's *Subodhinī*, Lokeśakāra's *Tattvadīpikā*, and editor's *Avyayārthamālā*, by Navkishore Jha. 2 volumes. KSS 91. Varanasi, 1931–1933.

KAVICANDRA (DATTA) (1600)

(NCat 3.274)

Dhātucandrikā

Dhātusādhana

(NCat 3.274)

Săralaharī (of Saṃkṣiptasāra school)

(NCat 3.274)

NĪLAKAṆṬHA VĀJAPEYIN (1605)

(YM 2.411–412)

Pāṇinīyadīpikā

Sukhabodhinī on Bhaṭṭoji's *Siddhāntakaumudī*

ŚEṢA VIṢṆU (1605)
Prakāśikā on Patañjali's *Mahābhāṣya*
Dhāturatnaprakāśa or *-mañjarī*
(NCat 9.292)
CANDRAKĪRTI (1607)
(Belvalkar, p. 82)
Subodhikā or *Dīpikā* on Anubhūti's *Sārasvataprakriyā*
See e960; e999; e1001.
G1135 : Edited KSS, 2 volumes. Varanasi, 1935–1936.
ŚRIVALLABHAVACANA ĀCĀRYA (1607)
(Belvalkar, p. 67)
Durgāpadaprabodha on Hemacandra's *Liṅgānuśāsana*
ACYUTA PIṢAROTI (1610)
Praveśaka
G1136 : Edited in Cochin Sanskrit Series 2. Cochin.
TARKATILAKA BHAṬṬĀCĀRYA (1614)
(Belvalkar p. 85)
Vṛtti on *Sārasvatasūtras*
(NCat 8.114)
Sabdabhāskara
(NCat 8.114)
GAṄGĀDHARA DĪKṢITA (1617)
Prabhā on Cidrūpāśrama's *Vyākaraṇadīpa*
(NCat 5.203, 9.66)
VARADARĀJA (1620)
(Belvalkar, p. 42; Cardona, p. 287)
Sārasiddhāntakaumudī
G1137 : Edited and translated by Govind Vinayak Devasthali. PCASS-C 4. Poona, 1968.
Madhyasiddhāntakaumudī
G1138 : *Liṅgānuśasana* section edited by Visvanatha Sarman. Varanasi, 1884.
G1139 : Edited with editor's commentary by Balakrsna Sarma Yogi with Jivarama Sastri Raikva. Bombay, 1895.
G1140 : Edited by Ganesha Datta Sastri. Lahore, 1899.
G1141 : Edited with editor's *Viṣamasthalaṭippaṇa* by Govindasimha. Bombay, 1900.
G1142 : Edited by Narayana Ram Acarya. Bombay, 1950.
G1143 : Edited by Sadasiva Sastri Joshi and Rama Candra Jha, with the former's *Sudhā*. HSS 213. Varanasi, 1960.
G1144 : Edited, with Viśvanātha Śāstri's *Prabhākara*, by Nigamananda Sastri. Delhi, 1964.
Laghusiddhāntakaumudī
G1145 : Edited Calcutta, 1827, 1874, 1877, 1883.
G1146 : Edited Agra, 1848.
G1147 : Edited Delhi, 1849, 1869.
G1148 : Edited and translated by James R. Ballantyne. Mirzapore, 1849; Varanasi, 1867, 1881. Reprinted Delhi, 1961. Edition and Hindi translation published Varanasi, 1856.
G1149 : Edited with editor's *Ṭīkā* by Rupacandra. Lahore, 1853.
G1150 : Edited Allahabad, 1873.
G1151 : Edited Varanasi, 1879, 1889, 1890.
G1152 : Edited Madras, 1880.
G1153 : Edited Bombay, 1881, 1890.

G1154 : Edited Lucknow, 1882.
G1155 : Edited by Vitthala Narayana Sarma Gore and Ramacandra Sarma Gunjikara. Bombay, 1885.
G1156 : Edited by Jivarama Sastri and Sitarama Sastri. Bombay, 1903.
G1157 : Edited, with editor's *Sārabodhinī*, by Shastri Rancchodji Odhavji. Bombay, 1905.
G1158 : Edited with editor's *Tiṅantapradīpikā* by Kalavati Devi. Lucknow, 1909.
G1159 : Edited with editor's *Saralā* by Jivarama Sarman. Moradabad, 1911; Vrindavan, 1918–1919.
G1160 : Edited with editor's *Ṭippaṇī* by Sivadatta Sarman. Bombay, 1915.
G1161 : Edited with editor's *Ṭīkā* by U. K. Venkatanarasimha Acarya. Madras, 1916.
G1162 : Edited by Kanakalal Thakur. HSS 2. Varanasi, 1924.
G1163 : Edited with editor's *Ṭippaṇī* by Jivanatha Raya. Moradabad, Varanasi, 1925.
G1164 : Edited Darbhanga, 1925.
G1165 : Part 1 edited and translated, with editor's *Bālabodhinī*, by Vasudev Visnu Mirashi. 1928. Reprinted Delhi, 1967.
G1166 : Edited, with Kanakalāla Śarman's *Saṃkṣiptabālabodhinī*, by Sadasiva Sarma Joshi. Varanasi, 1930.
G1167 : Edited by Narayana Ram Acharya. Bombay, 1948.
G1168 : Edited, with editor's *Bhaimī*, by Bhimasena Sastri. 3 volumes. Delhi, 1950–1980.
G1169 : Edited and translated by Kumudranjan Roy. Calcutta, 1957.
G1170 : Edited with Hindi commentary by Shridharananda Sarma Ghildiyal. Delhi, 1961.
G1171 : Edited with Hindi commentary by Taranisa Jha. 3 volumes. Allahabad, 1962–1965.
G1172 : Edited with Hindi commentary by Mahesh Singh Kushwaha. 2 volumes. Vidyabhavan Sanskrit Granthamala 131. Varanasi, 1965–1977.
G1173 : Edited, with Girija's *Ṭīkā* and editor's Hindi commentary, by Rajendra Chaudhuri. Allahabad, 1969.
G1174 : Edited with Hindi commentary by Sadasiva Sastri. HSS 119. Varanasi, 1977.

Ghirvarṇapadamañjarī

G1175 : Edited by Umakant Premanand Shah. Supplement to JOI 7.4, 1958, 1–18. Reprinted as MSUOS 4. Baroda, 1960.

Dhātukārikāvalī

G1176 : Edited in Grantharatnamala 3. Bombay, 1889.

General

G1177 : P. K. Gode, "Varadarāja, a Pupil of Bhaṭṭoji Dīksita, and His Works—Between 1600 and 1650," PVKF, pp. 188–199.

RAGHUNĀTHA (1620)
(Belvalkar, p. 86)
Laghubhāṣya on the *Sārasvatasūtras*

SAHAJAKĪRTI (1623)
Sārasvataprakriyāvārttika

SĀDHUSUNDARA GAṆI (1624)
Dhāturatnākara
(NCat, 9.293)

KOṆḌA or KAUṆḌA BHAṬṬA (1630)
(NCat 5.92; G1624, p. 285)
Vaiyākaraṇabhūṣaṇa on Bhaṭṭoji Dīkṣita's *Vaiyākaraṇamatonmajjana*, and *-sāra* thereon

G1178 : Edited by Taranatha Tarkavacaspati and Madana Mohana Tarkalamkara. Calcutta, 1849, 1872.

G1179 : Edited with Harivallabha's *Darpaṇa*. Varanasi, 1866.

G1180 : Edited Varanasi, 1890.

G1181 : Text only edited, with Koṇḍa Bhaṭṭa's *Padārthadīpikā*, by Ramakrsna Sastri Patavardhana. BenSS 15. Varanasi, 1899–1900.

G1182 : Edited, with Śrīkṛṣṇa's *Sphoṭacandrikā* and Bhairava Miśra's *Sphoṭaparīkṣā* by the Anandasrama pandits. ASS 43, Poona, 1901.

G1183 : Edited with editor's *Viṣamasthalaṭippaṇī* by Ramakrsna Sarma Tripathi. Varanasi, 1907.

G1184 : Edited, with Harivallabha's *Darpaṇa*, by Ratnagopala Bhatta. Varanasi, 1908.

G1185 : Text only edited, with Harirāma's *Kāśikā* by K.P. Trivedi. BSPS 70. Bombay, 1915.

G1186 : Edited with editor's *Saralā* by Gopala Sastri Nene. Varanasi, 1919.

G1187 : Edited, with Harivallabha's *Darpaṇa*, by Ananta Sastri Phadke. KSS 23. Varanasi, 1924.

G1188 : Edited, with Harivallabha's *Darpaṇa*, Bhairava Miśra's *Parīkṣā* and Kṛṣṇa Mitra's commentary, with Khuddi Jhā Śarmā's *Tiṅarthavādasāra*, by Sadasiva Sastri Joshi. KSS 133. Varanasi, 1939.

G1189 : Edited, with Bāla Kṛṣṇa Pañcoli's *Prabhā* and Harivallabha's *Darpaṇa*, by Tarakesvara Sastri, Caturvedi. AG 2. Varanasi, 1947.

G1190 : Edited, with Gopāla Śāstri Nene's *Saralā* and editor's *Subodhinī*, by Rama Prasada Tripathi HKNMM 7. Varanasi, 1952.

G1191 : P.K. Gode, "The Chronology of the Works of Koṇḍabhaṭṭa (a Nephew of Bhaṭṭoji Dīkṣita), Between A.D. 1610 and 1660," ALB 18, 1954, 62–67. Reprinted in SILH 6.2, 237–241.

G1192 : Edited, with editor's *Śaṃkarī*, by Śaṃkara Śāstri Marulkara. ASS 135. Poona, 1957.

G1193 : Shivaram Dattatray Joshi, "Koṇḍabhaṭṭa on the Meaning of Sanskrit Verbs." Ph.D. diss., Harvard University, 1960.

G1194 : *Sphoṭanirṇaya* (chapter 14) edited and translated by S.D. Joshi. PCASS-C 2. Poona, 1967.

G1195 : Partially edited, with editor's *Bhaimī*, by Bhimasena Sastri. Delhi, 1969. See a1109.

G1196 : *Nāmārthanirṇaya* edited and translated in Madhav Murlidhar Deshpande, "Kauṇḍabhaṭṭa on the Philosophy of Nominal Meanings." Ph.D. diss., University of Pennsylvania, 1972.

G1197 : *Lakārārthanirṇaya* edited and translated in Jayashri Achyut Gune, *Kauṇḍabhaṭṭa on the Meaning of Verbal Endings*. Poona, 1978.

G1198 : S.D. Joshi, "Kauṇḍa Bhaṭṭa on the Meaning of Case-endings," VIJ 18, 1980, 88–95.

G1199 : ———, "Kauṇḍabhaṭṭa on *sphoṭa*," in *Gaurinath Sastri Festschrift*, pp. 221–23,

G1200 : ———, "Kauṇḍa Bhaṭṭa on the Meaning of Compounds," ALB 44–45, 1980–1981, 369–389.

ABHINAVA NṚSIṂHĀŚRAMA, pupil of Rāmacandrāśrama (1630?)
(NCat 1.304)

Nāmakārthaprakāśasaṃgraha, a Sārasvata work
(NCat 1.304)

MALLAYA YAJVAN, father of Tirumala Yajvan (1630)
(YM 2.419–420)

Ṭippaṇī on Kaiyaṭa's *Mahābhāṣyapradīpa*

JINAVIJAYA, pupil of Kirtivijaya (1637)
Vākyaprakāśavārta on Udayadharma's *Auktika*
(NCat 3.97)
NĪLAKAṆṬHA ŚUKLA (1637) (pupil of Bhaṭṭoji Dīkṣita)
Śabdaśobhā
(NCat 7.152; 10.173, 177)
RĀMAKṚṢṆA DĪKṢITA, son of Govardhana Dīkṣita (1638)
Gaṇapāṭha
(NCat 5.255)
CANDRAŚEKHARA (1638?)
Commentary on Puruṣottama's *Prayogaratnamālā*
(NCat 6.368)
DURGĀDĀSA VIDYĀVĀGĪŚA or VĀCASPATI (1639)
Dhātudīpikā or *Paribhāṣāṭīkā* on Vopadeva's *Kavikalpadruma*
See e1010; e1014; e1020; e1021; e1023; e1027.
Subodhā on Vopadeva's *Mugdhabodha*
(NCat 9.78)
See e1015; e1017; e1022; e1024; e1030; e1031.
NĀRĀYAṆA BHAṬṬATIRI or VAINATEYA of Kerala (1640)
(NCat 10.72)
Apāṇinīyapramāṇatā or *Parapakṣakhaṇḍana*
G1201 : Edited by E.V. Raman Namputri. Trivandrum, 1942.
G1202 : Edited and translated by E.R. Sreekrishna Sharma. SVUOJ 8, Supplement 1965.
Prakriyāsarvasva
G1203 : Edited by K. Sambasiva Sastri. TSS 106. Trivandrum, 1931.
G1204 : *Uṇādisūtras* published MUSS 7.2. Madras, 1933.
G1205 : Part 3 edited by V.A. Ramaswami with an English introduction by S. Venkitasubramonia Iyer. TSS 152. Trivandrum, 1947.
G1206 : S. Venkitasubramonia Iyer, *Nārāyaṇabhaṭṭa's Prakriyāsarvasva: A Critical Study*. KUDSP 7. Trivandrum, 1972.
G1207 : K.V. Sarma, "A Vindication of non-Pāṇinian Systems of Sanskrit Grammar," VIZ. 13, 1975, 275–283.
Dhātukāvya
G1208 : Edited with the *Kṛṣṇārpaṇa* and Rāmapaṇivada's *Vivaraṇa*. KUDSP 6. Trivandrum, 1970.
General
G1209 : K. Kunjunni Raja, "Students of Melputtur Nārāyaṇa Bhaṭṭa," SPAIOC 15, 1949, 61–62.
G1210 : ———, "The Date of Nārāyaṇa Bhaṭṭa," PAIOC 13, 1951, 183–186.
See a1107.
AUTHOR UNKNOWN (1640)
Bhoja Vyākaraṇa
G1211 : P.K. Gode, "Chronology of *Dharmapradīpa* and *Bhoja Vyākaraṇa*, Composed Under the Patronage of Rao Bhojarāja of Kaccha (A.D. 1631 to 1645)," PO 16, 1952, 40–47.
KAMALĀKARA BHAṬṬA (1640?)
(NCat 3.165)
?Commentary on Rāmacandra's *Prakriyākaumudī*
(NCat 3.160)
Vibhaktyarthaprakāśa
(NCat 3.165)

Vyākhyādarśa on Patañjali's *Mahābhāṣya*
(NCat 3.165)
NĀRĀYAṆA (ŚĀSTRIN) (1640) (disciple of Dharmarājādhvarin, father of Rāmakṛṣṇa Yajvan
(NCat 10.87)
Vyākhyā or *Kaṭhinaprakāśika* on Kaiyaṭa's *Mahābhāṣyapradīpa*
See e1059.
Commentary on Haradatta's *Padamañjarī*
Dīpaprabhā on *Praiṣa*
(NCat 10.87)
Dīpaprabhā on Kātyāyana's *Vārttikas* or *Vararucasaṃgraha*
See e505.
KṚṢṆA (1645)
Laghubodha, an elementary grammar
(NCat 4.294)
JÑĀNATILAKA (1646)
(Belvalkar, p. 86)
Siddhāntacandrikā on the *Sārasvatasūtras*
BHAVADEVA (1649)
Taddhitakośa
(NCat 8.85)
TĀRAKA BRAHMĀNANDA SARASVATĪ (1650)
Vyākaraṇakroḍapattra
(NCat 8.151)
?*Citprabhā* on a *Paribhāṣenduśekhara*
(NCat 8.151)
RAṄGANĀTHA DĪKṢITA (1650)
(NCat 4.120)
Makaranda or *Parimala* on Haradatta's *Padamañjarī*
(NCat 4.120)
RĀMABHAṬṬA (1650)
(Belvalkar, p. 84)
Vidvatprabodhinī or *Rāmabhaṭṭī*
NṚSIṂHA (1650)
Prakriyākalpavallarī on Dharmakīrti's *Rūpāvatara*
(NCat 10.190)
KEŚAVA (1650)
(NCat 5.60)
Manoramākhaṇḍana (vs. Bhaṭṭoji Dīkṣita)
(NCat 5.60)
RĀMANĀTHA VIDYĀVĀCASPATI (1650?)
(GOS 134, 1961, 324)
Rahasya or *Ṭīkā* on *Kātantra*
(NCat 3.314, 318)
JAYANTA (1650)
(Belvalkar, p. 51)
Tattvacandra on Rāmacandra's *Prakriyākaumudī*
(NCat 7.180)
COKKANĀTHA DĪKṢITA (1650)
(NCat 7.85)
Śabdakaumudī
(NCat 7.85)

Ratnāvalī on Patañjali's *Mahābhāṣya*
(NCat 7.85, 9.293)
G1212 : *Dhātu* section edited JSML 27, 1975, 1–16.
ĀPADEVA (1650)
Sphoṭanirūpaṇa
(NCat 2.125)
HAṂSAVIJAYAGAṆI (1650)
(Belvalkar, p. 84)
Śabdārthacandrikā on Anubhūti's *Sārasvataprakriyā*
JAGANNĀTHA PAṆḌITARĀJA TAILIṄGA (1650)
(NCat 7.137; G1624, p. 280)
Prauḍhamanoramākucamardana (vs. Bhaṭṭoji Dīkṣita)
(NCat 7.138)
Śabdakaustubhakhaṇḍana (vs. Bhaṭṭoji; lost?)
General
See a1127
VINAYAVIJAYAGAṆI (1652)
(Belvalkar, p. 66)
Haimalaghuprakriyā
KṢEMAṄKARA (1653)
(Belvalkar, p. 85)
Pratyayodbhedapaddhati
(NCat 5.162)
UDAYAKĪRTI, pupil of Sādhusundara (1654)
Vivṛti on Vimalakīrti's *Padavyavasthākārikā*
(NCat 11.102)
LAKṢMĪNṚSIṂHA (1660)
Vilāsa on Bhaṭṭoji's *Siddhāntakaumudī*
(MS listed in Adyar D, vol. 6, no. 353)
TIRUMALA YAJVAN or DVĀDAŚAHĀDHVARIN (1660)
(NCat 8.182; YM 2.413)
Sumanoramā on Bhaṭṭoji's *Siddhāntakaumudī*
(MS listed in Adyar D, vol. 6, no. 355)
?*Anupāta* on Patañjali's *Mahābhāṣya* (cf. ALB 3.1, 1939, 28)
ŚIVARĀMENDRA SARASVATĪ (1660)
Siddhāntaratnaprakāśa on Patañjali's *Mahābhāṣya*
See e1059.
G1213 : Pierre Filliozat, "Śivarāmendra Sarasvatī's Interpretation of 'sthānivad ādeśaḥ,' Pāṇini I.1.56," ABORI 58–59, 1978, 619–626.
Ratnākaraṭīkā on Bhaṭṭoji's *Siddhāntakaumudī*
(RĀMA) NĀRĀYAṆA (ŚARMAN) (VANDYOPĀDHYĀYA) (1664)
(NCat 10.85)
Śuddhi (tattva) kārikā
(NCat 10.85)
Sārāvalī and *Vṛtti* thereon
(NCat 10.94)
Dhāturatnākara
(NCat 10.85)
Kārikāvalī
(NCat 3.384)
VIDYĀVĀGĪŚA BHAṬṬĀCĀRYA (1665)

Vivṛti on Vararuci's (= Kātyāyana's?) *Kṛdākhyātavṛtti*
(NCat 4.281)

NĀRĀYAṆA (SĀDHU) of Didvana in Marwar (1667)
Nirṇaya or *Anuvṛttyavabodhaka* on the *Sārasvatasūtras*
(NCat 10.94)
G1214 : K.M.K. Sarma, "*Sārasvatasūtranirṇaya* of Nārāyaṇa Sādhu," IHQ 23, 1947, 334–335.

APPAYYA DĪKṢITA III or CINNA APPAYYA (1670)
Prasiddhaśabdasaṃskāra
(NCat 1.267)

HARI DĪKṢITA, grandson of Bhaṭṭoji, teacher of Nāgeśa (1670)
(G1624, p. 284; Cardona, p. 287)
Bṛhat Śabdaratna on Bhaṭṭoji Dīkṣita's *Prauḍhamanoramā*
See e1118; e1129.
G1215 : Kashinath Vasudev Abhyankar, "Date and Authorship of the *Śabdaratna* and the *Bṛhatśabdaratna*," ABORI 32, 1951, 258–262.
See e1122; e1123.
(?) *Laghu Śabdaratna* on Bhaṭṭoji Dīkṣita's *Prauḍhamanoramā* (authorship disputed; may be by Nāgeśa Bhaṭṭa)
See e1114; e1115; e1116; e1117; e1118.
G1216 : Edited, with Bhāgavata Hari Śāstrī's *Citraprabhā*, by Tata Subbaraya Sastri. Andh University Series 6. Waltair, 1932.
See e1119; e1120.
G1217 : K. V. Abhyankar, "Authorship of the *Laghuśabdaratna*," ABORI 45, 1964, 152–158.
G1218 : M. S. Bhat, "Authorship of the *Laghuśabdaratna*," HDVCV 1965, 203–206.
G1219 : V. S. Joshi, "Authorship of the *Laghuśabdaratna*," VJSPG, pp. 107–161.
General
G1220 : G. H. Khare, "Hari Dīkṣita and His Works," PO 9.1–2, 1944, 62–67.

JAGAN MOHANA PAṆḌITA (1670?)
(NCat 7.144; JBRS 4, 1918, 14ff.)
Prabodhacandrikā
(NCat 7.144)

SADĀŚIVA (1670?)
(YM 2.416)
Gūḍhārthadīpanī on Patañjali's *Mahābhāṣya*
(NCat 6.96)

SUDHĀNANDASŪRIŚIṢYA (1671)
Jalpamañjarī
(NCat 7.206)

GOPĀLA CAKRAVARTIN (BĀNARJI) (1672)
Arthadīpikā on Kramadīśvara's *Saṃkṣiptasāra*
(NCat 6.137)
Vasudhātukārikā
(NCat 6.137)

NĪLAKAṆṬHA DĪKṢITA [cf. N. Ramesan, *Sri Appayya Diksita* (Hyderabad, 1972), pp. 137–139] (1675)
Prakāśa on Kaiyaṭa's *Mahābhāṣyapradīpa*
(NCat 10.172)

HARI BHĀSKARA AGNIHOTRA (1677)
(YM 2.295) (NCat 11.221)
Paribhāṣābhāskara

G1221 : Edited in *Paribhāṣāsaṃgraha*, pp. 317–324.
DVĀDAŚĀHAYĀJIN BĀLAPATAÑJALI (1680)
Śābdikarakṣā on Cokkanātha's *Śabdakaumudī*
(NCat 9.20)
LOKEŚAKĀRA (1683)
(Belvalkar, p. 86)
Tattvadīpikā on Rāmāśrama's *Siddhāntacandrikā*
See e1133.
RĀMACANDRA VIDYĀBHŪṢAṆA (1688)
(Belvalkar, p. 90)
Paribhāṣāvṛtti, a Mugdhabodha work
(NCat 2.294)
RĀMACANDRA PAṆḌITA (1690)
Svaraprakriyā and autocommentary
G1222 : Edited by K. V. Abhyankar. ASS 138. Poona, 1974.
RĀMAKṚṢṆA BHAṬṬA (1690)
Siddhāntaratnākara on Bhaṭṭoji's *Siddhāntakaumudī*
(NCat 1.430)
RĀMABHADRA DĪKṢITA (1692)
Uṇādimaṇidīpikā
G1223 : Edited by K. Kunjunni Raja. AOR 21–23, 1966–1971. Reprinted Madras, 1972.
Ṣaḍdarśinisiddhāntasaṃgraha (grammar section)
(MS listed in TD no. 7631)
G1224 : Edited by A. Thiruvengadathan as part of his doctoral dissertation.
Śabdabhedanirūpaṇa
(MS listed in TD no. 5301)
See e1224.
Vyākhyā on Sīradeva's *Paribhāṣāvṛtti*
(NCat 11.224)
Prabhāvalī
G1225 : K. Kunjunni Raja, "*Prabhāvalī*, a Rare Work Dealing with Sanskrit Roots," JOR 19, 1949, 289–290.
"*Tarapatamapau gha*" *sūtravicāra*
(NCat 8.110)
MAHĀDEVA VEDĀNTIN (1694)
(NCat 2.292)
Uṇādikośa
G1226 : Edited by K. Kunjunni Raja. MUSS 21. Madras, 1956.
RĀMAPRASĀDA (1694)
Ṭīkā on Rāmanārāyaṇa's *Kārikāvalī*
ḌHUṆḌIRĀJA (1700)
Gīrvāṇapadamañjarī
G1227 : Edited, with Ḍhuṇḍirāja's *Gīrvāṇavanmañjarī*, by Umakant Premanand Shah. JOI Supplement to volumes, 7–9. Reprinted MSUOS 4. Baroda, 1960.
Gīrvāṇavanmañjarī
See e1227.
DHARMASŪRI (1700)
(YM 2.311; NCat 2.387)
Paribhāṣārthaprakāśikā
(NCat 9.221, 274)
RĀMACANDRA (1700?)

(NCat 3. 312; Belvalkar, pp. 74, 75)

Kalāpatattvabodhinī on Trilocana's *Kātantravārttikapañjikā*

(NCat 3.312, 316)

MEGHAVIJAYA (1700)

(NCat 6.362) (Belvalkar, p. 66)

Haimakaumudī or *Candraprabhāvyākaraṇa*

See e921.

Śabdacandrikā on Hemacandra's *Śabdānuśāsana*

(NCat 4.283)

VAIDYANĀTHA DĪKṢITA or ŚĀSTRIN (1705)

Vyākhyā on Cokkanātha's *Śabdakaumudī* (MS listed in Adyar D, vol. 6, no. 177)

Paribhāṣārthasaṃgraha or *Paribhāṣāvṛttivyākhyā*

(NCat 11.222)

Paribhāṣopanyasa (lost)

NĀGEŚA or NĀGOJI BHAṬṬA (1714)

(Cardona, p. 287; G1624, p. 290)

(*Bṛhat*) *Śabdenduśekhara* on Bhaṭṭoji Dīkṣita's *Siddhāntakaumudī*

G1228 : Edited by Sitaram Shastri. 3 volumes. SBGM 87. Varanasi, 1960.

Laghu Śabdenduśekhara on Bhaṭṭoji Dīkṣita's *Siddhāntakaumudī*

G1229 : Edited, with Bhairava Miśra's *Candrakalā*, by Ganesadatta Sarma Miśra. Varanasi, 1866.

G1230 : Edited by Ramasastri Manavalli and Narayana Sastri Bharadvaja. Varanasi, 1887.

G1231 : Edited, with Bhairava Miśra's *Candrakalā*, by Sita Rama Sastri Sendiy. Varanasi, 1911.

G1232 : Edited with editor's *Dīpaka* by Nityananda Panta Parvatiya. Varanasi, 1918.

G1233 : Edited, with Bhairava Miśra's *Candrakalā*, by Narahari Sastri Pendse. 2 volumes. KSS 5. Varanasi, 1922, 1927.

G1234 : Edited up to Avyayi section, with Nityananda Panta Parvatiya's *Dīpaka*, by Gopal Shastri Nene. KSS 27. Varanasi, 1925.

G1235 : Edited with editor's *Guruprasāda* by Tata Subrahmanya Sastrin. Madras, 1926.

G1236 : Edited, with an *Abhinavacandrikā*, Vaidyanātha Paiyaguṇḍa's *Cidasthimālā*, Sadāśiva Bhaṭṭa's *Sadāśivabhaṭṭī*, a *Viṣamapadavivṛti*, Udayankar Nānapāṭhaka's *Jyotsnā*, a *Vijayā* and a *Varṇinī*, by Guru Prasad Shastri. RSCG 14. Varanasi, 1936.

G1237 : Edited, with Khuddi Jhā Śarmā's *Nāgeśoktiprakāśa*, by Sudama Miśra Sastri and Sadasiva Sastri Joshi. KSS 128. Varanasi, 1938.

Vaiyākaraṇa (*laghu*) *siddhāntamañjūṣā*

G1238 : Edited, with Durbala's *Kuñjikā* and Balambhaṭṭa's *Kalā*, by Madhava Sastri Bhandari, Madan Mohan Pathak and Nityananda Panta Parvatiya. CHSS 44. Varanasi, 1913–1926.

G1239 : Edited up to the end of the *Tātparyanirūpaṇa* section, with editor's *Ratnaprabhā*, by Sabhapati Sarma Upadhyaya. KSS 163. Varanasi, 1963.

G1240 : Edited by Kalika Prasada Shukla. Varanasi, 1977.

Paramalaghumañjūṣā

G1241 : Edited Varanasi, 1887.

G1242 : Edited by Nityananda Panta Parvatiya. Varanasi, 1913.

G1243 : Edited, with Śivānanda Pāṇḍeya's *Ratnadīpikā*. Varanasi, 1933.

G1244 : Edited, with editor's *Arthadīpikā* and notes by Nityananda Pant Parvatiya, by Sadasiva Sarma Sastri (Joshi). HSS 43. Varanasi, 1946, 1974.
G1245 : Edited, with editor's *Jyotsnā*, by Kalika Prasad Shukla. MSURS 7. Baroda, 1961.
G1246 : Kapil Deva Shastri, "On the Authenticity of *Parama-laghu-mañjūṣā*," CDSFV 1974, 299–304.
G1247 : Edited in Kapil Deva Shastri, *A Critical Study of the Paramalaghumañjūṣā*. Kurukṣetra, 1975.

Uddyota on Kaiyaṭa's *Mahābhāṣyapradīpa*
See e521.
See e524; e529; e550.
G1248 : Edited by Bahuvallabha Sastri. 4 volumes. BI 142. Calcutta, 1901–1910.
See e552; e574; e575; e582; e598; e611; e622.

Paribhāṣenduśekhara
G1249 : Edited Varanasi, 1854.
G1250 : Edited by F. Kielhorn. BSPS 2, 7, 9, 12. Bombay, 1868, 1874. Revised edition by K.V. Abhyankar, with V.S. Abhyankar's *Tattvadarśa*. Poona, 1962.
G1251 : Edited by Taranatha Tarkavacaspati. Calcutta, 1872.
G1252 : Edited, with editor's *Ṭippaṇīsārāsāraviveka*, by Balasastrin Ranade. Varanasi, 1885.
G1252A : Edited, with editor's *Ambākartrī*, by Govinda Bharadvaja Sastri. Poona, 1885.
G1253 : Edited, with Bhairava Miśra's *Vivṛti*. Varanasi, 1886.
G1254 : Edited with editor's *Bhūti* by Ramakrsna (Tatyasastri). Varanasi, 1897, 1912, 1926.
G1255 : Edited with Viśvanātha Bhaṭṭa's commentary. Tanjore, 1910–1915.
G1256 : Partly edited by Balakrsna Sastri. Varanasi, 1912.
G1257 : Edited, with Vaidyanātha Payaguṇḍe's *Gadā*, by Ganesa Sastri Gokhale. ASS 72. Poona, 1913.
G1258 : Edited, with Bhairava Miśra's *Bhairavī* and editor's *Tattvaprakāśikā*, by Lakshmana Tripathi. KSS 31. Varanasi, 1915, 1931.
G1259 : Edited, with Jayadeva Miśra's *Vijaya*, by Madhusudana Sarma Misra. Varanasi, 1915.
G1260 : Edited, with Raghunātha Śāstrī Vyākaraṇācārya's *Laghuṭīkā*, by Ananta Saṣtri Phadke. KSS 19. Varanasi, 1924.
G1261 : Edited, with Venimādhava's *Bṛhadaśāstrārthakalā*, by Rajanarayana Sastri. KSS 137. Varanasi, 1943.
See a972.
G1262 : Hartmut Scharfe, "Kleine Nachlese zu Kielhorns Übersetzung von Nagojibhaṭṭa's *Paribhāṣenduśekhara*," *Asiatica* 1954, 570–574.
G1263 : Louis Renou, "Études paninéennes : Le *Paribhāṣenduśekhara*... L'arrangement des *paribhāṣā* chez Nagojibhaṭṭa," PICI 2. Paris, 1956, pp. 132–149.
G1264 : Edited, with Jayadeva Sarma Misra's *Jayā*, by Umesa Misra Sarma. Allahabad, 1968.

Viṣamapadī on Bhaṭṭoji Dīkṣita's *Śabdakaustubha*
(NCat 10.21)

Vaiyākaraṇakārikā
(NCat 10.22)

Śabdānantasāgarasamuccaya
(NCat 10.22)

Suptiṅantasāgarasamuccaya
(NCat 10.22)
Prabhākaracandra on a *Tattvadīpikā*
(NCat 8.48)
Sphoṭavāda
G1265 : Edited, with editor's *Subodhinī*, by V. Krsnamacarya. ALS 55. Madras, 1946.
Jñāpakasaṃgraha
G1266 : Edited, with editor's *Vivṛti*, by N.S. Ramanuja Tatacarya. KSVS 18. Tirupati, 1972.
General
G1267 : M.V. Mahashabde, "The Penetrating Style of Nāgoji Bhaṭṭa," SPAIOC 15, 1949, 53–54.
G1268 : P.K. Gode, "The Relative Chronology of Some Works of Nāgojibhaṭṭa Between c. A.D. 1670 and 1750," OT 1.2, 1955, 45–52. Reprinted in SJS 38, 1956, 212–219.
G1269 : Paul Thieme, "The Interpretation of the Learned," FVSKB pp. 47–62. Reprinted in Budruss, pp. 596–611.
G1270 : S.D. Joshi, "Nāgeśa on the Guiding Principles of Constructional Meaning," SPAIOC 21, 1959, 198–199.
G1271 : Ludo Rocher and Rosane Debels, "La Valeur des termes et formules techniques dans la grammaire indienne, d'après Nāgeśabhaṭṭa," AIPHOS 15, 1960, 129–151.
G1272 : Uma Sankar Sarman, "Nāgeśa's treatment of *lakṣaṇāvṛtti*," SPAIOC 23.1, 1966, 57.
G1273 : Vidyadhar Dharmadhikar, "Nāgeśa: His Life and Works and Contribution to Sanskrit Grammar." Ph.D. diss., Allahabad University, 1966.

ŚRĪVALLABHAVĀCAKA or ŚRĪVALLABHAVĀCĀRYA (1718)
(GOS 134, 1961, 198; NCat 9.75; Belvalkar, p. 66)
Durgaprabodha on Hemacandra's *Liṅgānuśāsana*
(NCat 9.75)

(MAHĀBHĀṢYA) GOPĀLA KṚṢṆA ŚĀSTRIN (1720)
(NCat 6.136, 1.259)
Śābdikacintāmaṇi on Patañjali's *Mahābhāṣya* (MSS available)
Commentary on *Uṇādisūtras*
Lalita on Bhaṭṭoji Dīkṣita's *Siddhāntakaumudī*, completed by his son Anantanārāyaṇa
(NCat 6.136)

TIRUMALA BUKKAPATTANAM ŚRĪNIVĀSĀCĀRYA (1720)
Gajāsūtravāda
(NCat 5.231)

VEṄKAṬEŚVARA (1722)
Uṇādighaṇṭu
(NCat 2.293)

KĀŚĪNĀTHA (1725)
Dhātumañjarī
G1274 : Edited by Charles Wilkins. 1815.

APPA SŪRI or SUDHI (1730)
(NCat 1.270)
Śabdaratnāvalī
Vyākhyā on Vaidyanātha Śāstrin's *Paribhāṣārthasaṃgraha*.
(NCat 11.222)
Paribhāṣāratna
(Adyar D, vol. 6, no. 480)

JÑĀNENDRA SARASVATĪ (1730?)
(Cardona, p. 286; G1624, p. 278)
Tattvabodhinī on Bhaṭṭoji Dīkṣita's *Siddhāntakaumudī*, completed by Jayakṛṣṇa Maunin as *Subodhinī*
See e1074; e1082; e1083; e1100.
DHARAṆĪDHARA (1730)
(NCat 9.237)
Bodhapaddhatī MSS (available)
KĀŚĪŚVARA ŚARMAN (1739)
Jñānāmṛta
(NCat 4.142)
SVAYAMPRAKĀŚĀNANDA (1740)
Candrikā on Vaidyanātha Śāstrin's *Paribhāṣārthasaṃgraha*
(NCat 6.378, 11.222)
VAIDYANĀTHA PAIYAGUṆḌA or BALAMBHAṬṬA (1740)
(NCat 1.389)
Arthasaṃgraha
(NCat 1.389)
Prabhā on Bhaṭṭoji Dīkṣita's *Śabdakaustubha*
Bhāvaprakāśikā on Nāgeśa Bhaṭṭa's *Bṛhacchabdenduśekhara*
Cidasthimālā on Nāgeśa Bhaṭṭa's *Laghuśabdenduśekhara*
See e1236.
Kāśikā or *Gadā* on Nageśa Bhaṭṭa's *Paribhāṣenduśekhara*
See e1257.
Bhāvaprakāśikā on Hari Dīkṣita's *Śabdaratna*
Chāyā on Nāgeśa's *Mahābhāṣyapradīpoddyota*
See e622.
Kalā on Nāgeśa Bhaṭṭa's *Vaiyākaraṇasiddhāntamañjūṣā*
See e1238.
Bhāvaprakāśa on Bhaṭṭoji Dīkṣita's *Prauḍhamanoramā*
See e1120.
RĀMACANDRA (1744)
(GOS 134, 1961, 323)
Vṛttisaṃgraha on Pāṇini's *Aṣṭādhyāyī*
(NCat 1.472)
SATYAPRIYA TĪRTHA SVĀMIN (1745)
Vivaraṇa on Patañjali's *Mahābhāṣya* (MSS available)
JAYAKṚṢṆA MAUNIN (1745)
Sāramañjarī or *Śābdabodhaprakāśa*
(NCat 7.169)
Śabdārthatarkāmṛta
(NCat 7.160)
Subodhinī, completion of Jñānendra Sarasvatī's *Tattvabodhinī* on Bhaṭṭoji Dīkṣita's *Siddhāntakaumudī*
See e1074; e1082; e1083.
Ṭīkā on Varadarāja's *Madhyasiddhāntakaumudī*
(NCat 7.169)
Ṭīkā on Varadarāja's *Laghusiddhāntakaumudī*
(NCat 7.169)
(*Sphoṭacandrikā*: this work actually by Jayakṛṣṇa's brother Śrīkṛṣṇa. See below.)
HARI VALLABHA (1747)
Darpaṇa on Koṇḍa Bhaṭṭa's *Vaiyākaraṇabhūṣaṇasāra*

See e1179; e1187; e1188; e1189.

ŚIVARĀMA TRIPĀṬHIN (1750)

Vidyāvilāsa on Bhaṭṭoji Dīkṣita's *Siddhāntakaumudī*

G1275 : P.K. Gode, "*Vidyāvilāsa*, a Commentary on the *Siddhānta-kaumudī* by Śivarāma Tripāṭhin (Between A.D. 1700 and 1775)," ALB 15, 1951, 62–67. Reprinted in SJS 37, 1953, 237–241.

Uṇādikośa or *Lakṣmīnivāsābhidhāna*

G1276 : Edited Varanasi, 1873.

ŚRĪKṚṢṆA (BHAṬṬA) (MAUNIN) (1750)

Sphoṭacandrikā

See e1125; e1182.

Tarkacandrikā

(NCat 8.112)

Vṛttidīpikā

G1277 : Edited by Gangadhara Sastri Bharadvaja. POWSBT 29. Varanasi, 1930.

G1278 : Edited RPG 7. Jodhpur, 1956.

Ākhyātārthacandrikā (*nirṇaya*)

(NCat 2.11)

Kārakavāda or *Vibhaktyarthanirṇaya*

G1279 : Edited Bombay.

Lakārārthanirṇaya

(NCat 4.292)

Prakāśa on Rāmacandra's *Prakriyākaumudī*

See e1053.

(VARKHEDI) TIMMAṆĀCĀRYA (1750)

Pratyāhārasūtravicāra

(NCat 8.180)

VĀSUDEVA DĪKṢITA (1750)

(Cardona, p. 286; G1624, p. 279)

Bālamanoramā on Bhaṭṭoji Dīkṣita's *Siddhāntakaumudī*

See e1080; e1087; e1095; G1100; G1101.

(RĀJA ŚRĪ) VEṆĪMĀDHAVA (ŚŪKLA) (1750)

Kaumudīkalpalatikā

G1280 : Edited by Sri Rajanarayana Sukla. HSS 28. Varanasi, 1934.

Bṛhadaśāstrārthakalā on Nāgeśa Bhaṭṭa's *Paribhāṣenduśekhara*

See e1261.

NĪLAKAṆṬHA DĪKṢITA (1750?)

(NCat 10.173)

Paribhāṣāvṛtti

G1281 : Edited by T. Ganapati Sastri. TSS 46. Trivandrum, 1915.

G1282 : Edited in *Paribhāṣāsaṃgraha*, pp. 293–316.

Tattvaviveka on Patañjali's *Mahābhāṣya*

(NCat 10.173)

Gūḍhārthadīpikā on Jñānendra's *Tattvabodhinī*

(Adyar D, vol. 6, p. 117)

Laghuśabdakaustubha

(Adyar D, vol. 6, p. 117)

Kṛtprakāśa

(NCat 4.273)

Vyākhyā on Rāmacandra's *Prakriyāsarvasva*

(NCat 10.373)

ABHINAVA KĀLIDĀSA or UMĀMAHEŚVARA (1750)
Pāṇinīyavādanakṣatramālā
(NCat 1.298, 9.317)
ŚEṢĀDRISUDHI (1750)
(GOS 134, 1961, 394; NCat 11.22)
Paribhāṣābhāskara
G1283 : Edited in *Paribhāṣāsaṃgraha*, pp. 378–465.
KUPPU ŚĀSTRIN (1750)
(GOS 134, 1961, 126)
Critique of a *Paribhāṣābhāskara*
(NCat 4.197)
ANANTANĀRĀYAṆA ŚĀSTRIN (1750)
Continuation of Gopālakṛṣṇa Śāstrin's *Mahābhāṣya-Śābdikacintāmaṇi*
(NCat 6.136)
Continuation of Gopālakṛṣṇa Śāstrin's *Siddhāntakaumudī-Lalita*
(NCat 6.136)
LAKṢMINṚSIṂHA (1750)
Triśikhā on Nāgeśa Bhaṭṭa's *Paribhāṣenduśekhara*
(NCat 11.227)
NĀRĀYAṆA (SUDHI) (1750)
Pradīpa or *Śābdabhūṣaṇa* on Pāṇini's *Aṣṭādhyāyī*
(NCat 10.75)
Śabdabhedanirūpaṇa
(NCat 10.75)
Śabdamañjarī
(NCat 10.75)
PERUSŪRI (1755)
(NCat 3.98)
Auṇādikapadārṇava on *Uṇādisūtras*
G1284 : Edited by T.R. Chintamani. MUSS 7.4. Madras, 1939.
APPAYYA DĪKṢITA, pupil of Gopālakṛṣṇa Śāstrin (1760)
(NCat 1.259, 269)
Pāṇinīyasūtraprakāśa
(NCat 1.471)
RĀDHĀKṚṢṆA ŚARMAN (1764) (probably of the Jumara school)
(NCat 9.293)
Dhāturatnāvalī
(NCat 9.293)
ĀŚĀDHARA BHAṬṬA (1770?)
(NCat 2.19; 8.268)
Pūrvapakṣapraśnottarī or *-mañjarī*
(NCat 2.19; 8.268)
Padasaṃjñāvicāra
Śabdatriveṇikā
G1285 : Edited by Batuka Natha Sarma. POWSBT 14. Varanasi, 1925.
G1286 : Edited by Kaliprasad Sukla. Varanasi, 1957.
General
G1287 : Umakant P. Shah, "A Note on Āśādhara Bhaṭṭa and His Works," VRFV 1975, 351–359.
RĀMASEVAKA (1770)
(YM 2.423)
Vyākhyā on Kaiyaṭa's *Mahābhāṣyapradīpa* (mss. available)

ŚAṂKARA BHAṬṬA (1770)
Ṭikā on Nāgeśa Bhaṭṭa's *Laghuśabdenduśekhara*
(Adyar D, vol. 6, no. 347)
Vyākhyā or *Śaṃkarī* on Nāgeśa Bhaṭṭa's *Paribhāṣenduśekhara*
(NCat 11.228)

NĀGOBA PAṆḌITA (1775)
Sadbhāṣāsubantarāpadarśā
(NCat 10.23)

SADĀŚIVA BHAṬṬA (1780)
(GOS 134, 1961, 412)
Commentary on Nāgeśa Bhaṭṭa's *Paribhāṣenduśekhara*
(NCat 11.228)
Sadāśivabhaṭṭī on Nāgeśa Bhaṭṭa's *Laghuśabdenduśekhara*
See e1236.

KṚṢṆA MIŚRA (1780)
(NCat 4.344)
Kṛṣṇamiśraprakriyā
(NCat 4.344)

ŚIVARĀMENDRA YATI (1780)
Commentary on Pāṇini's *Aṣṭādhyāyī* 1.3.67 (= *Gajāsūtra*)
(NCat 5.231)

VEṄKATADĀSA or VEṄKATĀCĀRYA III (1780)
Gajāsūtravāda or *Neranāvatīsūtravyākhyā*
G1288 : Edited by R.V. Krishnamachariar. 1909.

KALYĀṆA SARASVATĪ (1790)
(Belvalkar, p. 86)
Laghusārasvata
(NCat 3.259)

BHĪMĀCĀRYA GALAGALI (1796)
Arthamañjarī on Nāgeśa Bhaṭṭa's *Paribhāṣenduśekhara*
(NCat 110.222, 227)

HARIRĀMA KALĀ (1797)
(NCat 4.116)
Kāśikā on Koṇḍa Bhaṭṭa's *Vaiyākaraṇabhūṣaṇasāra*
See e1185.

BHAVADEVA MIŚRA (1799)
Commentary on Hari Dīkṣita's *Śabdaratna* (lost?)

KULAMUNI (1800)
Samāsārṇava
(NCat 4.239)

INDRADATTA UPĀDHYĀYA (1800)
(NCat 2.251–252)
Śabdatattvaprakāśa (MSS available)
Śabdakaustubhaguṇa (lost)
Gūḍhaphakkikaprakāśa on Bhaṭṭoji Dīkṣita's *Siddhāntakaumudī*
G1289 : Edited by Indra Dutt Sharma. KSS 47. Varanasi, 1906.

GOPĀLĀCĀRYA or ŚRĪRĀMĀCĀRYA or GOPĀLADEVA VIDYĀVĀGĪŚA (1800)
Kāntimālā on Puruṣottama Vidyāvāgīśa's *Prayogaratnamālā*
(NCat 6.155)

DURBALĀCĀRYA or KṚṢṆA MITRA (ĀCĀRYA) (1800)
Kuñcikā on Nāgeśa Bhaṭṭa's *Vaiyākaraṇasiddhāntamañjūṣā*
See e1238.

Ṭīkā on Koṇḍa Bhaṭṭa's *Vaiyākaraṇabhūṣaṇa*
See e1188.
Commentary on Nāgeśa Bhaṭṭa's *Paribhāṣenduśekhara* (MSS available)
Bhāvapradīpa on Bhaṭṭoji Dīkṣita's *Śabdakaustubha*
(Adyar D, vol. 6, nos. 133–136)
Kalpalatā on Bhaṭṭoji Dīkṣita's *Prauḍhamanoramā*
G1290 : Edited in Vyakaranagrantharatnavali 7–12. Tanjore, 1910–1915.
Ratnārṇava on Bhaṭṭoji Dīkṣita's *Siddhāntakaumudī*
(NCat 4.344)
Yuktiratnākara
(NCat 4.343)
Vādacūḍāmaṇi
(NCat 4.344)
KĀRTTIKEYA SIDDHĀNTA BHAṬṬĀCĀRYA (1800?)
Subodhā on the *Mugdhabodha*
(NCat 4.7)
GAṄGĀDHARA (1800?)
(NCat 5.198)
Induprakāśa on Nāgeśa Bhaṭṭa's *Laghuśabdenduśekhara*
(NCat 5.198)
Induprakāśa on Nāgeśa Bhaṭṭa's *Paribhāṣenduśekhara*
(NCat 5.198)
DHARAṆĪDHARA (1809)
(NCat 1.472, 9.237)
Vaiyākaraṇasarvasva on Pāṇini's *Aṣṭādhyāyī*, completed by Kāśinātha
See e26.
ŚIVABHAṬṬA (1810)
(GOS 134, 1961, 391)
Kusumavikāsa on Haradatta's *Padamañjarī*
(NCat 4.120)
MANNU or MANYU or GOPĀLA DEVA (1815)
(NCat 6.142)
Laghubhūṣaṇasārakānti on Koṇḍa Bhaṭṭa's *Vaiyākaraṇabhūṣaṇasāra*
(NCat 6.142)
Doṣoddhāra on Nāgeśa Bhaṭṭa's *Laghuśabdenduśekhara*
(NCat 6.142)
Arthavatsūtravāda
(NCat 1.386)
Gajāsūtravādārtha or *-vicāra*
(NCat 5.231)
Kāṇṭakoddhāra or *Doṣoddhāra* on Nāgeśa Bhaṭṭa's *Paribhāṣenduśekhara*
(NCat 5.231, 6.142, 11.227)
UDAYAṄKARA NĀNAPĀTHAKA (1800)
(NCat 8.377)
Jyotsnā on Nāgeśa Bhaṭṭa's *Śabdenduśekhara*
See e1236.
Anekamanyapadārthasūtravicāra
(NCat 2.326)
Mitāvṛttyarthasaṃgraha on Pāṇini's *Aṣṭādhyāyī*
(NCat 2.326)
Paribhāṣāpradīpārcis
(NCat 2.326; 11.220)

Bahuvrīhyarthavicāra
(NCat 2.326)
KĀŚINĀTHA (1820?)
Completion of Dharaṇīdhara's *Vaiyākaraṇasarvasva*
See e26.
BHAIRAVA MIŚRA (1824)
Sphoṭaparīkṣā on Koṇḍa Bhaṭṭa's *Vaiyākaraṇabhūṣaṇasāra*
See e1182; e1188.
Candrakalā on Nāgeśa Bhaṭṭa's *Laghuśabdenduśekhara*
See e1229; e1231; e1233.
Gadā on Nāgeśa Bhaṭṭa's *Paribhāṣenduśekhara*
See e1253; e1258.
Bhairavī on Hari Dīkṣita's *Śabdaratna*
See e1118; e1120.
General
G1291 : M.S. Bhat, "Bhairava Miśra Circa 1780–1840 A.D.," IHQ 35, 1959, 76–78
DHARĀNANDA (1825)
Phakkikadarpaṇa
(NCat 9.239)
KOCCA SANKARAN SUSAD (1825)
Dhātupāṭhakārikā
Arthaprakāśikā on Bhaṭṭoji Dīkṣita's *Siddhāntakaumudī*
KUMĀRA TATĀYA (1825)
(YM 2.415)
Pārijātam Nāṭakam on Patañjali's *Mahābhāṣya* (MSS available)
GOVINDA BHĀRADVĀJA ŚĀSTRIN (1835)
Ambākartrī on Nāgeśa Bhaṭṭa's *Paribhāṣenduśekhara*
See e1252A.
BHĀRATA MALLIKA or BHĀRATASENA MALLIṢENA (1836? But NCat 3.379 says 1750)
Upasargavṛtti
(NCat 2.375)
Kārakollāsa
G1292 : Edited by Janakinatha Sahityasastri. SSPS 8. Calcutta, 1924.
Ekavarṇārthasaṃgraha
G1293 : Edited by Suresh Chandra Banerji. ISH 36, 1960, 29, 34.
Gaṇapāṭha (according to Mugdhabodha principles)
(NCat 5.256)
Drutabodha and *Drutabodhinī* thereon
(NCat 9.187)
GOKULACANDRA (1839)
(YM 1.496)
Vṛtti on Pāṇini's *Aṣṭādhyāyī*
(NCat 1.472, 6.110)
SATĀRĀ RĀGHAVENDRĀCĀRYA (GAJENDRAGADKAR) (1840)
(YM 2.417; BNK Sarma 2.358; NCat 3.379, 10.166)
Candrikā on Nāgeśa Bhaṭṭa's *Laghuśabdenduśekhara*
(MS at 594)
Tripathagā on Nāgeśa Bhaṭṭa's, *Paribhāṣenduśekhara*
(NCat 11.227)
Prabhā on Bhaṭṭoji Dīkṣita's *Śabdakaustubha*
Tripathagā on Patañjali's *Mahābhāṣya* (MSS available)

Prabhā on the *Kāraka* section of Hari Dīkṣita's *Śabdaratna*
G1294 : Edited by R.V. Krishnamachariar in Vyakaranagrantharatnavali 19–21. Tanjore, 1912.
VIPRARĀJENDRA (1845)
Maṇiratnaprabhā on Patañjali's *Mahābhāṣya*
See e537.
VIŚVANĀTHA DAṆḌIBHAṬṬA (1850?)
(GOS 134, 1961, 363)
Candrikā on Nāgeśa Bhaṭṭa's *Paribhāṣenduśekhara*
(NCat 6.178, 11.228)
LĀLĀ VIHĀRIN (1850)
(Abhyankar, p. 332)
Commentary on Nāgeśa Bhaṭṭa's *Paribhāṣenduśekhara*
(NCat 11.227)
HARIRĀMA (1850?)
Candrikā or *Vyākhyāsāra*
G1295 : Edited Calcutta, 1905.
Taddhitacandrikā
(NCat 13.85)
Commentary on Haribhāskara's *Paribhāṣābhāskara*
(NCat 11.221)
HARINĀTHA DVIVEDIN (1850)
(Abhyankar, p. 444)
Akāṇḍatāṇḍava on Nāgeśa Bhaṭṭa's *Paribhāṣenduśekhara*
DAYĀNANDA (SVĀMIN) SARASVATĪ (1850)
(GOS 134, 1961, 196)
Bhāṣya on Pāṇini's *Aṣṭādhyāyī*
See e63.
G1296 : Edited by Raghuvira Jijnasu and Brahmadatta Jijnasu. 2 volumes. Ajmer, 1940–1962.
See a121, a125, e241.
Bhāṣya on Pāṇini's *Uṇādisūtras*
See e416, e420.
Commentary on Pāṇini's (?) *Pāṇinīyaśikṣā*
See e429.
Avyayārtha
G1297 : Edited Ajmer, 1919.
Kārakīya
G1298 : Published in Vedangaprakasa 6. Allahabad, 1891.
General
G1299 : S.K. Gupta, "A Study of Dayānanda," PO 13.1–2, 1948, 30–33; 13.3–4, 1948, 3–9.
G1300 : ———, "Nature and Authorship of the Grammatical Work Attributed to Maharṣi Dayānanda Sarasvatī," PAIOC17, 1953, 93–94.
Ṭippaṇī on Patañjali's *Mahābhāṣya*
See e522; e547.
BĀLA ŚĀSTRIN RĀṆADE (1850)
(Abhyankar, p. 427)
Sārāsāraviveka on Nāgeśa Bhaṭṭa's *Paribhāṣenduśekhara*
See e1885 e1252.
GAṄGĀDHARA KAVIRĀJA (VAIDYA) (1850)
(NCat 5.202–203)

Trikāṇḍaśabdaśāsana
G1301 : Published.
Trisūtravyākaraṇa
G1302 : Published.
Setusaṃgraha on the *Mugdhabodha*
See e1012.
Commentary on Kātyāyana's *Vārttika*
Chandaprakāśa on Pāṇini's *Aṣṭādhyāyī*
(NCat 5.206)
RŪPACANDRA (1853)
Ṭīkā on Varadarāja's *Laghusiddhāntakaumudī*
See e1149.
SUBRAHMAṆYAM NAMBUTTIRIPAD (1860)
Prasāda on Nāgeśa Bhaṭṭa's *Laghuśabdenduśekhara*
Dhātusaṃgraha
(NCat 7.92)
TĀRĀNĀTHA TARKAVĀCASPATI (1867)
Āśubodhavyākaraṇa
G1303 : Published Calcutta, 1867, 1873.
(*Tarka*) *Ratnamālā*
(NCat 8.123)
Saralā on Bhaṭṭoji Dīkṣita's *Siddhāntakaumudī*
See e1075.
Dhāturūpādarśa
G1304 : Published Calcutta, 1869.
JARANĀTHA TARKAVĀCASPATI (1870)
Commentary on Bhaṭṭoji Dīkṣita's *Siddhāntakaumudī*
See e1077.
RAGHURĀMA 1871
(NCat 3.62)
Ekadaśakārikā
G1305 : Published Bombay, 1871.
YAJÑEŚVARA BHAṬṬA (1874)
(YM 2.139)
Gaṇaratnāvalī
G1306 : Published Baroda, 1874.
DEVĪDIN (1875)
Commentary on Pāṇini's *Aṣṭādhyāyī*
(NCat 1.472)
CANDRAKĀNTA TARKĀLAṂKĀRA (1880)
Ṭīkā on Trilocanadāsa's *Kātantrapañjikā*
See e644.
Chandaḥprakriyā on Śarvavarman's *Kātantrasūtras*
See e651.
?*Kaumudīsudhākara*
G1307 : Published Calcutta, 1888.
RĀMATARAṆA ŚIROMAṆI (1883)
Kāracakra
G1308 : Published 1883–1886, 1888.
KĀLĪCARAṆA VIDYOPĀDHYĀYA (1887)
Pāṇinīyatattvadarpaṇa (with Sūrya Prasāda Miśra)
G1309 : Published Varanasi, 1887.

MĀDHAVA (1887)
Mādhavī on Anubhūti's *Sārasvataprakriyā*
See e996.
GOVINDA PARAŚURĀMA BHAṬṬA (1888)
Ṭippaṇī on Anubhūti's *Sārasvataprakriyā*
See e997.
ŚRĪDHARA ŚARMAN (1889)
Vyākhyā on Nāgeśa Bhaṭṭa's *Laghuśabdenduśekhara*
G1310 : Published Varanasi, 1889.
BHAGAVAT PRASĀDA ŚARMAN (1890)
Ṭippaña on Jayāditya/Vāmana's *Kāśikā*
See e846.
BĀLAKṚṢṆA ŚARMAN YOGI (1895)
Commentary on Varadarāja's *Madhyasiddhāntakaumudī*
See e1139.
SETUMĀDHAVĀCĀRYA NADITIRAM (1895)
Bhāvabodhinī on Nāgeśa Bhaṭṭa's *Laghuśabdenduśekhara*
(Adyar D, vol. 6, p. 107)
RĀMAKṚṢṆA (TĀTYĀŚĀSTRIN) (1897)
Bhūti on Nāgeśa Bhaṭṭa's *Paribhāṣenduśekhara*
See e1254.
DVĀRAKĀNĀTHA NYĀYABHŪṢAṆA (1899)
Avyayakośa
G1311 : Published Calcutta, 1899.
RĀMA PAṆḌITAVARA (SĀHIBHA) (1900?)
Commentary on Kashmiri recension of *Kātantra*
(NCat 3.317)
YĀGEŚVARA (1900)
Haimavatī on Nāgeśa Bhaṭṭa's *Paribhāṣenduśekhara*
MAHENDRANĀTHA BHAṬṬĀCĀRYA (1900)
Ṭīkā on Śarvavarman's *Kātantrasūtras*
See e652.
HARI ŚARMAN (1900)
(NCat 2.98)
Vākyārthacandrikā on Nāgeśa Bhaṭṭa's *Paribhāṣenduśekhara*
(NCat 4.128, 11.228)
Citraprabhā on Hari Dīkṣita's *Śabdaratna*
G1312 : Edited by Tata Subbaraya Sastri. Andhra University Series 6. Waltair, 1932.
GAṆAPATI ŚĀSTRĪ (1900)
(NCat 5.248)
Gajāsūtravādārtha
(NCat 5.231)
ANANTĀCĀRYA (1900)
(NCat 1.186)
Commentary on the *Tiṅanta* portion of Nāgeśa Bhaṭṭa's *Śabdenduśekhara*
(NCat 1.286)
GOVINDASIṂHA (1900)
Viṣamasthalaṭippaṇa on Varadarāja's *Madhyasiddhāntakaumudī*
See e1141.
RĀMAKIŚORA ŚARMAN (1905)
Aṣṭamaṅgala on Śarvavarman's *Kātantrasūtras*
See e653.

NAVACANDRA NYĀYARATNA (1905)

Pāṇinisāra

G1313 : Published Dacca, 1910, 1925; Calcutta, 1915, 1918.

RAÑCCHOḌJI OḌHAVJI (1905)

Sārabodhinī on Varadarāja's *Laghusiddhāntakaumudī*

See e1157.

ANANTĀCĀRYA of Musarapakkam (1906?)

Śaraṇaśabdārthavicāra

G1314 : Published in Srivaisnava Grantha Mudrapaka Sabda Series. Madras, 1906.

RĀMAKṚṢṆA ŚARMĀ TRIPĀṬHĪ (1907)

Viṣamasthalaṭippaṇī on Koṇḍa Bhaṭṭa's *Vaiyākaraṇabhūṣaṇasāra*

See e1183.

DURGĀDĀSA VIDYĀVĀGĪŚA ŚRĪRĀMA TARKAVĀGĪŚA (1908)

Ṭīkā on Vopadeva's *Mugdhabodha*

See e1024.

BĀLACANDRA ŚĀSTRIN (1908)

Bālacandrī on Bhaṭṭoji Dīkṣita's *Siddhāntakaumudī*

See e1086.

KALĀVATĪ DEVĪ (1909)

Tiṅantapradīpikā on Varadarāja's *Laghusiddhāntakaumudī*

See e1159.

VIṢṆUPRASĀDA ŚARMAN (1910)

Ṭippaṇī on Anubhūti's *Sārasvataprakriyā*

See e1002.

ŚYĀMĀCARAṆA KAVIRATNA (1910)

Tippaṇī on Vopadeva's *Mugdhabodha*

See e1025.

KHUDDI JHĀ (ŚARMAN) (1910)

Nāgeśoktiprakāśa on Nāgeśa Bhaṭṭa's *Laghuśabdenduśekhara*

G1315 : Published Varanasi, 1899.

See e1237.

Tiṅarthavādasāra on Koṇḍa Bhaṭṭa's *Vaiyākaraṇabhūṣaṇasāra*

See e1188.

KĀLŪRĀMA ŚĀSTRIN (1910)

Avyayārthamīmāṃsā

G1316 : Published Allahabad, 1910.

HARENDRANĀRĀYAṆA DEVAŚARMAN (1912)

Parimala on Vopadeva's *Mugdhabodha*

See e1028.

BRAHMADATTA (1914)

Avyayavṛtti

G1317 : Published Lahore, 1914.

ŚIVADATTA ŚARMAN (1914)

Sāradarśinī on Bhaṭṭoji Dīkṣita's *Siddhāntakaumudī*

See e1090.

Ṭippaṇī on Varadarāja's *Laghusiddhāntakaumudī*

See e1160.

GAṄGĀPRASĀDA ŚĀSTRIN (1914)

Paṅkticandrikā on Bhaṭṭoji Dīkṣita's *Siddhāntakaumudī*

See e1089.

BRAHMĀNANDA SARASVATĪ (1915?)

Citprabhā on Nāgeśa Bhaṭṭa's *Paribhāṣenduśekhara*
(NCat 11.226)
DEVENDRAKUMĀRA VIDYĀRATNA (1915)
Pāṇinipariśiṣṭavyākaraṇa
G1318 : Dacca, 1915; Calcutta, 1916.
LAKṢMAṆA TRIPĀṬHIN (1915)
Tattvaprakāśikā on Nāgeśa Bhaṭṭa's *Paribhāṣenduśekhara*
See e1258.
U.K. VEṄKAṬANARASIṂHA (1916)
Ṭīkā on Varadarāja's *Laghusiddhāntakaumudī*
See e1916.
NITYĀNANDA PANTA PARVATĪYA (1918)
Dīpikā on Nāgeśa Bhaṭṭa's *Laghuśabdenduśekhara*
See e1232; e1234.
Commentary on Nāgeśa Bhaṭṭa's *Paramalaghumañjūṣā*
See e1242; e1244.
GOPĀLA ŚĀSTRĪ NENE (1919)
Saralā on Koṇḍa Bhaṭṭa's *Vaiyākaraṇabhūṣaṇasāra*
See e1186; e1190.
Vyākaraṇapūrvapakṣāvalī
G1319 : Edited in HSS 5. Varanasi, 1927.
Vyākaraṇa Uttarapakṣāvalī
G1320 : Edited by Brahmashankar Misra. HSS 16. Varanasi, 1931.
ŚĀRADĀRAÑJAN RAY VIDYĀVINODA (1920)
Mitabhāṣiṇī on Bhaṭṭoji Dīkṣita's *Siddhāntakaumudī*
See e1091.
MĀDHAVA ŚĀSTRIN BHAṆḌĀRĪ (1920)
Prabhā on Bhaṭṭoji Dīkṣita's *Prauḍhamanoramā*
See e1117.
Sphoṭavimarśinī
See e639.
NĀNAKARĀMA ŚĀSTRIN (1924)
Paṅktipradīpa on Bhaṭṭoji Dīkṣita's *Siddhāntakaumudī*
See e1092.
JĪVANĀTHA RĀYA (1925)
Ṭippaṇī on Varadarāja's *Laghusiddhāntakaumudī*
See e1163.
KARAPUTUGALA DHARMA ŚRĪ (1925)
Bhāvabodhinī on Bhaṭṭoji Dīkṣita's *Siddhāntakaumudī*
See e1093.
TĀTA SUBRAHMAṆYA ŚĀSTRIN (1926)
Guruprasāda on Nāgeśa Bhaṭṭa's *Laghuśabdenduśekhara*
See e1235.
VĀSUDEVA VIṢṆU MIRĀSHĪ (1928)
Bālabodhinī on Varadarāja's *Laghusiddhāntakaumudī*
See e1165.
JĪVARĀMA ŚARMAN (1928)
Commentary on Pāṇini's *Aṣṭādhyāyī*
G1321 : Published Moradabad, 1928.
HARI ŚAṂKARA JHĀ (1929)
Kuñcikā on Patañjali's *Mahābhāṣya*
See e566.

VĀSUDEVA ŚĀSTRI ABHYAṄKAR (1929)
Tattvādarśa on Nāgeśa Bhaṭṭa's *Paribhāṣenduśekhara*
See e1250.
Vṛtti on (*Jainendra*) *Paribhāṣā*, based on Abhayanandin's commentary
G1322 : Edited in *Paribhāṣāsaṃgraha*
NAVKISHORE JHĀ (1931)
Avyayārthamālā on Rāmacandrāśrama's *Siddhāntacandrikā*
See e1133.
RĀMA ŚARAṆA ŚĀSTRĪ (1931)
Kaumudīkathakallolinī
G1323 : Edited by Gayacarana Tripathi. VBGSM 54. Varanasi, 1961.
SŪRYANĀRĀYAṆA ŚUKLA (1937)
Bhāvapradīpa on book 1 of Bhartṛhari's *Vākyapadīya*
See e648.
Vādaratna
G1324 : Edited by R.G. Sukla. 2 volumes. KSS 80. Varanasi, 1932–1949.
P.S. ANANTANĀRĀYAṆA ŚĀSTRĪ (1940)
Vākyatattva
G1325 : Published Trichur, 1940.
SADĀŚIVA ŚĀSTRĪ (ŚARMAN) JOSHĪ (1946)
Arthadīpikā on Nāgeśa Bhaṭṭa's *Paramalaghumañjūṣā*
See e1244.
Sudhā on Varadarāja's *Madhyasiddhāntakaumudī*
See e1143.
Commentary on Rāmacandrāśrama's *Siddhāntacandrikā*
See e1133.
BRAHMADEVA (1943)
Vaiyākaraṇasiddhāntamañjūṣā
V. KṚṢṆAMĀCĀRYA (1944)
Sphoṭavāda Upodghāta
See e1265.
BĀLA KṚṢṆA PAÑCOLĪ (1947)
Prabhā on Koṇḍa Bhaṭṭa's *Vaiyākaraṇabhūṣaṇasāra*
See e1189.
RUDRA PRASĀDA ŚARMĀ (1948)
Pradīpa on Pāṇini's (?) *Pāṇinīyaśikṣā*
See e428.
GAṄGĀDATTA ŚĀSTRĪ (1950)
Tattvaprakāśikā on Pāṇini's *Aṣṭādhyāyī*
See e119.
MADHUKĀNTA ŚARMĀ JHĀ (1950)
Prakāśa on Patañjali's *Mahābhāṣya*
G1326 : Published HSS 199. Varanasi, 1950.
SOMANĀTHA ŚARMAN (1952)
Viśeṣavivṛti on Bhaṭṭoji Dīkṣita's *Siddhāntakaumudī*
See e1096.
RĀMA PRASĀDA TRIPĀṬHIN (1952)
Subodhinī on Koṇḍa Bhaṭṭa's *Vaiyākaraṇabhūṣaṇasāra*
See e1190.
RUDRADHARA JHĀ ŚARMAN (1954)
Tattvāloka on Patañjali's *Mahābhāṣya*
See e598.

ŚAṂKARA ŚĀSTRIN MARULAKĀRA (1957)
Śaṃkarī on Koṇḍa Bhaṭṭa's *Vaiyākaraṇabhūṣaṇasāra*
See e1192.
KĀLIKĀ PRASĀDA ŚUKLA (1961)
Jyotsnā on Nāgéśa Bhaṭṭa's *Paramalaghumañjūṣā*
See e1245.
ŚRĪDHARENDRA SHARMĀ GHILDAYĀL (1962)
Commentary on *Vibhaktyartha* section of Bhaṭṭoji Dīkṣita's *Siddhāntakaumudī*
See e1103.
K. A. SUBRAMANIA IYER (1963)
Commentary on the *Brahmakāṇḍa* of Bhartṛhari's *Vākyapadīya*
See e710.
ACYUTĀNANDA ŚĀSTRIN (1963)
Sugandha on Bhaṭṭoji Dīkṣita's *Siddhāntakaumudī*
See e168.
RAGHUNĀTHA SHARMĀ (1963)
Ambākartrī on Bhartṛhari's *Vākyapadīya*
See e711.
Vyākaraṇadarśanabindu
G1327 : Published Varanasi, 1971.
ŚABHĀPATI ŚARMAN UPĀDHYĀYA (1963)
Ratnaprabhā on Nāgeśa Bhaṭṭa's *Paramalaghumañjūṣā*
See e1239.
BRAHMADATTA JIJÑĀSU (1964)
Aṣṭādhyāyībhāṣyaprathamavṛtti
G1328 : Edited by Yudhisthira Mimamsaka. 3 volumes. Amritsar, 1964–1968.
BHĪMASENA ŚĀSTRĪ (1969)
Bhaimī on Koṇḍa Bhaṭṭa's *Vaiyākaraṇabhūṣaṇasāra*
See e1195.
SATYAKĀMA VARMĀ (1970)
Commentary on Bhartṛhari's *Vākyapadīya*, book 1
See e737.
N. S. RĀMĀNUJA TĀTĀCĀRYA (1972)
Vivṛti on Nāgeśa Bhaṭṭa's *Jñāpakasaṃgraha*
See e1266.
MURALĪDHARA MIŚRA (1977)
Raśmī on Rāmacandra's *Prakrīyākaumudī*
See e1053.

Part 2: Authors and Works Whose Dates Are Unknown

ĀDENNA
(YM 1.428)
Sphūrti on Kaiyaṭa's *Mahābhāṣyapradīpa*
(YM 1.428)
AJITASENA ĀCĀRYA
(Belvalkar, p. 60; YM 1.603; NCat 1.86)

(*Maṇi*)*Prakāśikā* on Yakṣavarman's *Cintāmaṇi*
(NCat 1.86)
ĀNANDADATTA
(Abhyankar, p. 60)
Cāndravyākaraṇapaddhati
(NCat 2.105; 7.18)
ĀNANDA SIDDHĀNTAVĀGIŚA
Kārakānanda or *Kārakādyarthanirṇaya*
(NCat 2.96; 3.378)
ANANTA (perhaps more than one)
Kārakacakra
(NCat 1.159)
Vākyamañjarī
(NCat 1.169)
ANANTA BHAṬṬA (perhaps more than one)
Jātiśaktivāda
(NCat 1.176)
Śabdasudhā
ANANTASŪRI
Prayogaśikṣā
(NCat 1.184)
Liṅganirṇayacandrikā
(NCat 1.184)
APPAYYA DĪKṢITA
Vṛttivārttika on the *Vyañjananirṇaya* of Nāgeśa Bhaṭṭa's *Vaiyākaraṇasiddhāntamañjūṣā*
G1329 : Edited by Sivadatta and K. P. Parab. Kavyamala 38. Bombay, 1893.
BALARĀMA
Dhātuprakāśa (*saṃgraha*) and *Ṭippaṇī* thereon
(NCat 9.291)
BETARĀYA
Dhātumālikā
(NCat 9.292)
BHAGAVATBHAKTA
Bhāṣya on Bhaṭṭoji Dīkṣita's *Siddhāntakaumudī*
G1330 : (Mrs.) Saroj Gune, "Bhāshā Siddhānta Kaumudi of Bhagavatbhakta," SPAIOC 27, 1974, 248–249.
BHĀSKARA (perhaps more than one)
Vilāsa on Bhaṭṭoji Dīkṣita's *Siddhāntakaumudī*
(NCat 5.111)
Dhātupāṭha
(NCat 9.288)
BHAṬṬA ŚIROMAṆI (or ŚIROMAṆI BHAṬṬA or ŚIVĀNANDAYOGASVĀMIN)
Taddhitakośa
(NCat 8.85)
BHĀVA MIŚRA or ŚARMAN
Vṛtti on (*Kātantra*) *Paribhāṣā*
G1331 : Edited by K. V. Abhyankar in *Paribhāṣāsaṃgraha*, pp. 67–75.
BHAVANĀTHA
Dhātupallava
(NCat 9.286)
BILVEŚVARA or VILVEŚVARA
Kalāpacandra on Śarvavarman's *Kātantrasūtras*
See e653; e657; e658.

(PEDDINTI) BRAHMADEVA
Vyākhyā on Varadarāja's *Madhyasiddhāntakaumudī* (completed by his pupil Agnihotra)
(NCat 1.45)
CAKRIN
(Abhyankar, p. 160)
Jāgrahitetivāda (defending Mādhava against Bhaṭṭoji Dīkṣita)
(NCat 6.290)
CANDRADATTA JHĀ
Paribhāṣāmaṇimālā
(NCat 6.354)
CANDRAKĀNTA VIDYĀLAṂKĀRA of Gamerimuri
Dhātumañjarī
(NCat 6.346; 9.292)
CANDRAŚEKHARA
Paribhāṣenduśekhara (or commentary on it?)
(NCat 6.368)
CANDRAŚEKHARA VIDYĀLAṂKĀRA
(YM 1.626)
Arthabodhinī on Goyīcandra's *Saṃkṣiptasāraṭīkā*
(NCat 6.370)
CAṄGADĀSA or CAKADĀSA or CĀRCĀDĀSA
(GOS 134, 1961, 151)
Sambandhoddeśa or *Sambandhopadeśa*
(NCat 7.1; 6.402)
Vaiyākaraṇajīvatu or *Caṅgasūtra*
(NCat 7.2)
CHICCHU or CHUCCHU or CHUCHUKE BHAṬṬA
(GOS 134, 1961, 158)
Laghuvṛtti on Kashmiri recension of *Kātantra*
(NCat 3.317)
CUDĀMIŚRA
Pāṇinisūtrasūcī or *Aṣṭādhyāyīsūtrasūcī*
(NCat 7.70)
DĀMODARA
Dhātuvṛtti on the *Mugdhabodha*
(NCat 9.19)
DĀMODARA DEVAŚARMAN
Commentary on Jumara's *Saṃkṣiptasāra*
NCat 9.19)
DĀMODARA ŚARMAN
Pratyayamauktikamālā
(NCat 9.23)
Bālabodha or *Bālabodhinī*
(NCat 9.23)
DANO(KĀCĀRYA)
Dhātulakana or *Daśadhātusādhana*
(NCat 8.320)
DAŚABĀLA
(Abhyankar, p. 197, NCat 8.346)
Daśabālakārikā (of Saṃkṣiptasāra or Jaumara school)
G1332 : Edited Katantraganmala, Calcutta, 1924.

DATTA RĀMA BHAṬṬA
Vṛtti on Pāṇini's *Aṣṭādhyāyī*
(NCat 1.472; 2.294)
DAYĀŚAṂKARA
Anubandhakhaṇḍanavāda
(NCat 8.324)
DEVADATTA
Kātantravṛtti
(NCat 3.313; 9.107)
DEVADATTA
Anvayadīpikā (Jain work)
(NCat 1.241)
DEVAKĪNANDANA
Avyayārthalaharī
(NCat 1.431)
Kārakādibodhinī
(NCat 3.378)
DEVASAHĀYA
(YM 1.502)
Laghu(vṛtti) vivṛti on Pāṇini's *Aṣṭādhyāyī*
(NCat 1.472)
DEVAŚARMAN
(GOS 134, 1961, 200)
Samanvayapradīpasaṃketa, metrical recast of Kudaka's work
(NCat 4.176)
DEVĪDATTA ŚĀSTRIN
Ekagotra sūtraparāmarśa
(NCat 9.135)
DEVĪDĀSA
Pāṇinisūtrārthasaṃgraha
(NCat 9.135)
DEVĪDĀSA CAKRAVARTIN
(YM 1.637)
Commentary on the *Mugdhabodha*
(NCat 9.135)
DHANAJIT
(Abhyankar, p. 206)
Dhātukalpalatikā
(NCat 9.284)
DHANAÑJAYA
Kramakaumudī on a Sanskrit *Dhātupāṭha*
(NCat 9.216)
DHANAÑJAYA BHAṬṬĀCĀRYA
Paryāyaśabdaratna
(NCat 9.218)
DHANAPRABHĀ SŪRI, a Jain
Dhuṇḍhikā on Durgasiṃha's *Kātantravṛtti*
(NCat 3.312)
Dhuṇḍhikā on Trilocanadāsa's *Kātantrapañjikā*
(NCat 9.222)
DHARMADĀSA

Commentary on Candra's *Cāndravyākaraṇa*
(NCat 9.248)
DHARMADEVA
Pañjikā on Anubhūtisvarūpa's *Sārasvataprakriyā*
(NCat 9.248)
(RĀJAKUMĀRA) DHARMAŚĀSTRIN
Laghuvṛtti on Pūjyapāda's *Jainendravyākaraṇa*
G1333 : Edited Varanasi, 1924.
DIVYASIṂHA MIŚRA
Kārikābhāṣya
(NCat 9.51)
DRAVYEŚA JHĀ
Pratyekārthaprakāśikā on Bhartṛhari's *Vākyapadīya*
See e656.
ELEŚVARĀGNIHOTRA
Lakṣyamālā
(NCat 3.77–78)
GADĀDHARA
Ṭīkā on Nāgeśa Bhaṭṭa's *Paribhāṣenduśekhara*
(NCat 11.226)
GAṆEŚA
Vṛtti on Nāgeṣa Bhaṭṭa's *Paribhāṣenduśekhara*
(NCat 5.267)
GAṄGĀDĀSA (PAṆḌITA)
(YM 2.410)
Vākyapadī
(NCat 5.195)
GAṄGĀDĀSĀCĀRYA
Kātantra Vyākhyālekha
(NCat 3.309)
GAṄGĀDATTA
Nyāsasaṃgraha
(NCat 5.194)
GAṄGĀDATTA ŚĀSTRIN
Commentary on Pāṇini's *Aṣṭādhyāyī*
G1334 : Edited Jullundur, 1905, 1962.
G1335 : Edited Hardwar, 1950.
GAṄGĀDHARA (YM 2.181)
Commentary on Vardhamāna's *Gaṇaratnamahodadhi*
(NCat 5.200, 257)
GAṄGĀDHARA NĀTHA
Vāgīśāmata
(NCat 5.203)
GAṄGĀDHARA ŚARMAN
Vyākaraṇasaṃgraha (of the Vopadeva system)
(NCat 5.206)
GAṄGĀRAMITRA PĀṬHIN (MĀLAVA)
Śabdasudhānidhi
(NCat 5.213)
GAṄGEŚA MIŚRA UPĀDHYĀYA
Sumanoramā
(NCat 5.226)

GAṄGEŚA ŚARMAN
Kātantrakaumudī
(NCat 3.317)
GAURAMOHANA BHAṬṬA (VIDYĀRATNA)
Ratnāvalī (of Saṃkṣiptasāra school)
(NCat 6.234)
GAUTAMA
Kātantradīpikā
(NCat 3.309; 6.223)
GEYADEVA
(*Prātipadika*) *Gaṇapāṭhasaṃgraha*
(NCat 5.256)
GHANAŚYĀMA
Varṇaprakāśa
(NCat 6.275)
Dhātukośa
G1336 : Edited JTSML 26.2–3, 1974.
GIRIJA
Ṭīkā on Varadarāja's *Laghusiddhāntakaumudī*
See e1062, G1173.
GOLHĀṆA
Ṭippaṇikā on *Haimacatuṣkavṛtti*
(NCat 6.182)
GOPĀLA
Commentary on Nāgeśa Bhaṭṭa's *Śabdenduśekhara*
(NCat 6.133)
GOPĀLĀCĀRYA
Sthemadarpaṇa
(NCat 6.155)
GOPĪNĀTHA
Śabdavyākhyā
(NCat 6.161)
GOPĪNĀTHA BHAṬṬA
Kārakavyutpattirahasya
(NCat 3.378)
GOSVĀMI ŚRĪ ŚIVĀNANDABHAṬṬA
Padavyavasthākośa
(NCat 11.102)
GOVARDHANA BHAṬṬA
(GOS 134, 1961, 145)
Kātantrakaumudī
(NCat 3.317)
Commentary on Vardhamāna's *Gaṇaratnamahodadhi*
(NCat 5.257)
GOVINDA BHAṬṬA
Commentary on *Kātantra Dhātupāṭha*
(NCat 3.315; 6.190)
Śiṣyaprabodhikā on *Kātantra*
(NCat 6.201)
GOVINDA MIŚRA
Commentary on Sīradeva's *Paribhāṣāvṛtti*
(NCat 6.203)

GOVINDA PAṆḌITA
Kātantrapariśiṣṭa
(NCat 6.200)
GOVINDARĀMA VIDYĀŚIROMAṆI
Śabdadīpikā on *Mugdhabodha*
(NCat 6.205)
GOVINDA SENA
Paribhāṣāpradīpa
G1337 : Edited (3d edition), Calcutta, 1906.
(SIDDHA) GUṆAKĀRA
Vyākaraṇaṭīkā
(NCat 6.58)
GURUWARA BĀLA ŚĀSTRĪ
Ṭippaṇī on Patañjali's *Mahābhāṣya* (?)
See e542.
HARAGOVINDA VIDYĀVĀCASPATI
Jñāpakāvalī (Saṃkṣipta work)
(NCat 7.350)
HARANĀTHA VIDYĀRATNA
Dhātupradīpa on Vopadeva's *Mugdhabodha*
G1338 : Edited by Madhavacandra Tarkacudamani.
HARIDATTA (DAIVAJÑA?)
Uṇādisūtra
(NCat 2.294)
Upasargārthadīpikā
(NCat 2.376)
HARIKṚṢṆA
Avyayārtha
(NCat 1.431)
HARI PAṆḌITA
Commentary on Pāṇini's *Aṣṭādhyāyī*
(NCat 1.472)
HARIRĀMA BHAṬṬĀCĀRYA
Sāra on Śarvavarman's *Kātantrasūtras*
See e663.
(BHAGAVAT) HARI ŚĀSTRĪ
Citraprabhā on Hari Dīkṣita's? *Laghuśabdaratna*
See e1100.
HARṢAKĪRTI SŪRI
(YM 2.129)
Vivaraṇa on Hemacandra's *Śabdānuśāsana-Dhātupārāyaṇa*
(NCat 9.290)
HAYAGRĪVĀCĀRYA
Candrikā or *Arthamañjarī* on Nāgeśa Bhaṭṭa's *Śabdenduśekhara*
(NCat 6.379, 11.222)
Arthamañjarī on Nāgeśa Bhaṭṭa's *Paribhāṣenduśekhara*
(NCat 11.228)
ĪŚVARAKAṆṬHA
Dhātumālā
(NCat 2.273, 9.292)
ĪŚVARAMIŚRA

Rūpataraṅgiṇī
(NCat 2.277)
ĪŚVARĪPRASĀDA
Śabdakaustubha
(NCat 2.280)
JAGADDHARA
Commentary on Haradatta's *Padamañjarī*
See e918.
JAGADĪŚA
Pāṇinīyasāra
(NCat 7.126)
JAGANNĀTHA
(GOS 134, 1961, 159; YM 1.633–634)
Sārapradīpikā on Anubhūti Svarūpācārya's *Sarasvatīprakriyā*
(NCat 7.134)
(MAHĀMAHOPĀDHYĀYA) JAGANNĀTHA
Siddhāntatattva
(NCat 7.134)
JANĀRDANA ŚARMAN
Śabdaratna (of Kātantra school)
(NCat 7.153)
JAYANTA BHAṬṬA
Vādighātamudgara on Anubhūtisvarūpācārya's *Sārasvataprakriyā*
(NCat 7.181)
JINADEVASŪRI
Kriyākalāpa
(NCat 5.130; 7.256)
JÑĀNEŚVARA
Śabdabhāṣā
(NCat 7.349)
KĀLADHARA
Śaktisphuṭa
(NCat 3.223)
KĀLĪDĀSA CAKRAVARTIN
Dhātuprabodha
(NCat 9.291)
KĀLĪ KUMĀRA ŚARMAN
Vyākaraṇādarśa
G1339 : Published.
KALYĀṆAMALA
(GOS 134, 1961, 113)
Dīpa on Hari Dīkṣita's *Śabdaratna*
(NCat 3.256)
KĀMADEVA GHOṢA
Śabdaratnākara
(NCat 3.349)
KANAKALĀLA ŚARMAN
Saṃkṣiptabālabodhinī on Varadarāja's *Laghusiddhāntakaumudī*
See e1166.
KĀNTA NĀTHA
Śabdārtharatnāvalī
(NCat 3.340)

KĀŚĪNĀTHA (perhaps several different)
Kṛdvivaraṇa
(NCat 4.126)
Dhātuprayogāvalī
(NCat 4.127)
Viśeṣyavāda
(NCat 4.127)
Śiśubodha
(NCat 4.127)
Prakriyāsāra on Ramacandra's *Prakriyākaumudī*
(NCat 4.527)
KĀŚĪNĀTHA DEVAŚARMAN
Pradīpa
(NCat 4.133)
KĀŚĪNĀTHA MIŚRA
Dhātusaṃgraha
(NCat 4.133)
KĀŚĪRĀJA
Commentary on *Kātantra*
(cf. YM 1.519)
KĀŚĪŚVARA
(Belvalkar, p. 94; YM 1.639)
Dhātupāṭha (of Saupadma school)
(NCat 4.141)
KĀŚYAPA
Bālāvabodhana on *Cāndravyākaraṇa*
See e797.
KAVI KAṆṬHAHĀRA
? (*Kalāpa*) *Carkaritarahasya*
G1340 : Edited Calcutta, 1905.
KAVĪNDRANANDANA
Vṛtti on *Kṛdvṛtti*
(NCat 4.281)
KAVISĀRAṄGA
Prayuktākhyātamañjarī
(NCat 3.287)
KAVI VALLABHA
Aparaviṣayapramāṇāni
(NCat 3.285)
KEDĀREŚVARA ŚARMAN
Dhātvāvalī
(NCat 9.296)
KEŚARI MIŚRA
Rapratyāhāramaṇḍana
(NCat 5.75)
KEŚAVA
(YM 2.417)
Sphoṭapratiṣṭhā
(NCat 5.61)
KEŚAVADEVA TARKAPAÑCĀNANA BHAṬṬĀCĀRYA
(Belvalkar, p. 92)

Vyākaraṇadurghaṭodghāta on Goyīcandra's *Saṃkṣiptasāravivaraṇa*
(NCat 5.64)
KHANA NṚPATI
Śabdaprakāśa
(NCat 5.184)
KODAṆḌARĀMA
(Abhyankar, p. 129)
Śabdasiddhāntamañjarī
(NCat 5.93)
KOLĀHALA
Paribhāṣāpradīpa
(NCat 5.95)
KṚPĀLA PAṆḌITA
Kātantrakaumudī
(NCat 9.317; 4.283)
KṚPĀRĀMA
Kārakārtha
(NCat 4.282)
Commentary on a *Ṣaṭpadī*
(NCat 4.282)
KṚṢṆA BHAṬṬA
Commentary on Nāgeśa Bhaṭṭa's *Paribhāṣenduśekhara*
(NCat 4.335)
KṚṢṆA BHAṬṬĀCĀRYA or ŚARMAN
Prabhāvatī on the Sārasvata *Vṛttipañjikā*
(NCat 4.340)
KṚṢṆĀCĀRYA (more than one?)
Candrikā
(NCat 4.9)
Yuktiratnākara
(NCat 4.9)
KṚṢṆA DVIVEDIN
Sphoṭatattva
(NCat 4.324)
KṚṢṆA PAṆḌITA
Gūḍhabhāvavivṛti on Rāmacandra's *Prakriyākaumudi*
(NCat 6.95)
KṚṢṆA ŚĀSTRIN
(NCat 4.364)
Sudhākara on Bhaṭṭoji Dīkṣita's *Siddhāntakaumudī*
(NCat 4.364)
Subantaprakāśa
(NCat 4.364)
KṚṢṆASUDHI or KṚṢṆAMĀCĀRIAR
Tārāvalī on Pāṇini's *Aṣṭādhyāyī* 7.2.115
(NCat 8.159)
KṚṢṆĀVADHŪTA
Kārakanirūpaṇa
(NCat 3.375)
KUDAKĀCĀRYA
Samanvayapradīpa
(NCat 4.176)

KULLUKA BHAṬṬA
Rūpaprakāśa following *Dhātupradīpa*
(NCat 4.248)
LAKṢMAṆA DVIVEDIN
Dvikarmavāda
(NCat 9.205)
LAKṢMĪDATTA, son of Kṛṣnamitra
Padārthadīpikā
(NCat 11.108)
LAKṢMĪDHARA, son of Nṛsiṃhodgātṛ, lived in Puri
Nāmanirmaladarpaṇa
(NCat 10.44)
LAKṢMĪKĀRA or LAKṢMĪŚRĪ of Nepal
(*Candra*) *Tiṅanta*
(Cordier 3.460)
LAKṢMĪNĀRĀYAṆA VYĀSA
Aṣṭādhyāyīsūtrakośa
(NCat 1.471)
LOKEŚVARA ŚARMAN ŚUKLA
Siddhāntaratnāvalī on Anubhūti's *Sārasvataprakriyā*
See e998.
MAHĀLIṄGA ŚĀSTRIN
Uṇādirūpāvalī
(NCat 2.293)
MAHEŚA JHĀ
Dhātuparyayamaṇimālā
(NCat 9.286)
MĀNALUR VIRARĀGHAVĀCĀRYA
Commentary on Pāṇini's *Aṣṭādhyāyī*
G1341 : Edited MGOML 33 (1954), 47 (1955)
(ŚRĪ) MĀNAŚARMAN of Campahatti, son of Lakṣmīpati
Vijaya on Siradeva's *Paribhāṣāvṛtti*
G1342 : Edited in *Paribhāṣāsaṃgraha*, pp. 273–292.
MAṄGARASA
(Belvalkar, p. 60)
Pratipadā on Yakṣavarman's *Cintāmaṇi*
MĀṆIKYADEVA
(Belvalkar, p. 45; GOS 134, 1961, 306)
Vṛtti or *Daśapadī* on (Jain) *Uṇādisūtras*
(NCat 8.345)
MAUNIŚEKHARA, pupil of Rājaśekhara
Commentary on *Kātantra*
(NCat 3.224)
NANDAKĪRTI
Tyadyantasya prakriyāpadārohaṇa
(NCat 8.227)
NANDANA MIŚRA or NYĀYAVĀGIŚA, son of Bāneśvara Miśra
Tantrapradīpoddīpana on Jinendrabuddhi's *Nyāsa*
(NCat 4.119, 9.327)
NARAHARI
Prabodha on Trilocana's *Kātantravṛttipañjikā*
(NCat 3.311, 9.367)

NARAHARI, disciple of Nārāyaṇa Tīrtha
(Belvalkar, p. 97; YM 1.639)
Bāla(ka)bodha
(NCat 9.368)

NARAIN DATTA TRIPĀṬHIN
Prakāśa on Bhartṛhari's *Vākyapadīya*, Book 1
See e662.

NARASIṂHA SŪRI, son of Rudrācārya of Kauṇḍinya gotra
Saptasvarasindhu or *Svaramañjarī*
(NCat 9.364)

NĀRĀYAṆA BHĀRATĪ
(Belvalkar, p. 85)
Sārasvatasārasaṃgraha
(NCat 10.94)

NĀRĀYAṆA
(NCat 3.374)
Kārakacakra-Dīpaprabhā
G1343 : Edited TSS 33, 1913.

NĀRĀYAṆA of Kerala
Prakriyāsāra
(NCat 10.86)

NĀRĀYAṆA of Govindapura
Pradīpa or *Śabdabhūṣaṇa* on Pāṇini's *Aṣṭādhyāyī*
(NCat 1.472)

NAROTTAMA VIDYĀLAṂKĀRA BHAṬṬĀCĀRYA
Samksiptasārakarika
(NCat 9.372)

NAYASUNDARA, pupil of Dhanaratna
Rūparatnamālā or *Sārasvatavyākaraṇa*
(NCat 9.350)

NĪLĀMBARA MIŚRA
Manoramācandrikā
(NCat 10.184)

NṚSIṂHA (more than one?)
Sūktiratnākara on Patañjali's *Mahābhāṣya*
(NCat 10.190)
Rūpamālā
(NCat 10.190)

NṚSIṂHA TARKAPAÑCĀNANA
Gaṇamārtaṇḍa on *Saṃkṣiptasāra-Dhātupāṭha*
(NCat 9.290, 10.195)

ORAM BHAṬṬA
Vyākaraṇadīpikā on Pāṇini's *Aṣṭādhyāyī*
G1344 : Edited by Ganapati Sastri Mokate, *Pan* n. s. 29 (1907)–37 (1915). Reprinted Varanasi, 1916.

PADMADHARA
Indirā
(NCat 11.153)

(RĀJA) PADMANĀRĀYAṆA

Śiśubodha
(NCat 11.131)
PADMASUNDARA
Uṇādisādhana or *Sundaraprakāśaśabdārṇava*
(NCat 2.293)
PAÑCĀNANA KANDALĪ
Chandraka Bhāṣya on *Ratnamālā*
(NCat 11.72)
?*Varṇaviveka*
(NCat 11.72)
PAŚUPATI of Rādhā
Kārakaparīkṣā
(NCat 3.375)
PĪTĀMBARA VIDYĀBHŪṢAṆA
Kātantra-Dhātusūtrapatrikā or *Kavirājapatrikā*
See e656.
PRAVARTAKOPĀDHYĀYA
(Abhyankar, p. 271; YM 1.428)
Prakāśa or *Prakāśikā* on Kaiyaṭa's *Mahābhāṣyapradīpa*
(NCat 5.76)
PRAYOGAVEṄKAṬĀDRI
(YM 1.415)
Vidvanmukhabhūṣaṇa or -*Maṇḍana* on Patañjali's *Mahābhāṣya* (MS at Adyar Library)
PṚTHVĪCANDRA or PṚTHVĪDHARA
Daurgasiṃhavṛtti on Durgasiṃha's *Kātantravṛtti*
(NCat 3.313)
PṚTHVĪŚVARA
Sarvalakṣaṇa on Harṣavardhana's *Liṅgānuśāsana*
See e818.
PUṆYASUNDARAGAṆI
(Belvalkar, p. 66)
Dhātupāṭha (Hemacandra school)
(NCat 9.290)
PŪRṆACANDRA
Dhātupāṭha
G1345 : Biswanath Bhattacharya, "On the Sanskrit Restoration of Pūrṇacandra's *Dhātu-Pāṭha* from Tibetan Base," JBBRAS 52–53, 1977–1978, 88–91.
RĀDHĀKṚṢṆA GOSVĀMIN
Avyayārtha
(NCat 1.431)
RĀGHAVA JHĀ
Kārakārthavicāra
(NCat 3.379)
Dvandvaikaśeṣavāda
(NCat 9.189)
RĀGHAVA SŪRI (YM 2.329)
Arthaprakāśikā on Kātyāyana's *Vārttika* (MS in Madras)
RĀGHAVENDRĀCĀRYA
Candrikā on Nāgeśa Bhaṭṭa's *Laghuśabdenduśekhara*
(NCat 6.379)
RAGHUNANDA ŚIROMAṆI

(Belvalkar, p. 71)
Kātantratattvārṇava or *Kalāpatattvārṇava*
See e653.
RAGHUNĀTHA ŚĀSTRĪ VAIYĀKARAṆA
Laghuṭīkā on Nāgeśa Bhaṭṭa's *Paribhāṣenduśekhara*
See e1134.
RĀJARĀMA DĪKṢITA
Commentary on Hari Bhāskara's *Paribhāṣābhāskara*
(NCat 11.22)
RĀJĪVA ŚARMAN or VIŚVANĀTHA CAKRAVARTIN or RĀMADEVA ŚARMAN
?*Acakṣaṇaviveka*
(NCat 2.21)
RĀMACANDRA, son of Viśvanatha and disciple of Kṛṣṇa Paṇḍita
Kriyākośa, abridgment of Bhaṭṭamalla's *Ākhyātacandrikā*
G1346 : Edited Varanasi, 1876.
RĀMACANDRA
Kārakacandrikā
(NCat 3.374)
RĀMACARAṆA
Kartṛsiddhāntamañjarī
(NCat 3.187)
RĀMACARITRA TRIPĀṬHIN
Phakkikā Saralārtha
G1347 : Edited by Sadasiva Sastri Joshi. HSS 21. Varanasi, 1932.
Pañcasamāsīya
(NCat 11.60)
RĀMAJÑA PĀṆḌEYA
Vyākaraṇadarśanapratimā
G1348 : Edited by Ramagovind Sukla. POWSBST. Varanasi, 1979.
RĀMA KIṄKARA SARASVATĪ
(GOS 134, 1961, 323; YM 1.639)
Āśubodha
(NCat 2.198)
RĀMAKUMĀRA NYĀYABHŪṢAṆA, son of Rāmagati Vācaspati
(NCat 3.225)
Kalāpasāra (based on Mugdabodha, Sārasvata, and Kātantra systems)
(NCat 3.225)
RĀMADEVA MIŚRA
Vṛttipradīpa on Jayāditya/Vāmana's *Kāśikā*
(NCat 4.119)
RĀMĀNANDA TĪRTHA
Kalāpasaṃgraha, a brief exposition of Kātantra
(NCat 3.225)
RĀMANĀRĀYAṆA ŚARMAN
Bhāṣya on Anubhūti's *Sārasvataprakriyā*
See e1004.
RĀMANĀTHA CAKRAVARTIN
Śabdaratnāvali or *Kātantravṛttiprabodha* or *Śabdasādhyaprabodhinī*
(NCat 3.314)
RĀMAPANIVĀDA

Vivaraṇa on Nārāyaṇa Bhattari's *Dhātukāvya*
See e1002.
RĀMARSI
Avyayārthamañjarī on an *Avyayārthakośa*
(NCat 1.431)
RĀMASIṂHA (more than one?)
Commentary on Haradatta's *Padamañjarī*
See e918.
Dhāturatnamañjarī
(NCat 9.292)
RAMEŚVARA TARKAVĀCASPATI BHAṬṬĀCĀRYA
Kārakamālāṭīkā on a *Ratnamālā*
(NCat 3.376)
RATIDEVA SIDDHĀNTAVĀGĪŚA, son of Gaṅgādharācārya of the Catta family of Bengal
Kṛtpariśiṣṭā
(NCat 4.273)
RATNAMATI
Ṭīkā on Candragomin's *sūtras*
(NCat 7.19)
RATNAPĀṆI
(*Ṣaṭ*)*Kārakavivaraṇa*
(NCat 3.377)
G1349 : Edited by H.V. Nagaraja Rao. MO 9, 1976, 49–62.
RATNEŚVARA
Commentary on Haradatta's *Padamañjarī*
See e917; e918.
RŪPARĀMA NYĀYAPAÑCĀNANA
Kārakarahasya, a Saupadma work
(NCat 3.376)
ŚABARASVĀMIN
(Belvalkar, p. 44; GOS 134, 1961, 383; YM 2.264)
Sarvārthalakṣaṇa on Harṣavardhana's commentary on Hemacandra's *Liṅgānuśasana*
See e817.
SABHĀPATI ŚARMĀ UPĀDHYĀYA
Lakṣmī on Bhaṭṭoji Dīkṣita's *Siddhāntakaumudī*
See e1017; G1104.
SACCIDĀNANDA
Taddhitaguṇadīpikā
(NCat 8.85)
SADĀNANDA
Subodhinī on Anubhūti's *Sarasvatīprakriyā*
See e988; e1134.
Subodhinī on Rāmacandrāśrama's *Siddhāntacandrikā*
See e1041.
SAMANTABHADRA
(Belvalkar, p. 60)
Ṭippaṇī on Yakṣavarman's *Cintāmaṇi*
ŚAṂKARA
Ṭīkā on Puruṣottamadeva's *Mahābhāṣyalaghuvṛtti*
(YM 2.403)
ŚAṂKARA ŚARMAN

Kātantrapariśiṣṭaprabodhaprakāśikā
(NCat 3.316)
SANĀTANA TARKĀCĀRYA
(YM 1.509)
Ṭippaṇī on Pāṇini's *Aṣṭādhyāyī*
(NCat 1.472)
Prabhā on ?Jinendrabuddhi's *Nyāsa* (or ?Maitreyarakṣita's *Tantrapradīpa*)
(NCat 4.119, 8.90)
SARVADHARA UPĀDHYĀYA
Commentary on (*Kātantra*) *Uṇādisūtras*
(NCat 2.295)
Vanmayapradīpa on Durgasiṃha's *Kātantravṛtti*
(NCat 3.313)
Tyadayantasyaprakriyā or *Kalāpatyādivṛtti*
(NCat 8.227)
ṢAṢṬHĪDĀSA, son of Jayakṛṣṇa Tarkavāgīśa
Dhātumālā
(NCat 9.292)
SATYAVARYĀRYA
Commentary on some *Uṇādisūtras*
(NCat 2.295)
(KĀŚĪ) ŚEṢA ŚARMAN, patronized by King Kṛṣṇarāja III of Mysore
(Belvalkar, p. 45; YM 2.299)
Sarvamaṅgala on Nāgeśa Bhaṭṭa's *Paribhāṣenduśekhara*
(NCat 4.141, 11.228)
SIDDHANĀTHA VIDYĀVĀGĪŚA
Commentary on Puruṣottamadeva's *Prayogaratnamālā*
G1350 : Edited. Kuch Bihar, 1890–1903.
SĪTĀNĀTHA ŚĀSTRIN
Saṃjīvanī on *Ākhyāta* section of Śarvavarman's *Kātantrasūtras*
See e658.
ŚIVADĀSA or ŚIVARĀMA ŚARMAN (VĀCASPATI)
Kṛnmañjarī with autocommentary
G1351 : Edited Dacca, 1886.
G1352 : Edited Calcutta, 1905–1906.
See e647
ŚIVADĀSA CAKRAVARTIN
Commentary on *Saṃkṣiptasāra Uṇādisūtras*
(NCat 2.296)
ŚIVĀNANDA GOSVĀMIN or ŚIROMAṆI BHAṬṬA, a southerner who visited Bikaner during the reign of Anupsingh
Kārakakośa or *Vibhaktyarthavivaraṇa*
(NCat 3.372) (See DKRPV, p. 363.)
ŚIVĀNANDA PĀṆḌEYA
Ratnadīpikā on Nāgeśa Bhaṭṭa's *Paramalaghumañjūṣā*
See e1122.
ŚIVANĀRĀYAṆA ŚIROMAṆI
Ṭippaṇī on Vopadeva's *Mugdhabodha*
See e1916.
ŚIVA PAṆḌITA
Kusumavikāsa on Haradatta's *Padamañjarī*
(NCat 4.120)

SOMANĀTHA
Bṛhatī Candrikā
(NCat 6.380)
SOMAPRABHĀ, a Jain
Auktika
(NCat 3.97)
ŚRĪDEVA PAṆḌITA
Arthasaṃgraha
(NCat 1.389)
ŚRĪKĀNTA MIŚRA
Candrikā
(NCat 6.380)
ŚRĪKṚṢṆA ŚARMAN
Tiṅam Śaktiḥ or *Tiṅvicāra*?
(NCat 8.166)
ŚRĪNĀTHA ŚIROMAṆI
Manoramā on Śarvavarman's *Kātantrasūtras*
See e655.
ŚRĪNIVĀSA
Commentary on Haribhāskara's *Paribhāṣābhāskara*
(NCat 11.22)
ŚRĪPRABHĀ SŪRI
Kārakoktisamuccaya
(NCat 3.379)
SṚṢṬIDHARĀCĀRYA
Commentary on Puruṣottamadeva's *Bhāṣāvṛtti*
See e938.
ŚRUTASĀGARA, pupil of Vidyānanda
Dhātupārāyaṇa
(NCat 9.290)
SUDARŚANĀCĀRYA
Kārakārthapradīpikā
(NCat 3.379)
SUDARŚANA DEVA
Pradīpa on Santānava's *Phiṭsūtras*
See e644.
SUSENA KAVIRĀJA MIŚRA, son of Miśra Mahīdhara
Candra or *Vyākhyāsāra* on Trilocana's *Kātantravṛttipañjikā*
G1353 : "Ākhyātavirāja" portion edited Dacca, 1890.
See e656.
ŚVETAVANAVĀSIN, son of Āryabhaṭṭa of Gārgya gotra
(NCat 2.172, 294–295)
Vṛtti on *Uṇādisūtras*
G1354 : Edited by T.R. Chintamani, MUSS 7.1, 1933.
TALADEVASUDHI
Dhātupratyayapañcikā
(NCat 9.291)
TĀRĀNĀTHA, son of Kālidāsa of Vatsa family
Śabdārtharatna
G1355 : Edited Calcutta, 1951.
TĀRĀPADA NYĀYARATNA

Kārakacandrikā
G1356 : Edited Calcutta, 1902.
TARKĀLAṂKĀRA BHAṬṬĀCĀRYA
Dhātucandrikā
(NCat 8.135)
TEKNĀTHA (?)
Paribhāṣārthadīpikā
(NCat 8.3)
ṬHAKKURADĀSA NYĀYAPAÑCĀNANA, son of Mṛtyuñjaya Sarasvatī
Dhātucandrikā
(NCat 8.5)
TILAKA
Ṭīkā on Kṣīrasvāmin's *Nipātāvyayopasargavṛtti*
G1357 : Edited svos 28, 1951.
TRILOCANA (more than one?)
Avyayaśabdavṛtti
(NCat 8.261)
Dhātupārāyaṇa
(NCat 8.261)
Vaiyākaraṇakoṭipāttra
(NCat 8.262)
TRILOKANĀTHA, son of Vaidyanātha
Kārakārthanirṇaya or *Ṣaṭkārakanirūpaṇa*
(NCat 3. 378, 8.259)
UTSAVAKĪRTI, SĀRAṄGA UPĀDHYĀYA
Padasūryaprakriyā (Kātantra work)
(NCat 2.322, 3.309, 11.103)
VAIJALADEVA
Prabodhacandrikā
G1358 : G.V. Tagare, "Vaijadeva's *Prabodhacandrikā*," SPAIOC 19, 1956, 36–37.
VĀLĀBHIDATTA
Commentary on Nāgeśa Bhaṭṭa's *Paribhāṣenduśekhara*
(NCat 11.227)
VAṄGADĀSA
Taddhitopadeśa
(NCat 8.86)
VARENDRA CAMPAHATTIYA MĀNAŚARMAN, son of Lakṣmīpati
Commentary on Sīradeva's *Paribhāṣāvṛtti*
(NCat 1.203)
Anuhyasasāra?
(NCat 1.203)
VĀSUDEVA
Kāśikāvṛttisāra
(NCat 4.120)
VEDĀNTĀCĀRYA
Kaumudīsārasaṃgraha, summary of Bhaṭṭoji Dīkṣita's *Siddhāntakaumudī*
(NCat 5.111)
VIDYĀCAKRAVARTIN
Commentary on Bhartṛhari's *Vākyapadīya* (lost)
VIJAYAVIMALA
Avacūrī on Harṣakulagaṇi's *Kavikalpadruma*
(NCat 3.270)

VINĀSVARANANDIN
Kārakasambandhoddyota
(NCat 3.378)
(King) VĪRAPĀṆḌYA
Tiṅantaparyāyasaṃgraha (?)
(NCat 8.166)
VĪRARĀGHAVĀCĀRYA
(Cardona, p. 36)
Pāṇinisūtravyākhyā
G1359 : Edited by T. Chandrasekharan. 2 volumes. MGOMS 33 (1954), 47 (1955).
VIŚVANĀTHA NYĀYĀLAṂKĀRA
Dhātucintāmaṇi (Pāṇiniya work)
(NCat 9.285)
VIŚVANĀTHA ŚĀSTRĪ
Prabhākarī on Varadarāja's *Mādhyasiddhāntakaumudī*
See e1048.
VIŚVEŚVARA SŪRI
(*Vyākaraṇa*)*Siddhāntasudhānidhi*
G1360 : Edited by Dadhi Ram Sarma, Sita Rama Sastri Shende, and Madhava Sastri Bhandare. ChSS 45. Varanasi, 1924.
VIŚVEŚVARA TARKĀCĀRYA, a Kātantra writer
(NCat 2.10)
Ākhyātavyākhyāna or *-bodha* (MSS available)
Commentary on Trilocana's *Kātantravṛttipañjikā*
(NCat 3.312)
VRAJARĀJA
Uṇādisūtra
(NCat 2.294)
VURAMIŚRA, son of Harighala
Dhātudarpaṇa, composed in the city of Amritsar
(NCat 9.285)
YAŚOBHŪTI
Laghuvṛtti or *Śiṣyahita* on Kashmiri recension of *Kātantra* (Tibetan translation exists in Tanjur; see JASP 1907, 125.)
YATĪŚA
Avyayārthapradīpikā
(NCat 1.431)
AUTHOR UNKNOWN
Sādhutvādinirvacana (MS notice in Adyar D, vol. 6, p. 245)
AUTHOR UNKNOWN
Sphoṭasiddhi (MS notice in Adyar D, vol. 6. no. 655)
AUTHOR UNKNOWN
Varavarṇinī on Nāgeśa Bhaṭṭa's *Laghuśabdenduśekhara*
See e1116.
AUTHOR UNKNOWN
Vijaya on Nāgeśa Bhaṭṭa's *Laghuśabdenduśekhara*
See e1116.
AUTHOR UNKNOWN
Viṣamapadavivṛti on Nāgeśa Bhaṭṭa's *Laghuśabdenduśekhara*
See e1116.
AUTHOR UNKNOWN

Abhinavacandrikā on Nāgeśa Bhaṭṭa's *Laghuśabdenduśekhara*
See e1116.
AUTHOR UNKNOWN
Sabdarūpāvalī
G1361 : Edited by Kanaka Lal Sharma. HSS 3. Varanasi, 1925.
AUTHOR UNKNOWN
Samāsaśaṃkhā
G1362 : Edited by H.V. Nagaraja Rao. MO 12, 1979, 45–46.

PART 3: SECONDARY LITERATURE ON *Vyākaraṇa*

G1363 : Henry T. Colebrooke, "On the Sanskrit and Prakrit Languages," *Asiatic Researches* 7, 1803, 199-231. Reprinted HTCMR 2.1–32; Staal, pp. 33–45.

G1364 : Theodor Aufrecht, *De Accentu Compositorum Sanskritorum*. Bonn, 1847.

G1365 : N.L. Westergaard, *Radices linguae sanscritae ad decreta grammaticorum definivit atque copia exemplorum exquisitorum illustravit*. Bonn, 1841.

G1366 : Theodor Benfey, *Vollständige Grammatik der Sanskritsprache zum Gebrauch für Vorlesungen und zum Selbststudium*. Leipzig, 1852.

G1367 : William Dwight Whitney, "On the Nature and Designation of the Accent in Sanskrit," TAPA 1869–1870, 20–45.

G1368 : Otto Böhtlingk, "Das Verhalten der drei kanonischen Grammatiker in Indian zu den im Würzelverzeichniss mit *s* und *n* anläutenden Würzeln," ZDMG 29, 1875, 483–490.

G1369 : Franz Kielhorn, *Grammatik der Sanskrit-Sprache*. Ist edition 1870, translated 1881. Wiesbaden, 1965.

G1370 : R.G. Bhandarkar, "Wilson Lectureship: Development of Language and of Sanskrit," JBBRAS 16, 1883–1885, 245–274.

G1371 : Hjalmar Edgren, "On the Verbal Roots of the Sanskrit Language and of the Sanskrit Grammarians," JAOS 11, 1885, 1–55.

G1372 : William Dwight Whitney, "The Study of Hindu Grammar and the Study of Sanskrit," AJP 5, 1884; IA 14, 1885, 33ff.; Silverstein, pp. 287–305; Staal, pp. 142–154.

G1373 : O. Böhtlingk, "Haben *iti* und *ca* bisweilen die Bedeutung von *ādi*?" ZDMG 41, 1887, 516–520.

G1374 : Georg Bühler, "A Disputed Meaning of the Particles *iti* and *ca*," WZKM 1, 1887, 13–20.

G1375 : Bruno Liebich, "Die Kasuslehre der indischen Grammatiker verglichen mit dem Gebrauch der Kasus im Aitareya-Brāhmaṇa (ein Beitrag zur Syntax der Sanskrit-Sprache)," BB 10, 1886, 205–234; 11, 1887, 274–315.

G1376 : J.S. Peijer, *Sanskrit Syntax*. Leiden, 1886; reprinted Kyoto, 1968.

G1377 : Friedrich Knauer, "Zu *iti* und *ca*," *Festchrift Bohtlingk*, pp. 62–67.

G1378 : F. Kielhorn, "Scheinbare Citate von Autoritaten in grammatischen Werken," *Festschrift Bohtlingk*, pp. 52–53; reprinted Rau, pp. 256–257.

G1379 : William Dwight Whitney, *Sanskrit Grammar*. Cambridge, Mass., 1889.

G1380 : R. Otto Franke, "Was ist Sanskrit?" BB 17, 1891, 54–90.

G1381 : Ferdinand Kittel, "Dravidische Elements in den Sanskrit-*Dhātupāṭhas*," *Festschrift Roth*, William Dwight pp. 21–24.

G1382 : William Dwight Whitney, "On Recent Studies in Hindu Grammar," AJP 14, 1893, 171–197.

G1383 : G. Buhler, "The Roots of the *dhātupāṭha* not Found in Literature," WZKM 8, 1894, 122–136. Reprinted IA 23, 1894, 141–154, 250–255; G1625, pp. 194–204.

G1384 : F. Kittel, "On Some Sanskrit Verbs," IA 24, 1895, 81–82.

G1385 : Jakob Wackernagel, *Altindische Grammatik*, Volume 1, *Lautlehre*. Gottingen, 1896. Reprinted Wackernagel.

G1386 : F. Kielhorn, "The Jātakas and Sanskrit Grammarians," JRAS 1898, 17–21. Reprinted Rau, pp. 294–298.

G1387 : Otto Wecker, "Der Gebrauch der Kasus in der älteren Upaniṣad-literature Vergleichen mit der Kasuslehre der indischen Grammatiker," BB 30, 1906, 1–61, 177–207.

G1388 : Satischandra Vidyabhusana, "Sanskrit Works on Literature, Grammar, Rhetoric and Lexicography as Preserved in Tibet," JASBe 3, 1907, 121–132; 4, 1908, 593ff.

G1389 : Hermann Jacobi, "Was ist Sanskrit?" *Scientia* 14, 1911, 251–274.

G1390 : V.I. Kalyanov, "Classification of the Compound Words in Sanskrit" (in Russian), *Izvestiya of Academia of Sciences, USSR* 6.1, 1912, 77–84.

G1391 : Emil Abegg, "Die Lehre vom *sphoṭa* im Sarvadarśanasaṃgraha," *Festschrift Ernst Wondisch*, pp. 188–195.

G1392 : Jakob Wackernagel, "Indo-Iranica 15. Zur Bildung des 7. Aorists im Altindischen", KZ 46, 1914, 273–275. Reprinted in Wackernagel.

G1393 : V.S. Sowani, "The History and Significance of *upamā*," ABORI 1, 1918–1920 87–98.

G1394 : Gopinath Kaviraj, "The Doctrine of *pratibhā* in Indian Philosophy," ABORI 5, 1923–1924, 1–18, 113–132.

G1395 : Bruno Liebich, "Über den *sphoṭa* (ein Kapitel uber die Sprachphilosophie der Inder)," ZDMG 77, 1923, 208–219.

G1396 : Siddhesvar Varma, "Analysis of Meaning in Indian Semantics," JDL 13, 1926, 1–38.

G1397 : Umesh Mishra, "Physical Theory of Sound and Its Origin in Indian Thought," AUSt 2, 1926, 239–290.

G1398 : Otto Strauss, "Altindische Spekulationen über die Sprache und ihrer Probleme," ZDMG 81, 1927, 99–151.

G1399 : Vittore Pisani, *Grammatica dell'antico indiano*. 3 parts. Rome, 1929–1933.

G1400 : N.H. Purandhare, "A Few Thoughts on Semantics," ABORI 10, 1929, 127–146.

G1401 : Siddheshwar Varma, *Critical Studies in the Phonetic Observations of Indian Grammarians*. London, 1929. Reprinted New Delhi, 1961.

G1402 : Prabhat Chandra Chakravarti, *The Philosophy of Sanskrit Grammar*. Calcutta, 1930.

G1403 : Louis Renou, *Grammaire Sanscrite*. Paris, 1930.

G1404 : Albert Thumb, *Handbuch der Sanskrit*. 2d edition. Heidelberg, 1930.

G1405 : Jakob Wackernagel und Albert Debrunner, *Altindische Grammatik*, volume 3, *Nominalflexion-Zahlwort Pronomen*. Göttingen, 1930.

G1406 : Willem Caland, "A Rhythmic Law in Language," AO 9, 1931, 59–68.

G1407 : J. Mansion, *Esquisse d'une histoire de la language sanscrite*. Paris, 1931.

G1408 : A.M. Ipzzagalli, *Elementi di grammatica sanscrita*. Milan, 1931.

G1409 : P.S. Subrahmanya Sastri, "History of Grammatical Theories in Tamil and Their Relations to the Grammatical Literature in Sanskrit," JOR 5, 1931, 183, 271; 6, 1932, 30, 130, 236, 371; 7, 1933, 113, 255, 376. Reprinted Madras, 1934.

G1410 : Paul Thieme, "Grammatik und Sprache, ein Problem der altindischen Sprachwissenschaft," ZII 8, 1931, 23–32. Reprinted Budruss, pp. 514–523.

G1411 : A. Gawronski, *Podrecznik Sanskrytu*. Krakow, 1932.

G1412 : V.A. Ramaswami Sastri, "The Doctrine of *sphoṭa*", AUJ 1, 1932, 231–240; 2, 1933, 109–120.

G1413 : Paul Thieme, "Zur Geschichte der einheimischen indischen Grammatik," OLZ 35, 1932, 236–242. Reprinted Budruss, pp. 524–527.

G1414 : S.S. Suryanarayana Sastri, "Vacaspati's Criticism of the *sphoṭa* Theory," JOR 6, 1932, 311–321.

G1415 : P.C. Chakravarti, *The Linguistic Speculations of the Hindus*. Calcutta, 1933.

G1416 : K.C. Chatterji, "Some Technical Terms of Sanskrit Grammar," IHQ 9, 1933, 279–281; COJ 3, 1936, 105–132.

G1417 : ———, "The Critics of Sanskrit Grammar," JDL 24, 1934, 1–21.

G1418 : P.C. Chakravarti, "Spiritual Outlook of Sanskrit Grammar," JDL 25.1, 1934, 1–11.

G1419 : Kurt F. Leidecker, *Sanskrit: Essentials of Grammar and Language*. New York, 1934.

G1420 : C.R. Sankaran, "Five Stages of pre-Vedic Determinative-compound-accentuation as Surmised by the Historical Survivals of Their Representatives in Sanskrit," JOR 8, 1934, 335–351; 9, 1935, 119–133.

G1421 : K.C. Chatterji, "Some Rules of *sandhi*," COJ 2, 1935, 261–268; 3, 1935, 9–16.

G1422 : ———, *Phonetics in the Study of Classical and Sacred Languages in the East*. Calcutta, 1935.

G1423 : Thomas Burrow, "Indian Theories on the Nature of Meaning" (summary), TPS 1936, 92–93.

G1424 : S.K. Chatterji, "A History of Aryan Speech in India," CR 60, 1936.

G1425 : Barend Faddegon, *Grammar of the Indeclinables*. Amsterdam, 1936.

G1426 : B.K. Ghosh, "Sanskrit Noun Inflexion," IHQ 12, 1936, 53–66.

G1427 : S.M. Katre, "New Lines of Investigation in Indian Linguistics," ABORI 20, 1936.

G1428 : Gaurinath Sastri Bhattacharya, "A Study in the Dialectics of *sphoṭa*," JDL 29.4, 1937, 1–115. Reprinted Delhi, 1980.

G1429 : A. Carnoy, *Grammaire elementaire de la langue sanscrite comparée avec celle des langues indo-européennes*. 2d edition. Paris, 1937.

G1430 : B.K. Ghosh, *Linguistic Introduction to Sanskrit*. Calcutta, 1937.

G1431 : Sten Konow, "Future Forms Denoting Past Time in Sanskrit and Prakrit," NTS 9, 1937–1938, 231–239.

G1432 : Louis Renou, *Monographie sanskrites: I: La Decadence et la disparition du subjonctif*. Paris, 1937.

G1433 : Johann Schropfer, "Ein Werk über die Philosophie der Sanskrit-Grammatik", AO 9, 1937, 417–429.

G1434 : K.A. Subramania Iyer, "Who Are the *anityasphoṭavādinaḥ*?" PAIOC 8, 1937, 258–263.

G1435 : Isidore Dyen, *The Sanskrit Indeclinables of the Hindu Grammarians and Lexicographers*. Baltimore, 1939.

G1436 : S.P. Chaturvedi, "Scholastic Disquisition in the Pāṇinian System of Grammar," Bhv 2.1, 1940, 59–63.

G1437 : K.M.K. Sharma, "The Doctrine of the *sphoṭa*," KVRACV, pp. 509–516.

G1438 : Betty Heimann, "*Sphoṭa* and *artha*," PVKF, pp. 221–227.

G1439 : Louis Renou, "Les Connexions entre le rituel et la grammaire en Sanskrit", JA 233, 1941–1942, 105–165. Reprinted G1625, pp. 435–469.

G1440 : K.M.K. Sarma, "The Pāṇinian School and the Prātiśākhyas: Post-Pāṇinian Reciprocity of Influence," Bhv 2.2, 1941, 230–238.
G1441 : K. A. Subramania Iyer, "*Pratibhā* as the Meaning of a Sentence," PAIOC 10, 1941, 326–332.
G1442 : J. R. Ballantyne, *First Lessons in Sanskrit Grammar*. Point Loma, Calif., 1942; San Francisco, 1951.
G1443 : Louis Renou, *Terminologie grammaticale du sanskrit*. 3 volumes. BEPHE 280–282, Paris, 1942. Reprinted in 1 volume, Paris, 1957.
G1444 : J. P. Vogel, "De eerste 'grammatica' van het Hindoestansch," *Mededelingen der Koniklijke nederlandse Akademie van Wetenschappen* (Amsterdam) 4 (15), 1942.
G1445 : K. A. Subramania Iyer, "The Conception of *guṇa* among the *vaiyākaraṇas*," NIA 5, 1942, 121–130.
G1446 : S. Suryanarayana Sastri, "Word and Sense," ABORI 23, 1942, 424–430.
G1447 : Jan Gonda, *Kurze Elementargrammatik der Sanskritsprache*. Leiden, 1943.
G1448 : S. M. Katre, *Some Problems of Historical Linguistics in Indo-Aryan*. Bombay, 1943.
G1449 : Vittore Pisani, *Grammatica Sanscrita*. Milan, 1943–1944.
G1450 : K.M.K. Sarma, "*Vāk* Before Bhartṛhari," PO 8.1–2, 1943, 21–36.
G1451 : Jan Gonda, "Quelques Observations sur l'emploi du verbe simple' au lieu d'un composé', etc. dans la langue sanscrite," ActOD 20, 1944, 167–205.
G1452 : Alain Daniélou, "L'Alphabet Sanskrit et la langue universelle," *France-Orient* 5 (48), 1945; *Lotus bleu* 61.2, 51–68.
G1453 : Batakrishna Ghosh, "Aspects of pre-Pāṇinean Sanskrit Grammar", BCLV 1.344–345.
G1454 : T. V. Kapali Sastry, "*Sphoṭa* and the Spoken Word," *Sri Aurobindo Mandir Annual* 4, 1945.
G1455 : Gopinath Kaviraj, "*Nāda*, *bindu* and *kalā*," JGJRI 3, 1945–1946, 47–62. Also *Festschrift Rajeswar Sastri Dravid*, pp. 174–182.
G1456 : Adrian Scharpe, *Précis de grammaire du sanscrit classique I*. Louvain, 1945.
G1457 : K. A. Subramania Iyer, "The *vaiyākaraṇa* Conception of 'Gender,'" BharKau 1945, 291–307.
G1458 : William Dwight Whitney, *Roots, Verb-Forms, and Primary Derivatives of the Sanskrit Language*. New Haven, 1945.
G1459 : Franklin Edgerton, *Sanskrit Historical Phonology*. AOS Offprint Series 19, 1946, 31.
G1460 : Louis Renou, *Grammaire sanscrite élémentaire*. Paris, 1946.
G1461 : M. Scheller, "Ein weiterer Beleg für Accusitavus com Infinitive in Sanskrit?" AO 18, 1946, 248–250.
G1462 : I.J.S. Taraporewala, "Some Considerations of Sanskrit Syntax," NIA 9, 1946, 2–63.
G1463 : Betty Heimann, "Form Not 'Apart' but 'a Part' of Meaning as Exemplified in Sanskrit Literature," UCR 6, 1947, 23–28.
G1464 : K. A. Subramania Iyer, "The Doctrine of *sphoṭa*," JGJRI 5, 1947, 121–147.
G1465 : R. B. Athavale, "*Śābdabodha*—a Study," SPAIOC 14.1, 1948, 111–113.
G1466 : K. C. Chatterji, *Technical Terms and Techniques of Sanskrit Grammar*. Usha Memorial Series 1, Calcutta, 1948, 1964.
G1467 : Barend Faddegon, "The Semitic and Sanskrit Alphabets," *Orientalia Nederlandica* 1948, 261–272.
G1468 : O. Nazzari, *Elementi de Grammatica Sanscrita*. Torino, 1948.

G1469 : K. A. Subramania Iyer, "The Point of View of the *vaiyākaraṇas*," JOR 18, 1948, 84–96. Reprinted in G1625, pp. 393–400.
G1470 : Jan Gonda, "Dissimilation de mots entiers," AO 21, 1949, 267–279.
G1471 : Calvin Kephart, *Sanskrit, Its Origin, Composition, and Diffusion*. Strasburg, Va., 1949.
G1472 : Siddhesvar Varma, "Sanskrit as a Medium of Conveying the Concept of Abstraction," IL 11, 1949–1950, 138–141.
G1473 : V. S. Agrawala, "Pre-Pāṇinian Technical Terms," SB 2, 1950, 135–137.
G1474 : Vidhusekhara Bhattacharya, "Some Composite Roots in Sanskrit," SB 1, 1950, 21–22.
G1475 : K. C. Chatterji, "On the Cases Governed by Some Sanskrit Particles," SB 1, 1950, 23–30.
G1476 : Jan Gonda, "*Ca*," *Lingua* 4, 1950, 1ff.
G1477 : K. A. Subramania Iyer, "The Conception of Action Among the *vaiyākaraṇas*," JGJRI 8, 1950-1951, 165–188.
G1478 : John Brough, "Theories of General Linguistics in the Sanskrit Grammarians," TPS 1951, 27–46. Reprinted G1625, pp. 402–414.
G1479 : J. Lehman, "Randbemerkungen zu den grammatischen 'kategorien,'" IF61, 1951, 17–28.
G1480 : Murray B. Emeneau, *Sanskrit Sandhi and Exercises*. Berkeley, 1952.
G1481 : Jan Gonda, "Professor Burrow and the Pre-history of Sanskrit," *Lingua* 6, 1952, 297–300.
G1482 : ———, "A Critical Survey of the Publications on the Periphrastic Future in Sanskrit," *Lingua* 6, 1952, 158–179.
G1483 : ———, "On Nominative Joining or Replacing' Vocatives," *Lingua* 6, 1952, 89–104.
G1484 : V. A. Ramaswami Sastri, "*Mukhya* and *gauṇa* Words in Language," BDCRI 14, 1952, 1–15.
G1485 : A. F. Stenzler, *Elementarbuch der Sanskrit-Sprache*. Berlin, 1952.
G1486 : F. R. Adredos, *Vedico y sanscrito classico*. Madrid, 1963.
G1487 : William Sidney Allen, *Phonetics in Ancient India*. London, 1953, 1963.
G1488 : Ram Shankar Bhattacharya, "Senses of *ca*," PO 18, 1953, 1–18.
G1489 : John Brough, "Some Indian Theories of Meaning," TPS 1953, 161–176. Reprinted Staal, pp. 414–423.
G1490 : Thomas Burrow, "Some Remarks on the Formation of Nouns in Sanskrit," ABORI 32, 1953, 19–33.
G1491 : M. Mayrhofer, *Sanskrit-Grammatik*. Berlin, 1953.
G1492 : Louis Renou, "Les Grammariens sanskrits," in Renou and Filliozat, pp. 86–94.
G1493 : ———, "Les Speculations sur le language," in Renou and Filliozat, pp. 79–84.
G1494 : K. A. Subramania Iyer, "On the Concept of *upagraha* Among the *vaiyākaraṇas*," JOR 23, 1953–1954, 79–88.
G1495 : Rulon Wells, "Secondary Derivation from Sanskrit *i*-Stems," Lg 29, 1953, 237–241.
G1496 : R. S. Bhattacharya, "Importance of the First Words of the *gaṇapāṭhas*," BhV 15, 1954, 29–34.
G1497 : Thomas Burrow, "The Sanskrit Precative," *Asiatica* 1954, 35–42.
G1498 : A. Debrunner, *Altindische Grammatik*, volume 2, *Die Nominalsuffixe*. Göttingen, 1954.
G1499 : Reingold F. G. Muller, "Über ein Neutrum im Sanskrit," *Die Sprache* 6.1, 1954, 39–45.

G1500 : A. Schropfer, *Geistiger Wortsatz des Indischen und seine Geschichte*. Heidelberg, 1954.

G1501 : E. R. Sreekrishna Sharma, "The Theories of the Ancient Indian Philosophers about Word, Meaning, Their Mutual Relationships and Syntactical Connection," Ph. D. diss., Philipps-Universität Marburg, 1954.

G1502 : K. V. Abhyankar, "A Short Note on *Paribhāṣā* Works in Sanskrit Grammar," ABORI 36, 1955, 157–162.

G1503 : Franklin Edgerton, "An Often Neglected Aspect of Word Composition in Sanskrit and Indo-European," JAOS 75, 1955, 279.

G1504 : M. B. Emeneau, "India and Linguistics," JAOS 75, 1955, 145–153.

G1505 : Jan Gonda, "Use of the Particle '*ca*,'" *Vāk* 5, 1955, 1–73.

G1506 : P. Hartmann, *Nominale Ausdrucksformen im wissenschaftlichen Sanskrit*. Heidelberg, 1955.

G1507 : K. Kunjunni Raja, "Indian Theories on Homophones and Homonyms," ALB 19, 1955, 193–222.

G1508 : ———, "The Theory of Suggestion in Indian Semantics," ALB 19, 1955, 20–26.

G1509 : K. A. Subramania Iyer, "The Concept of *dravya* among the *vaiyākaraṇas*," SPAIOC 18, 1955, 54–56.

G1510 : Bishnupada Bhattacharya, "Contribution of Words: *sphoṭa* Theory and Its Opponents", OH 4, 1956, 217–226.

G1511 : Betty Heimann, "Why Study Sanskrit?" ABORI 28, 1956, 294–300.

G1512 : K. Kunjunni Raja, "*Sphoṭa*: The Theory of Lingusitic Symbols," ALB 20, 1956, 84–116.

G1513 : M. Mayrhofer, "Altindische Nominalbildung: Zum neuen Band der 'Altindischen Grammatik," OLZ 1956, 5–15.

G1514 : Louis Renou, "Sur l' Evolution des composés nominaux en Sanskrit," *Bulletin de la Societe de Linguistique de Paris* 52.1, 1956, 96–116.

G1515———, *Histoire de la langue sanskrite*. Paris, 1956.

G1516 : P. S. Sastri, "Meaning and the Word," OT 2.1, 1956, 99–130.

G1517 : K. V. Abhyankar, "Short e (*ardha ekāra*) and Short *o* (*ardha okāra*) in Sanskrit," ABORI 36, 1957, 154–157.

G1518 : R. S. Bhattacharya, "Some Broad Aspects on Indian Grammar and the Theory of *sphoṭa*," JGJRI 15, 1957–1958, 83–92.

G1519 : Jan Gonda, "A Note on the Functions of the Accusative as Described in the Handbooks," in FVSKB, pp. 72–80.

G1520 : ———, "The Character of the Sanskrit Accusative," in *Martinet Commemoration Volume*. Tenerife, 1957.

G1521 : Chandra Bhan Gupta, "*Vyañjanā* as Suggestive Power," PAIOC 19.2, 1957, 59–62.

G1522 : Betty Heimann, *Terminology*: *Significance of Prefixes*. London, 1957.

G1523 : K. Kunjunni Raja, "Diachronic Linguistics in Ancient India," JMU 29, 1957, 127–130.

G1524 : ———, "*Ākāṅkṣā*: The Main Basis of Syntactic Unity," ALB 21, 1957, 282–295.

G1525 : Louis Renou, "Grammaire et Vedānta," JA 245, 1957, 121–132.

G1526 : Bishnupada Bhattacharya, "Connotation of Words (a Comparative Study of the Viewpoints of Grammarians, Mīmāmsakas and Naiyāyikas)," OH 5, 1958, 147–167.

G1527 : Trilokanath Jha, "The Concept of the Fivefold *śabdānaucitya* in Earlier Grammarians," JBRS 44.3–4, 1958, 164–168.

G1528 : V. I. Kalyanov, "The Means of Expression of the Past Tense in Epic

Sanskrit, According to the Materials of the Mahābhārata" (in Russian). *Scientific Paper no.* 13 *of the Oriental Institute of the Academy of Sciences, USSR*, 1958.

G1529 : K. Kunjunni Raja, "The Indian Influence on Linguistics," JMU 30, 1958, 93–111.

G1530 : ———, "The Elliptic Sentence—Indian Theories," ALB 22, 1958, 25–31.

G1531 : David Seyfort Ruegg, "On the Term *buddhivipariṇāma* and the Problem of Illusory Change," IIJ 2, 1958, 271–283.

G1532 : Gaurinath Sastri, "Nature of Absolute in the Philosophy of Grammar," PO 31, 1958, 217–218.

G1533 : Sukumar Sen, *Histrory and Prehistory of Sanskrit.* Mysore, 1958.

G1534 : Satya Vrat, "Studies in Sanskrit Semantics," PO 23.3–4, 1958, 1–14.

G1535 : Thomas Burrow, *The Sanskrit Language.* London, 1959.

G1536 : Erich Frauwallner, "Das Eindringen der Sprachtheorie in die indischen philosophischen Systeme," *Indologung-Tagen*, 1959, 239–243.

G1537 : Gajanan Moreshwar Patil, "Case-Morphemes in Sanskrit Nominal Declension," SPAIOC 20, 1959, 120.

G1538 : D. S. Ruegg, *Contributions à l'histoire de la philosophie linguistique indienne.* PICI 7, Paris, 1959.

G1539 : E. R. Sreekrishna Sarma, "Syntactic Meaning—Two Theories," ALB 23, 1959, 41–61.

G1540 : K. Kunjunni Raja, "*Tātparya* as a Separate *vṛtti*," PAIOC 20.2, 1959, 319–332.

G1541 : Richard V. de Smet, "Language and Philosophy in India," PICP 12.10, 1960, 47–54.

G1542 : Bimal Krishna Matilal, "The Doctrine of *karaṇa* in Grammar and Logic," JGJRI 17, 1960, 63–69. Also PAIOC 20, 1961, 303–308.

G1543 : Kalika Charan Pandeya, "The Theory of *śabdabrahman* and *sphoṭa*," JGJRI 17, 1960–1961, 235–255. Also see Bh 6.2, 1962–1963, 102–104.

G1544 : Louis Renou, "La Theorie des temps du verbe d'apres grammariens sanskrits," JA 248, 1960, 305–337. Reprinted G1625, pp. 478–499.

G1545 : J. Frits Staal, "Correlations Between Language and Logic in Indian Thought," BSOAS 23, 1960, 109–122.

G1546 : K. V. Abhyankar, *A Dictionary of Sanskrit Grammar.* GOS 134, Baroda, 1961.

G1547 : W. S. Allen, *Sandhi, the Theoretical, Phonetic, and Historical Bases of Word-Junction in Sanskrit.* Janua Linguarum, series minor 17. The Hague, 1962.

G1548 : Bishnupada Bhattacharya, *A Study in Language and Meaning.* Calcutta, 1962.

G1549 : Arthur L. Herman, "*Sphoṭa*," JGJRI 19, 1962–1963, 1–21.

G1550 : S. D. Joshi, "Verbs and Nouns in Sanskrit," IL 23, 1962, 60–63.

G1551 : K. Kunjunni Raja, "*Prārthayanti*—a Ghost Word Discussed by the Grammarians," ALB 26, 1962, 26–28.

G1552 : Ram Adhar Pathak, "Origin and Development of Sanskrit Grammar." Ph.D. diss., Banaras Hindu University, 1962.

G1553 : Rosane Rocher, "The Hindu Grammarians and Linguistic Change," JOI 11, 1962, 260–268.

G1554 : J. Frits Staal, "Negation and the Law of Contradiction in Indian Thought: A Comparative Study," BSOAS 25, 1962, 52–71.

G1555 : Ram Chandra Pandeya, *The Problem of Meaning in Indian Philosophy.* Delhi, 1963.

G1556 : K. Kunjunni Raja, *Indian Theories of Meaning.* ALS 91, Madras, 1963, 1969.

G1557 : E.R. Sreekrishna Sharma, "Controversies over *śabda*," *Janamuktavali* 1963, 182–193.

G1558 : Madeleine Biardeau, *Théorie de la connaissance et philosophie de la parole dans la brahmanisme classique*. Paris, The Hague, 1964.

G1559 : S.S. Barlingay, "Theories of Language in Indian Logic," *International Philosophical Quarterly* 4, 1964, 94–109.

G1560 : T.N. Dave, "*Upakrama-upasaṃhāra*—as a Criterion for Textual Interpretation," SPP 4.1, 1964 4–17.

G1561 : Richard Hauschild *Register zur Altindischen Grammatik von. J. Wackernagel und A. Debrunner (Bd. I–III)*. Göttingen, 1964.

G1562 : Mukund Madhava Sharma, "Some Observations on the *sphoṭa* Theory," CIDO 26, summaries 1964, 228–229.

G1563 : K.V. Abhyankar, "Euphonic Combinations of *r* and *l* with *r* and *l*," IL 26, 1965, 1–7.

G1564 : Rosane Rocher, "Les Grammariens indiens, leurs buts et leurs methodes," RUB 18, 1965–1966, 77–78.

G1565 : V. Anjaneya Sharma, "The *śabda-brahman* and the *prasthānatraya*," SVUOJ 8, 1965, 31–35.

G1566 : J. Frits Staal, "Reification, Quotation and Nominalization", in *Festschrift Bochenski*, pp. 151–187.

G1567 : Sergiu Al-George, "La Fonction révélatrice des consonnes chez les phoneticiens de l'Inde antique," CLTA 3, 1966, 11–15.

G1568 : Saudamini Bahulikar, "The Construcions *stotaḥ pakaḥ* and *stokaṃ pakaḥ*," PAIOC 22, 1966, 93–98.

G1569 : T.N. Dave, "Śrī Śankarācārya and *sphoṭa*," SPP 6.1, 1966, 19–27.

G1570 : C.G. Hartman, *Emphasizing and Connecting Particles in the Thirteen Principal Upaniṣads*. Annales Scientiarum Fennicare, series B, no. 143.2. Helsinki, 1966.

G1571 : S.D. Joshi, "Adjectives and Substantives as a Single Class in the 'Parts of Speech,' " PCASS-A 9, 1966. Also JUP 25, 1967, 19–30.

G1572 : ———, "Word-integrity and Syntactic Analysis," SPAIOC 23.1, 1966, 143. PCASS-A 20, 1968 (=JUP 27, 1968), 165–173.

G1573 : G. Marulasiddaiah, *Śabdavṛttis, Power of Words*. Mysore, 1966.

G1574 : B.L. Matilal, "Indian Theorists on the Nature of the Sentence (*vākya*)," FL 2, 1966, 377–393.

G1575 : Bommakanti Srinivasacaryulu, "Language Spoken and Written," SPAIOC 23.1, 1966, 170.

G1576 : J. Frits Staal, "Indian Semantics, I," JAOS 86, 1966, 304–310.

G1577 : ———, "Room at the Top in Sanskrit: Ancient and Modern Descriptions of Nominal Composition," "IIJ 9, 1966, 165–198.

G1578 : R.N. Vele, "A Law About Nominal Suffixes Beginning with *a-* in Sanskrit," SPAIOC 23.1, 1966, 169.

G1579 : George Cardona, "*Anvaya* and *vyatireka* in Indian Grammar," ALB 31–32, 1967–1968, 313–352. Summarized in CIDO 27, 313–314.

G1580 : G.T. Deshpande, "On the Accent of the Vocative (*amantita*)," NUJ 18, 1967 113–120.

G1581 : Suresachandra Dyaneshwar Laddu "A pre-Patañjalian Grammatical Observation," IA 3d series 2.4, 1967, 40–41.

G1582 : Y. Ojihara, "Causerie vyākaraṇique (IV): *jāti* 'genus' et deux definitions pre-patañjaliennes," JIBSt 16, 1967, 451–459. Reprinted G1625, pp. 425–431.

G1583 : J. Frits Staal *Word Order in Sanskrit and Universal Grammar.* FLSS 5, Dordrecht, 1967.

G1584 : M.D. Balasubrahmanyam, "*Amavāsya*: An Accentual Study" JUP 27, 1968, 1–25.

G1585 : M.B. Emeneau, "Sanskrit Syntactic Particles—*kila, khalu, nūnam,*" IIJ 11, 1968–1969, 241–268.

G1586 : Jan Gonda, "Abbreviated and Inverted Nominal Compounds in Sanskrit," *Janua Linguarum Series* 34, 1968, 221–246.

G1587 : Siegfried Lienhard, "Einige Bemerkungen über *Śabdabrahman* and *Vivarta* bei Bhavabhūti," WZKSOA 12–13, 1968–1969, 215–220.

G1588 : T.S. Nandi, "The Problem of *śabdaśaktimūladhvani* or Suggestion Based on the Power of the Word," JOI 18, 1968–1969, 101–125.

G1589 : G.B. Palsule, "The Role of *kṛ* in the Sanskrit Grammatical terms," PCASS-A 24, 1968 (=JUP 29, 1969, 11–29).

G1590 : ———, "Some Primary Nominal Formations Missing in Pāṇini," PCASS-A 18, 1968 (=JUP 27, 1967, 145–151).

G1591 : J.D. Singh, The Bases of Sanskrit Phonology," KUI 2, 1968, 107–118. Also ACIL 10.4, 1970, 145–153.

G1592 : Paul Thieme, "*Ādeśa*," PICI 28, 1968, 715–723. Reprinted Budruss, pp. 259–267.

G1593 : Siddheshwar Varma, "Plurality—Philosophical and Grammatical—in Sanskrit Tradition," SVUOJ 11, 1968, 1–4.

G1594 : K.V. Abhyankar, "Accent in Sanskrit," ABORI 50, 1969, 41–55.

G1595 : M.D. Balasubrahmanyam, "*Ārya-*: An Accentual Study," IA 3d series 3, 1969, 112–127.

G1596 : ———, "The Accent of *Kṛt* Formations." Ph.D. diss., University of Poona, 1969.

G1597 : Thomas Burrow, "Sanskrit," *Current Trends in Linguistics* 5, 1969, 3–35.

G1598 : Govind Vinayak Devasthali, "*Paribhāṣā* (Introduction and General Survey)," IA 3d series 3, 1969 1–13.

G1599 : K. Doraswamy "Phonological Studies in Ancient India and Greece," KUJ 3, 1969, 394–397.

G1600 : F. Lambert, "Who Wrote the First Sanskrit Grammar?" BhV 29, 1969, 1–9.

G1601 : Harald Millonig, "Stumme Laute: Untersüchung einer Beschreibungstechnik altindischer Linguistik." Ph.D. diss., University of Würzburg, 1969.

G1602 M.S. Narayana Murti, "Two Versions of the *ekasaṃjñādhikāra*," SVUOJ 12, 1969, 75–83.

G1603 : B.P. Rajapurohit, "Some Parallels Between Indian and Western Semantics," JKU 13, 1969, 72–81.

G1604 : J. Frits Staal, "Sanskrit Philosophy of Language," *Current Trends in Linguistics* 5, 1969, 449–531.

G1605 : Veluri Subba Rao, *The Philosophy of a Sentence and Its Parts.* New Delhi, 1969.

G1606 : Siddheshwar Varma, "Object—Philosophical and Grammatical—in Sanskrit," SVUJO 12, 1969, 39–44

G1607 : Ashok Aklujkar, "Ancient Indian Semantics," ABORI 51, 1970, 11–29.

G1608 : Sergiu Al-George, "L 'Inde antique et les origines du structuralisme," ACIL 10.2, 1970, 235–240.

G1609 : H.S. Ananthanarayana, "The *kāraka* Theory and Case Grammar," IL 31, 1970, 14–27.

G1610 : Vidya Niwas Misra, "Structural Meaning: An Indian Standpoint," ACIL 10.2, 1970, 555–559.

G1611 : Ramananda Acharya, "A Peep into the concepts of Cause and Instrument," *Anvīkṣā* 5.2, 1971, 88–92.

G1612 : Sergiu Al-George, "*Lakṣaṇā*, 'Grammatical Role' " JGJRI 27.3–4, 1971, 213-221.

G1613 : Venkatesh Laxman Joshi, "Treatment of Loanwords in Sankrit Grammar," IL 32, 1971, 113–122.

G1614 : S.D. Laddu, "Ancient Sanskrit Grammarians and the Literary Records," VIJ 9, 1971, 315–322.

G1615 : B.K. Matilal, *Epistemology, Logic and Grammar in Indian Philosophical Analysis*. The Hague, Paris, 1971.

G1616 : S.G. Moghe, "*Paribhāṣās* of *vyākaraṇa* and the Mīmāṃsā Rules of Interpretation," *Festschrift Rajeswar Sastri Dravid*, English section, pp. 90–100.

G1617 : M.S. Narayana Murti, "Sanskrit Compounds, a Philosophical Study." Ph.D. diss., Tirupati, 1971.

G1618 : Michael Silverstein, ed., *Whitney on Language: Selected Writings of William Dwight Whitney*. Cambridge, Mass., 1971.

G1619 : P. Thirujnanasambandham, "Problems of Meaning," in *Dr. V. Raghavan Shashtyabdapurti Felicitation Volume*, Madras, 1971, pp. 183–187.

G1620 : Franz Bopp, "Vergleiehende Zergliderung des Sanskrits und der mit ihm Verwendten Sprachen. Erste Abhandlung von der Würzeln und Pronominem erster und zweiter Person," *Abhandlungender Koniglichen Akademie der Wissenschaften zu Berlin*, ph. -hist. Kl. 1972, 117–148. Reprinted in *Kleine Schriften zur vergleichenden Sprachwissenschaft*, Leipzig, 1972, pp. 1–32.

G1621 : Pradip Kumar Mazumdar, "A Philosophical Approach to the Meaning of Particles," PAIOC 26, 1972, 256–258.

G1622 : Vidhata Mishra, *A Critical Study of Sanskrit Phonetics*. ChSSt 83. Varanasi, 1972.

G1623 : M.D. Pandit, "A Comparative Study of All Sanskrit Grammars, with *special* Reference to Past Passive Participle Formations." Ph.D. diss., University of Poona, 1972.

G1624 : Kali Charan Sastri, *Bengal's Contribution to Sanskrit Grammar in the Paninian and Candra Systems*, part one, *General Introduction*. CSCRS 53. Calcutta, 1972.

G1625 : J. Frits Staal, ed., *A Reader on the Sanskrit Grammarians*. SIL 1. Cambridge, Mass., 1972.

G1626 : Paul Thieme, "The Sanskrit Language," JBRS 58, 1972, 197–223.

G1627 : Siddheshwar Varma, "The Concept of 'Agent'—Philosophical and Grammatical—in Sanskrit," JGJRI 28.1–2, 1972, 713–721.

G1628 : ———, "Purpose—Philosophical and Grammatical—in Indian Tradition," SVUOJ 15, 1972, 11–16.

G1629 : J.G. Arapura, "Some Perspectives on Indian Philosophy of Language," *University of Rajasthan Studies in Sanskrit and Hindi* 6, 1973–1974, 1–32.

G1630 : Veena Bhatnagar, "Un-Pāṇinian *Sandhi* and Syntax in Epic Sanskrit." Ph.D. diss., University of Delhi, 1973.

G1631 : John Brough, "I-Ching on the Sanskrit Grammarians," BSOAS 36, 1973, 248–260.

G1632 : George Cardona, "Indian Grammarians on Adverbs," *Festschrift Kahane*, pp. 85–98.

G1633 : B.K. Matilal, "The Notion of Substance and Quality in Ancient Indian Grammar," in ACUT 2, 1973, 384–405.

G1634 : M.S. Narayana Murti, "Philosophy of Grammar," SVUOJ 16, 1973, 37–54.

G1635 : K.S. Ramamurti, "Andhra's Contribution to Indian Culture: *vyākaraṇa*," SVUOJ 16, 1973, 25–36.

G1636 : Jag Deva Singh, "Study of Language," KUJ 7, 1973, 199–203.

G1637 : Pratap Bandyopadhyay, "Sanskrit Indeclinables (*upasargas* and *nipātas*) and Their Meaning," SPAIOC 27, 1974, 231–232.

G1638 : S. Datta Kharbas and Rama Nath Sharma, *Sanskrit Grammar: A Bibliography of Selected Western Language Materials*. Rochester, 1974.

G1639 : G.V. Devasthali, "*Vākya* According to the Munitraya of Sanskrit Grammar," CDSFV 1974, 206–215.

G1640 : Jan Gonda, "*Nimitta*," CDSFV 1974, 233–240.

G1641 : T.S. Gourypathy Sastry, "Quotative Nominals in Sanskrit," IL 35, 1974, 1–13.

G1643 : T.R.V. Murti, "Some Comments on the Philosophy of Language in the Indian Context," JIP 2, 1974, 321–331.

G1644 : G.B. Palsule, "Some Further Examples of the Occasional Sanskrit *saṇadahi u-v > v*," VIJ 12, 1974, 235–240.

G1645 : V. Raghavan, "How Many Grammars?" CDSFV 1974, 271–278.

G1646 : H.G. Ranade, "Parts of Speech in Sanskrit," IL 35, 1974, 129–138.

G1647 : J.M. Shukla, "Grammatical *paribhāṣās* of the Jaina Grammarians," JOI 24, 1974–1975, 128–138.

G1648 : P. Sriramamurti, "Some Secondary Roots in Sanskrit," SPAIOC 27, 1974, 235.

G1649 : J. Frits Staal, "The Origin and Development of Linguistics in India," in D. Hymes, ed., *Studies in the History of Linguistics*, Bloomington, 1974, pp. 63–74.

G1650 : Siddheswar Varma, "Separation, Philosophical and Grammatical, in Indian Tradition," VIJ 12, 1974, 468–471.

G1651 : George Cardona, "Paraphrase and Sentence Analysis: Some Indian Views," JIP 3, 1975, 259–282.

G1652 : Madhva Deshpande, "Phonetics of Short *a* in Sanskrit," IIJ 17, 1975, 195–209.

G1653 : ———, *Critical Studies in Indian Grammarians I: The Theory of Homogeneity (Sāvarṇya)*. Ann Arbor, 1975.

G1654 : Pierre-Sylvain Filliozat, "On the Analysis of Sanskrit Compounds," in AOR Silver Jubilee Volume, 1975, pp. 81–95.

G1655 : Manjulika Guha, "*Sphoṭa* Theory," JASBe 17, 1975.

G1656 : S.D. Joshi, "*Śābdabodha* and Theories of Verbal Denotation," SVUOJ 18, 1975, 21–32.

G1657 : K. Krishnamoorthy, "*Tātparya* and *dhvani*," in AOR Silver Jubilee Volume 1975, pp. 21–33.

G1658 : K. Kunjunni Raja, "*Vyañjanā*: Suggestive Function of Language," in AOR Silver Jubilee Volume 1975, pp. 602–607.

G1659 : Angelo Morretta, "Sanskrit and the Sacred Language," ITaur 3–4, 1975–1976, 339–352.

G1660 : Kenneth H. Post, "Śaṃkara's Objection to the *sphoṭavāda*," ABORI 56, 1975, 67–76.

G1661 : Satya Vrat Sastri, "Sanskrit Usage," ITaur 3–4, 1975–1976, 449–454.

G1662 : J. Frits Staal, "The concept of Metalanguage and Its Indian Background," JIP 3, 1975, 315–354.

G1663 : J.M. Shukla, "Particle in Sanskrit," JOI 25, 1975–1976, 252–259.

G1664 : S. Venkitasubramonia Iyer, "The Concept and Scope of *adhikaraṇa* in Sanskrit Grammar," VRFV 1975, 145–162.

G1665 : Ashok Aklujkar, "Sanskrit and the Linguistic Science," PISC 1.2.2, 1976, 85.

G1666 : Michael Coulson, *Sanskrit: An Introduction to the Classical Language*. London, 1976.

G1667 : S.D. Joshi, "Sanskrit Grammar," in R.N. Dandekar, ed., *Ramakrishna Gopal Bhandarkar as an Indologist: A Symposium*, Poona, 1976, pp. 113–142.

G1668 : S.G. Kantawala, "Some Remarks on the Teaching of the Sanskrit Grammar," JOI 26, 1976–1977, 164–169.

G1669 : Hari Mohan Mishra, "Sanskrit and Semantics," PISC 1.2.2, 1976, 86–90.

G1670 : Satya Swarup Mishra, "Contribution of Sanskrit to the Study of Linguistics," PISC 1.2.2, 1976, 98–101.

G1671 : K. Raghavan Pillai, "Sanskrit Linguistics in the Context of General Linguistics," PISC 1.2.2, 1976, 83–84.

G1672 : Hartmut Scharfe, "A Second 'Index fossil' of Sanskrit Grammarians," JAOS 96, 1976, 274–280.

G1673 : K.A. Subramania Iyer, "Sanskrit and the Philosophy of Language," PISC 1.2.2, 1966, 70–81.

G1674 : Satyakam Varma, "The Philosophy of Universal Grammar," SVSI, pp. 160–184.

G1675 : ———, "Brief Survey of Sanskrit Grammar," SVSI, pp. 103–132.

G1676 : ———, "Divisibility of Phoneme," SVSI, pp. 144–159.

G1677 : Siddhesvara Varma, "Relationship—Philosophical and Grammatical—in Indian Tradition," VIJ 14, 1976, 1–4.

G1678 : George Cardona, "A Note on Morphophonemic and Phonetic Rules in Sanskrit," MO 10, 1977, 1–6.

G1679 : S.D. Joshi and J.A.F. Roodbergen, "*Vākyasaṃskāra* and *padasaṃskāra*," JBBRAS 52–53, 1977–1978, 142–148.

G1680 : Pradipa Kumar Mazumdar, *The Philosophy of Language in the Light of Paninian and the Mimamsaka Schools of Indian Philosophy*. Calcutta, 1977.

G1681 : Hartmut Scharfe, *A History of Indian Literature: Grammatical Literature*. Wiesbaden, 1977.

G1682 : A. Seshakumar, "The *Paribhāṣās* in Sanskrit Grammar: A Study." Ph.D. diss., Andhra University, 1977.

G1683 : J.M. Shukla, "*Bhāva* and *abhāva* According to the Grammarians," JBBRAS 52–53, 1977–1978, 260–267.

G1684 : Madhva Deshpande, "Pāṇinian Grammarians on Dialectical Variation," ALB 40, 1978, 61–114.

G1685 : Pierre Filliozat, "L'école moderne des Vaiyākarana du Mahārāshṭra," ITaur 6, 1978, 143–150.

G1686 : G. Gren. Ecklund, *A Study of Nominal Sentences in the Oldest Upanishads*. Act. Universitatis Upsaliensus. Studia Indoeuropeae Upsaliensis 3. Uppsala, Stockholm, 1978.

G1687 : H.V. Nagaraja Rao, "The Scope and Necessity of *aṅgādhikāra*," JIP 6, 1978, 145–176.

G1688 : Mario Piantelli, "Śaṃkara's Treatment of *śabdaprabhāvatva* in BSBh I.3.28 and the Problem of a Nexus Between the So-called *śabdabrahman* and *sphoṭa*: Some Considerations," ITaur 6, 1978, 241–250.

G1689 : D.S. Ruegg, "Mathematical and Linguistic Models in Indian Thought the Case of *śūnyatā*," WZKSOA 22, 1978, 171–182.

G1690 : Krishna Sivaraman, "The Śaiva and the Grammarian Perspectives of Language," IPR 19–32.

G1691 : Satya Vrat, "Sanskrit grammar," in CHI 5, 1978, 312–320.

G1692 : Sh. Bira and O. Sukhbeatar, "On the Tibetan and Mongolian Translations of Sanskrit Grammatical Works," ITaur 7, 1979 127–138.

G1693 : Johannes Bronkhorst "Yāska's Classification of *nipātas*" ABORI 60, 1979 137–149.

G1694 : Richard Gombrich "He Cooks Softly: Adverbs in Sanskrit Grammar" BSOAS 42, 1979, 244–256.

G1695 : Wilhelm Rau "Grammatik" in H. Bechert and G. von Simonson eds. *Einführung in die Indologie*. Dharmstadt 1979 pp. 159–161. 118ff.

G1696 : J. Frits Staal "Oriental Ideas on the Origin of Language" JAOS 99, 1979 1–14.

G1697 : M.M. Deshpande *Evolution of Syntactic Theory in Sanskrit Grammar: Syntax of the Sanskrit Infinitive -tum UN*. Linguistica Extrema Studia 10. Ann Arbor, 1980.

G1698 : V.S. Joshi, " '*Parā vāk*' and Sanskrit Grammarians" VJPSG 1980, 34–35.

G1699 : ——— "An Introduction to the Last Age in Pāṇini's School, VJPSG 1980, 79–90.

G1700 : ——— "Treatment of Loan Words in Sanskrit Grammar" VJPSG 1980 1–19.

G1700A : Harold Coward, *The Sphoṭa Theory of Language*. Delhi, 1980.

G1701 : Bernfried Schlerath, *Sanskrit Vocabulary*. Leiden, 1980.

G1702 : E.R. Sreekrishna Sarma, "*Sphoṭa* and Śaṃkara," ALB 44–45, 1980–1981, 223–228.

G1703 : T. Venkatacharya. "Significance of the Dictum 'yata evakāras tato nyātra niyamaḥ,' " VIJ 18, 1980, 80–87.

G1704 : Alex Wayman, "Notes on Metaphoric Transfer," ALB 44–45, 1980–1981, 272–285.

G1705 : M.M. Deshpande, "Sanskrit Gerund Constructions: Syntactic Disputations," IIJ 23, 1981, 167–185.

G1706 : K. Meenakshi, "Sanskrit Grammar as Model for Writing Tamil Grammar" (summary). SWSC 5, Delhi, 1981, pp. 49–50.

G1707 : J. Ouseparampil, "The Problem of Gender in Sanskrit and Indo-European Language" (summary). SWSC 5, Delhi, 1981, pp. 59–60.

G1708 : A.C. Sarangi, "Ancient Grammarians and Their 'Correct' Interpretations," BhV 40.4, 1981, 26–31.

G1709 : M.S. Narayana Murti, "Causality in Sanskrit Grammar" (summary). SWSC 5, Delhi, 1981, p. 58.

G1710 : J. Bronkhorst, "On the History of Pāṇinian Grammar in the Early Centuries Following Patañjali," JIP 11, 1983, 357–412.

G1711 : S.D. Laddu, "On the Earliest Handbooks on Derivation (*prakriyā*) in Sanskrit Grammar," DNSFV 1982, 83–90.

G1712 : V.N. Jha, "The Structure of a *śābdabodha*," DNSFV 1982, 77–82.

G1713 : M.S. Narayana Murti, "Divisions of Time According to Indian Grammarians," ALB 46, 1982, 12–24.

G1714 : J. Frits Staal, "Ritual, Grammar, and the Origins of Science in India," JIP 10, 1982, 3–36.

NOTES

"G" references are to the Bibliography in this Volume, "RB" refers to Volume I: Bibliography (Revised Edition) of the *Encyclopedia of Indian Philosophies.* Other abbreviations are identified in the Bibliography.

1 : Historical Resume

1. Kumārila, *Tantravārttika*, translated by Ganganatha Jha (RB155), p. 306.

2. Bṛhaddevatā, ed. A.A. Macdonnell, Harvard Oriental Series 5 (Cambridge, Mass., 1904), 2.117.

3. Leonard Bloomfield, *Language* (New York, 1933), p. 5.

4. See, part two, summary 4.

5. Gautama, *Nyāyasūtra* 2.2.65.

6. Pāṇini, *Aṣṭādhyayī* 2.1.1: "samarthaḥ padavidhiḥ." See Kunjunni Raja (G1556), pp. 154–156.

7. Yāska, *Nirukta* 1.1: "indriyanityaṃ vacanam audumbarāyaṇaḥ." See also Brough (G8).

8. Yāska, *Nirukta* 1.2. The six stages are "a thing comes into existence, exists, changes, grows, decays, and ceases to exist."

9. *Kṛṣṇa Yajurveda* 6.4.7.

10. Patañjali, *Mahābhāṣya* 1.1.1.

11. Bhartṛhari, *Vākyapadīya* 2.347.

12. Nāgeśa Bhaṭṭa, *Sphoṭavāda*, concluding verse. See part two, summary, 45 on *Sphoṭavāda.*

13. Thieme (G458), pp. 23–24.

14. Cardona, p. 273 (cf. abbreviation list in the bibliography).

15. See part two, summary 13.

16. See Gode (G1128).

17. Also called *Vaiyākaraṇamatonmajjinī*. It is quoted under that title in Nāgeśa Bhaṭṭa's *Sphoṭavāda.*

18. Ganganatha Jha (RB9473), p. 189.

19. Bhartṛhari, *Vākyapadīya* 2.3. See also Kunjunni Raja (G355), pp. 165–170.

20. See Jagadīśa's *Śabdaśaktiprakāśikā.*

21. This subsection was written by Shoryu Katsura.

22. For Dignāga's theory of *anyāpoha* and references to previous studies of the subject, see S. Katsura, "The *Apoha* Theory of Dignāga," *Journal of Indian and Buddhist Studies.* 28.1 (1979): 16–20.

23. Masaaki Hattori, "The Sautrāntika Background of the *Apoha* Theory," in *Buddhist Thought and Civilization: Essays in Honor of Herbert V. Guenther on His Sixtieth Birthday* (Emeryville, Calif., 1977), pp. 50–52.

24. Dignāga, *Pramāṇasamuccayavṛtti* (Vasudharakṣita's version) 70b^8; M. Hattori, "A Study of the Chapter on *Apoha* of the Mīmāṃsāślokavārttika (II)" (in Japanese), *Memoirs of the Faculty of Letters, Kyoto University* 15, 1975: 25, n. 20.

25. *Pramāṇasamuccayavṛtti* 169a2–4 = 83a6–8; See also Iyengar (G795), pp. 147–149.

26. Apoddhāre padasyāyāṃ vākyād artho vivecitaḥ / Vākyārthaḥ pratibhākyo yaṃ tenādāv upajanyate."

27. John Ruskin, *Sesame and Lilies unto This Last* (London, 1952).

2: Metaphysics

1. Hiriyanna (RB11464), pp. 182–183.
2. Staal (G1662), p. 319.
3. See, for example, the critique of modern language theories by Klaus Klostermaier in "Man Carries the Power of All Things in His Mouth," in *Revelation in Indian Thought*, ed. H. Coward and K. Sivaraman (Emeryville, Calif., 1977), p. 8.
4. Hans-Georg Gadamer, "Man and Language," in *Philosophical Hermeneutics*, trans. D.E. Linge (Berkeley, 1976), pp. 59–68.
5. *Vak* 1 (1958): 10–14.
6. Ibid., pp. 1–2.
7. *Ṛg Veda* 1.164.35 "brahmāyaṃ vācaḥ paramaṃ vyomaḥ."
8. As translated by K.A. Subramania Iyer (G721), p. 14.
9. See Murti (G1643), pp. 321–331.
10. Sri Aurobindo, *The Secret of the Veda* (Pondicherry, 1971), p. 8.
11. Bhartṛhari, *Vākyapadīya* 1.11.
12. See Frauwallner (RB12160).
13. See part two, summary 3, of Pāṇini's *Aṣṭādhyāyī*, *sūtras* 1.1.21, 1.1.65.
14. See, for example, the fine critical survey of modern biblical scholarship presented by Harvey McArthur in his introduction to *In Search of the Historical Jesus* (New York, 1969). The survey of form criticism is found on pp. 6–7. Although this analysis focuses on biblical studies, the same points would generally apply to all modern western literary criticism.
15. The Vedas also offer their own speculations regarding time. Time is described in one hymn as the first god, existing in many forms. Time generates the sky and the earth and sets in motion the past, the present, and the future. Time is the lord of all and the father of Prajāpati. The universe is set in motion and sustained by time. Indeed, in the *Atharva Veda* 19: 53 and 54, time (*kāla*) is celebrated as the primordial power and unifying principle of the universe. In *kāla* lie the worlds and the sun. By *kāla* was the universe urged forth. *Kāla* is Brahman. "Time contains and conquers all, and still continues onward" (W. Norman Brown, "Veda and Religion," in *India and Indology*, ed. R. Rocher [Delhi, 1978] , p. 45). But the high place accorded *kāla* in the *Atharva Veda* is seldom repeated in the Upaniṣads, and in the *Śvetāśvatara* the view that everything came out of time is regarded as a heretical doctrine (S.N. Dasgupta [RB11488,] 66). In the *Maitrī Upaniṣad*, though, time is given the same high status as in the *Atharva Veda*. In *Maitrī* 6 : 15 we read:

> There are, assuredly, two forms of Brahma: Time and the Timeless. That which is prior to the sun is the Timeless (*akāla*), without parts (*akāla*). But that which begins with the sun is Time, which has parts. Verily, the form of that which has parts is the year. From the year, in truth, are these creatures produced. Through the year, verily, after having been produced, do they grow. In the year they disappear. Therefore the year, verily, is Prajāpati, is Time, is food, is the Brahma-abode, and is Ātman. For thus has it been said :
>
> Tis Time that cooks created things,
> All things, indeed, in the Great Soul (*mahātman*)
> In what, however, Time is cooked—
> Who knows that, he the Veda knows.

(Translation by R.E. Hume, *The Thirteen Principal Upanisads* [Oxford, 1968], p. 434.) As in the *Atharva Veda*, time is here given the highest status of being identified with Prajāpati, but now also with Brahman and Ātman. Verse sixteen goes on to describe embodied Time as the great ocean of creatures, planets, and all things.

16. As translated by Peri Sarveswara Sharma (G738), p. 42.
17. Sastri (G706).
18. Subramania Iyer (G734).
19. G738, p. 50.
20. See Mahadevan (RB5466), pp. 236–251.
21. See Śaṃkara, introduction to *Brahmasūtrabhāṣya*, trans. G. Thibaut (RB243), 3ff.
22. RB5466, p. 229.
23. An English translation of Helārāja's *Ṭīkā* has been included by Peri Sarvesvara Sharma in G738. The date indicated is the one proposed by Sharma, p. 12.
24. Bhartṛhari, *Vākyapadīya* 3.9.62. See the translations in G738 and G748A.
25. K.A. Subramania Iyer's paraphrase of Helārāja's commentary on *Vākyapadīya* 3.9.62. See G748A, p. 54.
26. *Vākyapadīya* 1.142.
27. Ibid. 3.9.4. Translated by Subramania Iyer (G748A).
28. Ibid. 3.9.5.
29. Ibid. 3.9.23.
30. Ibid. 3.9.24. This balance, says Helāraja in his comment on 3.26, is Bhartṛhari's meaning of the term *vivarta*, which appears in *Vākyapadīya* 1.1 and 3.3.81.
31. Ibid. 3.9.74.
32. Ibid. 3.9.37.
33. Ibid. 3.9.41.
34. Ibid. 3.9.45, and *Ṭika* thereon.
35. Ibid. 3.9.46.
36. Ibid. 3.9.52.
37. Patañjali, *Yogasūtra* 3.13, translated by Rama Prasada (New Delhi, 1978), pp. 190ff.
38. *Vākyapadīya* 3.9.52.
39. Ibid. 3.9.53.
40. Ibid. 3.9.74.
41. Patañjali, *Mahābhāṣya* 4.2.3.
42. See introduction to G738, p. 37.
43. Potter (RB9446), pp. 91–93.
44. Ibid.
45. See introduction to G738, p. 19.
46. See Subramania Iyer (G719), pp. 112–113.
47. SVSI, p. 242.
48. Subramania Iyer, (G734), p. 58.
49. Sastri (G1428), 1980 ed., p. 82.
50. *Vākyapadīya* 3.9.46.
51. Ibid. 3.9.4.
52. Ibid. 3.9.74.
53. For a full analysis of the function of time see Coward (G777).
54. Cf. Klaus Klostermaier, cited in n. 3 above.
55. Subramania Iyer (G721), p. 119.
56. T.S. Eliot, *Murder in the Cathedral* (London, 1955), p. 44.
57. *Vākyapadīya* 1.142 with *vṛtti*.
58. Ibid. 1.143, *vrtti*. See also ibid. 1.14.

59. Ibid. 1.14.
60. Sastri (G1428), 1980 ed., p. 85.
61. *Vākyapadīya* 1.120 and *vrtti.*
62. Ibid. 1.120 and *vṛtti.*
63. Ibid. 1.5 and 1.14.
64. Ibid. 1.137.
65. Ibid. 1.89.
66. Subramania Iyer (G872), *kārikās* 19–20.

3. Epistemology

1. See, for example, Russell Fraser, *The Language of Adam* (New York, 1977), especially chapt. 4, "Mysticism and the Scientific Doom."
2. Ernst Cassirer, *Language and Myth*, trans. S.K. Langer (New York, 1953), pp. 8–9.
3. *Vākyapadīya* 1.123 as translated by T.R.V. Murti in his foreword to Coward (G1700A), p. vii.
4. Murti, (G1643), p. 321.
5. Ibid., p. 322.
6. Datta (RB10134), pp. 27–28.
7. See *Sāṃkhyakārikā* 4, *Sāṃkhyasūtras* 1.88, and *Yogasūtras* 1.7.
8. See Ganganatha Jha (RB9473), p. 80. Prabhākara accepts only five *pramāṇas.*
9. See Dharmarājādhvarīndra, *Vedāntaparibhāṣā,* trans. S. Suryanarayana Sastri (RB6306), chaps. 1–6.
10. In Subramania Iyer (G721), p. 45.
11. Translation in Murti (G1643), p. 325.
12. Ibid.
13. Ibid., p. 326.
14. Ibid.
15. The following discussion regarding the Platonic parallel with *vyākaraṇa* is based on Murti (G1643), p. 327.
16. *Sarvadarśanasaṃgraha* of Mādhava trans. E.B. Cowell and A.E. Gough, (London, 1892–1894), p. 219.
17. Subramania Iyer (G734), p. 163.
18. Subramania Iyer (G872), *karikā* 19. Similar arguments are offered to show how the progressively clearer perception cannot be attributed to defects of the senses or memory through resemblance, p. 49.
19. Mahadevan (RB5466), p. 62.
20. Sastri (G706), p. 50.
21. Pandy (RB4131), pp. 400–427.
22. G872, *sūtra* 20, pp. 51–52; and *Vākyapadīya* 1.88 and *vṛtti.*
23. Ibid.
24. G872, *sūtra* 24, p. 64. See also Subramania Iyer (G1445), in which he makes clear that from the *sphoṭa* viewpoint whatever distinction of degree or part is made in an object must be done through a *guṇa* (quality or particular). For the grammarians it is the *guṇa* and never the universal that serves to express degrees in objects. It should also be noted that of the many possible ways of interpreting the universal, Bhartṛhari prefers the following. A movement like lifting the hand consists of a series of movements. As these movements are transitory they cannot coexist and form a whole of which they would be the parts and in which the universal of the movement of lifting the hand would inhere. Now such a universal is more specific than the wider universal

of movement in general. Although it inheres in each moment of movement, it is not cognizable in them alone due to too much similarity between moments of lifting and those of the moments of each movement, such as turning the hand. The moments of each movement are the result of a special effort to make that movement, and they are the substrata of the universal of that movement. But that universal cannot be cognized until a series of moments has been cognized. One or two moments of movement are not enough, but after a series of moments is cognized the cognition of the universal inherent in each movement becomes clear. Lifting, for example, may be identified, and other movements such as turning excluded. The process is similar in the manifestation of *sphoṭas*. Each is manifested by a series of special efforts to utter letters. One or two utterances of the series are not enough to eliminate other words with similar sounds. But as the complete series of letters is cognized, the cognition of the *sphoṭa* or universal of the particular word is clearly perceived, and meaningful usage of it in speech becomes possible. (*Vākyapadīya* 2.20-21 as interpreted by Subramania Iyer [G734] , pp. 168–169.)

25. Ibid.

26. *Vākyapadīya,* 1.52.

27. Moving beyond Sanskrit itself and into the world of languages, I would take the universal error as referring to the necessity of going from the differentiated letters (the error) to the whole *sphoṭa* (meaning or ultimate reality). The fixed sequence and form of differentiation for a particular word-*sphoṭa* would only be a constant error within each language (such as Sanskrit).

28. *Vākyapadīya* 1.85.

29. *Sphoṭasiddhi, sūtra* 22.

30. Kaviraj (G1394), pp. 1-18 and 113-132.

31. K.A. Subramania Iyer's introduction to G872, p. 26.

32. *Vākyapadīya* 1.78-84. Among the analogies offered to explain the process, Bhartṛhari's favorite seems to be that the sounds leave impression seeds (*saṃskāra, bhāvanā,* or *bīja*), which, as they mature in the mind, are conducive to an increasingly clear perception of the *sphoṭa*—to which they finally offer a perfect "fitness" or identity. A literal rendering of *yogyatā* could be "to fit in a frame"—the "fit" of the "matured' series of letters into the "frame" of the *sphoṭa*. See also the *vṛtti* on *Vākyapadīya* 3.1.8.

33. The phrase "function of the mind" here is intended to indicate that *pratibhā* is not a function of the ordinary senses of the *buddhi* stage of consciousness, but is characteristic of the pre-*buddhi* or *śabdatattva* stage.

34. It should be clearly understood here that perfect perception of *pratibhā*, however valid in itself, remains outside the realm of *pramāṇa* (which is characterized by *sensory* perception and discursive cognition). With regard to language, therefore, it is *sphoṭa* when manifested as speech that is *pramāṇa* (and not *sphoṭa* at the unified level of *pratibhā*). The point made above, however, still stands. The cognition of *sphoṭa* at the level of either *śabda pramāṇa* or *pratibhā* is via direct perception, not via inference.

35. *Sphoṭasiddhi, sūtra* 23, as translated by Subramania Iyer (G872), p. 60.

36. Saṃkara, *Brahmasūtrabhāṣya,* as translated in Thibaut (RB243), vol. 1, p. 210.

37. *Vākyapadīya* 1.142.

38. Ibid., 1.123.

39. The following summary depends mainly on Subramania Iyer's presentation of Bhartṛhari's position in G734, pp. 144–146.

40. Patañjali, *Yogasūtra* 2.53.

41. There is considerable debate in current scholarship over whether there should or should not be a fourth level of language, *parā vāk*. Bhartṛhari himself seems to leave open that possibility. The *vṛtti* on *Vākyapadīya* 1.142 does quote among numerous other passages *Ṛg Veda* 1.164.45, which refers to four levels of *vāc*. Cardona, p. 302, seems to

contradict himself, suggesting four levels in the main text—*paśyantī* being divided into two aspects—but in the footnote observing "that Bhartṛhri did not recognize an absolute fourth level called *parā vāc.* 'supreme speech,' which was recognized by later thinkers, especially in the Kashmir Śaiva school of thought" (p. 369).

4: Word Meaning

1. See K. Kunjunni Raja, "Paṇini's Attitude Towards Lakṣaṇā," *Adyar Library Bulletin* (1965) : 177–187.
2. *Sarvadarśanasaṃgraha* of Mādhava, trans. E.B. Cowell and A.E. Gough (London 1892–1894, pp. 210ff.
3. See Chakravarti (G1402).
4. Patañjali, *Mahābhāṣya* 1.1.
5. Kumārila, *Ślokavārttika, sphoṭavāda* section, verse 5.
6. Patañjali, *Mahābhāṣya* 1.4.109.
7. Ibid.
8. See Chakravarti (G1402), p. 100.
9. *Vākyapadīya* 1.44.
10. Ibid. 1.45–46.
11. Ibid. 1.47.
12. Ibid. 1.49.
13. Subramania Iyer (G721), p. 58.
14. *Vākyapadīya* 1.1 and *vṛtti.*
15. Subramania Iyer (G872), p. 2.
16. Ibid., p. 3.
17. Subramania Iyer (G1464), p. 124.
18. A summary of part of Maṇḍana's answer to Kumārila in Maṇḍana's *Sphoṭasiddhi, kārikā* 3, as presented by Gaurinath Sastri in G706, p. 105.
19. *Sphoṭasiddhi, kārikā* 4.
20. Ibid.
21. Ibid.
22. Unlike the subsequent discussion, the preceding debate assumes no invisible trace or *saṃskāra.* Kumārila holds that the last phoneme, helped by the more visible going before of the other phonemes in the word, causes the understanding of meaning.
23. Subramania Iyer (G872), p. 14.
24. *Sphoṭasiddhi, kārikā* 5, G872, p. 16.
25. Ibid.
26. Ibid., *kārikā* 6, G872, p. 16.
27. Ibid., G872, pp. 17-18.
28. Ibid., *kārikā* 10, G872, p. 30.
29. Ibid., G872, p. 31.
30. Ibid., *kārikā* 11, G872, p. 34.
31. Ibid.
32. Ibid., *kārikā* 18, G872, p. 44.
33. Subramania Iyer (G1464), p. 136.
34. Subramania Iyer's introduction to G872, p. 13.
35. Ibid., *kārikā* 20, and *Vākyapadīya* 1.88 with *vṛtti.*
36. It should be noted that no less a person than Śaṃkara argued against the *sphoṭa* theory (in *Brahmasūtrabhāṣya* 1.3.28). See also the recent analysis of Śaṃkara's objection *sphoṭa* in Herman (G1549). Śaṃkara and Kumārila both base their criticism on *ācārya* Upavarṣa, and their objections are somewhat different from the debate between Vācaspati and Maṇḍana.

37. This passage and the following ones are taken from the translation by S.S. Suryanarayana Sastri in G1414, reprinted in *Collected Papers of S.S Suryanarayana Sastri* (Madras, 1961), p. 296.
38. Ibid.
39. Ibid.
40. Ibid., p. 301.
41. Ibid.
42. Ibid., p. 293.
43. See Subramania Iyer's introduction to G872, p. 17.
44. *Sphoṭasiddhi, kārikā* 24, G872, p. 64. See also Subramania Iyer (G1445), in which he makes clear that from the *sphoṭa* viewpoint whatever distinction of degree or part is made in an object must be done through a *guṇa* (quality of particular).
45. *Vākyapadīya* 1.85. For more on this topic see chapter 3 part 2 of this introduction.

5. Sentence Meaning

1. See *Sphoṭasiddhi, kārikā* 23.
2. For detailed discussion see Kunjunni Raja (G355).
3. See Kunjunni Raja (G1556), pp. 154–156.
4. Kumārila, *Ślokavārttika.*
5. See K. Kunjunni Raja, "The Role of *Tātparya* in Understanding the Sentence," in *Ancient Indian Theories on Sentence Meaning* (Poona, 1980).
6. Noan Chomsky, *Language and Mind* (New York, 1968), chap. 3.

NOTES TO SURVEY

1. Philosophical Elements in Vedic Literature

1. Nāgeśa Bhaṭṭa has interpreted this verse as referring to the fourfold manifestation of *vāc* into *parā, paśyantī, madhyamā,* and *vaikharī.*

2. Philosophical Element in Yāska's *Nirukta*

1. See B. Bhattacharya, *Yāska's Nirukta and the Science of Etymology* (Calcutta, 1952); Siddheswar Varma, *The Etymology of Yāska* (Hoshiarpur, 1953); Kunjunni Raja (G696).
2. Thieme (G458), pp. 23-24.
3. Cardona, pp. 270-273.
4. "Bhāvapradhānam ākhyātaṃ, sattvapradhānāni nāmāni."
5. "Ṣaḍ bhāvavikāra, bhavantīti vārṣāyaṇir jāyate 'sti vipariṇamate vardhate pakṣīyate vinaśyatīti."
6. "Prāptakrama viśeṣeṣu kriyā saivābhidhīyate kramarūpasya saṃhāre tat sattvam iti kathyate," *Vākyapadiya* 3.1.35.
7. "Pūrvāparībhūtaṃ bhāvam ākhyātenācaṣṭe."
8. "Kṛdabhihito bhāva dravyavad bhavati."
9. "Indriyanityaṃ vacanam audumbarāyaṇaḥ," *Vākyapadīya* 2.347.
10. Cf. Brough (G8).
11. "Nāmānyākhyātajānīti śākaṭāyano nairuktasamayaśca; na sarvāṇīti gārgyo vaiyākaraṇānāṃ caike," *Nirukta* 1.12.
12. "Bhāvapradhānam ākhyātam, sattvapradhānāni nāmāni."

3. Philosophical Elements in Pāṇini's *Aṣṭādhyāyī*

1. Generally taken to be later than Yāska; but Thieme takes him to be earlier. See the extended discussion summarized in Cardona.

2. "Śiṣṭaḥ śabdeṣu pramāṇam."

3. "Lokavijñānāt siddham," see *sūtras* 1.1.21, 1.1.65.

4. "Tad aśiṣyaṃ saṃjñāpramāṇatvāt," *sūtra* 1.2.53. "Siddhe śabdārthasambandhe lokataḥ," *Vārttika*.

5. "Avyutpanna prātipadika." See also the discussion in Yāska's *Nirukta*.

6. "Prātipadikavijñānācca Pāṇineḥ siddham / Uṇādayo vyutpannāni prātipadikāni."

7. "Arthaikatvād ekaṃ vākyaṃ sākāṅkṣaṃ ced vibhāge syād," Patañjali, *Mahābhāṣya* 3.2.41.

8. See Kunjunni Raja (G355); also Devasthali (G327), pp. 206–215.

9. *Nyāsa* on *Kāśikā*, edited by S.C. Chakravarti in G851, p. 423. See Brough (G1478), pp. 28-29; also Staal (G1566), pp. 164-167. Nārāyaṇa Bhaṭṭatiri elucidates this point in his *Prakriyāsarvasva*.

10. Nāgeśa Bhaṭṭa discusses *lakṣaṇā* at length in his *Mañjūṣā* and says in the *Paramalaghumañjūṣā* that according to the grammarians there is no necessity to accept *lakṣaṇā* as a separate function of words.

4. Philosophical Elements in Patañjali's *Mahābhāṣya*

1. The Mīmāṃsakas take *śabda* to be the sound only, while to the grammarians meaningfulness is an essential feature of a linguistic sign. See Maṇḍana Miśra's *Sphoṭasiddhi*, verse 3: "a *śabda* is the cause for creating the understanding of the meaning" ("arthāvasāyaprasavanimittaṃ śabda iṣyate").

2. *Mahābhāṣya* 1.1.

3. Kumārila, *Ślokavārttika*, *sphoṭavāda* section, verse 5.

4. See the discussion in chapter 5 of Bhartṛhari. Among the followers of Pāṇini, Vājapyāyana considered the meaning to be *ākṛti* or *jāti*, while Vyāḍi took it to be the individual or *dravya*. Among other scholars of philosophy, the Mīmāṃsakas took *ākṛti* to be synonymous with *jāti*, while the Nyāya school took it to be the structural form, as distinct from the universal. Cf. Gautama, *Nyāyasūtra*, "Jātyākṛtivyaktaas tu padārthaḥ."

5. *Vārttika* 1: "siddhe śabdārthasambandhe lokataḥ. . . ."

6. *Mahābhāṣya* 1: "arthavanto varṇāḥ. . . ."

7. Kātyāyana's *vārttika* on 1.2.64: "dravyābhidhānaṃ vyāḍiḥ" and "ākṛtyabhidhānād vaikaṃ vibhaktau Vājapyāyanaḥ."

8. "Jātyākhyāyām akasmin bahuvacanam anyatarasyam."

9. "Sarūpānām ekaśeṣa ekavibhaktau."

10. *Mahābhāṣya* 1.

11. "Pāṇinidarśane jātidravyau śabdenābhidhīyete."

12. "Yasya guṇāntareṣvapi prādurbhavatsu tattvaṃ na vihanyate tad dravyam" (on 5.1.119).

13. On Pāṇini's *sutra* 1.4.109.

14. *Mahābhāṣya* 1.35.5.

15. Buddhau kṛtvā sarvaś ceṣṭāḥ kartā dhīras tanvannītiḥ. Śabdenārthānvacyān dṛṣṭvā buddhau kuryāt paurvāparyam."

16. "Dhvaniḥ sphoṭaś ca sabdānāṃ dhvanis tu khalu lakṣyate Alpo mahāṃś ca keṣāṃcid ubhayam tat svabhāvataḥ." Also: "sphoṭah śabdaḥ dhvaniḥ śabdaguṇaḥ."

17. "Varṇasya grahaṇe hetuḥ prākṛto dhvanir iṣyate. Vṛttibhede nimittatvaṃ vaikṛtaḥ samapadyate."

18. "Avasthitā varṇā vaktuś ciráciravacād vṛttayo viśiṣyante."

19. *Mahābhāṣya* 1.181.

20. "Kṛpo ro laḥ," Pāṇini's *sūtra* 8.2.18.

21. "Stanakeśavatī strī syāl lomaśaḥ puruṣaḥ smṛtaḥ. Ubhayor antaraṃ yacca tadabhāve napuṃsakam."

22. "Na vaiyākaraṇais śakyaṃ laukikaṃ liṅgam āsthātum."

23. "Saṃstyānavivakṣāyāṃ strī, prasavavivakṣāyāṃ pumān ubhayavivakṣāyāṃ napuṃsakam."

5. Bhartṛhari

1. Cf. Frauwallner (RB12599), pp. 134–135.

2. The title *Vākyapadīya* could have referred originally to the second of the three *kāṇḍas* (chapters or books) that make up the work. It is definite that about A.D. 1000 *Vākyapadīya* was generally regarded as applying only to the first two books; *Trikāṇḍī* was the term that included all three books. The use of the title *Vākyapadīya* to speak of even the third book, the *Padakāṇḍa* or the *Prakīrṇaka* (Miscellany) seems to be no older than the sixteenth century (cf. Aklujkar [G733] , pp. 547–555). It is this use that is most common at present. The first two books, according to one manuscript tradition, consist of verses (*kārikās*) as well as a prose commentary (*vṛtti*). The other manuscript traditions have only the *kārikās*, or *kārikās* accompanied by a prose commentary (*ṭīkā*) evidently authored by someone other than the *kārikā* author. A long line of writers in the Sanskrit tradition has consistently held that the *Vṛtti* too is Bhartṛhari's work and is an integral part of the *Vākyapadīya* (cf. Aklujkar [G743] . In their understanding the reference of the title *Vākyapadīya* is not confined to the *kārikās*. For many modern students of Bhartṛhari's works, however, that title stands for the *kārikās*, primarily as well as exclusively. The *Vṛtti* is not generally viewed as included when references such as "*Vākyapadīya* 1.5" are made.

3. The word *nitya* is not intended here in the sense "eternal" (as in "God is eternal"). Even as signifying "permanent" it has two or three shades of meaning, depending on the theoretical context. See Aklujkar (G735), p. 82.

4. See the preceding note.

5. Cf. Aklujkar (G762), p. 12, n. 12.

6. When an expression is mentioned, as distinct from when it is used, it is thought to convey its own form as meaning. A theoretical distinction is made between an expression and its own form in cases of mention, and the former is said to be the signifier and the latter the signified; that is, when self-referring or quoted expressions are compared with the expressions having an external reference, the distinction is not seen in the mode of employment ("use-mention") of the two, but in what they convey—what the outcome is.

7. The concept *varṇasphoṭa*, as understood by the Pāṇinīyas, differs from "phoneme" as generally understood by linguists in one important respect. *A*, *a*, and *a*-—that is, short (*hrasva*), long (*dīrgha*), and prolonged (*pluta*) *a*—are regarded as different realizations of *varṇasphoṭa a*; in other words, the *varṇasphoṭa* here is an abstracted or generalized common factor form.

8. The implication is that linguistic units are assumed to be individuals or particulars in the discussion summarized in the preceding paragraph. One of Bhartṛhari's commentators (Puṇyarāja/Helārāja, at 2.1–2, 19, 39–40) systematizes the *sphoṭa* view of linguistic expressions as follows: (a) *bāhya sphoṭa*: individuals (*vyakti*) and universals

(*jāti*); (b) *abhyantara sphoṭa*: *śabdatattva*. This systematization is confirmed by the sequence of statements in 1.84–97.

9. The foregoing interpretation of 1.148–154 is conjectural, for the passages do not contain an explicit statement to this effect: "The following/preceding is the justification of the claim that knowledge or *śāstra*-based use of grammatical expressions can lead to merit." I have assumed that such a statement was intended by Bhartṛhari, because the context (1.144–147 and 1.158–174) is one of pointing out the importance of grammar and because the immediately following verses (1.155–157) are concerned with the relation between *sādhu śabda* and *dharma*. It is, however, possible that 1.148–157 are not at their original place in the *Brahmakāṇḍa*.

10. *Anvitābhidhāna-vādins* of the later works.

11. The last three correspond, respectively, to *madhyamā*, *paśyantī*, and *parāpaśyantī-rūpa*. Speech (*vaikharī*) is marked by an observable presence of breath and sequence in both its *upāṃśu* and non-*upāṃśu* varieties.

12. As will be apparent from this summary, the link among verses 112–115 is not clear.

13. There is some overlap in the list that follows by the very nature of the matter involved and because the list evolved through the efforts of generations of thinkers. For the latter reason, there is also an element of variation in the understanding or definition of terms involved. For example, *prakaraṇa* and *sāmarthya* obviously had wider meanings in addition to their specific meanings determined on the basis of other factors included in the list(s).

14. The Vaiyākaraṇas understand *dravya* in two senses: first, the everlasting substance that underlies all transient physical shapes; and, second, what a demonstrative pronoun (equivalent to "variable" of modern logic) can refer to. The second chapter, a summary of which begins at this point, expands on the first sense. The second sense is given in chapter 4.

15. In the first chapter of the third book, all expressions are said to refer, in the final analysis, to Existence. This Existence is then viewed as a universal pervading everything. Here in the second chapter a similar conclusion is reached, but the Existence is said to be a particular. Thus, there are two currents of thought, roughly corresponding to ontological reduction (a) to classes or (b) to individuals in recent western philosophy.

16. Most, if not all, common sentences would be logically problematic (internally inconsistent) if the words in them were viewed as referring to actually existing entities (for example, in the case of "sprout is born," one could ask: How is the sprout said to be born when it existed?). Explanations of how these sentences are possible vary. One involves distinction between reference and sense (or meaning). Another advocates acceptance of another kind of (verbal or linguistic) existence. The third rests on the observation that words cannot refer to entities in their entirety—in all of their aspects—or purely in themselves. The following summary alludes to this variety of explanations.

17. The intention behind calling the arising of an effect a miracle could be of two sorts: either the becoming of the effect cannot be expressed without giving rise to unintended implications—without realizing the inadequacy of language, as in the description of a miracle—or we cannot determine the point of transition—the exact moment or phase in which the cause ceases to exist and the effect comes into being. The transition seems to take place in a flash like a miracle. Helārāja (3.3.81) is aware of both interpretations, and there is contextual support for both. Verses 3.3.78–80 and 82–86 suggest that Bhartṛhari located the logical problems of cause-and-effect relationship in the expression of that relationship and in being not aware of general truths about language's relation to reality in understanding that expression. In other words, he seems to have dissolved the problems rather than solved them. Thus, the first

interpretation is contextually justified. Support for the second interpretation can be seen in the adjectives *abhāgam*, "partless," and *akramam* "sequenceless," which are used in 3.3.81.

18. The entity need not be explicity qualified. All that is necessary is a presupposition that *x* can be qualified if necessary (*bhedyatvena vivakṣita*). Second, qualification is to be understood as including predication, even of the simple type such as "*x* is/exists." The present definition allows us to view universals and the like as particulars and permits characterization of all word meanings as particulars or individuals. Thus, all words are said to refer to *dravya* in two ways: the one stated in chapter 3.2 (see the preceding note) and the one stated here in chapter 3.4.

19. This excelling can also be in such negative respects as being disliked, being despised, and so on (for example, *kutsitatara*, "more censured of the two").

20. The intended characterization of *sādhana* or *kāraka* should be clear from the summary of the following chapter. The important points to remember are, first, that they are viewed as supports of the action *as expressed in the sentence*; second, that their actual relation to the action as seen in the physical world does not matter—what matters is the capacities in which the speaker places them—and, third, that the action mentioned in this context is not necessarily physical, observable action characterized by a series of moments; even the meaning of "is" or "exists" is action.

21. As Helārāja (p. 209.12–13) observes here, while the definitions of *sādhana*, *kriyā*, and so on, like those of the preceding *dravya* and *guṇa*, are established by studying Pāṇinian rules, the characterization of space, time, and so on is a result of a direct attempt to understand their nature; the rules do not provide clues as in the other cases. For Bhartṛhari, *ākāśa* does not seem to be any positive, physical entity. It is nowhere distinguished from *diś* in his writings. He seems to have used the word conventionally in the sense "visible, perceptible space," which, in view of his final rejection of space as an actually existent entity, ultimately comes to mean "space that is *generally thought to be* perceptible."

22. Vaiśeṣikas, according to Helārāja, pp. 239.3–4, 243.9.

23. (a) Helārāja (p. 315.18) labels this view in verse 107 as *svasiddhānta*, "Bhartṛhari's own thesis," according to the available editions. But the view in verse 109 is also *svasiddhānta*, according to Helārāja (p. 316.12). (b) There are no words such as *atha vā*, *keṣāṃcit*, or *anyeṣāṃ*, indicating *pakṣāntara*, in verses 108 and 109. That these verses express views different from the one contained in 106–107 is something one has to accept on the authority of Helārāja, who, in turn, seems to have (rightly) noticed that the wording of 108–109 indicates different philosophical assumptions.

24. The assumption here is that an agent must really exist to appear as an agent in a sentence. In the view expressed in verse 105, real existence is not held to be necessary; a tentative, imagined existence is held to be sufficient. Among the thinkers advocating necessity of "real existence" there are two groups: one (probably Sāṃkhya) locates such real existence in the cause, maintaining that cause and effect are essentially identical; the second explains real existence as existence as a universal, clearly implying that the universals are real (as in the Nyāya view) and beyond question (which, of course, is not the case, as the questions of Buddhist logicians show). Although Bhartṛhari can accommodate these views (three in all: *buddhyavasthānibandhana* or *vivakṣānibandhana*, existence; *satkārya*; and *jātivyakti*) as well as the *upacārasattā* (secondary, derivative existence) view expressed in 3.3.45, his first preference is the *śabdārtho 'rtha* view, expressed in 3.7.109 110. Meaning (*śabdārtha*) and reference (*vastvartha* or *bāhyārtha*) are to be distinguished. In understanding usage, attention to what is reflected in language is sufficient. Whether the entity spoken of actually exists (a worthwhile concern if the purpose of inquiry is something else) need not be considered to account for usage, such as "As sprout comes into being." For words carrying out denotation in

sentences like this, all existent entities are no different from nonexistent entities. To put the point differently, it is improper to see contradictions in a sentence by asking questions like: "Did the sprout exist before coming into being? If it did, how can it newly come into being? If it did not, how can it perform the action of coming into being?" The use of the word "sprout" is in no way predicated on there being an actual sprout or a referent. The sentence with "sprout" as the subject can proceed as long as there is meaning or sense (*śabdārtha*) for "sprout."

25. In the original, verses 109-110, the observation about language (specifically, denotation) is said to hold good also in the case of *prajñā* or *buddhi*, "intellect" (specifically, a cognition reflecting an entity). Just as denotation implies acceptance of (some kind of) existence, cognition implies conceding (some kind of) existence. I have left out this mention of intellect and cognition here in order not to obscure the present discussion and also because language and intellect turn out to be ultimately identical in Bhartṛhari's philosophy.

26. (a) Actions such as putting the pot on the stove, pouring water into the pot, adding rice to the water, lighting the stove, and more, are subsumed under the one action denoted by "cooks." See summary of the eighth chapter (*Kriyāsamuddeśa*). (b) Helārāja points out that this way of accounting for "A sprout comes into being" differs from the first way (a), in that here the identity of cause and effect is based on a feature of usage called *upacāra* ("extended application" of a verbal root like "cook" to cover subsidiary actions leading to cooking), while in (a) the identity of cause and effect is held to be factual (*vāstava*).

27. The examples indicated by Bhartṛhari are: "yavāgū mūtrāya saṃpadyate," "suvarṇapiṇḍaḥ kuṇḍale bhavataḥ," "brāhmaṇāḥ saṃgho bhavati," "brāhmaṇāḥ saṃghībhavanti," "tvad-bhavasi," and "rājan arājā saṃpadyase/bhavasi." To them Helārāja adds: "kṣīraṃ dadhi saṃpadyate," "bījād aṅkuro jāyate," "yavāgvā mūtraṃ jāyate," "mahadbhūtaś candramāḥ," and "mahadbhūta brāhmaṇī." The discussion of these examples is determined to some extent by the peculiarities of the Sanskrit language. For this reason, as well as to indicate the relationship of the point here with the preceding, I have preferred simpler examples.

28. At the beginning of this section, a verse giving the definition of *apādāna* is expected, as in the case of sections on other *kārakas* in this Samuddeśa. But the first statement we see at present in it deals with the varieties of *apādāna*. It seems, therefore, that at least one verse has been lost in the known manuscripts. The form of the lost verse is likely to have been "apāye yad udāsīnaṃ calaṃ vā yadi vācalam / dhruvam evatadāveśāt tad apādānam ucyate," that is, essentially the same as the verse quoted by Bhoja (*Śṛṅgāraprakāśa*, chapter 4), Haradatta (*Padamañjarī* 1.4.24), Bhaṭṭoji Dīkṣita (*Śabdakaustubha* 1.4.24), and others.

29. As the last example indicates, the action of moving away associated with the concept of *apādāna* is not necessarily the actual or physical action of moving away. In conformity with the Vaiyākaraṇas *śābda* (conceptual or semantic, as distinct from *artha*, actual, physical) concept of action (see summary of the *Kriyāsamuddeśa*, book 3, section 8 instances in which the movement is only imagined or intellectually entertained are also relevant here.

30. Cf. Joshi (G1194) pp. 29, 39–40, etc.

31. Swaminathan (G780), pp. 3–4.

32. "Dvau śabdātmanau nityaḥ karyaś ceti kaiścid nityā iti dṛṣṭaḥ kaiścid anitya iti. Athavā jātir vyaktiś ceti athavā sphoṭo dhvaniś ca," ibid. p. 13.

33. Subramania Iyer (G734), p. 171.

34. Swaminathan (G780), p. 28; also Subramania Iyer (G734), p. 74.

35. "Sākṣāt pratipatter anumānapratipattir garīyasī."

9. Maṇḍana Misra

1. In this logical argument, it seems clear that Kumārila's attempt to identify *śabda* with the uttered phonemes is effectively discredited by the reasoning of Maṇḍana, who at the same time has vindicated the identification of *śabda* with *sphoṭa*. Although the logical groundwork has largely been completed, Maṇḍana still has to describe in detail exactly how *śabda* as *sphoṭa* may be comprehended using only ordinary memory traces of the phonemes to reveal the *sphoṭa*. He must also show the *sphoṭa* to be not a mere postulation but a perceivable reality, otherwise much of his logical argument simply collapses. These tasks he undertakes in *kārikās* 18–19 of the *Sphoṭasiddhi*.

10. Helārāja

1. See Subramania Iyer (G734), pp. 39–40.
2. Cf. G709, G747.
3. Aklujkar (G750), pp. 165–188.
4. Ibid.
5. Subramania Iyer (G734), p. 38.

12. Puṇyarāja

1. Subramania Iyer (G734), p. 41.

13. Kaiyaṭa

1. Cf. Sarma (G907).
2. "Yathottaraṃ munināṃ prāmāṇyaṃ" *sūtra* 1.1.29.
3. "Munitraya matenādyatva sādhvasādhu pravibhāgaḥ," *sūtra* 5.1.21.
4. Kaiyaṭa's views on different problems connected with language are found scattered in different parts of the commentary. Many of them have been noted and discussed in Koṇḍa Bhaṭṭa's *Bhūṣaṇa*(*sāra*).

21. Śeṣa Cintāmaṇi

1. Cf. Yudhisthira Mimamsaka, *Saṃskṛta vyākaraṇa-śāstra kā itihāsa* (Sonipat, 1973), vol. 1, pp. 418–419.

28. Annambhaṭṭa

1. Yudhisthira Mimamsaka, *Saṇskṛta vyākaraṇa-śāstra kā itihāsa* (Sonipat, 1973), vol. 1, p. 422.
2. P.P.S. Sastri's introduction to G587.

32. Śivarāmendra Sarasvatī

1. Theodor Aufrecht, *Catalogus Catalogorum: An Alphabetical Register of Sanskrit Works and Authors,* 3 pts. (Wiesbaden, 1962), pt. 1, pp. 718, 440,

33. (ŚEṢA) CAKRAPĀṆI (DATTA)

1. Yudhisthira Mimamsaka, *Saṇskṛta vyākaraṇa-śāstra kā itihāsa* (Sonipat, 1973), vol. 1, pp. 540–541.

2. Cf. *New Catalogus Catalogorum,* vol. 3, p. 275a, and Mimamsaka, *Saṇskṛta vyākaraṇa-śāstra*, pp. 487–495.

35. NĪLAKAṆṬHA ŚUKLA

1. See *New Indian Antiquary* 5 (1942): 177–183; also *Journal of the Tanjore Sarasvati Mahal Library* (1955 1956).

37. KOṆḌA (OR KAUṆḌA) BHAṬṬA

1. See volume 1 of this encyclopedia, *Bibliography of Indian Philosophies*, 2d ed., p. 387.

2. *Descriptive Catalogue of the Manuscripts of the Adyar Library*, vol. 9, no. 575.

3. Volume 1 of this encyclopedia, *Bibliography of Indian Philosophies*, 2d ed., p. 422.

4. The summary of this section was prepared through consultation of the dissertation of Gune (G1197).

5. The summary of this section is based on the unpublished dissertation of Deshpande (G1196).

40. TIRUMALA YAJVAN

1. See Yudhisthira Mimamsaka, *Saṇskṛta vyākaraṇa-śastra kā itihāsa* (Sonipat, 1973), vol. 1, pp. 413ff.

42. SADĀŚIVA

1. See Yudhisthira Mimamsaka, *Saṇskṛta vyākaraṇa-śāstra kā itihāsa* (Sonipat, 1973), vol. 1, pp. 416–417.

45. NĀGEŚA (OR NĀGOJI BHAṬṬA)

1. For a relative chronology of his works see Gode, (RB6813); also P.V. Kane, *History of Dharmaśāstra* Volume One (Poona 1930), 453–456.

57. ĀŚĀDHARA BHAṬṬA

1. Shah, RB4735.

66. SATĀRĀ RĀGHAVENDRĀCĀRYA GAJENDRAGADAKAR

1. B.N.K. Sharma, *A History of the Dvaita School of Vedānta and Its Literature* (Bombay, 1961), vol. 2, p. 358; Theodor Aufrecht, *Catalogus Catalogorum*: *An Alphabetical Register of Sanskrit Works and Authors*, 3 pts. (Wiesbaden, 1962), pt. 1, p. 500.

CUMULATIVE INDEX

References are to pages unless preceded by "G", in which case the reference is to numerical entries in the Bibliography. This cumulative index combines indices of names, titles, and topics into one alphabetized guide. Abbreviations used are the following:

a = article
b = book
d = dissertation
e = edition
t = translation

Abegg, Ernst a: G1391
ābhāsa. See reflection
abhāva. See absence
ABHAYACANDRA (ĀCĀRYA) (1329) 484
ABHAYANANDIN (750) 17-18, 474
abhidhā. See primary meaning
abhihitānvaya (verbal comprehensive theory) 9-10, 66, 92, 98
ABHINAVAGUPTA (1014) 28, 91, 193, 476
ABHINAVA KĀLIDĀSA (1750) 371, 507
ABHINAVA NṚSIṂHĀŚRAMA (1630) 496
abhinnarūpa. See adjective
ABHIRĀMA VIDYĀLAṂKĀRA (1500) 487
abhivyakti. See revelation
Abhyankar, Kashinath Vasudev 128. a: G242, G322, G519, G573, G726, G1215, G1217, G1502, G1517, G1563, G1594, e: G536, G781, G858, G1331, b: G1546
abhyanujñā. See permission
abhyāsa. See practice
ablative (*apādāna*) 168, 270, 337, 338, 560
absence (*abhāva*) 54, 127, 149, 288, 334, G1683
absolute G1532. *See also* Brahman
—consciousness. *See* consciousness
—eternality. *See* eternal, absolute
Acakṣaṇaviveka (of Rājiva Śarman) 530
ĀCĀRYA DĪKṢITA 239
ACCĀN DĪKṢITA 239
accent (*svara*) 15, 149, G185, G199, G298, G324, G397, G457A, G1367, G1580, G1584, G1594
Vedic G117, G1420
accomplisher (*uddeśya*) 330
accusative case 259, 272, G1461, G1519, G1520
Acharya, K. C. a: G366
Acharya, Mrityunjay a: G16
Acharya, Narayana Ram e: G1167
Acharya, Ramananda a: G1611
Achyatan, Mavelikara b: G493
action (*kriyā*) 168-70, 196-97, 256-58, 261-62, 264, 268, 337, 559, G1477
means to (*sādhana*) 25, 163-68, 262
miraculous course of (*atadbhūtavṛtti*) 161, G748
activity (*pravṛtti*) 169
activity (*rajas*) 44-45, 120, 275
activity (*spanda*) 328
ACYUTĀNANDA ŚĀSTRI (1963) 517, e: G168
ACYUTA PISHAROTI (1610) 494
ĀDENNA 517
adhikaraṇa. See locative

adhiṣṭhāna. *See* basis
adhiyajña. *See* ritualistic interpretation of the Veda
ādhunika. *See* technical term
adhyāsa. *See* superimposition
adhvan. *See* path of being
Ādityas 104
adjective (*abhinnarūpa*) 292, G1571
Adredos, F. R. b: G1486
adṛṣṭa 146, 186
Advaita Vedānta 20, 41-43, 54, 56-57, 59-60, 82, 216, 239-40, 255, 287, 305, 341, 369-71, 375, 397, G790, G809
Advaitaviveka (of Āṣādhara Bhaṭṭa) 375
Advayasiddhi (of Helārāja) 193, 475
adverb G1632
Adyar Library 211, 240
aesthetic experience 32-33
āgama. *See* scripture, tradition
agent (*kāraka*) 269-70, 336-37
  (*kartṛ*) 98, 16-167, 255-60, 268, 559, G259, G324, G1627
  prompting agent, see prompter
  reflexive agent 268
Agni 104-5
Agrawala, Vasudev Sharan a: G95, G112, G468, G469, G472, G572, G577, G1473, b: G476, G485
agreement (*anvaya*) G1579
  and difference (*anvayavyatireka*) 146, 275, 290
agriculture 12
Aindra school 13, G1, G5, G6, G7
Aitareya Brāhmaṇa 234, G1375
ajahatsvārtha 279-80
ājānika. *See* permanence of word
AJITASENA ĀCĀRYA 518
ākāṅkṣā. *See* expectancy
ākāra. *See* form
ākāśa 162, 168
akhaṇḍapada. *See sphoṭa*
akhaṇḍavākya. *See sphoṭa*
ākhyāta. *See* verb
Ākhyātacandrikā (of Bhaṭṭamalla) 530
  —*Kriyākośa* (of Rāmacandra) 530
Ākhyātārthacandrikānirṇaya (of Śrīkṛṣṇa Bhaṭṭa Maunin) 506
Ākhyātavāda (of Raghunātha Śiromaṇi)
  —*Arthanirṇaya* (of Jayakṛṣṇa Maunin) 361, 367
Ākhyātavyākaraṇa (of Vaṅgasena) 481
Ākhyātavyākhyāna (of Viśveśvara Tarkācārya) 534
Aklujkar, Ashok 123-73, 179, 193, 201, 559, 563, a: G731, G733, G736, G741, G743, G750, G762, G764, G765, G769, G774, G782, G806, G1607, G1665, d: G735
ākṛti. *See* configuration
akṣara. *See* syllable
AKṢAYASŪRI 371
ālambana. *See* supporting object
Alaṃkāra literature 239
Alaṃkārasarvasva (of Ruyyaka) 203
alaṃkāraśāstra, Ālaṃkārikās 31, 83, 91-2, 240
ālātacakra. *See* fire-wheel
Al-George, Sergiu a: G142, G212, G228, G243, G367, G491, G1567, G1608, G1612
Allen, William Sidney a: G132, b: G1478, G1547
alphabet G1467
AMARACANDRA (1250) 481
Amoghavarṣa I G883
  (*Śabdānuśāsana*) *Amoghavṛtti* (by Śakaṭāyana) 17, 474, G884, G890, 476
  —*Nyāsa* (of Prabhācandra) 476
Amṛtataraṅginī (of Kṣirasvāmin) 476
analogy. *See* comparison
ĀNANDADATTA 518
ĀNANDAPŪRṆA VIDYĀSĀGARA (1350) 484
ĀNANDA SIDDHĀNTAVĀGĪŚA 518
ĀNANDAVARDHANA 8, 12, 28-32, 66, 83, 91
ANANTA 518
ANANTA BHAṬṬA 518
ANANTĀCĀRYA (1900) 23, 518
ANANTĀCĀRYA of Musarapakkam (1906) 514
ANANTANĀRĀYAṆA ŚĀSTRIN (1750) 507
ANANTANĀRĀYAṆA ŚĀSTRI, P. S., *See* P. S. ANANTANĀRĀYAṆA ŚĀSTRI
ANANTA SŪRI 518
Ananthanarayana, H. S. a: G238, G1609, b: G350
ānantya. *See* infinity
Andhra G1635
Anekamanyapadārthasūtravicāra (of Udayaṅkara Nānapāthaka) 509
Anekārthasaṃgraha (of Hemacandra) 203
aṅgādhikāra G1687
aṅgirasa 30

anīpsitakarman 269
anirvacanīya. See indescribable
anityasphoṭavāda G1434
ANNAMBHAṬṬA (1540) 22, 223, 237, 249, 313, 489, 561
antaryāmin. See inner controller
anubandha G149, G417, G296, G619
Anubandhakhaṇḍanavāda (of Dayāśaṃkara) 520
ANUBHŪTI SVARŪPĀCĀRYA (1270) 20, 481-82
Anuhyasāra (of Varendra Campahattiya Mānaśarman) 534
anumāna. See inference
anuvāda 25
anuvṛtti G120
Anvayadīpikā (of Devadatta) 520
anvayavyatireka. See agreement and difference
anvitābhidhāna (*vāda*) 9-10, 91-2, 98, 558
aorist G1392
apabhraṃśa G804
apadāna. See ablative
ĀPADEVA (1650) 499
Apāṇinīyapramāṇatā (of Nārāyaṇa Bhaṭṭatiri) 22, 497
Aparaviṣayapramāṇāni (of Kavi Vallabha) 525
apaśabda 321-22
Apaśabdanirākarana (of Jagaddhara) 484
apavāda. See exception
āpekṣabuddhi. See enumerative cognition
APIŚĀLI 440
Apiśāliśikṣā (of Apiśāli) 440
apoddhāra. See meaning, abstracted
apoha (exclusion of others) 6, 27, 66, 125, 549
—*pariccheda* 28
APPAN NAINĀRYA (1510) 487
APPA SŪRI (1730) 504
APPAYYA DĪKṢITA 518
Appayya Dīkṣita, grandfather of Nīlakaṇṭha Dīkṣita 373
Appayya Dīkṣita, author of *Pāṇinisūtraprakāśa* 353, 507
APPAYYA DĪKṢITA I (1585) 239-40, 397
APPAYYA DĪKṢITA III (1670) 500
appearance (*vivarta*). *See* manifestation
application (*pravṛttinimitta*) 294
apposition 185
apraśastya. See impropriety
apūrva 74-9, 164, 184, 213, 265-67, 300, 344
Arapura, John G. 103, a: G1629
architecture 12
Arora, Sudarshan Kumari a: G618, d: G629
artha. See meaning; *See also* purpose
arthaikatva. See unity of purpose
arthāpatti. See presumption
Arthasaṃgraha (of Śrīdeva Paṇḍita) 533
Arthasaṃgraha (of Vaidyanātha Paiyaguṇḍa) 505
arthavāda. See supplementary description
Arthavatsūtravāda (of Manyudeva) 387, 509
artisans G234
Aryavaraguru, S.P.S. Jagannathaswamy e: G1067
ĀŚĀDHARA BHAṬṬA (1770) 23, 375, 507, 562
āsatti. See continuity
asatya. See unreal
Asiatic Society Library of Calcutta 207
Aśoka G504
aspect (*upagraha*) 173, G1494
āśrayāsiddhi. See fallacy of unestablished locus
association of word meanings (*saṃsargamaryādā*) 10, 98, 125, 161, 284, 304, 330, 333, 340, 344
Aṣṭādhyāyī (of Pāṇini) 4, 14, 16, 38, 86, 113-17, 257, 322, 441-54, 550, 556
—*Mitākṣara* (of Annambhaṭṭa) 237, 489
—*Prakāśa* (of Appayya Dīkṣita) 240, 507
Commentary (of Śivarāmendra Sarasvatī) 245, 508
—*Vārttikas* (of Kātyāyana). *See Vārttikas*
—*Laghubhāṣya* (author unknown) 459
—*Mahābhāṣya* (of Patañjali). *See Mahābhāṣya*
—*Vṛtti* G542
—*Kāśikā* (of Jayāditya and Vamana). *See Kāśikā*
Commentary (of Dharanīdhara) 509
Commentary (of Kāśīnātha) G26
—*Vṛtti* (of Mādhava) G35
—*Tattvaprakāśikā* (of Gaṅgādatta Śāstri) 516, 521
—*Vrtti* (of Jayanta Bhaṭṭa) 475
—*Prakīrṇaprakāśa* (of Helārāja) 475, 551
—*Rūpāvatāra* (of Dharmakīrti). *See Rūpāvatāra*
Commentary (of Govardhana) 478
—*Durghatāvṛtti* (of Śaraṇadeva) 480

—*Bhāṣāvṛtti* 480
Commentary (of Sṛṣṭidharācārya) G969
—*Prakriyākaumudī* (of Rāmacandra). *See Prakriyākaumudī*
—*Siddhāntakaumudī* (of Bhaṭṭoji Dīkṣita). *See Siddhāntakaumudī*
—*Vṛttisaṃgraha* (of Rāmacandra) 505
—*Pradīpa* or *Śabdabhūṣaṇa* (of Nārāyaṇa Sudhi) 507
—*Mitāvṛttyarthasaṃgraha* (of Udayaṅkara Nānapāthaka) 509
—*Vṛtti* (of Gokulacandra) 510
—*Bhāṣya* (of Dayānanda Sarasvatī) 511
—*Chandaprakāśa* (of Gaṅgādhara Kavirāja) 512
Commentary (of Devīdin) 512
Commentary (of Jīvarāma Śarman) 512
—*Bhāṣyaprathamavṛtti* (of Brahmadatta Jijñasu) 517
—*Sūcī* (of Cudāmiśra) 519
—*Vṛtti* (of Datta Rāma Bhaṭṭa) 520
—*Laghu(vṛtti)vivṛti* (of Devasahāya) 520
Commentary (of Hari Paṇḍita) 523
Commentary (of Mānalur Vīrāghavācārya) 527
—*Pradīpa* or *Śabdabhūṣaṇa* (of Nārāyaṇa) 528
—*Vyākaraṇadīpikā* (of Oram Bhaṭṭa) 528
—*Ṭippaṇī* (of Sanātana Tarkācārya) 532
—*Pāṇinisūtravyākhyā* (of Vīrāghavācārya) 535
Aṣṭādhyāyī-Dhātupātha (of Pāṇini) 14, 19, 113, G58, G59, G210, G236, G239, G240, G392
—*Kṣīrataraṅginī* (of Kṣīrasvāmin) 476
—*Śabdikābharaṇa* (of Hariyogin Śailāvācārya) 478
—*Mādhavīyadhātuvṛtti* (of Śayana) 484
—*Tārāvalī* (of Kṛṣṇasudhi) 526
Aṣṭādhyāyisūtrakośa (of Lakṣmanārāyaṇa Vyāsa) 527
āstika. *See* orthodox
astronomy (*jyotiṣa*) 12, 107
Aśubodha (of Rāma Kiṅkara Sarasvatī) 530
Aśubodhavyākaraṇa (of Tārānātha Tarkavācaspati) 512
Aśvins 104
Asyavāmīya hymn 37, 103-4
Athalekar, S. L. a: G294
Atharva Veda 40, 105-6, 550
Athavale, R.B. a: G1465
atideśasūtra. *See* extension rule
ātman. *See* self
atom 148
aucitya. *See* suitability
AUDAMBARĀYAṆA 10, 13, 68, 110, 123, 342, 440
AUDAVRAJI 440
Aufrecht, Theodor 393, 561. a:G29, G432, G434, G1040, b:G364
Auktika (of Kulamaṇḍana Sūri) 485
Auktika (of Somaprabhā) 533
Auktika (of Udayadharma or Dharmasūri) 486
—Commentary (of Harṣakūlagaṇi) 489
—*Vākyaprakāśavarta* 497
aum 37, 68, 106
(Śrī) Aurobindo (Ghose) 37-8, 550
autpattika. *See* original relation of word to meaning
avadhi. *See* limit
(King) Avantivarman 28
āvaraṇa. *See māyā*, obscuring
avasthā. *See* phase
avidyā. *See* ignorance
Avinīta. *See* Durvinīta
Avyayakośa (of Dvārakanātha Nyāyabhūṣaṇa) 513
Avyayārtha (of Dayānanda Sarasvatī) 511
Avyayārtha (of Harikṛṣṇa) 523
Avyayārtha (of Rādhakṛṣṇa Gosvāmin) 529
Avyayārthakośa
—*Mañjarī* (of Rāmarsi) 531
Avyayārthalaharī (of Devakīnandana) 520
Avyayārthanirṇaya (of Kālurāma Śāstrin) 514
Avyayārthapradīpikā (of Yatīśa) 535
Avyayaśabdavṛtti (of Trilocana) 534
Avyayavṛtti (of Brahmadatta) 514
Ayachit, S. M. a:G151, G156

Bahulikar, Saudamin a:G310, G319, G1568, d:G293
Bahuvrihyarthavicāra (of Udayaṅkara Nānapāthaka) 510
bāhyārtha. *See* reference
Bakre, M. Gangadhara 216, 268
Bala, Indu d:G360
Bāla (ka) bodha (of Narahari) 528
BĀLACANDRA ŚĀSTRI 514, e:G1086

BĀLA KṚṢṆA PAÑCOLI 24, 417, 516
BĀLAKṚṢṆA ŚARMĀ YOGI 513
BĀLAṂBHAṬṬA. *See* VAIDYANĀTHA PAIYAGUṆḌA
BĀLARĀMA 518
Bālaśarman, son of Nāgeśa Bhaṭṭa 323
BĀLAŚĀSTRIN RĀṆADE 511
Balasubrahmanyam, M. D. a:G163, G185, G198, G199, G270, G291, G292, G320, G351, G375, G379, G619, G1584, G1595, G1596, d:G213
Bālāvabodha (of Dāmodara Śarman) 519
Bālāvabodha (of Kāśyapa) 18, 480
Bali, Surya Kant b:G1130, d:G1129
Ballantyne, James R. b:G1442, e:G521, et:G1148
Banaras 215, 237, 241, 247, 255, 357, 399
Bandhu, Visva b:G308
Bandini, Giovanni a:G776
Bandyopadhyay, Pratap a:G1637
Banerji, Priyatosh a:G133
Banerji, Suresh Chandra e:G1132, G1293
Bannerji, S. R. 203-4
Barlingay, S. S. a:G1559
Barua, Anandaram e:G915
Basavaraju, C. N. a:G964
basis (*prakṛti*, *gaṇa*) 15, 113
(*adhiṣṭhāna*) 216
nominal (*prātipādika*). *See* nominal stem
verbal. *See* roots
Bechardas, Shravak Pandit e:G979
becoming (*bhava*) 12, 109-10, 169
modification of (*vikāra*) 169
Belvalkar, Shripad Krishna 17
Benaraji, Satya Ranjan e:G914
Benfey, Theodor b:G1366
Bengal 19, 207 209, 211
BETARĀYA 518
Bhaga 105
Bhagavadgītā G115
Bhagavat, Vamana Balakrishna e:G725
BHAGAVATBHAKTA 518
BHAGAVATPRASĀDA ŚARMAN (1890) 513, e:G846
BHAIRAVA MIŚRA (1824) 12, 389, 510 G1088
bhakti G62
BHĀMAHA G873, G874, G875
Bhāmatī (of Vācaspati Miśra I) 302
Bhandare, Madhava Sastri e:G1360
Bhandarkar, R. G. a:G32, G53, G523, G524, G525, G532, G539, G541, G546, G1370
Bhānujī Dīkṣita 241, 319
BHARADVĀJA 440
Bharadvaja, Damodara Sastri e:G433, G849
Bharadvaja, Gangadhara Sastri e:G1277
Bharadvāja lineage 239
Bhārata 28, 30-31
BHĀRATA MALLIKA (1836) 493, 510
BHĀRATA MIŚRA (1550) 22, 231-35, 488
BHARTṚHARI (530) 6-7, 10-13, 17-18, 22, 26-29, 36, 38, 40-62, 68-70, 77, 82-87, 93-95, 107, 110, 118-76, 181-82, 193-97, 203, 231, 242, 270, 286-89, 293, 295, 297, 307, 323-31, 334, 342, 476-81, 557-60
(*Aṣṭādhyāyī*) *Bhāṣāvṛtti* (of Puruṣottamadeva) 203-9, 480
—Commentary (of Sṛṣṭidharācārya) 533
BHĀSKARA 518
Bhaskara, Paramesvarananda Sarma e:G1100
Bhat, M. S. 389. a:G18, G200, G744, G1064, G1218, G1291
Bhate, Saroja V. a:G407, d:G258
Bhatnagar, Veena d:G1630
Bhatta, Govinda Parasurama e:G997
Bhāṭṭa Mīmāṃsā 6, 25-26, 66, 89-93, 97-98, 181, 213, 255, 273, 301, 336
Bhatta, Ratnagopala e:G1115, G1184
Bhattacharjee, Umesha Chandra e:G60
Bhattacharya, Bishnupada 557; a:G1510, G1526. b:G1548
Bhattacharya, Biswanath a:G1345
Bhattacharya, Dinesh Chandra a:G968, e:G971
Bhattacharya, Gaurinath Sastri 551-52, a:G1428
Bhattacharya, Gurunatha Vidyanidhi e:G651, G653, G656, G1027
Bhattacharya, Madhavacandra Tarkacudamani e:G643
Bhattacharya, Prasanna Kumara e:G657
Bhattacharya, Ram Shankar a:G118, G122, G129, G130-31, G134, G139-40, G369, G470, G473-74, G499, G591, G595-96, G1488, G1496, G1518
Bhattacharya, Siddheswar a:G484
Bhattacharya, Sitanatha Siddhantavagisa e:G658
Bhattacharya, Siva Prasad a:G843
Bhattacharya, Trilokyanatha G1046

Bhattacharya, Vidhusekhara a:G71, G1474
Bhattacharya, Visvanatha e:G921
BHAṬṬAMALLA 530
Bhattanathaswamy, Acharya e:G1067
Bhaṭṭanayaka 32, 66-67
BHAṬṬA ŚIROMAṆI 518
BHAṬṬOJĪ DĪKṢITA (1590) 17, 20-22, 227, 240-42, 247, 251, 280, 319, 323, 335, 490-93, 560, G555
bhāva. *See* becoming
BHAVADEVA (1649) 498
Bhavadeva Misra 389
BHAVADEVA MIŚRA (1799) 508
bhāvakatva 65, 67
BHĀVA MIŚRA (or ŚARMAN) 518
BHĀVAN 458
bhāvanā 67, 98, 336, 553
arthī- and *śābdī*- 25, 98
BHAVANĀTHA 518
Bhāvanāviveka (of Maṇḍana Miśra) 98
BHAVASENA TRAIVIDYEŚA (1250) 481
Bhave, D. G. a:G579
Bhawe, Shrikrshna a:G123
bheda. *See* difference
Bhikshu, Bhadanta Shanti a:G1097
Bhikshu, Narada e:G661
BHĪMĀCĀRYA GALAGALI (1796) 508
BHĪMASENA (550) 113, 472
BHĪMASENA (ĀCĀRYA) (1350) 484
BHĪMASENA ŚĀSTRĪ 517, G1168, e:G1195
bhoga. *See* experience
Bhoja 560, G889
BHOJADEVA or BHOJARĀJA (1055) 477
bhojakatva 65, 67
(Rao) Bhojarāja G1211
Bhoja Vyākaraṇa 497
Bhusari, R. M. a:G62
bhūtārthavāda 25
Bhūtirāja 193
Biardeau, Madeleine b:G720, et:G722, G871, G1558
Bible 39
bīja. *See* seed
Bikaner 243
Bilhana 205
BILVEŚVARA 519
bindu 328, G1455
Bira, Sh. a:G1692
birth 46, 127, 129, 169, 196
Birwe, Robert a:G135, G147, G157, G201, G833, G932
bliss 32
Bloomfield, Leonard 4, 549. a:G64
Bodhapaddhati (of Dharanīdhara) 23, 355, 505
Bohtlingk, Otto a:G47, G436, G441, G502, G548, G648, G1368, G1373, e:G50A, G410, G1013, eb:G27, et:G38
BOPADEVA. *See* VOPADEVA
Bopp, Franz a:G1620
Boudon, Pierre a:G90
BRAHMADATTA (1914) 514
BRAHMADATTA JIJÑASU (1964) e:G511
BRAHMADEVA (1943) 24, 411, 516
(PEDDINTI) BRAHMADEVA 519
Brahman (Absolute) 31-33, 36-37, 41-43, 45, 47, 56, 60, 68, 93, 99, 106-7, 128-30, 148, 194-97, 216, 308, 328, 341, 348-49, 551
BRAHMĀNANDA SARASVATĪ (1915) 514-15
Brāhmaṇas 13, 24, 104-5, 107-9, 234
Brahmasiddhi (of Maṇḍana Miśra) 181
Brahmasūtrabhāṣya (of Śaṃkara) 60, 551, 553
Brahmasūtramitākṣara (of Annambhaṭṭa) 237
Brahmins 39
breath (*prāṇa*) 39, 43, 49-50, 62, 197, 558
Breloer, B. a:G76
Bṛhadāraṇyaka Upaniṣad 37, 105-6
Bṛhaddevatā (of Śaunaka) 4, 82-83, 86, 108, 549
Bṛhaspati 13, 104
Bṛhatīcandrikā (of Somanātha) 533
Bṛhatmañjuṣā (of Nāgeśa Bhaṭṭa) 23
Bronkhorst, Johannes a:G376, G381, G392-93, G495, G818, G1693, G1710
Brough, John 557-58, a:G8, G809, G1478, G1489, G1631
Brown, W. Norman 550
buddhi. *See* intellect
BUDDHISĀGARA SŪRI 476
Buddhism 3, 6, 45, 55, 66, 190-91, 209, G445, G787, G789, G793, G807
Buddhist Logic 27-28, 65, 559
Bühler, J. George a:G44, G535, G678, G879, G962, G1374, G1383, b:G962
Buiskool, Hermann b:G73
Burnell, A. C. b:G1

Burrow, Thomas a:G1423, G1481, G1490, G1497, G1535, G1597

caitanya. *See* consciousness
CAKADĀSA. *See* CAṄGADĀSA
(ŚEṢA) CAKRAPANI (DATTA) (1595) 247, 493, 562
CAKRAVARMAN 440
CAKRIN 519
Caland, Willem a:G69, G1406
Candra (school) 17, G1624
CANDRA (GOMIN) (470) 17, 471-72
CANDRADATTA JHĀ 519
CANDRAKĀNTA TARKĀLAṂKĀRA (1880) 512
CANDRAKĀNTA VIDYĀLAṂKĀRA 519
CANDRAKĪRTI (1607) 494
Candraprabhāvyākaraṇa (of Meghavijaya) 502
CANDRASEKHARA (1638) 497
CANDRAŚEKHARA 519
CANDRAŚEKHARA VIDYĀLAṂKĀRA 519
Candrasūtras or *-vyākaraṇa* (of Candragomin) 18, 471-72
—*Pañjikā* (of Pūrṇacandra) 475
—*Ṭīkā* (of Ratnamati)
—Commentary (of Śariputta) 479
—*Paddhati* (of Ānandadatta) 518
Commentary (of Dharmadāsa) 520
—*Bālāvabodhana* (of Kāśyapa) 525
CANDRIKĀ (of Harirāma) 511
Candrikā (of Kṛṣṇācārya) 526
Candrikā (of Śrīkānta Miśra) 533
CAṄGADĀSA 519
Caṅgasūtra. *See Vaiyākaraṇajīvatu*
CANNAVĪRAKAVI 440
capacity (*sāmarthya*) of words 8-9, 86, 149, 329
=*śakti* 127
CĀRCĀDĀSA. *See* CAṄGADĀSA
Cardona, George 14-16, 20, 109, 549, 553-55, a:G13, G259-61, G280, G311, G323-24, G342-43, G380, G394, G637, G1579, G1632, G1651, G1678
CARITRASIṂHA (GAṆI) (1569) 490
(*Kalāpa*) *Carkaritarahasya* (of Kavi Kaṇṭhahāra) 525
Carnoy, A. b:G1429
Cārvāka 55
case-ending (*kāraka*) 115, 267-72, 559, G277, G318, G323-24, G331, G334, G338, G1375, G1387, G1609
accusative case. *See* accusative case
dative case 270
genitive case. *See* genitive case
case-inflected words 276-77
Cassirer, Ernst 53, 552
category (*padārtha*) 213
Caturveda, Giridhara Sarma e:G1100
catuṣkoṭi. *See* negation, fourfold
cause (*hetu*) 164-67, G1611
(*kāraṇa*) 65, 90, 125, 131, 161, 559, G260, G1709
auxiliary (*sahakārikāraṇa*) 129
material (*prakṛti*) 167, 170, 196
Chacko, I. C. e:G137
Chakravarti, Prabhat Candra 554, a:G561, G1418, b:G1402, G1415, t:G558
Chakravarti, Srish Chandra 556, e:G851, G934, G970
Chandamāruta 239
chandas. *See* metrics
Chāndogya Upaniṣad 106
Chandrasekhara, S. e:668
Chandrasekharan, T. e:G590, G1359
change, illusory G1531
Chatterji, Kshitish Chandra a:G19, G72, G74, G77-78, G111, G454, G477, G571, G600, G842, G928, G1127, G1416, b:G1466, e:G830, et:G601
Chatterji, S. K. a:G136, G1424
Chattopadhyaya, Kshetresh Chandra a:G325, G461, G465, G562
Chaturvedi, Mithilesh a:G746, G766, G810-12, G814
Chaturvedi, Saraswati Prasad G466, a:G79-80, G89, G96-98, G103-5, G108, G114, G120, G124, G460, G463, G471, G581, G1436
Chaudhuri, Rajendra e:G1173
CHICCHU BHAṬṬA 519
Chidambara 239
Chinna Bomma 239
Chinna Timma 239
Chintamani, T. R. a:G413, e:G1354
Chitari, Saroja Sadashiv a:G186
Chitrao, Siddhesvar Shastri b:G82, G564
Chomsky, Noan 96, 555
Choudhari, A. N. a:G666
CHUCCHU BHAṬṬA. *See* CHICCHU BHAṬṬA
CIDRŪPĀŚRAMA 494

CINNA APPAYYA. *See* APPAYYA DĪKṢITA III
cit. *See* consciousness
coalescence, rules of (*saṃdhi*) 4, 39, G1421, G1480, G1547, G1630
=*saṃsarga*. *See* association of word meanings
cognition (*jñāna*) 54
extraordinary 126
final 216
COKKANĀTHA DĪKṢITA (1650) 22, 311, 321, 498-99
Colebrooke, Henry T. a:G1363
collection (*samudaya*) of words 145, 185
(*samūha*) of parts 169
communication 263
comparison (*upamāna*) 54, 170, 213, G178, G723, G751
complexity. *See* fallacy of complexity
composition, nominal. *See* nominal composition
compound (*samāsa*) word 4, 125, 173, 276-86, 292, 334, 339-40, G166, G810, G1390, G1503, G1617, G1654
(*dvandva*) 283, G814
genitive. *See* genitive case, compound
conceptual construction (*vikalpa*) 6, 27, 66, 128, 147, 325
concomitance (*anvayavyatireka*). *See* agreement and difference
condition (*nimitta*) 128. *See* also *upādhi*
configuration (*ākṛti*) 6, 26, 131, 553
conjunction or contact (*saṃyoga*) 195
connection (*sāmarthya*). *See* capacity
syntactic. *See* syntactic connection
connotation G1526
consciousness (*cit, caitanya, saṃvid*) 33, 35, 43, 57, 93, 126, 128, 163
consistency (*yogyatā*) 5, 7-9, 14, 27, 59, 67, 83, 88, 125, 131, 195, 286-88, 329, 553
capacity restricted by convention (*yogyatānityatā*) 7
consonants, order of G167
construction, mental 171
construction-free (*nirvikalpaka*) perception 27-8
context (*prakaraṇa*) 149, 175, 268, 322
contextual factors 7, 26, 30, 82-3, 326-27
sensitive features, rules G195
contiguity (*āsatti, saṃnidhi*) 5, 8-9, 27, 88-89, 114, 329-30
continuity 46, 196
contradiction (*virodha*) 149, 288, G1544
convention, conventional (*saṃketa, saṃketika*) 7, 26, 55-56, 65, 77, 90, 163, 194, 286, 292
conventional (*rūḍhi*) power of words 325, 368-69
conventional-derivative (*yogarūḍhi*) power 325-26, 368-69
corrupt word (*melcchaśabda*) 263, 287, 325
cosignified (*dyotya*) 125
cosmic order (*ṛta*) 37, 105
Coulson, Michael b:G1666
Coward, Harold G. 182-91, 550, a:G757, G777, b:G813, G1700A
Cowell, E. B. 552, 554
creation of the world 3, 40
creativity 48
CUDAMIŚRA 519

Daiva (of Deva) 480
—*Puruṣakāra* (of Kṛṣṇalīlāśukamuni) 483
Daivakarana, Virajananda e:G365
daivī vāk. *See* language
Dalal, Chimanlal D. e:G368
DĀMODARA 519
DĀMODARA DEVAŚARMAN 519
DĀMODARA ŚARMAN 519
Daṇḍin 107, 177, G875
Dange, Sadashiv Ambadas a:G262
Danielou, Alain a:G1452
Danielson, P.A. a:540
DANO (KĀCĀRYA) 519
darkness. *See* inertia (*tamas*)
darśana. *See* (Indian) philosophy
Darśapūrṇamāsamantrabhāṣya (of Mallaya Yajvan) 249
Das, Govinda a:G549
Das, Karuna Sindhu a:G296, G395
DAŚABĀLA 520
Daśabālakārikā (of Daśabāla) 520
Daśadhātusādhana [of Dano (kācārya)] 520
Dasgupta, Surendra Nath 550
Dash, Prafulla Chandra a:G838
Datta, Dhirendra Mohan 552
DATTA RĀMA BHAṬṬA 520
Dattātreya 317
Dave, T. N. a:G1560, G1569
DAYĀNANDA SARASVATĪ 511, e:G63, G241, G416, G429
DAYĀPĀLA (MUNI) (1025) 476
DAYĀŚAṂKARA 520
De, Sushil Kumar a:G829

death 45, 127
Debels, Rosane a:G1271
Debrunner, Albert b:G1405, G1498
decay (*jarā*) 43-44, 47, 171
definition (*saṃjñāsūtra*) 15
deity (*devatā*) 42, 294-95, 302
Della Casa, Carlo a:G745
demon (*rākṣasa*) 132, 146
denotation (*śakti*) 263, 274, 285, 287-88
  direct 271-72
  (*vācya*) 125, 147
denotative (*vācaka*) 146, 289, 301, 343
Deo, Kapil d:G152
dependence, mutual (*vyāpekṣa*) 277-84, 329
derivation (*vyutpatti*)
  of words 7, 146
  derivative power of words (*yogayaugika*) 325-26, 368-69
  (*prakrīya*) G1711
deśa. *See* place
Deshpande, Gangesh Tryambak a:G153, G187, G202, G216, G271-75, G1580
Deshpande, Handerao e:G861
Deshpande, Madhav Muralidhar 562, a:G25, G263, G297, G344-45, G836, G1652-53, G1684, G1705, b:G1697, etd:G1196
designative. *See* denotative
De Smet, Richard V. a:G1541
destruction 169, 196
  of the world 40
deva. *See* god (s)
DEVA (1200) 480
Deva, Kapil a:G171, G805, b:G218
DEVADATTA 520
DEVAKĪNANDANA 520
Devalekara, Bapu Hara Set a:G987
DEVANANDIN. *See* PUJYAPĀDA
DEVASAHĀYA 520
DEVAŚARMAN 520
Devasthali, Govind Vinayak 556, a:G326-27, G361, G481A, G487-88, G512, G517, G588, G1598, G1639, b:G217, et:G667, G1137
devatā. *See* deity
Devayaśas, father of Vṛṣabhadeva 179
DEVENDRAKUMĀRA VIDYĀRATNA (1915) 515
DEVENDRASŪRI (1210) 481
Devi, Prajna e:G177
deviation. *See* false, deviation
DEVĪDĀSA 520
DEVĪDĀSA CAKRAVARTIN 520
Devidatta, grandfather of Kṛṣṇamitrācārya 381
DEVĪDATTA ŚĀSTRIN 520
DEVĪDIN (1875) 512
DHANACANDRA (1533) 488
DHANAJIT 520
DHANAÑJAYA 520
DHANAÑJAYA BHAṬṬĀCĀRYA 520
DHANAPĀLA (1100) 478
DHANAPRABHĀ SŪRI 520
DHANEŚVARA (1250) 211, 481
Dhanika 91
DHARĀNANDA (1825) 510
DHARAṆĪDHARA (1397) 485
DHARAṆĪDHARA (1730) 505
DHARAṆĪDHARA (1809) 23, 355, 375, 385, 485, 505, 509
dharma 54, 175, 234, 342. *See* also merit
  literature 239
  = truth. *See* truth
DHARMADĀSA 520
DHARMADEVA 521
Dharmadhikar, Vidyadhar d:G1273
DHARMAKĪRTI (640) 18, 203, 476
DHARMAPĀLA (625) 177, 472
Dharmapradīpa G1211
DHARMARĀJĀDHVARĪNDRA (1615) 87, 253, 552
(RĀJAKUMĀRA) DHARMAŚĀSTRIN 521
DHARMASŪRI (1700) 501
DHARMASŪRI. *See* UDAYADHARMA
Dharmottarapradīpa (of Durveka Miśra) 177
dhātu. *See* (verbal) root
Dhātucandrikā (of Kavicandra Datta) 493
Dhātucandrikā (of Tarkālaṃkāra Bhaṭṭācārya) 534
Dhātucandrikā (of Ṭhakkuradāsa Nyāyapañcānana) 534
Dhātucintāmaṇi (of Viśvanātha Nyāyālaṃkāra) 535
Dhātudarpana (of Vuramiśra) 535
Dhātukalpalaṭīkā (of Dhanajit) 520
Dhātukārikāvalī (of Varadarāja) 495
Dhātukāya (of Nārāyaṇa Bhaṭṭatiri) 497
  —*Kṛṣṇārpana* 497
  —*Vivaraṇa* (of Rāmapaṇivāda) 530
Dhātukośa (of Ghanaśyāma) 522
Dhātulakṣaṇa (of Dano (kācārya)) 519

Dhātumālā (of Īśvarakaṇṭha) 523
Dhātumālā (of Ṣaṣṭhidāsa) 532
Dhātumālikā (of Betarāya) 518
Dhātumañjarī (of Candrakānta Vidyālaṃkāra) 519
Dhātumañjarī (of Kāśīnātha) 504
Dhātupallava (of Bhavanātha) 518
Dhātuparāyaṇa (of Śrutasāgara) 533
Dhātuparāyaṇa (of Trilocana) 534
Dhātuparyayamaṇimālā (of Maheśa Jhā) 527
dhātupātha G126, G143, G149, G150, G1383
Dhātupātha (of Bhāskara) 518
Dhātupātha (of Candra school) 18
Dhātupātha (of Kāśīśvara) 525
Dhātupātha (of Narendrapūri) 483
Commentary (by Kṣemendra) 488
Dhātupāṭha (of Pāṇini). *See Aṣṭādhyāyī-Dhātupāṭha*
Dhātupāṭha (of Puṇyasundaragaṇi) 529
Dhātupāṭha (of Pūrṇacandra) 529
Dhātupāṭhakārikā (of Kocca Sankaran Susad) 510
Dhātupāṭhakramakaumudī (of Dhanañjaya) 520
Dhātuprabodha (of Kālīdāsa Cakravartin) 524
Dhātupradīpa (of Maitreya Rakṣita) 207, 478
Dhātuprakāśa (*saṃgraha*) and *Ṭippanī* (of Bālarāma) 518
Dhātupratyayapañcikā (of Taladevasudhi) 533
Dhātupratyayapañjikā (of Hariyogin Śailavācārya). *See Aṣṭādhyāyī-Dhātu-Śabdikābharaṇa*
Dhātuprayogāvalī (of Kāśīnātha) 525
Dhāturatnākara (of Nārāyaṇa) 315, 499
Dhāturatnākara (of Sādhusundara Gaṇi) 495
Dhāturatnamañjarī (of Rāmasiṃha) 531
Dhāturatnaprakāśa (of Śeṣa Viṣṇu) 494
Dhāturatnāvalī (of Rādhakṛṣṇa Śarman) 507
Dhāturūpa (of Vaṅgasena). *See Ākhyātavyākaraṇa*
Dhāturūpadarśā (of Tārānātha Tarkavācaspati) 512
Dhātusādhanā (of Kavicandra [Datta]) 493
Dhātusādhanā (of Rāmakānta) 487
Dhātusaṃgraha (of Kāśīnātha Miśra) 525
Dhātusaṃgraha (of Subrahmanyam Nambuttiripad) 512
Dhātuvṛtti (of Kāśyapa) 440
Dhātvāvalī (of Kedareśvara Śarman) 525
DHUṆḌIRĀJA (1700) 501
dhvani. *See* sound
Dhvanikāra 92
Dhvanyāloka (of Ānandavardhana) 28, 32
DHYĀNAKĀRA 465
difference (*bheda*) 6, 125, 145, 149, 197, 278
DIGNĀGA (480) 6, 27-28, 66, 123, G794, 549
dik. *See* space
Dikshitar, V. R. Ramachandra a:G509
Dikshitulu, R. B. d:G362
Dīrghatamas 103-4
disjunction (*vibhāga*) 268
dispositional tendency (*saṃskāra*, *vāsanā*), or latent disposition. *See* trace
distortion. *See* false: deviation (*viparyāsa*)
Divanji, Prahlad C. a:G115
diversity 42-43
DIVYASIṂHA MIŚRA 521
Doraswamy, K. a:G305, G1599
Doshi, Bechardas Jivaraj e:G1034
Dravidian G1381
dravya. *See* substance
DRAVYEŚA JHĀ 403, 521
Drutabodha with *Drutabodhinī* thereon (of Bhārata Mallika) 510
Dube, Harinatha e:G981
duration (*sthiti*) 304
DURBĀLĀCĀRYA. *See* KṚṢṆAMITRĀCĀRYA
DURGĀ (SIṂHA) or DURGĀDĀSA (950-1050) 17, 19, 475, 477, G641-42, G645, G656-58
DURGĀDĀSA VIDYĀVĀGĪŚA (1639) 497
DURGĀDĀSA VIDYĀVĀGĪŚA ŚRĪRĀMA TARKAVĀGĪŚA (1908) 514
Durgaprasad, Kedarnath e:G918
Durghaṭavṛtti (of Maitreya Rakṣita) 207, 478
DURVEKA MIŚRA (1020) 177
DURVINĪTA (550) 177, 471
Dutt, Nomita a:G422
DVĀDAŚAHĀDHVARIN. *See* TIRUMAL YAJVAN
(BĀLAPATAÑJALI) DVĀDAŚĀHAYAJIN (1680) 311, 501
Dvaita Vedānta 240
dvandva. *See* compound, *dvandva*
Dvandvaikaśeṣavāda (of Rāghava Jhā) 529

DVĀRAKANĀTHA NYĀYABHUṢAṆA (1899) 513
Dvikarmavāda (of Lakṣmana Dvivedin) 527
Dvivedi, H. P. a:G347, G396, b:G363
Dvivedin, Vindhyesvari Prasada e:G673, G1125, G1131
Dyen, Isidore b:G1435
dyotaka. See suggestive meaning
dyotya 125

Ecklund, G. Green b:G1686
economy, principle of 76
Edgerton, Franklin a:G1503, b:G1459
Edgren, Hjalmar a:G1371
effort, speaker's (*yatna*) 187, 258, 330, 332
Eggeling, Julius e:G642, G938
Ekadaśakārikā (of Raghurāma) 512
Ekagotrasūtraparāmarśa (of Devīdatta Śāstrin) 520
ekārthībhāva. See meaning, single
ekaśeṣa. See reduction of two verbs to one
ekavākyatā. See syntactic analysis
Ekavarṇārthasaṃgraha (of Bhārata Mallika) 493, 510
ELEŚVARĀGNIHOTRA 521
Eliot, T. S. 49, 551
elite, spiritual (*śiṣṭa*) 132
elliptical sentence 149, G530
Emeneau, Murray B. a:G1504, G1585, b:G1480
emotion, emotive meaning 12, 28-30, 67
(case-) ending (*vibhakti*) 163-64
personal 257-58, 263-64
primary 260
verbal 255, 262
energy, inner (*kratu*) 70
enumerative cognition (*āpekṣabuddhi*) 173
epic Sanskrit G1630
epistemology. *See* knowledge, theory of
error. *See* false
essence (*rasa*) 28-33, 130
(*svarūpa*) 188
eternal (*nitya*) 169, 175, 216
absolute (*kuṭastha*) 7, 118
as preserved by speakers (*pravāhanityatā*) 7, 118, 130-31
etymology (*nirukta*) 3, 8, 14, 38, 107-9, 111, 555
etymological meaning (*samākhya*) 83, 175
etymological words (*yaugika*) 368-69
Euclid G196
eulogy 83
excellence imparted by phonemes 235
exception (*apavāda*) 150
exclusion. *See apoha*
existence (*sattā*) 127, 169, 183, 234, 330-31, 558
(mutual) expectancy (*ākāṃkṣā*) 5, 8-9, 27, 85-88, 114, 124, 149, 300, 329, 343-44, G1524
experience (*bhoga*) 129
expressional (*saṃvyavahārika*) 194
extension rule (*atideśasūtra*) 15

Faddegon, Barend a:G66, G1467, b:G85, G1425
fallacy, of complexity 93
of interdependence 93
of unestablished locus (*āśrayāsiddha*) 189-90
of unknown qualificandness 189
"pathetic" 31
false, falsity, error 5, 54, 59, 187-89, 213, 217, 233, 236, 553
theory of error 56-60
—deviation (*viparyāsa, vyabhicāra*) 149, 273
feasibility (*kṛtisādhyatva*) 265-66
feature. *See* configuration (*ākṛti*)
feminine bases G265
function G238
figurative meaning. *See* meaning, figurative
Filliozat, Jean a:G800
Filliozat, Pierre-Sylvain a:G1213, G1654, G1685
Finot, L. ae:G659
fire-wheel (*ālātacakra*) 169
fitness. *See* consistency
form (*ākāra*) 129
(linguistic) (complex) formation (*vṛtti*) 173, 295-96, 329
Form Criticism 39
Foucher, A. a:G442
Fowler, Murray a:G190, G312
Franke, R. Otto a:G42, G45, G437, G1380, e:G840, et:G940
Fraser, Russell 552
Frauwallner, Erich 123, 550, 559, a:G607, G1536
function, operation (*vyāpāra*) 11, 67, 75-76, 98, 165, 169, 255-56, 258-61, 266, 330-31, 336

Gadadhara (1660) 521
Gadamer, Hans-Georg 36, 550
Gadgil, Dinkar Keshava Shastri e:G1083
Gaidani, M. G. a:G593
Gajāsūtravāda (of Tirumala Bukkapattanam Śrīnivasācārya) 504
Gajāsūtravāda (of Veṅkatadāsa) 508
Gajāsūtravādārtha (of Ganapati Sastri) 513
Gajāsūtravādārtha (of Mannu Deva) 509
GALAVA 440
Gaṇadarpaṇa (of Kumārapāla) 486
gaṇapāṭha 14, G1496
Gaṇapāṭha (of Bhārata Mallika) 510
Gaṇapāṭha (of Candra school) 18
Gaṇapāṭha (of Pāṇini) 113, G129, G151-52, G156-57, G161, G227, G278, G630
Gaṇapāṭha (of Rāmakṛṣṇa Dīkṣita) 497
Gaṇapāṭhasaṃgraha (of Geyadeva) 522
GAṆAPATI ŚĀSTRI (1900) 513
Gaṇaratnamahodadhi and *Vṛtti* (Vardhamāna) 478
Commentary (of Gaṅgādhara) 521
Commentary (of Govardhana Bhaṭṭa) 522
Gaṇaratnāvalī (of Yajñeśvara Bhaṭṭa) 512
Gaṇavṛtti (of Puruṣottamadeva) 209
GAṄEŚA 521
GAṄGĀDĀSA (PAṆḌITA) 521
GAṄGĀDĀSĀCĀRYA 521
GAṄGĀDATTA 521
GAṄGĀDATTA ŚĀSTRI 521, e:G119
GAṄGĀDHARA (1800) 509
GAṄGĀDHARA 521
GAṄGĀDHARA DĪKṢITA (1617) 494
GAṄGĀDHARA KAVIRĀJA (1850) 23, 395, 511-12
Gangadhara, Mahadeva Sarma e:G1061
GAṄGĀDHARA NĀTHA 521
GAṄGĀDHARA ŚARMAN 521
GAṄGĀPRASĀDA ŚĀSTRIN 514, e:G1089
GAṄGĀRAMITRA PĀṬHIN (MĀLAVA) 521
GAṄGEŚA (1350) 91, 96, 273
GAṄGEŚA MIŚRA UPĀDHYĀYA 521
GAṄGEŚA ŚARMAN 521
Ganguli, Hemanta Kumar a:G729, b:G713
Gani, Vinaya Vijaya b:G950
Garbe, Richard t:G50A
GĀRGYA 13, 110, 112, 114, 140
gauṇa, *gauṇi* words 65-66, 326, G1484
GAURAMOHĀNA BHAṬṬA (VIDYĀRATNA) 522
GAUTAMA (150) 97, 522, 549, 556
Gawronski, A. b:G1411
Geiger, Bernhard a:G551
gender (*liṅga*) 12, 15, 83, 115, 120, 149, 173, 196, 262, 273-75, 339, G712, G1457, G1707. *See* also person
genitive case 271, 339
compound 285
gerund G1705
GEYADEVA 522
GHANAŚYĀMA 522
Ghat(a)ge, Amrit Madhav a:G230, G516
Ghosh, Amalananda a:G570
Ghosh, Batakrishna a:G102, G109, G455, G466, G1426, G1453; b:G1430
Ghosh, Manumohan et:G427
GIRIJA 522
GIRĪŚACANDRA VIDYĀRATNA G1019
Gīrvaṇapadamañjarī (of Dundhirāja) 501
Gīrvaṇapadamañjarī (of Varadarāja) 495
Gītāsundara (of Sadāśiva Dīkṣita) 311
God (*īśvara*) 26, 32, 52, 55, 65, 90, 237, 286-87, 324, 330, 334-45, 557
god(s) (*deva*) 108, 132
Gode, P. K. a:G839, G1057, G1060, G1128, G1177, G1191, G1211, G1268, G1275
Godes, B. S. a:G313
Gokhale, Pratibha P. a:G352-53, G1111
Gokhale, V. N. a:G94
GOKULACANDRA (1839) 510
Goldstucker, Theodor a:G32, G430-31, e:G529-30
GOLHĀṆA 522
Gombrich, Richard a:G1694
GOṆĀRDIYA 458
Gonda, Jan a:G314, G1451, G1470, G1476, G1481-83, G1505, G1519-20, G1686, G1640, b:G1447
GOṆIKAPUTRA 458
Goonatilleke, William e:G820, etb:G34
Gopal, Ram a:G860
GOPĀLA 522
GOPĀLA BHAṬṬA (1590) 490
GOPĀLA CAKRAVARTIN (BANERJI) (1672) 500
GOPĀLĀCĀRYA 522. *See also* GOPĀLADEVA VIDYĀVĀGĪŚA
GOPĀLADEVA. *See* MANYUDEVA

GOPĀLADEVA VIDYĀVĀGĪŚA (1800) 508
GOPĀLAKṚṢṆA ŚĀSTRIN (1720) 23, 353, 504
GOPĀLĀNANDA YATI 309
GOPĀLA ŚĀSTRI NENE (1919) 24, 407, 515, e:G1048, G1094, G1101, G1120, G1186
GOPĪCAṆḌA. *See* GOYĪCANDRA
GOPĪNĀTHA 522
GOPĪNĀTHA BHAṬṬA 522
GOPĪNĀTHA TARKĀCĀRYA (1550) 488
Gore, Vitthala Narayana Sarma e:G1155
(Christian) gospels 39
GOSVĀMI ŚRĪ ŚIVĀNANDABHAṬṬA 522
Gough, A.E. 552, 554
GOVARDHANA (1100) 478
GOVARDHANA BHAṬṬA 522
Govardhana Bhaṭṭa, grandfather of Jayakṛṣṇa Maunin 361
GOVINDA BHARADVĀJA ŚĀSTRI (1835) 510
GOVINDA BHAṬṬA 522
GOVINDA MIŚRA 522
GOVINDA PAṆḌITA 523
GOVINDA PARAŚURĀMA BHAṬṬA (1888) 513
GOVINDARĀMA VIDYĀŚIROMAṆI 523
Govindārṇava (of Śeṣa Nṛsiṃha) 215
GOVINDA SENA 523
GOVINDASIṂHA (1900) 513
GOYICANDRA (1400) 19, G912, 485
grammar (*vyākaraṇa*) 3-4, 6-7, 12-14, 35, 128, 161, 163, 170, 196, 233, 323
grammatical analysis G767
grammatical derivation (*pratipādaka*). *See* nominal stem
grammaticality (*sādhutva*) 161
Grantovskij, E. A. a:G169
Greece G1599
Grierson, George a:G50
grouping (*sāhitya, sāmagri, samūha*) 127
growth (*krama*) 43-44
Guha, Dinesh Chandra e:G1106
Guha, Manjulika a:G1655
Guleri, Chandradhar a:G554
guṇa G1445, 120
  in Pāṇini G186
  in Sāṃkhya 44, 120, 173
  quality (in Vaiśeṣika, etc.). *See* quality
GUṆACANDRA (1210) 481
(SIDDHA) GUṆAKĀRA 523
GUṆANANDIN (890) 475
GUṆARATNA SŪRI (1411) 486
Gune, Jayashri Achyut 564, etb:G1197
Gune, Saroj a:G1330
Gunjikara, Ramacandra Sarman G1079, e:G1155
Gupta, Chandra Bhan a:G1521
Gupta, Rajanikanta e:G1022
Gupta, Suddhir Kumar a:G121, G125, G1299, G1300
GURUWARA BĀLA ŚĀSTRI 523

Hahn, Michael a:G834-35
Haimacatuṣkavṛttiṭippanikā (of Golhaṇa) 522
Haimalaghuprakrīyā (of Vinayavijayagaṇi) 499
HAṂSAVIJAYAGAṆI (1650) 499
HARADATTA (1059) 19, 203, 279-80, 477, 560, G849, G857, G877
HARAGOVINDA VIDYĀVĀCASPATI 523
HARANĀTHA VIDYĀRATNA 523
HARENDRANĀRĀYAṆA DEVAŚARMAN (1912) 514, e:G1028
hare's horn 325
Hargovindass, Shravak Pandit e:G979
HARI BHĀSKARA AGNIHOTRA (1677) 500-01
HARIBHAṬṬA (1801) 383
HARIDATTA (DAIVAJÑA) 523
HARI DĪKṢITA (1270) 21-22, 241, 319, 500
HARIKṚṢṆA 523
HARINĀTHA DVIVEDIN (1850) 511
HARI PAṆḌITA 523
HARIRĀMA (1850) 511
HARIRĀMA BHAṬṬĀCĀRYA 523
HARIRĀMA KALĀ (1797) 508
HARI ŚAṂKARA JHĀ (1929) 515, e:G566
HARI ŚARMAN or ŚĀSTRI (1900) 513, 523
HARISIDDHĀNTAVĀGĪŚA 91
HARIVALLABHA (1747) 4, 23, 363, 505-6, G118
HARI VṚṢABHA. *See* VṚṢABHADEVA
HARIYOGIN ŚAILĀVĀCĀRYA (1150) 478
HARṢAKĪRTI SŪRI 523
HARṢAKULAGAṆI (1557) 489
HARṢAVARDHANA (630) 472

Hartman, C.G. b:G1570
Hartmann, P. b:G1506
HARYAKṢA (350) 465
Hattori, Masaaki 27, 549
Hauschild, Richard b:G1561
HAYAGRĪVĀCĀRYA 523
Hazra, Rajendra Chandra a:G141
hearing (*śravaṇa*) 106
heaven (*svarga*) 46-47, 342
Heimann, Betty a:G1438, G1463, G1511, b:G1522
Hejib, Alaka a:G382
HELĀRAJA (980) 11, 40-44, 193-97, 203, 292, 475, 551, 557-61, G776
HEMACANDRA (1150) 203, 479, G889
HEMAHAṂSAVIJAYAGAṆI (1457) 486
Henry, Thomas 385
Herman, Arthur L. 554, a:G1549
Hertel, Johannes a:G443
Herzberger, Hans G. a:G773
Herzberger, Radhika a:G773
hetu. *See* cause
  in grammar G184
Hiriyanna, Mysore 550, a:G501, G778
Hoffman, Karl a:G328-29
homogeneity G1653
Hume, R. E. t:551

icchā. *See* will
I-ching. *See* I-tsing
identity (*tādātmya*) 129, G324
  syntactic identity 271
ignorance (*avidyā*) 42, 51, 54, 58, 61, 128, 147, 197. *See also* falsity
imitation word 276
imperative, Vedic G301
imperceptibility (*parokṣatva*) 264
implication 273
impropriety (*apraśastya*) 288
incompatibility or inconsistency of meaning 66-67, 148, 346
indeclinable particle. *See* particle
independence (*svātantrya*) 167
indescribable, inexpressible (*anirvacanīya*) 42, 60, 147-48
India, nation of 39
indication (*liṅga*) 149
indicator (*upalakṣaṇa*) 115, 183, 186, 273, 339
  dyotaka. *See* suggestive meaning
  jñāpaka 186
indices, referential G307, G348
Indira (of Padmadhara) 528
indirect object (of dative) (*sampradāna*) 167, 270-71, 337-38
individual. *See* particular
Indra 13, 17, 104, 295
INDRA (GOMIN) 439-40
INDRADATTA UPĀDHYĀYA (1800) 23, 379, 508
Indravyākaraṇa (of Indra) 439-40
indriya. *See* sense-organ
INDU (MITRA) (1070) 477-78
Indurāja 193
inertia (*tamas*) 44-45, 120, 275
inference (*anumāna*) 27, 51, 54, 59-60, 126, 132, 175, 213, 273
infinitive 262
infinity (*ānantya*) 273
inflection G1426
inherence (*samavāya*) 195, 268
injunction. *See* prescription
inner controller (*antaryāmin*) 129, 132
inseparable existence (*svarūpasat*) 274
insight. *See* intuition
Insler, Stanley a:G613
instigation (*pravartanā*) 265, 336-37
instrument of knowledge (*pramāṇa*) 25, 54-56, 59-60, 175, 553
instrumental case-ending. *See* means
integration (*vṛtti*) 278-79
intellect (*prajñā*, *buddhi*) 62, 146, 551, 560
intention of the speaker (*tātparya*) 9, 27, 65-66, 89-93, 145, 165, 300, 322, 327, 329-30, 344-46, 557, G1540, G1657
interdependence. *See* fallacy of interdependence
intuition (*pratibhā*) 10, 28, 31-32, 49-50, 59, 62-66, 94-95, 125, 130, 146, 327, 553, G763, G771, G1394, G1441
īpsitakarman 268-69
Ipzzagalli, A. M. b:G1408
iṣṭasādhanatva. *See* means to a desired result
īśvara. *See* God
ĪŚVARAKAṆṬHA 523
ĪŚVARAMIŚRA 523
ĪŚVARĀNANDA or ĪŚVARĪDATTA SARASVATĪ (1550) 22, 219, 229, 488
ĪŚVARĪPRASĀDA 524
itihāsa 108
itikartavyatā 25, 87
I-tsing 177, G689, G803, G1631
Iyengar, H. R. Rangaswami a:G795
Iyer, K. A. Subramania 41, 59, 79, 128, 182, 201, 213-14, 517, 550-55, 561,

a:G65, G670, G693, G728, G732, G751, G767-68, G804, G1434, G1441, G1445, G1457, G1464, G1469, G1477, G1494, G1509, G1673, b:G734, e:G709-10, G721, G727, G747, et:G 872, t:G742, G748A, G758
Iyer, S. Venkatasubramania a:G397, G421, G1107, G1205, G1664, b:G1205

Jacobi, Hermann a:G961, G1389
JAGADDHARA (1325) 484
JAGADDHARA 524
JAGADIŚA 524, 549
JAGAN MOHĀNA PAṆḌITA (1670) 500
JAGANNĀTHA 524
(MAHĀMAHOPĀDHYĀYA) JAGANNĀTHA 524
JAGANNĀTHA PAṆḌITARĀJA TAILAṄGA (1650) 23, 32, 83, 215, 241, 370, 499
Jāgrahitetivāda (of Cakrin) 519
jahatsvārtha 279
JAIMINI (25 A.D.?) 25, 114
Jain, Jainism—3, 17-19, 54, 123, G1647
Jainendravyākaraṇa 17, 466
—*Mahāvṛtti* (of Abhayanandin) G673, G676
—*Śabdārṇavacandrikā* (of Somadeva) G985
—*Vṛtti* (of Vāsudeva Śāstri Abhyaṅkar) 516
—*Laghuvṛtti* (of Dharmaśāstrin) 521
Commentary (of Guṇanandin) G674
Jaiyaṭa Upādhyāya 203
JĀJALI. *See* UJJVALADATTA
Jalpamañjarī (of Sudhānandasūriśiṣya) 500
Janacek, Adolf a:G603
Jānakīpariṇayananāṭaka (of Rāmabhadra Dīkṣita) 311, 321
JANĀRDANA ŚARMAN 524
Jani, A. N. a:G170, G203, G276
jarā. *See* decay
JARANĀTHA TARKAVĀCASPATI (1870) 512, G1020
Jāṭakas G1386
jāti. *See* universal
Jātiśaktivāda (of Ananta Bhaṭṭa) 518
jātisphoṭa. *See sphoṭa, jāti*
jātiviśiṣṭavyakti, see particular qualified by a universal
Jaumara school 19
JAYADEVA MIŚRA G1259, G1264
JINADEVASŪRI 524
JAYĀDITYA (650) 18, 203, 472-73
JAYAKṚṢṆA MAUNIN (1745) 23, 351, 361, 367, 505
JAYANTA (1650) 498
JAYANTA BHAṬṬA (870) 66, 91, 93-94, 97, 475
JAYANTA BHAṬṬA 524
Jayaswal, Kashi Prasad a:G444, G506, G560
Jesus 39, 550
Jha, Ganganatha 549, 552
Jha, Govinda d:G866
Jha, Krishna Deo d:864
Jha, Subhadra a:G128
Jha, Sukheswar a:G298
Jha, Taranisa e:G1171
Jha, Triloknath a:G1527
Jha, V. N. a:G1712
Jhajjar, Vedananda Vedavagisa e:G668
Jijnasu, Brahmadatta e:G177
Jijnasu, Raghuvira e:G1296
JINAPRABHĀ SŪRI (1280) 483
JINASĀGARA. *See* DHANACANDRA
JINAVIJAYA (1637) 497
Jinavijaya, Muniraja e:G663
JINENDRABUDDHI (725) 18, 115, 474
JĪVĀNANDA VIDYĀSĀGARA (1894) G917, e:G645, G991, G1023, G1041
JĪVANĀTHA RĀYA (1925) 515
JĪVARĀMAN ŚARMAN (1928) 515
jñāna. *See* cognition
Jñānāmṛta (of Kāśīśvara Śarman) 23, 505
JÑĀNATILAKA (1646) 498
JÑĀNENDRA SARASVATĪ (1730) 351, 373, G1100, 505
JÑĀNEŚVARA 524
jñāpaka. *See* indicator
Jñāpakasaṃgraha (of Nāgeśa Bhaṭṭa) 504
—*Vivṛti* (of N. S. Rāmānuja Tātācārya) 517
Jñāpakasamuccaya (*bhāṣya*) (of Puruṣottamadeva) 209, 480
Jñāpakāvalī (of Haragovinda Vidyāvācaspati) 523
jñāpana G128
JONARĀJA or JOGARĀJA (1450) 486
Joshi, Bechardas e:G832
Joshi, Bhargavasastri Bhikaji e:G582
Joshi, Dayashankar Madhusudan a:G277, d:G245
Joshi, Shivarama Dattatreya 174 255-

308 340, 560, a:G172, G246, G330-31, G354, G370, G398, G614, G620, G763, G1198, G1200, G1270, G1550, G1571-72, G1656, G1667, G1679. d:G1193, et:G625, G627, G632-34, G1192
Joshi, Venkatesha Laxman G1122
Joshi, Venkatesha Shastri a:G346, G383-89, G975, G1219, G1699-1700
JUMARANANDIN (1350) 19, 488, 484, G912
Junankar, P. B. b:G364
Jvalananda of Tiksnajnatiya 355
JYEṢṬHAKALĀŚA (1060) 205, 477
jyotiṣa. *See* astronomy

KAIYAṬA (1030) 19, 21-22, 86, 174, 203-4, 278-80, 289, 293-94, 304,339-42, 476, 561, G551, G877
kāla. *See* time
KĀLADHARA 524
Kalāpasaṃgraha (of Rāmānanda Tīrtha) 530
Kalāpasāra (of Rāmakumāra Nyāyabhūṣaṇa) 530
Kalāpatyādivṛtti (of Sarvadhara Upādhyāya) 532
KALĀVATI DEVĪ (1909) 514
KĀLICARAṆA VIDYOPĀDHYĀYA (1887) 512
Kālidāsa G475
KĀLIDĀSA CAKRAVARTIN 524
KĀLIKA PRASĀDA ŚUKLA (1961) 24, 324, 423, 517, e:G857, G1245, G1286
KĀLĪ KUMĀRA ŚARMAN 524
Kalpa (a Vedanga) 107
KĀLURĀMA ŚĀSTRIN (1910) 514
KALYĀṆAMĀLA ŚARMAN 524
KALYĀṆA SARASVATĪ (1790) 508
Kalyanov, V. I. a:G1390, G1528
KĀMADEVA GHOṢA 524
KAMALĀKARA BHAṬṬA (1640) 497-98
Kamalākara Dīkṣita 317
KAMALAŚĪLA (770) G775
Kāmarūpa school G1070
Kaṃsa 196
KANAKALĀLĀ ŚARMAN 524
KAṆAKAPRABHĀ (1240) 481
Kane, Pandurang Varman a:G584, G873
Kansara, N. M. a:G904
KĀNTA NĀTHA 524
Kantawala, S. G. a:G1668
kāraka. *See* agent; case-ending; syntactic function
Kārakacakra 528
—*Dīpaprabhā* (of Nārāyaṇa) 528
Kārakacakra (of Ananta) 518
Kārakacakra (of Dharmakīrti) 476
Kārakacakra (of Rāmatarana Śiromaṇi) 512
Kārakacandrikā (of Rāmacandra) 530
Kārakacandrikā (of Tārapada Nyāyaratna) 533-34
Kārakādibodhinī (of Devakīnandana) 520
Kārakakośa (of Śivānanda Gosvāmin) 532
Kārakānanda (of Ānanda Siddhāntavāgīśa) 518
Kārakanirūpaṇa (of Amaracandra). *See Satkarakalaksana*
Kārakanirūpaṇa (of Kṛṣṇāvadhuta) 526
Kārakaparīkṣā (of Paśupati) 529
Kārakarahasya (of Rūparāma Nyāyapañcānana) 531
Kārakārtha (of Kṛpārama) 526
(*Ṣaṭ*) *Kārakārthanirṇaya* (of Trilokanātha) 534
Kārakārthapradīpikā (of Sudarśanācārya) 533
Kārakārthavicāra (of Rāghava Jhā) 529
Kārakasambandhoddyota (of Rabhasanandin) 475
Kārakasambandhoddyota (of Vināsvaranandin) 535
Kārakatattva or *Kārakavicāra* (of [Śeṣa] Cakrapaṇi) 247, 493
Kārakavāda (of Śrīkṛṣṇa Bhaṭṭa Maunin) 506
(*Ṣaṭ*) *Kārakavivaraṇa* (of Ratnapāṇi) 531
Kārakavyutpattirahasya (of Gopīnātha Bhaṭṭa) 522
Kārakiya (of Dayānanda Sarasvatī) 511
Kārakoktisamuccaya (of Śrīprabhā Sūri) 533
Kārakollāsa (of Bharata Mallika) 510
karaṇa. *See* means
kāraṇa. *See* cause
KARAPUTUGALA DHARMA ŚRĪ (1925) 515, e:G1093
Kārikābhāṣya (of Divyasiṃha Miśra) 521
Kārikāvalī (of Nārāyaṇa) 499
—*Ṭīkā* (of Rāmaprasāda) 501
KARMADHARA (1501) 487
karman. *See* object (of action)
karmapravacanīya. *See* postposition
kartṛ. *See* agent
kartṛsiddhāntamañjarī (of Rāmacaraṇa) 530

KĀRTTIKEYA SIDDHĀNTA BHAṬṬĀCĀRYA (1800) 509
KĀŚAKṚTSNA 440-41
Kashmir, 28, 203, 205, G535
Kashmir Śaivism 57, 124, 324, 342, 554
Kāśī. *See* Banaras
(*Aṣṭādhyāyī*) *Kāśikā* (*vṛtti*) (of Jayāditya and Vamana) 18, 271, 472-73, G586, G596, G821, G863
—*Ṭippanī* (of Bhagavatprasāda Śarman) 513
—*Padamañjarī* (of Haradatta) 477, 560
—*Kusumavikāśa* (of Śiva Paṇḍita) 551
—*Nyāsa* (of Jinendrabuddhi). *See Kāśikānyāsa*
—*Prakriyāmañjarī* (of Ānandapūrṇa Vidyāsāgara) 484
—*Ṭīkā* (of Puṇḍarīkākṣa Vidyāsāgara Bhaṭṭācārya) 487
—*Vṛttipradīpa* (of Rāmadeva Miśra) 531
—*Sāra* (of Vāsudeva) 534
Kāśikānyāsa (of Jinendrabuddhi) 474
—*Anunyāsa* (of Indu) 478
—*Tantradīpa* (of Maitreya Rakṣita) 207, 478
—(*Vyākaraṇa*) *Prakāśa* (of Narapati Mahāmiśra) 486
—*Prabhā* (of Sanātana Tarkācārya) 532
KĀŚĪNĀTHA (1725) 504
KĀŚĪNĀTHA (1810) 510
KĀŚĪNĀTHA 525
KĀŚĪNĀTHA BHAṬṬA (1500) 487
KĀŚĪNĀTHA DEVAŚARMAN 525
KĀŚĪNĀTHA MIŚRA 525
KĀŚĪRĀJA 525
KĀŚĪŚVARA 525
KĀŚĪŚVARA BHAṬṬĀCĀRYA (1550) 489
KĀŚĪŚVARA ŚARMAN (1739) 23, 505
KĀŚYAPA 18, 440
KĀŚYAPA (1200) 480
KĀŚYAPA 525
Kātantra commentary (of Kumāralabdha) 465
Commentary (of Rāma Paṇḍitavara) 513
Kātantra system 17, 19-20, G664
Kātantrakaumudī (of Gaṅgeśa Śarman) 522
Kātantrakaumudī (of Govardhana Bhaṭṭa) 522
Kātantrakaumudī (of Kṛpala Paṇḍita) 526
Kātantrapariśiṣṭa (of Govinda Paṇḍita) 523
Kātantrapariśiṣṭa (of Śrīpatidatta) 486
—*Vaktavyaviveka* (of Puṇḍarīkākṣa Vidyāsāgara Bhaṭṭācārya) 487
—*Prabodha* (of Gopīnātha Tarkācārya) 488
—*Prakāśikā* (of Śaṃkara Śarman) 532
—*Siddhāntaratnākara* (of Śivarāma Cakravartin) 493
—*Candrikā* (of Rāmadāsa Cakravartin) 493
Kātantrasūtras (of Śarvavarman) 17, 464-65
—*Vṛtti* (of Durghasiṃha). *See Kātantravṛtti*
—*Kṛnmañjarī* (of Śivarāma Śarman) G647
—*Pariśiṣṭa* (of Śrīpattidatta). *See Kātantrapariśiṣṭa*
—*Ṭīkā* (of Mahendranātha Bhaṭṭācārya) 513
—*Aṣṭamaṅgala* (of Rāmakiśora Śarman) 513
—*Kalāpacandra* (of Bilveśvara) 518
—*Sāra* (of Harirāma Bhaṭṭācārya) 523
Kātantravṛtti (of Durghasiṃha) 475, 477, G641, G642, G645, G653
—*Pañjikā* (of Trilocanadāsa). *See* TRILOCANADĀSA
—*Ṭīkā* (of Durghasiṃha) 477
—*Vistara* (of Vardhamāna) 478
—*Ṭīkā* (of Pradyumna Sūri) 480
—*Tattvaprakāśikā* (of Guṇacandra) 481
—*Rūpamālā* (of Bhavasena Traividyeśa) 481
—*Bālaśikṣā* (of Saṃgramasiṃha) 483
Commentary (of Mokṣeśvara) 484
—*Bālā*(*va*)*bodhinī* (of Jagaddhara) 484
—*Nyāsa* (of Śitikaṇṭha) 486
—*Bālāvabodha* (of Merutunga) 485
—*Pariśiṣṭa* (of Śrīpattidatta). *See* ŚRĪPATTIDATTA
—*Padaprakaraṇasaṃgati* (of Jonarāja) 486
—*Prakāśa* (of Karmadhara) 487
—*Pradīpa* (of Puṇḍarīkākṣa Vidyāsāgara Bhaṭṭācārya) 487
—*Manoramā* (of Rāmanātha Śarman) 488
Commentary (of Rāma Tarkavāgīśa) 489
—*Durgāvākyaprabodha* (of Kulacandra) 489

—*Avacūri* (of Caritrasiṃha) 490
—*Uttarapariśiṣṭa* (of Trilocana) 493
—*Vyākhyasāra* (of Rāmadāsa Cakravartin) 493
—*Rahasya* or *Ṭīkā* (of Rāmanātha Vidyāvācaspati) 498
—*Chandaḥprakriyā* (of Candrakānta Tarkālaṃkāra) 512
—*Paribhāṣavṛtti* (of Bhāva Miśra) 518
—*Laghuvṛtti* (of Chicchu Bhaṭṭa) 519
—*Vṛtti* (of Devadatta) 520
—*Dhuṇḍika* (of Durgāsiṃha) 520
—*Vyākhyalekha* (of Gaṅgādāsācārya) 521
—*Dīpikā* (of Gautama) 522
—*Dhātupāṭha* (of Govinda Bhaṭṭa) 522
—*Śiṣyaprabodhikā* (of Govinda Bhaṭṭa) 522
—*Sāra* (of Harirāma Bhaṭṭācārya) 523
Commentary (of Kāśirāja) 525
Commentary (of Mauniśekhara) 527
—*Dhātusūtrīya* (of Pitambara Vidyābhūṣaṇa) G656
—*Daurgāsiṃhavṛtti* (of Pṛthvīcandra) 529
—*Tattvārṇava* (of Raghunanda Ācārya) 529
—*Prabodha* (of Rāmanātha Cakravartin) 530
—*Vanmayapradīpa* (of Sarvadhara Upādhyāya) 532
—*Saṃjīvanī* (of Sitānātha Śāstrin) 532
—*Manoramā* (of Śrīnātha Śiromaṇi) 533
—*Kalāpacandra* (of Susena Kavirāja Miśra) G656
—*Ākhyātaṭīkā* (of Vidyāsāgara) G653
—*Laghuvṛtti* or *Śiṣyahita* (of Yaśobhūti) 535
Kātantra (sūtra) vṛtti-Pañjikā (of Trilocana dāsa) G643, G656-58, 475-76
—*Uddyota* (of Trivikrama) 478
—*Pradīpa* (of Kuśala) 480
—*Durgā (pada) prabodha* (of Jinaprabhā) 483
—*Kalāpatattvabodhinī* (of Rāmacandra) 502
—*Ṭīkā* (of Candrakānta Tarkālaṃkāra) 512
—*Dhuṇḍikā* (of Dhanaprabhā Sūri) 520
—*Prabodha* (of Narahari) 528
—*Candra* or *Vyākhyāsara* (of Susena Kavirāja Miśra) 533
Commentary (of Viśveśvara Tarkācārya) 535
Kātantrottara (of Vijayānanda) 478
Katre, Sadashiv Lakshmidhar a:G24
Katre, Sumitra Mangesh a:G1427, b:G219, G231, G278, G483A, G1448
Katsura, Shoryu 549
KATYA 458
KĀTYĀYANA (250 B.C.) 6, 16, 18, 26, 85-86, 97, 114, 117, 119-20, 193, 204, 261, 277, 283, 293, 322, 558, G444, G446-47, 458-59, G593, G618
Kaumudīsudhākara (of Candrakānta Tarkālaṃkāra) 512
KAUṆḌA BHAṬṬA. *See* KOṆḌA BHAṬṬA
KAUṬILYA G1493
KAUTSA 441
Kavi, M. Ramakrishna a:G686
KAVICANDRA (DATTA) (1600) 493
KAVIDARPANA RĀGHAVA (1375) 485
Kavikalpadruma (of Hemacandra)
versification (of Harsakulagani) 489
—*Avacūrī* (of Vijayamala) 534
Kavikalpadrumaskandha Upasargamaṇḍana (of Maṇḍana Kavi) 485
KAVI KAṆṬHAHĀRA 525
KAVI KUÑJARA 371
KAVĪNDRANANDANA 525
Kaviraj, Gopinatha 553, a:G1394, G1455
Kavirājapātrikā (of Pitāmbara Vidyābhūṣaṇa) 529
Kaviratna, Syamacarana G1025, e:G555
KAVISĀRAṄGA 525
KAVI VALLABHA 525
Kāvyadarśa (of Daṇḍin) 107
Kāvyālaṃkārasūtravṛtti G852
Kāvya literature G557
KEDAREŚVARA ŚARMAN 525
Keith, Arthur Berriedale G559, a:G110, G459
Kenghe, C.T. a:G700
Kephart, Calvin b:G1471
KEŚARI MIŚRA 525
KEŚAVA (1650) 498
KEŚAVA 525
KEŚAVADEVA TARKAPAÑCĀNANA BHAṬṬĀCĀRYA 525
KHANA NṚPATI 526
Kharbas, S. Datta b:G1638
Khare, G. H. a:G1220
Kharwandikar, D. K. a:G926-27, d:G925
KHUDDI JHĀ (ŚARMAN) (1910) 23-24, 399, 514

Kielhorn, Franz G549, a:G14, G46, G425, G434, G535, G542-43, G545, G671, G677, G679, G785, G821, G848, G880, G882, G941, G1378, G1386, b:G2, G503, G1369, e:G536, et:G665
Kiparsky, Paul a:G247, G377
Kirātārjunīya (of Bhāravi) 175
Kiurste, J. e:G942, G944
Kiuttel, F. a:G1381, G1384
Klostermaier, Klaus 550-51
Knauer, Friedrich a:G1377
knowledge, theory of 5, 43, 53-63, 68-69, 126, G720, G1558, G1615. *See also* cognition
=*pramā* 54
=*vidyā* 128, 147
KOCCA SANKARAN SUSUD (1825) 510
KOLAHALA 526
KODANDARĀMA 526
KOṆḌA BHAṬṬA (1630) 21-22, 241, 255-308, 324, 369, 495-96, 562
Konow, Sten a:G106, G1431
Koparkar, D. G. a:G423, G895
Kotbhaskara, Ramachandra Sastri e:G680
krama. *See* growth; sequence
KRAMADĪŚVARA (1050) 19, 477
kratu. *See* energy, inner
kṛdanta. *See* primary derivative
Kṛdvivaraṇa (of Kāśīnātha) 525
Kṛdvṛtti (of Kavīndranandana) 525
Krishnamachariar, R.V. e:G1095, G1294
Krishnamacharya, V. 342, 363
Krishnamoorthy, K. a:G1657
kriyā. *See* action; verb
Kriyākalāpa (of Jinadevasūri) 524
Kriyānighaṇṭu (of Bhaṭṭoji Dīkṣita) 492
Kriyāratnasamuccaya (of Guṇaratna Sūri) 486
Kriyāviveka (of Helārāja) 193, 475
Kṛnmañjarī (of Śivadāsa) 532
KṚPĀLA PAṆḌITA 526
KṚPĀRĀMA 526
(God) Kṛṣṇa 195, G532
KṚṢṆA (1645) 498
KṚṢṆA BHAṬṬA 526
KṚṢṆA BHAṬṬĀCĀRYA 526
KṚṢṆĀCĀRYA 526
KṚṢṆĀCĀRYA II (1430) 486
KṚṢṆADVAIPĀYANA 146
KṚṢṆA DVIVEDIN 526
KṚṢṆALĪLĀŚUKA (1280) 483
KRSNAMĀCHARIAR. *See* KṚṢṆASUDHI
KṚṢṆA MIŚRA (1780) 508
Kṛṣṇamiśraprakriyā (of Kṛṣṇa Miśra) 508
KṚṢṆAMITRĀCĀRYA or DURBALĀCĀRYA (1800) 23, 377, 381, 508-9
KṚṢṆA PANDITA 526
KṚṢṆA ŚĀSTRIN 526
KṚṢṆASUDHI 525
KṚṢṆĀVADHŪTA 526
Kṛṣṇa Yajurveda 549
kṛti. *See* volition
kṛtisādhyatva. *See* feasibility
Kṛtpariśiṣṭa (of Ratideva Siddhānta Vāgīśa) 531
Kṛtprakāśa (of Nīlakaṇṭha Dīkṣita) 506
KṢAPAṆAKA (1650) 472
KṢEMANKARA (1653) 499
KṢEMENDRA (1525) 487-88
Kshirsagar, V. K. a:G370
KṢIRASVĀMIN (1050) 19, 476
Kudala, S.D. e:G552
KULACANDRA (1550) 489
KULAKĀCĀRYA 526
KULAMAṆḌANA SŪRI (1394) 485
KULAMUNI (1800) 508
KULLUKA BHAṬṬA 527
Kumar, Avanindra b:G399
KUMĀRALABDHA or KUMĀRALĀTA (200) 465
KUMĀRAPĀLA (1461) 486
KUMĀRA TATĀYA (1825) 23, 391, 510
Kumari, Sudesh d:G332
KUMĀRILA BHAṬṬA (660) 4, 18, 25-26, 71-77, 81, 88-89, 97, 181, 189-190, 213, 237, 282, 549, 554-56, 561, G682, G786
KUNĀRABADAVA 458
kundalinī 328
KUNI 458
KUPPU ŚĀSTRIN (1750) 507
KUŚALA (1200) 480
Kushwaha, Mahesh Singh e:G1172
kuṭasthanityatā. *See* eternal

Laddu, Sueshacandra Dhyaneshwar a:G180, G220, G264, G279, G299, G482A, G487A, G492, G513, G515, G621, G640, G1581, G1614, G1711
Laghubodha (of Kṛṣṇa) 498
Laghumañjuṣā (of Nāgeśa Bhaṭṭa) 23
—*Kalā* (of Vaidyanātha Paiyaguṇḍa) 23, 357

Laghuśabdakaustubha (of Nīlakaṇṭha Dīkṣita) 373, 506
Laghuśabdaratna (of Nāgeśa Bhaṭṭa) 323, 367
Laghusārasvata (of Kalyāṇa Sarasvatī) 508
Laghusiddhāntakaumudī (of Varadarāja) 494-95
—*Ṭīkā* (of Jayakṛṣṇa Maunin) 505
—*Ṭīkā* (of Rūpacandra) 512
—*Sārabodhinī* (of Rancchodji Odhavji) 514
—*Tiṅantapradīpikā* (of Kalāvati Devī) 514
—*Ṭippaṇī* (of Śivadatta Śarman) 514
—*Ṭīkā* (of U. K. Veṇkaṭanarasiṃha) 515
—*Ṭippanī* (of Jīvanātha Rāya) 515
—*Bālabodhinī* (of Vāsudev Viṣṇu Mirāshi) 515
—*Ṭīkā* (of Girija) 522
—*Saṃkṣiptabālabodhinī* (of Kanakalāla Śarman) 524
—*Sāralā* (of Jīvarāma Śarman) G1159
—*Bhaimī* (of Bhīmasena Śāstri) G1168
Laghusiddhāntamañjuṣā (of Nāgeśa Bhaṭṭa) 323
—*Kuñcikā* (of Kṛṣṇamitrācārya) 381
Lahiri, Prabodh Chandra b:G81
Lakārārthanirṇaya (of Śrīkṛṣṇa Bhaṭṭa Maunin) 367, 506
Lakṣaṇa (=King Muktapīda of Kashmir) 193
Lakṣaṇā. *See* secondary meaning
Lakṣmaṇa, 12th cent. ruler in Bengal 209
LAKṢMAṆA DVIVEDIN 527
LAKṢMAṆA TRIPĀṬHI (1915) 515
Lakṣmī 341
LAKṢMĪDATTA 527
Lakṣmīdhara 241
LAKṢMĪKĀRA 527
LAKṢMĪNĀRĀYAṆA VYĀSA 527
Lakṣmīnivāsābhidhā (of Śivarāma Tripāṭhin). *See Unādikośa*
LAKṢMĪNṚSIṂHA (1660) 499
Lakṣyamālā (of Eleśvarāgnihotra) 521
Lalamani Upadhyaya 379
Lambert, F. a:G1600
Langer, Susan K. 554
(spoken) language (*śabda*) (*vāc*) 3-4, 37, 94, 103-7, 114, 118, 124-25
—acquisition G763
as means of release (*śabdapūrvayoga*) 46-47, 49-50, G755
daivī vāk 37
—learning 93
levels of 61-63
parā vāk 63
philosophy of 27, 36, G720
—principle (*śabdatattva*) 95, 128, 553
Laṅkā 322
LĀTĀ VIHĀRIN (1850) 511
La Terza, Ermanagilda a:G681, G788
Lehman, J. a:G1479
Leidecker, Kurt F. b:G1419
LEŚAPRABODHA. *See* JINAPRABHĀ (SŪRI)
letter. *See* phoneme
Levi, Sylvain a:G48, G498, G504, G826
lexicography G1388
liar's paradox. *See* paradox
liberation (*mokṣa*) 18, 46-47, 49, 51, 99, 130, 342, G719
Liebich, Bruno a:G823-24, G1375, G1395, b:G57, G59, G67, G438, G822, G828, e:G58, G825, G827, et:G660, t:G847, G923
Lienhard, Siegfried a:G1587
Limaye, V. P. 128, a:G205, G221-22, G372, G669, b:G635, e:G726, G781
limit (*avadhi*) 132
liṅga. *See* gender; indication
Liṅganirṇayacandrikā (of Anantasūri) 518
Liṅgānuśāsana
of Candra school 18
Commentary (by Harṣavardhana) 472
—*Sarvalakṣaṇa* (of Pṛthivīśvara) 529
of Vāmana 473
rules 15
Liṅgānuśāsana (of Hemacandra) 504
—*Durgāprabodha* (of Śrīvallabhavācārya) 504
—*Sarvārthalakṣaṇa* (of Śabarasvāmin) 531
Liṅgānuśāsanavṛtti (of Utpāla) 479
Linge, D. E. 550
linguistic element (*śabda*) 5-6, 182-85
linguistic monism (*śabdādvaita*) 193
linguistics, diachronic G1523
linguistics, modern G314
literary criticism (*sāhitya*) 3-5, 28-33, 67. *See also alaṃkāraśāstra*
loan words G1613
Locana (of Abhinavagupta) 91
locative (case-ending) (*adhikaraṇa*) 168, 270, G1664, 337-39

absolute 262
logic G563, G1545, G1559
propositional G243
logos 37, 105-6
LOKEŚAKĀRA (1683) 501
LOKEŚVARA ŚARMAN ŚUKLA 527
Lüders, H. e:G664

Macdonnell, A. A. 549
MĀDHAVA or ŚAYANA (1350) 56, 68, 484, 554, 556
MĀDHAVA (1887) 513
(ARRA or ERRA) MĀDHAVA BHAṬṬA (1450) 486
MĀDHAVA BHAṬṬA (1520) 487
MĀDHAVA SARASVATĪ (1550) 489
MĀDHAVA ŚĀSTRĪ BHANDĀRĪ (1920) 515, e:G565, G1117
MADHUKĀNTA ŚARMĀ JHĀ (1950) 24, 516
MADHVA (1280) 266
Mādhyamaka Buddhism 45, 60
madhyamā vāc 43, 47, 49-50, 52, 61-62, 95, 99, 121, 124, 328-29, 342, 555, 558
Madhyasiddhāntakaumudī (of Varadarāja) 494
—*Ṭīkā* (of Jayakṛṣṇa Maunin) 505
Commentary (of Bālakṛṣṇa Śarmā Yogi) 513
—*Visamasthalaṭippanī* (of Govindasiṃha) 513
—*Sudhā* (of Sadāśiva Śāstrī Joshī) 516
—*Vyākhyā* (of Brahmadeva) 519
—*Prabhākara* (of Viśvanātha Śāstri) 535
Magha G873
Mahābhārata 146, G264, G1568
Mahābhāṣya (of Patañjali) 16-17, 19-22, 38, 45-47, 55, 68, 117-21, 124, 165, 167, 182-83, 196, 242, 264, 267, 271, 278, 325, 327, 334-35, 340-42, 345, 459-64, 549, 553, 551, 556-57, G181, G502, G515, G586
—*Dīpikā* or —*Tripādi* or *Ṭīkā* (of Bhartṛhari) 18, 22, 54, 124, 174-76, 470
—*Bhāgavṛtti* (of Vimalamati) 472, G791
—*Pradīpa* (of Kaiyaṭa). *See Mahābhāṣyapradīpa*
Commentary (of Jyeṣṭhakalāśa) 205, 477
—*Ṭīkā* (of Maitreya Rakṣita) 207, 478
—*Prāṇāpana* or —*Laghuvṛtti* (of Puruṣottamadeva) 209, 480
—*Ṭīkā* (of Śaṃkara) 531
—*Cintāmaṇi* (of Dhaneśvara) 211, 481
—*Ratnaprakāśa* (of Śivarāmendra Sarasvatī) 22, 245, 487
—*Sūktiratnākara* (of [Śeṣa] Nārāyaṇa Bhaṭṭa) 22, 225, 488
—*Sphūrti* (of Sarveśvara) 489
—*Prakāśikā* (of Śeṣa Viṣṇu) 22, 243, 494
—*Vyākhyādarśa* (of Kamalākara Bhaṭṭa) 498
—*Siddhāntaratnaprakāśa* (of Śivarāmendra Sarasvatī) 499
—*Ratnāvalī* (of Cokkanātha Dīkṣita) 22, 311, 499
—*Anūpāta* (of Tirumala Yajvan) 277, 499
—*Gūḍhārthadīpanī* (of Sadāśiva) 22, 317, 500
—*Prakāśa* (of Nīlakaṇṭha Dīkṣita) 500
—*Śābdikacintāmaṇi* (of Gopāla Kṛṣṇa Śāstrin) 23, 353, 504
—*Vivaraṇa* (of Satyapriya Tīrtha Svāmin) 23, 359, 505
—*Tattvaviveka* (of Nīlakaṇṭha Dīkṣita) 373, 506
—*Parijātam Nāṭakam* (of Kumāra Tatāya) 23, 391, 510
—*Tripāṭhaga* (of Satārā Rāghavendrācārya) 23, 393, 510
—*Maṇiratnaprabhā* (of Viprarajendra) 511, G37
—*Ṭippanī* (of Dayānanda Sarasvatī) 511
—*Prakāśa* (of Madhukānta Śarmā Jhā) 214, 516
—*Kuñcikā* (of Hari Śaṃkara Jhā) 515, G566
—*Tattvāloka* (of Rudhradhara Jhā Śarman) 24, 421, 516
—*Ṭippanī* (of Guruwara Bāla Śāstrī) 523
—*Sūktiratnākara* (of Nṛsiṃha) 528
—*Vidvanmukhabhūṣaṇa* (of Prayogaveṅkaṭādri) 529
Mahābhāṣyapradīpa (of Kaiyaṭa) 19, 22, 174, 203-4, 476
—*Laghuvivaraṇa* (of Satyānanda or Rāmacandra Sarasvatī) 219, 487
—(*Bṛhad*) *Vivaraṇa* (of Īśvarānanda) 22, 219, 229, 488
—*Uddyotana* (of Annambhaṭṭa) 22, 237, 489

—*Sphūrtī* (of Sarveśvara) 489
—*Ṭippanī* (of Mallaya Yajvan) 249, 496
—*Vyākhyā* (of Nārāyaṇa [Śāstrin] 22, 353, 498
—*Prakāśa* (of Nīlakaṇṭha Dīkṣita) 500
—*Uddyota* (of Nāgeśa Bhaṭṭa) 23, 340-42, 503
—*Chāyā* (of Vaidyanātha Paiyaguṇḍa) 23, 357, 505
—*Ṭippanī* (of Bāla Śāstrin) G522, G547
—*Vyākhyā* (of Rāmasevaka) 23, 377, 507
—*Sphūrtī* (of Ādenna) 517
—*Prakāśa* (of Pravartakopādhyāya) 529
—*Prakāśa* (of Seṣa Cintāmaṇi) 22, 221
Mahācārya 239
MAHĀDEVA (1270) 482
Mahādeva, father of Vaidyanātha Paiyaguṇḍa 357
Mahādeva Dīkṣita, father of Vāsudeva Dīkṣita 365
Mahadevan, T. M. P. 551-52
MAHĀDEVA VEDĀNTIN (1694) 501
MAHĀLIṄGA ŚĀSTRIN 527
Maharashtra 20, 241, 323, G1685
Mahashabda, M. V. a:G1267
Mahāvārttika (of Kātya or Bhāvan) 458
Mahavir a:G333, G400-01, G406, b:G373
Mahāvīra 17
MAHENDRANĀTHA BHAṬṬĀCĀRYA (1900) 513, e:G652
MAHEŚA JHĀ 527
Maheśvara, teacher of Kaiyaṭa 203
Maheśvara Sūri 203
Maheśvarasūtras of Pāṇini's *Aṣṭādhyāyī* 14, G65, G341. *See also Aṣṭādhyāyī*
Maitrayanī Saṃhita a:G433
MAITREYA RAKṢITA (1109) 19, 207, 478
Maitrī Upaniṣad 40, 45, 550
Majumdar, Baradaprasada e:G1021
MALAYAGIRI (1280) 483
MALLAYA YAJVAN (1630) 34, 496
Mammaṭa 83, 203, 370
MĀNALUR VIRARĀGHAVĀCĀRYA 527
manana. *See* thinking
(SRI) MĀNAŚARMAN 527
Manavalli, Gangadhara Sastri e:G680
Manavalli, Rama Sastri e:G1114
MAṆḌANA (1330) 484
MAṆḌANA KAVI (1400) 485
MAṆḌANA MIŚRA (690) 5, 11, 18, 22, 51, 56-59, 70-80, 82, 98, 181-91, 231 233-35, 266, 331, 473-74, 554, 556, 561
Māṇḍūkya Upaniṣad 37, 106
MAṄGARASA 527
manifestation (*vivarta, vyañjaka*) 93, 129, 216, 236, G1587
MĀṆIKYADEVA 527
Mañjuṣā (of Nāgeśa Bhaṭṭa) 323
Manoramācandrikā (of Nīlāmbara Miśra) 528
Manoramākhaṇḍana (of Keśava) 498
Mansion, J. b:G1407
mantra 24, 51-52, 107-8, 148, 188, 234
—*samādhi* 52
Manu G493
MANYUDEVA or MANADEVA (1815) 23, 387, 509
Marathi 287
marker (*it*) 16
Marulasiddaiah, G. b:G1573
Mātariśvara 104
mathematics G208, G1689
Matilal, Bimal Krishna a:G204, G1542, G1574, G1633, b:G1615
matter, material thing (*mūrti*) 162
MUNIŚEKHARA 527
Maurya G548
māyā 41-43, 60, 105
obscuring (*āvaraṇa*) 42
projective (*vikṣepa*) 42
Mayrhofer, M. a:G1513, g:G1491
Mazumdar, B. C. a:G52
Mazumdar, Pradip Kumar a:G1621, b:G1680
Mazumdar, Surendra Nath a:G850
McArthur, Harvey 550
meaning, theory of 5, 8-10, 18, 27-30, 90, 145, 186, 232-34, 324, G1396, G1555-56. *See also* connotation, *sphoṭa*
abstracted (*apoddhāra*) 13
=*artha* 5-6, 26, 94, 114, 118-19, 149, 559
figurative G5, 370
nominal. *See* nominal meaning
relation of word to 7-8
secondary. *See* secondary meaning
sentence. *See* sentence meaning
single (*ekārthībhava*) 277-84, 340
stable 131
verbal. *See* verbal meaning

word-meaning. *See* word
means or instrument (*karaṇa*) 25, 87, 163, 165, 168, 270, 337-38, G1542
=*sādhana* 145, 162-68, 195-96
=*upāya* 148
to a desired result (*iṣṭasādhanatva*) 265-66
measure (*parimāṇa*) 115
Meenakshi, K. a:G1706
MEGHARATNA (1400) 485
MEGHAVIJAYA (1700) G952, 502
Mehendale, M. A. a:G408
Meisezahl, R. O. a:G1007
memory, recollection (*smṛti*) 30, 184, 216, 235, 303, 321, 324
—traces (*samskara*) 43-44, 48, 74-78, 81. *See also* dispositional tendency
(inner) mental word 231, 234
merit (*dharma*) 121, 132
MERUTUṄGA (1388) 485
metalanguage G266, G286, G323, G1662
metaphor (*upacāra*) 5, 8, 11, 29-30, 67-68, 91, 194, 258
faded 66
metaphoric transfer 26, G1704
metaphysics 35-52
metarule (*paribhāṣā*) 14-15, G326, G352, G1502, G1598, G1616, G1647, G1682
metrics (*chandas*) 3, 39, 107
Millonig, Harald a:G1601
(Pūrva) Mīmāṃsā 3-6, 9, 12, 21, 25-28, 54-55, 60, 66, 69, 71, 73, 76, 79, 83, 85-91, 95-98, 118-19, 181, 184, 186, 190, 213, 233, 237, 240-41, 255-57, 260-63, 271-72, 282, 284-87, 292-93, 295-96, 324, 328, 331, 334, 339-40, 344, 346, 556, G797, G802, G1526, G1616, G1680. *See also* Bhāṭṭa; Prabhākara
Mimamsaka, Yudhisthira 205, 207, 211, 225, 241, 247, 249, 313, 359, 373, 561-62, a:G844, b:G285, ce:G23, e:G315, G420, G909, G977, G1328, t:G20
Mīmāṃsāsūtras (of Jaimini) 25, 86, 92, 114, 213, 230 233
—*Ślokavārttika* (of Kumārila). *See Slokavarttika*
—*Tantravārttikā* (of Kumārila). *See Tantravarttika*
—*Kutūhalavṛtti* (of Vāsudeva Dīkṣita) 365
miracle (*atadbhūta*). *See* action, miraculous course of
Misra, Adya Prasada G1052
Mishra, Avadh Bihari e:G690
Misra, Brahmashankara e:G1320
Mishra, Hari Deo a:G608
Mishra, Hari Mohan a:G402, G490A, G1669
Misra, M. P. e:G906
Misra, Narayana e:G862
Mishra, Ramasakala e:G885
Mishra, Satya Svarup a:G1670
Misra, Sobita e:G853
Misra, Sri Narayana a:G250
Misra, Sudama Sarman e:G1048
Mishra, Umesh a:G1397
Mishra, Vidhata b:G1622
Misra, Vidya Niwas a:G181-82, G1610, b:G206
Misra, Vir Bhadra a:G390
Mitākṣaravṛtti (of Balambhaṭṭa) 357
Mitra 104
Mitra, Rajendralal a:G497
mlecchaśabda. *See* corrupt word
Moghe, R. G. a:G1616
Mohana Lala, grandfather of Indradatta Upadhyaya 379
Mokate, Ganapati Sastri e:G1125, G1344
mokṣa. *See* liberation
MOKṢEŚVARA (1350) 484
Mongolian G1692
monism 61, G730
mood 263-67, 335-37
different permanent moods (*sthayībhāva*) 33
Mookerji, Radhakumud a:G446-47
moral power 47-48
morpheme 4, 6, G1537
analysis G176
morphophonemics G336, G1678
Morretta, Angelo a:G1659
motion, movement 552-53
motivating force (*prayojana*) 204
Mugdhabālāvabodha (of Kulamandana Sūri). *See Auktika*
Mugdhabodha (of Vopadeva) 20, 482-83
—*Pariśiṣṭa* (of Nandakiśora Bhaṭṭācārya Cakravartin) 485
—*Pramodajananī* or —*Kāraka* (of Rāma Tarkavāgīśa) 489
Commentary (of Kāśīśvara) 489
—*Subodha* (of Durgādāsa Vidyāvāīśa) 497
—(*Kavikalpadruma*) *Dhātudīpikā* or —*Paribhāṣāṭīkā* (of Durgādāsa Vidyāvāgīśa) 497

—*Subodha* (of Kārttikeya Siddhānta Bhaṭṭācārya) 509
—*Setusaṃgraha* (of Gaṅgādhara) 512
—*Ṭippanī* (of Śyāmacaraṇa Kaviratna) 514
—*Parimala* (of Harendranārāyaṇa Devaśarman) 514
—*Dhātuvṛtti* (of Dāmodara) 519
Commentary (of Devīdāsa Cakravartin) 520
—*Ṭippanī* (of Girīśacandra Vidyāratna) G1019
—*Śabdadīpikā* (of Govindarāma Vidyāśiromaṇi) 523
—*Dhātupradīpa* (of Haranātha Vidyāratna) 523
—*Ṭippanī* (of Śivanārāyaṇa Śiromaṇi) 532
Mugdhabodha school 19
Mugdhapariśiṣṭa (of Kāśīśvara Bhaṭṭācārya) 489
Mukhabhūṣaṇa 487
Mukhopadhyaya, Sunjit Kumar a:G1051
mukhya words G1484
Muktikalāśa, grandfather of Jyeṣṭhakalāśa 205
(King) Muktipāda of Kashmir. *See* Lakṣaṇa
Müller, F. Max a:G39, G520, G845
Müller, Reingold F. G. a:G1499
Muni, Jambuvijaya a:G794
Municandravijaya e:G959
Muralīdhara, greatgrandfather of Indradatta Upādhyāya 379
MURLĪDHARA MIŚRA (1977) 517, e:G1053
Murder in the Cathedral (of T. S. Eliot) 49
mūrta. *See* matter
Murti, M. S. Narayana a:G225, G249, G770, G772, G783, G1109, G1602, G1634, G1709, G1713, d:G1617
Murty, Parasuram Gopala Krishna a:G481
Murti, T.R.V. 53, 55, 550, 552, a:G1643
music G203
mystical experience 32, 47
mysticism 65

nāda 69-70, G1455
NĀGEŚA BHAṬṬA (1714) 21, 23, 68, 83, 87, 203, 319, 323-49, 357, 379, 387, G1081, G1084, 502-4, 549, 555-56, 562
NĀGOBA PAṆḌITA (1775) 508
Nakamura, Hajime a:G697, G745, G803, G807
Nalla Perumal Diksita 311
nāmadhātu. *See* verb, nominal
Nāmakārthaprakāśasaṃgraha (of Abhinava Nṛsiṃhāśrama) 496
nāman. *See* noun
Nāmanirmaladarpana (of Lakṣmīdhara) 527
name and form (*nāmarūpa*) 107
Namputiri, E. V. Raman e:G1201
nañ. *See* negation, negative particle
NĀNAKARĀMA ŚĀSTRIN (1924) 515, e:G1092
NANDAKĪRTI 527
NANDAKIŚORA ŚARMAN BHAṬṬĀCĀRYA CAKRAVARTIN (1398) 485
NANDASUNDARA. *See* DHANACANDRA
NANDASUNDARA GAṆI 528
Nandi, T. S. a:G1588
NARAHARI 528
NARAIN DATTA TRIPĀṬHIN 528
NARANĀRĀYAṆA. *See* PURUṢOTTAMA VIDYĀVĀGĪŚA BHAṬṬĀCĀRYA
Narang, Satya Pal a:G978
NARAPATI MAHĀMIŚRA (1425) 486
Narasimhacarya, M. S. e:G1059
NARASIṂHA SŪRI 528
NĀRĀYAṆA 528
NĀRĀYAṆA BHĀRATĪ 528
(ŚEṢA) NĀRĀYAṆA (BHAṬṬA) (1546) 22, 215, 225, 243, 488, G1107
NĀRĀYAṆA BHAṬṬATIRI (1640) 22, 497
NĀRĀYAṆA DANDANĀTHA (1100) 478
NĀRĀYAṆA NYĀYAPAÑCĀNANA (1550) 488-89
NĀRĀYANA (SADHU) (1667) 500
(RĀMA) NĀRĀYAṆA (SARMAN) (VANDYOPĀDHYĀYA) (1664) 315, 499
NĀRĀYAṆA (ŚĀSTRIN) (1640) 498
NARAYANA (SASTRIN) 22, 253, G1059
NĀRĀYANA SUDHI (1750) 507
NĀRENDRAPURI (1300) 483
NĀROTTAMA VIDYĀLAṂKĀRA BHAṬṬĀCĀRYA 528
Nath, Narendra Candra a:G265, b:G251
natural (*svabhāva*) intuition 146

Nāṭyaśāstra (of Bharata) 28
NAVACANDRA NYĀYARATNA (1905) 514
NAVKISHORE JHĀ (1931) 516
Nawathe, P. D. a:G300
NAYASUNDARA 528
Nazzeri, O. b:G1468
negation 262, 288-89, 291-92, 334, G124, G1554
  fourfold (*catuṣkoṭi*) 60
  negative compound G815
  negative particle G815
  paryudāsa 334
  prasajyapratiṣedha 60, 334
Neranāvatīsūtravyākhyā. *See* *Gajāsūtravāda* (of Veṅkatadāsa)
neuter G1499
New Catalogus Catalogorum 215
nididhyāsana 106
Nighaṇṭu (list of words) 4, 109
NĪLAKAṆṬHA DĪKṢITA (1675) 500
NĪLAKAṆṬHA DĪKṢITA (1750) 239, 317, 321, 351, 373, 506
NĪLAKAṆṬHA ŚUKLA (1637) 251, 497, 562
NĪLAKAṆṬHA VĀJAPEYIN (1605) 373, 493
NĪLAKAṆṬHA VYĀSA 393
NĪLAMBARA MIŚRA 528
nimitta. *See* condition; occasion
nipāta. *See* particle
Nipātavyayopasargavṛtti (of Kṣīrasvāmin) 477
  —*Ṭīkā* (of Tilaka) 534
nirukta. *See* etymology
Nirukta (of Yāska) 4, 10, 14, 108-12, 234, 258, 330-31, 549, 556, G393, G422, G605
nirvikalpaka (*pratyakṣa*) 27-28
niṣedha. *See* prohibition
Nītiśataka section of *Subhāṣitatrīsatī* 124
nitya. *See* eternal
NITYĀNANDA PANTA PARVATĪYA (1918) 24, 401, 515
niyojya (person enjoined to act) 25
nominal
  composition G1577, G1586
  formations G232, G1590
  meaning (*nāmārtha*) 272-76
  stem or suffix (*pratipādika*) 15, 115, 131, 258, 275-76, 284, 291, 325, 339, 343, G1513-14, G1578
  quotative G1641
  sentence. *See* sentence, nominal
  verb (*nāmadhātu*). *See* verb, nominal
nominalization G1566
nominative case 257, G1483
nonapprehension. *See* absence
noun (*nāman*) 110, 112, 114, 121, 149-50, 256-57, 339, G696, G1550
  abstract 292
  formation of G1490
novelty 83. *See also apūrva*
NṚSIṂHA (1650) 498
NṚSIṂHA 528
NṚSIṂHĀŚRAMA (1559) 237
NṚSIṂHA TARKAPAÑCĀNANA 528
number (*saṃkhyā*) 115, 127, 149, 172-73, 188, 213, 273, 275, 284, 335, G130
  singular/plural 163, 257, 261-62, 295-97, G1593
nuns G445
Nyāya 3, 5-6, 9-11, 21, 26-29, 45, 55, 60, 65-66, 85, 87-88, 90-93, 96-98, 237, 255, 258-59, 263, 265, 268, 272, 274, 282-92, 298-301, 303, 306, 324-40, 344-45, 368-69, 381, 397, 556, G1526
Nyāyabhūṣaṇa (of Bhāsarvajña) 262, 264-65, 296, 369
Nyāyamañjarī (of Jayanta Bhaṭṭa) 91, 97
Nyāyasaṃgraha (of Gaṅgādatta) 521
Nyāyasaṃgraha (of Hemahaṃsavijayagaṇi) 486
  —*Nyāyārthamañjuṣā* (autocommentary) 486
Nyāyasudhā (of Someśvara Bhaṭṭa)
  Commentary (of Annambhaṭṭa) 237
Nyayasūtras (of Gautama) 85, 97, 549, 556
(grammatical) object (of action) (*karman*) 164-65, 255, 257-62, 267, G1606
  —*kāraka* 337-38

occasion (*nimitta*) 147
Ojihara, Yutaka a:G148, G154, G158, G192, G226-27, G281, G518, G609, G615, G630, G638, G855, G859, G1582, t:G854
old age (*jarā*). *See* decay
onomatapoeia (*śabdānukṛti*) 111
ontology 127
operation. *See* function (*vyāpāra*)
operational rule (*vidhisūtra*) 15
Oppert, Gustav e:G881
opposition. *See* contradiction
option G378
ORAM BHAṬṬA 528

Orara, E. de Guzman a:G623
original relation of word to meaning (*autpattika*) 7, 90
orthodox (*āstika*) 37
Ousaparampil, J. a:G1707

pada. See word
Padacandrikā (of Śeṣa Kṛṣṇa) 488
—*Kṛṣṇakautūhula* (autocommentary) 488
Padamañjarī (of Haradatta)
Commentary (of Nārāyaṇa) 498
—*Makaranda* or —*Parimala* (of Raṅganātha Dīkṣita) 498
—*Kusumavikāśa* (of Śivabhaṭṭa) 509
Commentary (of Jagaddhara) 524
Commentary (of Rāmasiṃha) 531
Commentary (of Ratneśvara) 531
Padapāṭha (of Śākalya) 4, 13
padārtha. See category
Padārthadīpikā (of Konda Bhaṭṭa) 255, G1181
Padārthadīpikā (of Nāgeśa Bhaṭṭa) 323
Padasaṃjñāvicāra (of Āṣādhara Bhaṭṭa) 375, 507
padasphoṭa. See sphoṭa: pada
Padasūryapvakriyā (of Utsavakīrti) 534
Padavyavasthā (sūtra) kārikā (of Vimalakīrti) 488
—*Vivṛti* (of Udayakīrti) 499
Padavyavasthākośa (of Gosvāmi Śrī Śivānandabhaṭṭa) 522
Padhye, D. G. e:G861
PADMADHARA 528
PADMANĀBHADATTA (1375) 484-85
(RĀJA) PADMANĀRĀYAṆA 528
PADMASUNDARA 529
Paik, T. S. d:G316
painting 58
Palsule, Gajanan Balkrishna 182-91, 215-17, 231-36, 367-70, a:G21-22, G116, G149-50, G207, G232-33, G266, G301-02, G1589, G1590, G1099, G1644, d:G143, e:G1033
Pañcagranthī (of Buddhisāgara Sūri) 476
Pañcamatabhañjana (of Śrī Tātācārya) 239
PAÑCĀNANA KANDALĪ 529
Pañcapādikāvivaraṇa (of Prakāśātman) 287
Pañcasamāsīya (of Rāmacaritra Tripāṭhin) 530
Pancholi, Bala Krishna 417, G1189, e:G1104-5
Pandey, Chandra Kant a:G604, b:G173
Pandeya, Harisankara e:G91
Pandeya, Kalika Charan a:G1543
Pandeya, Kesava Deva a:G1035
Pandeya, Kshitish Chandra 552
Pandeya, Ram Chandra b:G1555
Pandeya, Umesh Chandra e:G159
Pandit, M. D. a:G165, G174-5, G208-9, G252, G283, G303, G317, G488A, d:G1623
Pandye, Ram Awadh d:G418
PĀṆINI (350 B. C.?) 4, 6, 9, 13-21, 36, 38, 45, 55, 66-68, 85-86, 97, 108-19, 165, 167, 194, 204, 261-64, 267-72, 276-77, 284, 293-97, 322, 331-45, 441-58, 549-50, 554, 556-57, G4, G503
Pāṇinipariśiṣṭavyākaraṇa (of Devendrakumāra Vidyāratna) 515
Pāṇinipradīpa (of Sundareśvara Yajvan) 373
Pāṇinisāra (of Navacandra Nyāyaratna) 514
Pāṇinisūtrārthasaṃgraha (of Devidasa) 520
Pāṇinīyadīpikā (of Nīlakaṇṭha Vājapeyin) 493
Pāṇinipradīpa (of Sundareśvara Yajvan) 373
Pāṇinīyamatadarpana (of Kavidarpana Rāghava) 485
Pāṇinīyasāra (of Jagadīśa) 524
Pāṇinīyaśikṣā 15, 455
—*Pañjikā* (of Dharaṇīdhara) 485
Commentary (of Dayānanda Sarasvatī) 511
—*Pradīpa* (of Rudra Prasāda Śarmā) 516
Pāṇinīyatattvadarpana (of Kālīcaraṇa Vidyopādhyāya and Sūrya Prasāda Miśra) 512
Pāṇinīyavādanakṣatramālā (of Umāmaheśvara) 371, 507
Pansikar, Vasudev Laxman Shastri e:G918, G1001, G1083
Parab, Kashinath Pandurang e:G943
paradox 60-61, G773
paragraph 61
Paramalaghumañjuṣā (of Nāgeśa Bhaṭṭa) 21, 23, 323-40, 342, 502-3, 556
—*Arthadīpikā* (of Sadāśiva Śāstrī Joshī) 24, 415, 503
Commentary (of Nityānanda Panta Parvatīya) 24, 401, 515
—*Jyotsna* (of Kālika Prasāda Śukla) 24, 324, 423, 517

—*Ratnaprabhā* (of Śabhāpati Śarman Upādhyāya) 24, 425, 517
—*Ratnadīpikā* (of Sivānanda Paṇḍeya) 503, 532
pāramārthika. *See* real
Paramatakhaṇḍana (of Cakrapaṇi) 247
(ṚṢIPUTRA) PARAMEŚVARA II (1410) 22, 213-14, 485-86
Paranjpe, Vasudeva Gopala b:G507
Paranjpe, Vinayak Wasudeo a:G144, G856
Parapakṣakhaṇḍana (of Nārāyaṇa Bhaṭṭatiri). *See Apāṇinīyapramāṇatā*
paraphrase G1651
parā vāk. *See* language
paribhāṣā. *See* metarule
Paribhāṣā (of Vyāḍi) 458
Paribhāṣābhāskaṛa (of Hari Bhāskara Agnihotra) 500-01
Commentary (of Śrīnivāsa) 533
Paribhāṣābhāskara (of Śeṣādrisudhi) 507
—*Paribhāṣābhāskara* (of Kuppu Śāstrin) 507
Commentary (of Harirāma) 511
Commentary (of Rājarāma Dīkṣita) 530
Paribhāṣāmaṇimālā (of Candradatta Jhā) 519
Paribhāṣāpradīpa (of Govinda Sena) 523
Paribhāṣāpradīpa (of Kolāhala) 526
Paribhāṣāpradīpārcis (of Udayaṅkara Nānapāṭhaka) 509
Paribhāṣāratna (of Appa Sūri) 504
Paribhāṣārthadīpikā (of Teknātha) 534
Paribhāṣārthaprakāśikā (of Dharmasūri) 501
Paribhāṣārthasaṃgraha (of Vaidyanātha Dīkṣita) 502
—*Vyākhyā* (of Appa Sūri) 504
—*Candrikā* (of Svayamprakāśānanda) 505
Paribhāṣāvṛtti (of Gopīnātha Tarkācārya) 488
Paribhāṣāvṛtti (of Puruṣottamadeva) 209, 480
Paribhāṣāvṛtti (of Nīlakaṇṭha Dīkṣita) 373, 506
Paribhasavṛtti (of Ramacandra Vidyabhusana) 501
Paribhāṣāvṛtti (of Siradeva) 480-81
—*Vyākhyā* (of Rāmacandra Dīkṣita) 501
Commentary (of Govinda Miśra) 522
—*Vijaya* (of Mānaśarman) 527, 535
Paribhāṣenduśekhara (author unknown) 503, 519
Visami (of Cidrūpāśrama) 490
Citprabhā (of Tāraka Brahmānanda Sarasvatī) 498
Paribhāṣenduśekhara (of Nāgeśa Bhaṭṭa) 323, 503, G972
—*Kāsikā* or —*Gadā* (of Vaidyanātha Paiyaguṇḍa) 357, 505
—*Bṛhadaśāstrārthakalā* (of Venimādhava) 506
—*Triśikhā* (of Lakṣmīnṛsiṃha) 507
—*Vyākhyā* or —*Śaṃkarī* (of Śaṃkara Bhaṭṭa) 508
—*Arthamañjarī* (of Bhīmācārya Galagali) 508
Commentary (of Kṛṣṇamitrācārya) 381, 509
—*Induprakāśa* (of Gaṅgādhara) 509
—*Bhairavī* or —*Vivṛti* (of Bhairava Miśra) 510
—*Ṭippanīsārasāraviveka* (of Bālaśastrin Rānade) 511
—*Candrikā* (of Viśvanātha Doṇḍibhaṭṭa) 511
Commentary (of Lālā Vidārin) 511
—*Akhaṇḍatāṇḍava* (of Harinātha Dvivedin) 511
—*Bhūti* (of Rāmakṛṣṇa Tātyaśāstrin) 513
—*Haimavatī* (of Yāgeśvara) 513
—*Vākyārthacandrikā* (of Hari Śarman) 513
—*Citprabhā* (of Brahmānanda Sarasvatī) 514-15
—*Tattvaprakāśikā* (of Lakṣmaṇa Tripāṭhi) 515
—*Ṭīkā* (of Gadādhara) 521
—*Vṛtti* (of Gaṇesa) 521
—*Arthamañjarī* (of Hayagrīvācārya) 522
Commentary (of Kṛṣṇa Bhaṭṭa) 526
—*Laghuṭīkā* (of Raghunātha Śāstrī Vaiyākaraṇā) 530
—*Sarvamaṅgalā* (of Śeṣa Śarman) 532
Commentary (of Vālābhidatta) 534
Commentary (of Viśvanātha Bhaṭṭa) G1255
—*Vijaya* (of Jayadeva Miśra) G1259, G1264
—*Tattvadarśa* (of Vāsudeva Śāstrī Abhyaṅkar) 516

Paribhāṣopanyāsa (of Vaidyanātha Dīkṣita) 502
(*Vedantakalpataru*) *Parimala* (of Appayya Dīkṣita I) 297, 304
parimāṇa. *See* measure
pariṇāma. *See* transformation
parokṣatva. *See* imperceptibility
PĀRTHIVA G506
particle (*nipāta*) 110, 112, 118, 121, 147, 289-92, 337, 333-35, G319, G1425, G1435, G1570 G1585, G1621, G1637 G1663
particular or individual (*vyakti*) 6, 10, 26, 82, 118-19, 145, 161, 185, 194, 231-36, 273, 334, 556
  qualified by a universal (*jātiviśiṣṭavyakti*) 6, 27, 92
  śabda-vyakti 126
  unique (*svalakṣaṇa*) 27
parts and wholes 131, 215, 235, 552
  parts of a sentence 191
Paryayaśabdaratna (of Dhanañjaya Bhaṭṭacārya) 520
paryudāsa. *See* negation
PAŚUPATI 529
paśyantī vāc 43, 47, 49-52, 61-63, 95, 99, 121, 124, 197, 328, 554-55, 558
  parā vāc 5, 121, 124, 558
Patanjal, Deo Prakas Shastri b:G486, e:G193
PATAÑJALI (150 B.C.) 5-6, 12-13, 16-22, 36, 38, 45-47, 55, 66, 69, 71, 110, 114-21, 124, 174-75, 182, 204, 261, 272, 275, 277-80, 283, 289, 297, 321-22, 329, 338-42, 459-64, 549, 551, 554, 556, G81, G220, G446-47, G502-3, G513
PATAÑJALI (author of *Yogasūtras*) 551, 553
Patañjalicarita (of Rāmabhadra Dīkṣita) 321
Patavardhan, Ramakrishna Shastri e:G680, G1181
path of being (*adhvan*) 44, 171
Pathak, K. B. a:G411, G414, G451-52, G553, G568, G672, G675, G682, G786-87, G874-77, G883-84, G887-88
Pathak, Ram Adhar d:G1532
Pathak, Shridhar Shastri b:G82, G564
"pathetic" fallacy. *See* fallacy, "pathetic"
Patil, Gajanan Moreshwar a:G155, G284, G1537
PAUṢKARASĀDI 16, 440
Pavolini, P. E. a:G692
Pawte, I. S. b:G83
Pāyaguṇḍe Balakṛṣṇa 387
Payyur family 213
PEDDINTI BRAHMADEVA. *See* BRAHMADEVA
Peijer, J. S. b:G1376
Pendse, Narahari Shastri e:G1006
perception (*pratyakṣa*) 59, 126, 175, 188, 196, 213, 232-33, 236
  erroneous 56-57
  valid 54
Peri, N. 203
periphrastic future G1482
permanence of linguistic units 125-26
permanence of word (*ājānika*) 118
permanence of word-meaning relation (*pravāhanityatā*). *See* eternal, as preserved by speakers
persmission (*abhyanujñā*) 43, 47
person (*puruṣa*) 172
personal ending. *See* ending, personal
PERUSŪRI (1755) 507
Peterson, Peter G532, G539, a:G439, G538
Phadke, Ananta Sastri e:G1038, G1187
Phakkikadarpana (of Dharānanda) 510
Phakkika Saralārtha (of Rāmacaritra Tripāṭhin) 530
phala. *See* result
  phalāśraya. *See* Substratum of the result
phase (*avasthā*) 127
(Indian) philosophy (*darśana*) 3-4, 18, 31, 35-37
Phirinda, King. *See* Pirinda
Phitsūtras (of Santānava Ācārya) 14, 465, G242
  —*Pradīpa* (of Sudarśanadeva) 533
phoneme or letter (*varṇa*) 4-5, 10-11, 57-61, 69-81, 94-95, 99, 108, 118-19, 124-25, 147, 182-91, 213-14, 216-17, 232-36, 242, 302, 304-8, 329, 347-48, 367-68, 561, G1676
phonetics (*śikṣā*) 107, 275, G337, G345, G359, G1401, G1422, G1487, G1591, G1599, G1622, G1652, G1678
Pillai, K. Raghavan 128, a:G1671, et: G739
Pillai, N. Gopala a:G694
Pillai, S. Vaiyapuri a:G585
Pinatelli, Mario a:G1688
Pirinda, King 225
Pisani, Vittore a:G11, G75, b:G1399, G1449

PĪTĀMBARA VIDYĀBHŪṢAṆA 529
place (*deśa*) 83
Plato, Platonic 55
poetry 30-32, 35, 65-67
polysemy 7-8
position (*sthāna*), a means of proof 83
Post, Kenneth H. a:G1660
Postal G489A
postposition (*karmapravacanīya*) 147
Potter, Karl H. 128-73, 182-91, 551
power (*śakti*) 128, 162-64, 195, 233, 286-88, 324-26, 369
  of complete freedom (*svātantryaśakti*) 42, 196
  sentence-power (*vākyaśakti*) 344
PRABHACANDRA (ĀCĀRYA) (1040) 476
PRABHĀKARA (700) 25-26, 87, 92, 554
Prabhākara Mīmāṃsā 6, 25-26, 87-93, 97-98, 265-67, 273-74, 300-01, 336, 346
Prabhāvalī (of Rāmabhadra Dīkṣita) 501
Prabodhacandrika (of Jagannatha Panpita) 23, 500
Prabodhacandrikā (of Vaijaladeva) 534
practice (*abhyāsa*) 54, 132, 146
pradhāna. *See* principal element
Pradīpa (of Kāśīnātha Devaśarman) 525
PRADYUMNA SŪRI (1170) 479-80
Praiṣadīpaprabhā (of Nārāyaṇa) 498
Prajāpati 551-52
prajñā. *See* intellect
PRAJÑĀNASVARŪPA. *See* NARENDRAPURI
prakāra 98
prakaraṇa. *See* context; subject-matter
Prakash, Buddha a:G224, G253
Prakrit language 19-20, G71, G543, G1431
prakriyā. *See* derivation
Prakriyādīpikā (of Appan Nainārya) 487
(*Aṣṭādhyāyī*) *Prakriyākaumudī* (of Rāmacandra) 19-20, 485
  —*Prasāda* (of Viṭṭhala) 486
  —*Gūḍhabhāvavivṛti* or =*Prakāśa* (of Śeṣa Kṛṣṇa) 448
  —*Sudhā* (of Mādhava Sarasvatī) 489
  Commentary (of Kamalākara Bhaṭṭa) 497
  —*Tattvacandra* (of Jayanta) 498
  —*Prakāśa* (of Śrīkṛṣṇa Bhaṭṭa Maunin) 506
  —*Vyākhyā* (of Nīlakaṇṭha Dīkṣita) 506
  —*Raśmī* (of Muralīdhara Miśra) 517
  —*Prakriyāsāra* (of Kāśīnātha) 525
  —*Vimarśa* (of Ādya Prasāda Miśra) G1052
  —*Siddhāntakaumudī* G1051
Prakriyāpradīpa (of Cakrapaṇi) 493
Prakriyāratnamaṇi (of Dhaneśvara) 211, 481
Prakriyāsaṃgraha (of Abhayacandra) 484
Prakriyāsāra (of Nārāyaṇa) 528
Prakriyāsarvasva (of Nārāyaṇa Bhaṭṭatiri) 497, 556
prakṛti. 128-30, 146 *See also* basis; cause, material
pramā. *See* knowledge
pramāṇa. *See* instrument of knowledge
Pramāṇasamuccaya and =*Vṛtti* (of Dignāga) 27, 123, 549
prāṇa. *See* breath
Prasada, Rama t:G553
prasajyapratiṣedha. *See* negation
Prasiddhaśabdasaṃskāra (of Appayya Dīkṣita III) 500
prasthānatrayī G724, G1565
pratibandha. *See* prevention
pratibhā. *See* intuition
prātipadika. *See* nominal stem
Prātiśākhyas 17, 39, 107, G86, G449, G461-64
pratiṣedha. *See* prohibition
pratyāhāra sūtras of *Aṣṭādhyāyī* 14, 204
Pratyāhārasūtravicāra (of Timmanācārya) 506
pratyakṣa. *See* perception
pratyaya. *See* suffix
Pratyayamaukikamālā (of Dāmodara Śarman) 519
Pratyayodbhedapaddhatī (of Kṣemaṅkara) 499
(*Siddhāntakaumudī*) *Prauḍhamanorāma* (of Bhaṭṭoji Dīkṣita) 20, 247, 367, 492
  —(*Paramata*) *Khaṇḍana* (of Cakrapani) 247, 493
  —*Kucamardana* (of Jagannātha Paṇḍitarāja Tailaṅga) 499
  —(*Bṛhat*)*Śabdaratna* (of Hari Dīkṣita) 21, 23, 323, 500
    —*Bhāvaprakāśikā* (of Vaidyanātha Paiyaguṇḍa) 357, 505
    Commentary (of Bhavadeva Miśra) 389, 508
    —*Bhairavī* (of Bhairava Miśra) 389, 510
    —*Dīpa* (of Kalyāṇamala) 524

—(*Laghu*) *Śabdaratna* (of Hari Dīkṣita) 319, 500
—*Prabhā* (of Sātāra Rāghavendrācārya) 511
—*Citraprabhā* (of Hari Śarman) 513, 523
—*Bhāvaprakāśa* (of Vaidyanātha Paiyaguṇḍa) 357, 505
—*Kalpalatā* (of Kṛṣṇamitrācārya) 381, 509
—(*Śabdaratna*)*Bhairavī* (of Bhairava Miśra) 510
—*Prabhā* (of Mādhava Śāstrin Bhandārī) 515
—*Sāralā* (of Gopāla Śāstrī Nene) 515
pravāhanityatā. *See* eternal, as preserved by speakers
PRAVARTAKOPĀDHYĀYA 529
pravartana. *See* instigation
Praveśaka (of Acyuta Pisharoti) 494
pravṛtti. *See* activity
pravṛttinimitta. *See* application
prayoga. *See* use
Prayogamukha (of Dharmakīrti). *See Kārakacakra*
Prayoga (*uttama*) *ratnamālā* (of Puruṣottama Vidyāvāgīśa Bhaṭṭācārya) 490
Commentary (by Candraśekhara) 497
—*Kantimālā* (of Gopāladeva Vidyāvāgīśa) 508
Commentary (of Siddhanātha Vidyāvāgīśa) 532
Prayogaśikṣā (of Anantasūri) 518
PRAYOGAVEṄKAṬĀDRI 529
prayojaka. *See* prompter
prayojana. *See* motivating force
Prayuktākhyātamañjarī (of Kavisaraṅga) 525
precative G1497
predicate G356
prefix or preposition (*upasarga*) 110, 112, 121, 146, G400, G1522, G1637
prescription or injunction (*vidhi*) 24, 26, 265, 336
Vedic 96
present time 45, 336
presumption (*arthāpatti*) 54, 213, 235, 273
prevention (*pratibandha*) 43, 47
preverb 4, 11, 289-90, 333
primary derivative (*kṛdanta*) 173, 292
primary meaning or denotative power (*abhidhā*) 27, 65, 91-92, 273-74, 301, 322, G732
principal element (*pradhāna*) 162
probability (*sāmarthya*). *See* capacity
product (*vikāra*) 167
production (*utpatti*) 302, 304
prohibition (*niṣedha*, *pratiṣedha*) 15, 24, 150
PROLANĀCĀRYA. *See* HARIYOGIN ŚAILĀVĀCĀRYA
prolation, ritualistic G300
prompter (*prayojaka*) 268-69
prompting (*pravartana*). *See* instigation
pronoun (*sarvanāman*) 112
prose passages of the Vedas. *See Brāhmaṇas*
PṚTHVĪCANDRA 529
PṚTHVĪŚVARA 529
P. S. ANANTANĀRĀYANA ŚĀSTRI (1940) 24, 409, 516
PUJYAPĀDA or DEVANANDIN (500) 17, 466
PUṆḌARĪKA VIDYĀSĀGARA BHAṬṬĀCĀRYA (1520) 487
PUNJARĀJA (485) 486-87
PUṆYARĀJA (1000) 22, 193, 201, 476, 557, 561
PUṆYASUNDARAGAṆI 529
Purandhara, N. H. a:G1400
Puratam Tirumal Devanarayana of Ambalappuzha 373
PŪRṆACANDRA (950) 475
PŪRṆACANDRA 529-30
purpose (*artha*) 26, 82, 108, G1628
puruṣa. *See* person
PURUṢOTTAMADEVA (1175) 19, 203, 209, 480
PURUṢOTTAMA VIDYĀVĀGĪŚA BHAṬṬĀCĀRYA (1560) 490
Pūrvapakṣapraśnottarī or =*mañjuṣā* or =*mañjarī* (of Āṣādhara Bhaṭṭa) 375, 507
Pūṣān 105

qualificandness, fallacy of unknown. *See* fallacy of unknown qualificandness
quality (*guṇa*) 127, 161-62, 171, 195, 213, 552 555, G1633
quotation G1566

RABHASANANDIN (950) 475
RĀDHAKṚṢṆA GOSVĀMIN 529
RĀDHAKṚṢṆA ŚARMAN (1764) 507
Radicchi, Anna a:G837
RĀGHAVA JHĀ 529
Raghavan, V. a:G899, G905, G930, G1645

Raghavan, V. K. S. N. 340-42
RĀGHAVĀNANDA ĀCĀRYA 529
Raghava Somayaji 237
RĀGHAVA SŪRI 529
RĀGHAVENDRĀCĀRYA 530
RAGHUNANDA ŚIROMAṆI 529-30
RAGHUNĀTHA (1620) 495
Raghunātha Bhaṭṭa 361
RAGHUNĀTHA ŚARMĀ (1963) 24, 427, 517, e:G711
RAGHUNĀTHA ŚĀSTRĪ VYĀKARAṆĀCĀRYA 530, G1260
RAGHURĀMA (1871) 512
Raja, C. Kunhan 201, G145, a:G689
Raja, K. Kunjunni 103, 109, 203-4, 321-22, 324-40, 342-49, 549, 554-56 G191, G355, a:G696, G715, G1058, G1209-10, G1225, G1530, G1540, G1551, G1658, b:G1556, e:G1223, G1226
Rajagopalan, N. V. a:G334
Rajakalasa, father of Jyesthakalasa 205
RĀJA KUMĀRA DHARMAŚĀSTRIN. *See* (RĀJAKUMĀRA) DHARMAŚĀSTRIN
Rajapurohit, B. P. a:G1603
RĀJARĀMA DĪKṢITA 530
rajas. *See* activity
RĀJĪVA ŚARMAN 530
rakṣasa. *See* demon
Ram, Kanshi d:G419
Ram, Sadhu a:G702, G796
RĀMABHADRA DĪKṢITA (1692) 23, 311, 321-22, 373, 501
RĀMABHAṬṬA (1650) 498
RĀMACANDRA (1400) 19-20, 485
RĀMACANDRA (1700) 501-2
RĀMACANDRA (1744) 505
RĀMACANDRA 530
RĀMACANDRA PAṆḌITA (1690) 501
RĀMACANDRA SARASVATĪ. *See* SATYĀNANDA
RĀMACANDRĀŚRAMA (1600) 493
RĀMACANDRA VIDYĀBHŪṢAṆA (1688) 501
RĀMACARAṆA 530
RĀMACARITRA TRIPĀṬHIN 530
Ramachari, C. a:G234, G705
RĀMADĀSA CAKRAVARTIN (1600) 493
RĀMADEVA MIŚRA 530
RĀMADEVA ŚARMAN 530
RĀMAJÑA PĀṆḌEYA 24, 431, 530
RĀMAKĀNTA (1489) 487
RĀMA KIṄKARA SARASVATĪ 530
RĀMAKIŚORA ŚARMAN (1905) 513
RĀMAKṚṢṆA ADHVARIN (1650) 351
RĀMAKṚṢṆA BHAṬṬA (1690) 501
RĀMAKṚṢṆA DĪKṢITA (1638) 497
RĀMAKṚṢṆA ŚARMĀ TRIPĀṬHĪ (1907) 514
RĀMAKṚṢṆA TĀTYĀŚĀSTRIN (1897) 513
Rāmakṛṣṇa Yajvan 253
RĀMAKUMĀRA NYĀYABHUṢAṆA 530
Ramamurti, K. S. a:G1635
RĀMĀNANDA TĪRTHA 530
RĀMANĀRĀYAṆA ŚARMAN 530
RĀMANĀTHA CAKRAVARTIN 530
RĀMANĀTHA ŚARMAN RĀYI (1546) 488
RĀMANĀTHA VIDYĀVĀCASPATI (1650) 498
RĀMA PAṆḌITAVARA (SĀHIBHA) (1900) 513
RĀMAPANIVADA 530
RĀMAPRASĀDA (1694) 501
RĀMA PRASĀDA TRIPĀṬHI (1952) 24, 419, 516, e:G1190
RĀMARṢI 531
RĀMA ŚARANA ŚĀSTRĪ (1931) 516
RĀMASEVAKA (1770) 23, 377, 381, 507
RĀMASIṂHA 531
RĀMĀŚRAMA. *See* BHĀNUJĪ DĪKṢITA
RĀMATARAṆA ŚIROMAṆI (1883) 512
RĀMA TARKAVĀGĪŚA (1550) 489
Rāmavarman of Śṛṅgaverapura 323
Rāmāyaṇa G533
RĀMEŚVARA. *See* ŚEṢA VĪREŚVARA
RĀMEŚVARA TARKAVĀCASPATI BHAṬṬĀCĀRYA 531
Ranade, H. G. a:G1646
RANCCHODJI ODHAVJI (1905) 514
Rangacharya, Kandur e:G1036
Rangacharya, M. e:G901, G903
RANGANĀTHA DĪKṢITA (1650) 498
Raṅgarājadhvarīndra 239
Rangaswami, O. P. a:G791
Raṅgoji Bhaṭṭa 241, 255
Rao, H. V. Nagaraja a:G1687, e:G1349
Rao, K. V. Lakshmana a:G445
Rao, P. S. a:G801
Rao, S. K. Ramachandra a:G482

Rao, Veluri Subba b:G1605
Rapratyāhārakhaṇḍana (of Vaidyanātha Payaguṇḍa) 357
Rapratyāhāramaṇḍana (of Keśari Miśra) 525
rasa. *See* essence
Rasagaṅgādhara (of Jagannātha Paṇḍitarāja) 32
Rasamañjarīvyākhyā (of Śeṣa Cintāmaṇi) 215
RATIDEVA SIDDHĀNTAVĀGĪŚA 531
(*Tarka*) *Ratnamālā* (of Tārānātha Tarkavācaspati) 512
Ratnamālā
 —*Chandraka Bhāṣya* (of Pañcānana Kandali) 529
 —*Kārakamālāṭīkā* (of Rāmeśvara Tarkavācaspati Bhaṭṭācārya) 531
RATNAMATI 479
RATNAPĀṆI 531
Ratnāvalī (of Gauramohana Bhaṭṭa) 522
RATNEŚVARA 531
Rau, Wilhelm a:G707, G716, G760-61, G819, G1695, b:G740, e:G759, G900
Rāvana G366
real (*pāramārthika*) 194-95
reality (*sattā*) 110, 195
recognition (*pratyabhijñā*) 302, 306
reduction of two verbs to one (*ekaśeṣa*) 173
reference (*vastvartha, bāhyārtha*) 115-16, 559-60
reflection (*ābhāsa*) 57
reflexive passive 259
reification G1566
relation (*sambandha, saṃsarga*) 125, 127, 149, 195, 278, 328
 syntactic. *See* syntactic relation
relational seam (*saṃsargamaryādā*) 300
relationship G1677
remembered scripture (*smṛti*) 54, 132
Renou, Louis G975, a:G127, G138, G417, G486A, G578, G594, G831, G967, G972-73, G982, G1439, G1492-93, G1514-16, G1525, G1544, b:G1403, G1432, G1443, G1460, et:G966, t:G113, G854
renunciation G705
replacement technique in Pāṇini G223
representation, simultaneous 283-84
result (*phala*) 11, 83
revealed scripture (*śruti*) 54, 87, 98, 255-59, 262, 330
revelation (*abhivyakti*) 302
Ṛg Veda 3-4, 14, 31-32, 35, 37, 50, 103-6, 108, 234, 341, 550, 553, G222, G486, G481A
rhetoric, rhetoricians 3, G1388
rhythm G1406
ritualistic interpretation of Vedas (*adhiyajña*) 108, G1439, G1714
Rocher, Ludo a:G160, G1271
Rocher, Rosane a:G183-84, G236, G254, G1553, G1564, b:G235
Rogers, David Ellis d:G255
Roodbergen, J. A. F. a:G1679, d:G631, et:G627, G632-34
(verbal) root (*dhātu*) 4, 7, 10-15, 19, 98, 113-14, 118, 146, 255-64, 268, 330-33, 335, 337, G254, G294, G353, G387, G1458
Roy, Kumudranjan et:G1167
ṛṣi. *See* sage
ṚṢIPUTRA PARAMEŚVARA II. *See* (ṚṢIPUTRA) PARAMEŚVARA II
ṛta. *See* cosmic order
rudhi. *See* conventional powers of words
Rudra 105
RUDRADHĀRA JHĀ ŚARMAN (1954) 24, 421, 516
RUDRA PRASĀDA ŚARMĀ (1948) 516, e:G428
Rudras 104
Ruegg, David Seyfort a:G1531, G1689, b:G1537
rule
 negative (*niṣedha*). *See* prohibition
 Paninian 559
RŪPACANDRA (1853) 512
Rūpamālā (of Nṛsiṃha) 528
Rūpamālā (of Vimala Sarasvatī) 483
Rūpaprakāśa (of Kulluka Bhaṭṭa) 527
RŪPARĀMA NYĀYAPAÑCĀNANA 531
Rūparatnamālā (of Nayasundara) 528
Rūpataraṅginī (of Īśvaramiśra) 523-24
Rūpavatāra (of Dharmakīrti) 203, 476
 —*Prakriyākalpavāllarī* (of Nṛsiṃha) 498
Ruskin John 31, 550
Ruyyaka 92, 203

Śabarabhāṣya (on *Mīmāṃsāsūtras*) 73, G584, G588
ŚABARASVĀMIN 531
śabda. *See* language; linguistic element; sound; (verbal) testimony

Śabdabhāskara (of Tarkatilaka Bhaṭṭācārya) 494
Śabdabhedanirūpaṇa (of Nārāyaṇa Sudhi) 507
Śabdabhedanirupaṇa (of Ramabhadra Dikṣita) 321-22, 501
śabdabodha. See verbal cognition
Śabdabodha (of Jñāneśvara) 524
Śabdabodhaprakāśa (of Jayakṛṣṇa Maunin). *See Sāramañjarī*
Śabdabodhataraṅginī (of Īśvarānanda) 23, 299, 488
śabdabrahman 12, 36-43, 45-50, 54, 56, 95, 99, 132, 216, 341, 369-70, G724, G1543, G1565, G1587, G1688
Śabdadhātusamīkṣā (of Bhartṛhari) 124, 470
śabdādvaita. See linguistic monism
Śabdāhāraṇa (of Śeṣa Kṛṣṇa) 215, 488
śabdajñāna. See verbal knowledge
Śabdakaumudī
Commentary (of Nalla Perumal Dīkṣita) 311
Śabdakaumudī (of Cokkanātha Dīkṣita) 311, 321, 498
—*Śābdikarakṣā* (of Dvādaśahayājin) 311, 501
—*Vyākhyā* (of Vaidyanātha Dīkṣita) 502
Śabdakaustubha (of Bhaṭṭoji Dīkṣita) 21, 240-42, 492, 560
—*Visampadī* (of Nāgeśa Bhaṭṭa) 323, 503
—*Prabhā* (of Vaidyanātha Paiyaguṇḍa) 357, 505
—*Bhāvapradīpa* (of Kṛṣṇamitrācārya) 381, 509
—*Prabhā* (of Sātāra Rāghavendrācārya) 393, 510
Śabdakaustubha (of Īśvarīprasāda) 524
Śabdakaustubhaguṇa (of Indradatta Upādhyāya) 508
Śabdakaustubhamaṇḍana (of Jagannātha Paṇḍitarāja Tailaṅga) 499
Śabdalakṣaṇa (of Buddhisāgara Sūri). *See Pañcagranthī*
Śabdālaṃkāra (of Śeṣa Kṛṣṇa) 215, 488
Śabdamañjarī (of Nārāyaṇa Sudhi) 507
Śabdānantasāgarasamuccaya (of Nāgeśa Bhaṭṭa) 503
śabdānaucitya G1527
Śabdanirūpaṇa (of Rāmabhadra Dīkṣita) 23
śabdānukṛti. See onomatapoeia
Śabdānuśāsana (of Śakaṭāyana) 17, 19, 474-75, G908
—*Amoghavṛtti* (of Śakaṭāyana). *See Amoghavṛtti*
—*Cintāmaṇi* (of Yakṣavarman) 476
—*Prakāśikā* (of Ajitasena Ācārya) 517-18
—*Pratipadā* (of Maṅgarasa) 527
—*Ṭippanī* (of Samantabhadra) 531
—*Rūpasiddhi* (of Dayāpāla) 476
Śabdānuśāsanabṛhadvṛtti (of Hemacandra) 19, 479
—*Laghuvṛtti* (of Hemacandra) 479, G946
—*Avacūrikā* (of Dhanacandra) 488
—*Nyāsa* (of Udayacandra) 480
—*Laghuvyākhyā* (of Devendrasūri) 481
—*Nyāsasāra* (of Kanakaprabhā) 481
—*Vṛtti* (of Malayagiri) 483
—*Duṇḍhika* (of Dhanacandra) 488
—*Durgāprabodha* (of Śrīvallabhavacana Ācārya) 494
—*Haimakaumudī* or *Candraprabhāvyākaraṇa* (of Meghavijaya Gaṇi) 502, G952
—*Vivaraṇa* (of Harṣakīrti Sūri) 523
Śabdaprabhā (Chapter one of Helārāja's commentary on *Trikāṇḍī*) 193
Śabdaprakāśa (of Khana Nṛpati) 526
śabdapūrvayoga. See language as means of release
Śabdaratna (of Janārdana Śarman) 524
Śabdaratnākara (of Kāśīśvara Bhaṭṭācārya) 489
Śabdaratnākara (of Kāmadeva Ghoṣa) 524
Śabdaratnaprabhā (of Sātāra Rāghavendrācārya) 393
Śabdaratnāvalī (of Appa Sūri) 504
Śabdaratnāvalī (of Kānta Nātha) 524
Śabdaratnāvalī (of Rāmanātha Cakravartin) 530
Śabdārtharatna (of Tārānātha) 533
Śabdārthasāramañjarī (of Jayakṛṣṇa Maunin) 23, 361, 505
Śabdārthatarkāmṛta (of Jayakṛṣṇa Maunin) 23, 361, 505
Śabdarūpāvalī 536
Śabdasādhyaprabodhinī (of Rāmanātha Cakravartin) 530
Śabdaśaktiprakāśikā (of Jagadīśa) 549
Śabdasiddhāntamañjarī (of Kodaṇḍarāma) 526
Śabdasiddhi (of Mahādeva) 482

Śabdaśobhā (of Nīlakantha Śukla) 251, 497
Śabdasudhā (of Ananta Bhaṭṭa) 518
Śabdasudhānidhi (of Gaṅgāramitra Pāṭhin) 521
śabdatatta. *See* language-principle
Śabdatattvaprakāśa (of Indradatta Upādhyāya) 23, 379, 508
Śabdatriveṇikā (of Āṣādhara Bhaṭṭa) 23, 375, 507
Śabdāvatāra (of Durvinīta) 177, 471
Śabdavṛtti G1573
Śabdavyākhyā (of Gopīnātha) 550
(*Bṛhat*) *Śabdenduśekhara* (of Bhaṭṭoji Dīkṣita) 343, 502
—*Bhāvaprakāśikā* (of Vaidyanātha Paiyaguṇḍa) 505
(*Laghu*) *Śabdenduśekhara* (of Nāgeśa Bhaṭṭa) 323, 367, 502, G1081
—*Cidasthimālā* (of Vaidyanātha Paiyaguṇḍa) 505
—*Sadāśivabhāṭṭī* (of Sadāśiva Bhaṭṭa) 508
—*Ṭīkā* (of Śaṃkara Bhaṭṭa) 508
—*Jyotsna* (of Udayankar Nānapāṭhaka) 509
—*Induprakāśa* (of Gaṅgādhara) 509
—*Doṣoddhara* (of Mannu Deva) 509
—*Candrakalā* (of Bhairava Miśra) 510
—*Candrikā* (of Sātāra Rāghavendrācārya) 510
—*Prasāda* (of Subrahmanyam Nambuttiripad) 512
—*Vyākhyā* (of Śrīdhara Śarman) 513
—*Bhāvabodhinī* (of Setumādhavācārya Nadatiram) 513
Commentary (of Anantācārya) 513
—*Nāgeśoktiprakāśa* (of Khuddi Jhā Śarman) 514
—*Guruprasāda* (of Tāta Subrahmanya Śāstrin) 515
Commentary (of Gopāla) 522
—*Candrikā* (of Rāghavendrācārya) 529
—*Varavarṇinī* 535
—*Vijaya* 535
—*Viṣamapadavivṛti* 535
—*Abhinavacandrikā* 536
SABHĀPATI ŚARMAN UPĀDHYĀYA (1963) 24, 425, 517, 531
Śabharañjanaśataka (of Kavikuñjana) 371
SACCIDĀNANDA 532
sacrifice 183, 267, 336-37
SADĀNANDA 531
SADĀŚIVA (1670) 22-23, 317, 500, 562
SADĀŚIVA BHAṬṬA (1780) 508
Sadāśiva Dīkṣita 311
SADĀŚIVA ŚĀSTRI JOSHI or ŚARMĀ (1946) 24, 415, 516, e:G1038, G1119, G1166, G1188, G1347
Sadāśivendra Brahmendra 351
Sadbhāṣāsubantarāpadarśa (of Nāgoba Paṇḍita) 508
Ṣaḍdarśinīsiddhāntasaṃgraha (of Rāmabhadra Dīkṣita) 23, 321-22, 501
sādhanā. *See* means
SĀDHUSUNDARA GAṆI (1624) 495
sādhutva. *See* grammaticality; nominal stem
Sādhutvādinirvācana 535
sādhya 25
sādṛśya. *See* similarity; simultaneity
SĀGARAMATTI. *See* ŚĀRIPUTTA
sage (*ṛṣi*) 36, 38, 52, 54, 63, 103
SAHĀJAKĪRTI (1623) 495
Sahāji, King of Tanjore 321
sahakārikaraṇa. *See* cause, auxiliary
sāhitya. *See* grouping; literacy criticism
Sāhityadarpana (of Harisiddhāntavāgīśa) 91
Sahityasastri, Janakinatha e:G1292
sāhṛdaya 31
Śaiva G1690
Kashmir Śaivism. *See* Kashmir Śaivism; Trika
ŚĀKALYA 4, 440
ŚAKAṬĀYANA (850) 14-16, 19, 110, 112, 114, 440, G876, 474-75
śakti. *See* denotation; power; significative power
Śaktisphuṭa (of Kāladhara) 524
ŚALIKANĀTHA MIŚRA (925) 87
Salus, Peter H. b:G489A
samādhi 328
sāmagrī. *See* grouping
samākhya. *See* etymology, etymological meaning
sāmanādhikaraṇya G717
SAMANTABHADRA (650) 531
Samanvayapradīpa (of Kudakācārya) 526
sāmāṇya. *See* universal
sāmarthya. *See* capacity
samāsa. *See* compound
Samāsārṇava (of Kulamuni) 508
Samāsaśaṃkhā 536
samavāya. *See* inherence
Samavāyapradīpasaṃketa (of Devaśarman) 520

sambandha. *See* relation
Sambandhoddeśa (of Gaṅgadāsa) 519
Sambasiva Sastir, K. 232
sambodhana. *See* vocative
Saṃgraha (of Vyāḍi) 117, 119-20, 458
SAṂGRAMASIṂHA (1279) 483
saṃjñā. *See* use
saṃjñāsūtra 15
ŚAṂKARA (ĀCĀRYA) (710) 41-43, 56, 59-60, 531, 551, 553-54, G1569, G1660, G1688, G1702
ŚAṂKARA BHAṬṬA (1770) 241, 508
ŚAṂKARA ŚARMAN 531
ŚAṂKARA ŚĀSTRI MARULKĀR (1957), 517, e:G574, G1192
saṃketa. *See* convention
Sāṃkhya 21, 44-45, 54, 381, 397, 559
saṃkhyā. *See* number
Saṃkhyāsūtra (of Kapila) 552
—*Laghuvṛtti* (of Nāgeśa Bhaṭṭa) 323
Saṃkṣiptasāra (of Kramadīśvara) 19, 477
Commentary (of Jumaranandin) 484, G912
Commentary (of Dāmodara Devaśarman) 519
—*Vivaraṇa* (of Goyīcandra) 485
—*Kaumudī* (of Abhirāma Vidyālaṃkāra) 487
Commentary (of Nārāyaṇa Nyāyapañcānana) 489
—*Arthabodhinī* (of Candraśekhara Vidyālaṃkāra) 519
—*Vyākaranadurghatodghāta* (of Keśavadeva Tarkapañcānana Bhaṭṭācārya) 525
—*Dīpikā* or —*Prakāśa* (of Nārāyaṇa Nyāyapañcānana) 489, 502
—*Arthadīpikā* (of Gopāla Cakravartin) 500
—*Dhātupāṭha-Sāra* (of Nṛsiṃha Tarkapañcānana) 528
—*Uṇādisūtra*—commentary (of Śivadāsa Cakravartin) 532
—*Rasavatī* G912
Saṃkṣiptasārakārikā (of Nārottama Vidyālaṃkāra Bhaṭṭācārya) 528
saṃnidhi. *See* contiguity
sampradānakāraka. *See* indirect object (of dative)
saṃsargamaryādā. *See* association of word meanings
saṃskāra. *See* trace
samudaya. *See* collection of words
samūha. *See* collection of parts; grouping
saṃvid. *See* consciousness
saṃvyavahārika. *See* expressional
saṃyoga. *See* conjunction
SANĀTANA TARKĀCĀRYA 532
sandhi. *See* coalescence, rules of
Sanghvi, Ratnalal e:G955
Sañjaya 146
Sankaran, A. e:G587
Sankaran, C. R. a:G1420
Sanskrit 237, 287, 321
SANTĀNAVA ĀCĀRYA (350) 15, 465
ŚĀNTARAKṢITA (750) G775
Saptasvarasindhu (of Nārasiṃha Sūri) 528
ŚĀRADARAÑJAN RAY VIDYĀVINODA (1920) 515, et:G1091
Sāralāharī (of Kavicandra) 493
Sāramañjarī (of Jayakṛṣṇa Maunin) 505
ŚARAṆADEVA (1172) 480
Śaraṇaśabdārthavicāra (of Anantācārya) 514
Sarangi, Aneka Chandra a:G335, G636, G1708
Sārasiddhāntakaumudī (of Varadarāja) 494
Sārasvataprakriyā (of Anubhūti Svarupācārya) 20, 481-82
—*Saṃdhiprakaraṇa* (of Maṇḍana) 484
Commentary (of Puñjarāja) 486-87
—*Subodhika* (of Amṛtabhāva) 487
—*Bhāṣya* (of Kāśīnātha Bhaṭṭa) 487
—*Pradīpa* (of Dhaneśvara Bhaṭṭa) 487
—*Sārasvataprasāda* (of Vāsudeva Bhaṭṭa) 490
—*Viṣamapadārthadīpikā* or *Gopālabhaṭṭī* (of Gopāla Bhaṭṭa) 490
—(*Vaiyākaraṇa*) *Siddhāntacandrikā* (of Rāmacandrāśrama) 493
Commentary (by Kṣemendra) 488
—*Tattvadīpikā* (of Lokeśakara) 501
Commentary (of Sadāśiva Śāstri Jośi) 516
—*Avyayārthamālā* (of Navkishore Jhā) 516
—*Subodhinī* (of Sadānanda) 531
—*Vṛtti* (of Tarkatilaka Bhaṭṭācārya) 494
—*Subodhikā* (of Candrakīrti) 494
—*Laghubhāṣya* (of Raghunātha) 495
—*Vārttika* (of Sahājakīrti) 495
—*Siddhāntacandrikā* (of Jñānatilaka) 498
—*Śabdārthacandrikā* (of Haṃsavijayagaṇi) 499
—*Nirṇaya* or —*Anuvṛttyavabodhaka* (of Nārāyaṇa Sudhā) 500

—*Mādhavī* (of Mādhava) 513
—*Siddhāntaratnāvalī* (of Mādhava Bhaṭṭa) 513
—*Ṭippanī* (of Govinda Paraśurāma Bhaṭṭa) 513
—*Ṭippanī* (of Viṣṇuprasāda Śarman) 514
—*Pañjikā* (of Dharmadeva) 521
—*Sārapradīpikā* (of Jagannātha) 524
—*Vādighatamudgara* (of Jayanta Bhaṭṭa) 524
—*Bhāṣya* (of Rāmanārāyaṇa Śarman) 530
—*Subodhinī* (of Sadānanda) 531
Sārasvatasārasaṃgraha (of Nārāyaṇa Bhāratī) 528
Sārasvata school 19
Sārasvatavyākaraṇa (of Nayasundara) 528
Sārasvatavyākaraṇadhuṇḍhika or —*Dīpikā* (of Megharatna) 485
Sarasvatī 105
Sarasvatīkaṇṭhābharaṇa (of Bhoja) 477
—*Hṛdayahariṇī* (of Nārāyaṇa Daṇḍanātha) 478
—*Ṭīkā* (of Jagaddhāra) 484
Commentary (of Jīvānanda Vidyāsāgara) G917
Commentary (of Rāmasiṃha) G918
Commentary (of Ratneśvara) G917, G918
Sarasvatī Makhin 313
Sarasvati river 104
Sārāvalī (of Nārāyaṇa) 315, 499
—*Vṛtti* 315, 499
ŚĀRIPUTTA (1150) 479
Sarma, see Sharma
Sarvadarśanasaṃgraha (of Mādhava) 56, 68, 552, 554, G1391
SARVADHĀRA UPĀDHYĀYA 532
sarvanāma. *See* pronoun
SARVĀNANDA PĀṆḌEYA G1243. e:G1243
SARVARAKṢITA 480
SARVAVARMAN (50) 17, 464-65
SARVEŚVARA (1555) 489
ṢAṢṬHIDĀSA 532
śāstra. *See* scientific treatise
Sastri. See Shastri
Śatapatha Brāhmaṇa 108, G452
SĀTĀRA RĀGHAVENDRĀCĀRYA GAJENDRAGADKAR (1840) 23, 393, 510-11, 562
Ṣaṭkārakalakṣaṇa (of Amaracandra) 481
Ṣaṭkārakavāda (of Rabhasānandin) 475
Ṣaṭpadī
Commentary (of Kṛpārāma) 526
sattā. *See* existence; reality
sattva 120, 275 (*See* also serenity)
satya. *See* truth
SATYAKĀMA VARMĀ (1970) 24, 429, 517
SATYĀNANDA or RĀMACANDRA SARASVATĪ (1500) 22, 219, 229, 487
SATYAPRĪYA TĪRTHA SVĀMIN (1745) 23, 359, 505
SATYAVARYĀRYA 532
SAUBHAVA (350) 465
ŚAUNAKA 4, 108
Sautrāntika 549
ŚAYANA. *See* MĀDHAVA
Scharfe, Hartmut a:G391, G483, G1672, b:G286, G610, G1681
Scharpe, Adrian b:G1456
Scheller, M. a:G1461
Schlerath, Bernfried b:G1701
Schroeder, Leopold Von a:G433
Schropfer, A. b:G1500
Schropfer, Johann a:G1433
science G616
scientific treatise (*śāstra*) 132
scripture (*āgama*) 235
secondary derivative (*taddhita*) 111, 173, 292, G1495
secondary meaning (*lakṣaṇa*) 6, 8-12, 26-28, 65-67, 89-92, 111-12, 115, 217, 272-73, 282-86, 322, 324, 326-27, 334, 343, 346, 554, 556, G191, G243, G732, G1612
based on common quality (*gauṇī*). *See gauṇī*
pure 326
secondary nature 195
secondary roots G1648
seed (*bīja*) 555
self, soul (*ātman*) 42, 130, 550
Great Self (*mahātmā*) 46-47
semantics 5, G1669
generative G318
semantic relations G247
Sen, Malati a:G852
Sen, Sukumar a:G166, G592. b:G267, G1533
SENAKA 440
Sengupta, Devendranatha e:G1031
Sengupta, Sailendranath a:G171, G210, G889, G958
Sengupta, Upendranatha e:G1031

sense-organ (*indriya*) 56, 189, 214, 286
sentence (*vākya*) 4, 10, 26-29, 61, 65, 83, 85-99, 108, 114, 124-25, 149-50, 216, 233, 304, 348, G204, G246, G355, G768, G1574
definition of G715
—formation 163
—meaning (*vākyārtha*) 9-10, 28, 146, 148, 191, 343, 346-47
nominal G1686
parts of 233
—*sphoṭa* 62, 95. *See also sphoṭa*
separation G1650
sequence (*krama*) 50, 94, 161, 169, 171, 184-86, 191, 196-97, 216, 232, 235-36, 303, 558
suppression of 49, 81
serenity (*sattva*) 44-45
ŚEṢA CINTĀMAṆI 22, 215, 221
ŚEṢĀDRISUDHI (1750) 507
ŚEṢA GOPINĀTHA 247
ŚEṢA KṚṢṆA (1540) 22, 78, 215-17, 221, 223, 237, 241, 247, 488
ŚEṢA NĀRĀYAṆA. *See* (ŚEṢA) NĀRĀYAṆA (BHAṬṬA)
Śeṣa Nṛsiṃha 215
Śeṣa Puruṣottama 247
Śeṣa Rāmacandra 215
(KĀŚĪ) ŚEṢA ŚARMAN 532
Śeṣa Vīreśvara 215, 223, 225, 237
ŚEṢA VIṢṆU (1605) 22, 243, 494
Seshakumar, A. d:G1682
SETUMĀDHAVĀCĀRYA NADITIRAM (1895) 513
Shah, Neelanjana S. a:G931
Shah, Umakant Premananda 375, a:G1287, e:G1175, G1227
Sarma, Arvind a:G382
Sharma, Aryendra e:G861
Sarma, Batuka Natha e:G1285
Sharma, B. N. Krishnamurti 393, 562, a:G4
Sarma, Dadhi Ram e:G1360
Sharma, Dipti a:G403
Sarma, E. R. Sreekrishna a:G602, G708, G712, G1539, G1557, G1702, et:G1202, t:G1501
Sharma, Indra Datta e:G1289
Sharma, Jagdish P. a:G963
Sharma, Krishna Kumar a:G336
Sarma, Kanakalala e:G239
Sharma, K. Madhava Krishna a:G99-101, G415, G467, G485A, G511, G580, G583, G695, G783, G792-93, G897, G929, G1214, G1437, G1440, G1450
Sarma, K. V. a:G1207
Sharma, Mukund Madhava a:G1562
Sharma, Mahesh Dutt a:G404, G863, G1108
Sharma, Mangal Deva a:G586
Sharma, Peri Sarvesvara 561, a:G748, G907, t:G738, 551
Sarma, Ram Nath a:G307, G348, b:G1638, d:G282
Sarman, Rudradatta Jha e:G598
Sharma, Uma Shankara a:G1272, e:G164
Sarman, V. Anjaneya a:G724, G1565
Sarma, Virendra d:G752
Sharma, V. Venkatarama e:G841
Sastri, A. Mahadeva e:G1036
Sastri, Bahuvallabha e:G550, G1248
Sastri, Bala e:G31, G522
Sastri, Bala Krishna e:G1116
Shastri, Bhim Sen b:G878
Shastri, Biswanarayana a:G1070
Sastri, Bommakanti Ramalinga a:G176
Shastri, Charudeva a:G685, e:G611, G687, G692
Sastrin, C. Samkara Rama e:G1095
Sastri, Damodara e:G35, G922, G1037
Shastri, Dharmendra Nath a:G484A
Shastri, Dwarikadas e:G1039
Sastri, Gangadhara e:G35, G49, G1114
Sastri, Gaurinath 41, 57, 542, 552, 554, a:G699, G701, G730, G1532, b:G706
Sastri, Gosvami Damodara e:G680
Sastri, Guru Prasada e:G575
Shastri, Haraprasad 201, G892
Sastri, Jivarama e:G1156
Sastri, K. A. Nilakantha a:G902
Sastri, K. A. Sivaramakrishna a:G357
Shastri, Kali Charan a:G935-36, G983, b:G1624
Shastri, Kapil Deva a:G717-18, G1246, eb:G1247
Sastri, Karnataka Kṛṣṇa e:G1084
Sastri, K. Sambasiva e:G488, G497, G688
Shastri, Lallurama Jivarama e:G650
Shastri, Mangala Deva a:G464, et:G86
Sastri, Patavardhana Narayana e:G1082
Sastry, P. C. Naganatha b:G1110
Sastri, P. P. Subrahmanya 237, 561, a:G1409, b:G589, e:G587
Sastri, P. S. a:G1516

Sastri, Sada Siva Sarma (Joshi) e:G1118, G1174, G1244
Sastri, Samkara Rama e:G88
Sastri, Santi Bhiksu ta:G714
Shastri, Satya Vrat a:G799, G1661, b:G399
Sastri, Sitarama e:G1123, G1156, G1228
Shastri, Sitaramacari e:G683
Sastri, S. K. Ramanatha e:G870
Sastri, S. S. Suryanarayana 80-82, 552, 555, a:G924, G1414, G1446
Sastri, Sulavatanka Kalyana Sunvamba-samkara e:G1003
Sastri, Tarakesvara e:G1189
Sastri, T. Ganapati 235, e:G505, G965, G976, G1065, G1281
Sastri, Tata Subbaraya e:G1216
Sastry, T. S. Gourypathy a:G1641
Sastry, T. V. Kapali a:G1454
Sastrio, V. A. Ramaswami a:G698, G789-90, G1412, e:G1205
Sastrigal, S. Chandrasekhara e:G1087
Shaw, J. L. a:G356
Shefts, Betty b:G162
Shembavnakar, K. M. a:G107
Shende, Sita Rama Sastri e:G1360
Shukla. *See* Sukla
SIDDHANĀTHA VIDYĀVĀGĪŚA 532
siddhānta. *See* view
Siddhāntakaumudī (of Bhattoji Dīkṣita) 17, 20, 240, 319, 367, 490-92
—*Prauḍhamanorāma* (autocommentary) *See* (*Siddhāntakaumudī*)-*Prauḍhamanorāma*
—*Sukhabodhinī* (of Nīlakaṇṭha Vājapeyin) 493
—*Vilāsa* (of Lakṣmīnṛsiṃha) 499
—*Ratnākaraṭīkā* (of Śivarāmendra Sarasvatī) 499
—*Sunamanoramā* (of Tirumala Yajvan) 499
—*Siddhāntaratnākara* (of Rāmakṛṣṇa Bhaṭṭa) 501
—(*Bṛhat*)*Śabdenduśekhara* (of Nāgeśa Bhaṭṭa) 323, 502
—*Bhāvaprakāśikā* (of Vaidyanātha Paiyaguṇḍa) 357
—*Cidasthimālā* (of Vaidyanātha Paiyaguṇḍa) 357, 505
—*Dūṣaṇoddhara* (of Manyudeva) 387, 509
—*Candrakalā* (of Bhairava Miśra) 387, 509
—*Candrikā* (of Sātāra Rāghavavendrācārya) 393, 510
Notes (of Khuddi Jhā) 399, 514
—*Dīpikā* (of Nityānanda Pānta Parvatīya) 401, 515
—(*Laghu*)*Śabdenduśekhara* (of Nāgeśa Bhaṭṭa). *See* (*Laghu*)*Śabdenduśekhara*
—*Lalita* (of Gopālakṛṣṇa Śastrin) 504, 507
—*Tattvabodhinī* (of Jñānendra Sarasvatī) 351, 505
Subodhinī (of Jayakṛṣṇa Maunin) 351 361, 505
—*Vidyāvilāsa* (of Śivarāma Tripāṭhin) 506
—*Kalpalāṭīkā* (of Venimādhava) 506
—*Bālamanoramā* (of Vāsudeva Dīkṣita) 365, 506
—*Gūḍhaphakkikaprakāśa* (of Indradatta Upādhyāya) 508
—*Ratnārṇava* (of Kṛṣṇamitrācārya) 381, 509
—*Arthaprakāśikā* (of Kocca Sankaran Susad) 510
—*Ratnaprakāśikā* (of Bhairava Miśra) G1088
—*Saralā* (of Tārānātha Tarkavācaspati) 397, 512
—*Bālacandrī* (of Bālacandra Śāstri) 514
—*Paṅkticandrikā* (of Gaṅgaprasāda Śāstrin) 514
—*Saradarśanī* (of Śivadatta Śarman) 514
—*Mitābhāṣinī* (of Śaradarañjan Ray Vidyāvinod) 515
—*Paṅktipradīpa* (of Nānakarāma Śāstri) 515
—*Bhāvabodhinī* (of Karaputugala Dharma Śrī) 515
—*Kathakollolinī* (of Rāma Śaraṇa Śāstrī) 516
—*Viśeṣavivṛti* (of Somanātha Śarman) 516
—*Sugandha* (of Acyutananda Śāstrin) 517
Commentary (of Shrīdharenda Sharmā Ghildiyāl) 517
—*Bhāṣya* (of Bhagavatbhakta) 518
—*Vilāsa* (of Bhāskara) 518
—*Sudhākara* (of Kṛṣṇa Śāstrin) 526
—*Lakṣmī* (of Sabhāpati Śarmā Upādhyāya) 531
—*Sārasaṃgraha* (of Vedāntācārya) 534

(*Vyākaraṇa*)*Siddhāntasudhānidhi* (of Viśveśvara Sūri) 535
Siddhāntatattva (of Jagannātha) 524
Sieg, E. e: significative power (*śakti*) 6-7, 26, 42, 45, 65-68, 90-91, 330-31, 346
svātantryaśakti. See power of complete freedom
śikṣā. *See* phonetics
Śikṣāprakāśa G427
śilpaśāstra. *See* architecture
Silverstein, Michael e:G1618
Simenscly, Th. b:G146
Simhasuragani 123
similarity (*sādṛśya*) 288. *See also* analogy; comparison; simultaneity
Siṃhasūrigaṇi 123
Simonsson, Nils a:G9
simultaneity (*sādṛśya*) 184-85, 289
Singh, Jag Deva a:G287, G304-5, G337-38, G1591, G1636
Sinha, Anil C. a:G318
SĪRADEVA (1250) 481
Sircar, Dinesh Chandra a:G576
ŚIROMAṆI BHAṬṬA. *See* BHAṬṬA ŚIROMAṆI
ŚIROMAṆI BHAṬṬA 532
śiṣṭa. *See* elite
Śiśubodha (of Kāśīnātha) 525
Śiśubodha (of Padmanārāyaṇa) 528-29
Śiṣyahitanyāsa (of Ugrabhūti) 476
ŚĪTIKAṆṬHA (1450) 486
SĪTĀNĀTHA ŚĀSTRIN 532
Śiva G554
Śiva Bhaṭṭa, father of Nāgeśa 323
ŚIVABHAṬṬA (1810) 509
ŚIVADĀSA 532
ŚIVADĀSA CAKRAVARTIN 532
ŚIVADATTA PĀṆḌEYA 533
ŚIVADATTA ŚARMAN (1914) 514, e:G943
ŚIVĀNANDAYOGASVĀMIN. *See* BHAṬṬA ŚIROMAṆI
ŚIVA NĀRĀYAṆA ŚIROMAṆI 532
ŚIVA PAṆḌITA 532
ŚIVARĀMA CAKRAVARTIN (1600) 493
Sivaraman, Krishna 550, a:G1690
ŚIVARĀMA ŚARMAN (VĀCASPATI) 532
ŚIVARĀMA TRIPĀṬHIN (1750) 506
ŚIVARĀMENDRA SARASVATĪ (1660) 22, 227, 245, 499, 561
ŚIVARĀMENDRA YATI (1780) 508
Śivasūtras (of the *Aṣṭādhyāyī*) 14, 203-4, G74, G145, G203, G244, G453
Skold, Hannes a:G449, b:G448
sleep, deep 37, 106
(*Mīmāṃsā*)*Ślokavārttika* (of Kumārila Bhaṭṭa) 181, 189-90, 213, 549, 554-56
smallness (*tadalpatā*) 288
smṛti. *See* memory; remembered scripture
Smrtiratna, Taranatha Gosvami e:G1069
ŚOKANĀTHA DĪKṢITA. *See* COKKANĀTHA DĪKṢITA
soma 105
SOMADEVA (1250) 17, 481
Somananda 124
SOMANĀTHA 533
SOMANĀTHA ŚARMAN (1952) 516, e:G1096, G1102
SOMAPRABHĀ 533
SOMAYĀJIN DĪKṢITA. *See* SARVEŚVARA
Someśvara Bhaṭṭa 237
sound (*dhvani*) 28, 30, 37, 55, 69, 91, 119-20, 132, 153, 187-88, 231, 303, 308, 329, 342, G728, G1637
physical theory of G1397
prākṛta 94-95, 120, 174-75, 236, 329, G1588
vaikṛta 94-95, 120, 174-75, 236, 329
sound (*śabda*) 183, 308, 558
Sowani, V. S. a:G1393
space, spatial direction (*dik* or *diś*) 43, 45, 127, 149, 162-63, 184, 195, 559 a:G703
spanda. *See* activity
specification (*viśeṣavidhi*) 150
speech (*vāc* or *vāk*) 49, 93-94, 103, 341, 555
= *bhāṣā* 113
daivī 37
madhyamā. *See madhyamā vāk*
parā 63, 121, 328, 553-55
—*principle* (*śabdatattva*). See language principle
—*vaikharī*. *See vaikharī vāk*
sphoṭa, theory of 5, 10-11, 14, 18-21, 29, 42-43, 49, 51, 56-62, 68-82, 110, 232-36, 242, 298-99, 303-08, 324-29, 342-43, 347, 367-70, 552-55, G1391, G1394, G1412, G1428, G1454, G1464, G1510, G1512, G1518, G1543, G1549, G1562, G1569, G1655, G1688, G1700A, G1702, 552-55
akhaṇḍasphoṭa 242, 298, 305, 348-49
jātisphoṭa 306-8
padasphoṭa 6, 242, 298-99, 303, 305, 328

vākyasphoṭa 6, 93-95, 242, 298-300, 305, 328, 369-70
varṇasphoṭa 242, 298, 308, 557
vyaktisphoṭa 306-7
Sphoṭacandrikā (of Śrīkṛṣṇa Bhaṭṭa Maunin) 23, 36, 215, 367-70, 506
Sphoṭanirūpaṇa (of Āpadeva) 499
Sphoṭanirūpaṇa (of Śeṣa Kṛṣṇa) 22, 78, 215-17, 488
Sphoṭaparīkṣā (of Bhairava Miśra) 23, 389, G1182
Sphoṭapratiṣṭha (of Keśava) 526
Sphoṭasiddhi (of Bhārata Miśra) 22, 231-36, 489
Sphoṭasiddhi (of Maṇḍana Miśra) 5, 18, 22, 56, 70-80, 82, 181-91, 213, 232-36, 473-74, 553-56, 561
—*Gopālika* (of [Ṛṣiputra] Parameśvara II) 22, 213-14, 486
Sphoṭasiddhi (author unknown) 535
Sphoṭasiddhinyāyavicāra 22, 231, 235-36, 489
Sphoṭatattva (of Kṛṣṇa Dvivedin) 526
Sphoṭatattvanirūpaṇa (of Śeṣa Kṛṣṇa) 22, 78, 215-17, 488
Sphoṭavāda (of Nāgeśa Bhaṭṭa) 242, 342-49, 504, 549
—*Subodhinī* or —*Upodghāta* (of V. Kṛṣṇamācārya) 24, 413, 516
Sphoṭavimarśinī (of Mādhava Śāstrin Bhandāri) 515
SPHOṬĀYANA 13, 68, 349, 440
śravaṇa. *See* hearing
ŚRĪDEVA PAṆḌITA 533
ŚRĪDHARĀNANDA ŚARMĀ GHILDIYAL (1962) 517, e:G1103
ŚRĪDHARA ŚARMAN (1889) 513
ŚRĪKĀNTA MIŚRA 533
ŚRĪKṚṢṆA BHAṬṬA MAUNIN (1750) 23, 361, 367-70, 506
ŚRĪKṚṢṆA ŚARMAN 533
Sri Lanka 18
ŚRĪNĀTHA ŚIROMAṆI 533
ŚRĪNIVĀSA 533
Srinivasacaryulu, Bommakanti a:G1575
ŚRĪPATIDATTA (1450) 486
ŚRĪPRABHĀ SŪRI 533
ŚRĪRĀMĀCĀRYA. *See* GOPĀLADEVA VIDYĀVĀGĪŚA
Sriramamurti, P. a:G771, G1648
ŚRĪ TĀTĀCĀRYA (1580) 239
ŚRĪVALLABHAVACAKA or =ĀCĀRYA (1718) 504
ŚRIVALLABHAVACANA ĀCĀRYA (1607) 494
Śṛṅgāraprakāśa (of Bhoja) 560
Śṛṅgāraśataka section of *Subhāṣitatriśatī* 124
SṚṢṬIDHARĀCĀRYA 533
ŚRUTASĀGARA 533
śruti. *See* revealed scripture
Staal, J. Frederick (Frits) 550, 556, a:G167, G195-96, G211, G247, G1545, G1554, G1566, G1576-77, G1604, G1649, G1662, G1696, G1714, b:G1583, G1625
state (*bhāva*) 129
statement, direct (*śruti*), a means of proof 83
stem 4, 118, 146, 348. *See also* nominal stem
Stenzler, A. F. b:G1485
sthāna. *See* position, a means of proof
sthayībhāva. *See* mood
Sthemadarpana (of Gopālācārya) 522
Sthiroratna, Loharam G1018
sthiti. *See* duration
Strauss, Otto a:G563, G1398
structure, deep/surface G306
Subantaprakāśa (of Kṛṣṇa Śāstrin) 526
SUBHAŚILA GAṆI (1425) 486
Subhāṣitatriśatī (of Bhartṛhari) 124
subject-matter (*prakaraṇa*) 82-83, 108
subjunctive G1432
sublation (*bādha*) 188, 214
Subrahmanyam, K. G. a:G61, G412, G450, G508, G557, G559-560, G684
Subrahmanyam, P. S. a:G306
SUBRAHMANYAM NAMBUTTIRIPAD (1860) 512
substance (*dravya*) 6, 119, 161, 164, 170, 194-95, G1509, 558-59, G1633
substantive G1571
substratum of the result (*phalāśraya*) 267
of agency 269
subtle body (*sūkṣmaśarīra*) 132
SUDARŚANĀCĀRYA 533
SUDARŚANADEVA 533
Śuddhicandrikā (of Jayakṛṣṇa Maunin) 361
Śuddhi(tattva)kārikā (of Nārāyaṇa) 315, 499
SUDHĀNANDASŪRIŚIṢYA (1671) 500
suffix (*pratyaya*) 4, 10, 12, 15, 98, 118, 146, 257-58, 262, 266, 292-95, 335, 343, 348, G198, G292, G335
inflectional 276
nominal. *See* nominal stem

personal 331
primary 4, 261, 297-98
secondary 4, G347, G349, G396
suggestion (*vyañjanā*) 11, 27-30, 65, 92, 287, 324, 327, 341, G1508, G1521, G1658
suggestive meaning (*dyotaka*) 112, 146-47, 289, 322, 333
suitability (*aucitya*) 83, 149
Sukhbeatar, O. a:G1692
Sukhthankar, Vishnu S. e:G486
Shukla, J. M. a:G798, G891, G960, G1647, G1663, G1683
Shukla, Karunesha a:G809
Sukla, Rama Govind e:G324, G1348
Sukla, Sri Rajanarayana e:G1280
sūkṣmaśarīra. *See* subtle body
Sūktiratnākara (of [Śeṣa] Nārāyaṇa [Bhaṭṭa]) 215
Sumanoramā (of Gaṅgeśa Miśra Upādhyāya) 521
Sundaraprakāśaśabdārṇava. *See Uṇādisādhana*
SUNDAREŚVARA YAJVAN 373
śūnyatā G1689
Supadma (of Padmanābhadatta) 484-85
—*Makaraṇḍa* (of Viṣṇumiśra) G1043, G1044
—*Vivaraṇapañcikā* G1045
—*Ṭippanī* (of Trilokyanātha Bhaṭṭācārya) G1046
superimposition (*adhyāsa*) 42, 65, 126, 216-17, 306, 324
supplementary description (*arthavāda*) 24
supporting object (*ālambana*) 189
Suptiṅantasāgarasamuccaya (of Nāgeśa Bhaṭṭa) 504
Suri, Chandra Sagara e:G953
Suri, Vijayalvani e:G954
Suryanarayana, S. e:G691
SŪRYANĀRĀYAṆA ŚUKLA (1937) 24, 405, 516
SŪRYA PRASĀDA MIŚRA (1887) 512
SUSENA KAVIRĀJA MIŚRA 533
svabhāva. *See* natural
svara. *See* accent
Svaramañjarī. *See Saptasvarasindhu* (of Nārasiṃha Sūri)
Svaraprakriyā and autocommentary (of Rāmacandra Paṇḍita) 501
svarga. *See* heaven
svarūpa. *See* essence
svarūpasat. *See* inseparable existence
svātantrya. *See* independence
svātantryaśakti. *See* power of complete freedom
SVAYAṂPRAKĀŚĀNANDA (1740) 505
ŚVETANIVASIN 533
Śvetāśvatara Upaniṣad 550
Swaminathan, V. 560, a:G605, G779, G802, G1047, e:G780, G898
Syadisamuccaya (of Amaracandra) 481
ŚYĀMACARAṆA KAVIRATNA (1910) 514
syllable (*akṣara*) 104, 128
syntactic analysis. *See* syntactic unity
syntactic connection (*parasparā vyāpekṣā*) 114, 330
a means of proof (*vākya*) 83
syntactic function (*kāraka*) 16, 87, 164, 195, G215
syntactic identity. *See* identity
syntactic relation 8-9, G247, G257
syntactic unity (*ekavākyatā*) 26, 29, 86, G1572
syntax 4, 114-15, G1539

tādātmya. *See* identity
taddhita. *See* secondary meaning, derivative
Taddhitacandrikā (of Harirāma) 511
Taddhitakośa (of Bhaṭṭa Śiromaṇi) 518
Taddhitakośa (of Bhavadeva) 498
Taddhitakośa (of Bhaṭṭa Śiromaṇi) 518
Taddhitaungadipika (of Saccidananda) 531
Taddhitopadeśa (of Vaṅgadāsa) 534
Tagare, G. V. a:G1358
Taittirīya Āraṇyaka G858
Taittirīya Brāhmaṇa 105
Taksan G234
TALADEVASUDHI 533
tamas. *See* inertia
Tamil (Nadu) 321, G1409, G1706
Tantravārttika (of Kumārila) 213, 549
Commentary (of Annambhaṭṭa) 237
Tantric works 324
Tantrism 342
TĀRAKA BRAHMĀNANDA SARASVATĪ (1650) 309, 498
TĀRANĀTHA 533
TĀRANĀTHA TARKAVĀCASPATI (1867) 397, 512, e:G30, G1178
TĀRAPADA NYĀYARATNA 533-34
Taraporewala, I. J. S. a:G1462
tarka 132
Tarkabhāṣāyuktimuktāvalī (of Nāgeśa Bhaṭṭa) 323

Tarkacandrikā (of Śrīkṛṣṇa Bhaṭṭa Maunin) 23, 367, 506
Tarkacudamani, Madhavacandra e:G933
TARKĀLAṂKĀRA BHAṬṬACĀRYA 534
Tarkalamkara, Madana Mohana e:G1178 G1014
Tarkapancanana, Navakumara e:G641
Tarkapradīpa (of Koṇḍa Bhaṭṭa) 255
Tarkaratna (of Koṇḍa Bhaṭṭa) 255
Tarkaratnamālā (of Tārānātha Tarkavācaspati) 397
Tarkasaṃgraha and —*Dīpikā* (of Annambhaṭṭa) 237
TARKATILAKA BHAṬṬĀCĀRYA (1614) 494
Tarkavagisa, Durgadasa Vidyavagisa Srirama e:G1024
Tarkikas 369
Tarpatam apau gha sūtracvicāra (of Rāmabhadra Dīkṣita) 501
TĀTĀCĀRYA, N. S. RĀMĀNUJA (1972) 517, e:G1266
TĀTA SUBRAHMANYA ŚĀSTRIN (1926) 515
tātparya. *See* intention of the speaker
Tattvabindu (of Vācaspati Miśra) 80
Tattvabindu (of Jñānendra)
—*Gūḍhārthadīpikā* (of Nīlakaṇṭha Dīkṣita) 373, 506
Tattvadīpikāprabhākaracandra (of Nāgeśa Bhaṭṭa) 323, 504
Tattvamīmāṃsā (of Kṛṣṇamitrācārya) 381
Tattvasaṃgraha (of Śāntarakṣita) G775
Tattvaviveka (of Nṛsiṃhāśrama)
Commentary (of Annambhaṭṭa) 237
technical terms (*ādhunika*) 118
TEKNĀTHA 534
Telang, Kashinath Trimbak a:G531
Telugu 237, 241
tense 149, 263-64, 331, 336, G302, G1528
termination 4
(verbal) testimony (*śabda*) 54-56, 126, 175, 324
THAKKURADĀSA NYĀYAPAÑCĀNANA 534
Thakur, Kanakalal e:G1162
Thibaut, Georg 553
Thieme, Paul 14, 109, 549, 555-56, a:G84, G409, G458, G462, G465, G479-80, G490, G617, G1269, G1410, G1413, G1592, G1626, b:G457
thinking (*manana*) 106
Thirujnanasambandham, P. a:G1619
Thumb, Albert b:G1404
Tibet 18
Tibetan G368, G397, G1007, G1051, G1692
TILAKA 534
time (*kāla*) 12, 40-49, 83, 93-94, 119, 127, 129, 149, 162, 164-65, 170-72, 196-97, 257-58, 261, 263-64, 335, 550, G624, G694, G704, G772, G777, G798-99, G1455, G1544, G1713
limiting function of time (*kālaśakti*) 45, 129, 164
(VARKHEDI) TIMMANĀCĀRYA (1750) 506
Tiṅam Śaktiḥ (of Śrīkṛṣṇa Śarman) 533
(*Candra*)*Tiṅanta* (of Lakṣmīkāra) 527
Tiṅantaparyayasaṃgraha (of Vīrapāṇḍya) 535
Tiṅantaśeṣasaṃgraha 240
Tiṅvicāra (of Śrīkṛṣṇa Śarman) 533
Tirumala Ācārya 237
TIRUMALA BUKKAPATTUNAM ŚRĪNIVĀSĀCARYA (1720) 504
TIRUMALA YAJVAN (1660) 313, 499, 562
Tiwari, Kapil Muni a:G288, d:G237
Tolkappiyam G305, G585
trace (*saṃskāra*) 184, 186-88, 213, 216, 233, 235, G1679, 553-54
tradition (*āgama*) 132
Traividyādeva, Bhavasena G650
transformation (*pariṇāma*) 129
transitive 259
Trapp, Valentin t:G569
Trikāndaśabaśāsana (of Gaṅgādhara Kavirāja) 23, 395, 512
Trikāṇḍī (of Bhartṛhari). *See Vākyapadīya*
Trika system. *See* Kashmir Śaivism
TRILOCANA (1600) 493
TRILOCANA 534
TRILOCANADĀSA (1000) 475-76
TRILOKANĀTHA 534
Tripādoddyotinī (of Mādhava Bhaṭṭa) 486
Tripathi, Bhaviratprasada b:G197, e:G40
Tripathi, Gayacarana e:G1323
Tripathi, Kailas Patil a:G337
Tripathi, Ram Suresh a:G606
Tripathi, Shambhu Nath e:G890
Trisūtravyākaraṇa (of Gaṅgādhara Kavirāja) 23, 395, 512
Trivedi, Kamalasankara Pranasankara e:G1050, G1185

TRIVIKRAMA (1118) 478
truth (*satya*) 5, 54, 106
=*dharma* 51
Tvaṣṭṛ 105
Tyadyantasyaprakriyā (of Sarvadhara Upādhyāya) 532
Tyadyantasyaprakriyāpadārohana (of Nandakīrti) 527

U. K. VEṄKATANARASIṂHA (1916) 515
UDAYACANDRA (1180) 480
UDAYADHARMA (1451) 486
UDAYAKĪRTI (1654) 499
UDAYAṄKARA NĀNAPĀTHAKA (1800) 509-10
UDAYASAUBHAGYA. *See* DHANACANDRA
Uddālaka 106-7
uddeśya. *See* accomplisher
Udipi 240
UGRABHŪTI (1000) 476
UJJVALADATTA (1350) 484
UMĀMAHEŚVARA (1750) 371, 507
Umarji, Varadaraja a:G5-7
Uṇādigantu (of Veṅkateśvara) 504
Uṇādikośa (of Mahādeva Vedāntin) 501
Uṇādikośa (of Śivarāma Tripāṭhin) 506
Uṇādimamamālā (of Śubhaśīla Gaṇi) 486
Uṇādimaṇidīpikā (of Rāmabhadra Dīkṣita) 501
Uṇādipariśiṣṭa (of Kramadīśvara) 477
Uṇādirūpāvalī (of Mahāliṅga Śāstrin) 527
Uṇādisādhana (of Padmasundara) 529
Uṇādisūtras 4, 13-14, 16, 108, 110, 113-14, 434-35, G242
  Commentary (of Puruṣottamadeva) 209
  —*Uṇādimaṇidīpikā* (of Rāmabhadra Dīkṣita) 321
  Commentary (of Gopālakṛṣṇa Śāstrin) 353, 504
  Commentary (of Kṣapanaka) 472
  —*Vṛtti* (of Ujjvaladatta) 484
  —*Uṇādikapadārṇava* (of Perusūri) 507
  —*Bhāṣya* (of Dayānanda Sarasvatī) 511
  Commentary (of Sarvadhāra Upādhyāya) 532
  Commentary (of Satyavaryārya) 532
  —*Vṛtti* (of Śvetanivāsin) 533
Uṇādisūtras (of Haridatta) 523
Uṇādisūtras (of Vrajarāja) 535
Uṇādisūtras (Jain)
  —*Vṛtti* or *Daśapadī* (of Māṇikyadeva) 527
understanding. *See* knowledge
unestablished locus. *See* fallacy of unestablished locus
union (*yoga*) 138
unity of purpose (*arthaikatva*) 86
unity, syntactic. *See* syntactic unity
universal (*jāti*, *sāmānya*) 6, 10, 26, 28, 82, 92, 118-19, 125-27, 131, 145, 148, 161, 169, 183, 185, 191, 194, 231-32, 234, 236, 273-74, 339, 552-53, 556, 558, G226, G602, G606, G723, G1582
  great universal (*mahāsāmānya*) 194
  =*śabdākṛti* 125
  sphoṭa-universal (*jātisphoṭa*) 349
  universal word (*jātiśabda*). *See* word, universal
unnecessary assumption 216, 280
unreal (*asatya*) 129
upacāra. *See* metaphor
upādhi 145, 162, 171, 305
Upadhyaya, Krishnadeva a:G87
upagraha. *See* aspect
upakrama-upasaṃhāra G1560
upalakṣaṇa. *See* indicator
upamā. G1393
upamāna. *See* comparison
Upaniṣads 105-6, 161, 342, 348, G1387, 550
upasarga. *See* prefix
Upasargārthadīpikā (of Haridatta) 523
Upasargārthasaṃgraha (of Kṛṣṇācārya II) 486
Upasargavṛtti (of Bhārata Mallika) 510
Upasargavṛtti (of Candra school) 18
UPAVARṢA 234, 554
upaya. *See* means
use, usage (*prayoga*) 145
  (in) correct 47-48
  =*saṃjñā* 114-15
UTPĀLA (1170) 479
UTPĀLĀCĀRYA (930) 24
utpatti. *See* production
UTSAVAKĪRTI SARAṄGA UPĀDHYĀYA 534
utthita. *See* expectancy: natural
UVAṬA G86

vac. *See* speech
  paśyantī. *See paśyantī vāc*
vācaka. *See* denotative
VĀCASPATI MIŚRA I (960) 80-81, 240, G1414, 554
vācya. *See* denotation
Vādacudāmaṇi (of Kṛṣṇamitrācārya) 509

Vādaratna (of Sūryanārāyaṇa Śukla) 516
Vādārthasaṃgraha (of M. G. Bakre) 216
VĀDAVA 458
VĀDIRĀJA (1571) 240
VĀGAMBHṚNI 103
Vāgīśāmata (of Gaṅgādhara Nātha) 521
Vaidya, Uma C, d:G378
Vaidyanātha, father of Gopālakṛṣṇa Śāstrin 353
VAIDYANĀTHA DĪKṢITA (1705) 502
VAIDYANĀTHA PAIYAGUṆḌA, (1740) 23, 323, 327, 387, 505
VAIJALADEVA 534
vaikharī vāk 43, 47, 49-51, 61-62, 95, 99, 121, 124, 328-29, 342, 555, 558
VAINATEYA. *See* NĀRĀYAṆA BHAṬṬATIRI
Vairāgyaśataka section of *Subhāṣitatrīśatī* 124
Vaiśeṣika 82, 163, 194, 196, 213, 559. *See also* Nyāya
Vaiyākaraṇabhūṣaṇa and *—Sāra* (of Koṇḍa Bhaṭṭa) 21-22, 255-308, 324, 367, 495-96
—*Darpana* (of Hari Vallabha) 23, 363, 383, 505-06
—*Kāśikā* (of Harirāma Kalā) 508
—*Ṭīkā* (of Kṛṣṇamitrācārya) 23, 381, 509
—*Kāntī* (of Manyudeva) 23, 387, 509
—*Sphoṭaparīkṣā* (of Bhairava Miśra) 389, 510
—*Tiṅarthavādasāra* (of Khuddi Jhā) 23, 399, 514
—*Viṣamasthalaṭippaṇī* (of Rāmakṛṣṇa Śarmā Tripāṭhi) 514
—*Sāralā* (of Gopāla Śāstri Nene) 24, 407, 515
—*Prabhā* (of Bāla Kṛṣṇa Pañcoli) 417, 516
—*Subodhinī* (of Rāma Prasāda Tripāṭhi) 419, 516
—*Śaṃkarī* (of Śaṃkara Śāstrin Marulacakāra) 517
Vaiyākaraṇadarśa (of Kāli Kumāra Śarman) 524
Vaiyākaraṇadarśanabindu (of Raghunātha Śarmā) 24, 517
Vaiyākaraṇadarśanapratimā (of Rāmajña Pāṇḍeya) 24, 530
Vaiyākaraṇajīvatu (of Gaṅgadāsa) 519
Vaiyākaraṇakārikā (of Nāgeśa Bhaṭṭa) 503
Vaiyākaraṇakoṭipāttra (of Trilocana) 534
Vaiyākaraṇamatonmajjana (of Bhaṭṭoji Dīkṣita) 21, 255, 492
—*Vaiyākaraṇabhūṣaṇa* (of Koṇḍa Bhaṭṭa). *See Vaiyākaraṇabhūṣaṇa*
Vaiyākaraṇapūrvapakṣāvalī (of Gopāla Śāstrī Nene) 515
Vaiyākaraṇasaṃgraha (of Gaṅgādhara Śarman) 521
Vaiyākaraṇasarvasava (of Dharanīdhara) 385, 509
Vaiyākaraṇasiddhāntadīpikā or *—kārikā* (of Bhaṭṭoji Dīkṣita). *See Vaiyākaraṇamatonmajjana*
Vaiyākaraṇasiddhāntamañjuṣā (of Brahmadeva) 24, 411, 516
Vaiyākarana (laghu) siddhāntamañjuṣā (of Nāgeśa Bhaṭṭa) 502
—*Kalā* (of Balambhaṭṭa) 505
—*Kuñjikā* (of Durbāla) 508
—*Vṛttivārttika* (of Appayya Dīkṣita) 518
Vaiyākaraṇa Uttarapakṣāvalī (of Gopāla Śāstrī Nene) 515
VĀJAPYĀYANA 6, 16, 119, 194, 273, 458, 556
Vājasaneyī Saṃhitā G452
vākya. *See* sentence; syntactic connection
vākyārtha. *See* sentence meaning
vākyaśakti 345. *See also* power
vākyasphoṭa. *See sphoṭa*
Vākyakāntaṭīkā (of Helārāja) 193
Vākyamañjarī (of Ananta) 518
Vākyapadī (of Gaṅgadāsa) 521
Vākyapadīya and *—Vṛtti* (of Bhartṛhari) 18, 22, 27, 36, 38, 40-51, 54, 56, 60-61, 69-70, 77, 83, 95, 107, 120, 123-74, 242, 270-271, 302, 307, 326, 341, 466-70, 549, 551-55, 557-60
—*Prakīrṇavṛtti* (of Dharmapāla) 177, 472
—*Paddhatī* (of Vṛṣabhadeva) 22, 178, 472
—*Śabdaprabhā* (of Helārāja) 475
—(*Prakīrna*) *Prakāśa* (of Helārāja) 22, 193-97, 203, 292, 475, G776
—*Prameyasaṃgraha* 199, 475
—*Prakīrnavivaraṇa* (of Abhinavagupta) 476
—*Prakāśa* or —*Ṭīkā* (of Puṇyarāja) 22, 201, 476
—*Bhāvapradīpa* (of Sūryanārāyaṇa Śukla) 24, 405, 516
Commentary (of Satyakāma Varma) 517
Commentary (of K. A. Subramania Iyer) 517

—*Pratyekārthaprakāśikā* (of Dravyeśa Jhā) 403, 521
—*Prakāśa* (of Narain Datta Tripāṭhin) 528
Commentary (of Vidyācakravartin) 534
Vākyapradīpa (of Helārāja) 193
Vākyaprakāśa (of Udayadharma) 486
Vākyatattva (of P. S. Anantanārāyaṇa Śāstri) 24, 409, 516
VĀLĀBHIDATTA 534
VALLABHĀCĀRYA. *See* RABHASĀNANDIN
Vallabha Utprabatiya 363
VĀMANA (650) 19, 203, 472-73
Vāmendrasvāmin 351
VAṄGADĀSA 534
VAṄGASENA (1250) 481
Van Nooten, Barend A. a:G223, G248, G268, G514. et:G12
VARADARĀJA (1620) 494-95
Varadarajiengar, M. B. e:G901
Varadeśvara Dīkṣita 373
Varanasi. *See* Banaras
VARARŪCI. *See* KĀTYĀYANA
VARDHAMĀNA (1088) 478
VARDHAMĀNA (1140) 478
VARENDRA CAMPAHATTIYA MĀNAŚARMAN 534
VARKHEDI TIMMANĀCĀRYA. *See* TIMMANĀCĀRYA
Varma, K. C. a:G496
Varma, L. A. Ravi e:G688
Varma, Satyakarma 46, a:G15, G17, G340-41, G358-59, G755-56, G816-17, G1674-76, e:G737
Varma, Siddheswar 555, a:G117, G478, G616, G1098, G1472, G1593, G1606, G1627-28, G1650, G1677, b:G374, G1401
varṇa. *See* phoneme
varṇasphoṭa. *See sphoṭa*, *varṇa*
Varṇaprakāśa (of Ghanaśyāma) 522
Varṇasūtras of Candra school 18
Varṇaviveka (of Pañcānana Kaṇḍalī) 529
VĀRŚĀYANĪ 12, 110, 196
Vārttākṣa 110
(*Aṣṭādhyāyī*) *Vārttikas* (of Kātyāyana) 16-17, 117, 297, 458-59, 556
—*Vṛttikonmesa* (of Helārāja) 193, 475
—*Dīpaprabhā* (of Nārāyaṇa) 498
—*Vivṛti* (of Vidyāvāgīśa Bhaṭṭācārya) 500
—*Arthaprakāśikā* (of Rāghava Sūri) 529
Varuṇa 104
vāsanā. *See* dispositional
Vasiṣṭha 146
vastvartha. *See* reference
Vasu, Srisa Chandra et:G41, G1085
Vasu, Vaman Das et:G1085
VASUBANDHU (360) 123
Vasudeva G60, G553
VĀSUDEVA 534
VĀSUDEVA BHAṬṬA (1567) 490
VĀSUDEVA DĪKṢITA (1750) 365, 506
VĀSUDEVA ŚĀSTRY ABHYAṄKAR (1929) 516, e:G573
VĀSUDEVA VIṢṆU MIRASHI (1928) 515
Vasudhatukarika (of Goapala Cakravartin) 500
Vasurāta 123
Vasus 104-8
Vāṭeśvara 223
Veda, Vedic texts 5, 24, 26, 32, 35, 37-39, 45, 48-51, 66, 68, 73, 82, 91, 111, 113, 121, 128-30, 146, 148, 175, 183-84, 188, 204, 231-32, 234, 265, 284, 321, 330, 336, 341-43, 346, 550, 555, G199, G213, G351, G361, G489A, G594, G817-18, G860, G1098, G1486
Vedic accent. *See* accent
Vedic language 321, G270, G279, G291
Vedic prescription. *See* prescription
Vedic sages. *See* sage
Vedāṅga 3, 107-9, 188, 321, 343
Vedāṅgaśikṣāpañjikā G427
Vedāntabhāṣyapradīpoddyota (of Nāgeśa Bhaṭṭa) 323
VEDĀNTĀCĀRYA 534
VEDĀNTA DEŚIKA (1330) 239
Vedāntaparibhāṣā (of Dharmarājadhvarīndra) 87, 552
Vedantatirtha, Girisacandra e:G969
Vedavati, Vyakaranopadhyaya e:G869
Vedavrata 340, e:G611
Veer, Yajan a:G405
Vele, R. N. a:G1578
VENIMĀDHAVA (1750) 506
Venkatacharya, T. a:G1703
VEṄKATADĀSA (1780) 508
Veṅkatārya, father of Umāmaheśvara 371
Venkatasubbiah, A. a:G662
Venkateśa, father of Tirumala Yajvan 313
VEṄKATEŚVARA (1722) 504
verb (*ākhyāta*) 110, 112, 121, 149, 256-57, 333, G223, G1384

verb (*kriyā*) 321, G696, G1549
nominal verb (*nāmadhātu*) 173
verbal cognition (*śabdabodha*) 26, 89-90, 95-99, 300, 346, G1465, G1656, G1712
verbal comprehension. *See abhihitānvaya*
verbal ending. *See* (case)-ending
verbal knowledge (*śabdajñāna*) 27
verbal meaning G248
verbal testimony (*śabda, āgama*). *See* testimony
vibhāga. See disjunction
vibhakti. See (case)-ending
Vibhaktyarthanirṇaya (of Śrīkṛṣṇa Bhaṭṭa Maunin) 361, 506
Vibhaktyarthaprakāśa (of Kamalākara Bhaṭṭa) 497
Vibhaktyarthavivaraṇa (of Śivānanda Gosvāmin) 532
vidhi. See prescription
vidhisūtra. See operational rule
Vidhiviveka (of Maṇḍana Miśra) 266
Vidvatprabodhinī (of Rāmabhaṭṭa) 498
vidyā. See knowledge
Vidyabhusana, Satischandra a:G1388
VIDYĀCAKRAVARTIN 534
VIDYĀNANDA. *See* VIJAYĀNANDA
Vidyanidhi, Vipinacandra e:G1004
Vidyaratna, Govindacandra e:G1016
Vidyavacaspati, Veda Prakasa e:G639
VIDYĀVĀGĪŚA BHAṬṬĀCĀRYA (1665) 499-500
Vidyavaridhi, Syamacarana Kaviratna e:G1032
view, final true (*siddhānta*) 16
Vijaya, Manohara e:G957
VIJAYAMĀLĀ 534
Vijayanagara empire 238
VIJAYĀNANDA (1140) 478
Vijaya Raghunatha Tondaiian I, King of Pudukottah 353
VIJAYĪNDRA BHIKṢU (165) 240
vikalpa. See conceptual construction
vikāra. See becoming; product
Vikarmāṅkadevacarita (of Bilhaṇa) 205
vikṣepa. See māyā
VIMALAKĪRTI (1550) 488
VIMALAMATI (648) 472
VIMALA SARASVATĪ (1300) 483
VINĀSVARANANDIN 535
VINAYAVIJAYAGAṆI (1652) 499
Vinodamañjarī (of Vallabha Utprabaṭiya) 363
viparyāsa. See false
VIPRAJENDRA (1845) 511, e:G537
Vira, Raghu a:G10, G70, G426, G453
VĪRAPĀNDYA 535
VĪRARĀGHAVĀCĀRYA 535
VĪREŚVARA 241, 247, 319
virodha. See contradiction
Visalakshy, P. a:G867
Viśeṣyavāda (of Kāśīnātha) 525
viśeṣavidhi. See specification
Viśiṣṭādvaita 240
(King) Viṣṇugupta 179
VIṢṆUMIŚRA G1043-44
VIṢṆUMITRA (1547) 227, 488
VIṢṆUPRASĀDA ŚARMAN 514, e:G1002
VIŚVANĀTHA BHAṬṬA G1255
VIŚVANĀTHA CAKRAVARTIN 530
VIŚVANĀTHA DAṆḌIBHAṬṬA (1850) 511
VIŚVANĀTHA NYĀYALAṂKĀRA 535
VIŚVANĀTHA NYĀYASIDDHĀNTA PAÑCĀNANA (1640) 91
VIŚVANĀTHA ŚĀSTRĪ 535
Viśvedevas 104
Viśveśvara Dīkṣita 365
VIŚVEŚVARA SŪRI 535
VIŚVEŚVARA TARKĀCĀRYA 535
VIṬṬHALA (1460) 486, G1050
Vivaraṇa school of Advaita 41-42
vivarta. See manifestation
V. KṚṢṆAMĀCĀRYA (1944) 24, 413, 516, e:G1265
vocative (case) (*sambadhana*) 168, 262, 337, G1483
Vogel, J. P. a:G1444
voice (active/passive) 258, G235
volition (*kṛti*) 257-58, 332
VOPADEVA (1275) 20, 211, 482-83
VRAJARĀJA 534
Vart, Satya a:G624, G703-4, G1534, G1691
(HARI) VṚṢABHADEVA (1650) 22, 50, 179, 201, 472
Vrtākṣa 13
vṛtti. See formation; integration
Vṛttidīpikā (of Jayakṛṣṇa Maunin) 361, 367
Vṛttidīpikā (of Śrīkṛṣṇa Bhaṭṭa Maunin) 23, 506
Vṛttipañjikā
—*Prabhāvatī* (of Kṛṣṇa Bhaṭṭācārya) 526

VURAMIŚRA 535
vyabhicāra. *See* false, deviation
VYĀḌI 6, 16, 117, 119-20, 194, 273, 458, 556
vyākaraṇa. *See* grammar
Vyākaraṇadarśanapratimā (of Rāmajña Pāṇḍeya) 431
Vyākaraṇadīpa (of Cidrūpāśrama)
—*Prabhā* (of Gaṅgādhara Dīkṣita) 494
Vyākaraṇakrodapāttra (of Tāraka Brahmānanda Sarasvatī) 309, 498
Vyākaraṇaṭīkā (of Guṇakara) 523
Vyākhyasāra (of Harirāma). *See Candrikā*
vyakti. *See* particular
vyaktisphoṭa. *See sphoṭa*
vyañjanā. *See* suggestion
vyāpāra. *See* function
vyāpekṣa. *See* dependence
parasparāvyāpekṣa. *See* syntactic connection
VYĀSA 44
vyatireka G1579
vyutpatti. *See* derivation
Vyutpattivāda (of Gadādhara) 370

Wackernagel, Joseph a:G93, G1392, b:G1385, G1405
Wadegaonkar, Narayana Dadaji e:G1121
Wayman, Alex a:G775, G1704
Weber, Albrecht a:G431, G526-28, G533
Wecker, Otto a:G1387
Wells, Rulon a:G1495
Westergaard, N. L. b:G1365
Wezler, Albrecht a:G309, G749, b:G256, G749
Whitney, William Dwight a:G440, G1367, G1372, G1382, b:G379, G1458
whole. *See* part and whole
Wilkins, Charles e:G1274
will (*icchā*) 90
word (*pada*) 5-6, 10, 26-27, 47, 55, 58, 61, 71-73, 94, 99, 108, 119, 124-25, 147, 149, 183, 187, 189-90, 216, 232-34, 276, 303, 345-46, 348, 369, G187, G272
compound word. *See* compound
word derivation. *See* derivation
divine word 46
noncompound word 125
word-meaning (*padārtha*) 11-12, 65-83, 146, 161, 194, 343, G732
(inner) mental word. *See* mental
word-order 47, G1583
universal word (*jātiśabda*) 28

Yādavābhyudaya (of Vedānta Deśika) 239
YAGEŚVARA (1900) 513
Yajñarāma Dīkṣita 321
YAJÑEŚVARA BHAṬṬA (1874) 512
Yājurveda 86, G514
Yājuṣmantra 26
YAKṢAVARMAN (1050) 476, G840, G885-86
Yāma 104
YĀSKA 4, 7, 10-11, 13-14, 36, 68, 107-12, 169, 196, 333, 342, 549, 555-56, G422, G450, G621, G696, G1693
YAŚOBHUTI 535
Yasovijaya, Muni e:G959
YATĪŚA 535
yatna. *See* effort
yaugika. *See* derivation; see also etymology
Yāvanas 237, G533
yoga. *See* derivation; see also union
yoga of the word (*śabdayoga*) 47, 50-52
Yoga 21, 44-45, 54
Yogācāra 177
yogarūḍhi. *See* convention
Yogasūtras (of Patañjali) 16, 44, 46, 551-53
—*Vṛtti* (of Nāgeśa Bhaṭṭa) 323
yogic intuition 146
yogin 31-32
yogyatā. *See* consistency
Yuktiratnākara (of Kṛṣṇācārya) 526
Yuktiratnākara (of Kṛṣṇamitrācārya) 509

zero G143, G165, G209, G212
Zgusta, Ladislav a:G257